THE GREATEST OF ALL PLAGUES

The Greatest of All Plagues

HOW ECONOMIC INEQUALITY
SHAPED POLITICAL THOUGHT
FROM PLATO TO MARX

David Lay Williams

PRINCETON UNIVERSITY PRESS

PRINCETON & OXFORD

Published by Princeton University Press
41 William Street, Princeton, New Jersey 08540
99 Banbury Road, Oxford OX2 6JX

press.princeton.edu

Library of Congress Cataloging-in-Publication Data

Names: Williams, David Lay, 1969- author,
Title: The greatest of all plagues : how economic inequality shaped political
    thought from Plato to Marx / David Lay Williams.
Description: Princeton : Princeton University Press, [2024] | Includes
    bibliographical references and index.
Identifiers: LCCN 2023048805 (print) | LCCN 2023048806 (ebook) |
    ISBN 9780691171975 (hardback) | ISBN 9780691255514 (ebook)
Subjects: LCSH: Income distribution. | Distributive justice. | Equality—Economic
    aspects. | Political stability. | Philosophers. | BISAC: PHILOSOPHY /
    Political | BUSINESS & ECONOMICS / Economic History
Classification: LCC HB523 .W55 2024 (print) | LCC HB523 (ebook) |
    DDC 339.2—dc23/eng/20240214
LC record available at https://lccn.loc.gov/2023048805
LC ebook record available at https://lccn.loc.gov/2023048806

British Library Cataloging-in-Publication Data is available

Editorial: Rob Tempio and Chloe Coy
Production Editorial: Ali Parrington
Jacket Design: Karl Spurzem
Production: Erin Suydam
Publicity: Kate Hensley and Carmen Jimenez
Copyeditor: Joyce H.-S. Li
Jacket art and frontispiece: Heinrich Aldegrever, *Lazarus Begging for Crumbs from Dives's Table*, 1552, pen and brown ink, brown wash, traces of black chalk, incised for transfer. Courtesy of the J. Paul Getty Museum Collection

This book has been composed in Miller

Printed on acid-free paper. ∞

Printed in the United States of America

10 9 8 7 6 5 4 3 2 1

In memory of Lawrence A. Weiser

CONTENTS

CONTENTS

ACKNOWLEDGMENTS

IT IS IMPOSSIBLE TO WRITE a book of this nature without incurring many debts. These fall into two large categories—academic and emotional supports. Regarding the former, I have been overwhelmed by the generosity of many scholars who have taken the time to engage early chapter drafts. One of the greatest benefits of working on a book with contemporary resonance has been a large number of kind invitations to speak at workshops and colloquia. I have presented chapters of this research at Aarhus University, Cambridge University, Columbia University, Dartmouth College, Fordham University, Kansas State University, Northern Illinois University, Northwestern University, Texas State University, University of Chicago, University of Houston, University of North Carolina–Chapel Hill, University of Notre Dame, University of Texas at Austin, Vanderbilt University, University of California–Davis, University of California–Los Angeles, University of Wisconsin–Madison, and Yale University. I have benefited greatly from each one. Among the many valuable commentators on my chapters from these events and at related conference presentations were Richard Avramenko, Alyssa Battistoni, Steven Bilakovics, Christopher Brooke, Naomi Choi, Christian Christiansen, Jeffrey Church, Susan Collins, Andrew Day, Mary G. Dietz, Zachary Durec, Jeffrey Flynn, Alin Fumuresc, Emre Gercek, Ayten Gündoğdu, Samir Haddad, Ryan Patrick Hanley, Eileen M. Hunt, David Chambliss Johnston, Daniel J. Kapust, Mary Keys, David Konstan, Glory Liu, Karuna Mantena, Luke Mayville, Michael Morrell, Emily Nacol, Frederick Neuhouser, Emma Planinc, Andrea Radasanu, Geneviève Rousselière, Andy Sabl, Malcolm Schofield, Melissa Schwartzberg, Howard Schweber, Sidney Simpson, Steven Smith, Noah Stengl, Nick Tampio, Maurizio Viroli, Paul Weitman, Reed Winegar, Catherine Zuckert, and John Zumbrunnen. I am embarrassed by the names I have forgotten but grateful to all for taking the time to engage the ideas in this book.

I want to especially thank Devin J. Vartija, who invited me to participate in what will always be a career highlight—a workshop on the history of equality at the University of Utrecht on May 25–27, 2022. It was my first "normal" academic activity in a world cautiously emerging from the COVID-19 pandemic, and it reminded me of everything I love about academia but especially the shared love of engaged inquiry. This workshop brought together numerous accomplished humanists working on equality and inequality, including Teresa Bejan, Annelien de Dijn, Lynn Hunt, Shiru Lim, Anne Phillips, and Siep Sturrman. I am grateful to them and all the workshop participants for stimulating me to think more deeply about important issues in this book and for providing an infusion of energy to embark on an important round of revisions.

Many others read chapters independent of such events out of the goodness of their hearts. Among these are Alec Arellano, Andreas Avgousti, Deborah Baumgold, Adrian Blau, Jonathan Bloch, Terrell Carver, Arturo Chang, Devin Christensen, Robin Douglass, Jill Frank, Alan J. Kellner, Steven Kelts, Al Martinich, Helen McCabe, John P. McCormick, William Clare Roberts, David Stasavage, Devin Stauffer, John Warner, Matthew H. Young, and Samuel Garrett Zeitlin.

Still others engaged me in valuable conversations about important themes and tricky questions arising in the course of writing this book. Among those I can recall are Tyler Brown, Blake Hestir, Jared Holley, Michael Morrell, Timothy Raynor, Doug Thompson, Todd Wenzel, and Scott Williams.

I have benefited immensely from the support of my colleagues at DePaul University, especially my chairs, Scott Hibbard and Valerie Johnson, but also Noel Barker, David Barnum, Larry Bennett, Susan Burgess, Giuseppe Cumella, Will Denton, Ben Epstein, Joey Mello, Michael Naas, Phillip Stalley, Wayne Steger, Joe Tafoya, Erik Tillman, and Harry Wray. I was deeply fortunate to have received two sabbaticals over the course of writing this book, as well as a Wicklander fellowship at DePaul's Institute for Business and Professional Ethics. I am also grateful to DePaul's Faculty Scholarship Collaborative, which hosted informal brown bag presentations for most early chapter drafts.

I owe a special debt of gratitude to those who took the time to read my entire manuscript. On June 28–29, 2022, DePaul hosted a book workshop with seven gifted scholars, who offered detailed feedback, including Mike Budde, James Farr, Sam Fleischacker, Sean Kirkland, Matthew W. Maguire, Ricky Rivard, and Dana Villa. This event was generously funded by the Institute for Humane Studies with additional support from DePaul's Political Science department. Michael Locke McLendon read the first draft of every chapter and improved the manuscript in countless ways in addition to discussing nearly every argument of the book over the course of almost a decade. He is a dear friend and a brilliant scholar of Rousseau and inequality. I also especially want to thank Darrin McMahon and Michelle Schwarze for their remarkable reviews on behalf of Princeton

University Press. Although no author is initially excited about many detailed singled-spaced pages of suggested revisions, only a fool would fail to acknowledge the degree to which such feedback can improve a manuscript. I am deeply honored by their thoughtful suggestions that have improved this book in countless ways.

This book would likely not exist were it not for my editor, Rob Tempio, at Princeton University Press. He not only helped me conceive it, but he remained interested and engaged with this project at every stage—for nearly a decade. I have been fortunate to work with great editors over the years. It is difficult to imagine, however, anyone better at his job than Rob.

I have relied extensively on emotional support from friends and family. Among friends, I have benefited greatly from Doug Belkin, Darren Carlton, David Chan, Richard Galvin, Ben Gregg, Marcel and Dawn Grdinic, Mark Hawley, Jesper Hede, Tim Johnson, Chris Kuzawa, Andy Kuusisto, Anna Law, Charles Lockhart, Brad Mapes-Martins, Jonathan Marks, Jason Maloy, Sean Phillips, Jon Rosenblatt, Rixey Ruffin, and Frank Thames. I also enjoyed significant support from my many music friends, including Todd Burrer, Alan Burton, Skip Dolt, Trent Evans, Dave Fodor, Leo Kawczinski, Tom Laney, Derek Layes, Eric Perney, Michael Petterson, Drew Ruiz, Jonathan Singer, Curt and Kay Wilson, Gordon Wright, Tony and Ashley Yarbrough, and all the members of the Chicago Jazz Dads, In Full Swing, and the Curt Wilson Alumni Jazz Band.

I would not have been able to complete this project without a very tolerant family, who have long been asking, "So when are you actually going to finish this book?" I'm grateful to my in-laws, Julia Weiser, Mike Weiser, Maggie Weiser, and Ken Stevenson, as well as to my mother, sister, and relatives scattered between the coasts. I owe more than I can express to my patient wife, Jen Weiser, who has assisted throughout the book-writing process—providing not only the time and space needed to write but also for innumerable conversations and regular inspiration. I have spent the vast majority of my son's life writing this book. He makes me proud every day. Ben can now look forward to the part of his childhood that will be free from his father's obsession.

When it takes a decade to write a mid-career book like this, there is a great danger of losing important people along the way. I have lost a handful of dear friends and mentors. This includes my cousin, Scott Lay, the California politics junkie who liked to joke that while I had the theoretical inclinations in the family, he was the one who understood "real politics." I'd like to think that he would have enjoyed this attempt to bridge that gap. My good friend in Stevens Point, Doug Forbes, passed away early during this project, but he inspired me to seek joy, camaraderie, and balance throughout. I also lost my undergraduate mentor, Gregg Franzwa, at Texas Christian University. Gregg picked me up off the scrap heap and almost single-handedly decided he would make something out of me. His devotion to his students was legendary and serves as a constant reminder to give all I have to my own students. He introduced me to many of the thinkers in this book for the first time. My dissertation advisor, T. K. Seung, at the University of Texas at Austin, passed away as I approached completion of my final chapters. Tom read my Plato chapter and offered typically penetrating feedback, even at the age of eighty-five. He will always be my Platonic idea of a scholar and a reminder to push myself harder to be bold. I also lost my early-career mentor and beloved friend, Patrick Riley. Patrick has been a constant inspiration throughout this project and the model of how to interrogate an idea over a large time span. Closer to Chicago, I lost my friend and DePaul colleague, Cathy May, whose enthusiasm for teaching political theory was never lost on me or on her students. We discussed many of the ideas in this book and she remains an inspiration. Finally, I lost my father-in-law, Larry Weiser. Before he was my father-in-law, Larry was an economist and my colleague at the University of Wisconsin–Stevens Point. Even after he retired, he remained intellectually engaged. His love of inquiry was the source of countless long conversations that had me looking forward to every family gathering. Not long before I took his daughter and grandson with me to Chicago, Larry and I formed a discussion group (with Dick Feldman, Wayne McCaffrey, and Scott Wallace) at Emy J's to read and discuss every page of Adam Smith's *Theory of Moral Sentiments*. It was participating in this reading group that the first ideas for this book emerged. Because of Larry's enthusiasm for these ideas but also, more consequentially, his modeling of how to be a good husband and father, I dedicate this book to him.

Significant portions of chapter 3 were published as "Hobbes on Wealth, Poverty, and Economic Inequality," *Hobbes Studies* 34, no. 1 (2021): 9–57. I am grateful to Brill for granting permission to include this in the book.

Works of Thomas Hobbes

Behemoth	Behemoth, or the Long Parliament, 1688
Citizen	On the Citizen, 1642
Elements	Elements of Law: Human Nature and De Corpore Politico, 1640
Leviathan	Leviathan, or the Matter, Form, and Power of a Commonwealth Ecclesiastical and Civil, 1651
Man	On Man, 1658
Rhetoric	The Whole Art of Rhetoric, 1637
Tacitus	"Discourse upon the Beginning of Tacitus," 1620

Works of Jean-Jacques Rousseau

d'Alembert	Letter to d'Alembert on the Theater, 1758
Corsica	Plan for a Constitutional Project for Corsica, 1767
Dialogues	Rousseau, Judge of Jean-Jacques: Dialogues, 1772–1776
Emile	Emile, or On Education, 1762
EOL	Essay on the Origin of Languages, 1781
FD	Discourse on the Sciences and Arts, or First Discourse, 1751
Julie	Julie, or the New Heloise, 1761
Last Reply	Last Reply, 1751
LF	"Letter to M. de Franquières," March 25, 1769
LT	"Letter to Robert Tronchin," November 26, 1758
Mountain	Letters Written from the Mountain, 1764
Narcissus	"Preface to Narcissus," 1752–1753
Observations	Observations by Jean-Jacques Rousseau of Geneva, 1751
PE	Discourse on Political Economy, 1756
PF	"Political Fragments," 1994
Poland	Considerations on the Government of Poland, 1772
SC	Of the Social Contract, 1762

SD	*Discourse on the Origin and the Foundations of Inequality among Men*, or *Second Discourse*, 1755
SF	"Separate Fragments" from *Plan for a Constitutional Project for Corsica*, 1767
WFT	"On Wealth and Fragments on Taste," 1749–1756

Works of Adam Smith

Astronomy	*History of Astronomy*, 1795
LJ	*Lectures on Jurisprudence*, 1763
TMS	*Theory of Moral Sentiments*, 1759–1790
WN	*An Inquiry into the Nature and Causes of the Wealth of Nations*, 1776

Works of John Stuart Mill

Autobiography	*Autobiography*, 1873
Bentham	*Bentham*, 1838
Blessings	*Blessings of Equal Justice*, 1823
Coleridge	*Coleridge*, 1840
Considerations	*Considerations on Representative Government*, 1861
French News	"French News," 1834
Income and Property	*The Income and Property Tax*, 1852
Labour	*The Claims of Labour*, 1845
Liberty	*On Liberty*, 1859
Newman	"Newman's Political Economy," 1851
Notes	*Notes on Newspapers*, 1834
Principles	*Principles of Political Economy*, 1849–1871
Rationale	*Rationale of Representation*, 1835
Religion	*Three Essays on Religion*, 1874
Remarks	*Remarks on Bentham's Philosophy*, 1833
Socialism	*Chapters on Socialism*, 1879
State of Society	*State of Society in America*, 1836
Subjection	*The Subjection of Women*, 1869
Thornton	"Thornton on Labour and Its Claims," 1869
TOA, I	*M. de Tocqueville on Democracy in America*, I, 1835

TOA, II	*M. de Tocqueville on Democracy in America, II,* 1840
Utilitarianism	*Utilitarianism,* 1861
Vindication	*Vindication of the French Revolution of February 1848,* 1849

Works of Karl Marx and Friedrich Engels

AD	*Anti-Dühring: Herr Eugen Dühring's Revolution in Science,* 1878–1894
Capital	*Capital: A Critique of Political Economy,* vol. 1, 1867
Capital 3	*Capital,* vol. 3, 1894
Chartism	"Chartism," 1853
Civil War	*The Civil War in France,* 1871
CFL	"Condition of Factory Laborers," 1857
CM	*The Communist Manifesto,* 1848
Condition	*The Condition of the Working Class in England,* 1845
EPM	*Economic and Philosophic Manuscripts,* 1844
GI	*The German Ideology,* 1845
Gotha	"Critique of the Gotha Program," 1875
Grundrisse	*Grundrisse: Foundations of the Critique of Political Economy,* 1857–1858
Introduction	Introduction to *The Civil War in France,* 1891
JQ	*On the Jewish Question,* 1843
LQ	"The Labor Question," 1853
Lunacy	"The Increase of Lunacy in Great Britain," 1858
Possibility	"The Possibility of Non-violent Revolution," 1872
Poverty	*The Poverty of Philosophy,* 1845
WLC	*Wage Labour and Capital,* 1849

THE GREATEST OF ALL PLAGUES

Introduction

ECONOMIC INEQUALITY HAS BEEN STEADILY growing for the past few decades—in the United States and in much of the developed world. According to a database maintained by the economists Thomas Blanchet, Emmanuel Saez, and Gabriel Zucman, whereas the poorest 50 percent of Americans have seen their wealth grow an average of $12,000 per household since 1976—scarcely enough to cover a single major medical crisis without insurance, far less than one year of college tuition—those occupying the top 10 percent have seen their wealth grow by nearly $3 million. Those in the top 1 percent have seen their wealth grow by $16 million. Those in the top 0.1 percent have seen theirs grow by $85 million. And those occupying the top 0.01 percent have seen their net wealth grow by $440 million per household.[1] If anything, the pace of inequality's growth appears to be accelerating. Per Oxfam, over a recent two-year period, billionaires across the globe have seen their fortunes grow more than they did in the previous twenty-three years combined, such that now the world's wealthiest ten individuals have more than the poorest 40 percent of humanity.[2] Elon Musk alone saw his wealth grow from $25 billion to more than $200 billion over the course of a few years.[3] Per data available from the Federal Reserve, the top 1 percent of Americans in 2020 held more than fifteen times the wealth of the bottom 50 percent of all Americans.[4]

The French economist Thomas Piketty has documented economic inequality's steady rise over the past five decades.[5] After a period of lower inequality following World War II, changes in taxation, regulation, and other policies led to a significant shift of resources from the poorest citizens to the wealthiest. From the 1980s to the 2000s, almost the entire growth in household wealth belonged to the richest 20 percent of

Americans, two-thirds of that to the top 1 percent alone.[6] By 2018, economic inequality in the United States was greater than any time since the 1920s.[7] And as even casual observers have noted, this growth in inequality has corresponded to a growth in authoritarian populist movements, social distrust, and political instability.

Yet as historian Walter Scheidel notes, although extreme inequality may feel relatively new, it has historically been the norm: "Inequality either grew or held fairly steady for much of recorded history, and significant reductions have been rare."[8] Or as political scientist Charles Lindblom observed a generation earlier, "Historically, all societies, market or not, have preserved economic inequality."[9] Despite this, relatively little attention has been drawn to what historical sources have been saying about inequality all along. Although it may feel to some that consciousness of inequality and its dire effects is recent in origin, the fact is that it extends back as long as philosophers have been thinking about politics. Philosophers, including the most canonical ones in the Western tradition, have expressed concerns about inequality this whole time, often right underneath our noses. While almost every undergraduate philosophy major knows about Plato's philosopher rulers, for example, few realize that he identifies economic inequality as among the greatest threats to any thriving republic. While almost everyone who has taken an introduction to political theory course in college knows that Thomas Hobbes advocated for absolute sovereignty as the best path to a peaceful commonwealth, few know that, for him, inequality is one of the commonwealth's greatest threats. While almost everyone knows Adam Smith's role as an early advocate of market economies, few know that, for him, inequality threatens to divide citizens anywhere it is allowed to exist. And while many know John Stuart Mill as the definitive champion of individual liberty, few know that, for him, liberty needs to be balanced with a healthy degree of economic equality. We have been reading these thinkers for a long time, yet there is so much still they can teach us about what many consider to be the defining economic, social, and political challenge of our age. Recovering their largely forgotten wisdom about inequality is the aim of this book.

Inequality's persistence and effects on social and political stability is, as Sigmund Freud once observed, both "flagrant" and has "always been recognized." Indeed, as the Viennese psychiatrist continued, "It is to be expected that . . . underprivileged classes will envy the favored ones their privileges and will do all they can to free themselves from their own surplus of privation. Where this is not possible, a permanent measure of discontent will persist within the culture concerned and this can lead to dangerous revolts."[10] For Freud, this was common sense and had long been understood as such.

The escaped slave and orator Frederick Douglass expressly acknowledged this tradition by citing the mythical ancient Spartan lawgiver Lycurgus (treated in chapter 1 of this book), who was "fully justified in the extreme measures he adopted," including in his confiscation and equal redistribution of all private wealth to secure his citizens' liberties. Drawing on his knowledge of this tradition within Western thought, Douglass observed, "Wherever the palaces tower highest, and enclose within their walls the greatest accumulations of luxury and wealth, there does the peasant grovel lowest in ignorance and misery; there is tyranny most secure and freedom most hopeless."[11] Economic inequality, for him, was the foundation of abject poverty, mass ignorance, and despotism. For Douglass, this meant, among other things, that the freedom of American slaves would have to be accompanied by real economic equality rather than gestures to mere legal equality—a point also found in the same Plutarch's *Lives* where Douglass discovered Lycurgus: "for a mere law to give all men equal rights is but useless, if the poor must sacrifice those rights to their debts, and, in the very seats and sanctuaries of equality, the courts of justice, the offices of state, and the public discussions, be more than anywhere at the beck and bidding of the rich."[12] For Plutarch's ancient Greek lawgivers and for Douglass, legal, social, and political equality must proceed from a foundation of economic equality.

The point, however, is this: both Douglass and Freud were fully aware of this long Western tradition of criticizing economic inequality. Yet much of this tradition has been neglected, to our own detriment. Those who find economic inequality troubling today would benefit from an awareness of this tradition, as did Freud and Douglass. Not only would standing on the shoulders of giants offer greater confidence, but the tradition furnishes powerful arguments against inequality—arguments largely unknown today. This book traces the history of inequality through seven central figures in this tradition—Plato, Jesus,[13] Thomas Hobbes, Jean-Jacques Rousseau, Adam Smith, John Stuart Mill, and Karl Marx[14]—and in doing so, promises not only to provide a richer intellectual history but also to enrich our understanding of inequality more generally.

A book of this nature requires justifying the choice of texts under consideration. Why these seven figures and not others? I choose them primarily for the most obvious reason: they are familiar. Almost everyone across the world has heard of Jesus. And much of the educated world has some passing familiarity with some combination of the rest. Anyone who has taken an undergraduate introductory course in philosophy, political theory, or intellectual history has likely read some of them. Yet despite their familiarity, most of these figures are known for reasons other than their attention to economic inequality. Plato, for example, is familiar mostly as an advocate of philosopher rulers and political hierarchy, as found in his *Republic*. Thomas Hobbes is mostly familiar for his depiction of the state of nature as "solitary, poor, nasty, brutish, and short." Adam Smith is familiar to most as the "godfather of capitalism." These are three of the most celebrated thinkers in the Western intellectual tradition. And despite this, even as they continue to be read and discussed broadly, vanishingly little consideration is given to what they have to say about inequality despite the issue's pressing contemporary salience.

We have been reading these philosophers and figures for hundreds if not thousands of years, and in many cases we have not yet begun to appreciate how remarkably relevant they remain. I say this because they do not merely declare that inequality is "bad" and move on to their next point. They rather take pains to explain exactly *why* inequality is problematic. In explaining their reasoning, these seven figures perform a remarkable service for those grappling with inequality—a critical disposition too often assumed and unargued. Take, for example, Thomas Piketty's magisterial *Capital in the 21st Century*. He condemns inequality as "excessive," "shameful," "beyond all reasonable limits," "terrifying," engendering a "feeling of dispossession," threatening "democratic sovereignty" and "the values of social justice," risking a "drift toward oligarchy," and in some regions representing "unprecedented levels of injustice."[15] Yet other than passing references to John Rawls and Amartya Sen, he does not elaborate. In this respect, he follows a pattern adopted by many activists, journalists, and public officials. Although many condemn inequality, few elaborate substantially on *why* it might be problematic. This is not a critique of Piketty's accomplishments, which represent essential descriptive work on inequality's trajectory over time and its tendency to emerge in capitalist economies. But it is to suggest the work left undone—or rather ignored and unappreciated.

The fact that many contemporary opponents of inequality have failed to outline *why* inequality is problematic has become fodder for a presumption that inequality's critics are merely giving vent to their *resentment* against and *envy* of the wealthy—that they express the vices of small-minded people more than legitimate moral or political concerns.[16] For economist Deirdre McCloskey, efforts to ameliorate inequality are merely manifestations of "an insatiable envy."[17] On such accounts, inequality's critics might be better served in getting counsel from a therapist or a clergy member, who might cure them of their envy, than in wasting their efforts on critiquing inequality.

This is reason enough to return to canonical texts. Because even though it may be possible for some to dismiss various frustrations expressed about inequality, it would be more difficult and perhaps irresponsible to ignore the arguments of the figures in this book. This is true for at least two reasons: first, precisely because *they provide arguments* and second, because we have already been taking these thinkers seriously for centuries. Their objections to inequality are difficult to dismiss as expressions of resentment or envy. They are, rather, anchored in profoundly influential political theories (and in Jesus's case, theology). And they argue with striking consensus that excessive inequality threatens to divide communities, pit citizens against one another, undermine democratic legitimacy, and, in the most extreme cases, even foment revolution. Rather than dismissing complaints about inequality as expressions of the vice of envy, they argue that inequality results from other vexing vices, including greed (*pleonexia*), injustice, intemperance, selfishness, and impiety. If they are right, then maybe contemporary scholars have been focusing on the wrong vices.

Further, these canonical texts put us in conversation with much contemporary political philosophy and economics, especially the school known as "sufficientarianism," which holds that although poverty is a genuine moral problem, concentrated wealth and inequality are morally irrelevant. Scholars and journalists such as Steven Pinker, Tyler Cowen, and David Brooks, among others, argue that so long as the poor are fed, housed, and clothed, there should be little concern with the wealthy. The economist Cowen, for example, has recently insisted that we should "fight poverty, not inequality."[18] Yet Cowen has elsewhere venerated Plato and Mill, apparently unaware that these two thinkers are among the most strenuous objectors not merely to poverty but to excessive wealth and inequality. Similarly, while *New York Times* columnist David Brooks acknowledges that something should be done to help the poor, he insists that attention to inequality is distracting and "*needlessly polarizes*" current political debates. Yet elsewhere he has pleaded that more people should be reading Plutarch for instructive lessons today—the same Plutarch who depicted harrowing stories of economic inequality in the ancient world and inspired Frederick Douglass to fight inequality in his own times.[19] Careful study of the history of political thought reveals arguments that squarely challenge many today, especially the sufficientarians. If sufficientarians are to maintain their claim that inequality is morally unproblematic, they should have to confront and refute the arguments of the canonical philosophers that, in many cases, they claim most to admire.

Much of what follows will be surprising to some on both the political right and left. Many conservatives casually assume that the Western canon uniformly endorses concentrated wealth as the result of just exchanges over time. Free-market economist and advocate Milton Friedman, for example, treated economic egalitarianism as largely an invention of twentieth-century liberals.[20] It had not occurred to him that there was an extended tradition of serious objections to inequality extending back to antiquity. Friedrich Hayek similarly describes socialism and egalitarianism as representing a "sharp . . . break not only with the recent past but with the whole evolution of Western civilization . . . as it has grown from the foundations laid by Christianity and the Greeks."[21] For Hayek, the Western canon, if anything, uniformly supports inequality. Many on the left, for related reasons, too often assume that the canon stands opposed to egalitarian principles. If the "great books" have failed adequately as critics of inequality on other dimensions, so the argument goes, what reasons do they offer to believe that those books provide worthy insights into the economic sphere? Who is *Plato*, of all people, to teach contemporary liberals about *equality*? Scrupulous examination of these texts with an eye to economic inequality suggests Plato and others can teach a great deal. In coming to appreciate this, we have fresh reasons to read these familiar books yet again.

Examining these texts on inequality reveals a general and undeniable pattern: inequality is not incidental to any of these thinkers. I have not written a book to draw attention to scattered and disconnected observations on inequality. I am arguing something much more. For these thinkers, inequality threatens their greatest moral, political, and sometimes theological ambitions. Furthermore, this trend persists despite their disparate ambitions or goals. The seven figures under consideration here represent a philosophically diverse group, including a classical republican, the founding figure of Christianity, an early modern republican, a classical liberal, a utilitarian, and a communist, as well as Hobbes, who seems to defy labels. Plato, for example, aims to create a community of civic harmony and friendship. Jesus seeks to promote the love of God and love of neighbor. Hobbes sought to secure peace. Rousseau's republic aims to realize the general will. Smith ardently desires mutual sympathy. Mill pursues utility. And Marx seeks to free the proletariat from bourgeois domination.

Remarkably, they all want something different in their political and moral theories, yet they all clearly understand inequality as a threat to their respective goals. Although Rousseau and Marx are surely the best-known critics of inequality in this book, their concerns about inequality are hardly historically unique. They are instead part of a larger tradition that understands inequality to be socially and politically disruptive, if not downright antagonistic, to thriving states. It thus becomes harder to dismiss their concerns about inequality as idiosyncratic musings. Rather, this suggests that thinking about inequality has been intrinsic to political philosophy itself. The nature of inequality requires that political philosophy engage and address it lest its effects undermine the greatest ambitions for political communities, almost regardless of what those ambitions might be. To proceed otherwise, indifferent to inequality, would be to dismiss canonical wisdom.

It is important to establish what this book is and what it is not. This is a book about *economic* inequality in the history of political thought. It is not a book about all forms of inequality. A larger work on inequality would necessarily have to address social, political, gender, racial, religious, and other inequalities in addition to economic inequality. In writing this book, I do not want to argue that those inequalities are somehow less important or even independent of economic inequality. Economic equality often coexists with other pervasive inequalities.[22] It is no secret, for example, that Plato and Hobbes embrace antidemocratic political inequalities. Yet one can be a committed economic egalitarian while holding inegalitarian views on other dimensions. I restrict my inquiry in this book to *economic inequality* only in order to highlight a largely ignored theme in the history of political thought. It is my hope that other scholars will explore the important connections among these various forms of inequality. These relationships are complex and deserve greater study.

Why this *humanistic* account of inequality when there are countless impressive and important empirical studies on inequality by political scientists, sociologists, and economists? Should that not be enough?[23] Why study the *historical ideas* associated with inequality? As Siep Stuurman has pressed, "ideas matter and canonized ideas matter a lot."[24] Ideas often communicate elements of the experience of inequality unexamined in quantitative studies.[25] It is one thing to know the extent of inequality. It is another thing to contemplate how it affects rich and poor alike and, further, how it affects political communities more broadly. A benefit of humanistic approaches is the attempt to flesh out the quantitative accounts of inequality with portraits of unequal societies, such as those discussed in the texts studied in this book. A further benefit to humanistic approaches to inequality is the range of arguments available to critique it. An empirical study can tell readers *how much* inequality might exist, but humanistic accounts can reveal whether that degree of inequality is *morally* or *politically alarming* and *why*. Through these canonical thinkers, we are compelled to ponder inequality not just empirically but as it affects our morals, our religious commitments, our relationship with the rule of law, our democratic institutions, and our connections with our neighbors, employers, and coworkers. As Piketty has himself rightly insisted, economics must be supplemented by other disciplinary approaches when studying inequality: "Social scientific research is and always will be tentative and imperfect." A broad approach, however, drawing on sources from across the social sciences and humanities, can "help to redefine the terms of debate, unmask certain preconceived or fraudulent notions, and subject all positions to constant critical scrutiny."[26] This book explores a range of humanistic accounts across a vast historical span that helps to round out our understanding of inequality and perhaps even better grasp the lived experience of inequality. To the extent that thinkers from Plato to Marx provide a normative vocabulary to account for the experience of inequality, their voices are worth hearing.

Further, even though my book studies seven varied historical figures, it is not comprehensive. I realize there is much more to be said about and learned from the history of political thought on this topic. Much can be said about inequality in Aristotle, Cicero, More, Bodin, Harrington, Bacon, Hume, Grouchy, Wollstonecraft, Freud, Rawls, and many others. The fact that I have not written about them here does not suggest otherwise. But one must draw lines somewhere to make a scholarly project manageable. I have selected thinkers who provide some diversity in viewpoints, points of emphasis, and epochs. I hope this book provides a sense of the range of engagements with inequality over a significant period of time, but I remain fully aware that it is merely a sampling of a much greater range of studies. In short, there is more work to be done on economic inequality in the history of political thought.

Moreover, this is a book on Western political thought and not a book on political thought more globally. This limitation is for practical reasons: to engage in a study of inequality across cultures would be to expand its scope beyond my present scholarly abilities. There is much to be learned from engaging with non-Western writings on inequality, as even a small sampling makes clear. Confucius observed, for example, that a wise ruler "worries not about poverty but about uneven distribution"; Lao Tzu cautioned against those "possessed of too much wealth"; Gandhi lamented that "the contrast between the rich and the poor today is a painful sight."[27] There has already been some engagement with their ideas, and doubtless these inquiries should expand in the coming years.

Although this book addresses various remedies for economic inequality, this is not a book of policy prescriptions for at least two reasons. First, in some cases the remedies are beyond what the current political climate can entertain. While Rousseau's proposal for the island nation of Corsica to abolish currency might succeed in radically reducing inequality, for example, such a proposal would almost surely fall on deaf ears. Second, it is difficult to know to what degree the prescriptions advocated by various figures in this book rely on underlying inequalities rightfully rejected today. For example, although Plato's arguments in the *Laws* for greater equality through trade restrictions might surely appeal to some, his solution assumed an underlying slave class. I do not know to what degree his conception of equality rested on that underlying inequality, but I know enough to suggest that at the very least we ought to confront his acceptance of slavery before adopting his prescriptions for addressing economic inequality. This being said, it is not wrong to entertain some of the remedies more broadly. Would it make sense to raise luxury taxes, as Rousseau recommended? Would it make sense to impose a steep estate tax, as Mill suggested? Would it help to educate children vigorously against the dangers of the base selfishness that exacerbate inequality, as advocated by Plato, Hobbes, Rousseau, and Mill? These remedies merit consideration. And to this degree, it is not out of place to evoke historical ideas in pondering our own problems. One must draw from the past with caution, but at the same time it is not implausible that some of those ideas might very well inform contemporary discussions. And even if we did not think any of their remedies were especially applicable today, current debates about inequality would be richer if we endeavored to understand them. Even if we know that Rousseau's plan to eliminate currency and commerce is impracticable in today's large societies, understanding his engagement with inequality can inform a deeper understanding of the nature and experience of inequality. And deeper understandings, one hopes, ultimately inspire more thoughtful remedies.

A common question I encountered while writing this book is why I have sometimes focused on the problematization of *concentrated wealth* rather than *inequality* specifically. Are not wealth and inequality two separate matters? I do not think that they are, for three reasons. First, "economic inequality" was not a term in broad use until after Rousseau. If one were to address only thinkers who used that term, it would exclude almost everyone before him. Such a book could surely be written. But it is also clear that many thinkers preceding Rousseau addressed inequality, only with slightly different vocabulary, often speaking of the related matters of poverty and concentrated wealth. They belong in this history.

The second reason also relates to Rousseau, who once observed, "money is a sign which has a genuine effect only by the inequality of distribution. . . . It is useful only as a sign of inequality" (*Corsica*, 140). "Money" as Rousseau uses the term here is wealth, which is useful primarily as it distinguishes the rich from the middle class or the poor. Or as he explains elsewhere, "the words poor and rich are relative, and wherever men are equal there is neither rich nor poor" (*Observations*, 45).[28] Noted political theorist and Rousseau scholar Judith Shklar has echoed, "Wealth is a relative notion whose meaning depends on the existence of poverty."[29] I often focus on concentrated wealth in these texts as a marker of inequality, just as Rousseau and Shklar assume, because "wealth" only makes sense where some have much and others do not. To speak of haves and have-nots in this fashion is to speak of inequality. Although Plato, Jesus, and Hobbes, for example, do not use the term "inequality," we should not assume they are unconcerned with inequality. Rather, for reasons that will emerge, they very much are.

The third reason I often focus on concentrated wealth, even more than on desperate poverty, is that it is the defining feature of inequality for much of the developed world today. In the United States, for example, Lyndon Johnson announced a War on Poverty in 1964, endeavoring to eradicate desperate poverty. Although this program has been subjected to steady criticism, it is largely inarguable that this series of antipoverty measures coincided with a significant decrease in the desperate poverty associated with malnourishment, homelessness, and lack of access to health care. Medicaid and school lunches, for example, have alleviated some of the worst burdens of absolute poverty. And perhaps resulting from these programs, the rate of absolute poverty in the United States has dropped from 22.4 percent in 1959 to somewhere between 11 percent and 15 percent since the War on Poverty was declared.[30] Yet inequality has nevertheless soared over this same period. As an example, in 1965, the average CEO earned 21.1 times as much as a typical worker at the same company. By 1978, that number grew to 31.4 times; by 1989, it was 61.4 times. The average CEO in 2021 earned 351.1 times as much as a typical worker at the same company.[31] As legal scholar Daniel Markovits has recently insisted, "Economic inequality now distinctly concerns not poverty but wealth."[32] Although I certainly address poverty as described by various thinkers, their descriptions of excessive wealth are arguably even more relevant when pondering inequality today.

I note here that unless otherwise expressly stated, when speaking of "economic inequality," I mean what economists sometimes call "wealth inequality," as opposed to "income inequality." Although income and wealth are often strongly correlated, sometimes they are not. For example, one reason that many billionaires pay relatively low taxes today is because they technically have little income. Rather, their wealth is tied to unrealized capital gains (such as large stock holdings) and enjoyed by borrowing against those assets to fund lavish lifestyles. Although they are surely wealthy by any other definition, they are not "high-income earners," at least in any fashion that meaningfully reflects their vast assets. Further and perhaps most relevant to this book, for much of the tradition of political thought, the notion of "income" is insignificant in comparison with wealth. Those thinkers addressed here are unconcerned with how much money anyone has earned over a single year compared with overall financial standing. Finally, accumulated wealth is simply more consequential than annual income insofar as it considers the compounding effects of inequality over generations. Rousseau was the first major philosopher to comment on this in his *Discourse on Inequality*, but it remains salient today, especially among those interested in understanding how economic and racial inequality interact and reinforce each other.[33] Income provides a proxy for inequality, perhaps, but wealth reveals inequality's structural and enduring impacts.

A final general consideration in this introduction: Why speak of a "plague" in the title? Some readers, in the wake of a historic global pandemic, might object to this book's title, *The Greatest of All Plagues*, hyperalert to the unpleasant realities of an actual plague rather than a metaphorical one. The book title comes from Plato's Athenian Stranger in the *Laws*, and it requires clarification. Strictly speaking, the "greatest of all plagues" for Plato is civil war, which he understands to be the inevitable outcome of significant economic inequality (*Laws*, 744d). Since civil war is a necessary consequence of extreme economic inequality in Plato's account, I do not draw a sharp distinction between them. This connection between inequality and political divisions with the possibility of those divisions degenerating into civil strife is a persistent theme throughout Western political thought— from Plato to Jesus's "house divided" all the way to Marx's class antagonisms culminating in revolution. Although Plato was the first to describe inequality as resulting in this kind of plague, he was far from the last.

Why would Plato refer to the effects of inequality as the greatest of all plagues, especially as an ancient Athenian citizen, who as a child witnessed a historic plague himself? To answer this, we should examine Thucydides and the history of Plato's Athens. To be sure, the plague was physiologically devastating, but arguably more dramatic was its effect on Athenian society itself, which became a community in which citizens abandoned moral restraint and remorselessly turned on one another. Thucydides's readers know that Athens was characterized by economic inequality during the Peloponnesian War, as manifested in a series of class-based revolutions, even though it was less economically divided than most other Greek city-states at the time. It is quite possible that a plague of this nature, though miserable in any context, was worse in an economically and socially divided society. Recall that for Plato, who was raised during the war, cities marked by radical inequality are two cities rather than one—"a city of the poor and one of the rich" (*Republic*, 551d). In this context, it may be easier to understand or at least contextualize the particular failures of Athens during the plague. Indeed, many suspect that this relationship of inequality and political turmoil has been true in the United States and other unequal societies throughout the COVID-19 pandemic. Consider the tumult of the past decade—police killings of citizens, protests, riots, fights over vaccine and masking policies, heightened partisanship, flirtations with authoritarianism, and even insurrection. Would America have been spared all of this were it not already suffering from significant inequality? I cannot say for certain. But neither do I see any reason to ignore Plato's admonition that inequality fosters pathological divisiveness—the worst of plagues, as it makes every other setback, including pandemics, more burdensome.

My chapters follow a general pattern. I first sketch some historical background for each thinker to provide context and perhaps some insight into what might have made inequality salient. Then I identify the general ambitions of those figures and their respective moral, political, and, in the case of Jesus, religious thought. I next depict the nature and effects of inequality as understood by each figure studied in this book. This includes attention to the effects of inequality on the rich and poor as individuals and then a description of inequality's broader social and political effects. Finally, I outline what they think could or should be done about inequality. In some cases, as with Plato, Rousseau, Mill, and Marx, these solutions will have been expressly presented as such by the authors themselves. In other cases, I draw from their arguments to see what resources they offer—in the context of their own thought—to combat the problems

they have described. I have labored not to take excess liberty in constructing their remedies.

The first substantive chapter addresses Plato, since he is the first major
political philosopher in the Western tradition. He will be among the most
unexpected figures included in this book because he is typically understood as radically inegalitarian. This is not wrong, at least insofar as one
considers Socrates's politics in Plato's *Republic*—a city-state in which all
political power is concentrated in the hands of a few supremely virtuous
philosophers. Yet embedded throughout this familiar text is a systemic critique of economic inequality. To appreciate why inequality worries Plato, it
is necessary to understand what I take to be his overarching goal, as shared
in his two major political dialogues, the *Republic* and the *Laws*. The primary interlocutors in those dialogues, Socrates and the Athenian Stranger,
respectively, both insist on the centrality of civic harmony, friendship, and
fraternal bonds. Understanding his commitment to civic harmony in the
dialogues reveals how Plato's exploration of inequality discloses myriad
moral and social concerns. His *Republic* is peppered with passages detail-
ing these problems. Yet it is in his later dialogue, the *Laws*, where he
most extensively interrogates the pathologies of inequality, according to
his Athenian Stranger, which extend to faction, disharmony, and civil war.
The Stranger considers many measures to treat the malady of inequality,
broadly divided into two approaches: ideal and practical. The ideal solution, applicable primarily to unsettled, new communities lacking a history of
inequality, is to distribute wealth such that the richest citizens have no more
than four times the wealth of the poorest. But for settled cities, already
burdened by inequality, such measures would alienate and divide citizens
more than they would harmonize them. This does not lead Plato to argue,
however, that inequality is off-limits for legislators. It *must* be reduced but
only gradually and incrementally by patient persuasion of the wealthiest
citizens that their city would be improved if only wealth were more widely
dispersed.

The second chapter addresses what can be learned about economic
inequality from the New Testament. Understanding its lessons requires
understanding the nature of inequality as found in Jesus's Roman Palestine, a community characterized by extreme wealth contrasted with
extreme poverty. It further necessitates understanding the Hebrew laws
of Sabbatical and Jubilee, which required, among other measures, that all
debts be forgiven once every seven years and all property restored to an
equitable distribution once every half century. Emerging from this Jewish
context, Jesus insists on the love of God as the highest aspiration for his

disciples. Yet the love of money hinders divine love—one can love God *or* mammon. He appeals to Jewish law and tradition to celebrate the poor and scorn the rich, culminating in his pronouncement of a "year of the Lord's favor" (Luke 4:19), a Jubilee year in which debts must be forgiven and property be redistributed.

The third chapter treats Thomas Hobbes, who like Plato is rarely understood as an egalitarian. He is typically interpreted as a philosopher desperate to distance society from the unhealthy equality in the state of nature that is synonymous with civil war. The state of nature is after all a state of "equality," which gives rise to competition, diffidence, and ultimately war—Hobbes's greatest evil. His highest good, therefore, such as it is, is his first law of nature, peace, which can only be achieved by concentrating all civic authority in the hands of a sovereign or "Leviathan." Yet this Leviathan, to protect subjects, must fend off all competitors for sovereign authority—and among the greatest threats to that authority are the wealthy, riches "gathered in too much abundance in one or a few private men" (*Leviathan*, 29.19). For Hobbes, great poverty results in "*resentment* and *envy*," which in turn "are the sources of sedition and war" (*Citizen*, 5.5); concentrated wealth generates a "presumption of impunity" inconsistent with the rule of law (*Leviathan*, 27.30). He allows that the Leviathan may distribute or redistribute property to prevent these extremes, hence protecting the peace that is his ultimate goal.

The inclusion of Jean-Jacques Rousseau in chapter 4 will be less surprising to most readers since he authored the celebrated *Discourse on the Origin of Inequality*. The Genevan autodidact diagnosed inequality in the context of an emerging market economy, where myriad inequalities are ultimately reduced to the inequality of wealth, since it is with riches that one can purchase all other sources of distinction, such as power and public esteem. Perhaps more than anyone, Rousseau probes what he takes to be the pathologies of economic inequality, which makes "all men competitors, rivals, or rather enemies." The inevitable outcome of inequality, as he understands it, is a "handful of powerful and rich men at the pinnacle of greatness and fortune, while the masses grovel in obscurity and misery." The former soon find that their greatest pleasures come from flamboyantly enjoying things they know to be beyond the reach of others (*SD*, 184). This inequality is a direct affront to Rousseau's highest political value, the general will, which tends "to equality" (*SC*, 2.1, 59).[34] It is therefore one of the chief objectives of civil government, according to Rousseau, to distribute wealth such that no citizen has either too much or too little. But like Plato, he understands that some communities will be better

prepared for equality than others. For those republics relatively uncorrupted by both luxury and inequality, like Corsica, currency and commerce
can be mostly banned to obviate inequality. But even for societies already
corrupted by commerce and inequality, stringent capitation and luxury
taxes must be employed to slowly promote greater equality. "Taxes such as
these, which relieve poverty and burden riches," he insists, "are the way to
forestall the ever-widening inequality of fortunes" (*PE*, 36).

For many readers, the inclusion of Adam Smith in a book about historical criticisms of poverty and inequality will be a surprise. Yet in chapter 5,
I draw on a growing body of literature of Smith studies to sketch the Scottish
philosopher and political economist as among the most powerful critics of
both poverty and inequality, as they tend to undermine his declared goal
of promoting "mutual sympathy," as described early in his *Theory of Moral
Sentiments*. Not only does poverty rob its victims of necessities, but he also
insists that it demoralizes them, making them feel shame, rendering them
objects "nobody thinks it is worth while to look at" (*TMS*, 63, 68). Smith
worries that inequality emboldens the rich, marginalizes the poor, and fosters both legal and moral codes structured to benefit the rich and punish the
poor systematically. Great wealth inflames the rich with vanity and inspires
an unhealthy selfishness. At the same time, as he observes in his *Wealth of
Nations*, the "affluence of the rich excites the indignation of the poor, who
are often driven by want, and prompted by envy, to invade his possessions"
(*WN*, 710). Smith's concerns about inequality are indisputable. Yet his solutions to inequality raise questions about whether they are adequate to the
problems he outlined. Although he allows a degree of progressive taxation
and other modest measures, he ultimately invests greater effort in ameliorating poverty through a growing economy and presumably growing wages,
even as wealthy employers grow richer.

John Stuart Mill is another British political economist with a reputation
for free market enthusiasm, who yet represents a stern critic of inequality.
He is perhaps best known as a proponent of the principle of utility that
prioritizes promoting the greatest happiness of the community. I explore
his critique of inequality and his analysis of how it undermines utility in
chapter 6. For him, inequality corrupts the rich and poor alike, rendering
the former selfish brutes and the latter desperate, malnourished victims,
increasingly tempted by circumstances to satisfy their needs through
crime. At the root of these problems, for Mill, is how inequality inflames
selfishness. As he laments in his *Principles of Political Economy*, "All
privileged and powerful classes, as such, have used their power in the interest of their own selfishness, and have indulged their self-importance in

despising, and not in lovingly caring for, those who were, in their estimation, degraded, by being under the necessity of working for their benefit."
The selfishness bred in unequal societies turns rich and poor against
one another, such that it "will sooner or later become insupportable to
the employing classes, to live in close and hourly contact with persons
whose interests and feelings are in hostility to them" (*Principles*, 760, 767).
Mill explores several solutions to address the maladies he associates with
inequality, including worker cooperatives, an education program to dis-
courage the underlying selfishness, and a steep inheritance tax aimed at
the radical redistribution of resources.

The final philosopher under consideration is Karl Marx, who represents
the logical culmination of this narrative insofar as he is broadly understood
to be the West's greatest critic of inequality. He is surely the most obvious
figure to appear in this book. Yet there has never hitherto been a systematic
study of his treatment of economic inequality—its origins, causes, effects,
and remedies. Chapter 7 begins by acknowledging his highest political
aspiration, which is to free the proletariat from domination by the bourgeoisie, and proceeds to explain how intrinsic economic inequality is to
maintaining that domination. I focus on many passages largely ignored by
nonspecialists, including his discussion of the myth underlying inequality
that justifies capitalism—that the rich are industrious and virtuous while
the poor are lazy and shiftless—as well as the brutally violent acts involved
in colonialism and slavery that ignited bourgeois inequality. The chapter
further explores, through careful exposition of *Capital*, the ways in which
inequality affects both rich and poor, physically and morally. It also untan-
gles the sometimes-confusing fact that Marx often speaks ill of "equality,"
associating it with bourgeois notions of legal equality that are perversely
used to justify radical economic inequality in capitalist economies. The
chapter concludes with careful attention to his remedy, arguably the most
radical one offered by any figure treated in this book: overturning the
economic system itself. Although it is wrong, as some have suggested, to
assume that Marx endorses violent revolution in all cases as a means for
shaking off capitalism and the inequalities inevitably attached to it, he nevertheless is committed to overturning the economies and the societies they
support—and sometimes, for Marx, this will require force.

The various approaches to understanding, problematizing, and addressing inequality will of course vary from figure to figure. Plato, for example,
is deeply concerned about the effects of inequality on individual souls.
Marx is concerned about how inequality leads to domination and, further,
inhibits individual freedom. Each thinker needs to be understood in his

own terms. This being said, there are many themes that recur throughout. Prominent among these is greed or *pleonexia*, which is found in Plato and Marx, as well as in most of these thinkers. The insatiable greed they describe plays a significant role in the growth of inequality, and for many thinkers in this book, its suppression represents a significant goal. Another recurrent theme is the importance of achieving what is variously described as civic friendship, harmony, fraternity, or what John Stuart Mill calls, "unity with our fellow creatures" (*Utilitarianism*, 32). Nearly every thinker discussed at length in this book has an objective along these lines, and virtually all of them understand extreme inequality to threaten this goal. As Plato insisted, "If (as we presume) the city must avoid the greatest of all plagues, which has been more correctly termed 'civil war' than 'faction,' then neither harsh poverty nor wealth should exist among any of its citizens. For both these conditions breed both civil war and faction" (*Laws*, 744d). A necessary condition for escaping faction and civil war over the long run, for Plato and many others, is to limit inequality to foster a community of shared interests and affective bonds. The more inequality, the more at odds are the various citizens and the more unstable the political community.

This survey of canonical texts insists, contrary to those holding inequality to be benign today, that great wealth disparities cannot be dismissed. These concerns have been expressed from the very birth of Western political philosophy itself and can be found in its most venerated texts. These are not ancillary to the Western tradition—they represent much of that tradition's core. Further, these worries cannot be reduced to any single school of thought. They inform most of the major traditions of political thought from antiquity through the nineteenth century. Complaints about inequality cannot simply be dismissed as the unique concern of one branch of political philosophy.[35] The consensus found among these various schools and approaches suggests that inequality must be taken seriously, especially in the face of recent trends. Finally, the attention paid in these texts to wealth concentration and inequality, in addition to poverty, suggests that if "the canon" has anything to teach us about these matters, it is that although housing and feeding the poor is certainly important, this may not be an adequate policy response. To the degree that inequality stokes social and political divisions, inequality itself demands careful monitoring—or at least this is what significant voices from the Western tradition suggest. To the extent that we still take these texts seriously in the twenty-first century, we should hear them out.

CHAPTER ONE

Plato

"THE GREATEST OF ALL PLAGUES"

IT HAS OFTEN BEEN REMARKED that Plato ranks among the greatest elitists in Western civilization.[1] This reputation is largely associated with his celebrated *Republic* in which his Socrates elevates to political power "those few people who are born with the best natures and [who] receive the best education" (*Republic*, 431c). By virtue of their rare talents and training, his philosopher rulers assume godlike authority over their less gifted fellows in the names of justice and goodness.[2] It is for this reason that many philosophers, such as Karl Popper, have railed against Plato for his "hostility towards the equalitarian creed."[3] R.H.S. Crossman went so far as to characterize Plato's kallipolis as "but another variant of oligarchy."[4] To be sure, the *Republic* depicts a kind of inegalitarian society, whereby political power is exercised by a small elite. This characterization, however, fails to acknowledge another, profoundly egalitarian dimension of his thought. Despite the epistemic and political inequality underlying political institutions in what Socrates refers to as Glaucon's kallipolis, or beautiful city, Plato's major political works reveal a pervasive and even foundational economic egalitarianism,[5] outlined in the utopian *Republic* and in the later and more practical *Laws*. It is in the latter that he outlines in greatest detail the dangers of inequality and the foundational necessity of resolving the problem before commencing with legislation.

This chapter traces the concern with the problem of inequality in these dialogues by understanding the dangers of inequality in the ancient Greek world, before turning to Plato's problematization of it in his major political dialogues. As I argue below, Plato's desire for economic equality is fundamental and systemic—to the point of characterizing inequality as

[18]

fostering "the greatest of all plagues" (*Laws*, 744d), insofar as it hastens civic divisions ultimately fatal to republics. Although there are important differences in his treatment of economic inequality in the *Republic* and the *Laws*, they share central themes. Both dialogues suggest that economic inequality undermines the virtue and civic harmony required for thriving regimes. The greater this inequality, the less stable the regime. Plato's attention to inequality is hence fundamental, which makes it striking that scholars have not made it the focus of extended examination.[6] In the following pages, I explain that addressing economic inequality is, in fact, necessary and central to his political programs both in the *Republic* and the *Laws*.

The Ancient Greek Experience of Inequality and Oligarchy

SOLON IN ATHENS

Book 8 of Plato's *Republic* outlines the various possible regime types, ordered both by their moral value and their chronological unfolding with aristocracy being both first and best, followed by timocracy, oligarchy, democracy, and tyranny. Readers are often drawn to the transition from oligarchy to democracy:

> Since the rulers rule in it [oligarchy] because they own a lot, I suppose they are not willing to enact laws to prevent young people who have become intemperate from spending and wasting their wealth, so that by buying and making loans on property of such people, the rulers themselves become even richer and more honored. (*Republic*, 555c)[7]

Socrates speculates that intemperance among the young and poor and greed among the rich and powerful inevitably culminate in extreme economic inequality, "some of them in debt, some disenfranchised, some both—hating and plotting against those who have acquired their property, and all the others as well; passionately longing for revolution" (*Republic*, 555d–e).

What relatively few appreciate about this passage from the *Republic* is that Socrates is merely recounting a history of Athens that would have resonated with his contemporaries—namely, how the Athenian lawgiver Solon (ca. 630 BCE–ca. 560 BCE) was required to rewrite the polis's fundamental laws.[8] On Plutarch's account, approximately two centuries prior to Plato's birth, Athens suffered a political crisis:

The Athenians . . . fell into their old quarrels about the government, there being as many different parties as there were diversities in the country. The Hill quarter favored democracy, the Plain, oligarchy, and those that lived by the Seaside stood for a mixed sort of government, and so hindered either of the other parties from prevailing. And the disparity of fortune between the rich and the poor, at that time, also reached its height; so that the city seemed to be in a truly dangerous condition, and no other means for freeing it from disturbances and settling it to be possible but a despotic power. All the people were indebted to the rich; and either they tilled the land for their creditors, paying them a sixth part of the increase, and were, therefore, called Hectemordii and Thetes, or else they engaged their body for the debt, and might be seized, and either sent into slavery at home, or sold to strangers; some (for no law forbade it) were forced to sell their children, or flee their country to avoid the cruelty of their creditors; but the most part and the bravest of them began to combine together and encourage one another to stand to it, to choose a leader, to liberate the condemned debtors, divide the land, and change the government.[9]

Just as Plato's Socrates describes oligarchic decline in book 8 of the *Republic*, ancient Athens, well before either Plato or Socrates, had striking economic inequality. The rich were not content with their wealth, seeking to expand it at the expense of the poor. As Aristotle observes, Solon "always attaches the overall blame for the strife to the rich."[10] When the poor's debts exceeded their cash holdings, they were compelled to sell themselves and their children into slavery, which hastened the appeal of revolution. What is there to lose when one is squarely confronting a life of slavery for oneself - and one's children?

It was in such dire straits that the Athenians appealed to Solon, who was chosen not only because he was "the wisest of the Athenians" but also because he was "the only one not implicated in the troubles, that he had not joined in the exactions of the rich, and was not involved in the necessities of the poor."[11] Solon was therefore uniquely capable of winning the confidence of both factions. The wealthy championed him as an aristocrat who would protect their holdings. The poor saw him as an ally because of his reputation for honesty, who would redistribute all property on the principle of numerical or absolute equality. He took a middle course, which secured the peace. To achieve this, he neither protected the credit of the wealthy nor redistributed property but rather remitted the remaining debts of the poor (*seisacthea*) and prohibited the practice of selling oneself into slavery as a debt security. As Plutarch reports, "In this he pleased neither party, for the rich were angry for their money, and the poor that the land was not divided."[12] Plutarch suggests this solution was imperfect but that in such cases the ideal would have been the enemy of the good: "And, therefore, when he [Solon] was afterward asked if he had left the Athenians the best laws that could be given, he replied, 'The best they could receive.'"[13] An ideal solution for either the rich or poor—whether it amounted to enforcing the debts owed to the creditors or enforcing absolute equality—would have alienated enough citizens that no lasting social harmony could likely follow.

Plutarch subsequently elaborates that the relative economic equality Solon introduced via the *seisacthea* was necessary for securing democratic liberty. For Solon, liberty requires more than mere legal equality but also a degree of economic equality: "for a mere law to give all men equal rights is but useless, if the poor must sacrifice those rights to their debts, and, in the very seats and sanctuaries of equality, the courts of justice, the offices of state, and the public discussions, be more than anywhere at the beck and bidding of the rich."[14] Legal equality is necessary but insufficient for political liberty since liberty requires a degree of economic equality. Equality need not be absolute, but the poor must have enough to be secure in their persons, enjoy equality under the law, and have a meaningful voice in policy deliberations. Plutarch suggests that Solon was able to achieve all this with his reforms. Citizens reclaimed their liberty, meaningful legal equality, and political equality. But perhaps above all, Solon's reforms dissolved the looming threats of a violent class-based revolution.

LYCURGUS IN SPARTA

Athens was not the only ancient city-state burdened by significant economic inequality. Its ultimate vanquisher in the Peloponnesian War, Sparta, faced a similar challenge in the seventh century BCE.[15] Plutarch, again, describes the conditions:

> There was an extreme inequality amongst them [the Spartans], and their state was overloaded with a multitude of indigent and necessitous persons while its whole wealth was centered upon a very few.

This inequality engendered "arrogance and envy, luxury and crime,"[16] resulting in "anarchy and confusion,"[17] necessitating the return of its native son, Lycurgus, who had been traveling throughout the Mediterranean, absorbing the constitutional principles and lessons of Crete, Persia, and Egypt. It was with the benefit of his worldly observations that he implemented the radical reforms necessary to refound Sparta.

Whereas Solon chartered a middle course between stasis and radical egalitarianism in Athens, Lycurgus's reforms were radically egalitarian. The latter's view was not merely that economic inequality threatened Sparta's political stability but that it also threatened the very character of its citizens.[18] Plutarch describes the principles underlying Lycurgus's reforms:

> To the end, therefore, that he might expel from the state arrogance and envy, luxury, and crime, and those yet more inveterate diseases of want and superfluity, he obtained of them to renounce their properties, and to consent to a new division of the land, and that they should live all together on an equal footing; merit to be their only road to eminence, and the disgrace of the evil, and credit of worthy acts, their one measure of difference between man and man.[19]

His reforms fell into four categories: (1) the redistribution of land, (2) the elimination of currency, (3) the expulsion of luxury, and (4) the institution of common meals. Perhaps the most striking of Lycurgus's reforms was his confiscation of all property and subsequent division of Sparta into equal plots of land to be distributed to all households, a measure unthinkable for Solon in Athens. Each lot was large and fertile enough to produce sufficient food, oil, and wine to maintain the strength and good health for its respective families. Lycurgus is reputed to have remarked on observing this equal distribution in practice, "Methinks all Laconia looks like one family estate just divided among a number of brothers."[20]

Another measure was equalizing wealth through the expulsion of gold and silver coins. The point of precious metals, according to Lycurgus, was to facilitate "odious distinctions of inequality."[21] He mandated that all such coins be rendered to the state, and in return citizens would receive a commensurate amount of the new currency made of heavy iron. This currency reform had multiple beneficial effects, according to Plutarch. First, it dramatically reduced commerce since carrying and trading the heavy iron was hardly worth the trouble. Second, it reduced greed since one could hardly store massive quantities of a heavy metal. Third, it dramatically reduced theft since thieves could scarcely pilfer hundreds of pounds of metal without literally herculean efforts. Fourth, the intrinsic undesirability of iron tended to equalize wealth across households since there was little intrinsic incentive to accumulate it.

Another of Lycurgus's radical economic reforms was the elimination of luxuries more generally. This followed naturally from the banishment of silver and gold. Without easily transferrable currency, "there was now no more means of purchasing foreign goods and small wares; merchants sent no shiploads into Laconian ports; no rhetoric-master, no itinerate fortune-teller, no harlot-monger, or gold or silversmith, engraver, or jeweler . . . so that luxury, deprived little by little of that which fed and fomented it, wasted to nothing and died away of itself."[22] And without luxuries, to the extent that there were still rich people, there was little they could do to distinguish themselves. They could not adorn their homes with luxuries to inflame their neighbors' envy. As a result, the neighbors lived together more harmoniously, resembling the large family of brothers Lycurgus sought.

A final relevant reform was mandatory common meals for all citizens. Plutarch places special stress on this now seemingly remote and obscure practice of common meals, which Lycurgus conceived as a "blow against luxury and the desire of riches."[23] The point of the common meals was to minimize the advantages of wealth. The wealthy could not enjoy the advantages of their fortunes by eating refined meals in the privacy of their own homes. They had to eat the same food as their poorer neighbors. All of this had the effect of reducing their arrogance and also eliminating their neighbors' envy—again, rendering citizens more like siblings than the factious citizens who preceded Lycurgus's reforms.[24]

Although Plutarch reports that Lycurgus succeeded in gaining citizens' consent to these reforms, he also acknowledges that this consent was neither immediate nor universal. At an early stage of the reform process, a gang of wealthy citizens approached Lycurgus wielding stones "so that at length he was forced to run out of the market-place, and make to sanctuary to save his life." He escaped all of these aggrieved oligarchs, save one, Alcander, who got close enough to Lycurgus to poke out one of his eyes. The authorities thereafter caught the offender and brought him to Lycurgus for sentencing. Contrary to all expectations, Lycurgus brought Alcander into his circle, offering him the opportunity to observe his "gentleness and calmness of temper" as well as in his "extraordinary sobriety and indefatigable industry,"[25] such that Alcander ultimately became Lycurgus's most zealous admirer.

THE RETURN OF INEQUALITY
IN ATHENS AND SPARTA

Lycurgus's and Solon's reforms were surely familiar to educated Greeks of Plato's generation. Aristotle, for example, acknowledges that "laws were made by Solon and others prohibiting an individual from possessing as much land as he pleased."[26] Indeed, Aristotle would go on to describe Solon's reforms—economic and otherwise—in great detail in his *Constitution of Athens*. Despite this, the economic reforms of Lycurgus and Solon were not enduring. In Sparta, Lycurgus's reforms were largely undone by the Spartan king Agis II, who reintroduced gold and silver into the republic and subsequently "all those mischiefs which attend the immoderate desire of riches." His general, Lysander, with his victory in the Peloponnesian War brought to Sparta "rich spoils" along with "avarice and luxury," hence subverting "the laws and ordinances of Lycurgus."[27] With wealth and luxury once again attainable, records Plutarch,

> terror and the laws were now to keep guard over the citizens' houses, to prevent any money from entering into them; but their minds could no longer be expected to remain superior to the desire of it when wealth in general was thus set up to be striven after, as a high and noble object.[28]

When culture and circumstances conspire against wealth accumulation, Plutarch reasons, there is less need for imposing and threatening laws. By increasing inequality, the most effective restraints on citizens' rapacity becomes the threat of harsh punishment. He implies, to be sure, that it is much better to live without this looming threat of violent retaliation. Far better to be free of the temptations of wealth than to succumb to those temptations and await the attending severe sanctions.

The decline of economic equality in Athens was less dramatic, if only perhaps because its parity was less austere and demanding than Sparta's. But it is clear from the historical record that the relative economic equality that Solon sought to establish would not endure. By the time of Socrates and Plato in the fifth century BCE—which also coincided with the age of Agis and Lysander in Sparta—Athens also had distinct economic classes and some very wealthy citizens. In the case of Athens this was perhaps more likely than it was in Sparta because, again, Solon's reforms were less extreme than Lycurgus's—both regarding redistribution and in their respective attempts to remold civic values. Solon did not redistribute property; he did not banish currency; he did not banish luxury; he did not banish commerce. All of these facilitated the establishment and maintenance of economic disparity. It was on the basis of his great wealth and the connections it afforded, for example, that Nicias ascended to power in Athens during the Peloponnesian War. According to Plutarch, the wealthy had a clear sense of its identity and interests as a class by this time and promoted Nicias as one of their own to check the less predictable and more populist Cleon.[29] It was obvious enough by this time, according to Josiah

Ober, that "the unequal distribution of wealth among citizens was perhaps the most problematic condition of social inequality pertaining in democratic Athens."[30]

Athens experienced a resurgence of inequality in its extended war with Sparta. And with the growth of inequality came a greater sense of *class* identity, as contrasted with *civic* identity. One voice to emerge in this period was the anonymous "Old Oligarch," who expressed a genuine frustration with the poor majority who exercised democratic control of the polis. The Athenian constitution, as he understood it, "assign[s] more to the worst persons, to the poor, and to the popular types than to the good men."[31] Such people are defined not only by their lack of money but also by a corresponding lack of education. The latter, however, does not imply that the poor misunderstand their own interests. They understand their interests as diametrically opposed to their wealthy fellow citizens. They therefore use their democratic authority to impose laws "not so much concerned with justice as with their own advantage."[32] Given the opportunity, according to the oligarch, they would "disenfranchise the aristocrats, take away their money, expel and kill them, whereas they promote the interests of the lower class."[33] This sometimes manifests itself, the oligarch notes incredulously, in the people possessing finer public baths and other amenities than the wealthy can afford for themselves. Further, the poor get drunk on their own power, mocking those of wealth and high birth, while prohibiting mockery of the poor in dramas and comedies. As political theorist Ryan K. Balot has observed, the oligarch does not object to the raw selfishness of the poor, so much as the fact that the oligarchs lack the power to oppose them. Old Oligarch assumes that everyone is fundamentally greedy and selfish rather than charitable or generous.[34] For him, inequality is a natural fact of civic life, along with the greed, selfishness, and social tensions it engenders. The aim of politics, as he understands it, is to seize power so that one enjoys the benefits it confers. This represents a significant departure from Solon's and Lycurgus's goals.

Late fifth-century Athens experienced repeated revolutions, including two forged by oligarchs to protect and advance their financial interests against the poor. The first occurred in 411, when a group of wealthy citizens had grown weary of democracy. Upon seizing power, they limited political power to four hundred wealthy citizens, effectively excluding the poor. As Balot has suggested, these oligarchs "were self-consciously enacting the ideals of those who promoted the politics of greed and self-interest."[35] One of their first tasks was to kill the democratic leader of Athens, Androcles. By all accounts, their primary ambitions were to consolidate oligarchic power and reduce their own taxes. Indeed, Antiphon, one of the revolution's primary architects, advocated using justice for one's "own advantage" rather than treating it as an ideal to which all must be held equally accountable.[36]

A second oligarchic revolution commenced seven years later at the close of the Peloponnesian War. Sparta had just defeated Athens, after which a group of thirty oligarchs—known simply as "the Thirty"—seized power and ruled tyrannically. They were more extreme than their predecessors, murdering up to 5 percent of the Athenian population over their thirteen-month rule, terrorizing survivors with further threats to win submission. Among their targets were not only the poor who opposed their rule but even other democratically sympathetic oligarchs, confiscating their possessions to enhance their own personal wealth. As the classicist Andrew Wolpert has observed, the Thirty understood establishing oligarchy required refounding Athens's political culture through "fear, force, and intimidation."[37] Scholars estimate that the two oligarchic revolutions produced thousands of casualties.[38] Thus the hard-earned lessons of Solon and Lycurgus had been largely lost to their respective cities. Those lessons, however, registered with Plato.

Plato's Republic

Plato's political works reveal acute awareness of the economic challenges burdening Athens and Sparta, as well as general sympathy with Solon and Lycurgus. Inequality is not to be celebrated as the happy result of growing economies and prospering societies, nor is it an inevitable fact of nature. It rather represents an avoidable pathology threatening to undermine thriving communities. Plato's observations on inequality emerge in his two longest dialogues—the *Republic* and the *Laws*—as outlined respectively by Socrates and the Athenian Stranger. The former sketches some of the difficulties associated with inequality and, to a limited degree, some measures for addressing it. The latter elaborates significantly on the burdens of inequality and the means of suppressing it.

THE FOUNDATIONS OF THE KALLIPOLIS: VIRTUE AND FRATERNITY

Plato's most celebrated dialogue, the *Republic*, outlines a just city in order that its characters might ultimately understand what it means to be just individuals.[39] The city and soul parallel each other in their components and virtues. Plato's Socrates outlines a city populated by three classes of citizens: workers, soldiers, and philosopher rulers. The city's four virtues reside in understanding their respective roles and relationships. Courage, for example, is exemplified in the temperament and actions of the soldiers, who have the "power to preserve through everything its belief that the things, and the sorts of things, that should inspire terror are the very things, and sorts of things, that the lawgiver declared to be such in the course of educating it" (*Republic*, 429bc). Courageous soldiers are neither deterred nor distracted from this course by the fear of pain or the allure of pleasures. They pursue their mission with a single-minded determination cultivated by their carefully crafted education. The virtue of calculative rationality (*logismos*) is located in the ruling class—those called philosopher rulers.[40] To the extent that rulers possess wisdom, they will "not deliberate about some particular thing in the city, but about the city as a whole, and about its internal relations and its relations with other cities" (*Republic*, 428cd).[41] A city possesses the virtue of moderation or temperance insofar as "the appetites of the masses—the inferior people—are mastered by the wisdom and appetites of the few—the best people" (*Republic*, 431cd). Finally, a city exercises the virtue of justice to the degree that all citizens perform the jobs for which they are suited without encroaching on the proper tasks of others.

A thriving city possesses all of the above virtues. One might ask, however, how to identify a successful city? Plato's interlocutors identify two measures: fraternal bonds and the happiness of the whole. Regarding the latter, Socrates specifies,

> in establishing our city, we are not looking to make any one group in it outstandingly happy, but to make the whole city so far as possible. For we thought that we would be most likely to find justice in such a city, and injustice, by contrast, in the one governed worst. And we thought that by observing both cities, we would be able to decide the question we have been inquiring into for so long. At the moment, then, we take ourselves to be forming a happy city—not separating off a few happy people and putting them in it, but make the city as a whole happy. (*Republic*, 420bc)

Following Lycurgus's model, a flourishing city therefore does not elevate and prioritize the happiness of a single class of citizens. Cities benefiting individuals or classes of citizens at the expense of others are, by definition, unhappy failures.

A thriving city also promotes fraternal bonds between fellow citizens.[42] The greatest good of any city, Socrates insists, is that which "binds it together and makes it one." To achieve this, he describes a community of pleasures and pains in which "all the citizens feel more or less the same joy or pain at the same gains and losses" (*Republic*, 462b).⁴³ He subsequently explains that a state should be evaluated as an "entire partnership" akin to a biological organism (*Republic*, 462c). The pain I might suffer when stepping on a rusty nail cannot be dismissed as merely my foot's problem; it is a problem for my whole being. The same should be true, Socrates suggests, when some segment of the kallipolis suffers insult or injury. A just community cannot dismiss offenses and injustices against particular parties and classes as "someone else's problem"; it is *everyone's* problem. This is the disposition he seeks to cultivate in his ruling class, who in turn are to transmit it to their citizens.

This principle explains some of the *Republic*'s otherwise vexing elements. Consider, for example, the noble lie, which includes the myth of autochthony—the myth that all citizens were born out of the earth's soil, effectively from the same mother, such that all must "regard the other citizens as their earthborn brothers" (*Republic*, 414e).⁴⁴ Socrates also aggressively promotes the community of pleasures and pains in his abolition of private families for the ruling class. Philosopher rulers are prohibited from having their own families in order to promote the sense that the entire community is their family: a ruler "will regard everyone he meets as a brother or a sister, a father or a mother, a son or a daughter, or some ancestor or descendant of these" (*Republic*, 463c). Socrates introduces these measures to promote the fraternal bonds that thriving states require.

The opposite of fraternity is factions, clusters of like-minded citizens who understand that their interests differ from their fellow citizens'. There are many possible proximate causes of factions, but early in the *Republic*, Socrates identifies injustice as a fundamental source: "Injustice causes faction, hatred, and quarrels among men, while justice brings friendship and a sense of common purpose." He continues, "If the function of injustice is to produce hatred wherever it occurs, then whenever it arises, whether among free men or slaves, won't it make them hate one another, form factions, and be unable to achieve any common purpose?" (*Republic*, 351de). So whatever contributes to injustice often produces factions.

ECONOMIC INEQUALITY AND ITS CIVIC COSTS IN THE *REPUBLIC*

Knowing the priority of fraternity contextualizes Socrates's remarks about economic inequality in the *Republic*. The most detailed discussion occurs in book 4, where he describes "two [cities] . . . which are at war with one another: the city of the poor and that of the rich" (*Republic*, 422e–423a). This is specifically with regard to the prospects of success in warfare—one of those common enterprises to which he elsewhere alludes (e.g., *Republic*, 351de). Indeed, undoubtedly reflecting on Athens's recent loss to Sparta in the Peloponnesian War, Socrates observes that economically unequal cities are easier to conquer than those characterized by relative equality.[45] Extreme economic inequality, for Socrates, divides cities, inflaming private interests while muting the common good. The wealthy understand their interests as opposed to the poor; the poor understand their interests as opposed to the wealthy. This is why rich and poor citizens alike crave "revolution" (*Republic*, 422a).[46]

The greatest inequality emerges under oligarchy, where "the rich rule and the poor man does not participate in ruling" (*Republic*, 550d). Such regimes are effectively two cities rather than one. Their disparate classes are so opposed, according to Socrates, that they fear one another more than they fear external enemies. And because oligarchies establish the rule of the wealthy, they arguably violate all of Plato's civic virtues. Since the ruling class is wealthy and promotes its own interests, it violates the virtue of wisdom, which requires that rulers prioritize "the city as a whole, and . . . its internal relations." It violates the virtue of temperance insofar as the city's worse elements rule its better ones. Indeed, as Socrates clarifies, "you cannot honor wealth in a city and maintain temperance in the citizens at the same time" (*Republic*, 555c). Oligarchy violates justice insofar as citizens fail to perform the jobs for which they are suited and meddle with others—manifested in the fact that oligarchs effectively prevent philosophers from ruling. As such, an oligarchy invites unsavory characters, such as thieves, "pickpockets, temple robbers, and craftsmen of all sorts of evil" (*Republic*, 552d). Finally, oligarchies lack courage to the degree that in unequal cities, the rich fear arming the poor to fight their wars, "having more to fear [from] them than [from their] enemy" (*Republic*, 551d).

Oligarchies ultimately culminate in the circumstances described at the opening of this chapter—the wealthy collecting the last pennies from the pockets of the poor through unsavory high-interest loans since they have "neglected everything except making money" (*Republic*, 556b). This consuming desire of the rich to enhance their wealth at the expense of all other concerns is the vice of *pleonexia* (πλεονεξια), often translated as "greed." Those infected with *pleonexia* are reduced to desiring more without the possibility of satisfaction. No matter how much they acquire, they will want more. The desires for money and power are perhaps the most susceptible to *pleonexia*.[47] One can usefully contrast the lust for money with gluttony. The physical structure of the stomach limits the amount of food one can consume. But this is not true of wealth and power because there is no threshold beyond which one cannot want even more. The lure of boundless wealth means that one can be ruled by *pleonexia* for an entire lifetime.[48]

In the case Socrates describes, since the debtors cannot satisfy their creditors with money and eventually refuse to pay with their freedom, the poor begin plotting against the rich, thinking to themselves, "These men are ours for the taking; they are good for nothing" (*Republic*, 556de). Concealed factions become overt enemies, resulting in a violent revolution. And because they have numbers on their side, the poor are victorious, killing and expelling the rich, establishing a democracy in the embers of the fallen oligarchy.

EFFECTS ON THE SOUL

The effects of extreme wealth, poverty, and inequality are not limited to the collapse of political regimes, as bad as that is. These effects extend to individual souls, distorting one's character.[49] To understand how extreme inequality transforms souls, one must recall that Socrates's political philosophy is meant to parallel the soul. Like the city, the soul possesses three parts: the appetitive (*epithumetikon*), spirit (*thumos*), and reason (*logos*). In his initial presentation, the appetites represent animal desires—food, drink, shelter, sleep, and the like (*Republic*, 437b–439b). Socrates subsequently adds, however, that the appetite is "most insatiate" for wealth (*Republic*, 442a).[50] The second faculty of the soul, reason, is capable of taming the appetites when necessary. The third faculty, spirit, is the passionate part of the soul that aligns itself either with the appetites or reason, depending on circumstances. The attributes and relationships of these faculties facilitate the soul's virtues. Insofar as *thumos* can withstand the allures of pleasure and persist through fears, one is courageous. Insofar as a soul knows the "Forms" or "Ideas"—enduring, unchanging truths—then one possesses wisdom. Insofar as the better part of the soul rules the worse part—namely, that reason rules over the appetites—individuals possess temperance. Finally, to the extent that all faculties perform their respective jobs without interfering with the other faculties, individuals are just. The dialogue's greatest concern is injustice, where the appetites rule over reason.

Socrates's conceptions of these faculties and virtues clarify the effects of wealth, poverty, and inequality on individual souls. His most detailed account pertains to the wealthy with oligarchic souls. Unlike healthy souls ruled by reason, the appetites rule oligarchic souls. He provides a speculative origins story of oligarchs in book 8 in which the son of the honor-loving timocratic man witnesses his father suffer from poverty. "And humbled by poverty, he turns greedily to moneymaking and, little by little, saving and working, he amasses property. Don't you think that someone like that will then establish the appetitive and moneymaking element on that throne, and make it king within himself, adorned with golden tiaras and collars and Persian swords?" (*Republic*, 553a–c). Socrates stresses how the appetites seize authority within the soul. A fear of poverty facilitates this transition—a suggestion that the virtue of courage is already absent since courageous souls persevere through fears.[51] This transition to the oligarchic soul also suggests the absence of at least two other virtues. Oligarchic souls lack moderation insofar as the better part of the soul (reason) fails to rule over the worse (the appetites). They also lack justice insofar as the appetites meddle with reason's defined role of ruling the soul.

In some ways, oligarchs are functional citizens despite their disordered souls. This is because among available appetites, they elevate the pursuit of necessary rather than unnecessary or lawless appetites.[52] Specifically, it is this oligarchic component of the appetites that he calls money loving (*philochrematon*) or profit loving (*philokerdes*) (*Republic*, 581a). Everyone needs some money of course. Insofar as the desire for money rules the soul, it can check the lawless appetites, such as the desire for addictive substances, gambling, and the like. Earning money generally takes discipline. Money lovers are often thrifty. So oligarchs can appear respectable and self-controlled.[53] Yet this respectability endures only for so long. The oligarch will eventually have children. And those children, raised without regard to the virtues of courage, moderation, justice, and wisdom, will be ill-prepared for their circumstances. Whereas first-generation oligarchs are raised in relative poverty and fear returning to it, their children lack this fear. They have few incentives to maintain their parents' habits of discipline and relative self-control. As Socrates elaborates, when these children are exposed to the unnecessary and lawless pleasures that their parents had refused, they will often yield to them (*Republic*, 559d–560a).

SOLUTIONS TO INEQUALITY IN THE *REPUBLIC*?

Socrates's discussions of wealth, poverty, and inequality in the *Republic* are striking. Oligarchy is not merely a stop along the path of regime decline but a regime with distinctive faults. Despite this, there is a relative absence of concrete and practical solutions for grappling with them in this dialogue. There are no detailed accounts of the kallipolis's economic regime, the role of commerce, modes of taxation, currency, and other measures employed by Solon and Lycurgus—and certainly nothing like those found in Plato's *Laws*. This being noted, it would be mistaken to suggest the *Republic* offers nothing to confront at least some of the ills associated with extreme inequality. Socrates is most specific when it comes to the ruling class, which is prohibited from possessing any private property.[54] The gold in their souls, he suggests, is an ample divine gift. They therefore "have no need of human gold in addition." In fact, echoing Lycurgus, Socrates elaborates, rulers will be prohibited from handling or even touching gold or silver: "They must not be under the same roof as these metals, wear them as jewelry, or drink from gold or silver goblets." To be in the metals' presence would inflame a latent appetite for wealth. Once that latent appetite manifests, he laments, guardians "will spend their whole lives hating and being hated, plotting and being plotted against, much more afraid of internal than of external enemies—already rushing, in fact, to the brink of their own destruction and that of the rest of the city as well" (*Republic*, 416e–417b). Socrates then demands that these propertyless guardians prevent wealth and poverty "in every way from slipping into our city undetected" since they are the source of bad work, illiberality, idleness, and political instability culminating in revolution (*Republic*, 421e–422a). He does not detail how this might be accomplished, choosing rather to trust the propertyless rulers' judgment, one imagines, because of their exceptional nature and training.

There is one other mechanism Socrates introduces potentially to mitigate the effects of great wealth. There is precisely one character in the *Republic* specifically defined by his wealth: Cephalus. By all accounts, Cephalus was a real person, who emigrated from Sicily to Athens to engage in commerce and did so with great financial success.[55] Notably, it is clear from his temperament that he possesses the composure and self-control of the oligarchs described above. What explains this? Interestingly, it is not—like the oligarchs of book 8—because he is a first-generation oligarch, who fears returning to poverty. He inherited money from his father, who had inherited it from his father. But Cephalus does fear something: Hades. He explains,

What I have to say would not persuade the masses. But you are well aware, Socrates, that when someone thinks his end is near, he becomes frightened and concerned about things he did not fear before. It is then that the stories about Hades, that a person who has been unjust must pay the penalty there—stories he used to make fun of—twist his soul this way and that for fear that they are true. And whether because of the weakness of old age, or because he is now closer to what happens in Hades and has a clearer view of it, or whatever it is, he is filled with foreboding and fear, and begins to calculate and consider whether he has been unjust to anyone. (*Republic*, 330e–331a)

Cephalus continues to explain that his potentially fateful encounter with eternity has motivated upright behavior, as he understands it, by speaking the truth and paying his debts.

Socrates immediately criticizes what he takes to be Cephalus's simplistic account of justice. But one might argue that Cephalus has also planted a seed that Socrates subsequently harvests in his Myth of Er.[56] Broadly speaking, the Myth of Er speaks to the possibility of divine rewards and sanctions. The myth recounts the story of a soldier, Er, who was killed in battle but has returned from death to report on the afterlife. He has learned that the gods "will never neglect anyone who eagerly wishes to become just and, by practicing virtue, to make himself as much like a god as a human being can" (*Republic*, 613a). As for the unjust, the gods will render them like those who "become wretched and are showered with abuse by foreigners and citizens, beaten with whips, and made to suffer those punishments . . . such as racking and burning." More specifically, for each injustice they commit, Er reports, they pay "the penalty for every one in turn, ten times over for each" (*Republic*, 613d, 615a). After a thousand years, each soul must choose a new life and its associated principles. Socrates emphasizes that if the myth were persuasive, "it would save us" (*Republic*, 621b).

While the myth addresses many concerns at once, there is reason to believe Socrates hopes it might especially resonate with the wealthiest citizens. First, it is Cephalus—the wealthiest interlocutor in the *Republic*—who first references the afterlife and its power to influence his behavior and control his appetites. Second, when faced with the choice of the next life, the myth specifically counsels that we must consider the effects of "wealth or poverty" on our souls (*Republic*, 618c), with Socrates especially counseling that we ought not be "dazzled by wealth and other such evils." We would be wisest, he suggests, to "choose the middle life . . . and avoid either of the extremes" (*Republic*, 619a).[57]

The final reason that the Myth of Er might have been devised to mitigate the effects of enormous wealth is built into its underlying moral psychology. Whereas much of the argumentation found throughout the *Republic* is intended to inspire positive visions associated with the joys of knowledge and virtue for its own sake, the myth operates on different terms—by relying on brute fear. Consider that Cephalus fears that the stories about Hades might be true, awaking from sleep "in terror" that he faces divine judgment (*Republic*, 330e). Consider also the role of fear in Socrates's account of oligarchic souls. What keeps them relatively ordered, compared with democratic and tyrannical souls, is the *fear* of poverty.[58] Oligarchs resemble nobler souls, he speculates, not because reason is ascendant in their souls but rather because of the powerful forces of "compulsion and fear" (*Republic*, 554d). The fear of poverty compels a kind of discipline that keeps them from indulging in the worst kinds of appetites and injustices. Their responsiveness to the fear of poverty, one might deduce, suggests a susceptibility to fear more generally. In this case, oligarchic souls fearing poverty might also be motivated to virtue by a fear of divine punishment. To be sure, however, the extraconstitutional appeal to a myth about divine sanctions represents a broad measure intended to abate vices of all kinds, not just those associated with great wealth.

If Plato's Socrates intended this as a curb on the abuses associated with wealth, power, and inequality, however, there are obvious limitations— namely, the constraints Cephalus experiences come to him only as an old man. Cephalus concedes that he did not feel them as a younger man. Nor does his wealthy son, Polemarchus, suggest that he is constrained in this way. Such myths, thus, are likely to have a belated and minimal effect, if any, on the abuses perpetrated by the wealthiest citizens.

Plato's Laws *and Economic Inequality*

THE FOUNDATIONS OF MAGNESIA: HARMONY AND VIRTUE

Whereas the *Republic* provides a framework for pondering wealth, poverty, and economic inequality, it is in his *Laws* that Plato defines inequality as a central problem of politics. As in the *Republic*, the *Laws* stresses the importance of fraternal bonds. If anything, these ties become even more important in this later political work, which is evident from the dialogue's opening paragraphs. Plato's Athenian Stranger, the primary character of the *Laws*, engages this question by asking his Spartan and Cretan interlocutors, Megillus and Kleinias, respectively, about the purpose of the laws. Kleinias instinctually suggests it is to promote the cause of winning wars. The Stranger offers some sympathy to Kleinias, particularly when comparing external warfare to the warfare that takes place within one's soul: the combat between the lesser and greater faculties of the soul. But it seems to him that the laws serve a much higher purpose than to support warfare. The point is not defeating others "but rather reconciling them by laying down laws for them for the rest of time and securing their friendship with one another. Such a judge and lawgiver would be better by far" (*Laws*, 627e). The laws should "bring harmony to the city" to promote "friendship" and "reconciliation" (*Laws*, 627e). As he summarizes, "the best . . . is neither war nor civil war . . . but rather peace and at the same time goodwill toward one another" (*Laws*, 628c). The Stranger's early emphasis on friendship, reconciliation, and harmony weaves its way throughout the entire dialogue.[59]

One way to secure civic friendship and harmony is to promote virtue. This is why virtue also plays a central role throughout the *Laws*.[60] As the Stranger observes, Kleinias's problem—and the problem with warrior cultures generally—is his myopic focus on a single virtue: courage. Courage remains a virtue for the Stranger, but it comes last in importance among the four primary virtues of wisdom, moderation, justice, and courage (*Laws*, 630b-d). To the extent that these virtues prevail among citizens and governments alike, friendship and social harmony are likely to follow.

The Stranger's definitions of the virtues lay the foundation for their political importance. As in the *Republic*, the virtue of moderation requires that individuals have mastery over "two opposed and imprudent counselors, which we call pleasure and pain" (*Laws*, 644c). To the extent that individuals can resist the allures of pleasures or can persist through fears of pain, they possess moderation. He adds, however, that there are certain things we would be right to fear—most importantly, shame. The fear of shame has the capacity to "save us from many great evils" (*Laws*, 647b).

The political importance of moderation becomes clearer after exploring the Stranger's understanding of justice and wisdom, as depicted in the *Laws*. His conception of justice here, at first glance, seems to differ considerably from Socrates's in the *Republic*. It emerges, however, in familiar fashion—in response to the claim that justice is "the interest of the stronger" (*Laws*, 714c). Plato's interlocutors subject this definition of justice to extensive scrutiny in both his *Gorgias* (483e-484a) and his *Republic* (338b-339a). His Stranger in the *Laws* counters this doctrine insofar as just laws "are laid down for the sake of what is common to the whole city." By contrast, he continues, "where the laws exist for the sake of some, we declare the inhabitants to be 'partisans' rather than citizens, and declare that when they assert their ordinances to be the just things they have spoken in vain" (*Laws*, 715b). Anticipating Rousseau's "general will," Plato's conception of justice is general rather than particular.

A corollary of the Stranger's conception of justice is the sovereignty of the laws themselves. A just republic requires that no individual or group ever stands above the laws:

> I have now applied the term "servants of the laws" to the men usually said to be rulers, not for the sake of innovation in names but because I hold that it is this above all that determines whether the city survives or undergoes the opposite. Where the law is itself ruled over and lacks sovereign authority, I see destruction at hand for such a place. But where it is despot over the rulers and the rulers are slaves to the law, there I foresee safety and all the good things which the gods have given to cities. (*Laws*, 715d)

By insisting that rulers become "slaves" to the laws, he means that they must be held accountable to the same laws binding on others. This represents a rejection of arbitrary rule. Plato elaborates on this doctrine in his Eighth Letter, where he praises Lycurgus for having made law the "rightful lord and sovereign of men," such that "men no longer ruled the laws with arbitrary power" (354c).[61]

Practical wisdom (*phronesis*) is the final virtue essential for flourishing polities outlined in the *Laws*. The Stranger identifies it as the highest virtue and the "leader among all the divine goods" (*Laws*, 631c). If it is the highest virtue in general, it is also certainly the greatest virtue of rulers, as he confirms in book 3: "the man who is a statesman-lawgiver must always look to this [wisdom] in setting up the orderings of the law" (*Laws*, 688a). It is important, in fact, for lawgivers to possess all the virtues, but wisdom is clearly foremost: "what should be done was to look to the whole of virtue, and especially at the first part, the leader of all virtue, which would be prudence, and intelligence, and opinion" (*Laws*, 688b). And if wisdom is the greatest virtue, the greatest vice is surely ignorance. In his account of the failed cities of Argos and Messene, the Stranger observes, "The corruption was caused by all the rest of vice [beyond cowardice], and especially ignorance regarding the greatest of human affairs" (*Laws*, 688c). As such, legislators have an obligation in framing laws to "try to instill as much prudence as possible in the cities and drive out the lack of intelligence as much as possible" (*Laws*, 688e).[62] The worst ignorance, for the Stranger, is "when someone doesn't like, but rather hates, what in his opinion is noble or good, and likes and welcomes what in his opinion is wicked or unjust" (*Laws*, 689a). This is ignorance about the good, as discussed in the *Republic*. But it is also different. The suggestion here is not simply that people fail to know the good. The Stranger here assumes people *do* know the good and do not like it, presumably because it is not serving their private advantage. So they instead pursue selfish ends.

PROBLEMATIZING INEQUALITY IN THE *LAWS*

The Stranger's account of harmony and virtue contextualizes his frequent protestations against extreme wealth and economic inequality.[63] One can make no mistake: he detests both concentrated wealth and inequality as the origins of nothing less than "the greatest of all plagues" (*Laws*, 744d), which is social disharmony and civil war.[64] His attention to this "plague" is neither fleeting nor incidental. It upends the friendship, harmony, and virtue necessary for sustaining a just republic. So just as with Solon and Lycurgus, any act of lawgiving—particularly regarding the writing of a constitution or what some call "fundamental law"—requires sustained attention to preventing elevated economic inequality.

The Stranger first turns his attention to economic equality in book 3, where he outlines what early modern philosophers would subsequently call the "state of nature"—a kind of origins story of government and the laws. He describes a great flood wiping out the vast majority of civilization, leaving scattered mountain shepherds as the only survivors. One might think, having just witnessed the destruction of nearly all civilization that these shepherds would be distraught. But the Stranger describes them as "delighted with one another and full of goodwill," never engaging in the fights that presumably consumed their ancestors. Although this is surely due in part to their good fortune in surviving, he remarkably attributes their happiness to the flood's destruction of all the world's collections of gold and silver. The absence of these markers of wealth fostered among the shepherds "the most well-bred dispositions," where "neither wealth nor poverty" resided. In the metals' absence, the Stranger celebrates, is "neither insolence nor injustice, nor again jealousies and ill will" (*Laws*, 679bc).[65]

Plato's Stranger expands on the effects of extreme wealth and inequality in his account of Persian history. Persia benefited initially from the relatively enlightened rule of Cyrus, who promoted a spirit of equality, which fostered both freedom and friendship (*Laws*, 694b). Despite Cyrus's best efforts, his work was soon undone by his own son. Too consumed with ruling to raise his own children, he left them in others' hands, who showered the offspring with luxury and flattery. One of these children was the future king, Cambyses. It should not have been surprising, on Plato's reading, that when he ascended to the throne that he was "bursting with luxury and lack of restraint." He continues, reporting that Cambyses killed his brother "because he couldn't bear to share equally; after this the one who remained, maddened by drunkenness and lack of education, had his rule destroyed by the Medes and by the fellow they, at that time, called 'the Eunuch,' who had nothing but contempt for the silliness of Cambyses" (*Laws*, 694b).

The story of Cyrus and his sons is followed immediately by one of another Persian ruling family: Darius and his son, Darius Xerxes.

> Let's observe as we follow the argument. For Darius was not the son of a king, and was not brought up under a luxurious education. He came into the rule and seized it as the seventh member of a group, and divided it into seven parts. . . . He saw fit to govern by establishing laws, through which he introduced a sort of general equality and regulated by law the tribute promised to the Persians by Cyrus; thus he brought about friendship and a sense of community among all the Persians, and won over the Persian populace with money and gifts. That's why his army was well disposed to him and gave him additional territories, no less than those left by Cyrus. But then after Darius Xerxes was once again educated in a royal and luxurious education: "O Darius!" it's perhaps very just to say, "you have failed to learn from the vice of Cyrus and have brought up Xerxes in the same habits as Cyrus did Cambyses!" Anyway, as he was an offspring of the same sorts of education, so he wound up suffering just about the same things as Cambyses. And since that time there has arisen among the Persians hardly a single truly "great" king, except in name. The cause of this is not chance, my argument goes, but rather the evil life led for the most part by children of exceptionally rich and tyrannical men. No child or man or old man will ever become outstanding in virtue if he has been brought up in such a way. (*Laws*, 695c–696a)[66]

The Stranger's conclusions from Persian history could not be bolder: great wealth corrupts souls. It disables their capacity to exercise self-control. This is why Darius Xerxes had been Callicles's hero in Plato's *Gorgias*. In arguing against Socrates that a powerful man ought to "shake off all . . . controls, burst his fetters, and break loose," Callicles finds his greatest exemplar in Darius Xerxes (*Gorgias*, 484de).[67] Xerxes had abandoned the virtue of moderation. Why would wealthy children, praised for their unearned fortunes, ever consider cultivating moderation? They have no incentives to do so. Furthermore, in the cases of Xerxes and Cambyses, they had no one teaching them self-control.

The lack of restraint fosters other vices, notably injustice and igno-rance. For the Stranger, justice requires attention to the whole community. Injustice, by contrast, elevates one person or group above the whole. To the extent that wealth corrupts citizens, people assume that they *deserve* a greater share. Excessive wealth, to this extent, inflames self-love:

> The truth is that excessive friendship for oneself is the cause of all of each man's wrong-doings on every occasion. Everyone who cares for something is blind when it comes to the thing cared for, and hence is a poor judge of what is just and good and noble, because he believes he should always honor his own more than the truth. Yet a man who is to attain greatness must be devoted not to himself or to what hap-pens to belong to him, but to what is just—whether it happens to be done by himself or by someone else. This same failing is the source of everyone's supposing that his lack of learning is wisdom. As a result, we think we know everything when in fact we know, so to speak, nothing: and when we refuse to turn over to others what we don't know how to do, we necessarily go wrong, by trying to do them ourselves. So every human being should flee from excessive self-love. (*Laws*, 731e–732b)

To be sure, the Stranger acknowledges everyone tends to love themselves. Self-love "grows naturally in the soul" (*Laws*, 731d). The difference, presum-ably, is that most encounter enough frustrations in life that they are regularly reminded of their own limitations. Things are different, however, for the wealthy and powerful, who scarcely encounter these obstacles. As such, their egoism grows unabated. This unrestricted self-love manifests in ignorance and injustice. They are unjust insofar as they assume their own concerns transcend or even define the common good. They are ignorant insofar as they come to assume they are wise in all things when they clearly are not.

When the ruling class embraces these vices—immoderation, injustice, and ignorance—it is disastrous. This is why Cambyses was quickly van-quished (see *Laws*, 688e, 689d). It is the Stranger's unrelenting conviction that great wealth and power produce precisely these immoralities:

> Then isn't it clear that it was the kings of that time [Cambyses and Darius Xerxes] who were first seized by this—the desire to have more than the established laws allowed—and that they weren't in conso-nance with themselves as regards what they praised in speech and in their oath? The dissonance—which we have asserted to be the greatest ignorance but which seems [to them] to be wisdom—corrupted every-thing. (*Laws*, 691a)

Thus, great wealth and luxury frustrate the virtues. This is why he repeatedly asserts, "It is impossible that those who become very rich also become good" (*Laws*, 742e).[68]

Empowering vice ultimately undermines civic friendship and harmony. Those placing themselves above others call their ignorance "wisdom" and repeatedly flaunt their lack of restraint. They sabotage the friendship essential to thriving regimes. The Stranger expressly draws this connection in his conclusions about Persia's failures. The vices of its luxurious leaders

> destroyed friendship and community within the city. Once this is corrupted, the policy of the rulers is no longer made for the sake of the ruled and the populace, but instead for the sake of their own rule; if they suppose just a little more will accrue to themselves each time, the rulers are willing to overturn and destroy with fire friendly nations, and as a result, they give and receive bitter, pitiless hatred. (*Laws*, 697c)

Persia's history confirms a principle that Plato's Stranger expresses later in more general terms when aiming for a middle point between extremes. Although the dangers of inattention to one's body, for example, are problematic, excessive attention to one's physique is also dangerous insofar as it "makes souls boastful and rash." He next applies this principle to wealth and property:

> The same holds true for the possession of money and property: honor should be bestowed on this according to the same scheme. Excess of each of these [wealth and property] create enmities and civil strife both in cities and in private life, while deficiencies lead . . . to slavery. (*Laws*, 728e–729a)

As the Stranger notes later, quoting an ancient proverb, "equality produces friends" (*Laws*, 757a).[69] It stands to reason, therefore, that inequality produces enemies. The vices fostered by enormous wealth and luxury ultimately culminate in hatred, civil war, and regime collapse. While the extremely wealthy grow egoistic and *pleonectic*, the poor grow destitute, embittered, desperate, and angry.

SOLVING THE PROBLEM OF INEQUALITY IN THE *LAWS*

If great wealth, luxury, and inequality represent the problem, the Stranger's solution is to reduce wealth and eliminate poverty, greatly restricting inequality's scope. To be sure, while Plato's Socrates had implied this was necessary in the *Republic*, the Stranger is strikingly specific in his means to achieve these goals for Magnesia in the *Laws*.

The Stranger's program of reducing inequality in the *Laws* reflects a larger awareness of empirical considerations generally in this dialogue. In the *Republic*, Socrates was less concerned with limitations introduced by history and human nature, among other concerns, since he assumed morally perfect philosophers would have free rein to shape the citizens needed to create his community of pleasures and pains. But in the *Laws*, the Stranger understands the limitations imposed by real-world circumstances. For this reason, he frequently contrasts ideal conditions for promoting equality with more realistic ones. He shifts between the two, often presenting the ideal immediately before the practical so that legislators might know what is possible under the best circumstances.[70]

The Stranger's initial account of an ideal community in regard to economic equality emerges in his story of the shepherd community emerging from the great flood. The great advantage of the flood, as previously noted, was that it wiped out all property and wealth, which freed the new society to choose the optimum policies for economic equality.

> When the lawgivers were arranging . . . some sort of equality in property they were not subjected to that very great reproach raised in many other cities during the time of the establishment of laws, whenever someone seeks to change land tenure and dissolve debts because he sees that otherwise a sufficient degree of equality will never be possible. When a lawgiver tries to change such things, everyone raises against him the cry, "Do not move the immovable!" and curses him for introducing the redivision of land and dissolution of debts, and thus putting every man at his wit's end. But for the Dorians there was this further advantage, that the process went along in a fine way and was free from blame, because they could divide up the land without disputes and, in addition, there were no large ancient debts. (*Laws*, 684de)

Plato here likely has in mind the contrast between the Spartans and Athenians. For the Athenians, with their long history of great fortunes and property attachments, such a redistribution would have triggered significant upheaval. And even if it were achieved, it would have created enduring resentments that would have hobbled the resulting community. Solon rejected confiscating and redistributing property, seeking a middle course between radical equality and inequality, liquidating debts and prohibiting the use of debtors' bodies as collateral. Lycurgus, by contrast, pursued the radical path, confiscating wealth and property and redistributing it equally. The radical path is surely better for Plato, everything else being equal. But it would be unwise to impose Lycurgus's equality on those unprepared for it.

The Stranger's economic reforms are mindful of the people's receptivity to radical change. But in the immediate case of legislating in the *Laws*, the Stranger and his interlocutors are writing laws for the new colony of Magnesia. Its colonists have no previous property claims, with no property to be confiscated and redistributed. Plots will be distributed de novo. Hence they enjoy the same circumstances that favored the mountain shepherds, receptive to the best property laws any city might enjoy. The Stranger begins legislating Magnesia's laws by reminding readers of the importance of economic equality:

> We assert that if (as we presume) the city must avoid the greatest of all plagues, which has been more correctly termed "civil war" than "faction," then neither harsh poverty nor wealth should exist among any of its citizens. For both these conditions breed both civil war and faction.

To this extent, Plato's Stranger reaffirms Persia's lessons as well as those of Athens and Sparta. But since his immediate circumstances permit an ideal solution, he recommends the following:

> So let the limit of poverty be the value of the allotment, which must be maintained, and which no magistrate, and none of the others who desires to be honored for virtue, should ever allow to be diminished in the case of anyone. Taking this as the measure, the lawgiver will allow citizens to acquire twice again, and three times again, and up to four times again this amount. But if anyone acquires more than four times this amount—by finding something or by being given something, or by money-making, or some other such stroke of luck—let him dedicate the surplus to the city and to the gods who possess the city. (*Laws*, 744d–745a)

There will be four resulting economic classes corresponding to property holdings. But those classes will be tightly restricted. The wealthiest class of citizens will have no more than four times the property of the poorest citizens.[71] To enforce this, the state must maintain meticulous property and wealth records to prevent anyone from exceeding these limits. Anyone caught violating this law will be subjected to public censure and confiscation of their excess wealth (*Laws*, 745a). The Stranger subsequently adds that violators are subjected to greater penalties. Any citizen suspicious that another has exceeded four times the wealth of the poorest citizens may bring that wealthy man to trial. If the wealthy man is found guilty of possessing excessive and illicit wealth, he is to lose not only his excess wealth but all of his wealth, save for his original allotment, meaning he returns to the poorest class of citizens. Furthermore, his name will be permanently scarred by public shame (*Laws*, 754e–755a).[72]

The impossibility of becoming exceedingly rich or poor achieves many of the Stranger's ambitions. Insofar as no one can become too poor, one can expect less suffering, less starvation, fewer citizens being tempted to rob, steal, covet, or revolt out of desperation. On the opposite end, insofar as no one can become extremely wealthy, citizens will avoid the many vices associated with great fortunes. They will be less likely to think themselves above the law. They will be less susceptible to *pleonexia*, immoderation, injustice, and ignorance. By solving all these problems at once, he hopes to promote the very purpose of republics—the friendship and harmony of all citizens.

This relatively equal wealth distribution is, to be sure, the most striking policy innovation in the *Laws*, but it is far from the only means by which the Stranger hopes to promote equality and social harmony. He also imposes limitations on inheritances: "let no one be a lover of money for the sake of his children, so that he may leave them as wealthy as possible: this is better neither for them nor the city. A portion that will not attract flatterers around the young but will avoid neediness is the most musical and the best of all; for this brings us consonance, and through harmony makes life painless in all respects."[73] Rather than leaving children wealth, one should rather bequeath to them "an abundance of awe" and a sense of shame (*Laws*, 728ab). He does not specify a particular formula for restricting the monetary portion of one's inheritance, but the laws generally place a cap on wealth. So presumably a child could inherit no money exceeding four times the wealth of the poorest citizens. The remainder would presumably return to the state.[74]

Another innovation meant to inhibit growing economic inequality concerns marriage. As social scientists have observed, marriage patterns tend to exacerbate economic inequality. The wealthy tend to marry one another and have children. Poorer citizens tend to do the same. This perpetuates and exacerbates preexisting inequalities, as children from wealthy families gain all the benefits from their parents' assets, while poor children experience the opposite.[75] The Stranger acknowledges much the same: "It is according to nature that everyone always be somehow attracted to what is most similar to himself." But he continues, "And because of this the city as a whole becomes uneven as regards wealth and the disposition

of characters. The consequences of this, which we wish to avoid for ourselves, are very prevalent in most cities" (*Laws*, 773bc). Insofar as marriages
tend to partner rich with rich, they not only intensify inequalities, but they
also produce exceedingly wealthy heirs, like Darius Xerxes and Cambyses,
who reject the virtues required for thriving republics. To this extent, Plato's Stranger recommends that citizens marry according to "what is in the
interest of the city" rather than what might enhance their private wealth.[76]
This presumably means that marriages should cross class boundaries. But
he does not go so far as to regulate this by law since he recognizes the practical limits of impositions on marriage choices.[77]

Another regulation intended to curb the accumulation of wealth is the
Stranger's prohibition on the kinds of economic activities that commonly
produce wealth, including a ban on interest-bearing loans. This likely follows from Plato's awareness of Athenian history, where high-interest loans
produced extreme economic inequality and debt slavery. Wishing to avoid
this fate, if anyone is caught loaning money at interest, debtors will not
only be relieved of the interest charged, but they may also keep the principal (*Laws*, 742c). Although not being threatened with imprisonment or
other sanctions, creditors lose all incentives to loan money for profit.

Along these lines, Plato's Stranger also prohibits the buying and selling of landed property. He describes the initial property distribution as
deliberately promoting equality, friendship, and harmony. To the extent
that citizens exchange property, they endanger this careful balance by facilitating wealth accumulation. Prohibiting such exchanges, he adds, fosters
a system where "great money-making is impossible, and the consequence
is that there should not and cannot be anyone who makes money in any
way from illiberal pursuits. No one needs to accumulate money from the
sort of occupation that receives the contemptible epithet 'gross vulgarity'
and that can distort the character of a free man" (*Laws*, 741e). This prohibition, hence, simultaneously protects the initial equality bequeathed at
the city's founding, and it also prevents the "vulgarities" generated by great
fortunes.

In a further measure of preserving character against the temptations
of great wealth, Plato's Stranger adopts Lycurgus's currency guidelines:
"no one is to be allowed to possess any gold or silver in any private capacity" (*Laws*, 742a). This is not a ban on currency altogether but rather a
ban on the kinds of currency that promote *pleonectic* accumulation. The
Magnesian currency used for daily transactions—which he acknowledges as necessary—should lack value beyond its borders. This being
said, Plato's Stranger allows the government to hold precious metals for

ambassadors and other necessary foreign engagements. But if the Magnesian emissary should return home with any remaining gold or silver, it must immediately be returned to the state coffers.[78]

Further limits on luxury and wealth accumulation can be found in the regulations of retail trade. Although it is possible for the virtuous to engage in fair trade, he laments that the "bulk of human beings are entirely the opposite. . . . They want without measure, and when it's possible for them to gain measured amounts, they choose to gain insatiably" (*Laws*, 918d). Commercial society, in other words, exacerbates problems inherent in human nature by transforming mere selfishness into fully realized *pleonexia*. To quell this development, Plato's Stranger counsels the following:

> Now it has been correctly said of old that "against two from opposite quarters it is difficult to fight," in the cases of diseases and many other things; and indeed the present battle about and around these matters is against two, poverty and wealth, one of which corrupts the soul of human beings through luxury, and the other which urges it to shamelessness through pains. What aid would there be then for this disease, in a city that possessed intelligence? The first is to make use of the class of retail traders as little as one can; then, human beings ought to be assigned to a retail trade whose corruption would least affront the city; in the third place, a device should be found to prevent the dispositions of soul in those who partake of these practices from easily becoming unrestrainedly shameless and illiberal. (*Laws*, 919bc)

To this effect, he implements a series of reforms intended to promote fair commercial exchanges, where no one can exploit another party, including special attention to the menace of price gouging. The Stranger comments that overcharging represents an "injustice," born from "a desire for a small gain," threatening to loosen the "great ties of community." As such, the government is obliged to legislate, coming "to the defense of the bond that holds the city together" (*Laws*, 921c). In these pages, Plato's Stranger repeatedly connects his commercial exchange laws to his fundamental principles. Commerce must be regulated to protect against wealth, poverty, and inequality, which in turn must be avoided to preserve social harmony.[79]

To be sure, even though the Stranger's proposals ameliorating economic inequality are earnest and might even be effective under ideal conditions, many of them would strike twenty-first-century readers as unrealistic. It is highly unlikely, for example, that a large commercial society would embrace a currency lacking value beyond its borders. Nor are such communities likely to employ the kind of radical property redistribution outlined in the *Laws*. But it is one of the hallmarks of this dialogue, as contrasted with the *Republic*, that it entertains and explores second-best solutions.[80] Plato appears to acknowledge here that if conditions permitted, he would surely prefer a regime resembling the kallipolis outlined in the *Republic*, where "every sort of property is common" and "every device has been employed to exclude all of what is called the 'private' from all aspects of life." Yet his Stranger concedes in the *Laws* that such a city requires its citizens be "gods or children of gods," with the capacity and willingness to abandon selfishness in the service of the common good. Lacking gods and their descendants, however, does not release lawgivers from endeavoring to come "as close as possible to such a regime" within the bounds of what circumstances permit (*Laws*, 739c–e). Thus the pursuit of "a second-best city" (*Laws*, 739a).

Constructing a second-best city requires careful attention to empirical circumstances, including human nature and history, as well as existing social, cultural, political, religious, and economic practices. Plato is keenly aware of such empirical circumstances and the limitations they impose on well-intentioned lawmakers. As T. K. Seung has emphasized, "It is hard to overstate the importance of empirical and historical knowledge in the *Laws*."[81] It matters, for example, that the shepherds emerging from the great flood have no property or an accumulated wealth. Without this history, Magnesia's lawgivers are free to employ ideal economic legislation. It is similarly helpful that they are legislating for a society with no preexisting history and practices—it is a colony of immigrants. So the Athenian Stranger is at liberty to place strict caps on economic inequality.

But the Stranger's sensitivity to empirical circumstances also means that he knows Magnesia is unique. Most legislation is not written for new polities; it is written for those already living under other laws, with their peculiar circumstances, prejudices, and expectations. This is particularly true regarding economic legislation. The fact is that most legislators encounter a populace characterized by preexisting inequalities. Were they to ignore this fact, it would be at their own peril.[82] For this reason, he stresses that ideal economic laws cannot be employed except under ideal circumstances. Elsewhere, lawgivers must proceed cautiously. It is worth parsing Plato's words carefully. The Stranger begins by stressing Magnesia's great advantage in lacking a previous history of property distribution. "Let us not, by the way, overlook the good fortune that has befallen us, the same luck that we said befell the colony founded by the descendants of Heracles: they avoided the terrible, dangerous strife occasioned by the redivision of land, cancelling of debts, and redistribution." He continues, however, acknowledging that Magnesia is unique in this regard. Most cities have a preexisting unequal property distribution. These inequalities demand rectification, but this transformation must proceed slowly. Doing so requires wise reformers, drawn from both the wealthy and debtor classes, motivated by a "sense of fairness" (*di' epieikeian*).[83] They should introduce moderate reforms intended not only to redistribute property but also to create a culture that shames *pleonexia*.

> When a city with ancient roots is compelled to legislate about this, it finds that it cannot leave things as they are, unchanged, nor is it able to change them in any way; the only thing left, so to speak, is prayer, and small, careful transformation that gradually produces a small result over a long period of time. For this to happen there must be a continual supply of reformers from among those who possess an abundance of land and many debtors. These reformers must be willing, out of a sense of fairness, to share in some way what they have with any of their debtors who are in distress, forgiving some of the debts and parceling out some of their land. Thus they bring about a kind of measure and show that they believe poverty consists not in a lessening of one's property but in an increase of one's avarice. (*Laws*, 736de)

This legislation is essential to maintain a functioning city, which cannot long be sustained without a degree of economic equality. Beyond this, citizens must recognize that avarice is unseemly.

> This is the most important source of a city's preservation, and provides a sort of sturdy foundation upon which someone can later build whatever political order befits such arrangements. But if this foundation is rotten, political activity would always encounter difficulties in the city. This danger, as we assert, we're avoiding; nevertheless, it is more correct to discuss it, at any rate, and show how we might find a way out if we were not escaping it. It's been said that what would be needed is an absence of the money-loving that goes with justice: there is no other way of escape, broad or narrow, besides this device. So let this stand now as a kind of buttress for our city. (*Laws*, 736e–737b)

This being said, he again emphasizes that such reforms require caution. If legislators simply cancel all debts and redistribute property, without regard to how this might affect civic harmony, they risk stirring resentment and creating a permanent class of embittered citizens.

> Somehow or other things must be arranged so that they don't have dis-
> putes over their property, because those who have even a little intel-
> ligence won't voluntarily go ahead with the rest of the arrangements as
> long as ancient property disputes remain unsettled among themselves.
> But for men in a new situation like ours now, where a god has given a
> new city to found, and where there are as yet no hatreds against one
> another; no human ignorance, even if combined with complete evil,
> would lead men to set up a division of land and houses that would
> introduce these hatreds among themselves. (*Laws*, 736b)

The Stranger concludes this long paragraph by returning to the dialogue's
foundational principles. Abrupt and extreme legislation—even where well
intentioned—threatens to undermine the harmony and friendship required
in thriving states. Confiscating great estates and redistributing them
according to strict egalitarian principles embitters the wealthy. One might
argue that such radical reallocation programs as employed in the Russian
Revolution, for example, created a permanent angry class—an anger that
could only be quelled by credible threats of brutal violence, scarcely conducive to social harmony and friendship.[84] This is perhaps a lesson that
Plato learned from Solon, who sought to resolve the problem of Athenian
inequality without alienating the rich. Solon's reforms not only protected
and satisfied the poor, hence staving off revolution, but also—in not confiscating and redistributing property—kept the rich from overtly challenging
the laws' legitimacy. Montesquieu, a careful reader of Plato's *Laws*, once
remarked along these lines, "By abruptly removing wealth from some and
increasing wealth of others, they [legislators] make a revolution in each
family and must produce one generally throughout the state."[85]

This being stated, egalitarian reforms nevertheless remain essential. Stark economic inequality subverts filial bonds. Permitting extreme
inequality emboldens the wealthy and embitters the poor, especially since
these inequalities tend to expand over time as the wealthy grow increasingly *pleonectic*.[86]

Notably, the Stranger's arguments regarding ideal and nonideal circumstances parallel two conceptions of equality he outlines in a passage
that does not immediately address *economic* equality but rather *political*
equality:

> For there are two equalities, the same in name, but in many respects
> almost diametrically opposed in deed. Every city and every lawgiver is
> competent to assign honors to the other sort—the equality that con-
> sists in measure and weight and number—and by the use of the lot

applies it in distributions. But it's not so easy for everyone to discern the truest and best equality. For it is the judgment that belongs to Zeus, and it assists human beings only to a small degree, on each occasion; still, every bit of assistance it does give to cities or private individuals brings all good things. By distributing more to what is greater and smaller amounts to what is lesser, it gives due measure to each according to their nature: this includes greater honor always to those who are greater as regards virtue, and what is fitting—in due proportion—to those who are just the opposite in regards to virtue and education. It is for this that we should now strive, and to this equality we should now look, Kleinias, to found the city that is now growing. The same holds in the case of another city someone might found sometime: it is to this that one should look while giving laws. . . .

Nonetheless necessity compels every city to blur sometimes the distinction between these two, if it is to avoid partaking of civil war in some parts. For equity and forgiveness, whenever they are applied, are always enfeeblements of the perfection and exactness that belong to strict justice. Because of the discontent of the many they are compelled to make use of the equality of the lot, but when they do, they should pray both to the god and to good luck to correct the lot in the direction of what is most just. Thus, of necessity, both equalities ought to be employed, though the type that depends on chance as rarely as possible. A city that is going to last is compelled, for these reasons, to do things this way, my friends. (*Laws*, 757b–758a)[87]

The Stranger suggests that among the many real-world circumstances that wise lawgivers must consider is the people's capacity to tolerate inequality. In this particular passage, he is concerned that if citizens feel that they are excluded from political decision making, they will sense injustice on their own terms and foment factions and political instability. The same reasoning should also apply to economic inequality. Even if one were to argue that some citizens *deserved* more money than others on the basis of talent, intelligence, originality, or efforts, then a radical inequality—or a departure from what the Stranger above calls the "equality of the lot"— would nevertheless offend commonsense understandings of justice and undermine the republic by turning citizens against one another. Lawgivers ignore such considerations at their own peril.

One might ask whether it is inequality itself or merely the perception of inequality responsible for the social pathologies that worry Plato. Because if it is more the perception than the fact of inequality, then one could plausibly adapt Plato's "noble lie" to conceal material inequalities, thereby maintaining civic order. Consider, for example, that the presence of a first-class cabin significantly increases incidents of air-rage episodes on commercial flights.[88] But for this effect to take place, passengers must load the plane from the front, with coach passengers walking through the cozy first-class section, after the first-class passengers have already preboarded the plane. When coach passengers, by contrast, enter the planes from the middle, beyond the first-class sections, air-rage incidents significantly drop. Could not Plato, in this spirit, direct his rulers to lie to the poorest citizens in order to maintain his desired civic harmony?[89] Although some benefit might be achieved from such measures, it is doubtful that Plato, especially the late Plato, would have endorsed this stratagem. First, as I have argued elsewhere, Plato seems to have distanced himself from the idea of a "noble lie" by the time he wrote the *Laws*.[90] Second and more fundamentally, such a policy would do nothing to curb the behavior of the wealthiest citizens, who would doubtless remain aware of their relative privileges. The only way such inequalities could conceivably be concealed would be to eliminate every advantage that accrues to those at the top of the economic structure, which would undermine the very point of those striving to achieve or maintain great wealth. Such a strategy, it seems, would defeat the very point of inequality in the first place.

The Inequality Underlying Plato's Egalitarianism

Plato's egalitarianism is striking enough that it is tempting to overlook the inequality on which it is built. Most obviously, despite a general willingness to challenge the conventions of his time, he largely accepted the Greek institution of slavery and clearly assumed as much in constructing his otherwise egalitarian republic of Magnesia. It has been estimated that there were approximately 125,000 slaves, or two to three slaves per citizen, in Athens at the time the Peloponnesian War started. These slaves were employed in a variety of tasks, most of which were domestic—such as errand running, cooking, cleaning, and childcare—rather than in agriculture or other modes of commerce or business.[91] A minority were employed in other tasks, up to and including the very unpleasant chore of mining, often resulting in the slaves' premature deaths. But even when they performed domestic duties, they were surely helpful for the citizens to tend to their farms, businesses, and civic responsibilities.

In the definitive study of Plato's treatment of slavery in the *Laws*, classicist Glenn R. Morrow observed that the philosopher's laws regarding slavery are "no creation of his philosophical imagination" but rather "an adaptation of positive Greek law, and more particularly the law of Athens."[92] This includes express references to employing slaves on private farms (*Laws*, 805e, 806d), in the master's house (*Laws*, 808ab), tending to the master's children (*Laws*, 808e), as well as their employment in any number of public works (*Laws*, 760e, 763a).[93] This is, Morrow speculated, because Plato had come to accept the constraints of certain empirical realities—for example, that no people was likely to submit itself to a small band of philosopher rulers but also that no Greek people of his time would consider establishing a republic without a substantial slave class to handle many of its most onerous duties. But as Morrow carefully explained in his study of Plato's treatment of slavery, this fact cannot be plausibly used to argue that Plato secretly or otherwise opposed the institution of slavery. This is because where Plato's *Laws* depart from Athenian law regarding slavery, it is often to be harsher, rather than gentler, in the treatment of slaves. To the degree that Plato can be perceived as progressive on economic issues, and even on gender issues, the same does not apply to his views on slavery.

Plato's acceptance or embrace of slavery complicates his vision of economic equality. While a 4:1 ratio of richest to poorest households is very progressive by contemporary standards, it emphatically applies *only to citizens*. The slaves do not count as the poorest citizens. They stand in all respects—in wealth, law, and dignity—significantly below the lowest class. Since the number of slaves in Magnesia was likely to be equal to if not much greater than the number of citizens, it is arguable that Plato's second-best city is scarcely egalitarian at all.[94] In this important regard, the Stranger undeniably sketches an egalitarian regime for citizens that stands on a larger inegalitarian slave-holding foundation. This may have been less bothersome to most of Plato's contemporaries, Aristotle among them, but it is obviously jarring to contemporary eyes.

The remaining question, then, is whether Plato's acceptance of slavery renders his thinking about inequality largely irrelevant. Or to put it another way, does Magnesia's egalitarianism for citizens require a slave class? Is equality, for Plato, only possible with inequality? One may well assume it is. But it is worth giving the matter serious thought before jumping to conclusions. Consider what the Athenian citizens "gained" in employing slaves. For the classicist H.D.F. Kitto, slavery was not the primary source of the free time that citizens could dedicate to their civic life. He speculates that slavery was prevalent more so from habit than from essential lifestyle support.

The real source of the leisure Athenians cherished, on his account, was their relatively modest lifestyle. According to Kitto, it was the "extremely simple standard of life on which even the wealthy Athenian lived" that made leisure possible, much more than the slaves they employed.[95] If this was true of the Athenians, it is even more true of Plato's Magnesians, for whom simplicity of lifestyle is a defining feature. I have already detailed that the Athenian Stranger expelled precious metals from the city—something never considered in Athens. He also largely prohibited foreign luxuries through trade. He insisted on simple meals. And as is already known by this point, he placed strict caps on wealth. The Athenian Stranger's prohibition on precious metals alone, for example, would have obviated the need for the many thousands of slaves Athens employed in its deadly mines. If Kitto is right, much of what Plato sought for his citizens in Magnesia could likely have been accomplished without slavery, so long as they did not complicate their lives with desires for abundant luxuries.

To be sure, Kitto's "simplicity thesis" raises another set of questions about whether contemporary peoples are willing to make the trade-off implicit in the ancient world—trading luxury and comfort for equality. Insofar as people keep their desires modest, they can live in a more egalitarian fashion. Indeed, Socrates almost seems to imply this in the *Republic*, when he balks at Glaucon's "city of pigs," which includes perfumes, pastries, gold, ivory, embroidery, and other luxuries (*Republic*, 372e–373a). Embracing the kinds of luxuries to which many have been accustomed can be difficult to sacrifice, as Glaucon attests and as Socrates reluctantly allows. But the Spartan elements of Plato's *Laws* at least have the virtue of impressing on readers the drawbacks of luxurious cities—limits increasingly acknowledged by people today who advocate for decreased energy consumption, the elimination of single-use plastics, and the reduction of luxuries such as automobiles. But perhaps the greatest drawback of luxurious cities, for Plato, is the degree to which they seem destined to suffer inequality and its effects—a conclusion Rousseau would reaffirm some two thousand years later. It may yet be that Plato's ideas have an audience receptive to the simplicity that his egalitarianism might require.

Conclusion

In his *Social Contract*, Jean-Jacques Rousseau relates two anecdotes about Plato's brief career as a would-be legislator. He likely read about these accounts in the works of the ancient historians Diogenes Laertius and Plutarch, admittedly several centuries removed from Plato and of uncertain historical accuracy. According to the former, the Arcadians and Thebans both invited Plato to legislate at the founding of Megalopolis, roughly two hundred kilometers southwest of Athens, in 371 BCE. Yet Diogenes reports that "when he discovered that they were opposed to equality of possessions, he refused to go."[96] Plutarch reports a similar tale in his life of Lucullus in which Plato is reported as once having had the opportunity of legislating for the Cyrenians (in modern-day Libya) but declined because they were abounding "in wealth and plenty."[97] As Rousseau would summarize these historical accounts, Plato refused to legislate for both because he "knew that these two peoples were rich and could not tolerate equality" (SC, 2.8, 74).

Although the authenticity of these stories may be questioned, they nevertheless raise important issues largely overlooked in the scholarship. Most important, as Rousseau had emphasized, they point to the centrality of economic equality for Plato's political project. Without sufficient commitment to the principle of equality, neither Megalopolis nor Cyrene stood a chance of long-term political success. They would presumably suffer the same fate that concerned Plato in both the *Republic* and the *Laws*. Whereas equality breeds friendship, inequality breeds faction, civil strife, and civil war.

What is also notable in these anecdotes, however, is the suggestion that Plato thought it was pointless to legislate for them. This seems inconsistent with the Athenian Stranger's willingness to work toward equality in unequal societies, forging "small, careful transformation that gradually produces a small result over a long period of time." There is a ready explanation for this refusal, however. The Stranger allows that every republic requires a "sturdy foundation" on which legislators can build. He continues, however, "If this foundation is rotten, political activity would always encounter difficulties in the city" (*Laws*, 736e–737a). In particular, the sturdiest foundation, for him, is a people unburdened by extreme inequality and an insatiable lust for wealth. The presence of money loving and inequality in Cyrene and Megalopolis was likely the "rotten" foundation that rendered laws futile. This is Rousseau's own interpretation of Plato, and it becomes an important premise of his own political theory.

It does not seem, however, that Plato's Athens was so unequal as these other cities.[98] This discovery in recent scholarship suggests that perhaps I have made too much of the inequality in Athens during the Peloponnesian War. But I would like to offer an alternative reading. Although Athens enjoyed greater equality than its neighbors, it nevertheless maintained sharp social classes—a fact manifest in the class-based revolutions of the period. Taking this into account, one can imagine that Athens was precisely the kind of city that was ripe for those gradual reforms that would bring about greater equality and civic harmony over generations precisely so that it could avoid such revolutions in the future. That is, the Athenian Stranger has Athens itself in mind in his reforms. As the Stranger suggests, one condition of such progress is the presence of a "continual supply of reformers from among those who possess an abundance of land" who are animated by a "sense of fairness." Indeed, Plato's best evidence for the possibility of progress in Athens along these lines is himself. More than any other figure in subsequent chapters of this book, Plato was born into a family of significant wealth and high social standing. Among the ancestors his family claimed were Solon on his mother's side and the god Poseidon on his father's side. Even though such mythical ancestry should not be taken too seriously, the fact that such stories were passed down by generations of historians itself suggests the degree of his family's privilege and status. Despite his wealth and social standing, of course, Plato was one of the greatest critics of wealth and inequality in the ancient world. This confirms the Athenian Stranger's faith that egalitarian reformers could be found among the upper classes.

It is well known, however, that Plato shunned real-world politics. I have already cited his reported refusal to legislate for Megalopolis and Cyrene. But if Plato's reputed Seventh Letter is accepted as an authentic Platonic text, he also abandoned an attempt to tutor the Syracusian prince Dionysius due to the prince's luxury and lack of restraint. This would represent Plato's third pass on engaging real-world politics. What are egalitarians to do to promote his cause, then, if they are unable to engage politically in good conscience? In Plato's case, he founded the Academy, the first institution of higher learning in the West, where he spent his final decades writing and teaching. Among his most prominent students was a young philosopher from Macedonia, Aristotle, who would eventually become one of Plato's greatest critics. Aristotle would come to reject Plato's views on many subjects, from his understanding of women and the family to his metaphysics. Yet Aristotle exempts one important element of his teacher's doctrines from his critiques: Plato's critique of economic inequality. The pupil largely accepted his teacher's view that it is problematic when some "own too much wealth and others very little."[99] Aristotle's acceptance of Plato's critique of inequality helped cement this criticism in Western political thought, which would then inform not only Christianity but also early modern thinkers such as Thomas More, Jean Bodin, Montesquieu, and especially Jean-Jacques Rousseau. Plato may not have been a political reformer in the manner outlined by his Athenian Stranger, but his work as a teacher and scholar assured an enduring egalitarian legacy.

CHAPTER TWO

The New Testament

"THE EYE OF A NEEDLE"

POPE FRANCIS HAS MADE HEADLINES with his public pronounce-
ments on the moral and spiritual problems of wealth and inequality. In
a concise Tweet sent in 2014, he asserted, slightly modifying 1 Timothy
6:9–10, "Inequality is the root of all social evil."[1] This was neither an impul-
sive nor a fleeting sentiment. It rather summarizes his extensive thought
on matters of economics and justice in their relationship to the fundamental principles of Christianity. In his *Evangelii Gaudium* (*The Joy of the
Gospel*), he singles out a pervasive "crude and naïve trust in the goodness
of those wielding economic power" and an economic system grounded
in base selfishness. This economy based on egoism and the substantial
economic inequality it engenders, for Francis, tends to replace God with
an "idolatry of money" and replaces a proper common-good-oriented ethics with bald selfishness.[2] Such a system, he continues, justifies itself by
blaming the poor for their circumstances, and it even fosters class tensions
and violence. He extends his thoughts subsequently in his *Encyclical on
Climate Change and Inequality*,[3] which explains how extreme inequality
effectively excludes considerations of the poor in important policy debates.
This inequality further produces a "numbing" effect on the conscience of
the wealthy, who tend to exploit the poor for their own purposes.[4] In light
of the far-reaching effects of inequality, the moral and spiritual imperative of Christians, according to the pope, is to curb excessive wealth and
inequality. He goes so far as to appeal for divine intervention in this cause:
"Why not turn to God and ask him to inspire their [government leaders']
plans? I am firmly convinced that openness to the transcendent can bring
about a new political and economic mindset which would help to break

down the wall of separation between the economy and the common good of society."[5]

Francis's bold attack against excessive wealth and inequality has surprised some. But it should not. Although he has occasionally been associated with politically liberal causes, even his reputedly conservative predecessor, Pope Benedict XVI, has similarly observed that the economy is driven by "purely selfish ends," where the market is a "negative force" undermining friendship, solidarity, and reciprocity. As such, Benedict insists, while approvingly citing Pope Leo XIII's *Rerum Novarum* (*On Labor and Capital*), modern economies require, at a minimum, "intervention from the State for purposes of redistribution."[6]

To be sure, these assertions upset many generations of self-identifying American Christians, extending back at least as far as the American advertising executive Bruce Barton, who characterized Jesus as the "Founder of Modern Business."[7] Indeed, this tradition of American Christians condemning the poor, embracing the rich, and celebrating inequality was established well before Barton. As the economist Benjamin M. Friedman has outlined, there were popular preachers throughout the late nineteenth and early twentieth centuries who did precisely this. The Congregationalist pastor Henry Ward Beecher, for example, preached that God "has meant that the great shall be great and that the little shall be little" and further that "no man in this land suffers from poverty unless it be more than his fault—unless it be his *sin*." An Episcopal bishop in Massachusetts, William Lawrence, wrote, "Godliness is in league with riches." And a Philadelphia Baptist pastor, Russell Conwell, implored his congregants, "I say that you ought to get rich. . . . It is your Christian and godly duty to do so."[8] And this legacy persists today, as one relatively recent study suggests that 61 percent of American Christians believe that "God wants people to be prosperous."[9]

Yet one of the aims of this chapter is to suggest that the pope's attacks on wealth, greed, and inequality hew closer to scripture than this American pastoral tradition suggests. This concern can readily be traced to the earliest figures of the religion: Jesus, Paul, and James. I seek here to contextualize, depict, and elucidate their understandings of these phenomena for multiple reasons. First, as is evidenced in the twenty-first-century popes, the biblical critiques of wealth, greed, and inequality cast a long shadow in Western moral and political thought. And this influence is not limited to popes or even Catholics. The New Testament's repeated skepticism about and even condemnation of wealth, greed, and inequality has permeated Western moral sentiments more broadly. Any historical understanding of these phenomena in the West, therefore, requires engaging the Bible. Second, the critiques of wealth and greed in the New Testament call for serious attention in their own right. Jesus's critique of wealth, in particular, represents a serious argument about the nature of money and its effects on character. James's arguments against wealth push Jesus's arguments even further into an explicitly political realm—suggesting that economic inequality necessarily fuels political domination and tyranny. Third, since these arguments are sometimes underemphasized or even ignored among some professed Christians, it is important to highlight them as part of the religious tradition. The critiques of wealth and greed are not to be dismissed as merely curious passing references. They occur with great frequency and as such are integrated into understanding what it means to be a good Christian. This has, in fact, been the mission of the above-cited popes. My work here clarifies this ambition but with more sustained attention to the texts and contexts of the central characters of the New Testament.[10]

This being said, the New Testament itself presents some ambiguities on matters of wealth, greed, and inequality. I argue that this is most evident in the various approaches to understanding the effects of wealth on the soul. Whereas Jesus and his brother James are particularly concerned about the corrosive effects of wealth on souls, Paul is strikingly silent about the moral effects of great fortunes. His emphasis is rather on the related problem of greed and its tendency to warp souls, a concern he shares with Jesus. But inattention to wealth itself raises important questions about the distinction between the effects of wealth and greed on the soul. It also raises questions about Paul's and Jesus's understandings of wealth. To appreciate their approaches to wealth and greed, it is especially useful to know Jesus's and Paul's respective audiences— which differed in relevant respects. Whereas Jesus largely preached to poor and illiterate Jewish peasants in Galilee, Paul addressed himself to wealthier, educated, and Hellenized peoples in the greater Roman world. Much of what follows here fleshes out these contexts and audiences so that readers might better appreciate their aims. This difference in emphasis between Jesus and James, on the one hand, and Paul, on the other, has given rise to competing understandings among Christians about the ultimate lessons of the New Testament for subsequent interpreters of the religion that persist to the present. Articulating these differences sheds some light on why readers of the New Testament vary greatly on their understanding of the text's teachings regarding wealth and inequality.

Contextualizing the Gospels

While scholars debate various elements of Jesus's life and doctrines, one fact is unquestioned: he was Jesus *of Nazareth*. Nazareth was a real place with historically verified and distinct circumstances. The more one learns about those circumstances, the easier it becomes to understand the frequent attention to matters of wealth, poverty, greed, and inequality throughout the Gospels, and the more difficult it becomes to read the Gospels without considering these issues.

GALILEE

Nazareth was itself part of the larger region of Galilee, specifically in lower Galilee. Shortly before Jesus's birth, upon King Herod's death, Rome divided the Jewish world into three regions to be ruled by Herod's three sons. One of these divisions, which encompassed Galilee and Peraea, fell under the rule of Antipas. Galilee was north of Jerusalem and consisted of many villages, towns, and even some cities. Although little is known about Nazareth's history, scholars know that the village was poor, lacking in basic infrastructure, such as roads, public buildings, or any semblance of sewage systems and waste removal.[11] Homes were built of mud and loose brick. Most residents were peasant farmers engaged in agriculture, animal husbandry, and small craftwork. Among peasants, illiteracy was the norm. The natives spoke Aramaic; Hebrew was largely only known to scholars. Any natives possessing artisan skills would scarcely be able to practice their craft in town and would instead have to travel to the closest city of Sepphoris.

As scholars have noted, the region's heavily agrarian economy was exceptionally vulnerable to drought and famine.[12] Indeed, excepting rare bumper crops, food scarcity predominated. Peasant farmers throughout Galilee endured perpetual poverty and hunger. Farming techniques were primitive in important respects, and population density added further pressures on food supplies. Moreover, there is evidence that in seeking to penetrate the emerging market of wealthy neighbors in places like Sepphoris, there was a degree of "speculative agriculture," such as viticulture, which exposed local farmers to market fluctuations and periodically left them on the brink of starvation.[13] Adding to the existing economic stress, the Roman practice of "liberating" Hellenized cities of Palestine in the second century BCE had driven significant numbers of Jewish refugees into the provinces, which had the effect of increasing the labor pool and driving down compensation.[14]

More dramatic than these sources of poverty in Galilean villages, however, were the social sources of this poverty. The historian Martin

Goodman has argued that much of their poverty can be attributed to the practice of predatory lending and subsequent land seizures.[15] In violation of the Jewish law banishing loans with interest (Exodus 22:25; Leviticus 25:36–37),[16] wealthy and enterprising citizens issued high-interest loans to the provincial poor and desperate landowners, who lacked other options amid impending starvation. Lenders understood from the outset that the peasant farmers were unlikely to raise the funds to repay the loans. This did not, however, deter them. It was, in fact, precisely their inability to pay off the loans that made them attractive to the wealthy lenders, who would then be able to seize the land on nonpayment. As such, they could expand their property holdings at a relative bargain and then convert the farmers into tenants[17] or, in many cases, slaves.[18] As the New Testament scholar John Dominic Crossan has commented, wealthy lenders did "much better by heavy fines for nonpayment" than they ever could have done with conventional loans where they expected timely payments.[19]

The effects of this poverty were compounded when considering their social, psychic, and even religious effects. It was common, for example, for many poor Galilean farmers to lack the resources to host proper Shabbat dinners and Passover seders, which required meat, fish, and eggs as well as ceremonial bread. To fail in this regard was not merely disappointing but was also considered "socially and religiously demeaning." Similar problems also attended poor clothing, which would sometimes have the effect of excluding the poor from important religious ceremonies.[20]

Poverty in rural Galilee stood in stark relief when compared to the region's largest and wealthiest city of Sepphoris. As Galilee's administrative center, Sepphoris was close enough to Nazareth—about three miles—that it was possible for many rural craftsmen to commute for work. What they would have seen there during the life of Jesus would represent a striking contrast with their hometowns. The regional governor of Galilee, Antipas, had invested enormous sums to make the city worthy of its distant Roman patrons as the "ornament of all Galilee."[21] The city was lined with lavish mosaics adorned by Greek inscriptions, as well as large and luxurious homes—the likes of which did not exist in places like Nazareth.

JERUSALEM

Farther from Nazareth than Sepphoris but unquestionably at the center of the Jewish world during Jesus's life was Jerusalem, which had its own building boom two decades prior to Sepphoris under Herod's rule. Rome had appointed Herod as client king to impose order on its various Jewish sects. Herod achieved this by acquiring a reputation for tyrannical cruelty, suppressing all political opposition.[22] Thereafter, he embarked on a series of building projects signaling the city's jurisdiction under Hellenized Rome—with markets, theaters, and grand palaces for its elite. He funded these projects with high taxes, especially burdening Judaea's poor. When combined with tithes and other taxes, it is estimated that the overall tax burden on typical peasant farmers at this time could exceed 40 percent of their total harvest.[23]

One of the client king's central duties was appointing the high priest of the Temple, which was itself the epicenter of Jerusalem and the Jewish world.[24] Typical of the empire, the Romans insisted that the high priest be distinguished, above all, by personal wealth,[25] regardless of any natural connection to the Jewish people in Jerusalem, much less any claims to their affection. The high priests of this post-Herod era until the destruction of the Second Temple in 70 CE used their office to enhance their personal wealth as well as their friends'.[26] The construction of the Temple itself brought an influx of money into Jerusalem, which increased the wealth of the Jerusalem elites and placed additional financial pressures on the city's poor by increasing rents and land values.[27]

HEBREW SCRIPTURE BACKGROUND

The accumulation of wealth in the hands of a small elite was certainly not unusual in the larger Roman world. But the accumulation of wealth by a small subset of citizens was considered extremely unseemly and even ungodly among many in the Jewish community—a point to which the elite Romans and their beneficiaries were indifferent. If anything, much of Jewish scripture tended to promote the view that poverty, if anything, was noble. There is a prominent motif in the Hebrew Bible of the unjust sufferings of the poor, often at the hands of the rich, and of the obligations of others to do all in their power to alleviate the poor's condition. Among the most notable such occasions occurs in the book of Amos. By all accounts, Amos delivered his prophecy in the context of economic prosperity for Israel, generated largely by growth in commerce and trade. Amos's concern was that this prosperity was concentrated in a wealthy elite that was defined by its indifference to poverty.[28] Amos sketches a lifestyle of the rich that would be considered luxurious at any stage of history, featuring large and sumptuous homes. The wealthy slept on ivory beds, ate chateaubriand while being serenaded by the lute, and drank fine wines. This was bad enough for Amos. But the underlying source of this wealth made these luxuries especially intolerable. This wealth was largely extracted from the poor via dubious lending practices. And when the poor could not pay their debts, the wealthy went so far as to confiscate their clothing. In the face of such affronts, Amos insists that God condemns the wealthy who have sold their "righteous[ness] for silver" and have "trample[d] the head of the poor into the dust of the earth" (Amos 2:6–7).[29] Such deeds, Amos prophesizes, create an angry god bent on vengeance, specifying among other punishments that "the houses of ivory shall perish, and the great houses will come to an end" (Amos 3:15).[30] Throughout the book of Amos, the poor are associated with righteousness (e.g., Amos 5:12), whereas the wealthy are self-indulgent, avaricious, and oppressive. At best, the rich are simply indifferent to the predicament of the less fortunate (e.g., Amos 6:6). At worst, they revel in their gains at the poor's expense.

There is further scriptural background that clarifies Amos's perspective. The offenses of the rich in Amos's epoch were in direct violation of Mosaic law, as outlined in the Pentateuch. I refer here specifically to the practices of Sabbatical and Jubilee years. Although these laws are little discussed today and were inconsistently implemented in the past, they are known to have resonated deeply in ancient Jewish culture. Sabbatical years require several economic and agricultural reforms to occur every seven years, all intended to protect the interests of the poor and to manage encroaching inequality. They include the following three provisions:

- First, in the "seventh year you shall let it [your land] rest and lie fallow, so that the poor of your people may eat" (Exodus 23:11).
- Second, "every seventh year you shall grant a remission of debts. And this is the manner of the remission: every creditor shall remit the claim that is held against a neighbor, not exacting it of a neighbor who is a member of the community, because the Lord's remission has been proclaimed" (Deuteronomy 15:1).[31]
- Third, all community members who are slaves must be freed: "If a member of your community, whether a Hebrew man or Hebrew woman, is sold to you and works for you six years, in the seventh year you shall set that person free. And when you send a male slave out from you a free person, you shall not send him out empty-handed. Provide liberally out of your flock . . . thus giving to him some of the bounty with which the Lord your God has blessed you" (Deuteronomy 15:12–14).[32]

These provisions were to be followed every seven years. Beyond this, on the occasion of every seventh Sabbatical year, occurred a Jubilee year, or "year of the Lord's favor" (Luke 4:19). The Jubilee year required adherence to all Sabbatical laws with an additional radical provision:

- "You shall hallow the fiftieth year and you shall proclaim liberty throughout the land to all its inhabitants. It shall be a jubilee for you: you shall return, every one of you, to your property and every one of you to your family" (Leviticus 25:10).[33]

In effect, the Jubilee calls for a restoration of all property to its original owners.[34] And if the original owners cannot be found, then it should be returned to their legal heirs. God was said to have this right over all land ultimately since, as the scripture reports, "the land is mine; with me you are but aliens and tenants" (Leviticus 25:23).[35] Scholars have consistently observed that these provisions were expressly intended to hinder the kind of capital accumulation that characterized the days of Amos, not to mention those of the Second Temple.[36] Judging from the promised divine sanctions for violating Sabbatical and Jubilee year rules in Leviticus, one can assume that these rules were drafted with the utmost seriousness. As Moses reports his god's position on violators: "I will bring terror on you, consumption and fever that waste the eyes and cause life to pine away. . . . You shall be struck down by your enemies; your foes shall rule over you, and you shall flee though no one pursues you. And if in spite of this you will not obey me, I will continue to punish you sevenfold for your sins" (Leviticus 26:16–18).[37]

Although there is record of some of these laws being followed,[38] the wealthy in Jerusalem of the Second Temple period had requested and been granted exemptions from these laws in the form of a *prosbul*, especially those pertaining to remission of debts. The potential creditors had argued successfully to Hillel that the Sabbatical laws had frozen credit and therefore hindered poor farmers in gaining access to the funds required to sustain themselves and their families.[39] To be sure, there is little record of the Jubilee requirement of property redistribution being vigorously followed with regularity in Jewish history.[40] The irregular adherence to these laws, however, does not imply that they failed to excite the imaginations of many Jews, especially among the poor. Well after Moses, for example, Isaiah recovers the language of Jubilee in speaking to an impoverished and oppressed people, proclaiming, "The Lord has anointed me; he has sent me to bring good news to the oppressed to bind up the broken hearted, to proclaim the year of the Lord's favor, and the day of vengeance of our God to comfort all who mourn" (Isaiah 61:1–2), where the "year of the Lord's favor" specifically recalls the Jubilee year of Leviticus. And as theologian John Bergsma has detailed, traces of the Jubilee can be found in much of the rest of the Hebrew Bible, including Kings, Jeremiah, and Ezekiel.[41]

The persistence of this robust scriptural tradition of concern about moral effects of wealth and economic inequality no doubt informed one of the most prominent Jewish sects of Jesus's day: the Essenes.[42] This sect was so noted for its asceticism and strict morality that, by some accounts, it shunned sex of all kinds, insisting on purity. The condemnation of earthly pleasures extended to economic matters. The most detailed record of the Essene economic philosophy can be found in Josephus's *Jewish War*:

> Contemptuous of wealth, they are communists to perfection, and none of them will be found to be better off than the rest: their rule is that novices admitted to the sect must surrender their property to the order, so that among them all neither humiliating poverty nor excessive wealth is ever seen, but each man's possessions go into a pool as with brothers their entire property belongs to them all. . . . Among themselves nothing is bought or sold: everyone gives what he has to anybody in need and receives from him in return something he himself can use; and even without giving anything in return they are free to share the possessions of anyone they choose.[43]

To be sure, the Essenes were small and insular (an estimated four thousand members), but they were by Josephus's account distributed throughout the Jewish world.[44] It is virtually certain that Jesus and his followers would have encountered Essenes in Galilee, although perhaps not the most doctrinaire among them, who were to be found closer to the Dead Sea.[45] Scholars have also speculated that one of Jesus's closest associates, John the Baptist, had strong ties to the Essene community.[46]

Relatedly, one finds condemnation of concentrated wealth in the noncanonical book of Enoch, much of which was written in the century leading up to Jesus, during a period of growing economic inequality throughout the Jewish world. Enoch resembles the book of Amos with its stern judgment of those who have profited at the expense of the poor:

> Woe to you, ye rich, for ye have trusted in your riches,
> And from your riches shall ye depart,
> Because ye have not remembered the Most High in the days of your
>   riches.
>
> Ye have committed blasphemy and unrighteousness,
> And have become ready for the day of slaughter,
> And the day of darkness and the day of the great judgment.
>   (Enoch 94:8–9)

The book continues emphasizing God's uncompromising judgment when it comes to the wealthy:

> Woe unto you, ye sinners, for your riches make you appear like the
>   righteous,
> But your hearts convict you of being sinners,
> And this fact shall be a testimony against you for a memorial of (your)
>   evil deeds.
>
> Woe to you who devour the finest of the wheat,
> And drink wine in large bowls,
> And tread under foot the lowly with your might. (Enoch 96:4–5)

According to Enoch, the wealthy have the most to fear from a vengeful god. As one scholar has observed, for Enoch, the sin can neither be recanted nor forgiven: "Their judgment is certain with no chance for repentance. The prophetic announcements in the *Epistle* [of Enoch] function as a formal testimony to the deeds of the wicked while simultaneously warning the faithful community of the irreversible consequences of associating with the rich."[47]

CLASS ANTAGONISMS IN ROMAN PALESTINE

The growing gap between rich and poor in Roman Palestine was accompanied by increasing social tensions. There were frequent provocations, where the wealthy and powerful would abuse their power, stirring up resentment among the poor. Josephus observes, "Hostility and violent factionalism flared between the high priests on one side, and the priests and the leaders of the Jerusalem masses on the other."[48] These incitements found in poor Jewish peasants a people especially attuned to economic inequality and oppression. The poor knew of the Sabbatical and Jubilee laws and, further, recalled occasions on which they had resisted financial and political oppression, including the successful Maccabean revolt of 167–60 BCE in which peasant Jews ousted the Greek Seleucid Empire along with their wealthy collaborators in Jerusalem, an outcome that surely bolstered optimism that the peasants were not fated to suffer at the hands of wealthy oppressors.[49]

It was likely the confluence of high taxes, predatory lending, inescapable debt, drought, famine, and desperate poverty that was the most proximate cause of an angry peasant class. Among other consequences, this resulted in the proliferation of bandits throughout Roman

Palestine. They are noted in the Gospels, where Jesus is recorded as suspecting that his arrest was on charges of banditry (Mark 14:48) and where he is crucified between two accused bandits (Mark 15:27). As the historian Eric Hobsbawm has outlined, regardless of other factors, bandits typically emerge in agrarian societies from the peasant classes after a period of suffering at the perceived hands of elites.[50] The crucial variables in producing bandits are the underlying desperation of the indigent, as well as the ascendance of a wealthy class perceived to benefit at the poor's expense. Such conditions certainly characterized Roman Palestine.

The first wave of brigands, according to Josephus, emerged under the leadership of Hezekiah around 47 BCE and was violently quelled by Herod.[51] The violent response, however, did not suppress the movement of disgruntled peasants, who continued in subsequent decades to represent a significant thorn in the side of economic and political elites. Claiming to be agents of God, they plundered the homes of the wealthiest citizens and sometimes even redistributed their booty to the poor.[52] As the New Testament scholar Richard A. Horsley has observed, whereas the elites feared and detested the bandits, the poor regarded these thieves as "heroes," frequently hiding and protecting them when pursued by the authorities.[53] Josephus reports that by 50 CE, "the whole of Judaea was infested with brigands."[54]

The culmination of these tensions ultimately came in the form of a massive and failed revolt against the Roman occupation of Judaea, a conflict defined by its class dimensions.[55] Although tensions between the Roman occupiers and their wealthy collaborators, on the one hand, and the Jewish peasants and brigands, on the other, had endured for decades, by 56 CE, they had reached a fevered pitch. Frustrated by the continued occupation, the imposition of crushing poverty, unemployment, high taxes, and the seizure of private farms, the bandits grew desperate and bold. Among the various robbers inhabiting Jerusalem in this period were the Sicarii, who, on Josephus's account, "took their name from a dagger carried in their bosoms."[56] These uncompromising bandits relied on popular support in stabbing several high priests, then melting back "into the indignant crowd."[57] Their boldest measure in 66 CE was storming the house of the high priest Ananias, setting fire to his home. This was not mere random violence—Josephus notes that they had a particular goal in mind. The Sicarii "took their fire to the Record Office, eager to destroy the money-lenders' bonds and so make impossible the recovery of debts, in order to secure the support of an army of debtors and enable the poor to rise with impunity against the rich. The keepers of the records fled and the building was set on fire."[58] Destroying all official records of debts, they had hoped, would de facto reinstate the Sabbatical law of debt remittance.

Such moments of relative triumph for the bandits, however, were short lived. Although the rebels had seized the Temple, the Romans would win the war by effectively trapping them within it—cutting them off from food and water supplies. Those who escaped in search of food were immediately put down. By 70 CE, the Romans finally set the Temple ablaze, killing thousands of rebels inside. Afterward, the Romans forbade the Jews from rebuilding a temple to their God and rather constructed a temple to the Roman god of Jupiter as a final insult to the remaining Jews. The whole affair, which was the culmination of more than a century of economic, political, and religious division, was thoroughly demoralizing. Josephus aptly describes the aftermath of this protracted conflict:

> Somehow those days had become so productive of every kind of wickedness among the Jews as to leave no deed of shame uncommitted; and even if someone had used all his powers of invention, he could not have thought of any vice that remained untried; so corrupt was the public and private life of the whole nation, so determined were they to outdo each other in impiety towards God and injustice to their neighbors, those in power ill-using the masses, and the masses striving to overthrow those in power. One group was bent on domination, the other on violence and robbing the rich.[59]

Although Josephus was no philosopher, the barren remains of Jewish civilization he describes here reflect Plato's observations about persistent inequality in ancient Greece and Persia. When Persia elevated the wealthy ruling class well above its subjects, according to Plato's Athenian Stranger, it "destroyed friendship and community within the city" (*Laws*, 697c). According to Plato's Socrates in the *Republic*, such rule usually culminates in the people "hating and plotting against those who have acquired their property, and all others as well; passionately longing for revolution" (*Republic*, 555de). In the wake of said revolution, on this account, the citizens "return insolence, anarchy, extravagance, and shamelessness from exile in a blaze of torchlight, wreathing them in garlands and accompanying them with a vast chorus of followers. They praise the returning exiles and give them fine names, calling insolence good breeding, anarchy freedom, extravagance magnificence, and shamelessness courage" (*Republic*, 560de).

Jesus

It is easy to read the Gospels without considering Jesus's historical context. So much of what he says takes on the character of universal maxims
to appeal across cultures and generations. But context provides greater
resonance to his words particularly on economic matters. Jesus's immediate audience consisted of rural Galilean peasants, farmers, and fishers.
Compounding their material deprivations was the fact that only a few
miles away in Sepphoris were the ostentatious displays of wealth by those
who had made allies of their Roman occupiers. Exacerbating the sense of
oppression was the fact that this wealthy class engaged in a systematic confiscation of peasant lands through predatory lending practices, enabled by
the suspension of ancient Jewish laws established by Moses. If there ever
was an audience ready for Jesus's economic message, it was surely this one.

Even though there is obviously far more to Jesus's message in the Gospels, I highlight their economic themes. More specifically, I feature poverty, wealth, greed, and economically divided communities. Although any
reader of the Gospels will observe the presence of these themes, it is striking to observe their persistence,[60] their consistency with long-held Jewish
doctrine, and how much these themes resonated with Jesus's immediate
audience. With this background, one can begin to process Jesus's economic lessons.

JESUS'S AMBITIONS: LOVE OF GOD
AND LOVE OF NEIGHBOR

Every chapter of this book endeavors to sketch the ambitions or highest
goals of its respective thinkers. I argued in chapter 1, for example, that
Plato prioritized creating a republic characterized by civic harmony and
friendship. It will be apparent in the next chapter that Thomas Hobbes
sought peace above all. In both of those instances, I have argued that
significant economic inequality posed serious threats to these respective
priorities. I follow the same formula here, though I fully recognize the
contentious nature of this text insofar as many more people have opinions
about the Bible than about Plato or Hobbes and, further, that many readers' opinions about scriptural matters are likely to be categorically different from their opinions about secular texts. Further, opinions about these
matters will often be stronger. I fully recognize that the Bible is a deeply
personal text for each individual reader, and individual readers will surely
have their own opinions about Jesus's priorities.

Since I am not writing theology, however, and instead approach the Bible as I do other historical texts, I emphasize here that even though my assertions about Jesus's intentions have theological implications, I am primarily reading the books of the New Testament as a work of moral and political philosophy and simply as a "Great Book," which it surely is. This being said, I draw here from Augustine, a highly respected religious authority who insists in his *City of God* that God has commanded two things above all: love of God and love of neighbor.[61] Augustine's distilling of Jesus's most ardent wishes for humankind is well grounded in Scripture. He expressly references Jesus's own words in the book of Matthew. When asked "which is the commandment in the law that is the greatest?" Jesus responded,

> "You shall love the Lord your God with all your heart, and with all your soul, and with all your mind." This is the greatest and first command-
> ment. And a second is like it: "You shall love your neighbor as your-
> self." On these two commandments hang all the law and the prophets.
> (Matthew 22:36–40)

Of course, these commandments are anchored in the Hebrew Bible. In meditating on the Ten Commandments in Deuteronomy, Moses explains that the greatest of all commandments is "You shall love the Lord your God with all your heart, and with all your soul, and with all your might" (Deuteronomy 6:5). And in Leviticus, the Lord speaks to Moses, "You shall love your neighbor as yourself" (Leviticus 19:18). Jesus brings these together. For Augustine, these commandments are tightly related because if one *truly* loves God, one must necessarily love one's neighbor. A genuine love of God, in other words, fills one with a love of God's will, especially that everyone should love their neighbor. It is for this reason, Augustine elaborates, "he that loves God, loves His precepts. And what are the precepts of God? *A new commandment I give unto you, that you love one another.*"[62]

These two precepts—loving God and loving one's neighbor—should not be controversial, as they are anchored in Scripture and canonical interpre-tation as well as the practices of many Christians even today. But they also have profound implications for thinking about the Bible on inequality. As should soon become clear, much of what the Bible says about inequality's problems can be traced to how it complicates realizing these two central precepts. To accumulate massive fortunes is, for Jesus, to choose mam-mon over God; to enjoy great wealth while ignoring the needs of the poor is to disregard God's command to neighborly love. These are the simple reasons, I argue, that the Bible so frequently condemns excessive wealth and seeks to promote greater equality.

JESUS ON POVERTY

There is an extended tradition of Jewish Scripture addressing the poor's special status, beginning with Moses's Sabbatical and Jubilee laws, which are expressly crafted to serve the interests of the poor in the Jewish community. As Moses reports God telling him, "Since there will never cease to be some in need on the earth, I therefore command you, 'Open your hand to the poor and needy neighbor in your land'" (Deuteronomy 15:11). In the wisdom literature, "oppressing the poor in order to enrich oneself, and giving to the rich, will lead only to loss" (Proverbs 22:16). Amos speaks repeatedly of God's anger at those "who trample the head of the poor" (Amos 2:7).

Given this tradition, although Jesus's beatitudes may have been received by his adversaries as revolutionary with respect to contemporary practices, they were not *scripturally* revolutionary. They were rather the extension of familiar themes that were understood to have extended back to the very word of God. They are also themes that resonated with peasant farmers. Jesus clearly knows this. There are many indications throughout the Gospels that Jesus speaks to an audience specifically defined by its poverty. This is one reason that he repeatedly references the hunger that plagued impoverished peasant farmers in Galilee. The Gospel of Matthew, for example, specifically identifies his disciples as "hungry" (Matthew 12:1). This may have also been true in a metaphorical sense, but it was unquestionably true in the literal sense. This hunger was not limited to Jesus's immediate disciples. It was endemic throughout Galilee. This is why the theme of feeding hungry peasants occurs with regularity in the Scriptures and likely why it resonated so deeply with those who first learned of the legend of Jesus. Although Jesus performs many miracles, perhaps the most broadly appealing ones to his fellow Galileans were those in which he, for example, transforms seven loaves of bread and "a few small fish" into a meal for more than four thousand hungry peasants (Matthew 15:32–39). Mary's song of praise goes so far as to emphasize God's choice to serve the poor and hungry over the rich: "He has filled the hungry with good things, and sent the rich away empty" (Luke 1:53).

When Jesus speaks of the hungry poor he emphasizes their nobility. His privileging of the indigent over the rich extends throughout the Gospels, commencing with the Beatitudes:

Blessed are the poor in spirit, for theirs is the kingdom of heaven.

Blessed are those who mourn, for they will be comforted.

Blessed are the meek, for they will inherit the earth.

Blessed are those who hunger and thirst for righteousness, for they
   will be filled. (Matthew 5:3–6)

Some ambiguity accompanies this first presentation of the beatitudes insofar as Jesus speaks of the "poor in spirit" and those who "hunger and thirst for righteousness." But the second presentation of the beatitudes in Luke is more direct:

Blessed are you who are poor, for yours is the kingdom of God.

Blessed are you who are hungry now, for you will be filled.

   (Luke 6:20–21)

In this instance, Luke clarifies that although Jesus is surely concerned about those who are poor "in spirit," his most immediate concern is for those who literally hunger for food. They are the people of God whom Jesus has come to address and champion. To clarify, Luke continues, "But woe to you who are rich, for you have received your consolation. Woe to you who are full now, for you will be hungry" (Luke 6:24–25).

The fact that Jesus embraces the poor amid great inequality explains why he is confused with the bandits that populated Roman Palestine and menaced the wealthy ruling class in Judaea. When arrested, Jesus responds by asking the authorities, "Have you come out with swords and clubs to arrest me as though I were a bandit?" (Matthew 26:55; see also Luke 22:52). That Jesus might have been mistaken for a bandit due to his sympathy for the poor is confirmed by the Gospels' depiction of him being crucified between two bandits (Matthew 27:38; see also Mark 15:27).

Finally, Jesus's concern for the poor persists throughout his repeated exhortations to practice almsgiving. This affirms those portions of the Hebrew Bible that demand giving to the poor (e.g., Job 31:16–22; Proverbs 19:17, 31:20; Isaiah, 58:7, 58:10). This doctrine returns early in the Gospels with Jesus insisting that his followers must "give to everyone who begs from you" (Matthew 5:42). In speaking to a rich man, he commands, "Sell your possessions, and give alms" (Luke 12:33). Subsequently, he praises a tax collector for giving half of his possessions to the poor (Luke 19:1–10). He further explains that almsgiving is not to be practiced in a quest for praise: "So whenever you give alms, do not sound a trumpet before you, as the hypocrites do in the synagogues and in the street, so that they may be praised by others" (Matthew 6:2). This is self-exaltation, which contradicts the imperatives of loving God and one's neighbor.

JESUS ON WEALTH

Jesus's embrace of the poor stands in stark contrast to his portrait of the wealthy. Some Christians are reluctant to interpret Jesus as condemning great fortunes. But the fact is that he does so repeatedly and emphatically. The Gospel of Matthew draws attention to the problem of wealth when the devil tempts Jesus in the wilderness: "The devil took him to a very high mountain and showed him all the kingdoms of the world and their splendor; and he said to him, 'All these I will give you, if you will fall down and worship me.' Jesus said to him, 'Away with you, Satan!'" (Matthew 4:8–10). This is the first indication that the Gospels associate wealth with evil, but it is far from the last.

The most familiar of all biblical passages addressing wealth concerns the "eye of a needle" (Matthew 19:16; Mark 10:17–31; Luke 18:18–30), where a young, rich man approaches Jesus to ask what he must do to secure eternal life. Jesus initially responds by reminding him to "keep the commandments," specifically referencing a handful of the Ten Commandments, including the prohibitions against murder, adultery, theft, and lying. But when the rich man presses him,[63] Jesus responds that he should "go, sell your possessions, and give the money to the poor, and you will have treasure in heaven; then come follow me." The Gospel of Matthew continues, "When the young man heard this word, he went away grieving, for he had many possessions" (Matthew 19:21–22). But the most dramatic passage occurs immediately thereafter, where Jesus warns his disciples,

> Truly, I tell you, it will be hard for a rich man to enter the kingdom of heaven. Again I tell you, it is easier for a camel to pass through the eye of a needle than for someone who is rich to enter the kingdom of God. (Matthew 19:23–24)

There is scholarly consensus that Jesus employs this analogy expressly to emphasize the impossibility of the rich man entering God's kingdom.[64] That kingdom is foreclosed to him because he has placed a love of material wealth above his love of God. Diverted from what rightly deserves his love and attention, he treats his material fortune as his god.

To be sure, the "eye of a needle" is the best-known passage in which Jesus problematizes wealth, but it may not even be the most emphatic. This would likely be his account of Lazarus and the "rich man," sometimes known as "Dives."[65]

> "There was a rich man who was dressed in purple and fine linen who feasted sumptuously every day. And at his gate lay a poor man named Lazarus, covered with sores, who longed to satisfy his hunger with what fell from the rich man's table; even the dogs would come and lick his sores. The poor man died and was carried away by angels to be with Abraham. The rich man also died and was buried. In Hades, where he was being tormented, he looked up and saw Abraham far away with Lazarus by his side. He called out, 'Father Abraham, have mercy on me, and send Lazarus to dip the tip of his finger in water and cool my tongue; for I am in agony in these flames.' But Abraham said, 'Child, remember that during your lifetime you received your good things, and Lazarus in like manner evil things; but now he is comforted here, and you are in agony. Besides all this, between you and us a great chasm has been fixed, so that those who might want to pass from here to you cannot do so, and no one can cross from there to us.' He said, 'Then father, I beg you to send him to my father's house—for I have five brothers—that he may warn them, so that they will not also come into this place of torment.' Abraham replied, 'They have Moses and the prophets; they should listen to them.' He said, 'No, father Abraham; but if someone goes to them from the dead, they will repent.' He said to him, 'If they do not listen to Moses and the prophets, neither will they be convinced even if someone rises from the dead.'" (Luke 16:19–31)

This is striking because it confirms the "eye of a needle" passage that the wealthy will not be saved. In fact, Jesus insists not only will the wealthy fail to secure eternal life in God's kingdom, but they will rather be cast into Hades to suffer in burning agony. What is more, Jesus suggests that *there is no saving the wealthy*: "no one can cross from there to us." They have been given a lifeline in the laws of Moses and the prophets but have instead chosen material wealth. By contrast, lowly Lazarus, uncorrupted by wealth and material pursuits, is free to hear Moses and the prophets.[66]

Strikingly, the image of Lazarus enjoying heavenly bliss while the rich man suffers in Hades recalls Plato's account of the afterlife in the *Republic*'s Myth of Er.[67] Even though there are important differences between Plato's version of the afterlife and the book of Luke, Plato's Socrates stresses how wealth and greed merit divine sanctions. On the Athenian's account, vice is punished tenfold with whips, racks, and burning for each violation (*Republic*, 613d, 615a). After this punishment, each soul is allowed to select a new life when reincarnated. Socrates warns his interlocutors to consider the effects of "wealth or poverty" on their souls—with the assumption that great wealth burdens people with vices (*Republic*, 618c). We ought not, he cautions, be "dazzled by wealth and other such evils." We would be wisest to "choose the middle life, . . . and avoid either of the extremes" of wealth or poverty (*Republic*, 619a) since that would produce greater virtue in the reincarnated life and subsequent divine rewards.

Although Jesus outlines many sins meriting divine sanctions, I want to explain why wealth is prominent among them. In exploring this, one must first appreciate that it was common sense for many in Roman Palestine to assume that their wealth had effectively purchased them God's favor. Most obviously, the wealthy could readily afford to give to the Temple, host Shabbats, wear high priest–sanctioned clothing, and participate in Temple sacrifices. These expenses were out of reach for the poor. But the elite in cities like Sepphoris and especially Jerusalem at this time had more than enough to cover these matters with plenty left over for other luxuries. Jesus confronts this when describing the "widow's offering":

> He [Jesus] looked up and saw rich people putting their gifts into the treasury; he also saw a poor widow put in two small copper coins. He said, "Truly I tell you, this poor widow has put in more than all of them; for all of them have contributed out of their abundance, but she out of her poverty has put in all she had to live on." (Luke 21:1–2; see also Mark 12:41–44)

When Jesus praises the impoverished widow donating her last coins, while the wealthy comparatively contribute spare change, he identifies her as more pious. The wealthy keep most of what they have for their own purposes. The only occasion on which Jesus expressly praises a wealthy person is when Zacchaeus gives fully half of his possessions to the poor (Luke 19:8).[68] But Zacchaeus is notable precisely because he is the exception to the norm of modest giving by the wealthy.

Jesus perceives this reluctant benevolence to reveal a lack of commitment to God's laws. This falls under the well-known category of being unable to serve two masters: "No one can serve two masters; for a slave will either hate the one and love the other, or be so devoted to the one and despise the other. You cannot serve God and wealth" (Matthew 6:24; see also Mark 4:1–9 and Luke 8:4–8).[69] The parallel to the slave with two masters suggests that the rich man will come to love one—either God or wealth—and hate the other. If he has chosen to love God and hate wealth, he will presumably donate much of his money to the poor.[70] But if he has chosen wealth over God, we will know by the simple fact that he has kept most of his wealth.

Jesus elaborates on the impossibility of serving both God and wealth in his Parable of the Sower, which occurs in the first three Gospels, each account similar in relevant details. In the parable, he explains the ways in which seeds may fail to thrive. They may fall onto the path, in which case the birds will scoop them up. They may fall on rocky terrain, in which case they will lack the roots to endure the scorching sun. They may fall among thornbushes, in which case they will become "choked up." The only seeds likely to take root are those that fall on good soil. As Jesus subsequently explains, when it comes to the wealthy, his word is received as seeds among thornbushes: "As for what was sown among thorns, this is the one who hears the word, but the cares of the world and the lure of wealth choke the word, and it yields nothing" (Matthew 13:22; see also Mark 4:18–19 and Luke 8:14). The wealthy are too preoccupied with earthly matters to receive the word of God.[71]

JESUS ON GREED

It is already apparent that, for Jesus, wealth and greed are intimately connected. The Parable of the Sower makes this clear insofar as the "lure of wealth choke[s] the word." Yet it is also worth separating wealth and greed for at least two reasons. First, the Gospels employ distinct terms for wealth (*mamōnás*, Romanized as mammon) and greed (*pleonexia*). These are different terms with different definitions. Mammon originated from Jesus's Aramaic of *māmōn*, which originally meant wealth. In New Testament Greek it is *μαμωνᾶς*, which is simply "wealth." On occasion, however, it is modified as the more emphatic *μαμωνᾶς τῆς ἀδικίας*, such as at Luke 16:9, which is translated as "dishonest wealth." Over subsequent generations of interpretation, its meaning has sometimes been blended with greed. But its initial meaning was, in fact, brute wealth. *Pleonexia* (*πλεονεξία*) is a Greek word. Although commonly translated as "greed," usage by Plato and Aristotle suggests something more emphatic.[72] *Pleonexia* implies *insatiable greed*. Those who suffer from it can never satisfy their desires. It can only apply to inexhaustible objects, like wealth, status, and power. One cannot suffer, for example, from a *pleonexia* for food since the stomach can only hold finite quantities. But one can suffer from a *pleonexia* for wealth regardless of how much one already possesses.

Second, wealth and greed are analytically separable. One need not be rich to suffer from greed. The poor can also suffer from greed insofar as they covet the possessions of the rich. This is a problem in the tradition at least as old as Moses (Exodus 20:17). Indeed, it is arguable that one of Jesus's fundamental missions in the Gospels is to dissuade the poor from the belief that the good life means becoming wealthy. This was especially challenging in a world burdened by extreme inequality, where the wealthiest citizens ostentatiously enjoyed their luxuries in full view of the poor. The poor saw that wealth not only bought food, security, and stability, but it also purchased goodwill among religious authorities as well as political power. As is true in most epochs, there were myriad incentives for acquiring great wealth. So one does not need to be rich to be greedy. This being said, given how Jesus characterizes wealth, it is safe to assume that for him the wealthy especially suffer from *pleonexia*.

The best illustration of the problem of *pleonexia* is in Jesus's Parable of the Rich Fool in which he recounts the story of a family confronting a tricky inheritance.

Someone in the crowd said to him [Jesus], "Teacher, tell my brother to divide the family inheritance with me." But he said to him, "Friend, who sent me to be a judge or arbitrator over you?" And he said to them, "Take care! Be on your guard against all kinds of greed, for one's life does not consist in the abundance of possessions." Then he told them a parable. "The land of a rich man produced abundantly. And he thought to himself, 'What should I do, for I have no place to store my crops?' Then he said, 'I will do this: I will pull down my barns and build larger ones, and there I will store all my grain and my goods. And I will say to my soul, Soul, you have ample goods laid up for many years; relax, eat, drink, be merry.' But God said to him, 'You fool! This very night your life is being demanded of you. And the things you have prepared, whose will they be?' So it is with those who store up treasures for themselves but are not rich toward God." (Luke 12:13–21)

One brother is insulted upon learning that the other is to receive the bulk of their parents' inheritance. He appeals this insult directly to Jesus, hoping to win his support for a greater share. But Jesus simply cautions him to guard himself against his own greed. Jesus then recounts the story of a wealthy man whose primary concern is constructing an edifice large enough to hold his growing resources—a man dissatisfied simply because he could have even more, if only he had a structure large enough to contain it. The rich man is persuaded for the moment that if he could only have this much more, he could then "eat, drink, and be merry."

The inclination to "eat, drink, and be merry" itself has deeper roots in the Hebrew Bible. It references the book of Ecclesiastes, which explores the folly of prioritizing earthly pursuits, particularly wealth and vanity. It depicts someone dedicated to pursuing these ends in order that he might "eat and drink, and find enjoyment" (Ecclesiastes 2:24; see also 3:13 and 8:15). This pursuit originates in the "envy of one another," which inspires nothing less than "chasing after the wind" (Ecclesiastes 4:4) a metaphor pervasive throughout Ecclesiastes. The metaphor depicts the curse of *pleonexia*. "I saw vanity under the sun: the case of solitary individuals without sons or brothers; yet there is no end to all their toil, and their eyes are never satisfied with riches" (Ecclesiastes 4:7).[73] Indeed, Ecclesiastes suggests that the very pursuit of political power is also a futile effort to satisfy the insatiable: "On the side of their oppressors there was power—with no one to comfort them" (Ecclesiastes 4:1). There is no satisfying the pursuit of riches, social status, and power.

As Luke alludes, one seeks these ends in the pursuit of pleasure and merriment. But the reference to Ecclesiastes clarifies its futility: "There is an evil that I have seen under the sun, and it lies heavy upon humankind: those to whom God gives wealth, possessions, and honor, so that they lack nothing of all that they desire, yet God does not enable them to enjoy these things, but a stranger enjoys them. This is vanity, it is a grievous ill" (Ecclesiastes 6:1–2). In pursuing wealth, status, and power, one casts aside spiritual aims by the very nature of *pleonexia* or "chasing the wind." Because an all-consuming *pleonectic* quest forecloses the possibility of achieving sufficient wealth, power, or status, there is no opportunity for spiritual pursuits. There is no respite from acquisitive demands: "the surfeit of the rich will not let them sleep" (Ecclesiastes 5:12).

Much of what transpires in Ecclesiastes applies to Luke's Rich Fool, a man defined by his wealth and his greed. Despite his vast fortune, he feels compelled to seek still more. In constructing new barns to deposit larger harvests he intends to sell at great profit, he is in the grips of *pleonexia*. Indeed, this kind of wealth acquisition is precisely what led the wealthy in Roman Palestine to engage in predatory lending to impoverished farmers. Those already with vast properties and wealth could not resist the lure of greater property and wealth—directly at the expense of their poor neighbors. They "store up treasures for themselves but are not rich toward God" (Luke 12:21). The parable affirms the fateful nature of this choice, especially since this wealthy man here is apparently about to die. Choosing wealth over God and one's neighbors presents him with the same challenge facing the camel attempting to pass through the eye of a needle. His choice has foreclosed any possibility of eternity in God's Kingdom.

When considering the actions of Judas, readers are reminded that *pleonexia* is not merely a "rich person's problem." It is important to recall that as a disciple, Jesus had already instructed him to abandon all of his money (Matthew 9:8–9; Mark 6:8; Luke 9:3). Therefore, it is safe to assume that he is poor. Yet when offered a bribe to betray Jesus (Mark 14:11; Luke, 22:5), he immediately seizes it. So even though Judas is poor, he too is consumed with a greed that corrupts his judgment to the extent of collaborating in the arrest of his friend and teacher. As the philosopher T. K. Seung has suggested, "When a soul lives in poverty, it is always subject to the temptation of greed."[74] Indeed, the story of Judas's betrayal demonstrates the dangers of inequality and greed on both sides of the equation. On the one side, Judas's poverty and greed for money renders him morally vulnerable. On the other side, the priests offering the bribe—greedy to consolidate and extend their power by snuffing out apparent threats—enable this corruption of Judas by virtue of their fortunes. Further, one might argue that it is their love of power and the perceived threat of Jesus that initially inspires the plot. This reveals how the lust for both money and power—two of the main objects of *pleonexia*—conspire in summoning the central betrayal of the Gospels.

"A House Divided": Jesus versus the Pharisees

Along with the Essenes and the Sadducees, the Pharisees were one of the primary Jewish sects in Roman Palestine. Josephus describes them as "the most authoritative exponents of the Law"[75] and the dominant sect in the Jewish world. They emphasized the role of fate in human affairs, but somewhat paradoxically they also demanded stern divine judgment for poor earthly choices. While concentrated in Jerusalem with strong ties to Temple authorities, they had a reputation extending throughout Roman Palestine as "representatives of Jerusalem interests," known for "pressing the 'laws of the Judaeans' upon the inhabitants" of Galilee.[76] But although the Pharisees cultivated this reputation for legal fidelity, they were sometimes less committed to the precise letter of the law, at least when compared to the Sadducees.[77] They had their own prominent rabbis, including the celebrated Hillel, who adapted the Hebrew law to his times.

Jesus's difficulties with the Pharisees are well chronicled.[78] The overarching theme of his diatribe against them is hypocrisy. They presented themselves as being among the holiest of citizens in Jerusalem, when in his estimation they were the most corrupt. They cultivated a reputation for piety by tending to appearances. They spoke of God and Moses's laws, but they neither worship their God with genuine piety nor are they faithful to the spirit of his laws: "You tithe mint, dill, and cumin, and have neglected the weightier matters of the law: justice and mercy and faith" (Matthew 23:23). The underlying problem, for Jesus, was their wealth and greed. While they "clean the outside of the cup and of the plate," they are at the same time "full of greed and self-indulgence" (Matthew 23:25). This association with wealth and greed is clarified when Jesus suggests they have "swallow[ed] a camel" (Matthew 23:24)—allusion to the "eye of a needle." The allusion appears unambiguous since Jesus himself asks the Pharisees rhetorically, "How can you escape being sentenced to hell?" (Matthew 23:33).

Knowing this assessment of the Pharisees is essential for understanding Jesus's "house divided" (Matthew 12:22; Mark 3:24–25; Luke 11:17).

> Then they brought him [Jesus] to a demoniac who was blind and mute; and he cured him, so that the one who had been mute could speak and see. All the crowds were amazed and said, "Can this be the son of David?" But when the Pharisees heard it, they said, "It is only by Beelzebul,[79] the ruler of the demons, that this fellow casts out the demons." He knew what they were thinking and said to them, "Every kingdom divided against itself is laid to waste, and no city or house divided against itself will stand."

There is plenty transpiring here, much of it profoundly theological, as one might expect. But I want to emphasize its economic and political dimensions. Jesus had already identified Pharisees as "full of greed and self-indulgence." This is also a good moment to recall that Hillel—the rabbi who issued the *prosbul*, suspending the Sabbatical and Jubilee laws—was himself a Pharisee. The *prosbul*, as previously noted, had the likely unintentional effect of delivering peasant lands into the hands of the regional elite. Given this, peasants from Galilee likely understood the Pharisees as conspiring with the other wealthy citizens of Roman Palestine. It is accurate to call the Jewish people of Roman Palestine a "house divided" in economic terms.[80] There were two classes of citizens with virtually no middle class. The large gap between the classes had fomented distrust and even violence[81] that would culminate in the destruction of the Temple. Even though Jesus was doubtlessly concerned about perceived theological shortcomings of the Pharisees and their part in fracturing the Jewish community, it is easy to imagine that, as a Galilean peasant, he also worried about the radical economic inequality they had fostered through public policy and manipulation of Mosaic law.

What to Do about Inequality?

For Jesus, wealth, greed, and inequality had profound effects on at least two levels. First, concentrated wealth created an opulent class that had abandoned God and God's laws. They had effectively surrendered their souls in a *pleonectic* quest to enrich themselves at the expense of their less fortunate neighbors. As such, the rich exposed themselves to divine sanctions and exclusion from God's Kingdom. Second, the creation of a class towering above their impoverished neighbors created a "house divided" that would succumb to violence and be "laid to waste." The pressing question in the face of both civic and spiritual destruction is whether Jesus offers any solutions. I argue that he provides at least two: a restitution of the Mosaic Sabbatical and Jubilee laws and his ambitious doctrine of love of neighbor. Both seek to ameliorate the social and spiritual problems of wealth, greed, and inequality.

REINSTATING THE SABBATICAL AND JUBILEE LAWS

In one of the most striking passages in the Gospels, early in his ministry Jesus announces his mission to his neighbors in Nazareth:

> The Spirit of the Lord is upon me, because he has anointed me to bring good news to the poor. He has sent me to proclaim release to the captives and recovery of sight to the blind, to let the oppressed go free, to proclaim the year of the Lord's favor. (Luke 4:18–19)

This pronouncement references the Hebrew Bible's book of Isaiah, which had similarly announced,

> The spirit of the Lord God is upon me, because the Lord has anointed me; he has sent me to bring good news to the oppressed, to bind up the brokenhearted, to proclaim liberty to the captives, and release the prisoners; to proclaim the year of the Lord's favor. (Isaiah 61:1–2)

As scholars have observed, the reference to the "year of the Lord's favor" in both passages are to the Jubilee years described in Leviticus 25.[82] As discussed earlier, Jubilee years require (1) letting the lands go fallow so that the poor may eat from them, (2) remitting all debts, (3) freeing all slaves, and (4) restoring all property to its original equitable distribution as established in Exodus. According to the Pentateuch, the first three laws must be carried out once every seven years, and the fourth must happen once every half century. Hillel suspended these laws after wealthy land-owners appealed to him that the laws had frozen credit. In proclaiming this to be the "year of the Lord's favor," however, Jesus appears to call for restoring these very laws.

This interpretation of Jesus as calling for the restoration of Sabbatical and Jubilee laws is buttressed by the persistent theme of debts and debt remittance in the Gospels. It is easy to neglect, for example, the political significance of the Lord's Prayer, which demands that others "forgive us our debts, as we forgive our debtors" (Matthew 6:12; see also Luke 11:4).[83] But its significance would have been apparent to Jesus's immediate audience of impoverished peasant farmers in Nazareth, suffering under the burden of substantial, predatory, high-interest loans secured under economic duress. The forgiveness of debts, as required by Jewish law, was among the most hopeful messages they might have received during the Second Temple era. It was the one measure that might have forestalled generations of grinding poverty for them and their descendants.

The theme of debt remittance emerges subsequently in the Parable of the Unforgiving Servant. In this story, a slave owes his king ten thousand talents, an astronomical figure he cannot possibly afford. Jesus reports that the king takes pity on the slave, releases him from slavery, and then forgives the entire debt in accordance with the Sabbatical laws. Afterward, however, this released slave becomes an unforgiving creditor himself, demanding his debtor to "pay what you owe." When the debtor fails to raise the small amount owed, the creditor "threw him in prison until he would pay the debt" (Matthew 18:28). Upon discovering the deeds of the debtor-turned-unforgiving creditor, the king is enraged, condemning him to torture until the king recovers his original once-forgiven ten-thousand-talent debt. The parable clearly references the obligations of the Sabbatical laws, including the freeing of slaves and especially debt remittance. In this instance, the king has fulfilled the law, while the former debtor has flagrantly violated it. As Michael Hudson has observed, this parable "leaves little doubt that the poor should literally be forgiven their debts."[84]

There is still another reference to debt remittance in Luke in which Jesus dines in the house of Simon, one of the Pharisees. Shortly after sitting down to eat, a disreputable woman appears. She proceeds to weep, bathe Jesus's feet, dry them with her hair, and anoints them with oil. The Pharisee is outraged by this disruption, calling her a "sinner" (Luke 7:39). But Jesus replies with a story:

A certain creditor had two debtors; one owed five thousand denarii, and the other fifty. When they could not pay, he canceled the debts for both of them. Now which of them will love him more? (Luke 7:41–42)

Jesus's question is almost rhetorical, but Simon acknowledges that the greatest love comes from the debtor forgiven the most. This parable is especially important not only because it recalls the Sabbatical law of debt remittance, but it also hints at the law's social benefits: it builds goodwill. One may argue, as people did in these days, that remitting debts is bad for the credit industry. But its social benefits are significant. Not only does it mitigate the radical inequalities between the poorest and wealthiest citizens, but it also fosters a culture of forgiveness and love. Under such conditions, wealthier citizens no longer view their fellow citizens as wallets to be exploited but rather as human beings deserving of forgiveness. Similarly, the poor no longer view the wealthy as oppressors but rather as forgiving fellow citizens. These effects could be magnified by the enforcement of the Jubilee laws Jesus references in Matthew, requiring property redistribution. If such laws were enforced on a willing populace, one might argue, tensions between rich and poor would be diminished. A Jubilee every fifty years would prevent the accumulation of the kind wealth that requires generations to accumulate. It is, effectively, the biblical equivalent of a steep estate tax—a proposal with advocates from Plato to Mill—with the purpose of managing inequality to stave off "the house divided" that threatened and ultimately consumed Roman Palestine. Indeed, to the extent that citizens anticipate an impending Jubilee and the return of property to original owners, this would reduce the incentives for pursuing extreme wealth in the first place. That is, it represents a structural check on greed itself. As Rousseau observes in his *Emile*, "How much less greedy usurers were made by the Jubilee of the Hebrews, and how many miseries prevented!"[85] When one cannot accumulate limitless wealth, one is less susceptible to *pleonexia*. One may desire more wealth, just as one desires food and drink, but the fact that it must eventually be returned makes it less an object of an obsessive, all-consuming quest at others' expense.

LOVE OF GOD/LOVE OF NEIGHBOR/LOVE OF ENEMIES

While the reestablishment of Sabbatical and Jubilee laws represents a top-down strategy for coping with inequality, for Jesus this must be paired with a bottom-up strategy of reforming the human heart. This mission is so central to teachings of the Gospels that he describes it as representing the two greatest commandments:

> When the Pharisees heard that he had silenced the Sadducees, they gathered together, and one of them, a lawyer, asked him a question to test him: "Teacher, which commandment in the law is the greatest?" He said to him, "You shall love the Lord your God with all your heart, and with all your soul, and with all your mind. And a second is like it: 'You shall love your neighbor as yourself.' On these two commandments hang all the law and the prophets." (Matthew 22:34–40; see also Mark 12:30–34 and Luke 10:27)[86]

Notably, Jesus once again addresses the Pharisees, whom he associated with greed and the love of money, no doubt partly because of their role in the *prosbul* suspending the Sabbatical and Jubilee laws, as well as their general association with the growing inequality plaguing Roman Palestine.

There is much to unpack in the twin commandments to love God and to love one's neighbor. First, one must observe the pairing of these commandments. Commentary acknowledges that these two commandments are "inextricable."[87] Among the most thoughtful meditations on this relationship can be found in Benedict de Spinoza's *Theological-Political Treatise*, though broadly shared among scriptural interpreters, which identified all of divine law to be summed up in these twin commandments.[88] Since the Gospels do not themselves elaborate on the relationship of the commandments to love of God and to love of neighbor, Spinoza points to several passages in both the Old and New Testaments that do. For example, he locates a passage in which Jeremiah reports God contrasting righteous and unrighteous kings. The unrighteous king builds his kingdom by exploiting the poor while constructing a great palace for himself. The righteous king, by contrast, tends to the poor and needy. "Is this not to know me? Says the Lord" (Jeremiah 22:16). The scriptural implication, on Spinoza's reading, is that knowledge and love of God necessarily require love of one's neighbors, especially the neediest. He also points to 1 John, which emphasizes the command to love one another:

> Beloved, let us love one another, because love is from God; everyone who loves is born of God and knows God. Whoever does not love does not know God, for God is love. God's love was revealed among us in this way: God sent his only Son into the world so that we might live through him. In this is love, not that we loved God but that he loved us and sent his Son to be the atoning sacrifice for our sins. Beloved, since God loved

us so much, we ought to love one another. No one has ever seen God; if we love one another, God lives in us, and his love is perfected in us. (1 John 4:7–12)

This passage suggests that if one is to know and love God, then one must do what God wants most—to treat one another with love and kindness.

The command to neighborly love, as depicted in the Gospels, is notably detached from other kinds of worship that might have required money. In Mark's version of the fundamental commandments, Jesus is persuasive with his Pharisee interlocutor, who adds, "'to love one's neighbor as oneself.'—this is much more important than all whole burnt offerings and sacrifices." Jesus immediately approves: "You are not far from the kingdom of God" (Mark 12:33–34). It is especially notable here that the scribe is a Pharisee, who likely could have well afforded the costs associated with ritual sacrifices at the Temple. Those sacrifices were considered central to many Pharisees of this time and indeed many people throughout Roman Palestine. Yet prioritizing "love of neighbor" above ritual sacrifices is corrective in at least two respects. First, it implies that wealth does not purchase God's favor. Second, it insists that if one does have wealth, it is better—and infinitely more pious—to spend that money on helping others.

Indeed, if a rich person were to take the directive of loving neighbors seriously, it might suggest abandoning his wealth altogether. As legal scholar J. Duncan M. Derrett has suggested, "As we infer from instances in the Gospel, . . . a man could hardly be rich in those days without neglecting the command 'Love thy neighbor. . . .' Consequently, riches and unrighteous living were virtually synonymous."[89] This argument implies at least two important observations. First, Roman Palestine's wealthy often acquired their riches at the expense of the poor, in which case they had already sinned against their neighbors. Second, every moment that they failed to relinquish their fortunes without aiding the poor constituted additional violations of Jesus's command to love one's neighbors.

Of course, as previously noted, the command to neighborly love has a history extending far back in Jewish Scripture. To be sure, Jesus affirms this tradition, but he also extends it in the Sermon on the Mount:

You have heard it was said, "You shall love your neighbor and hate your enemy." But I say to you, Love your enemies and pray for those who persecute you, so that you may be children of your Father in heaven; for he makes his sun rise on the evil and on the good, and sends rain on the righteous and on the unrighteous. For if you love those who love you, what reward do you have? Do not even the tax collectors do

the same? And if you greet only your brothers and sisters, what more
are you doing than others? Do not even the Gentiles do the same? Be
perfect, therefore as your heavenly Father is perfect. (Matthew 5:43–48)

For Jesus, though the command to neighborly love is important and
necessary, it can also be relatively easy, especially when imagining these
"neighbors" to be friends and relatives. In these instances, it is scarcely
demanding to ask one to love them. That love exists regardless of God's
commands. The real challenge is to extend that love to those we are
inclined to hate—our enemies. The New Testament scholar N. T. Wright
suggests that the most likely enemies of Jesus's immediate and impoverished audience were their wealthy oppressors. It was a society, he notes,
"with a few becoming very rich and the majority being poor, some very
poor."[90] This context is essential for understanding that when a wealthy
creditor was suing his delinquent and impoverished debtor in court to
take his coat, Jesus counsels, "Give your cloak as well" (Matthew 5:40).
This passage revealing tensions related to economic inequality comes
immediately preceding the demand to love our enemies. The poor were
inclined to hate the rich, especially when they were confiscating property
for failed debt payments. The aim of Jesus's demanding reformulation of
"love of neighbor" was to defuse the tensions that inevitably arise in economically divided cities.

To be sure, scholars have commented on the difficulty of this command to love one's enemies. Many suggest that it is even impossible.
Among other implications, some argue, this is why Christians require Jesus
in order to overcome their own human limitations imparted to them via
original sin. Setting these theological considerations aside, however, even
if it is impossible to act on this imperative all the time, one imagines that
to the extent it is followed, it has the capacity to calm elevated tensions
in divided societies.

One might argue that loving one's enemies plays into the hands of
the wealthy. A wealthy oppressor can exploit this meek and forgiving philosophy to rack up the profits without resistance. But it is important to
understand that Jesus issues this command while also evoking the Sabbatical and Jubilee laws. As such, this is emphatically a two-pronged program of economic and social reform with each prong mutually reinforcing
the other. Insofar as people are inclined to love both their neighbors and
enemies, they might be less inclined to exploit them for profit. Insofar as
the Sabbatical and Jubilee laws are enforced, there will likely be fewer
oppressors tempted to exploit their neighbors. Thus, the poor are not

merely standing targets vulnerable to exploitation. The gap between rich and poor is systematically and regularly reduced and reset at something resembling equality such that the poor are not so vulnerable and the rich are not so powerful. Rousseau's reading of the Jubilee laws is especially insightful on this relationship between these laws and the neighborly love Jesus means to promote: "The brotherhood promoted by this law unified the whole [Jewish] nation, and not a beggar was to be seen among them."[91] The equality introduced by Jubilee laws, along with its powerful check on greed, for Rousseau, had the effect of promoting "brotherhood." In this context, one can appreciate how tightly related the Jubilee laws and neighborly love are as a unified strategy of promoting social harmony.

James

Many of Jesus's thoughts on greed, wealth, and inequality are amplified in the book attributed to his younger brother James. There are disputes among scholars on whether James himself might have written the letter. Some have speculated that as a poor Galilean Jew, James would have lacked the ability to write in Greek.[92] Others have argued that James could have dictated it to a scribe or secretary, who would have had Greek-language skills.[93] But even those scholars raising doubts about James's composition concede that the letter is likely a faithful account of a historically important figure of the early church.

Regardless of authorship, the themes in James cling remarkably close to Jesus, especially regarding economics and justice. Early on, James warns the rich,

> Let the believer who is lowly boast in being raised up, and the rich in being brought low because the rich will disappear like a flower in the field. For the sun rises with its scorching heat and withers in the field; its flower falls, and its beauty perishes. It is the same way with the rich; in the midst of a busy life, they will wither away. (James 1:9–11)

This passage recalls at least three key themes of the Gospels. First, its reference to a failed flower evokes the Parable of the Sower in which poorly planted seeds yield failed crops—just as God's word fails to take root among the rich. Second, it alludes to the "busy lives" of the rich. As discussed before, the biblical view is that the wealthy are too consumed with earthly pursuits to concern themselves with spiritual matters. Finally, the passage evokes the beatitudes' celebration of the poor and lowly in contrast to the wealthy. Even though the poor are not guaranteed salvation here, they are far better situated, in James's estimation, to receive God's word. They reside in the "good soil" that yields fruitful crops.

The most dramatic passage in James relevant to wealth and greed, however, follows shortly thereafter:

> Come now, you rich people, weep and wail for the miseries that are coming to you. Your riches have rotted, and your clothes are moth-eaten. Your gold and silver have rusted, and their rust will be evidence against you, and it will eat your flesh like fire. You have laid up treasure for the last days. Listen! The wages of the laborers who mowed your fields, which you kept back by fraud, cry out, and the cries of the har-vesters have reached the ears of the Lord of hosts. You have lived on the earth in luxury and in pleasure; you have fattened your hearts in the day of slaughter. You have condemned and murdered the righteous one, who does not resist you. (James 5:1–5)

Whereas James 1:9 is pessimistic about the prospects of the wealthy earning God's favor, this passage is exclusionary. Consistent with Luke 16:26, James holds the wealthy to be destined for divine punishment. They deserve this fate, he suggests, because of their myriad wealth-related sins. Instead of dedicating themselves to service of the needy, they have instead dedicated their time to accumulating private riches. Further, James suggests that their fortunes have been accumulated dubiously by exploiting the poor. His vituperation reflects the historical context, as the speculative rich were confiscating the lands of peasant farmers throughout Roman Palestine, especially in Galilee, where James grew up with his brother. Those indebted farmers were then converted into either slaves or tenant farmers with the suppressed wages referenced here. James reminds the oppressors that although they have enjoyed the fruits of their injustices in this world, they will not escape divine judg-ment in the next.

James concludes the above passage by referencing his brother's arrest and crucifixion. For him, it was surely not the poor who orches-trated Jesus's demise. It was those wealthy, "fattened" ones who wielded political power in Jerusalem. They did what the wealthy tend to do when threatened—they eliminated the threat. On this construction, Jesus was a poor Galilean, who championed the poor and oppressed throughout Roman Palestine. He questioned the morals and spiritual commitments of the rich and powerful. He cited inconvenient scripture. The natural response was to eliminate the man most responsible for challenging their wealth, status, and power.

Further, for the scholars who think that the book of James was not authored by James himself but was rather conceived as a tribute to "The Just One," as his followers called him, the reference to "condemnation" and "murder" assumes even greater relevance. This is because, like his brother before him, James was also condemned and executed. Evidence suggests that James had offended Jerusalem authorities, particularly the high priest Ananus, for exposing official corruption. The wealthy high priests in Jerusalem had been systematically seizing the tithes intended for lower level priests who were closer to the poor farmers. James condemned this act of greed by the wealthy against the poor and was subsequently sentenced to death by stoning.[94] As the sociologist and journalist of religion Reza Aslan has summarized, "James was likely killed because he was doing what he did best: defending the poor and weak against the wealthy and powerful. Ananus's schemes to impoverish the lower-class priests by stealing their tithes would not have sat well with James the Just."[95]

Another feature of James's teaching is his emphasis on the importance of justification by works, rather than by *sola fide*, or salvation by faith alone. Indeed, James's emphasis on the centrality of works over faith was so problematic for Martin Luther's doctrine of *sola fide* that the monk from Worms sought to marginalize the book of James, even calling it an "epistle of straw."[96] Setting aside soteriological questions, however, James's emphasis on works is essential for understanding the social message of early Christianity. He cautions his followers in this regard not to "deceive themselves" into thinking that one can merely hear "the word." They must, rather, be "doers of the word." And he is explicit that "doers" have obligations "to care for orphans and widows in their distress, and to keep oneself unstained by the world" (James 1:22–27).

Finally, it is worth emphasizing a dimension of James's thought less explicit in the Gospels: his emphasis on impartiality.

My brothers and sisters, do you with your acts of favoritism really believe in our glorious Lord Jesus Christ? For if a person with gold rings and in fine clothes comes into your assembly, and if a poor person in dirty clothes also comes in, and if you take notice of the one wearing the fine clothes and say, "Have a seat here, please," while to the one who is poor you say, "Stand there," or "Sit at my feet," have you not made distinctions among yourselves, and become judges with evil thoughts? Listen, my beloved brothers and sisters. Has not God chosen the poor in the world to be rich in faith and to be heirs of the kingdom that he has promised to those who love him? But you have dishonored the poor. Is it not the rich who oppress you? Is it not they who drag you into court? Is it not they who blaspheme the excellent name that was invoked over you? (James 2:1–7)

This passage inaugurates the intellectual tradition of the "general will" culminating in Jean-Jacques Rousseau's political philosophy.[97] As Rousseau subsequently elaborates, there is a great difference between what he calls the general will and a "private" or "particular" will. Whereas the general will privileges equality and the interests of the whole community, private wills represent the benefit of some smaller subset of the community—usually the moneyed interests. For Rousseau, once the common bonds between citizens are broken and neighborly love has dissolved, the impartiality of the general will is replaced by the ascendant partiality of private wills, which enables the rich to shape the laws to suit their selfish purposes. For James, the immediate relevance is the partiality that Roman Palestine had been giving to its wealthiest citizens. They already had the greatest fortunes. But because of this they also exercised all of the political power; they received the benefit of the doubt in courts of law; they occupied the best seats in the synagogues; and they got the presumption on the part of some of having received divine blessings. Meanwhile, the poor got none of the same. James's stress on impartiality assumes that the ordinary course of earthly affairs benefits the wealthy. With some modifications, Paul will also engage this question.

Paul

Differences between the teachings of Jesus and Paul have often drawn the attention of readers and theologians. There is notably a lack of references in Paul's many letters to specific teachings of Jesus, and there is a great deal of emphasis on atonement and the propitiation of sins—matters absent from the Gospels.[98] Paul himself was originally Saul, an educated Pharisee, who as a young man had participated in the persecution of Jesus's followers and even in the execution of the first Christian martyr, Stephen (Acts 7:58–8:3). But as recorded in Acts, Saul experienced a change of heart upon reportedly hearing the disembodied voice of Jesus, who appealed, "Saul, Saul, why do you persecute me?" The same voice then appeals to Ananias in Damascus to acknowledge Saul's role in the growth of Jesus's message—that Jesus has identified Saul as "an instrument whom I have chosen to bring my name before Gentiles and kings and before the people of Israel" (Acts 9:4, 15). Henceforth, Saul would be known as Paul.

THE NEW TESTAMENT [89]

Although Jewish and of the same generation as Jesus and James, Paul's background is dramatically different. Rather than originating from the impoverished province of Galilee, Paul grew up in Tarsus, now on the southern coast of Turkey. Being by the sea, it was a prosperous trading city, engaged in commerce, textiles, and learning.[99] Like Galilee, it was under Roman jurisdiction, but it was also more comfortable with this jurisdiction than Nazareth. The native tongue in Tarsus was Greek, so Paul was effectively Greco-Roman. Paul's writing abilities suggest some higher education and the family wealth to cover the associated expenses.[100] At the same time, as a Jew, Paul also enjoyed an extensive education in the Hebrew Scriptures that enabled him to cite long passages from memory. His education in both pagan philosophy and Hebrew Scripture facilitated the unique synthesis of Paul's letters.

Although Paul never met Jesus, he made at least two trips to Jerusalem, where he met the leader of the Jesus movement—James. Much has been written about these encounters, with an emphasis on how Paul would bring Jesus's lessons to the Gentile community. A source of contention between the two concerned how much the Jewish laws—especially kosher laws and circumcision—would be required of Jesus's followers. As a Jew in Jerusalem, James was eager to maintain the Hebrew laws. As a missionary to a Gentile audience keen to avoid adult circumcision, among other concerns, Paul downplayed the importance of those laws, placing more emphasis on faith in Jesus as the Son of God. The question of fidelity to the traditional Jewish laws was a constant source of tension between the two men, but James ultimately permitted Paul to downplay some of them, if only he would "remember the poor," which Paul reports he was "eager to do" (Galatians 2:10).

PAUL ON ALMSGIVING

To Paul's credit, he upheld his accord with James to raise significant alms for the poor—a radical mission of service to the indigent largely unprecedented at this time. Although Paul's delivery of these funds to the Temple in Jerusalem ultimately proved personally disastrous, likely because of the provocative way in which he delivered it,[101] he nevertheless raised substantial funds from his mission throughout the Aegean world for Jerusalem's poor. Of greater enduring importance, however, Paul also preached the centrality of almsgiving to the poor in general—obligations written into Christianity's canonical texts. The most extensive passage on almsgiving comes in the context of Paul's fundraising at James's request. In attempting to raise money for the poor in Jerusalem, Paul appeals to the Corinthians, citing the charity of the impoverished Macedonians, who in "their extreme poverty have overflowed in a wealth of generosity" (2 Corinthians 8:2). These Macedonians, he reports, gave beyond their means so that others might have enough to eat. Paul appeals to the comparatively wealthy Corinthians, not as a "command" but rather in a test of "the genuineness of your love against the earnestness of others" that they dig into their pockets and donate to the poor "according to your means" (2 Corinthians 8:8, 11). For Paul, this means finding a "fair balance" between one's own means and the needs of the impoverished, such that "the one who had much did not have too much, and the one who had little did not have too little" (2 Corinthians 8:15).[102] So Paul promotes voluntary sharing among members of his community so that the wealthier tend to the needs of the poorer. His appeals for almsgiving can be found elsewhere in his letters, where he, for example, stresses that the faithful will be "enriched in every way for your great generosity" (2 Corinthians 9:11). He subsequently counsels in Ephesians that Christians ought to labor hard "so as to have something to share with the needy" (Ephesians 4:28).

Scholars have noted that although Paul, with James's encouragement, promotes almsgiving, his measures fall short of Jesus's relative radicalism. Although "he calls for generosity . . . he does not call for a radical redistribution of wealth."[103] Paul, for example, neglects any hint of the Sabbatical and Jubilee laws, much less a release from financial debts, that were central in the Gospels. He also speaks of almsgiving as "generosity" rather than an obligation under a divine command. Further, he does not suggest that Christians should abandon all their earthly goods, so much as they should give "according to your means."[104] So even though it is proper to give alms, for Paul, followers do not appear to be under an obligation to make outsized gifts.

PAUL ON WEALTH

A further distinction between Jesus and James, on the one hand, and Paul, on the other, concerns the moral assessment of the wealthy. One of the most striking features of the New Testament is that whereas Jesus and James both sternly condemn the wealthy, Paul never does so. For Jesus and James, those clinging to their wealth have chosen their master: they prefer their money to their god. As such, both Jesus and James suggest divine sanctions await the rich. Paul makes no such suggestions.

To understand why Paul differs in this respect, it is important to recall their respective audiences. Jesus and James were poor Galileans who preached to the impoverished and oppressed. Their followers were eager to embrace the harsh judgment of their perceived oppressors. By contrast, Paul preached to the Hellenized, the literate, and often the rich. The historian E. A. Judge, for example, has assessed Paul's congregants as a "socially pretentious section of the population of big cities"—a very different set of people from poor Galileans.[105] Although this assessment of Paul's congregants as a whole is not universal,[106] most scholars agree that the wealthy and educated were certainly an important part of Paul's audience.[107] The German theologian Gerd Theissen, for example, has determined that of the seventeen known Corinthian Christians in the New Testament, at least nine of them belonged to the upper classes.[108]

If it is true that much of Paul's audience was wealthy, it makes sense that he might have downplayed Jesus's teachings that most alarmed them. It can be difficult to recruit followers to a religion by singling them out for divine sanctions (e.g., Luke 16:25). Such messages are likely to alienate and antagonize the wealthy. It is in this context that one can appreciate Paul's statement on appealing to particular audiences with idiosyncratically crafted messages:

> For though I am free with respect to all, I have made myself a slave to all, so that I might win more of them. To the Jews I became as a Jew, in order to win more Jews. To those under the law I became as one under the law (though I myself am not under the law) so that I might win those under the law. To those outside the law I became as one outside the law (though I am not free from God's law but am under Christ's law) so that I might win those outside the law. To the weak I became weak, so that I might win the weak. I have become all things to all people, that I might by all means save some. I do it all for the sake of the gospel, so that I may share in its blessings. (1 Corinthians 9:19–23)

For Paul, the most important mission is to "save some" souls. But to accomplish this, he acknowledges that he must appeal to the unique character of each audience. As he outlines above, this means appealing separately to those who do and do not follow the Hebrew laws, as well as to the weak with a message that might appeal specifically to them. The one unmentioned audience—but that we know existed in his congregations—was the wealthy. Given Paul's rhetorical strategy, it is reasonable to imagine that he often spoke and wrote in a way that would refrain from alienating his wealthiest congregants. As such, he could not emphasize those elements of Jesus's teachings that threatened the rich with damnation, nor could he speak in the way that James addressed the angry and impoverished peasants who made up his Jerusalem audience. To do so would undermine his apostolic mission.

PAUL ON GREED

Although Paul says little about wealth, he joins Jesus in condemning greed or *pleonexia*. His attacks are not so systematic or scathing as they are in the Gospels, but they regularly recur in his letters. In 1 Corinthians, three times he provides a list of sins in which greed accompanies sexual immorality, idolaters, revilers, drunkards, thieves, and the like. No such sinners, he insists, "will inherit the kingdom of God" (1 Corinthians 5:10). He repeats this judgment in Ephesians 5:5: "Be sure of this, that no fornicator or impure person, or one who is greedy (that is, an idolater), has any inheritance in the kingdom of Christ and of God." In Colossians 3:6, he identifies greed along with various modes of sexual immorality as meriting the "wrath of God." In light of his consistency, it is safe to conclude that Paul associated greed with idolatry, itself a violation of the Decalogue, and he unambiguously insists that unrepentant money lovers face divine sanctions.

To be sure, Jesus would largely agree with this assessment of the dangers of greed. What distinguishes Paul from Jesus and James on this matter, however, is the fact that Paul never suggests that the wealthy are necessarily greedy. That is, he reserves room for a category of those who are wealthy but not greedy. Jesus and James have no such category. For them, great fortunes are alone sufficient evidence of greed and idolatry. Paul, by contrast, carves out a category of the pious rich. As suggested above, this would have allayed the fears of some of his wealthier congregants who were reluctant to part with their fortunes.

Paul does not elaborate a theory of how one could be both wealthy and a Christian at the same time.[109] But he might have found inspiration elsewhere in the Roman world at this time in the form of Seneca the Younger. The Stoic philosopher Seneca (4–65 CE) was contemporaneous with Jesus, James, and Paul.[110] He was of noble Roman lineage and became notable enough a scholar to serve as Nero's tutor and valued adviser. Along the way, he accumulated a personal fortune that made him one of the wealthiest Roman citizens.[111] When accused of hypocrisy in promoting Stoic detachment from earthly pleasures while simultaneously enjoying all the luxuries that come with unimaginable riches, he composed a lengthy defense of a life that is characterized both by virtue and great wealth. For

Seneca, one can maintain a high standard of virtue along with a great fortune so long as one is not obsessed with maintaining that fortune. Seneca identifies himself as adopting precisely this attitude: "As for me, I shall pay no heed to Fortune, either when she comes or when she goes."[112] This being said, at the same time, he acknowledges that it is better to have great wealth than not. The wise man "does not love riches, but he would rather have them; he does not admit them to his heart, but to his house, and he does not reject the riches he has, but he keeps them and wishes them to supply ampler material for extending his virtue."[113] Just as it is unnecessary to be tall to be a good person, surely many would prefer to be taller all the same. He goes even further, however, to elaborate that his wealth has afforded him the opportunity to practice virtues unavailable to the poor, such as generosity, diligence, and orderliness.

Whether such claims are true is beyond my scope. But I want to make two points about Seneca's defense of wealth regarding the early figures of Christianity. First, Seneca represents the polar opposite of figures like Jesus and James. Among other things, unlike Seneca, Jesus was perfectly satisfied that the poor could exercise heroic generosity with their almsgiving (e.g., Luke 21:1–2). Further, both Jesus and James viewed wealth and virtue as mutually exclusive—the very possession of wealth was a sign of one's *pleonexia*. Second, Seneca's view that wealth and virtue were compatible was amenable to Paul, who allows that wealthy congregants could have a place in the Kingdom of God. It is even possible that both Paul and the better educated members of his community would be familiar with Seneca's arguments for this compatibility, as Seneca was perhaps the most celebrated intellectual of the Roman world at this time.

PAUL ON LOVE OF NEIGHBOR
AND THE GENERAL WILL

This difference between Jesus and Paul does not foreclose important agreements relevant to coping with the problems stemming from economic inequality. A teaching of Jesus especially important to Paul was the love of neighbor. Paul recalls this doctrine in contrast to the selfishness often associated with greed:

> For you were called to freedom, brothers and sisters, only do not use
> your freedom as an opportunity for self-indulgence, but through love
> become slaves to one another. For the whole law is summed up in a
> single commandment, "You shall love your neighbor as yourself." If,

however, you bite and devour one another, take care that you are not consumed by one another. (Galatians 5:13–15)

Paul is especially faithful here to Jesus's words, which emphasized the twin commandments to love God and one's neighbor (e.g., Mark 12:30–31). Further, along with Jesus, Paul understands this doctrine not merely as a theological imperative but also as a social doctrine. The social effect of loving one's neighbors, he hopes, is to calm tensions and improve social relations. Failing to heed the commandment, Paul intimates, inflames social divisions—or what Jesus might have called a "house divided." To be sure, it is less clear here with Paul than it was with Jesus that he might have intended this as a solution to social divisions emanating from economic inequality, although the effect would be the same.

Furthermore, when considering Paul on these matters, one cannot overlook his contribution to the general will tradition also located in James. Indeed, the historian of political thought Patrick Riley traces the origins of the general will tradition back to Paul's first letter to Timothy:[114]

> I urge that supplications, prayers, intercessions, and thanksgivings be made for everyone, for kings and all who are in high positions, so that we may lead a quiet and peaceable life in all godliness and dignity. This is right and is acceptable in the sight of God our Savior, who desires everyone to be saved and to come to the knowledge of the truth. (1 Timothy 1–4)

As Riley notes, this passage concerns salvation rather than political or economic matters. God wills universal salvation—or as subsequent philosophers and theologians will call it, God has a general will for everyone to be saved. Yet it is worth reading all of 1 Timothy to understand this message in its larger context. Although God wills universal salvation, some souls will fall short. Paul identifies greed as a particular threat in this context. Echoing Seneca, he cautions readers not to be "lovers of money" (e.g., 1 Timothy 3:3, 3:8). Succumbing to this sin, he warns, begets a host of others:

> Those who want to be rich fall into temptation and are trapped by many senseless and harmful desires that plunge people into ruin and destruction. For the love of money is a root of all kinds of evil, and in their eagerness to be rich some have wandered away from the faith and pierced themselves with many pains. (1 Timothy 6:9–10)

Although the letter does not elaborate, it is easy to speculate about the many ways that greed inspires dubious moral choices, such as cheating, stealing, and lying, not to mention idolatry. All of this presumably can undermine God's inclination to save all souls, as they are rather destined for "ruin and destruction."

The underlying problem with greed, for Paul, is that it obscures the imperative to love and tend to one's neighbors. As he clarifies in Philippians, acting on one's selfish private will undermines one's social obligations: "Do nothing from selfish ambition or conceit, but in humility regard others as better than yourselves. Let each of you look not to your own interests, but to the interest of others" (Philippians 2:3–4).

If one has heard Jesus's teachings correctly, Paul observes in 1 Corinthians, the wealthiest congregants will set aside their own private wills in favor of the neediest members of the community:

> The members of the body that seem to be weaker are indispensable, and those members of the body that we think less honorable we clothe with greater honor, and our less respectable members are treated with greater respect; whereas our more respectable members do not need this. But God has so arranged the body, giving the greater honor to the inferior member, that there may be no dissension within the body, but the members may have the same care for one another. If one member suffers, all suffer together with it. (1 Corinthians 12:22–26)[115]

This passage expressly acknowledges economic divisions within Corinthian congregations, and it implores the rich not to ignore the poor among them—acknowledging here, more than anywhere else in his letters, the beatitudes' message that the poor are the blessed. It is in this context that he introduces his often-recited poetic meditation on the nature of love. Sometimes forgotten in recitations of Paul's paean to love is that "when the complete [love] comes, the partial will come to an end" (1 Corinthians 13:10). This preference for a general over a "partial" will speaks to a broader concern for the good of the whole community—with an emphasis on tending to the needs of the poor.

Conclusion

Jesus, James, and Paul all share core commitments relevant to thinking about economic inequality. They are all committed to the dignity and special status of the poor. They all emphasize the importance of almsgiving. They all inveigh against greed. They all celebrate neighborly love. These values offer a consistency and coherence across the New Testament and speak to anyone reading these texts in search of insight and wisdom into the problem of inequality. Yet there are also clear and important differences. Whereas Jesus demands almsgiving as a divine imperative, Paul rather recommends it as an act of "generosity." Whereas Jesus demands almsgiving on a grand scale, Paul counsels almsgiving "according to one's means." Whereas Jesus and James understand the wealthy to be destined for divine punishment, Paul never addresses wealth in isolation as soteriologically consequential. Whereas Jesus and James believe that wealth equates to greed, Paul allows that one can be rich without necessarily being greedy.

These differences in New Testament Scriptures have afforded latitude to subsequent interpreters. The early Eastern Church, for example, emphasized the lessons of Jesus and James regarding the dangers of wealth, greed, and inequality. Prominent among the early Orthodox figures is Saint Basil of Caesarea (329–379 CE). Basil was born into a prominent wealthy Greek family in Caesarea, now in central Turkey. Although his wealth afforded him the luxury of an excellent education, he was never comfortable with his privilege, especially in the face of the numerous poor in his midst. For Basil, the very possession of great wealth violates Jesus's core moral teaching to love one's neighbor as oneself: "The more you abound in wealth, the more you lack in love." He continues, "If you had truly loved your neighbor, it would have occurred to you long ago to divest yourself of this wealth."[116] Echoing Jesus, Basil insists that the very possession of great wealth is evidence of greed or *pleonexia*. The fabulously rich cling to their wealth as if it were their most prized possession—more than their limbs, much less their souls. Once consumed with *pleonexia*, there is little hope of salvaging their souls—"those who love money will never be satisfied with what they have. Hades never says 'enough,' nor does the greedy person ever say 'enough.'"[117] As such, and in a fashion that resembles Plato, Basil characterizes *pleonexia* as a "tyranny" of the soul in which all other elements of our souls "cower at its dominion."[118]

Wealth and inequality are not merely problems for individual souls, however, according to Basil. They are also the source of social disorder:

> How long shall gold be the oppression of souls, the hook of death, the lure of sin? How long shall wealth be the cause of war, for which purpose weapons are forged and sword blades whetted? Because of wealth, kinsfolk disregard the bond of nature, and sibling contemplates murder against sibling. Because of wealth, the desert teems with murderers, the sea with pirates, and the cities with extortionists. Who is the father of lies? Who is the author of forgery? Who gave birth to perjury? Is it not wealth? Is it not the pursuit of wealth?[119]

Compounding these effects, for Basil, wealth and its relentless pursuit necessarily results in economic inequality. "Evil things come upon the people for the sake of a few; for one person's depravity the people are punished."[120] As such, Basil insists on dividing wealth between citizens: "Like a mighty river that is divided into many streams in order to irrigate the fertile soil, so also are those who give their wealth to be divided up and distributed in the houses of the poverty-stricken."[121] And, to be sure, Basil practiced what he preached. He pledged his own family's considerable fortune to create the *Basiliad*, a philanthropic foundation dedicated to leveling economic circumstances and providing for the poor with food, shelter, and medical care.[122] Over time, the foundation grew and took on the characteristics of a city that emphasized equality, simplicity, and neighborly love.

Similar views emerged in the West. The most dramatic condemnation of wealth in the period shortly following Basil can be found in the Pelagian work *De divitiis*, or *On Riches*, written ca. 410 CE. For its anonymous author, there is no such thing as unproblematic wealth. It is always a product of greed, which is a freely chosen disposition among the rich. This is most obviously true of those who amass the original fortune, but it also obtains to those who inherit it since, for the author, one was either the agent or the complicit beneficiary of evil deeds. The accumulation and possession of wealth were understood to be evil in the context of a zero-sum economy where every addition to a wealthy man's fortune came at the expense of the suffering poor. As the historian Peter Brown has summarized, "Every time someone overstepped the divinely ordained line of mere sufficiency by becoming rich, others were pulled down into poverty."[123] The very existence of economic inequality, in other words, implied the presence of evil. The solution, for the anonymous Pelagian, was simple: "Get rid of the rich and you will not find the poor."[124]

To be sure, much of what one finds in the New Testament regarding wealth, greed, and inequality parallels Plato's explorations on these matters. Both employ the same Greek word of *pleonexia* to describe a diseased soul incapable of satisfying its own expanding desires. Further, they both paint these diseased souls as wreaking havoc on society at large. Jesus, James, and Plato share the assumption that the very possession of wealth itself is an indication of the presence of greed and its ignoble effects on the soul. Finally, all three are determined that the solution to problems both of society and the soul require fairly radical measures, up to and including threats of divine punishment for acquiring too much wealth.

These similarities being observed, much separates Plato from the early Christian tradition—namely, that there are a great many more Christians in the world, self-understood, than there are Platonists. In a hypothetical world where Plato's dialogues constituted a predominant world religion, his thoughts on wealth, greed, and inequality would have played a significant role in public discussion of these matters. But this is actually true of the New Testament, and this fact distinguishes it from all the other texts addressed throughout the rest of this book.[125] The political philosopher Leo Strauss once characterized the division between Jerusalem and Athens as being one of the most enduring and defining problems of Western political thought.[126] For him, the two cities represent polar opposite claims to authority—God or reason. I need not resolve the question here of how these competing authorities might be reconciled. But what one can observe is that the New Testament has much broader reach than Plato's dialogues will ever have. There are more than two billion Christians worldwide, eager in their own way to embrace the principles found in those texts. And as Strauss suggests, for many of them, those texts speak to them with indisputable authority—it is, for them, the word of God. For various reasons, Jesus and James's condemnations of wealth and inequality are commonly downplayed at the expense of other teachings—by priests and pastors, by public interpreters, or by individuals at home with their Bibles. But it is also undeniable that those very same Bibles in the hands of billions of people draw stark and dramatic attention to these same problems.

The celebrated philosopher Jürgen Habermas, among others, has argued that the Enlightenment project has effectively stalled out and that "pure reason" is unlikely to motivate vast majorities of citizens to action on their important moral and civic responsibilities. This is in some ways the great shortcoming of a school of thought associated with thinkers like Immanuel Kant—that all one needs to do is to articulate reasoned arguments in a free society and then can witness the inevitable public enlightenment. Yet far too often the carefully reasoned arguments of philosophers are ignored because relatively few find themselves motivated by mere arguments. In this "postsecular" context, Habermas argues, it may be helpful to acknowledge and commandeer the motivational forces of religion insofar as they have the unique capacity to inspire the fulfillment of moral and civic duties.[127] To be sure, the record of religiously motivated actions is mixed, as even the future pope Benedict XVI concedes in his dialogue with Habermas on this matter.[128] Yet at the same time, if one acknowledges the inevitability of religious appeals in the public sphere, as Habermas suggests we might,[129] it would seem foolish to ignore the remarkable tradition of religious texts on questions so vital to contemporary debates.

CHAPTER THREE

Thomas Hobbes

"TOO MUCH ABUNDANCE"

IN CONSTRUCTING A POLITICAL SYSTEM culminating in the accumulation of all political power in the hands of a sovereign Leviathan, it can be argued that Thomas Hobbes is among the least egalitarian philosophers in the history of political thought. His politics is premised on the concentration of power preferably in the hands of a solitary figure. Insofar as he is associated with equality, scholars are drawn to his assertion of equality in the state of nature—that "Nature hath made men so equal in faculties of body and mind, as that . . . the weakest has the strength enough to kill the strongest" (*Leviathan*, 13.1).[1] Yet it is precisely this natural equality between human beings that eventually necessitates the profound inequality between sovereign and subjects that animates Hobbes's commonwealth.

Less attention, however, has been paid to Hobbes's thought concerning a different dimension of equality—economic equality. Indeed, with some notable exceptions, relatively little has been written about Hobbes's economic principles.[2] The most celebrated treatments of his economics largely labor to confirm the view that Hobbes is fundamentally inegalitarian, determined to defend the emerging market system and the unequal distribution of goods its principles yield. The most prominent interpreter of Hobbes along these lines is political theorist C. B. Macpherson, who determined that "Hobbes's morality is the morality of the bourgeois world and . . . his state is the bourgeois state."[3] Macpherson would subsequently elaborate that Hobbes's policies were "designed to increase the wealth of the nation by promoting the accumulation of capital by private enterprisers."[4] Another interpreter, philosopher Michael Levin, argues along related lines—that Hobbes's political theory demands the absence of economic regulations in a libertarian "minimal state."[5]

To be sure, Macpherson and his disciples have had their detractors. Prominent among them is historian Keith Thomas in his remarkable 1965 essay "The Social Origins of Hobbes's Political Thought." Also notable is philosopher Gregory Kavka, who argues, "Though it is rarely noticed, Hobbes is a bit of an economic liberal, that is, he believes in some form of the welfare state and in the redistributive taxation needed to support it."[6] This is correct insofar as, I argue, Hobbes's political theory authorizes significant redistribution of property. But Kavka's analysis has two significant flaws. First, it attends only to the poor. Although I agree that Hobbes worries about the poor, he dedicates arguably greater attention to the problems associated with excessive wealth. In fixating exclusively on ameliorating the financial condition of the poor, Kavka treats Hobbes as a kind of sufficientarian. His analysis of Hobbesian economics lingers almost exclusively on locating "the guaranteed economic minimum" in the Hobbesian state.[7] The second problem with Kavka's analysis is that it ignores Hobbes's rich moral psychology integral to his understanding of wealth, poverty, and inequality. Kavka, in other words, treats Hobbes as merely interested in alleviating poverty in quasi-mathematical terms— and unconcerned about the deeper psychological issues that pit the classes against one another.

Hobbes's texts suggest a more complicated story regarding economic inequality and the concentration of wealth, as even Macpherson himself once admits.[8] The Malmesburian likens the excessive concentration of wealth within a commonwealth to pleurisy—"when the treasury of the commonwealth . . . is gathered in too much abundance in one or a few private men" (*Leviathan*, 29.19) the commonwealth flirts with its own demise. The story of Hobbes's concern about inequality and the concentration of wealth is complex and largely untold.[9] To grasp his response to these phenomena, one must understand not only his political theory but also his historical context. Context is no stranger to Hobbes scholars, who have made much of the English Civil War. But much of what led to this war had important—indeed, transformational—economic dimensions. Exploring this history not only clarifies Hobbes's understanding of the eventual war but also the economic dimensions of his political theory specifically regarding inequality and wealth concentration.[10] Insofar as subjects can acquire limitless fortunes, according to Hobbes, they become insolent and presumptuous of impunity, eventually rising to threaten sovereign authority. As can be discerned from early modern English history, including Hobbes's own account of the Civil War in *Behemoth*, this growing concentration of wealth in the emerging merchant class was one of the country's fatal defects precipitating that violent war. Hence, for Hobbes, avoiding this "pleurisy" necessarily becomes paramount in managing the commonwealth.

Seventeenth-Century English Mercantilism: Between Feudalism and Capitalism

Historically minded Hobbes scholars often contextualize his work in the politics of the English Civil War. Yet that war itself occupied a particular economic environment, which played an important role in its politics. This section outlines the economic transformations emerging in Hobbes's England with an eye to how they shaped the politics that informed his social thought.

The defining economic feature of Hobbes's seventeenth-century England was its slow transformation from a feudal to a market economy. This process had already begun by the time Hobbes was born in 1588 but had not reached maturity until significantly after his death in 1679. Beginning with Adam Smith, economists referred to the economy of this period as "mercantilism." This was an economy in which serfs had largely left the old feudal estates, owned by lords, who in earlier times compensated their workers with room and board. But this was also before the ascendance of the free market. Monopolies were common, free trade and open markets by later standards were uncommon, and emerging merchants were often viewed with suspicion. It was a period of growing wealth but also great upheaval and uncertainty. The working class could no longer count on their lords to provide for them. Some members of the working class would succeed spectacularly. Many more would struggle to pay rent and secure food.

For the first time in anyone's memory, the working class would depend on wages. Despite feudalism's obvious drawbacks, it had largely protected working people from homelessness and starvation. Under mercantilism, workers needed jobs to secure their own necessities. As the nineteenth-century French aristocrat and social observer Alexis de Tocqueville would remark nearly two centuries after Hobbes, this exposed workers to new dangers. Market economies speculate "on secondary needs which a thousand causes can restrict and important events completely eliminate."[11] Consequently, workers who once enjoyed the security of necessities found themselves often living on the edge, especially in contrast with their landed and merchant neighbors. And given the relatively new economic structures along with the fluctuations they introduced, uncertainty about how to navigate the economy and secure basic needs fueled a general anxiety.[12]

Many factors conspired to impoverish sixteenth- and seventeenth-century English wage laborers. In addition to the vicissitudes of the speculative markets common in market economies, the poor had to contend with high taxes, rising rents, bad harvests, high inflation, and declining real wages. Inflation in the middle sixteenth to middle seventeenth centuries was so extreme that some later called it the "inflationary century."[13] The relatively stable feudal economy had rendered inflation largely unknown, especially to serfs, who had little need for money in any case. But in the sixteenth and seventeenth centuries, the price of grains—a staple in the English diet of this period—rose dramatically. Scholars remain uncertain about the precise causes of this inflation. As historian Keith Wrightson has observed, "contemporaries had a ready explanation: greed."[14] According to the moralists of the sixteenth and seventeenth centuries, the primary cause of inflation was the unchecked covetousness of land-owning farmers and their economic agents that priced the poor out of the grain market. In a world where markets were still poorly understood, citizens were drawn to the notion of "just prices"—the idea that prices should be set according to what seems "fair" to consumers, rather than from supply and demand.[15] Insofar as the price of grains exceeded the ability of many citizens to pay for them, it was understandable that they would have labeled the high prices "unjust."

A contributing factor to inflation was the English population boom of this period. Between the 1520s to the 1580s, England's population increased by approximately one-third.[16] As the population grew, so did the demand for grains, which would have inflated grain prices. But the increasing population had additional important economic effects. Just as wage laborers were for the first time having to secure their own lodgings with rent, rent prices began to skyrocket. As the eighteenth-century Dutch-English philosopher Bernard Mandeville subsequently noted, "as to the rents, it is impossible they should fall while you increase your numbers."[17] While the population grew, landlords began shortening leases to avoid being disadvantaged by inflation. Among other effects, this hastened a significant increase in evictions. Rental income between the late sixteenth to mid-seventeenth century, for example, grew anywhere from 100 percent to 1,000 percent across England. The increasing scarcity of rental properties also allowed landlords to impose hefty fees for late payments.[18] As one scholar has observed, this remarkable rise in rents had the effect of engendering "a massive redistribution of income in favour of the landed class."[19]

Another challenge confronting working people in this period was stagnant wages, which were radically declining when placed in their inflationary context. Between 1603 and 1640, as nearly half of England's population became reliant on wages to provide for their needs, the purchasing power of wage laborers dropped approximately two-thirds. As Hill has observed, "the real earnings of a worker born in 1580"—just eight years before Hobbes was born—"would never exceed half of what his great-grandfather had enjoyed."[20] Under these conditions, wage earners often resorted to a diet of simple "black bread." Unsurprisingly, wage laborers lacked unions that might have championed wage hikes in this inflationary period. Wages then were largely set by the regional justices of the peace, who, as themselves members of the employing class of citizens, according to Hill, sought to "fix wages at the lowest possible rates."[21] Wage-earning servants, for example, provide a particular lens on the plight of working people in this period. If servants wanted to leave an employer to work elsewhere, they had to purchase a "ticket of release" from their employer—presumably difficult to afford in the context of precipitously declining real wages. And if servants somehow earned a wage beyond the maximum set by the justice of the peace, they were subjected to punitive fines and even imprisonment. Employers paying those salaries, by contrast, were subject to very modest fines, if anything. Further, employees threatening to abandon their jobs because of low wages or poor working conditions were to be treated as vagabonds, subject to imprisonment and other sanctions.[22] This placed employers in positions of considerable power over their workers. As such, vast numbers of the working poor struggled throughout the seventeenth century with securing basic needs. To compensate for declining real wages, many had to work considerably longer hours than their ancestors. As Wrightson has observed, among craftsmen in Hull by the 1630s, workers had to work for 306 days to earn what once could have been achieved in 192 days. Laborers in the same town had to work 459 days to earn what once could have been achieved in 256 days.[23] Workers would surely have been poorer and more fatigued in the middle seventeenth century than their predecessors.

Hobbes was witness to this poverty. Although employed by the aristocratic Cavendish family as a tutor, he had been born into relative poverty. His father, Thomas Hobbes Sr., was a barely literate and pugnacious clergyman, who struggled with alcoholism. When young Thomas was fifteen, his father brawled with another preacher and fled town, never to be seen again. The Hobbeses' native Malmesbury had thrived as a wool producer up until the mid-1550s but then declined rapidly in the decades immediately preceding Thomas Jr.'s birth, as cotton supplanted wool. Although the family was far from the poorest in town, Hobbes biographer A. P. Martinich describes them as very much "lower middle class."[24]

As an adult, Hobbes recorded the plight of the working poor during a 1626 trip to the Peak District. He pointedly commented that "poverty has damned" locals to work in the lead mines, which rendered them "lean as a skeleton, pale as a dead corpse." Upon his arrival at the mines, he discovered that one had collapsed on and crushed two of the men who had dug it. He remarked, "They had dug their own sepulcher."[25] Mining was a backbone of the British economy in this period, and it is likely that such scenes were relatively common throughout the commonwealth.

Poverty was not merely problematic for individuals; it was also a social problem. As England transitioned from feudalism to mercantilism, the poor increasingly expressed discontent. This began as early as 1549 with Kett's Rebellion—a violent response triggered by frustrations with the enclosure laws that allowed wealthy landowners to fence off common land.[26] This left many poor farmers with no place to graze their animals and threatened their livelihoods. Ultimately following the command of a sympathetic yeoman farmer, Robert Kett, the rebels seized the city of Norwich before being overwhelmed by the Earl of Warwick. Three thousand farmers were killed, including Kett.[27] Similar revolts occurred throughout England in 1596, 1607, 1622, 1628–1631, and 1640–1643. These episodes had a class component, such as in the Gloucestershire rebellion of 1622, when the unemployed "went in groups to houses of the rich, demanding money and seizing provisions."[28] As the historian Julian Cornwall summarized the poor's frustrations, there was a growing sense that the "state had been taken over by a breed of men whose policy was to rob the poor for the benefit of the rich."[29]

Despite the relatively desperate condition of many in England, some did astoundingly well. The mercantilist age saw the extraordinary growth of wealth in a few hands.[30] Much of this wealth, as can be deduced from the rising rent, went into the hands of landowners, or the "gentry." By virtue of their land (recently acquired by the liquidation of the monasteries upon the establishment of the Anglican Church) and the exceptionally favorable conditions benefiting landlords, the gentry enjoyed soaring wealth[31] and engaged in what Hill has called "an orgy of conspicuous building, . . . housing themselves in greater comfort" throughout England but especially building large country estates.[32]

More remarkable perhaps was the sudden growth of the merchant class. Whereas under feudalism, wealth was almost exclusively attached to landed estates passed down the generations, clever entrepreneurs in the sixteenth and especially the seventeenth century discerned the rules of the new economy well before their peers, amassing extraordinary fortunes. The paths to great riches varied but included many of the so-called bourgeois virtues, such as thrift, careful bookkeeping, moderate consumption, attention to economic trends, and the like. Naturally, wealth accumulation often relied on luck, such as being well situated to exploit emerging markets for commodities like coal, salt, and textiles. Coal, in particular, was foundational for the new economy, as it stimulated production in cannon founding, sugar refining, papermaking, brickmaking, soap boiling, glassblowing, dyeing, salt refining, and brewing, as well as iron, steel, and copper production. Although the largest deposits were in Warwickshire, Staffordshire, and Shropshire, smaller mines were dispersed throughout England. The mining process itself was revolutionized by advancements in the division of labor, which presumably had the effect of reducing wages—by virtue of reducing the skill level required of miners, combined with England's rapidly growing population. In the century prior to the publication of Hobbes's *Leviathan*, coal production increased from 200,000 to 1.5 million tons a year.[33] As was typical throughout the mercantile economy, entry into the small world of coal-mine ownership was strictly limited by government-restricted grants of monopoly. For example, in the coal-rich Tyne region, there were only twenty coal-mine owners, who were known regionally as the "Lords of Coal."[34]

Some of the most spectacular fortunes of this period were generated in the burgeoning field of international trade, such as with the East India Company, founded in 1600 to facilitate the importation of spices from India. Privately owned by investors with a government charter, the company was a rapid and remarkable success, earning as much as 500 percent returns on investments by 1607. For a small handful of investors—primarily in London but some scattered throughout England—small fortunes grew exponentially.[35] Other companies arose in the same period, such as the Russia Company (1555) and the Turkey Company (1581), with similar purposes and profits. Once-modest merchants were for the first time acquiring massive wealth, which they would subsequently invest in government finance, usury, and land for rental income. These fortunes came to rival and even exceed those held by the gentry.

Prior to the mercantilist age, usury—defined as loaning money at interest with all risk assumed by the debtor—was condemned on moral and theological grounds. Such views rested on the Old Testament (specifically Leviticus 25:36) and Saint Thomas Aquinas, who condemned usury as unjust since it represented a fundamentally unequal exchange—for example, trading $10 for $12. As such, it violates what he called "commutative justice."[36] Hobbes's friend, the philosopher Francis Bacon, had written that "usury is the certainest means of gain, though one of the worst."[37] As recently as 1487 and 1495, England had passed a series of laws prohibiting usury. Yet half a century later, another series of laws effectively reversed this policy, at least tacitly permitting loans at up to 10 percent interest, by virtue of mild, unenforced penalties. By the end of the sixteenth century, 10 percent interest on loans had been broadly accepted as morally permissible, with "usury" being redefined loosely as charging "excessive" interest rates. Even then, these limits on excessive rates were increasingly ignored. This created new low-risk opportunities for those with capital to extend their fortunes.[38]

Many of these industries required significant resources; much of this money could be found in London, England's economic capital. By 1600, 87 percent of English commerce passed through the city. The newly rich were not only engaged in finance capital and usury but also in emerging industries such as cloth, which would employ as many as a thousand workers. Consequently, by 1640, London was home to most of England's wealthiest citizens. Of course, it was not only the rich who flocked to London. The city's population exploded, quadrupling in the sixteenth century and doubling again in the first half of the seventeenth century.[39]

It was not unusual for successful merchants to earn fortunes in the thousands or tens of thousands of pounds—enormous sums for the times. William Finch of the East India Company, for example, left an estate of over £80,000 to his heirs.[40] In a period when some merchants and members of the gentry saw their fortunes growing exponentially and members of the working class saw their purchasing power dramatically decline, inequality became the norm. It is difficult to imagine that any society replacing feudalism would be less egalitarian in economic terms, as the feudal system was premised on social and economic inequality. Yet economic historians are confident that this is precisely what happened. Hill has written of this period, there was "a redistribution of wealth as well as a rise in total national wealth. It was a great divide. Some of the rich and many of the middling sort grew richer; the poor . . . grew poorer."[41] Others have noted the parallel growth both in gross domestic product (GDP) and inequality throughout this time as inequality grew rapidly, even as they argue that absolute poverty was declining.[42] Wrightson highlights the "gross disparities which existed in the distribution of an expanding national income," adding, "there was nothing new about poverty or inequality. But the marked divergence in living standards and life chances between those who gained and those who lost in the decades around 1600, and the sheer growth in the numbers of the laboring poor have led many historians of England and Wales to view this period as one not only of economic expansion, but also of social polarization."[43]

As the gentry and merchants built their fortunes, their interests increasingly turned to politics. While they would butt heads with the monarch throughout much of Hobbes's lifetime, they found their entry into government through Parliament. The House of Lords belonged, more or less, to the propertied class, both old and new money. The House of Commons, however, is where new money especially made its mark. Merchants and members of the gentry not only sought the influence of a seat in the Commons, but they also sought the accompanying social esteem. Suffrage varied regionally at the time—from only enfranchising those with incomes of more than 40 schillings to universal male suffrage—but in most cases the results were the same: members of the House of Commons fervently defended the rights and interests of the emerging wealthy class. As Hill has noted, "the Lower House spoke for the prosperous gentry and the richer merchants."[44]

Emerging from a period in which political matters had been largely trusted to the monarch and a hierarchy of associated aristocrats, new wealth began to challenge old institutions and established laws. For monarchs, this emerging wealthy class was initially viewed as a new revenue source. One revenue stream along these lines was the sale of monopoly rights to operate state-sanctioned commercial enterprises, such as in bricks and glass, not to mention international trade. But monopolies were controversial from the beginning, as potential economic competitors viewed them as suppressing new economic opportunities.[45]

Relatedly, many merchants also objected to trade restrictions throughout the sixteenth and seventeenth centuries. Monopolies represented one state-imposed obstacle to free trade. Trade barriers between nations were still another. These impediments originated in early modern economic orthodoxy—that trade was zero sum. Profits earned by one nation were losses suffered by another. Whether or not such views were accurate, they exercised powerful influence on policymakers—to the great consternation of merchants whose business plans were thereby obstructed. By virtue of its growing influence, Parliament overturned some of these measures—such as the repeal of the 1606 dissolution of the Spanish Company, which permitted free trade between England, France, Spain, and

Portugal. But the process of opening markets was slow and a constant frustration to aspiring trade merchants.

Even where international trade was opening, the government permitted free trade primarily for its potential to raise tax revenues. It was increasingly important in the half century preceding the civil war to raise revenues, as government expenses were expanding due to war expenses and the growing costs of modernizing government bureaucracy. Initial attempts to raise revenue through property taxes failed miserably insofar as wealthy landholders were radically underassessed.[46] A subsequent solution was the sale of offices and titles. Shortly after ascending to the throne, James I began selling knighthoods as a source of revenue. Given the frequency of these sales, their abundance soon began reducing their price and their relative prestige. As English historian Lawrence Stone observed, "knighthood in its turn fell into contempt and men began seeking some further title of distinction."[47]

A more secure source of revenue was subsequently sought through the imposition of taxes known as "ship money." Ship money was effectively a wealth tax on coastal merchants. James I was drawn to it initially because it did not require Parliament's consent, as it was grounded in a feudal law that entitled the sovereign to claim ships or their financial equivalent from ports. It was also attractive because it targeted the growing class of wealthy merchants. Whereas this promised to improve the government's finance problems, it was despised by those merchants, who felt singled out. James I's successor, Charles I, extended the tax throughout the entire kingdom, not just on those in port cities. Wealthy merchants legally challenged the ship money tax in 1637. They lost their case, but the spectacle of the challenge rallied greater public scrutiny of the tax. As Hill has noted, "almost the whole propertied class united in opposition to Ship Money."[48] Whereas in 1636, the government collected 96.5 percent of assessed ship money taxes, two years later, it could collect only 39 percent.

Tensions between Charles I and Parliament persisted for decades leading up to the civil war and the publication of *Leviathan*. In an earlier dispute, in 1629 Charles I had dissolved Parliament for more than a decade. It was the absence of an active legislature, among other factors, that had required reviving the ship money taxes to finance the government. But the failure of the wealthy to comply with these taxes, combined with the pressing need to finance the Bishops' Wars with Scotland, finally forced Charles's hand to reconvene Parliament twice in 1640.[49] The first of these was the Short Parliament. As soon as Parliament met in April, they began by expressing grievances about the ship money taxes. Frustrated with

Parliament's unwillingness to consider new taxes, Charles dissolved it in less than a month. Yet by November, still pressed for financing, he reconvened Parliament. This would become known as the Long Parliament. Among its first acts was a law that prohibited the monarch from dissolving Parliament without its consent. Frustrated with a legislature that would neither fund the government nor could be dissolved, Charles began arresting lawmakers in 1642, thus precipitating the English Civil War.

The civil war broke out in 1642 with armies of between sixty thousand and seventy thousand fighting on both sides—the Royalists and Parliament. Parliament's initial stronghold was London and its wealthier surrounding regions, which had profited from growing commerce—citizens whose support for Parliament was consistent with their objections to ship money. Charles's support came mainly from the aristocratic families and the poor. The aristocrats had long been allied with the crown and had grown increasingly uncomfortable with the emergence of wealthy merchants in their midst, who did not share their backgrounds, values, or alliances. Parliament further angered them when it targeted them with new taxes to pay for the civil war. Parliament also targeted the poor with consumption taxes on beer, meat, salt, starch, and soap. These consumption taxes were Parliament's alternative to ship money, which has been assessed on the wealthy merchant class. These levies were imposed in a period of low wages, bad harvests, and rising food prices. So unsurprisingly the poor preferred to cast their lot with the crown.

With Scotland's assistance and after some early setbacks, Parliament won the first round of the civil war, with the king's surrender on May 5, 1646. Yet in 1648, Charles had persuaded the Scots to join the Royalist cause—with the Scots invading England in an attempt to rout Parliament. The invasion failed and Parliament ordered Charles's beheading, which took place on January 30, 1649. The Scots, now aligned with Charles's son, Charles II, made one further attempt to invade London in September 1651, which likewise failed, representing the final formal battle of the English Civil War. More than two hundred thousand lives were lost over the decade.

Hobbes's Quest for Peace

Hobbes begins his political theory in a "state of nature"—a thought experiment designed to grasp human nature, the origins of the state, and the proper functions of government. It is an imaginary condition absent of laws, government, or any discernible organized society. According to Hobbes, in the state of nature, human beings are equal. Although by default this is true in economic terms since there is no society to support currency, much less to manage its distribution, he suggests an equality in more fundamental terms. They are equal insofar as "the weakest has strength enough to kill the strongest, either by secret machination or by confederacy with others" (*Leviathan*, 13.1; see also *Citizen*, 1.2). This equality engenders competition. Those equally confident in their abilities tend to compete over scarce resources, which may include food but also other objects like glory. People only compete when they understand them- selves to have a reasonable chance of succeeding.

The knowledge that anyone can kill anyone else in a context of fierce competition over scarce resources produces diffidence—a mutual distrust characterizing the state of nature. Equality, competition, and diffidence, in turn, produce conflict and war. Hobbes suggests many possible manifesta- tions of conflict, including wars for gain, safety, and reputation (*Leviathan*, 13.7). But all wars, regardless of objectives, share something in common: they are to be avoided at almost all costs. Wars undermine everything that reasonable people seek: the opportunity to work, to engage in agriculture, navigate the high seas, science, arts, letters, philosophy, and society itself. The state of nature is thus infamously a state of war—a condition defined by "continual fear, and danger of violent death; and the life of man, soli- tary, poor, nasty, brutish, and short" (*Leviathan*, 13.9).

Hobbes's account of the state of nature is, among other things, an account of human nature. Specifically, he highlights humanity's egoism. As he confidently asserts, "of the voluntary acts of every man, the object is some *good to himself*" (*Leviathan*, 14.8; emphasis original).[50] This principle is sometimes amplified in his writings—for example, chapter 11 of *Levia- than*: there is "general inclination of all mankind a perpetual and restless desire of power after power that ceaseth only in death" (*Leviathan*, 11.2).

Much could be, and has been, said of Hobbes's principle of egoism. But most relevant is that it is *not* Hobbes's goal to unleash selfishness. In this respect, there is a decisive disjuncture in the Western tradition of egoism upon the arrival of Bernard Mandeville in the early eighteenth century. Whereas Hobbes allows some role for selfishness in exiting the state of nature and in obeying sovereign commands (and the attendant threats), he is generally inclined to constrain the various encroachments of selfishness, as with the laws of nature. Mandeville, by contrast, seeks to give that selfishness the widest possible latitude in the formation of social norms and laws. In this respect, it is Mandeville, rather than Hobbes, who is best understood as the intellectual forbearer of the free market. As will be seen, Hobbes was hardly one to endorse the mantra "Greed is good." For

Hobbes, greed is an unfortunate tendency in human nature and a violation of the laws of nature. It would be in Mandeville that greed would be celebrated and channeled.

Egoism is most usefully manifested for Hobbes in the fear of death insofar as individuals recognize that all prospects of satisfying the selfish desire to continue living and enjoy its pleasures. Hobbesian individuals realize that only a sovereign can protect them from the state of nature. The Leviathan represents a coercive power absent in the state of nature—a power strong enough to redirect humanity's fears from one another to the sovereign power. It is only when individuals fear the Leviathan that peace—the object of all individuals in the state of nature—becomes possible. Because once they fear the sovereign power, that sovereign can then legislate and enforce laws. And law facilitates peace.

Those civil laws enacted and enforced by the sovereign must correspond to what Hobbes calls the "natural laws" (see *Citizen*, 14.9–10; *Leviathan*, 26.8). He identifies as many as nineteen such laws. The first and most important of these laws is to seek peace (*Leviathan*, 14.4), which he defines as precisely the opposite of the state of nature (*Leviathan*, 13.8). Yet there are many looming threats to this peace. So each of the subsequent laws of nature, in turn, aim at supporting the fundamental natural law of peace by confronting and mitigating these various threats. This includes the laws of justice, gratitude, pardon, complaisance, and equity. For example, citizens lacking complaisance—which Hobbes defines as the ability of a subject to "accommodate himself to the rest"—threaten the peace insofar as they fail to acknowledge the rights and needs of fellow subjects. They are, for Hobbes, "stubborn, insociable, froward [obstinate], intractable" (*Leviathan*, 15.17). He elaborates elsewhere that the man lacking complaisance tends to keep "more than he needs for himself" and "takes the necessities of life from other people." Such individuals "will be to blame for the war which breaks out," according to Hobbes, since their resources will inevitably be needed—and when the commonwealth or the poor come for them, he won't surrender them without a fight (*Citizen*, 3.9). I argue later that some of these natural laws are central to Hobbes's solution to the problems of excessive wealth and inequality. It is a sovereign duty, above all, to preserve the peace, which can only be achieved by legislating and enforcing the natural laws. Failure to do so dissolves sovereign authority, returning the commonwealth to the state of nature, where everyone lives not in fear of the Leviathan but rather in fear of violent death at one another's hands. Because sovereign authority is central to the commonwealth's success— and indeed, its inhabitants' very survival—Hobbes invests it with absolute authority. But absolute authority on Hobbes's account should not, however, be mistaken for sovereign license, as the sovereign can only sustain authority by respecting the laws of nature.

Hobbesian Problems with Poverty, Concentrated Wealth, and Inequality

Hobbes's political program prioritizes peace above all. It is thus essential to understand how poverty, concentrated wealth, and inequality all obstruct it. This is one of the fundamental lessons Hobbes likely learned in the decades leading up to the English Civil War—a war at least partly facilitated by the economic upheaval, the impoverishment of many along with the enriching of a few. He acknowledges some of this in his own history of the civil war, *Behemoth*. Early in his account, he describes several factors contributing to the corruption of the people, such that they "would have taken any side for pay or plunder" in the wars. Two factors bear emphasis in this context. The first is London and the other "great towns of trade" where merchants have become envious of the "great prosperity" of places like the commercial Netherlands and have them "inclined to think that the like change of government here, would to them produce the like prosperity."[51] In other words, English merchants had learned from the Dutch that co-opting the political system was essential to increasing their profits. The second simultaneous source of corruption among the English was poverty, where many "saw no means how honestly to get their bread." These impoverished masses "longed for a war" insofar as any significant disruption to the existing order promised to be better than the one that had them on the brink of starvation (*Behemoth*, 2–3).

Hobbes's early attention to these matters in *Behemoth* suggests their roles in his broader political theory. Namely, they threaten his first law of nature—peace—and hence the possibility of a thriving, enduring commonwealth. But at this point, it is necessary to consider his systematic political philosophy to explore the ways in which greed, concentrated wealth, poverty, and inequality undermine the Hobbesian commonwealth.

HOBBES ON POVERTY

Among the relevant economic and moral categories cited previously, poverty receives less attention than the others. Yet it would be wrong to insist, as does political theorist Stephen Holmes, that Hobbes never "lost much sleep over poverty."[52] As already mentioned, he came from a lower middle–class family and was shocked to discover the conditions of poor English coal miners. His concern for the poor animated his political theory. For Hobbesian individuals, poverty threatens both their dignity and their very physical survival: "What grieves and discontents the human spirit more than anything else is poverty; or *want* of the essentials for the preservation of life and dignity" (*Citizen*, 12.9; emphasis original). Without these basic resources, citizens are often compelled to choose between the unappealing alternatives of begging or stealing.[53]

Poverty also has politically existential consequences. Early in part 2 of *Leviathan*, Hobbes remarks, "No king can be rich nor glorious nor secure, whose subjects are poor or contemptible or too weak through want" (*Leviathan*, 19.4).[54] In the immediate context, he suggests this is the case because the king's soldiers would be too weak to fend off foreign invaders. But he suggests a second underlying reason why poverty is problematic: the "discontent that arises from poverty." Poor and hungry citizens are envious, resentful, and angry. Even though he is not beyond blaming some of the poor for imprudent spending or idleness, he recognizes the legitimacy of their grievances. Beyond this, poverty emboldens the poor to commit crimes. As he records in his translation of Thucydides, "poverty will always add boldness to necessity."[55] Indeed, for Hobbes, discontent arising from poverty hastens "sedition" (*Citizen*, 13.10)[56]—rebellion against sovereign authority. Poverty fosters a restless desire for change, regardless of the consequences.

To be sure, Hobbes never condones sedition and rebellion. "Attaining sovereignty by rebellion," he insists, is "against reason" (*Leviathan*, 15.7) since it violates the social contract that holds together the social fabric. To be seditious is to reject the sovereign, government, and society itself. Yet he knows that subjects can nevertheless be driven by circumstances to sedition and rebellion. As he observes in his conclusion to part 2 of *Leviathan*, rebellion is the "natural punishment" of negligent princes who fail to uphold the peace. Although rebellion may be irrational, it is nonetheless a natural consequence of desperate circumstances, including poverty. This is why Hobbes endorses a Thomist doctrine that otherwise perplexes some readers—that the poor have the right to steal from the rich with relative impunity. Thomas Aquinas's political theory included a general prohibition against thievery, yet allowed exceptions in cases of necessity. For him, "the natural law requires that superfluous things in one's possession be used for the sustenance of the poor." So if the rich fail to share their surplus with the poor, the poor have a right to steal it—under the authority of the natural law. As Thomas insists, "if the necessity is so pressing and clear that one has an immediate need of things at hand, then one may lawfully alleviate one's necessity with the goods of another, whether one takes the goods openly or secretly."[57] As such, it cannot properly be called "theft" or "robbery" and is a morally permissible response to the sin of the rich who fail in their duties of benevolence.

Hobbes follows Thomas's lead,

> when a man is destitute of food or other things necessary for his life and cannot preserve himself any other way but by some fact against the law, as if in a great famine he may take the food by force or stealth, which he cannot obtain for money nor charity; or in defense of his life, snatch away another man's sword; he is *totally excused*. (*Leviathan*, 27.26; emphasis added)[58]

Hobbes's excuse of theft here is surprising on at least two levels. First is that despite his contempt for Scholastic philosophy,[59] his arguments here parallel Thomas's in *Summa Theologiae*. Second, and of greater immediate importance, however, is his exceptions to the law against theft. He is generally concerned about thievery. In addition to his approving citation to the Decalogue's prohibition of theft as binding commands because they are "drawn from the will of God our King, whom we are obliged to obey" (*Leviathan*, 25.10), he further insists that theft is "forbidden by the laws of nature." Yet even as he defines theft as both a sin and violative of the laws of nature, he allows that the definition of the term is "to be determined by the *civil*, not the *natural, law*" (*Citizen*, 6.16; emphases original). Upon recalling the purpose of the laws of nature as promoting peace—in addition to the fact that hunger and indignity fuel sedition—it is consistent with his larger principles to permit the kind of theft he describes at *Leviathan*, 27.26. A commonwealth tolerating needless hunger, especially when combined with the indignity of poverty he describes, flirts with its own demise. Indigent and indignant subjects ultimately pose a greater threat to the commonwealth than does periodic thievery by the poor. Given England's problems with peasant rebellions in the century leading up to the publication of *Leviathan*, such as Kett's Rebellion, one can understand how Hobbes arrived at this conclusion.[60]

HOBBES'S MORAL PSYCHOLOGY OF THE WEALTHY

Although Hobbes is concerned about the problems poverty poses for his commonwealth, he expresses even greater concerns about concentrated wealth. His earliest discussion of wealth can be found in his *Art of*

Rhetoric, written in 1637, a summary of Aristotle's *Rhetoric*.[61] For Aristotle's part, the wealthy are

> wantonly aggressive and arrogant, since they are affected somewhat by the possession of wealth (for their disposition is the same as if they possessed every good thing, since wealth is something like a standard value for other good things, which is why all of them appear purchasable by it). And they are luxurious and pretentious people: luxurious, because of their mode of life and their display of prosperity; pretentious and vulgar, because all of them are accustomed to spending their time on what they love and admire and to thinking that others are emulously jealous of the same things as themselves. . . . And they think they deserve to rule (for which they think they have the things on account of which one is worthy to rule). And, in sum, the character proper to wealth is that of a prosperous person who lacks understanding.[62]

Hobbes's summary of Aristotle echoes:

> *Rich* men are contumelious, and proud; this they have from their riches; for seeing everything may be had for money, having money they think they have all that is good. And effeminate; because they have wherewithal to subminister to their lust. And boasters of their wealth, and speak in high terms foolishly; for men willingly talk of what they love and admire, and think others affect the same that they do; and the truth is, all sorts of men submit to the rich. And think themselves worthy to command, having that by which men attain command. And in general they have the manners of fortunate fools. They do injury, with intention not to hurt, but to disgrace; and partly also through incontinence. (*Rhetoric*, 2.18; emphasis original)

For Hobbes and Aristotle, the wealthy are vain and arrogant; they tend to reduce the value of things to their cash value; they assume their superiority over others; they are selfish, lack self-control, and express a lust to dominate others; they assume that they, above all others, know best how to rule on account of their riches.[63] But as Hobbes's *Rhetoric* largely summarizes Aristotle's work, one can question whether he actually shares in Aristotle's assessments about the wealthy's character flaws. After all, he generally dismisses Aristotle as "vain and erroneous" (*Leviathan*, 44.3).

Despite Hobbes's *Rhetoric* being largely an exercise in translation and summary, there are good reasons to believe he agrees with Aristotle's moral psychology of the rich.[64] Some of his most developed thoughts along these lines can be found in his *On Man* (*De Homine*), which he completed several years after *Leviathan*. It is worth examining this text carefully:

> From the goods of fortune, that is from riches, nobility of birth, and civil power it happens that dispositions are in some measure made various; for dispositions are frequently made more proud by riches and civil power, for those who can do more demand that they be allowed more, that is, they are more inclined to cause injuries, and they are more unsuited for entering into a society of equitable law with those who can do less. (*Man*, 13.5)

For Hobbes, elevated wealth inflames pride and vanity. As he elaborates earlier in the text, "excessive self-esteem impedes reason; and on that account it is a perturbation of the mind, wherein a certain swelling of the mind is experienced because the animal spirits are transported" (*Man*, 12.9). In *Leviathan*, he characterizes pride as a kind of "madness," one that "subjecteth a man to anger, the excess whereof is the madness called RAGE and FURY" (*Leviathan*, 8.18–19). It also engenders arrogance— the wealthy think themselves wiser than others (*Man*, 11.8).[65] Arrogance has its own complications for Hobbes—namely, the arrogant are "unsuited for correcting their own faults. For they do not believe that anything in them needs correcting. On the contrary, they are inclined either to correct others' deeds, or to be vituperative or scornful about them, like those who believe that whatsoever they see being done contrary to their own opinion is being done improperly. And so they judge a state to be badly governed which is not governed as they themselves wish" (*Man*, 13.6).

The pride and arrogance Hobbes associates with great fortunes explains why the wealthy are so difficult to govern in a "society of equitable laws." On his reasoning, the rich assume they are better than their fellow citizens and even better than their government. Any law failing to please them only inflames their anger and rage.

One can imagine that Hobbes's frustrations with the wealthy reflect the problems that the wealthy merchants created in seventeenth-century England. As they grew richer, they became increasingly frustrated, angry, and ultimately rebellious with sovereign policies, such as with the ship money tax. Hobbes describes these frustrations in his account of the English Civil War. For him, "those great capital cities, when rebellion is upon pretense of grievances, must needs be of the rebel party: because the grievances are but taxes, to which citizens, that is, merchants, whose profession is their private gain, are naturally mortal enemies." As he explains, the wealthy merchants are thus "most commonly . . . the first encouragers of rebellion" (*Behemoth*, 126). The wealthy perceive taxation as an affront for which rebellion is the natural response. This explains a fundamental cause of the seventeenth century's tumults. As the government increasingly sought to tax the emerging merchants, that class, in turn, rejected sovereign authority to impose said taxes. It would rather upend the government itself than submit to sovereign authority. Hence, not only does poverty foster "sedition," but wealthy merchants are also prone to rebellion.

Leviathan contains Hobbes's most developed thoughts about the effects of wealth on moral psychology:

> Of the passions that most frequently are the causes of crime, one is vainglory or a foolish overrating of their own worth, as if difference of worth were *an effect of their wit or riches* or blood or some other natural quality, not depending on the will of those that have the sovereign authority. From whence it procedeth a presumption that the punishments ordained by the laws and extended generally to all subjects ought not to be inflicted on them with the same riguour they are inflicted on poor, obscure, and simple men, comprehended under the name of *vulgar*.
>
> Therefore it happeneth commonly that such as *value themselves by the greatness of their wealth* adventure on crimes, upon hope of escaping punishment by corrupting public justice or obtaining pardon by money or other rewards. (*Leviathan*, 27.13–14; emphases added)

As in *De Homine*, Hobbes worries about a tendency among the wealthy to vainglory. Elsewhere in *Leviathan*, he describes vanity as commonly the malady of the young, "corrected oftentimes by age" (*Leviathan*, 6.41). But his remarks above suggest that wealth and privilege have the effect of extending it throughout life, effectively rendering them overgrown adolescents.

One of the remarkable features of vanity born from wealth, according to Hobbes, is their presumption that the laws do not bind them, as they do the "poor, obscure, and simple." On his account, they feel exempt from the laws because they harbor expectations that the laws do not apply to them. Exceptions will be made; bribes can obtain pardons; justice can always be compromised. As such, for Hobbes, these men "take courage to violate the laws from a hope of oppressing the power to whom it belonged" (*Leviathan*, 27.15). This is precisely the revolutionary spirit of the burgeoning merchant class that so disturbs Hobbes in *Behemoth*. If the laws displease them, to their mind, they can always overturn the government. And threatening to change the government is an act of rebellion, undermining the rule of law and sovereign authority.

The dominant theme in Hobbes's moral psychology of the wealthy is their sense of impunity. In discussing the sources of lawlessness, he acknowledges many factors. As already noted, some of these are justifiable when committed by the poor, who are driven by an excusable desperation (*Leviathan*, 27.26). But he is less forgiving of lawless behavior when committed by the wealthy:

> The same fact done against the law, if it proceed from presumption of strength, riches, or friends to resist those that are to execute the law, is a greater crime than if it proceed from hope of not being discovered or of escape by flight; for presumption of impunity by force is a root from whence springeth at all times and upon all temptations a contempt of all laws; whereas in the latter case the apprehension of danger that makes a man fly renders him more obedient for the future. (*Leviathan*, 27.30)

Those with means, status, and connections, for Hobbes, presume an ability to evade all legal accountability. He had long speculated along these lines, as evidenced in his early "Discourse upon the Beginning of Tacitus," which included the remark, "Nothing is more proverbial than that Laws are like Spiders' webs, only to hold the small Flies." He continued that although other attributes, like favor or friendships can facilitate legal impunity, "money gave the easiest passage of all" (*Tacitus*, 49).[66] This presumption of impunity makes the rich a particular threat to the rule of law, which requires habits of obedience. Whereas vagabonds might occasionally violate the laws, they always fear the law since they tend to suffer its sanctions. But the presumptions of the wealthy render them indifferent to the law. Not worrying about the consequences of their lawbreaking, they represent a unique threat to the Hobbesian commonwealth. There can only be one figure in his commonwealth who legitimately acts with impunity—the sovereign (*Citizen*, 5.13).

Greed is an underlying element in the growing fortunes of the wealthy as well as their subsequent sense of impunity.[67] Hobbes's concern about greed extends back to his 1629 translation of Thucydides's *History of the Peloponnesian War* in which greed (*pleonexia*) represents a persistent menace to various parties consumed in the conflict. As Ryan Balot has observed, greed is a frequent theme of Thucydides's *History*,[68] as Hobbes well knew. The Corcyraeans, for example, ruled "out of avarice and ambition," resulting in the "most horrible outrages . . . without regard of justice or the public good."[69] Greed also features significantly in the Mytilenean debate in which Diodotus observes, "For poverty will always add boldness to necessity; and wealth, covetousness to pride and contempt."[70] Hobbes acknowledges the Greek origins of this concept by specifically employing the Greek word *pleonexia* in both *Leviathan* and *Elements*, which he defines as "a desire [of subjects] for more than their share" (*Leviathan*, 15.22; see also *Elements*, 17.2).[71]

Hobbes also would have been attuned to greed through Scripture. It is a frequent theme in both the Old and New Testaments, figuring prominently in the book of Ecclesiastes as well as the Gospels and Paul's epistles. Similar condemnations of greed could also be found widely in Hobbes's milieu. Published just ten years before Hobbes's birth, Philipp Caesar's *General Discourse against the Damnable Sect of Usurers* condemned the "so beastlie and poisoned wickednesse" of usury, as practiced by those who were "worse than pagans, which are without Religion, wicked, not beleeuyung there is a God." Caesar likens these money-driven agents to "poysoned serpantes, to greedie Wormes, to Wolues, Beares, and to such other rauening beastes."[72] Such views persisted throughout Hobbes's lifetime, as reflected in James Harrington's biblical insistence in 1656 that his readers remember "that covetousness is the root of all evil."[73] So it is unsurprising that Hobbes references biblical sources in *On the Citizen*, describing the commandment "*Thou shalt not covet*" as a natural law (*Citizen*, 14.14; see Exodus 20:17).

Hobbes sees avarice as ingrained in human nature. Indeed, in the epistle dedicatory of *On the Citizen*, he identifies two principles of human nature: greed and natural reason. Greed invites trouble; reason provides the best prospects for escaping it (*Citizen*, p. 6). He describes such difficulties in chapter 3 of *On the Citizen*:

> A man who keeps more than he needs for himself and, in the hardness of his heart, takes the necessities of life from other people, and is too temperamentally stubborn to be corrected, is normally said to be *inconsiderate* of others and difficult. Now since our basic principle is that every man is not only *right*, but *naturally compelled*, to make every effort to win what he needs for his own preservation, anyone who tries to thwart him for the sake of luxuries will be to blame for the way which breaks out, because he was the only one who had no need to fight; and is therefore acting against the fundamental law of nature [viz., peace]. (*Citizen*, 3.9; emphases original)[74]

The pursuit of greater riches, especially at the expense of the poor, triggers what Hobbes describes as the poor's natural and rightful defense of their modest resources. Those consumed with greed "are inclined to continue the causes of war and to stir up trouble and sedition" (*Leviathan*, 11.4).

Greed thus violates the natural law insofar as it threatens peace. He draws this connection in his *Behemoth* in which "rich subjects . . . never look upon anything but their present profit." He continues, "If they had understood what virtue there is to preserve their wealth in obedience to their lawful sovereign, they would never have sided with Parliament" (*Behemoth*, 142). In other words, the greed of the wealthy threatens to undermine the sovereign. Had they been less avaricious, they likely would have accepted sovereign authority and lived harmoniously with fellow subjects.[75]

INEQUALITY, ENVY, RESENTMENT, FACTIONALIZATION, AND DISSOLUTION

Hobbes elaborates that wealthy presumptions are the source of factions, which are best understood as a category of human association, as outlined in chapter 22 of *Leviathan*. Political theorist Richard Boyd has aptly summarized that Hobbes divides different groups into the classes: "subordinate" versus "independent," "public" versus "private," and "lawful" versus "unlawful."[76] The only independent system is the state itself. All other lawful groups are subordinate. Private groups not expressly authorized by the state cannot be tolerated as lawful insofar as they oppose sovereign authority. The most threatening groups are both private and unlawful, the category to which factions belong. Hobbes presents his own examples in chapter 22: "If the sovereign power be in a great assembly and a number of men, part of the assembly, without authority, contrive the guidance of the rest, this is a faction or conspiracy unlawful, as being a fraudulent seducing of the assembly for their particular interest" (*Leviathan*, 22.30). But factions extend, for Hobbes, well outside political institutions. They frequently pit subjects against one another. This is clear in his definition of factions in *On the Citizen*: "By FACTION I mean a crowd [*multitude*] of citizens, united either by *agreements* with each other or by the power of one man, without authority from the holder or holders of sovereign power. A *faction* is like a commonwealth within the commonwealth; for just as a commonwealth comes into being by men's union in a natural state, so a faction comes into being by a new union of citizens" (*Citizen*, 13.13; emphases original). The definitions of faction in *Leviathan* and *On the Citizen* emphasize the partiality of interests. Whereas the commonwealth, for Hobbes, must always seek the "common good" (e.g., *Leviathan*, 24.6; *Citizen*, 5.4; *Elements*, 19.8), factions elevate the "particular interest" and "private interest" of subsets within the broader population (*Leviathan*, 22.30).[77] It stands to reason, of course, that if factions promote their own particular interests, they frequently antagonize the interests of other subjects—this is what it means, after all, to prefer a private interest to the common good. Thus it follows that "*factions* are the source of sedition and civil war" (*Citizen*, 10.12; emphasis original).

There is a long tradition of associating factions with economic or class divisions. As American founder James Madison would observe more than a century after Hobbes, "the most common and durable source of factions, has been the various and unequal distribution of property. Those who hold, and those who are without property, have ever formed distinct interests in society."[78] But well before either Hobbes or Madison, Plato's Athenian Stranger in the *Laws* observed that the simultaneous presence of "harsh poverty" and great wealth "breed[s] both civil war and faction" (*Laws*, 744d).[79] Hobbes largely agrees. In listing the sources of factions, he identifies popular figures, who can recruit allies in their grievances against the sovereign. But he quickly adds, "The same is to be said of immoderate private wealth; for everything obeys money" (*Citizen*, 13.13).

As already suggested, inequality's factious nature, for Hobbes, manifests in the reluctance of the wealthy to pay their taxes. Where states depend on tax revenues to provide essential benefits—like protection against invasion and promotion of the peace more generally—it is easy to understand the existential danger of failed tax payments. But there is another dimension in which inequality generates Hobbesian problems: envy and resentment. He sketches this in chapter 10 of *Leviathan*:

> Riches joined with liberality is power, because it procureth friends and servants; without liberality, not so, because in this case they defend it not, but expose men to envy, as a prey. (*Leviathan*, 10.4)[80]

Wealth can be a source of great social power, for Hobbes, but especially when shared with the indigent. In the absence of regular acts of charity, the rich inspire envy, which Hobbes defines as a "grief arising from seeing one's self exceeded or excelled by his concurrent . . . joined with pleasure conceived in the imagination of some ill fortune that may befall him" (*Elements*, 9.12).[81] That is, envy engenders a desire to witness the suffering of one's betters, as it were and, as he explains in *Leviathan*, even to play a role in bringing about that suffering. Those hoarding great wealth inflame the poor's envy and thus subject themselves to becoming the deprived's prey. The presumptions of the rich thus inspire violence among the poor. Hobbes elaborates in chapter 30 of *Leviathan*: "Impunity maketh insolence; insolence, hatred, and hatred, an endeavor to pull down all oppressing and contumelious greatness, though with ruin of the commonwealth" (*Leviathan*, 30.16). The wealthy's presumption of impunity is readily apparent to the poor, who resent them for it. That resentment urges them to attack the rich, bringing down the commonwealth along with them. Hobbes may well have in mind moments in recent English history, such as the Gloucestershire rebellion of 1622 in which the poor's envy led them to forcibly seize the wealthy's possessions. Even though the commonwealth did not collapse on this occasion, Hobbes seems acutely aware that such episodes possess this potential. This is why "*resentment* and *envy* . . . are the sources of sedition and war" (*On the Citizen*, 5.5; emphases original; see also *Leviathan*, 17.7).

To be sure, many deny the legitimacy of this envy and resentment. Harvard cognitive scientist Steven Pinker has related a Soviet-era fable in which two poor peasants are distinguished only by the fact that one of them has a scrawny goat. When the goat-less peasant is granted a wish, he simply wishes that "Boris's goat should die." Pinker uses the fable to expose the gratuitous malevolence of envy in the context of inequality. The scrawny goat is not the source of the peasant's suffering, according to Pinker, so much as is his poverty. Amid a growing commercial economy, however, he argues, everyone's condition is improving, and residual envy can only be the source of needless strife.[82] But here is what Hobbes understands that Pinker does not: we cannot simply will envy and resentment away, however irrational it may be. For Hobbes, envy and resentment will always accompany inequality. It is no different from telling betrayed spouses not to experience jealousy. Yes, jealousy is powerfully destructive for everyone involved. One might even call it irrational. Yet simply telling the betrayed to not feel it does not resolve the problem. The feeling runs deep. Likely the best strategy in dealing with jealousy would be to prevent the betrayal in the first place by fostering healthy relationships. For Hobbes, the solution to inequality is not to tell the poor to stop feeling envy and resentment; the solution is rather to reduce the inequality that inflames it.

Economic Issues and State Failure

In chapter 29 of *Leviathan*, Hobbes addresses the sources of a commonwealth's dissolution. Among these are the failure to grant absolute authority to the sovereign, the division of governmental powers, lack of resources, and the like. But infrequently observed in Hobbes's discussion of failing states is how often these failures intersect with economic issues. Hobbes himself, however, is sometimes explicit in making this connection. In this section, I draw attention to these failures, connecting his attention to economic issues to at least five of these sources of state failure. These include (1) difficulty in raising public money, (2) private judgments of good and evil, (3) individual claims of private and absolute rights to private property, (4) excessive concentration of wealth, and (5) want of absolute sovereign power. There is much overlap among these, and they all relate to the economic issues already raised in this chapter.

A good place to begin understanding these factors is to reconsider the refusal of the wealthy to pay their ship money taxes in 1638.[83] The sovereign had imposed these taxes on merchants, as their growing wealth offered a new revenue stream. The merchants acquiesced for a time but subsequently refused to pay. In Hobbesian terms, this refusal posed multiple threats to the commonwealth. First and most obvious, insofar as subjects refused to pay their taxes, they made it difficult for the sovereign to raise revenue "for the necessary uses of the commonwealth, especially in the approach of war" (*Leviathan*, 29.18). In the immediate context of 1638–1640, this undermined the Bishops' Wars against Scotland. And with France's forces in Scotland, it raised questions for Hobbes about the crown's ability to maintain its sovereignty. Second, the refusal to pay the taxes represented a private judgment of evil. For Hobbes, individual subjects cannot have this right to judge a tax evil, just as they have no right to make any private judgments of evil (see *Leviathan*, 6.7, 18.10, 26.8, 46.32). All subjects surrender this right in the social contract. Violations of this prohibition against private judgments about good and evil, according to Hobbes, are "not only vain, but also pernicious to the public state" (*Leviathan*, 46.32). Third, their refusal to pay taxes represented a kind of absolute claim of private property, "such as excludeth the right of the sovereign." They effectively claimed that their money was, in fact, *their money* and ultimately not sovereign property. Yet Hobbes insists that private property is contingent. Hobbesian subjects have a right to exclude other subjects from seizing their property, but they do not have that right against the sovereign since the subject has property "only from the sovereign power, without the protection whereof every other man should have right to the same" (*Leviathan*, 29.10).

Fourth, the refusal to pay taxes came from the wealthiest merchants— merchants who were likely, to Hobbes's mind, a bit too wealthy. This is because

there is sometimes in a commonwealth a disease which resembleth the pleurisy; and that is when the treasury of the commonwealth, flowing out of its due course, is gathered in too much abundance in one or a few private men . . . in the same manner as the blood in a pleurisy, getting into the membrane of the breast, breedeth there an inflammation, accompanied with a fever and painful stitches. (*Leviathan*, 29.19)[84]

Hobbes's concern about concentrated wealth comes in the context of his worries about those who threaten to compete with the Leviathan for sovereign authority. This includes not only the rich but also "popular" figures, like Julius Caesar, "who was set up by the people against the Senate." The effect of such machinations is to challenge sovereign authority. As Hobbes understands, "this proceeding of popular and ambitious men is plain rebellion, and may be resembled to the effects of witchcraft" (*Leviathan*, 29.20). Such is the danger of powerful orators, who have "as much power as the *people* itself, and they have a kind of tacit agreement to turn a blind eye to each other's greed (*my turn today, yours tomorrow*)" (*Citizen*, 10.7; emphases original).

It is perhaps intuitive to connect the power of popular leaders to the power of wealth, as Hobbes himself acknowledges that the desire for wealth is, at bottom, a "desire of power" (*Leviathan*, 8.15). As he subsequently elaborates, "riches are honourable, for they are power" (*Leviathan*, 10.40; see also *Elements*, 8.5). To be wealthy, for Hobbes, is to be powerful, which immediately raises questions about the dangers private wealth poses to commonwealths. Thus, on his account, it must be carefully regulated by the sovereign:

> Private power has a certain limit beyond which it will ruin the commonwealth; because of it monarchs must sometimes take steps to see that no harm comes to the Country [*Respublica*] from that direction. When the source of that power has been wealth, they have decreased it by decreasing the wealth. (*Citizen*, 10.7)

Wealthy subjects can exercise this power in different respects. They may, for example, seize power for themselves, as did Sulla in the Roman Republic. Or they might work from the sidelines, as it were, undermining the existing sovereign whenever it threatens their private interests. Regardless of strategy, the very rich pose a looming threat of contesting and disrupting sovereign authority, which makes it prudent for the sovereign to pursue "decreasing the wealth." Failure to do so undermines the sovereign's absolute authority, where absolute authority is essential for the commonwealth's continued existence—the fifth category cited above. So managing economic inequality is a matter on which the commonwealth depends.

Hobbesian Solutions

Hobbes's problematizations of wealth, poverty, greed, and inequality demand solutions. There is ample evidence in his work to suggest he has them. What is more, these solutions are recognizably Hobbesian. The primary way to address these pathologies is to rely on the Leviathan, whose absolute powers are required to address these social maladies. His broadest measure is to authorize sovereign redistribution of property, where necessary, to establish an equitable balance of wealth and property, consistent with peace and the common good. But to support this, he institutes several natural laws aimed at addressing the maladies associated with wealth, greed, and inequality.

Most obvious among these measures is Hobbes's system of public charity to protect subjects, who by "accident inevitable, become unable to maintain themselves by their labour." He elaborates, "For as it is uncharitableness in any man to neglect the impotent; so it is in the sovereign of a commonwealth to expose them to the hazard of such uncertain charity" (*Leviathan*, 30.18). Hobbes clearly prefers public charity, presumably resembling the Elizabethan poor laws, to private charity, which is contingent on the goodwill and whimsy of the wealthy. To be sure, providing for the basic needs of the poor is for him a necessary measure not only for humanitarian reasons but also because the poor are prone to sedition, as has been noted. Thus tending to their most immediate needs should be high priority for any prudent sovereign.

This program of providing for the poor is likely connected to Hobbes's attention to the distribution of property in chapter 24 of *Leviathan*, as part of a larger discussion of the "nutrition and procreation of a commonwealth."[85] His discussion of property remarkably parallels one found in the Old Testament. Moses outlines the Jubilee laws, according to which God demands that all property changing hands over the past fifty years must be restored to the original distribution, as established in Numbers 26:52–54 and Joshua 13–19 (see Leviticus 25:28). Numbers, in particular, establishes a principle of equity in property distribution whereby "to a larger group give a larger inheritance, and to a smaller group a smaller one; each is to receive its inheritance according to the number of those listed" (Numbers 26:54). There is no principle of distributing land according to talent, merit, or industry. Leviticus explains the underlying authority for Jubilee as divine since the land ultimately belongs to God, whereas the Israelites merely "hold [it] as a possession" (Leviticus

25:23). God's ownership of the land thus authorizes this periodic property redistribution. There is no questioning Jubilee, even though the author of Leviticus understands that Jubilee will rankle feathers and that those benefiting from property exchanges since the last Jubilee will want to maintain their gains for themselves and their heirs. This is why God promises violent retribution against anyone violating Jubilee laws, including but not limited to the destruction of crops, attacks by wild animals, the death of children, plagues, famine, and the delivery of violators to their enemies (Leviticus 26:23–39).[86]

Hobbes's discussion of property distribution commences with a parallel assumption, that it is ultimately at the "mortal god's" discretion: "*propriety* [property] . . . belongeth in all kinds of commonwealths to the sovereign power" (*Leviathan*, 24.5; emphasis original).[87] For this reason and because of the sovereign's absolute authority, property distributions are unchallengeable. Hobbes connects his own theory of property and ancient Jewish law by expressly evoking the Hebrew division of land from Joshua 13–19 (*Leviathan*, 24.6).

Although sovereign authority to distribute property cannot be challenged, this does not mean that it can be arbitrary. Hobbes specifies that property should be distributed and redistributed according to "equity and the common good" (*Leviathan*, 24.6), or as he subsequently elaborates "the common peace and security" and "equity and the law of nature" (*Leviathan*, 24.7). Some will be surprised that Hobbes has a notion of "common good" at all.[88] But given context in these paragraphs of *Leviathan*, the "common good" can readily be reduced to peace, security, equity, and the law of nature—all of which share much in common. "Peace" and "security" amount to the same thing—the absence of war (*Leviathan*, 13.8)—constituting the first and foundational law of nature (*Leviathan*, 14.4). "Equity" is also a law of nature and, as such, is directed back to the first—to the preservation of peace.[89] Beyond this, however, Hobbes specifies that equity requires sovereigns to "deal equally" between subjects (*Leviathan*, 15.23). The opposite of equity, he notes, is partiality, which is a source of faction.[90] Equity also requires that subjects accept this equal dealing as authoritative for the sake of their peace and security (*Leviathan*, 15.24).

Hobbesian equity includes an underlying moral psychology. First, he notes that in treating subjects unequally, by "giv[ing] more or less to one than to the other, you are *insulting* the person who is not favored" (*Citizen*, 3.15; emphasis original).[91] Although he speaks here of distributing rights, one can imagine the same principle extending to property distribution. Where subjects possess radically unequal shares of land, one can imagine the perception of insult. Second, if subjects were to possess radically unequal shares of property, it could well incite envy and resentment, which, as Hobbes is at pains to suggest, is the source of political instability and even civil war (*Citizen*, 5.5; see also *Leviathan*, 17.7). Given sovereign authority to distribute and redistribute property at will; given that Hobbes insists that property should be distributed according to equity, peace, and security; and given that significant economic inequality fosters envy, resentment, factions, and ultimately sedition and civil war, it seems that Hobbes's assumptions demand fairly equal property distribution.[92] Anything less endangers the peace and security on which the commonwealth rests.

Finally, regarding Hobbesian sovereign authority to distribute and redistribute property, one might object that even though this is technically within the sovereign authority, it is not something he considered as a measure to confront specifically concentrated wealth and inequality. Yet Hobbes himself cites redistribution as a salutary practice of previous sovereigns: "when the source of that power has been wealth, they [sovereigns] have decreased it by decreasing the wealth" (*Citizen*, 10.7). Concentrated wealth is problematic for Hobbes; wealth redistribution is clearly his solution.

Hobbes's program for sovereign distribution of property is his primary mechanism for managing economic inequality. Yet this program of property redistribution itself points careful readers to other dimensions of his philosophy aimed at achieving the same—namely, his laws of nature against contumely, pride, and arrogance.

Hobbes associates pride with vanity: "The passion whose violence or continuance maketh madness is . . . great *vain-glory*, which is commonly called *pride* and *self-conceit*" (*Leviathan*, 8.18; emphases original).[93] One of the primary sources of pride, for him, is wealth: "Dispositions are frequently made more proud by riches" (*Man*, 8.5). The proud and vainglorious, he observes, "estimate their sufficiency by the flattery of other men or the fortune of some precedent action, without assured ground of hope from the true knowledge of themselves, are inclined to rash engaging" (*Leviathan*, 15.12). They also lack an underlying self-confidence. They seek their sense of self-worth in public applause. They may be rich, but that alone does not make them feel content. They use their wealth to effect the praise of others. If anyone should get the better of them on a given occasion, pride merely inspires them to take vengeance against their competitors, as "revenge . . . is motivated by vainglory" (*Citizen*, 3.11). Given that vengeance violates the natural law for Hobbes, one can appreciate that pride and vainglory can trigger a spiraling of offenses against the natural laws, culminating with threats to the first law of peace.[94]

Hobbes contrasts his natural law against pride with its opposite: the recognition of natural equality. By nature, as he emphasizes, all humanity is fundamentally equal, both in body and mind: "The question who is the better man has no place in the condition of mere nature" (*Leviathan*, 15.21). Yet he acknowledges that civil society introduces inequalities. Aristotle's error in this regard, for Hobbes, is assuming that social inequalities parallel natural inequalities. For Hobbes, Aristotle's presumption of natural inequalities inflates the pride of those occupying the top of social hierarchies. Hobbes presses even further, allowing that even if Aristotle were right—that some are naturally superior—that doctrine would have to be publicly denied: "*The pursuit of peace* requires *that they be regarded as equal*" (*Citizen*, 3.13; emphases original). So long as some are permitted to assume their natural superiority, they will seize greater privileges. That makes them a social menace. Hence, "the ninth law of nature . . . *that every man acknowledge another for his equal by nature*. The breach of this precept is *pride*" (*Leviathan*, 15.21; emphases original).

One implication of Hobbes's law of equality is his requirement that all citizens be equally liable to taxation: "To equal justice appertaineth also the equal imposition of taxes."[95] He elaborates that this equality of taxes "dependeth not on the equality of riches, but on the equality of the debt that every man oweth to the commonwealth for his defense." For contemporary readers, this might resemble what is now called a "flat tax," where everyone pays the same tax rate regardless of their economic class. But this is not Hobbes's position. Rather, he argues, all subjects have a debt to society for their protection. In the first place, this means that *all* subjects are liable to military service. But Hobbes notes that most rich people will simply "hire others to fight for them." So whereas the poor pay with their bodies, the rich must pay in cash. Beyond this, they are to pay this as a consumption tax—insofar as Hobbes seeks not to burden those who are working hard and saving, so much as he who is "living idly . . . spending all he gets" (*Leviathan*, 30.17). He targets those living extravagantly, rather than the working poor, who labor hard and save all they can. This suggests that he objected to making the poor pay consumption taxes on staples like beer, meat, salt, starch, and soap as Parliament had imposed with particularly damaging effects on the poor. His calculus suggests that the poor have likely already paid their taxes with their bodies, leaving the consumption taxes to fall on luxury items purchased by wealthier subjects.

Paralleling the natural law against pride is the law against arrogance. As with the proud, the arrogant seek to distinguish themselves over and above their fellow subjects. The law itself reads, "that at the entrance into conditions of peace, no man require to reserve to himself any right which he is not content should be reserved to every one of the rest" (*Leviathan*, 15.22). As previously noted, the wealthy, for Hobbes, tend to assume "that the punishments ordained by the laws and extended generally to all subjects ought not to be inflicted on them with the same rigour that they are inflicted on poor, obscure, and simple men" (*Leviathan*, 27.13; see also *Man*, 13.5). Arrogance presumes greater privileges for oneself over one's fellow subjects. For the arrogant rich, what is illegal for the poor is legal for them. This violates Hobbes's prohibition against arrogance. He continues, violating this law can also be called "*pleonexia*, that is, a desire of more than their share" (*Leviathan*, 15.22). As discussed in chapter 1, *pleonexia* is the Greek word for greed—an unquenchable thirst for more that, for the Greeks, often results in self-ruin. For Hobbes, the arrogant assume they are entitled to more than others. And because they are consumed by *pleonexia*, there is little reason to believe that their quest for greater money, status, and power will ever cease. More than perhaps any other character in Hobbes's oeuvre, the arrogant embody the "restless desire of power after power that ceaseth only in death" (*Leviathan*, 11.2). Indeed, as Hobbes elaborates, such figures present an existential threat to the commonwealth: "Competition of riches, honour, command, or other power inclineth to contention, enmity, and war, because the way of one competitor to the attaining of his desire is to kill, subdue, supplant, or repel the other" (*Leviathan*, 11.3). The aims of the arrogant and *pleonectic* cannot be broadly shared—it is their nature to be exclusive. This pits subjects against one another, fomenting enmity, sedition, and war. Hobbes speaks directly to the necessity of curbing greed in *On the Citizen*:

> Since our basic principle is that every man is not only *right*, but *naturally compelled*, to make every effort to win what he needs for his own preservation, anyone who tries to thwart him for the sake of luxuries will be to blame for the war which breaks out, because he was the only one who had no need to fight; and is hence acting against the *fundamental law of nature*. (*Citizen*, 3.9; emphases original)

The desire for more than one's share is, for Hobbes, not only inconsiderate regarding the needs of others. It undermines the fundamental law of nature—namely, seeking peace.

So fundamental are the natural laws against pride and arrogance, for Hobbes, that they inform the very title of his magnum opus: *Leviathan*. The figure of the Leviathan is a carefully considered reference to the book of Job.[96] The book of Job is best known for its depiction of the travails of Job, a wealthy and faithful man, who is tormented by Satan in a series of indignities to test his enduring love of God. He suffers these torments for a time but eventually grows weary, condemning God for having permitted these punishments despite his best efforts to lead a pious life. God responds to Job indignantly. In questioning God's actions, Job has presumed that he knows better than God. God's closing speech in the book of Job is an expression of his superiority over Job in every conceivable way, including in brute physical force. It is only God who can create a Leviathan, a great sea creature, capable of filling all with overwhelming, cowering fear.

> When it rises up, the mighty are terrified; they retreat before its thrashing. The sword that reaches it has no effect, nor does the spear or the dart or the javelin. Iron it treats like straw and bronze like rotten wood. Arrows do not make it flee; slingstones are like chaff to it. A club seems to it but a piece of straw; it laughs at the rattling of the lance. Its undersides are jagged potsherds, leaving a trail in the mud like a threshing sledge. It makes the depths churn like a boiling caldron and stirs up the sea like a pot of ointment. It leaves a glistening wake behind it; one would think the deep had white hair. Nothing on earth is its equal—a creature without fear. It looks down on all that are haughty; it is king over all that are proud. (Job 41:25–34)

The "haughty," those who think they know better than God, must be tamed by a power they cannot themselves resist—a physically overwhelming force that terrorizes them into submission. And, indeed, immediately after God presents the image of the Leviathan, Job submits to God's authority.

Scholars have long noted Hobbes's biblical source here, as Hobbes does himself in chapter 28 of *Leviathan*.

> Hitherto I have set forth the nature of man, whose pride and other passions have compelled him to submit himself to government, together with the great power of his governor, whom I compared to Leviathan, taking that comparison out of the two last verses of the one-and-fortieth of Job where God, having set forth the great power of Leviathan, calleth him king of the proud. *There is nothing*, saith he, *on earth to be compared with him. He is made so as not to be afraid. He seeth every high*

thing below him; and is king of all the children of pride. (Leviathan,
28.27; emphasis original)

The historian of political thought Christopher Brooke has rightly drawn
attention to Hobbes's concern to tame the pride and arrogance that
threaten the peace.[97] Yet there are additional insights to be derived from
further analysis of Hobbes's appeal to Job's Leviathan. First, one should
recall that for Hobbes the proud and arrogant are often very wealthy.
Second, he connects the wealthy's larger fortunes to their sense that they
are above the law. Third, he attributes to the proud and arrogant a tendency to "judge a state to be badly governed which is not governed as
they themselves wish" (*Man*, 8.6). To be sure, Job is wealthy; he is also
someone who, albeit briefly, thinks he knows better than God how to
rule. In broad terms, Job's presumptions here parallel the wealthy merchants in seventeenth-century England, who think they know better than
the king who should be paying taxes and how much. As Hobbes suggests,
it is surely the task of the sovereign to tame those individuals, particularly with respect to their pride and arrogance, so that the state might
secure the peace that had been so severely disrupted in the years leading
up to the wars.

Another natural law bears mentioning. This is Hobbes's law against
contumely, which amounts to "all signs of hatred or contempt" (*Leviathan*, 15.8). To be sure, here again economic circumstances play a role.
As previously discussed, the wealthiest subjects assume impunity, and for
Hobbes, "impunity maketh insolence; insolence, hatred, and hatred, an
endeavor to pull down all oppressing and contumelious greatness, though
with ruin of the commonwealth" (*Leviathan*, 30.16).[98] The causal arrow
also points in the other direction. The privileges enjoyed by the wealthy fill
the poor with jealousy and resentment since riches without charity "pro-
voke envy" (*Man*, 9.7). Thus economic inequality threatens Hobbes's natural law against contumely, given that it inspires insolence on the one hand
and envy and resentment on the other. The common failure of the wealthy
to heed these natural laws against pride, arrogance, and contumely, for
Hobbes, is well summarized in chapter 18 of *Leviathan*: "For all men are
by nature provided of notable multiplying glasses (that is their passions
and self-love) through which every little payment appeareth a great griev-
ance, but are destitute of those prospective glasses (namely moral and
civil science) to see afar off the miseries that hang over them and cannot
without such payments be avoided" (*Leviathan*, 18.20). Natural egoism is
magnified by wealth and power; and that wealth and power inclines them

to act even more selfishly, expressly against the natural laws, even where those laws uphold the society that nurtures them.

Of course, it is one thing to command subjects to follow the natural law. It is another to gain their compliance. In some instances, commanding and following the natural laws is relatively straightforward, such as in the laws of primogeniture and contract. But with other laws, Hobbes speaks to a state of mind, and as he subsequently acknowledges, the mind is difficult to govern (*Leviathan*, 46.37). Even though the Leviathan indeed possesses awesome political authority, it has no special access to individual consciences. It would be difficult to imagine, in other words, that a sovereign could meaningfully command that subjects abandon pride, arrogance, and contumeliousness with the expectation that this would resolve the problems associated with concentrated wealth.

To overcome this limitation of the mortal god's powers, Hobbes provides at least three measures. First, he supposes the existence of an immortal God, who has access to the thoughts of subjects. And he specifies that this God very much expects individuals to engage in acts of "charity and love" (*Leviathan*, 43.4). For Hobbes, Christians have a duty to give alms: "we should make friends with our riches of the poor, and thereby obtain their prayers whilst they live" (*Leviathan*, 45.38). Indeed, Hobbes suggests that almsgiving should extend well beyond token gifts: "To give great gifts to a man is to honour him, because it is buying of protection and acknowledging of power. To give little gifts is to dishonor, because it is but alms and signifies an opinion of the need of small helps" (*Leviathan*, 10.21). Indeed, as he adds, the "honour of great persons is to be valued for their beneficence and the aids they give to men of inferior rank, or not at all" (*Leviathan*, 30.16). To be sure, however, the practice of charity seems in many respects a religious or divine duty—to be enforced by an omnipotent God.

The second respect in which Hobbes can involve the mortal god, or Leviathan, is in rectifying the problems of concentrated wealth and inequality. If the problems of pride, arrogance, and contumely are in significant part attributable to concentrated wealth and inequality, the solution would seem to be to reduce that inequality—an authority Hobbes expressly authorizes. This is arguably a sovereign responsibility insofar as the Leviathan's primary responsibility is maintenance of the natural law, culminating in the first law of nature, the peace and security of the subjects (*Leviathan*, 30.1).

A third respect in which Hobbes attempts to address these problems is through education.[99] The civil laws should be, as he claims, coextensive with the laws of nature (e.g., *Leviathan*, 26.8). But as already noted, many natural laws are difficult to enforce since they pertain directly to the content of individual minds beyond the sovereign's reach. Hobbes intends for education to address this limitation of sovereign power. Indeed, as adherence to the laws of nature is essential for the commonwealth's survival, education in the laws of nature is a sovereign duty. Thus there needs be "a general provision contained in public instruction, both of doctrine and example; and in the making and executing of good laws to which individual persons may apply their own cases" (*Leviathan*, 30.2). The state is to reserve days for subjects to learn of their rights and duties according to the natural law. In doing so, he appeals to the Jewish tradition of a Sabbath—a day set aside each week to ponder God's laws (*Leviathan*, 30.10). To achieve this, Hobbes insists, universities must teach the same laws to their students. Among those, of course, are the laws against pride, arrogance, and contumely.[100]

Conclusions

While Hobbes's approach to the problems of poverty, excessive wealth, and inequality offers insights to readers of any generation, at least part of his solution is potentially threatened by a familiar objection. In his *Second Treatise on Government*, the philosopher John Locke objected to Hobbes's absolute monarchs since "absolute monarchs are but men."[101] In other words, if humanity is as selfish and violent as Hobbes depicts it in the state of nature, how would it make any sense to then grant all the political power to a single one among them? This objection, among other observations, has been at the foundation of the doctrines of separation of power and checks and balances, both of which Hobbes opposes. Yet Locke's objection can even be amplified when thinking about the problem of great wealth. Human nature is dangerous enough without great wealth. Hobbes adds that people are even more insufferable when they possess enormous wealth. Since it is difficult to imagine a Hobbesian sovereign as anything other than a wealthy monarch, would that not make the monarch even more dangerous?[102]

To be sure, this is a reasonable concern about the Hobbesian system that wants to concentrate all power in a small set of hands. Yet it is important to recall, for Hobbes, that much of what worries him about concentrated wealth and inequality is the threat it poses to sovereign power. Those with enormous fortunes, such as the emerging merchants of the seventeenth century, represented legitimate competitors for sovereign authority in Britain. The sovereign's wealth, by contrast, does not represent a threat in this respect. Another threat sovereign fortunes might pose would be a sense that the sovereign is above the law. This is, again, unproblematic for Hobbes since a sovereign is by definition above the law, according to his philosophy. The greatest threat posed by sovereign wealth is likely wealth's effects on one's character—the fostering of a sense of impunity. This could theoretically detach the sovereign from its obligation to heed the laws of nature. Insofar as the Leviathan possesses an enormous fortune, it may come to assume that it stands above the laws of nature. To be sure, there are powerful reasons to withhold from such presumptions, for Hobbes, most important among them that the sovereign's own position is endangered by violating those laws. At any rate, for Hobbes, the threat of sovereign wealth is far less than wealth found anywhere in the commonwealth.

Despite reasonable concerns regarding sovereign wealth, Hobbes's treatment of wealth, poverty, and inequality demonstrates the persistence of these phenomena in the modern world. Inequality is not simply a problem for those committed to the ancient virtues and their associated religious systems. Inequality is also a problem for peace and a threat to modern sovereignty regardless of the questions that bothered Plato and the authors of the New Testament. Concentrated wealth is not merely a problem because it blocks the path to a virtuous life or to the love of God. Poverty is not just a problem because it can make people hungry. Wealth is a problem because it inspires the wealthy to seize power for themselves. Poverty is a problem because it inspires insurrection. Inequality is not just a moral problem. It is, for Hobbes, fundamentally political, demanding political interventions. To be sure, this is not entirely new with Hobbes. Plato also understood the political dimensions of the problem, but his ambitions were higher than Hobbes's—fostering civic harmony and friendship, as opposed to securing peace. But what Hobbes teaches above all is that one's ambitions need not be so elevated as Plato or Jesus to be concerned about inequality. One can focus on simply keeping individuals from returning to a state of nature, and even this relatively modest ambition requires maintaining a degree of equality. The lowered ambitions of Hobbes's philosophy did not render inequality irrelevant—they merely offered new reasons to worry about it.

CHAPTER FOUR

Jean-Jacques Rousseau

"THE EVER-WIDENING INEQUALITY
OF FORTUNES"

THERE IS PERHAPS NO GREATER CRITIC of inequality than Jean-Jacques Rousseau. He is, after all, the author of the remarkable *Discourse on the Origin of Inequality* (also known as the *Second Discourse*), which explores the roots and pathologies associated with social and economic disparities. His *Discourse* engages myriad questions that bear on these matters in various ways—from human nature, to the origins of human society and government, to the nature of despotism. My focus here is on what I take to be the *Discourse*'s very core—namely, inequality itself. More specifically, I address the inequality he identifies as the proximate cause of illegitimate government: economic inequality. It is nothing less than the "usurpations of the rich" and the "banditry of the poor" that "gave way to the most horrible state of war," where "no one found safety in either poverty or wealth" (*SD*, 171, 172, 173). As readers of the *Discourse* are aware, the overt portion of this war of rich versus poor ceased with a social contract and the establishment of civil government, "which gave the weak new fetters and the rich new forces" and "forever fixed the Law of property and inequality"—a condition he subsequently defines as "despotism" (*SD*, 173, 186).

Some have argued that Rousseau actually opposes equality. His biographer Maurice Cranston has suggested that despite Rousseau's reputation as a "radical egalitarian," the Genevan is rather casually, if at all, committed to egalitarianism. According to Cranston, Rousseau's institutional preferences inclined toward aristocracy and his economic egalitarianism was more directed against ostentation than inequality: "The equality in question here [for Rousseau] ... is not equality of property or estates, but relative equality in the leading of a simple and austere *train de vie*."[1] Although Cranston allows that this may require some modest reduction of economic inequality for Rousseau, it hardly deserves the designation of "egalitarian." His Rousseau is aristocratic and comfortable with significant inequality, so long as the wealthy do not parade their fortunes.

The philosopher Paul Weirich argues perhaps for an even more inegalitarian Rousseau—one committed to an unequal distribution of resources, corresponding to unequal work among citizens—from each according to their abilities, to each according to their abilities, as it were. That is, Weirich's Rousseau embraces a quasi-Aristotelian principle of merit or desert as a principle of justice. Since different citizens are characterized by different talents and efforts, a republic's distributional scheme must reflect this in a community marked by broad economic inequality.[2]

Over the past decade, the political theorist John P. McCormick has argued that Rousseau is inegalitarian, especially in contrast to Niccolò Machiavelli. McCormick's Rousseau, much like Cranston's, is aristocratic at heart, attracted to the rigid social and economic hierarchies that characterized Rome's mature republic. McCormick argues that Rousseau's social structure, as outlined in book 4 of the *Social Contract*, "relies on significant inequality." In his account, Rousseau permits economic inequality precisely because wealth is "to be the preeminent marker of political worthiness."[3]

Regarding these readings of Rousseau as an inegalitarian, first, I should note that I do not address those arguments that his *politics* might have an aristocratic element. Even though I think these claims are somewhat overstated, my focus here is on the *economic* dimensions of Rousseau's thought, rather than those that are specifically political or institutional. Second, although I am not engaging in a detailed analysis of and response to the scholars cited immediately above, I am presenting what can be called the "preponderance of evidence." I undertake an extensive analysis of the reasons why Rousseau found economic inequality to be troubling and what he thought should be done about it. These arguments are so extensive both in their frequency and intensity that I am comfortable that this represents an adequate response to Cranston, Weirich, and McCormick. As should become clear, there is less textual ambiguity than these interpreters have suggested since, for Rousseau, "the wealth of an entire nation produces the opulence of a few private individuals to the detriment of the public, and the treasures of millionaires increase the misery of the citizens" (*PF*, 50). I save retorts to specific arguments for other occasions.

Others have adopted the contrary view that Rousseau was deeply concerned about the maldistribution of economic resources. Political theorist Sharon K. Vaughan, for example, insightfully addresses Rousseau's attention to the problem of poverty. But although she acknowledges that for Rousseau poverty is largely a "relative" condition,[4] her focus is mainly on the Genevan's treatment of the poor. Philosopher Sally Scholz also focuses on poverty but with more attention to its identity as a relative condition.[5] Yet her thoughtful analysis does not attempt to integrate Rousseau's discussion of poverty into his larger political theory. And neither reading prioritizes the effects of inequality on the wealthy themselves or on society beyond the conditions of those suffering at its bottom ranks.

Philosopher Frederick Neuhouser has authored the most ambitious treatment to date of Rousseau on inequality.[6] While his book addresses the various modes of inequality Rousseau outlines in his *Second Discourse*, economic inequality receives extended treatment in a chapter of its own. Neuhouser emphasizes the role of *amour-propre* (self-love) in the origins and consequences of economic inequality. For Rousseau, *amour-propre* is "only a relative sentiment, factitious, and born in society, which inclines every individual to set greater store by himself than by anyone else, inspires men with all the evils they do to one another" (*SD*, 218nxv).[7] Neuhouser insightfully clarifies how economic inequality emerges from *amour-propre* and how it subsequently exacerbates the problems of self-love. Yet his analysis is ultimately incomplete on three dimensions. First, he does not contextualize Rousseau's interest in inequality as one of the defining features of his age. Second, he does not connect it to Rousseau's most significant constructive political concept—the general will. Last, he does not elaborate on Rousseau's solutions to the problem of inequality. This chapter seeks to fill these gaps by placing Rousseau's interest in inequality in historical context, connecting his problematization of inequality to his general will, and exploring his strategies for addressing it.

Economic and Political Context: Eighteenth-Century Geneva

Any comprehensive account of Jean-Jacques Rousseau's understanding of economic inequality must situate him in his relevant cultural context since, as the Swiss literary critic Jean Starobinski has aptly noted, "before writing about inequality, Jean-Jacques of course experienced it in life."[8] Rousseau was born in 1712 in the city-state of Geneva. Like much of western Europe throughout the period, the shift from feudalism to capitalism was well under way in Geneva. Whereas the premodern Genevan economy had largely been agricultural, its growing bourgeois class had by Rousseau's birth generated significant private wealth, especially in international banking and the manufacturing of luxury goods. The city's reliance on luxury goods manufacturing, such as jewelry and watches, rendered its artisan workers vulnerable to the vicissitudes of the market. As intellectual historian Helena Rosenblatt has observed, the wars of Louis XIV and the War of Spanish Succession significantly curtailed demand for such goods, which displaced countless Genevan workers for much of Rousseau's youth. Among the eighty qualified master gold wire-drawers in 1721, for example, only six of them could find work.[9] Compounding the susceptibility to unemployment as well as the city's reliance on imports for necessities, Geneva was subjected to food scarcity and exceptionally high food prices. The city's poor often had difficulty in acquiring basic nourishment.

Not everyone suffered, however. The merchant-banking class did exceedingly well. When demand for luxury goods was high, they controlled production. When demand for luxury goods faltered, they simply ceased production (displacing workers) and turned their attention to banking, where they were able to grow existing wealth into even greater fortunes. The potential for enormous riches tempted some bankers to succumb to a "speculative fever," which led to the bursting of economic bubbles, the downfall of selected wealthy families, economic instability, and a growing sense among some that the city was gripped by decadence.

Upon acquiring their fortunes, the successful merchants would display their earnings ostentatiously before the less fortunate in newly fashionable quarters of town so as to *abandon themselves to arrogance*," as one critic railed.[10] They constructed mansions in the "upper town" as testaments to their opulence, in full sight of those unemployed and hungry artisans. Some even appropriated for themselves actual titles of nobility along with attendant seignorial rights.[11]

Geneva's political power was shared between two "councils."[12] The democratic General Council consisted of an assembly drawn from all citizens,[13] who theoretically exercised the right of legislation. The Small Council, by contrast, was composed of twenty citizens chosen by a wealthy elite. The two councils would clash throughout the eighteenth century, each staking its own claims to sovereignty. Originally conceived in the Middle Ages as a democratic voice, by the eighteenth century the General Council lacked authority to initiate laws. It also lacked the capacity to impose or calibrate taxation. Rather, its powers were largely limited to confirming policies already drafted by the city's elite, as manifested in the Small Council. Unsurprisingly, the Small Council prioritized wealthy interests. It would vigorously promote free trade and reducing luxury taxes since, it was argued, such taxes would "just drive the rich away from Geneva, which would not be good for business."[14]

The social, economic, and political transformations implemented by the Small Council met with some resistance, particularly from traditionally powerful religious authorities. The prominent pastor E. Gallatin, for example, published a sermon in 1724 condemning luxury, which threatened to "engulf" the city-state. In 1725, the Consistory of Pastors, created by John Calvin for the city's moral upkeep, condemned the indulgence of luxury as "a kind of epidemic illness."[15] But these critical voices were soon replaced with others more sympathetic to the city's financial elite. As Rosenblatt has commented, "by the eighteenth century, most prominent ministers came from Geneva's elite and had family relations in government."[16] This new generation of pastors would suggest the possibility of an "innocent" desire for wealth and luxury, detached from all vice. Further, they would alter existing teachings about Christian charity, downplaying wealthy obligations to the poor.

Rousseau's youth in Geneva afforded him the unique opportunity to witness these transformations and their effects on social life. His mother, née Suzanne Bernard, descended from a prominent Genevan family of wealth and status. Yet as she died in childbirth, Rousseau's upbringing fell to his father, Isaac, an artisan watchmaker with little personal wealth to sustain the comfortable lifestyle the family enjoyed before Suzanne's death. After Jean-Jacques's birth, the family moved from the fashionable quarters of Grande Rue no. 40 to the artisan quarter of St. Gervais, a locus of radical dissent against the ruling class.[17] Although Rousseau largely reported being happy in these years, he also could hardly help but observe the vast economic disparities that characterized the city.

After Rousseau's father abandoned him at age ten, he was placed in his maternal uncle's custody. Taken in by the family's wealthy branch, Rousseau briefly enjoyed its privileges—a delightful country estate and some formal schooling. But this abruptly ended when his uncle determined that Rousseau's mixed heritage best suited him to follow his father's artisanal career path.[18] So at age thirteen, he was contracted to apprentice under an engraver for a term of five years, where he was so viciously and repeatedly beaten by his master that he fled the shop and the city at age fifteen.

Inequality was not unique to Geneva in Rousseau's personal experience. As a young man, he briefly resided in Montpellier, which he described in a letter to a friend in the following way:

> These streets are lined by superb houses interspersed with wretched cottages filled with mud and dung. Half the inhabitants are very rich, the other half excessively miserable. But all are equally beggars for living in the vilest and filthiest manner imaginable.[19]

Such inequality was found in almost all the major cities of the eighteenth-century Francophone world. And it is on the basis of his life experiences that the political theorist Judith Shklar asserts, "the enduring source of Rousseau's insight into the condition of inequality was personal experience."[20]

Intellectual Context: Mandeville and Doux Commerce

Appreciating Rousseau's thoughts on inequality also requires intellectual context. Much of his analysis is a response to the growing popularity of the doctrine of *doux commerce*—the belief that commerce improves societies. Perhaps the central figure in this eighteenth-century doctrine was the physician philosopher Rousseau frequently cites in his *Discourse on Inequality*: Bernard Mandeville (1670–1733). Mandeville's magnum opus was his *Fable of the Bees*, published in two volumes in 1723 and 1728, approximately three decades before Rousseau's discourses. The book's thesis is present in its subtitle: *Private Vices, Public Benefits*. Drawing on the Jansenists Pierre Nicole and Pierre Bayle, Mandeville argued that human society did not require virtue. Rather, people can be directed to sociable behavior via their reliably selfish dispositions. That is, they will behave themselves and restrain their desires insofar as they are rewarded with public esteem in the form of honor, flattery, and praise.

Mandeville further argues that promoting the public good requires giving free rein to the human tendency to sin, including avarice, luxury, pride, envy, vanity, and opulence. This is because, for him, the more citizens exercise their vices, the more the economy grows. And with economic growth comes greater employment. And greater employment promotes the common good. Such are the foundations of *doux commerce*. As he clarifies in his preface, man's "vilest and most hateful Qualities are the most necessary Accomplishments to fit him for the largest, and, according to the World, the happiest and most flourishing Societies."[21] And continual commercial activity over decades or centuries would result in significant social improvements, on Mandeville's account. As he notes, if we were to compare the conditions of the poorest today with the wealthy of earlier generations, we would reflect on the early rich people as "destitute of a great many Comforts of Life."[22] By allowing the indulgences of the wealthy at one stage of history, he reasons, we ultimately chart a path to the subsequent enjoyment of those same benefits to everyone.

For this magic to work, Mandeville assumes significant inequality. There must be both rich and poor. Mandeville's portrait of a flourishing society requires that most workers hover just above subsistence. People must be induced to work—and poverty is the most effective catalyst of industry. Those with savings incline to being "Insolent and Lazy."[23] But further, the poor are capable of being motivated by "desires"—let them live alongside the rich to stimulate them with covetousness, pride, and envy. This will only encourage them to work harder, thus generating greater social wealth and its associated benefits. Of pride, for example, Mandeville observes that there is "no other Quality so beneficial to Society, and so necessary to render it wealthy and flourishing."[24] Pride accomplishes this because of people's natural desire to assume their relative superiority. But to *really* experience pride, one must *prove* oneself better—namely, by working hard, earning money, and then spending that money ostentatiously. One has to work hard to purchase the kind of jewelry that will turn heads, and that work, in turn, is good for society. Further, spending money on jewels or other luxuries further contributes to the public good by creating jobs in those luxury industries. So not only is pride good, for Mandeville, but so too is wealth since the wealthy are a blessing on their own terms insofar as they spend their fortunes on luxuries, which circulates money and creates jobs. Inequality is thus an essential feature of thriving economies and societies.

Mandeville's theories would be embraced and developed in subsequent decades by philosophers such as David Hume and the Baron de Montesquieu. Hume extended Mandeville by insisting that international trade should be promoted insofar as it promotes greater wealth, and consequently greater happiness. Montesquieu went further, arguing, "commerce cures destructive prejudices" and that most everywhere it is found, "there are more gentle mores." For him, this is not only true among citizens trading within the same state, but it is also true of different states trading with one another. "The natural effect of commerce" among states "is to lead to peace. Two nations that trade with each other become reciprocally dependent," where "all unions are founded on mutual needs."[25]

As will be clear in due course, Rousseau is doubtful that *doux commerce* will deliver the common good. Writing about a subsequent adherent to this philosophy, Jean-François Melon, Rousseau would describe it as a "poisonous doctrine," characterized by "odious maxims" that "make for rich people and wretches" (*Last Reply*, 86). That is, Rousseau would reject *doux commerce* specifically on the grounds that it fosters inequality.

Rousseau on the Origin of Inequality

Rousseau's Genevan upbringing left an imprint on his subsequent political philosophy and especially on his thoughts concerning inequality. Evidence can be found in the dedication of his *Discourse on the Origin on Inequality* "to the Republic of Geneva, Magnificent, Most Honored, and Sovereign Lords"—by which he specifically meant the General Council, not the Small Council. His dedication, in fact, extends for several pages in which he celebrates what he describes as Geneva's most prized virtues. Among these virtues are the rule of law (*SD*, 115), popular sovereignty (*SD*, 114–15, 116), and the absence of excessive wealth and poverty, respectively (*SD*, 118). Indeed, it was precisely these virtues that were threatened by the economic, social, and political transformations taking place in Geneva during Rousseau's youth. Growing inequality had robbed poor citizens of their sovereignty, raised the elites above the law, exacerbated existing imbalances, and alienated the classes from one another. The bulk of Rousseau's *Discourse* is dedicated to explaining the failure to attain his ideals. This is the story, true to its title, of the origins of inequality.

For Rousseau, inequality, economic and otherwise, is unnatural or artificial—it only emerges in society. Natural humanity, as he describes it in the "state of nature," is characterized by "scarcely perceptible" inequality (*SD*, 159). To be sure, physical inequalities exist, such as in size, strength, countenance, and the like. But they are irrelevant where needs are easily met and social interaction is minimal. A "natural man" in the state of nature could be strong enough to lift a tree, but in a world where such feats are unnecessary, no one is impressed.

Natural human beings, for Rousseau, are motivated by two inclinations. First, they possess *amour de soi-même*, which is commonly untranslated in English because the closest approximation, self-love, fails to convey his meaning adequately. "Self-love" is typically employed in English to imply unhealthy egoism or even vanity. But *amour de soi-même*, rather, is "a natural sentiment which inclines every animal to attend to its self-preservation and which, guided in man by reason and modified by pity, produces humanity and virtue" (*SD*, 218n15). Almost everyone instinctually and continuously acts on *amour de soi-même*. It manifests itself, for example, in simple acts of hygiene. Washing hands or brushing teeth are incidents of *amour de soi-même*—acts of self-preservation that have nothing to do with unhealthy egoism or vanity.

The second component of human nature is pity or compassion (*pitié*), which "precedes the exercise of all reflection." Pity inclines everyone to experience "restlessness," "agitation," "repugnance," and even "anguish" at the sight of others' suffering. Rousseau emphasizes that compassion is hardwired. Traces of it reside in everyone, regardless of how much they work to repress it—even for those with the "most depraved morals" (*SD*, 152). "It is pity," he suggests, "that carries us without reflection to the assistance of those we see suffer" (*SD*, 153).

Human nature, Rousseau reasons, inclines naturally toward peace and harmony. There is no innate desire to harm others. There is no innate desire to impress others. There is no innate desire to acquire more than others. This is why there is no meaningful inequality, economic or otherwise, in the state of nature.

Inequality, hence, can only come from external forces. These circumstances dramatically emerge from natural disasters—floods, earthquakes, tsunamis, volcanic eruptions, fires, and the like compel previously asocial human beings to band together (*EOL*, 284). Once they are drawn together, *amour-propre* emerges. Rousseau defines *amour-propre* as a relative sentiment by which people compare themselves, favorably or unfavorably, to others (*SD*, 218). Insofar as they are judged favorably, their *amour-propre* is stimulated; insofar as they are judged unfavorably, their *amour-propre* is injured. The dimensions on which people may be judged depend on what a community values. In early societies, for Rousseau, it might be very simple matters, such as strength and speed. But as societies evolve, it increasingly becomes marked by personal wealth. Once *amour-propre* emerges, the quest to satisfy it becomes the driving force of social history. It compels everyone to seek public admiration. Wealth is among the most durable of the sources of public esteem and hence *amour-propre*. Certain individuals, skilled in their peculiar ways, found themselves possessing talents that facilitated the accumulation of more wealth than their peers. Rousseau describes, for example, that in early societies "the more skillful used his work to better advantage; the more ingenious found ways to reduce his labor. . . . This is how natural inequality imperceptibly unfolds together with unequal associations, and the differences between men, developed by different circumstances, become more perceptible, more permanent in their effects, and begin to exercise a corresponding influence on the fate of individuals" (*SD*, 170). And because wealth, like *amour-propre* more generally, is a social and relative phenomenon, it meant the simultaneous creation of the poor.

Although the initial acquisition of wealth might have emerged innocently enough from idiosyncratic talents, for Rousseau, the subsequent pursuit of wealth assumed malevolent dimensions. For the rich in a developed economy, it pits them against their fellow citizens.

> Consuming ambition, the ardent desire to raise one's relative fortune less out of genuine need than in order to place oneself above others, instills in all men a dark inclination to harm one another, a secret jealousy that is all the more dangerous as it often assumes the mask of benevolence in order to strike its blow in greater safety: in a word, competition and rivalry on the one hand, conflict of interests on the other, and always the hidden desire to profit at another's expense. (*SD*, 175)

Wealth can only be acquired at others' expense. Drawing on the mercantilist orthodoxy of his day, wealth is, for Rousseau, a zero-sum game. For one person to acquire massively superior wealth, others must surrender it. As he first explains in his *Last Reply*,

> for every hundred paupers whom luxury feeds in our cities, it causes a hundred thousand to perish in our countryside: the money that passes between the lands of the rich and the Artists to provide for their superfluities is lost for the Husbandman's subsistence; and he is without a suit of clothing precisely because they must have piping. . . . Our dishes require gravies; that is why so many sick people lack broth. We must have liquors on our tables; that is why the peasant drinks only water. We must have powder for our wigs; that is why so many poor people have no bread. (*Last Reply*, 71n)

But as Rousseau elaborates in his *Discourse on Inequality*, this exploitation of the poor only enhances the wealthy's enjoyment of their luxuries. There is a kind of double payoff for *amour-propre* in acquiring great wealth since one's status rises not only from increased wealth but also in witnessing the suffering of others. *Amour-propre* means, in fact, that people perversely enjoy witnessing and especially inflicting others' pain because they gain in relative terms. The ability to harm others with relative impunity can be viewed as the greatest statement of power in deeply corrupt societies.[26]

The resulting danger is an intoxicating incentive to pursue boundless wealth and power. It is one kind of pleasure to be known for great business success. It is yet another, of potentially even greater magnitude, to drive one's competitors out of business. Upon achieving financial ascendance, Rousseau observes, the rich find a special pleasure in domination. The ability to control others is the ultimate mark of social status. And nothing facilitates such control better than outsized fortunes: "The rich, for their part, had scarcely become acquainted with the pleasure of dominating than they disdained all other pleasures, and using their old Slaves to subject new ones, they thought only of subjugating and enslaving their neighbors; like those ravenous wolves which once they have tasted human flesh scorn all other food, and from then on want to devour only men" (SD, 176).[27]

Effects of Inequality on Individuals

The effects of economic inequality on individuals are substantial. For Rousseau, pure human nature, as abstracted from social life, is absolutely good. It is important here to define "good." "Good," for Rousseau, is a natural disposition that he contrasts with virtue, which results from conscious effort and struggle: "This word virtue means *force*. There is no virtue without struggle, there is none without victory. Virtue consists not only in being just, but in being so by triumphing over one's passions, by ruling over one's own heart" (LF, 286). Goodness, by contrast, is the effortless inclination to not harm others. Goodness is ubiquitous in nature, for Rousseau, where virtue is in fact impossible. Virtue is only possible where goodness is lacking—namely, in the social world, where people are consumed with artificial but nevertheless powerful inclinations to pursue their own interests at others' expense.

Prompted by *amour-propre*, economic inequality effectively disables or obscures natural goodness. Great fortunes inflame self-interest. To protect that wealth and promote its growth, those selfish interests will predominate. One may choose to act against those interests, in theory, but it is no longer an act of goodness. It becomes an act of virtue—the outcome of a moral struggle where the wealthy individual chooses to sacrifice her wealth for the benefit of others. This may seem like a semantic matter for Rousseau. Indeed, it may even seem superior, as Rousseau consistently praises virtue. The problem, however, is that virtue is unreliable. In fact, it is even worse than unreliable, for him, when it comes to the wealthiest.

Can wealthy individuals be truly virtuous for Rousseau? There are suggestions in his writings that some wealthy people achieve moral nobility, such as in the character of Wolmar, a virtuous aristocrat in his novel *Julie*. Yet the greater body of Rousseau's works suggests that Wolmar is an exception to the rule. This is especially clear in his "On Wealth and Fragments on Taste"—originally composed as a letter to a fictional young man, who claimed to have been inspired by Rousseau's philosophy to earn a great fortune, which he would then dispense to the needy as charity. The would-be philanthropist pleads, "I aspire to fortune, but it is in order to atone for its injustices. . . . A benevolent rich man seems to me to be the great agent of the divinity here below, the glory of the human race" (WFT, 6).[28] Rousseau's response begins sympathetically, taking the young man's intentions to be sincere. But he reasons that his correspondent lacks the necessary wisdom to know precisely how the acquisition of wealth can change one's perspective. It is natural for a poor man to assume that upon attaining a great fortune, he would then employ that asset to serve the poor. But he is ignorant of the reality, Rousseau argues, that the acquisition of wealth itself will profoundly change one's priorities: "I suspect that there might very well be some causes that make me change systems upon changing situation, and that deprive them of the will to do good while giving them the power to do it" (WFT, 7). He pursues his suspicions with speculations about the path to wealth itself. The fact is that one cannot accumulate great fortunes without injustice. Becoming wealthy requires "years of hardening" oneself to the dignity of others in the name of profits (WFT, 8). "How is it possible to become wealthy without contributing to impoverishing someone else, and what would one say about a charitable man who would begin by despoiling all of his neighbors in order to have the pleasure afterwards of giving them alms?" he asks incredulously. Of course, to Rousseau's mind, in most instances the alms rarely follow after acquisitions of fortune. Once embarking on the path of great fortune, greed becomes the ruling muse.[29] The power of domination becomes a far greater pleasure than those of beneficence. The most likely outcome of this path is becoming "insatiable and harsh up to the end of your days, ceaselessly accumulating for lack of having enough to lavish and dying overburdened with gold, years, and avarice without ever having found time or means to do good for anyone" (WFT, 9). The rich cultivate the "canker of corrupted hearts," he reasons, losing all natural pity, and adopting values that rationalize their own opulence and the suffering of the poor (WFT, 14). It requires nothing less than to "harden your soul" (WFT, 12).[30]

Beyond hardening the soul, Rousseau observes, the wealthy find less pleasure in their riches than they anticipated. Great fortune brings new anxieties. The wealthy man must "multiply the iron doors, the locks, the chains, the guards and watchmen" to protect his property against the encroachments of the poor. Part of this protection of property requires a two-front ongoing public relations campaign "in order to make the poor man's theft even more infamous and the rich man's even more respected." The rich man must ensure that petty crimes are scandalized while his own usurpations are celebrated as triumphs. Further, he will find himself surrounded by servants who "will serve you at a great price with disguised manure" (*WFT*, 12). His wealth multiplies the number of parasites surrounding him, whom he requires but can never trust. He will be surrounded by the "flattery of scoundrels," but no one in the end admires him (*WTF*, 13).[31]

To the extent that they retain a sliver of conscience, Rousseau speculates, they will be tormented by "pangs of remorse." "Cruel anxieties will come to afflict your soul in the bosom of voluptuous pleasures. In your most tumultuous feasts a thousand bitter memories, a thousand fatal pangs of remorse will cry out at the bottom of your heart, louder than all your guests" (*WFT*, 13). The life of the rich, for Rousseau, is consumed by anxiety and misery.

Of course, there are also poor people in unequal societies. What of their lives? Rousseau's thoughts about the lives of the indigent initially appear ambivalent. Some have taken his ambivalence to suggest that he was relatively unconcerned about poverty per se and certainly less concerned than many of his contemporaries.[32] There is evidence to buttress this reading. Rousseau frequently praises the virtues of poverty, mostly when writing of societies on the whole. There is no question in Rousseau's mind that relative poverty is advantageous for nations insofar as it fosters civic virtue. Rome was virtuous in the early days of its Republic, to his mind, before it grew wealthy, idle, and soft. It was the Germans' relative poverty that proved to be their great advantage in ending the Roman Empire. Their "simplicity, innocence, and virtues" fostered a "rustic nation so vaunted for its courage" that it could subdue a wealthy empire (*FD*, 11). His praise of the early Germans follows a pattern of praising relatively poor societies, such as Sparta and the early Roman Republic. Great republics, he suggests, understand the dangers of wealth and luxury. By contrast, "countries rich in money must be poor in everything else" (*Emile*, 190). The Athenians cultivated commerce and gold to their detriment; the Spartans preferred a closed agricultural economy. It was no accident, to Rousseau's mind, that the Spartans won the Peloponnesian War, and it is one weighty reason why, when asked, he counsels the island of Corsica to avoid commerce and wealth.[33]

Such excerpts might suggest that Rousseau prefers poverty. But it requires clarification. The poverty he celebrates is a *relative* societal poverty—relative to the bloated, luxurious states of eighteenth-century Europe. He does not advocate or lionize absolute impoverishment and deprivation. There is nothing good about people living on the brink of starvation. Poverty of this kind is clearly bad for both body and soul. Most obviously, absolute poverty is a constant threat to bodily health. As he observes in his *Emile*,

> to care for a sick peasant, do not purge him, give him drugs, or send him a surgeon. These poor people need none of these things. They need better and more plentiful food. You others [of means] should fast when you have a fever. But when your peasants have one, give them meat and wine. Almost all their illnesses come from poverty and exhaustion. Their best herb tea is in your cellar; their only apothecary ought to be your butcher. (*Emile*, 436n)

Rousseau repeats these concerns in lamenting the plight of peasants "who do not have enough to live on while cultivating" the land (*Corsica*, 139).

Beyond the material threats of malnourishment and starvation, the destitute endure social and psychic insults to daily life. In societies characterized by great economic inequality, the wealthy man enjoys all the benefits of institutions established to protect and promote his interests, whereas the poor man must endure the opposite:

> The more humanity owes him, the more society denies him: all doors are closed to him, even when he has the right to have them opened; and if sometimes he obtains justice, it is with greater difficulty than another would obtain a pardon; if there are corvées to be done, a militia to be raised, he is the first to be called up; in addition to his own burden, he always bears the burden from which his richer neighbor has the influence to get himself exempted; at the least accident that befalls him, everyone avoids him; if his poor cart tips over, far from being helped by anyone, I consider him fortunate if in making his way he escapes being battered by some young duke's ruffians; in a word, all free assistance flees him when he needs it, precisely because he lacks the means to pay for it. (*PE*, 32)[34]

These indignities transcend mere physical want and deprivation. For Rousseau, the costs of poverty in unequal societies extend well beyond hunger and housing. These costs, he suggests, are not incidental to unequal societies—they are structural. The very point of the social contract as it emerged historically was to forever fix "the Law of property and inequality" such that it "gave the weak new fetters and the rich new forces"

(*SD*, 173). The rich invented the laws to protect themselves and punish the poor. The hardships of the poor were no accident of the social contract—they were one of its central purposes.

These burdens, for Rousseau, ultimately overwhelm impoverished souls. The longer they suffer, the more likely they are to lose their noble qualities—their freedom and virtue. Moral freedom—the ability to resist inclinations and heed the conscience—is one of humanity's defining features (*SD*, 140–41). Virtue acts on this freedom—deliberately following one's conscience, even where it means resisting passions, impulses, public opinion, and the temptations of wealth and privilege. As he defines virtue in his *Discourse on Political Economy*, it "is nothing but . . . conformity of the particular will to the general will" (*PE*, 13). In simplified terms, virtue requires setting aside one's personal interests in favor of the common good.

Rousseau argues that poverty amid great inequality inhibits freedom and virtue. Unmet needs, social barriers, lack of respect, and hopelessness all conspire to this effect. Radically unequal societies produce an effectively enslaved underclass. The poor man

> needs their [the wealthy class's] help, and moderate means do not enable him to do without them. He must therefore constantly try to interest them in his fate and to make them really or apparently find their own profit in working for his: which makes him knavish and artful with some, imperious and harsh with the rest, and places him under the necessity of deceiving all those he needs if he cannot get them to fear him and does not find it in his interest to make himself useful to them. (*SD*, 170–71)

To the extent that the poor require the wealthy both for their physical and psychic sustenance, they lose their freedom. Since virtue requires a free will, it follows that inequality also impedes the exercise of virtue. Inequality creates an underclass devoid of robust moral agency. The poor naturally detest the rich, but the indigent also come to disregard their peers' humanity. Although Rousseau does not elaborate substantially, in his *Second Discourse* he sketches the outlines:

> It is not part of my subject to show how such a disposition engenders so much indifference to good and evil altogether with such fine discourses on morality; how everything being reduced to appearances, everything becomes factitious and play-acting: honor, friendship, virtue, and often even vices in which one at length discovers the secret of glorying; how,

in a word, forever asking of others what we are, without ever daring to ask it of ourselves, in the midst of so much Philosophy, humanity, politeness, and Sublime maxims, we having nothing more than a deceiving and frivolous exterior, honor without virtue, reason without wisdom, and pleasure without happiness. It is enough for me to have proved that this is not man's original state, and that it is only the spirit of Society, together with the inequality society engenders, that changes and corrupts all our natural inclinations this way. (*SD*, 187–88)

Rousseau depicts poverty's effects on poor souls in introducing the "Profession of Faith of the Savoyard Vicar" from his *Emile*. The vicar speaks to a young man, who suffers "utter destitution" (*Emile*, 260). Over time, according to the vicar, his poverty stifled "his nature little by little . . . leading him rapidly to his destruction and heading him toward the morals of a tramp" (*Emile*, 263). His poverty was "the opprobrium to which fortune had reduced the boy [which] stifled every true sentiment of good and evil in him." It was a kind of "moral death" since "the inner voice [of conscience] cannot make itself heard to someone who thinks only of feeding himself" (*Emile*, 264). Although poverty had not erased the young man's conscience, it had obscured it in the face of unrelenting hardship. As Rousseau once wrote to Robert Tronchin, "everywhere it is the rich who are always the first to be touched by corruption, the poor follow" (*LT*, 160). Thus the effects of inequality on the poor and rich alike, for Rousseau, eviscerates humanity's capacity to exercise its most noble attributes of freedom and virtue.[35]

The Social Effects of Inequality

Inequality's effects on individuals do not exist in isolation. Rather, they are manifested in a complex social environment. The vices cultivated by extreme economic inequality wield myriad and enormous social consequences. Some of these have been cataloged elsewhere, most notably in Neuhouser's *Rousseau's Critique of Inequality*. Prominent among these is the unhealthy dependence it creates, especially of the poor on the rich, which undermines freedom. Neuhouser also alludes in passing to the social disorder resulting from inequality.[36] Here I amplify this suggestion, which turns out to be central to Rousseau's critique of economic inequality precisely because it undermines his conceptions of justice and the general will.

Understanding the forces inequality unleashes, for Rousseau, requires understanding his conceptions of justice and the general will. As Judith

Shklar commented, "the general will is Rousseau's most successful metaphor. It conveys everything he most wanted to say."[37] As Rousseau himself insists in his *Discourse on Political Economy*, "the first and the most important maxim of legitimate or popular government, that is to say of government that has the good of the people as its object, is ... in all things to follow the general will" (*PE*, 9). He reaffirms the primacy of the general will throughout his constructive political writings, especially *The Social Contract* in which he pronounces, it "alone can direct the forces of the State according to the end of its institution, which is the common good" (*SC*, 2.1, 59). Broadly, the general will is Rousseau's highest political value—the standard of right and wrong, of legitimacy, and of political morality.

There is, of course, an enormous literature on the general will,[38] and its interpretation—like much Rousseau scholarship—is characterized by diverse and sometimes contradictory readings. In what follows, I draw on my own established interpretation, acknowledging that others will deviate on important points. This being said, it perhaps goes without saying that I believe my interpretation to be grounded substantially in Rousseau's texts and his general political principles.

It is uncontroversial that Rousseau's general will requires a will.[39] For the general will to exist, it must issue from a free will. I have already discussed Rousseau's commitment to the notion of a free will. A general will emerging from coerced or otherwise unfree voices is illegitimate. A people coalescing around a unified but unfree will in no way establishes a general will. It merely affirms the determined opinions of external forces. It is illegitimate, on Rousseauean grounds, for a coerced citizen to vote for a policy whose purpose is to serve someone else's particular interests contrary to the common good. Citizens must arrive at and express their opinions fully of their own free wills.

Further, the general will must "issue from all in order to apply to all" (*SC*, 2.4, 64). That is, it cannot issue from a subset of the population, nor can it apply to only a subset. If the laws were determined merely by a subset or faction, they would incline toward benefiting the interests of that faction. Likewise, any law applying to some and not others is inherently dubious. That only some and not others, for example, would be accountable to factory emission standards represents an obvious violation.

Rousseau makes still broader claims about the nature of the general will, including that "one need only be just in order to be sure of following the general will" (*PE*, 12). That is, the general will must conform to the idea of justice.[40] He offers several textual clues to support this connection. In his *Letters Written from the Mountain*, he insists "the first and greatest public interest [and hence the object of law and the general will] is always justice" (*Mountain*, 301).[41] In his *Political Economy*, he insists "the most general will is also the most just" (*PE*, 8). Further, he frequently cites the general will as the guiding force of the law,[42] and at the same time, he insists that the laws of the state must also be just.[43]

Assuming this to be the case, what does Rousseau mean by "justice"? In his *Emile*, he defines justice and a crucially related idea: "The love of order which produces order is called *goodness*; and the love of order which preserves order is called *justice*" (282). Goodness and justice here can be understood as moral ideas. God creates the universe's moral order. It is humanity's responsibility to maintain it. Humanity's failure is revealed in the first sentence of *Emile*: "Everything is good as it leaves the hands of the Author of things; everything degenerates in the hands of man" (37). The same overarching narrative characterizes the *Second Discourse*, where naturally good human beings ultimately fail to maintain this order through war and despotism. The primary responsibility of any state, then, is to maintain order. But the fact that Rousseau clearly rejects despotism throughout his writings and especially in the *Second Discourse* suggests that not any order will suffice. Rather, as he defines it in his *Emile*, human goodness is "love of [one's] fellows" (285). Order requires that citizens actively love one another in the Christian sense—that they approach one another socially as if everyone's interests matter as much as their own.

Equal concern for fellow citizens required by Rousseau's sense of justice suggests a final and crucial element of his general will: equality. The concept of equality animates all his constructive political works. In his *Emile*, he writes that the general will "always tends toward equality" (463). In his *Government of Poland*, he characterizes equality as "the principle of the constitution" (215). In his *Social Contract*, he contrasts the particular will, which "tends, by its nature, to partiality," with the general will, which tends "to equality" (2.1, 59). And he clarifies in his *Letters Written from the Mountain*, "The first and greatest public interest is always justice. All wish the conditions to be equal for all, and justice is nothing but this equality" (301). So it is no surprise that Shklar would characterize Rousseau's general will as the "will against inequality."[44]

Justice, the General Will, and Economic Inequality

Understanding the centrality of justice and equality to the general will reveals the unsettling nature of economic inequality in Rousseau's political system. If what he suggests about the effects of inequality on the soul are true, it poses an existential threat to justice. One of the most consequential effects of economic inequality, for Rousseau, is its divisive tendency, the pitting of rich against the poor. Lacking anything in common with the poor, wealthy citizens exploit them and their dwindling resources, becoming "ravenous wolves" who are only satisfied with the blood of fellow citizens (*SD*, 171). It is not because they need the money in any material sense. It is because it inflames their insatiable *amour-propre*. As he subsequently elaborates, "if one sees a handful of powerful and rich men at the pinnacle of greatness and fortune while the masses grovel in obscurity and misery, it is because the former value the things they enjoy only to the extent that the others are deprived of them, and they would cease to be happy if, without any change to their own estate, the People ceased to be miserable" (*SD*, 184).

Insofar as the poor understand the reality, they despise their oppressors and develop a corresponding urge to raze the existing institutions. This precipitates the civil war Rousseau describes in his *Discourse on Inequality*. The radical economic inequality emerging in early societies, he suggests, ultimately gives way to the "most horrible state of war" (*SD*, 172). To end violence and to enjoy and extend the privileges of their wealth, the wealthy pit the poor against one another so they could never unite and direct their shared misery into a cause against their oppressors. Consider the following passage from the *Discourse on Inequality*:

> From the extreme inequality of Conditions and fortunes ... would arise masses of prejudices equally contrary to reason, happiness, and virtue; one would see Chiefs foment everything that can weaken assembled men by disuniting them; everything that can give Society an air of apparent concord while sowing seeds of real division; everything that can inspire mistrust and mutual hatred in different estates by setting their Rights and interests at odds, and strengthen the Power that contains them all. (*SD*, 185)

The wealthy turn the poor against one another, fostering a culture of "mutual hatred" that effectively insulates the rich from rebellion.

While these circumstances would be disruptive by any standard, they are particularly so for Rousseau. His account of justice is, again, "the love of order which preserves order," particularly manifested, as I have argued, as "love of [one's] fellows." Economic inequality, by contrast, fosters distrust and division. It is disruptive and disorderly. Taking seriously his insistence that the general will must embody the ideas of justice, order, equality, and mutual love means that excessive inequality undermines the general will itself.

But this is not the only regard in which economic inequality threatens Rousseau's general will. It also disrupts other forms of equality. To be sure, his idea of equality has multiple dimensions. Most scholars acknowledge that fundamental among these dimensions is a legal equality under the rule of law—such that no citizen might receive partial and preferential treatment by the laws. But what has been less appreciated is that equality before the law itself requires relative economic equality. As Rousseau worries in his *Political Economy*, the wealthy will deploy their resources under the "pretext of the public good" to seize others' assets. As such, just republics must pursue "strict integrity to render justice to all, and above all . . . [to] protect the poor against the tyranny of the rich." It accomplishes this by "prevent[ing] extreme inequality of fortunes" (*PE*, 19).

What exactly, for Rousseau, constitutes "extreme inequality"? The term, or something approaching it, occurs repeatedly in his works (e.g., *SD*, 137, 185; *d'Alembert*, 348; *Julie*, 17; *SC*, 2.11, 81n; *Corsica*, 131; *Poland*, 229). The closest he comes to defining it is in the *Social Contract*, when he acknowledges that although perfect economic equality is not his goal, a republic should provide that "no citizen be so very rich that he can buy another, and none so poor that he is compelled to sell himself." This evokes the inequality burdening Athens when Solon's legislative services were required—an inequality in which the poor's debts compelled them to sell themselves and their children into slavery.[45] He elaborates in a footnote, asking, "Do you want to give the State stability? bring the extremes as close together as possible; tolerate neither very rich people nor beggars. These two states, which are naturally inseparable, are equally fatal to the common good" (*SC*, 2.11, 81n). For Rousseau, while we cannot achieve "absolutely the same" in wealth among citizens, we must nevertheless "bring the extremes as close together as possible." What counts as "possible" here is an open question. Likely, the realm of the possible depends on a variety of circumstances that might be best discerned by either a lawgiver or the general will. Rousseau himself suggests in book 3 of the *Social Contract*, the more democratic a government, the more necessary a vigorous equality. It is also clear that the more virtue that reigns among citizens, the easier it would be to limit inequality. Virtuous citizens are less concerned with their private wealth and more concerned for the well-being of their neighbors, which explains why virtue is among his highest priorities (*PE*, 19–21).

Without meaningful equality, the laws will invariably favor the wealthy. This is most dramatically evident in the *Discourse on Inequality*, where Rousseau traces the historical origins of Western law to the machinations of its wealthiest parties. The rich, he speculates, scheme in the very terms of the social contract to give "the weak new fetters and the rich new forces" (*SD*, 173). They exploit the poor's desperation and ignorance to create laws permanently tilted in their own favor.[46] Insofar as the general will, as Rousseau insists, "always tends toward equality," there can be no question that economic inequality represents one of its most serious threats.

Rousseau's concerns about the effects of wealth on the exercise of political power simultaneously threatens the democratic dimensions of his political project. As political theorist James Miller has observed, although Rousseau rejects democratic governments (by which he really means democratic executives), he emphatically supports democratic sovereignty,[47] meaning for him that legislation must issue from democratic consent. This is what Rousseau means when he insists, "law is nothing but the declaration of the general will" (*SC*, 3.15, 117). Insofar as the laws merely express wealthy preferences, they are partial or private rather than general. They are certainly not democratic. So if he is correct in his assessment that the presence of extreme private wealth results in a public policy favoring that private wealth, it is fair to assume that it also undermines his requirement that legitimate societies operate on the principle of democratic sovereignty.[48]

Finally, economic inequality threatens the will of the general will. Insofar as "one has to be free in order to will" (*PE*, 9), it is crucial to safeguard freedom to cultivate the general will. Yet economic inequality has precisely the opposite effect, according to Rousseau. He connects freedom to equality in book 2, chapter 11 of his *Social Contract*:

> If one inquires into precisely what the greatest good of all consists in, which ought to be the end of every system of legislation, one will find that it comes down to these two principle objects, *freedom* and *equality*. Freedom, because any individual dependence is that much force taken away from the State; equality, because freedom cannot subsist without it.

Rousseau clarifies what he means by "equality" in the next paragraph:

> This word must not be understood to mean that degrees of power and wealth should be absolutely the same, but that, as for power, it stop short of all violence and never be exercised except by virtue of rank and the laws, and that as for wealth, no citizen be so very rich that he can buy another, and none so poor that he is compelled to sell himself: Which assumes moderation in goods and influence on the part of the great, moderation in avarice and covetousness on the part of the lowly. (*SC*, 2.11, 80–81)

Relative economic equality promotes freedom insofar as economic dependence suppresses individual wills. When a poor person depends on the wealthy for his subsistence, for example, his freedom is vulnerable. If his boss tells him, for instance, "I might have to fire employees if candidate X is elected," he must seriously weigh whether his own will matters at all. He needs to eat; he therefore needs to keep his job. And although he might have other ideas about politics, he is unlikely to sacrifice his job to advance other political ideas. His will, in other words, is surrendered to his economic superior. Where few citizens possess a robust free will, there is no functional general will.

As Rousseau clarifies in his essay on Corsica, in significantly unequal societies, all political power is exercised by the wealthy. In making this point, he distinguishes "legitimate" from "abusive" civil power. Legitimate authority issues from the general will and is oriented to serving the common good. But in societies where "wealth dominates," legitimate authority is separated from power. Right lacks might. Only money has might. In unequal societies, "the apparent power is in the hands of the magistrate and the real power is in those of the rich." In such abusive societies, those who seek public office do so only to "sell its use to the rich and to enrich themselves by this means." But for most, the straightest path to power is acquiring a great fortune, which is used to purchase magistrates (*Corsica*, 155). This is what Rousseau means in the *Emile*, when he observes that "wealth and influence mutually prop each other up. The one is always maintained with the other" (*Emile*, 457).[49] Needless to say, such societies lack a general will and are governed, rather, by the narrow private wills of its wealthiest citizens. As he observes in his *Letter to d'Alembert*, significant economic inequality is simply incompatible with republicanism or democracy. Societies hosting extremely wealthy individuals soon discover that "the rich are always the true sovereign" (*d'Alembert*, 336).[50]

Rousseau and the Birth of Meritocracy

A further consideration in Rousseau's analysis demands attention: he was the first to understand inequality specifically in the context of an emerging meritocracy. Consider, for example, that status in Plato's Athens was largely inherited from one's parents. The same was true in Jesus's Nazareth. This became especially true in the subsequent centuries of the extended feudal age in which parental lineage was the only significant variable determining one's wealth and social status. For anyone of significant wealth, land, and property, all of this was inherited from one's parents. No one could claim to merit their good fortune in any meaning-ful sense. The same was true of the poor. People were poor because their parents were poor.

What changed in modernity was the degree to which Europeans were freed from ascriptive status. This liberation was celebrated as the age of merit. Emancipated from the feudal farms, rather than inheriting wealth and status, individuals would increasingly have to *earn* it. There is ample reason why it was celebrated in the eighteenth century and beyond. It no longer meant that lazy and talentless individuals would be rewarded with wealth and status. It also provided the opportunity for those born to poor and low-status families to achieve great wealth and fame on the basis of their talents and efforts. Society would be the beneficiary, enjoying the cultural, economic, and intellectual achievements of those who never pre-viously enjoyed the opportunity to exploit their native abilities. This is the upside of meritocracy.

Yet more than anyone before him, and maybe better than anyone since, Rousseau understood meritocracy's drawbacks. For him, the same society that might successfully exploit its latent talent pool also instills its rich and poor with psychological and, ultimately, social baggage. In meritocratic societies, those at the top feel that they *belong* there.[51] They have earned their way to the top and should richly enjoy their well-deserved privileges. At the same time, they also feel that those who are at the bottom of the same hierarchy likewise *deserve* their place as a reflection of their meager efforts and talents. The poor deserve their suffering, so it is *misguided* to pity them. Although, as Rousseau insists, it is natural to feel for the suffer-ing of those less fortunate, a meritocratic society discourages this natural sentiment. It suggests that pity is misplaced. Those who suffer in poverty have deserved it through a just and fair system.[52] To pity them is to reject meritocratic justice. As he observes in his *Second Discourse*, modern soci-ety effectively "stifl[es] natural pity" (*SD*, 171).

To compound the misery, in meritocratic societies, the poor are com-pelled to confront and accept their failures. Their poverty, according to meritocratic principles, reflects their lack of talent, effort, and general worthiness. For the poor, such reflections are harsh realizations of their daily lives. This analysis of the underlying moral psychology of inequality of meritocratic societies is one of Rousseau's most novel and greatest insights.[53]

The emergence of meritocracy, as Rousseau diagnosed it, exacerbates all the effects of inequality detailed in my earlier chapters. Whereas a pauper in ancient Israel, for example, might have taken solace in the belief that his poverty was God's will and part of a divine plan, the same pauper in eighteenth-century Geneva or Paris would have been encouraged to understand that his poverty reflected his own worthlessness, making an already difficult material condition worse by defining it as a punishment and natural consequence. As Vaughan has rightly observed, in Plato's world, "being poor is nothing to be ashamed of."[54] But this view changes radically in modernity. To the difficulties of material struggle, the poor now had additionally to carry the burdens of existential concerns about their self-worth. For Rousseau, shame results from unfavorable comparisons with fellow citizens—or the negative judgment of *amour-propre*. The epidemiologists Richard Wilkinson and Kate Pickett confirm much of what the Genevan philosopher observed, suggesting that the shame associated with poverty characterizes both developing and developed nations that have embraced the market-society assumptions Rousseau sketches. Poverty is not experienced as a force of nature or even culture. Poverty is, rather, regarded as a *personal failure* in which the poor despise "themselves for being poor." But further, children despise their parents for their poverty, women despise their husbands, and students despise their poor classmates. Among other consequences, according to their study, are anger, resignation, despair, depression, and even suicidal thoughts.[55] Their research affirms an evolutionary inheritance of "aversion to low social status." Rousseau, however, adds an important cultural element to this experience of shame among the poor.[56] Modern people were beginning to be held to be squarely responsible for their poverty, adding psychological insult to material deprivation.

By contrast, those who have succeeded in accumulating large fortunes in the modern world do so in full confidence that they have *earned* their wealth. It is not simply that they had rich parents or that fortune smiled on them in other ways. It is that they have worked harder than others; it is that they have been smarter than others; it is that they *deserve* their largesses. So if they seem to take special satisfaction in savoring luxuries in their neighbors' full view, it is only because they want to confirm what they feel deeply in their hearts: their internal sense of superiority and merit, amplified by their *amour-propre*. Michael Sandel has found that those succeeding at the top levels of society have come to believe "that their success is their own doing," rather than a result of the advantages they have received from their families and social structures. As a consequence, he laments, there grew a "corrosive" effect on society, where it is harder "to learn gratitude and humility" and "care for the common good."[57] Rousseau is the first major Western philosopher to appreciate these characterological and

existential challenges brought about by economic inequality in meritocratic societies that persist to the present. I will return to this theme in
chapter 7 when considering Marx's myth of two kinds of people, and meritocracy's role in justifying modern inequality.

Rousseau's Solutions to the Problem of Inequality

Economic inequality represents one of the greatest threats to the establishment and maintenance of Rousseau's general will. It is unsurprising,
then, that he repeatedly demands that something be done about it. In his
Political Economy, for example, he insists, "What is most needful and perhaps most difficult in government is a strict integrity to render justice to
all, and above all to protect the poor from the tyranny of the rich. . . . It
is, therefore, one of the most important tasks of government to prevent
extreme inequality of fortunes" (19). In his *Social Contract*, he affirms,
"The social state is advantageous for men only insofar as all have something and none has too much of anything" (1.9, 58n). In his *Emile*, he
warns against "the inequality of fortunes" (468). In his *Government of
Poland*, he cautions against "the extremes of misery or opulence" (224).
In his *Corsica*, he prioritizes "diminish[ing] the extreme inequality" (131).
The persistence of this theme throughout his works leaves little doubt of
its importance to his larger political theory.

It remains to explore Rousseau's constructive solutions to ameliorate
inequality. I argue that these exist on a continuum of practicality but all
animated by his general will. His most radical proposals, such as the elimination of commerce and currency, surely qualify as the least practical. But
the same principles that animate these radical proposals also inform less
radical ones also found in his writings, such as tax reforms. I explore the
range of his solutions with an eye to the reasons for considering them and
how they reflect his larger political philosophy.

It is in his late writings that we find Rousseau's most utopian solutions
to the problem of extreme wealth and inequality. Their spirit is conveyed
by an excerpt from his autobiographical *Dialogues*. Early in the first of
three dialogues, the character "Rousseau" asks his interlocutors to "picture
an ideal world similar to ours, yet altogether different." In this world, he
suggests, these enlightened citizens will

> make light of opulence, and do nothing to acquire it, knowing the art of
> enjoyment too well to be ignorant of the fact that true pleasure cannot
> be bought for money. And as for the good a rich man can do, they also

know it is not the man but his wealth which does it; that the wealth would do better still without the man if it were divided among many or rather eliminated by this distribution; and that all the good a rich man thinks he does through this wealth rarely equals the real evil that must be done to acquire it. (*Dialogues*, 11)

The desire to distribute wealth relatively equally animates Rousseau's final two political texts concerning Poland and Corsica, both of which were commissioned to exploit his political wisdom for existing territories. Although the details vary, both recommend—insofar as it is feasible—eliminating commerce and currency altogether since they conspire to create inequality and its accompanying social ills. Needless to say, eliminating either commerce or currency seems impracticable by contemporary standards. But understanding the reasons why Rousseau sought to address inequality in this fashion reveals exactly how deeply rooted the problem is.

Commerce and currency are related pathologies, according to Rousseau, since the purpose of commerce is to generate revenue. Eliminate commerce, and one progresses toward reducing currency. But what is problematic about currency for Rousseau? "Money is a sign," he observes, "which has a genuine effect only by the inequality of distribution. . . . It is useful only as a sign of inequality" (*Corsica*, 140). Money merely exists, for him, to valorize the wealthy and shame the poor.[58] Inequality inflates unhealthy *amour-propre*, demoralizes the poor, and demotes what should be the real source of pride—moral virtue. Banning currency frees citizens from the temptation to impress others with their wealth. "The pecuniary interest is the worst of all [interests], the vilest, the most liable to corruption" (*Poland*, 231). Without money, individuals are freed from the temptation to act "like those ravenous wolves" he describes in the *Second Discourse*, who feed on fellow citizens. They are instead free, he hopes, to distinguish themselves by their patriotism and fraternal love.[59]

Rousseau flirts with a few strategies to eliminate the antisocial effects of money. The most dramatic of these is his proposal to eliminate currency altogether, which can be done, he argues, by attaining complete autarky, or economic independence. "If Corsica needed foreigners it would need money, but being able to be self-sufficient, it does not need it" (*Corsica*, 140). Nations serious about reducing inequality should withdraw from international commerce. They should instead turn their energies to cultivating their own land for their own purposes. Agriculture should be the national economy. Of course, some domestic trade will be necessary. But these transactions can proceed through traditional bartering such that "all the productions of the Island [of Corsica] being dispersed equally will take on the level of the population by themselves." Although unusual in eighteenth-century Europe, Rousseau is optimistic that such reforms were possible in Corsica because of its geographic isolation, like Swiss cantons of the medieval period, where large mountains and rushing rivers effectively cut off trade routes. The main purpose of these reforms, however, is crystal clear: "Everyone must live and no one get[s] rich" (*Corsica*, 142).

Along these lines, Rousseau specifies the state should own a substantial amount of land, while little is privately owned. Although his proposal is "not to destroy private property absolutely," he desires that "the property of the state . . . be as great, as strong and that of the citizens as small, as weak as possible" (*Corsica*, 148). In this way, the state harnesses the revenues necessary for its operations, presumably in the form of agriculture,[60] while citizens, in the absence of currency, cease to distinguish themselves by the size of their estates. Without incentives to accumulate either currency or property, the impetus for robust commerce is largely eliminated.

Beyond its own property holdings, the state will collect taxes primarily in the form of public service:[61] "by using their labor, their arms, and their heart, rather than their purse in the service of the fatherland," citizens give the state what it needs to sustain itself in the absence of currency (*Corsica*, 149).[62] Rousseau reiterates this in his *Government of Poland*, where he elaborates, "I should like always to have more taxes borne by men's arms, than by their purse; to have roads, bridges, public buildings . . . not paid for by money. This sort of tax is . . . the least burdensome and above all the one least liable to be abused" (229).

Despite his occasional optimism that currency could be eliminated, he frequently acknowledges that practical circumstances require some money. At these moments, he clarifies, "my object is not to abolish the circulation of specie, but only to slow it down" (*Poland*, 233). Its value for such exchanges seems necessary and inevitable. But he seeks to temper the negative effects he associates with money. In a healthy republic, money plays a modest role in exchanges without radical economic inequality and its accompanying *amour-propre*.

Money can coexist with a healthy society, he speculates, insofar as no accolades are attached to it. Public honor, rather, belongs to those distinguished by their virtue:

I should like that all grades, all employments, all honorific awards be marked by external signs, that no public figure be allowed ever to move about incognito, that the marks of his rank or dignity follow him everywhere, so that the people at all times show him respect, and that he himself at all times has self-respect; that he might thus always keep the upper hand over opulence; that a rich man who is nothing but rich, feeling forever eclipsed by Citizens who are titled and poor, find neither deference nor approval in his fatherland; that he be forced to serve it if he wishes to shine in it, to have integrity out of ambition, and to aspire, in spite of his riches, to ranks that can be reached only through public approbation, and from which disapprobation can at all times cause one to fail. This is how to drain the forces of riches, and how to make men who are not for sale. (*Poland*, 232–33)

Rousseau seeks a culture honoring those dedicated to civic virtue and the public good.[63] Insofar as it takes root, the remaining incentives to acquire great fortunes vanish. Money loses its corrupting powers.

The task of creating a society of civic-minded citizens is no small undertaking. This is in many ways one of the fundamental purposes of book 4 of Rousseau's *Social Contract*, where he worries, "when the social knot begins to loosen and the State . . . weaken[s]; when particular interests begin to make themselves felt, and small societies . . . influence the larger society, the common interest diminishes and meets with opposition, votes are no longer unanimous, the general will is no longer the will of all, contradictions and disagreements arise, and the best opinion no longer carries the day unchallenged" (*SC*, 4.1, 124–25). The state must, therefore, employ various tools to bind the citizens together so that they love one another more than themselves. This is the purpose of the various institutions he introduces in the final book of the *Social Contract*, such as the Tribunate, the Comitia, the Censor, and especially his civil religion, discussion of which transcends my scope here.[64] Beyond these, Rousseau expresses in his *Government of Poland* that education should cultivate a patriotism that "gives souls the national form, and so direct their tastes and opinions that they will be patriotic by inclination, passion, necessity. Upon opening its eyes, a child should see the fatherland, and see only it until his dying day. Every true republican drank love of fatherland, that is to say love of the law and of freedom, with his mother's milk" (189).[65] Insofar as citizens love their nation and their fellow citizens "by inclination" and "necessity," they no longer lust for great personal wealth to inflate their *amour-propre*. Their self-love is instead satisfied by praise received for acts of civic virtue. Similarly, much of Rousseau's treatise *Emile* targets the unnecessary desires for luxuries, cultivating citizens relieved from the burdens of the exhausting and dangerous pursuit of riches.

Where money and inequality have already taken root, however, such cultural transformations may well be quixotic. But the difficulty of achieving such ambitions does not deter Rousseau from exploring more moderate strategies to "forestall the ever-widening inequality of fortunes." Accordingly, he provides more practical suggestions in his *Political Economy*. Namely, he seeks to address inequality through two tax measures: capitation and luxury taxes.

To understand Rousseau's capitation tax, it is helpful to recall that the bulk of French taxes in this period were collected as part of the taille—a mode of taxation extending back to the medieval period, from which all clergymen and aristocrats were exempted. The taille was a direct or "personal tax," originally imposed on peasants but subsequently extended to all commoners in Rousseau's era until the French Revolution in 1789.[66] He approvingly cites Montesquieu in describing it as a tax "in keeping with servitude" (*PE*, 31).[67] Alexis de Tocqueville would later cite its aristocratic "exemption from taxation" as indicative of an "inequality of taxation [that] prevailed all over Europe"[68]—a tax burden falling disproportionately on the poor.

The capitation tax, by contrast, was relatively new, originally devised by Louis XIV in 1695 as a war-funding measure, becoming permanent in the eighteenth century. It was intended to be a proportional income tax, which subjects paid regardless of social rank and class, counterbalancing the undue tax burdens placed on the peasant and laboring classes.[69] Yet in practice, the burdens again fell disproportionately on those very classes. As Tocqueville notes, "as the capitation tax of *taille*-payers . . . was always heavier than the capitation of privileged persons, the very plan which seemed to favor uniformity kept up the inequality between the two."[70] Rousseau describes the combined effects of the taille and capitation taxes on the French poor:

> The scorned farmer, weighed down by taxes needed to support Luxury, and condemned to spend his life between labor and hunger, abandons his fields to go look in the Cities for the bread he should be taking to them. The more the stupid eyes of the People are struck with admiration by capital cities, the more one must bemoan to see the Countryside abandoned, the fields lie fallow, and the highways overrun by unfortunate Citizens turned beggars or thieves and destined someday to end their misery on the wheel or a dunghill. This is how the State, while it grows rich on the one hand, gets weak and depopulated on the other. (*SD*, 202 [III: 206])

The primary effect of these taxes, for Rousseau, was to redistribute resources from the poorest citizens to the wealthiest.

For Rousseau, the principle of taxation must derive from the general will (*PE*, 30). This has two important implications. First, taxes must be imposed by the people themselves in a majority vote. This would exclude taxation principles found in eighteenth-century France, where the clergy and the nobles effectively set the rates—to everyone else's detriment. Second, as already discussed, the general will is a principle of equality. So any tax that disproportionately burdens the poor flagrantly violates the general will.

This clarifies his rejection of the taille as practiced in France since "nothing would be more disproportionate than such a tax." As such, he inclines to a modified head tax, along the lines of the proportionate nature of the capitation tax, which in theory would be "the most equitable" because it would be "strictly proportioned to individual means." Of course, in practice the capitation tax frequently failed in its equitable ambitions due to the "greed, influence, and fraud" that allowed for the wealthy and well-connected to "find ways to elude" such revenue measures.[71] But Rousseau favored the general principle of equality that would have citizens with ten times the wealth paying ten times the taxes. In fact, he even entertains extending the tax even further—on both extreme ends of the economic spectrum. Those with only the "bare necessities" should pay no taxes, while those with an abundance should be prepared to "go up to the full amount that exceeds his necessities" (*PE*, 31).[72] In theory, his modified head tax could be used to impose a strict equality on all citizens at the level of subsistence, although there is enough textual evidence elsewhere to suggest that he did not find it either necessary or feasible, at least in his more practical reforms.

Beyond capitation taxes, Rousseau proposed equalizing corrupted societies with significant luxury taxes. To be sure, luxury taxes already existed in the eighteenth-century Francophone world, including Geneva. As with taille, sumptuary laws frequently exempted the very wealthy. "Some Genevans seemed to favor sumptuary ordinances," according to Rosenblatt, "precisely because they *maintained* the distinctions between the various orders of society."[73] Rousseau, by contrast, sought to reconceptualize sumptuary laws such that they would largely burden the very rich.

Rousseau's attitude toward luxuries parallels his attitude toward money itself insofar as both are markers of inequality. As he notes in *Emile*, "The importance given them [luxuries] by the rich does not come from their use but from the fact that the poor cannot afford them" (186).[74] So if they are to be tolerated at all, they should be subjected to steep taxation:

> Duties on the import of foreign merchandise which the population craves but the country does not need, on the export of domestic merchandise of which the country has no excess and which foreigners cannot do without, on the productions of the useless and excessively lucrative arts, municipal duties on pure amenities, and in general all luxury items, will achieve this twofold objective fully. Taxes such as these, which relieve poverty and burden riches, are the way to forestall the ever-widening inequality of fortunes. (*PE*, 36)

Rousseau consistently condemns luxuries, beginning with his *First Discourse*, where he describes how luxuries produce myriad social ills: "Granting that luxury is a certain sign of riches; that, if you like, it even serves to increase them: What conclusion is to be drawn from this paradox so worthy of being born in our time; and what will become of virtue, when one has to get rich at all costs?" (*FD*, 18).[75] The possibility of acquiring luxury goods stimulates greed. Taxing luxuries, therefore, has a double ameliorating effect on economic inequality. First, its burdens fall almost exclusively on the wealthiest, hence serving to reduce extreme inequality. Second, it disincentivizes fortune-building in the first place.

While Rousseau's guidance on tax policy threatens significant wealth penalties, he does not insist on perfect economic equality. Prominently, in his "Political Fragments," he admits that it is "a waste of time to stop at a supposition as chimerical as that of the equal distribution of riches. This equality cannot be conceded even hypothetically, because it is not in the nature of things" (49). Acknowledging the impossibility, Rousseau nevertheless wants to reduce inequality as much as possible: "Do you want to give the State stability? bring the extremes as close together as possible; tolerate neither very rich people nor beggars. These two states, which are naturally inseparable, are equally fatal to the common good" (*SC*, 2.11, 81n). Although he obviously does not require absolute economic equality, it is abundantly clear that he seeks a great deal more equality than what was typical in his times—and enough equality to put the general will within reach.

Equality for Women and Racial Minorities?

Economic egalitarianism does not always correspond with political, gender, or racial egalitarianism. Plato's Kallipolis, for example, highlights the threats of economic inequality, but nevertheless installs a political hierarchy where the republic is controlled by a small bevy of philosopher rulers. Similarly, although Plato's Magnesia is highly egalitarian in economic terms, its egalitarian principles do not extend to its substantial slave class, which is excluded from considerations of distributive justice. The one area in which Plato has a strong case to be called an egalitarian outside economics concerns equality between the sexes, since he insists that women have just as much right to rule as do men.[76] Insofar as these other intersecting inequalities exist, it is reasonable to raise questions about the effectiveness of anyone's egalitarian program in the economic sphere.

Similar questions emerge in reading Rousseau, especially regarding his writings on women. His approach to understanding women and their social roles has long been the object of considerable scrutiny, beginning with Mary Wollstonecraft, who describes Rousseau's program of education for women as aimed at producing "a fanciful kind of *half* being."[77] She was not wrong insofar as Rousseau conceived of the education of women who are, for him, "made specially to please man" (*Emile*, 358)—a point he would develop at disconcerting length throughout book 5 of his pedagogical novel. One need not rehearse this point by multiplying quotations from Rousseau's work—his failure to accept the equality of women is widely known and acknowledged.[78] The point is that Rousseau did not consider women in his project of economic egalitarianism except insofar as they were attached to households led by men. It is unclear, however, that his shortsightedness here implies that his economic doctrines are inconsistent with gender equality. After all, Rousseau's favorite ancient republic, Sparta, embraced significant economic *and* gender equality at the same time. So did Plato, arguably Rousseau's favorite philosopher. To the extent that Rousseau borrows from these sources, there is a path to build for equality on both of these dimensions simultaneously. It is unfortunate that Rousseau did not rise above his century's views about the capacities of women for full engagement in the economic and political dimensions of their communities, but there is reasonable ground to speculate that his economic doctrines leave room for greater inclusion of women.

On the question of whether Rousseau's inegalitarianism extended to members of other races, the evidence is more favorable. Unlike Plato, he rejected slavery. He identifies Plato's student Aristotle in the *Social Contract* as having defended slavery on dubious grounds. Aristotle had falsely deduced from the degraded condition of slaves in his midst that slaves were naturally deficient in their reasoning powers and hence best suited to lives of servitude. Rousseau explains that it was merely "force" that created slavery and nothing in the nature of the slaves themselves (*SC*, 1.2,

45). Elsewhere, in his novel *Julie*, in the voice of Saint Preux, the character with whom Rousseau most closely identified, he laments, "I have seen those vast and unfortunate countries that seem destined only to cover the earth with herds of slaves," continuing that in "seeing the fourth part of my equals turned into beasts for the service of others, I rued being a man" (340).[79] Even though he does not elaborate on his condemnation of chattel slavery here, this is enough to suggest his disapproval. No Rousseauean republic could likely tolerate slavery, whether race-based or otherwise. Yet because he is writing in the context of a deeply homogenous eighteenth-century Francophone world, he offers little guidance on how to construct institutions that might expressly consider the effects of deeply embedded racism on the distribution of social wealth.

Not only does Rousseau reject slavery, but he also celebrates Native peoples outside of Europe. It is the Europeans, for him, who have been most thoroughly corrupted by civilization. Native peoples, and he especially focuses on the Amerindians, have wisely avoided the trappings of civilization that stimulate *amour-propre*, inequality, and despotism. Rather than understanding the Amerindians to be living in anarchy and without rules, Rousseau finds that they have rational governments, and he adds, "they govern themselves . . . very well" (*SC*, 3.5, 95). He finds that the Mesoamerican state of Tlaxcala, for example, is a model republic insofar as it has consciously rejected dependence on the neighboring Aztecs, even sacrificing the luxury of salt in doing so: "The wise Tlaxcalans saw the trap. . . . They preserved their freedom" (*SC*, 2.8, 80n). Rousseau finds much to admire in Native peoples, and there is no reason to assume he saw any reason to entangle race with economic inequality.[80]

It is worth considering a further point regarding Rousseau and the nature of deeply embedded racial inequalities. One of the most important theorists of race and the social contract, Charles Mills, has celebrated Rousseau for his uniquely insightful understanding of the injustices of that tradition. Mills praises the *Discourse on the Origin of Inequality* for discerning that the social contract tradition has largely been "deceitful" insofar as it has established and legitimated exploitation, oppression, and immorality. For him, Rousseau "gives us a kind of X-ray vision into the real internal logic of the Racial Contract."[81] Mills acknowledges that Rousseau does not expressly address how racial inequalities are embedded through this process—for Rousseau these inequalities are fundamentally economic ones. But Rousseau, for Mills, explains better than anyone how racial inequalities could have been secured and protected by governments long after they are established, and how difficult it becomes to remove them. For Rousseau, as with

Mills, it is inadequate to establish a legal inequality on top of an underlying superstructure of economic or racial inequality. Mills acknowledges and praises Rousseau for discerning the structures of inequality, whether economic or racial. So even if Rousseau is not especially race conscious, for Mills, he remains one of the most valuable tools for interrogating racial inequality, including its connection to economic inequality.

Beyond Rousseau's critique of the existing social contract tradition, Jane Anna Gordon has pushed considerably further in her recent reading of the Genevan. She has argued that Rousseau's positive vision for politics, his general will, offers great promise in resolving problems of racial inequality. The general will, on Rousseau's account, must come from all and apply to all (*SC*, 2.4, 64), implying that in racially diverse societies minority races must have genuine input into legislation and, further, that all laws must apply to all races in a genuine fashion. The underlying ethos of the general will, for Gordon, is its insistence on achieving a genuine "common good" that transcends the interest of any economic class or race residing in the state. This means, for her, "minimizing the kinds of inequality that would lead to fundamentally antagonistic interests between members, which would make it impossible for them to see their fates as intertwined."[82] Rousseau's egalitarian principles, on her account, ultimately animate Frantz Fanon's political theory. So even though Rousseau may not have expressly envisioned a racially diverse or multicultural society from his vantage point in eighteenth-century France, his doctrines have inspired those later navigating this terrain.

Conclusion

Rousseau's approach to understanding inequality is an important landmark in the Western tradition. Among other things, unlike his predecessors who spoke of the problems of poverty and wealth concentration, he gives the simultaneous presence of these conditions a name: *inequality*. It is a term that will be appropriated by all those who later share his concerns. Further, he is especially determined to understand not only how inequality comes about, but also how it is *legitimated* through the social contract and its subsequent institutions. As Patrick Riley artfully demonstrates, legitimacy is one of the most important inventions of modern political thought. The first notable social contractarian, Thomas Hobbes, had insisted that "the right of all sovereigns is derived originally from consent, of everyone of those that are to be governed" (*Leviathan*, 40.123). Rousseau embraces the principle of legitimacy in his *Social*

Contract, which confirms, "I owe nothing to those to whom I have promised nothing" (2.6, 68).[83] This is the principle of legitimacy on which rests
the modern social contract tradition and much of the modern political
ethos to this day.

But what distinguishes Rousseau from Hobbes and his other
predecessors is his acknowledgment of how the principle of legitimacy can
be abused to secure inequalities and govern on the elite's behalf. The lesson of the *Discourse on Inequality* is that most of the social contract tradition has rationalized such inequalities. The point of the social contract, as it
had been practiced, was to secure a kind of faux legitimacy, which "forever
fixed the Law of property and inequality, transformed a skillful usurpation
into an irrevocable right, and for the profit of a few ambitious men" (*SD*,
178). The wealthy have been able to establish a system that guarantees their
advantages by tricking the poor and dispossessed into consenting to a social
contract that legitimizes their oppression.

Rousseau's concern informs the opening sentence of his *Social Contract*,
where "Man is born free, and everywhere is in chains." Those are the chains
of the faux contract—the despotism in which subjects are led to believe that
they had consented to extreme inequality. It is especially important, however, to read to the end of the opening paragraph: "What can make it [the
social contract] legitimate? I believe I can solve this problem" (*SC*, 1.1, 43).
As should be clear by now, making the social contract legitimate, for Rousseau, means gaining consent to live according to the terms of the general
will, and the general will requires a significant commitment to economic
equality. This is one of Rousseau's most striking contributions to the Western tradition. Consider that although Plato also desired economic equality,
it was not something to which citizens necessarily consented. For Hobbes,
although subjects consent to live in the state under the authority of the
Leviathan, they are not doing so to secure economic equality. Equality is,
rather, something that a wise sovereign will realize is necessary for achieving the peace to which the commonwealth is aimed. But for Rousseau,
the very terms of a legitimate social contract are this: "Each of us puts his
person and his full power in common under the supreme direction of the
general will" (*SC*, 1.6, 52), where the general will "always tends to equality"
(*Emile*, 463). A truly legitimate social contract means agreeing to significant
economic equality.

Rousseau's understanding of the faux social contract that has secured
illegitimate inequalities animates his successors. For Adam Smith, "laws
and government may [thus] be considered . . . in every case as a combination of the rich to oppress the poor, and preserve to themselves the

inequality of the goods which would otherwise be soon destroyed by the attacks of the poor, who if not hindered by the government would soon reduce the others to an equality with themselves by open violence" (*LJ*, 208). John Stuart Mill laments that the poor have been persuaded by the rich that their poverty is a "necessary evil," and consent to their condition has been "partly extorted from their fears" (*Socialism*, 227). For Friedrich Engels, the "legal system has been devised to protect those who own property from those who do not" (*AD*, 317). These subsequent thinkers have drawn from Rousseau's logic of the faux contract, sometimes with express acknowledgment. His approach to understanding inequality, thus, significantly raises the stakes. Inequality is more dangerous because it is more deeply entrenched, not only in the laws and institutions of Western societies but in the notion that popular consent legitimates it.

One final consideration. Rousseau is the last philosopher in this book for whom the economy is entirely "zero-sum," according to which one person's gain is another's loss. As he asks incredulously, "How is it possible to become wealthy without contributing to impoverishing someone else?" (*WFT*, 9; see also "Last Reply," 71n). The accumulation of wealth, for him and his predecessors, necessarily comes at others' expense. This makes the concentration of wealth dangerous twice over—both in what it does psychically to the wealthy but also in further impoverishing the poor.

The zero-sum view of the economy changes with Adam Smith, who will understand economic growth and wealth in different terms.[84] Commerce has the capacity, he will argue, to grow the overall wealth of a society. So it is possible, on his reasoning, that someone can grow rich without it coming at others' expense. In colloquial terms, this is sometimes known as "growing the pie"—if the pie is larger, then everyone gets a larger slice, and it explains why it is that although Smith will affirm Rousseau's criticisms of inequality, he does less to mitigate it. Growing the pie allows everyone to improve their material condition, even if their share of that pie is smaller in relative terms. John Stuart Mill and Karl Marx agree but only to a point. Growing the pie, on their accounts, enhances aggregate social wealth. They only see those benefits extending to a point, however, and even then at great cost. This is for two reasons. First, growth inevitably often comes at the price of enormous inequality. Second, economic growth is only desirable to a certain point, beyond which its benefits become greatly diminished or, in fact, counterproductive. Once the market has produced enough material wealth for everyone to live a good life, the priority then becomes to ensure that wealth benefits everyone.

CHAPTER FIVE

Adam Smith

"A COMBINATION OF THE
RICH TO OPPRESS THE POOR"

UP TO THIS POINT IN THE BOOK, I have examined economic observations and comments from various figures, but none of them could truly be called "economists"—not even Jean-Jacques Rousseau, who wrote a *Discourse on Political Economy*. This changes with Adam Smith and will become a theme for the remaining chapters since John Stuart Mill and Karl Marx thought of themselves as economists or at least political economists. Beginning with Smith, observations about the operations of economies become more frequent, detailed, and systematic. Political and economic matters become henceforth more entangled and mutually dependent. Scattered observations about economic relations in the works of Plato, Jesus, Hobbes, and Rousseau became one-thousand-page treatises in the age of Smith, Mill, and Marx. In the hands of these latter thinkers, economics became a science. But these intellectuals still share much in common with their predecessors—something that distinguishes them from many contemporary economists today. They are moral and political philosophers. Economics in their hands was not a "pure science" to be fenced off from moral and political philosophy—it was, rather, one branch of it. Growing wealth—or the critique thereof, as with Marx—was part of a larger endeavor to promote still greater ends. For Mill, this would be utility. For Marx, it would be the freedom from bourgeois domination.

It makes sense to read Smith in this same spirit, especially since he was actually a professional philosopher, who taught at the University of Glasgow. He had built his reputation on a work of moral philosophy titled the *Theory of Moral Sentiments*, so his better-known *Wealth of Nations* can also be read as philosophy, rather than a work of pure economics. As a philosopher, it is not enough to know that Smith wanted to make people richer—which he surely did—but to know *why* he sought to do so. To this end, he writes in the introduction to his most famous work, undeveloped nations "are so poor, that from mere want, they are frequently reduced, to the necessity sometimes of directly destroying, and sometimes abandoning their infants, their old people, and those afflicted with lingering diseases, to perish with hunger, or to be devoured by wild beasts" (*WN*, 10). It is easily overlooked that in Plato's *Republic*, for example, Socrates permits that many infants will be allowed to die and that health care would be limited to those whom society could afford to save (*Republic*, 460bc, 405c–408e). Part of what it meant to live in those times was making hard choices about how to allocate scarce resources. Adam Smith looks at such societies as places of needless suffering. "No society can surely be flourishing and happy," he insisted, "of which the far greater part of the members are poor and miserable" (*WN*, 96). The point of his *Wealth of Nations*, as he makes admirably clear, is to create a society in which "the produce of society is so great, that all are often abundantly supplied . . . even [those] of the lowest and poorest order" (*WN*, 10). This is the justification for the market economy he describes and advocates in the foundational work of capitalism. Although obscured by generations of economists, political philosophers and theorists have brought increasing attention to this core feature of Smith's work.[1]

But Smith was not only attuned to the problem of poverty; he was also, I argue, acutely aware of the dangers of inequality.[2] He worried about the moral corruption of the rich, their tendency to accumulate undue social and political power, their excessive and corruptive influence on the morals of poor people, and perhaps most of all, the corrosive effects of inequality on the ability of citizens to experience mutual sympathy across a broad class divide. "Wherever there is great property," he acknowledges, "there is great inequality." And with that inequality comes "indignation," "envy," and political instability (*WN*, 709–10). This chapter details Smith's concerns.

But there is something relatively unique in Smith's response to inequality that demands careful attention and scrutiny. Even though he is fully aware of the problems of inequality and articulates these problems in great and knowing detail, he largely demurs when it comes to addressing these problems.[3] That is to say, while he is concerned about both poverty and inequality, he appears to prioritize addressing poverty over inequality. Better that no one starves than that people get along well. This choice is apparent in his stadial theory of history in which he divides history according to four stages: hunters, shepherds, agricultural, and commercial. It is really only the hunter-gatherer stage of historical development, for Smith, that achieves extensive economic equality. As he quips in his *Wealth of Nations*, "universal poverty establishes their universal equality" (*WN*, 712). Yet this is the same stage of history that he describes as most punishing to the poor. This suggests that although he understands inequality's deleterious social effects, he is even more concerned about the poor. So even though market economies may not resolve the problem of inequality, their capacity to unburden the poor is enough to overlook its associated difficulties. This is not to suggest that Smith has *nothing* to offer regarding inequality. I address some of his measures later in this chapter. But his relatively modest measures, compared with others discussed throughout this book, as well as his prioritization of ameliorating the burdens of absolute poverty, distinguishes his approach.

Smith's Treatment of Inequality in Context

Eighteenth-century Britain underwent a period of unprecedented economic growth that surely colored Adam Smith's world. Much of Britain's wealth, to be sure, still resided in its aristocracy that persisted from feudal times. Although relatively few in number, their fortunes were great. There were some two hundred aristocrats of peerage heading the big Whig families of the age—the Russells, the Cavendishes, the Fitzwilliamses, the Pelhams, and the like. According to one study, the ten wealthiest families in 1760 had annual incomes of over £20,000. The next twenty wealthiest families earned £10,000, and the next 120 families earned between £6,000 and £8,000 a year. For comparison's sake, the wealthiest one thousand merchants averaged £600 a year and the wealthiest manufacturers earned approximately £200 a year.[4] While the last two categories certainly rose throughout the eighteenth century and beyond, this simple fact of wealth distribution offers context for understanding inequality in eighteenth-century Britain and in reading Smith. Often when Smith complains of inequality, he has these families in mind, not yet fully aware of how industrialization would redistribute wealth throughout Britain and much of the rest of the world. The aristocracy's wealth certainly manifested itself in British politics. The British political system was, by all accounts, an oligarchy in which the landed aristocracy still exercised its considerable influence over Parliament.[5]

As suggested, however, Britain in the eighteenth century was also host to two separate groups of emerging wealth—the merchants and the industrialists. Much merchant wealth was made in colonial trade, including the highly profitable triangular transatlantic slave trade. Britain would purchase slaves in West Africa, who would then, at great peril and with obscenely high mortality rates, be shipped to the Americas to live out their remaining days as slaves. Those slaves would be used to harvest raw materials, especially cotton, which would then be shipped to Britain. Britain would then use those to manufacture and sell materials such as textiles at great profit. Then the profits would be used to purchase more West African slaves. The practice was scarcely challenged and, as Christopher Hill has speculated, established a pattern of abusive relations with workers that eventually "would extend . . . to white labour in England."[6] The cotton industry experienced exponential growth in the eighteenth century, including a tenfold increase in the sale of British textiles from 1750 to 1769, when Adam Smith was professionally active. And it should be noted that Scotland and Glasgow, in particular, the city where Smith spent much of his academic career, participated in the slave trade, shipping somewhere between four thousand and five thousand Africans to the Americas for enslavement. Much of Glasgow's growing wealth in this period can be directly traced to the slave trade, especially among tobacco merchants, which was, according to a Smith biographer, "the city's flagship enterprise and the source of its enormous wealth." A vocal opponent of slavery, Smith was well aware of this foundation of Glasgow's growing wealth.[7]

Another source of merchant wealth was Britain's presence in India and through state-protected monopolies such as the East India Company. Trade with India, characterized by some as "plunder,"[8] which imported tea and spices to Britain, generated fortunes for British merchants sometimes large enough for them to purchase peerage and seats in Parliament. Tea imports from India to Britain alone rose from 54,000 pounds in 1706 to 2,325,000 pounds in 1750.

British manufacturing boomed when Abraham Darby discovered how to smelt iron ore with coke in 1708. This process allowed cast iron to be made cheaply on a large enough scale to replace wooden machines by the 1750s. This innovation accelerated industry and paved the way for subsequent industrial fortunes.

In some respects, life for the working poor was improving. Innovations in manufacturing reduced the prices of goods, and there were advances in public health and hygiene that better protected the working class from the plagues that decimated them in earlier centuries. Yet poverty was still very much a fact of life in eighteenth-century Britain. As John Locke would observe in 1697, "the multiplying of the poor, and the increase of the tax for their maintenance, is so general an observation and complaint that it cannot be doubted of. . . . It has been a growing burden on the kingdom these many years."[9] In 1700, more than 20 percent of Britons were receiving poor relief. Much of this came in the form of wage supplements from the state since employers had powerful incentives to keep wages low. The poor generally had little protein, relying extensively on potatoes for their calories. Although average real wages were growing for many working people throughout Britain, this conceals differences between skilled and unskilled labor. Whereas skilled labor saw wage growth adequate to cover growing inflation, especially in the second half of the eighteenth century, wages for unskilled labor tended to lag behind.

As Christopher Hill has observed, even where wages grew, the terms of those wages were often difficult to bear, most important in the degree to which workers surrendered their relative freedom. Before moving to the cities to work in factories, workers had greater ability to determine where they would work, under what conditions, and for how long. Although their incomes were modest, they nevertheless maintained what Hill calls "an aura of freedom."[10] But as technology and industry advanced, opportunities to work so freely were rapidly vanishing. Laborers would increasingly have to work in factories, and that meant living on the terms of wealthy factory owners.

Increasingly, as market innovations were introduced, inequality advanced. It was one of David Ricardo's fundamental arguments in his *Principles of Political Economy and Taxation* (1817) that as population rises, so too does rent, resulting in poorer laborers and wealthier landowners. Population in Glasgow boomed throughout the eighteenth century from around 14,000 in 1700 to 31,000 to mid-century to 81,000 by century's end,[11] surely creating upward pressure on the rent of working people. Economic historian Peter H. Lindert has further argued that inequality rose sharply in eighteenth-century Britain due to sudden price increases in staples, including grains, bread, and fuel, whereas the relative cost of luxury items held steady or actually decreased in the same period.[12] This decreased living conditions among the middle and lower classes while granting the wealthy greater purchasing powers. These observations confirm the findings of economist Lee Soltow, who has found that inequality in eighteenth-century Scottish land holdings was significant and greater than elsewhere in Britain or western Europe more broadly. He measures the 1770 Scottish Gini coefficient for land ownership at a striking 0.755.[13] Thomas Piketty reports that in 1780, the top 10 percent of wealthiest British citizens possessed 90 percent of total private property;

the top 1 percent possessed slightly more than 60 percent. The bottom 50 percent possessed less than 5 percent. This was significant inequality by almost any measure.[14]

It would have been difficult for Adam Smith not to notice this striking inequality. To be sure, he comments on the problems of economic inequality, collusion, class conflict, and labor violence in his *Wealth of Nations*. The wealthiest nations, he laments, commonly pay the lowest wages. "Masters," he notes, "are always and every where in a sort of tacit, but constant and uniform combination, not to raise the wages of labour above their actual rate." In response to these suppressed wages, laborers, he observes,

> have always recourse to the loudest clamour, and sometimes to the most shocking violence and outrage. They are desperate, and act with the folly and extravagance of desperate men, who must either starve, or frighten their masters into an immediate compliance with their demands. (*WN*, 83–84)

It is in this context that readers can better appreciate his lamentation, "Wherever there is great property, there is great inequality. For one very rich man, there must be at least five hundred poor, and the affluence of the few supposes the indigence of the many" (*WN*, 709–10). Smith knew this to be true because this was his Scotland. Casual observation doubtlessly confirmed this for him every day.

Industrial innovations introduced in this period in the form of new machines were often met with resistance and even violence by the working class. As early as 1675, London weavers in Spitalfields rioted for three days, smashing the machine looms that threatened to displace hand looms individually operated by workers. Repeated similar incidents persuaded Parliament in 1727 to make the destruction of industrial equipment a capital offense. The English industrial inventor John Kay, who had invented the flying shuttle used in weaving and which threatened to displace countless workers, was forced to flee Britain after his home was destroyed by an angry mob in 1753.

As Eric Hobsbawm has argued, industrial relations in the first half of the eighteenth century could largely be characterized as "collective bargaining by riot." Wealthy clothing industrialists complained to Parliament in 1718 and 1724 that workers "threatened to pull down their houses and burn their work unless they would agree with their terms." Labor disputes throughout early industrial Britain in 1726–1727 resulted in weavers "breaking into the houses (of masters and blacklegs), spoiling of wool, and cutting and destroying the pieces in the looms and the utensils of trade." A 1738 textile workers' riot in Melksham commenced with laborers "cut[ting] all the chains in the looms belonging to Mr. Coulhurst . . . on account of his lowering the prices." In 1740, Northumberland miners burned the pithead machinery in a protest that would eventually earn them a long-desired raise. Frame breaking was routine in the East Midlands hosiery trade throughout the middle eighteenth century.[15] None of this is to suggest that rich and poor were constantly at each other's throats in this period. But the conflicts were frequent and conspicuous enough.

Foundational Principles: Mutual Sympathy and Concord

In the search for foundational principles in Smith, it would seem, so far as the *Wealth of Nations* is concerned, that he prioritizes generating the greatest possible wealth. This would be true to a certain point, but it does not answer the question of why generating that wealth is important in the first place since it would not have been obvious to readers in 1776 that this would be a desirable goal. To grasp his larger principles and philosophical commitments, one must grapple with his earlier *Theory of Moral Sentiments*, where he comes closest to providing an underlying principle of his moral and political thought. I suggest that principle is "concord" or "mutual sympathy."

To be sure, concord or mutual sympathy is not what most casual readers take to be Smith's organizing principle. That most commonly identified principle is self-interest, which most readers learn from his account of the "invisible hand," as presented in his *Wealth of Nations*.[16] Yet the word "selfish" is actually the very second word in his *Theory of Moral Sentiments* in which he acknowledges the common assumption that humankind is self-interested. Smith does not deny that there is some truth in this assumption: "Every man is, no doubt, by nature, first and principally recommended to his own care. . . . Every man, therefore, is much more deeply interested in whatever immediately concerns himself, than in what concerns any other man" (*TMS*, 100; see also *TMS*, 258). Along with Hobbes, Smith concedes that this is a prominent component of human nature. But he refuses to concede that this constitutes the sole or defining principle of human nature. For Smith, self-interest can be either benign or malignant, depending on whether it is in the service of virtue or vice.[17] He dubs the latter "absurd self-love" and defines it as one imagines "that other people may be sacrificed at any time, to his conveniency or his humour"—a tendency characterized by "gross insolence and injustice" (*TMS*, 115). The pursuit of this malignant self-love rightfully earns one the condemnation of one's peers and hopefully, for Smith, of one's own conscience. By contrast, benign self-love does not injure or insult other citizens and includes the virtues of security, modesty, frugality, industry, probity, frankness, and the like.[18]

For a variety of reasons, many of Smith's greatest admirers, especially economists, have come to assume that selfishness is the sole principle of his moral psychology—a sentiment best represented by George Stigler, who once asserted, "*The Wealth of Nations* is a stupendous palace erected upon the granite of self-interest."[19] Yet Smith refutes any such reduction of his thought generally at the very opening of his *Theory of Moral Sentiments*—a book he wrote well before the *Wealth of Nations* and which he continuously revised throughout his career:

> How selfish soever a man may be supposed, there are evidently some principles in his nature, which interest him in the fortune of others, and render their happiness necessary to him, though he derives nothing from it except the pleasure of seeing it. Of this kind is pity or compassion, the emotion which we feel for the misery of others.

No individual is indifferent to the sufferings and joys of others. Indeed, "the greatest ruffian, the most hardened violator of the laws of society, is not altogether without" sympathy (*TMS*, 13). The degree to which individuals sympathize with others, however, differs according to several factors, including the wisdom and virtue of the spectator, the relationship of the parties, their physical proximity, and how much they have in common. Generally speaking, the powers of sympathy operate with the greatest force on those of great virtue (*TMS*, 265) and for those with whom we are close either by kinship or geography (*TMS*, 258–60).

Beyond mere sympathy for Smith, however, lies a goal more elevated and perhaps more elusive: mutual sympathy. It is not simply that people incline to sympathize with others—it is that the sympathies citizens feel for others should be mutual and, further, that this mutual sympathy is "sufficient for the harmony of society" (*TMS*, 28). He sometimes calls this mutual sympathy "concord," which he distinguishes from unison. It is not that everyone in society needs to think and feel the same things. Rather, in a harmonious society they should adopt the habit of placing themselves in their fellow citizens' shoes, so to speak. The practice of mutual sympathy, for Smith, "necessarily abates the violence of what he felt" prior to adopting this perspective—namely, what one might judge from a merely self-interested vantage point (*TMS*, 29).

Mutual sympathy produces many rewards for Smith. Notably, it is psychologically satisfying: "nothing pleases us more than to observe in other men a fellow-feeling with all the emotions of our own breast; nor are we ever so much shocked as by the appearance of the contrary" (*TMS*, 18). When others echo our sentiments, we feel validated. When others ignore or dismiss our feelings or predicaments, we feel scorned or rejected. But beyond our own personal feelings, mutual sympathy promises larger social benefits. Mutual sympathy reduces conflict, dissolves factions, and adds an element of impartiality or fairness to society. But again, perhaps most valuably, it fosters harmony. Insofar as mutual sympathy pervades society, citizens look to one another as vested partners in a joint mission rather than as competitors for scarce resources, material or psychological. Living in a community characterized by mutual sympathy means not having to look behind one's back. It means having the confidence of support. It means knowing that we are all in this together, so to speak.

Even though mutual sympathy or concord is clearly a high priority for Smith, he also worries about its fragility. This is because people are more inclined to feel sympathy for specific people with whom they share some connection (*TMS*, 105). It is easy to feel compassion for immediate family. It takes much greater effort to do so for strangers suffering a tragedy thousands of miles from home. It is easier to empathize with members of one's own social class than it is with those significantly below us. This particular obstacle to achieving mutual sympathy makes inequality particularly troublesome for Smith.

The Effect of Inequality on Individuals

The worst moral pathologies, for Smith, emerge most immediately from selfishness and the related drive for distinction. This is especially true in commercial societies, where distinction, as Rousseau had argued, is typically measured by wealth. As Smith suggests, "it is chiefly from this regard to the sentiments of mankind, that we pursue riches and avoid poverty" (*TMS*, 62).[20] In commercial societies where distinction is measured by wealth, the most obvious sign is opulence. Conversely, the most obvious sign of failure is poverty.

Complications follow from the fact that wealth becomes the measure of success. In particular, the pursuit and possession of wealth are accompanied by notable vices. Prominent among these are pride and vanity. Indeed, because of the drive for distinction and rank, Smith suggests that it is vanity, rather than material comforts, that inspire the pursuit of wealth. "The rich man glories in his riches, because he feels that they naturally draw the attention of the world" (*TMS*, 63).[21] Along with wealth and distinction, Smith reasons, numerous other largely unwarranted and dubious benefits arise. The wealthy enjoy broad admiration simply by virtue of their fortunes. The larger public "favour[s] all their inclinations" and even "wish[es] them immortal."[22] "Every calamity that befalls them," he observes, "excites in the breast of the spectator ten times more compassion and resentment than he would have felt had the same things happened to other men" (*TMS*, 64, 65).[23] The wealthy become the celebrities and role models. This constant adulation comes at the cost of their character. For the affluent man, Smith laments, public esteem—derived, he insists, *not* from his justice, wisdom, or virtue but merely from the possession of wealth itself—inflates the sense of "his own superiority" (*TMS*, 65).

Vanity, Smith subsequently argues, is self-consciously feigned. The vain often understand that this public adulation is unmerited. This does not, of course, mean that they cease their pretensions. Rather, it exacerbates them insofar as these pretensions promise the reward of even greater public esteem. The conceited man, he suggests, courts esteem "with the most anxious assiduity." Fearful of being exposed as a fraud, he "endeavors to bribe you into a good opinion of him" (*TMS*, 300).[24] This may occasionally include socially useful gestures, such as charity, but it is equally likely to inspire greater ostentation to overawe the public.

Another danger attached to vanity is that it might convert to pride. Pride differs from vanity in a crucial respect. Whereas the vain fear exposure as frauds, the proud actually believe in their own merit. "The proud man is sincere, and, in the bottom of his heart, is convinced of his own superiority; though it may sometimes be difficult to guess upon what that conviction is founded." Smith's own arguments suggest the moral psychology underlying this transition. Simply stated, the masses grant adulation to anyone who appears successful and wealthy. When granting esteem, the public naturally defaults "to admire, and almost to worship, the rich and powerful, and to despise, or, at least to neglect persons of poor and mean condition." This allocation of public affection and contempt is nothing less than, for Smith, "the great and most universal cause of the corruption of our moral sentiments" (*TMS*, 73).[25] This is corruption insofar as esteem should rather be granted to the wise and virtuous. But empirical observation seems to subvert the moral order: "We frequently see the respectful attentions of the world more strongly directed toward the rich and the great, than towards the wise and virtuous" (*TMS*, 74).

Insofar as the vain man acquires and displays greater wealth, he will win that public esteem. And the more esteem he acquires, the more his vanity evolves into pride. Because of the high opinion in which the proud man holds himself, "if you appear not to respect him as he respects himself, he is more offended than mortified, and feels the same indignant resentment as if he had suffered a real injury" (*TMS*, 300). The public may be amused or offended by the absurdity of the vain and proud insofar as their stations are so disproportionate with their dispositions. The student with a low GPA, for example, cannot long brag about his high IQ before being mocked by his classmates. But where there appears to be some plausible correlation between one's disposition and the accompanying attitude, "we thoroughly enter into and sympathize with the excessive self-estimation of those splendid characters" (*TMS*, 299). And one can surmise that for Smith, the wealthy and the proud are consumed by their own "natural selfishness and rapacity" (*TMS*, 215; see also, *WN*, 494).

The highest ranking members of society, insofar as they are proud or vain, are "constantly dissatisfied." The proud are "tormented with indignation at the unjust superiority, as he thinks it, of other people." The vain are similarly tormented by the "continual dread of the shame which, he foresees, would attend upon the detection of his groundless pretensions" (*TMS*, 307). In brief, although wealth in commercial society is rewarded with "trinkets of frivolous utility," it comes at the cost of deep personal dissatisfaction. Great wealth hardly delivers happiness to the ambitious.

The poor, by contrast, suffer the effects of shame. This embarrassment in poverty, as addressed in chapter 4, took on new meaning after the feudal age. Under feudalism, economic status was simply inherited. Poverty did not reflect one's talents or efforts. It merely reflected larger social institutions. But with the emergence of market society and its accompanying freedoms came the belief that those occupying the top of the hierarchy merited their high stations. This may be why the public eagerly celebrates their achievements. But for the poor, the corollary presumption is that they are talentless and lazy. The shame accompanying their poverty results from the perception of genuine life failures, rather than the inevitable outcome of institutional forces beyond their control. "The poor man," for Smith, "is ashamed of his poverty. He feels that it either places him out of the sight of mankind, or, that if they take any notice of him, they have, however, scarce any fellow-feeling with the misery and distress that he suffers" (*TMS*, 63).[26] This internal sense is confirmed by how the rich, in fact, regard the poor: "The fortunate and the proud wonder at the insolence of human wretchedness, that it should dare to present itself before them, and with the loathsome aspect of its misery presume to disturb the serenity of their happiness" (*TMS*, 64).

The poor's shame is compounded by their envy of the rich. Smith paints a vivid picture in part 4 of his *Theory of Moral Sentiments*:

> The poor man's son, whom heaven in its anger has visited with ambition, when he begins to look around him, admires the condition of the rich. He finds the cottage of his father too small for his accommodation, and fancies he should be lodged more at his ease in a palace. His is displeased with being obliged to walk a-foot, or to endure the fatigue of riding on horseback. He sees his superiors carried about in machines, and imagines that in one of these he could travel with less inconveniency. He feels himself naturally indolent, and willing to serve himself with his own hands as little as possible; and judges, that a numerous retinue of servants would save him from a great deal of trouble. . . . For this purpose he makes his court to all mankind; he serves those whom he hates, and is obsequious to those whom he despises. Through the whole of his life he pursues the idea of a certain artificial and elegant repose which he may never arrive at, for which he sacrifices a real tranquility that is at all times in his power, and which, if in the extremity of old age he should at last attain to it, he will find to be in no respect preferable to that humble security and contentment which he had abandoned for it. It is then, in the last dregs of life, his body wasted with toil and diseases, his mind galled and ruffled by the memory of a thousand injuries and disappointments . . . that he begins at last to find that wealth and greatness are mere trinkets of frivolous utility. (*TMS*, 211–12)

For the poor man who envies the wealthy and seeks his own fortune, little good comes of it. Indeed, as Smith continues, even if he should actually succeed in realizing his ambition of great fortunes, he will be constantly exposed to "anxiety, to fear, and to sorrow" (*TMS*, 213). These are the psychic consequences of the pursuit of wealth on which commercial society depends. But this striving is itself fueled by envy, which is only possible where great wealth is on display and theoretically available to those willing to work for it.

For Smith, the poor's psychic pain is an insult added to physical injury. As he laments in his *Wealth of Nations*, the life of the poor is physically debilitating. In market economies, wages sometimes drift downward. This is especially true in mature markets because the labor supply tends to be generous. Because "many workmen could not subsist a week" without a job, while employers can commonly endure "a year or two," the "masters must generally have the advantage" in all contracts (*WN*, 87, 85). If workers are fortunate enough to have a job, the division of labor tends to make the work monotonous and mind numbing:

> The man whose whole life is spent in performing a few simple operations, of which the effects too are, perhaps, always the same, or very nearly the same, has no occasion to exert his understanding, or to exercise his invention in finding out expedients for removing difficulties which never occur. He naturally loses, therefore, the habit of such exertion, and generally becomes stupid and ignorant as it is possible for a human creature to become. The torpor of his mind renders him, not only incapable of relishing or bearing a part in any rational conversation, but of conceiving any generous, noble, or tender sentiment, and consequently of forming any just judgment concerning many even of the ordinary duties of private life. (*WN*, 783)

The riches of commercial society, for Smith, come at a high price to laborers. By contrast, he observes, in "barbarous" societies presumably characterized by far greater economic equality, "invention is kept alive, and the mind is not suffered to fall into the drowsy stupidity, which in a civilized society, seems to benumb the understanding of almost all the inferior ranks of people" (*WN*, 787). He continues to describe the effects of modern poverty on the body as well, which he portrays as rendering the laborer "incapable of exerting his strength with vigour and perseverance" (*WN*, 783). Given the effects of poverty on the body and mind, it is unsurprising that he finds it "extremely unfavorable to the rearing of children" (*WN*, 97), lamenting the high mortality rate for indigent children and insisting on an ambitious program of education to stave off the effects of poverty on their minds.

The Social and Political Effects of Economic Inequality

While troubled by the effects of wealth, poverty, and inequality on individuals, Smith is also alert to their larger social effects. Notably, among these is the inability to relate to and sympathize with other classes. This is especially important insofar as some readers of Smith are inclined to believe that inequality's pathologies are mitigated by sympathy. Although it is true that Smith strongly desires that everyone experience mutual sympathy, such feelings are frequently absent in practice. Importantly, however, this deficit in compassion cuts primarily in one direction— downward. The poor are generally sympathetic toward those above them. This is strikingly different from accounts found elsewhere in the history of political thought. Smith is optimistic that all society—certainly including the poor—will admire the wealthy with great sympathy:

> The man of rank and distinction . . . is observed by all the world. Every body is eager to look at him, and to conceive, at least by sympathy, that joy and exultation with which his circumstances naturally inspire him. His actions are the objects of the public care. Scarce a word, scarce a gesture, can fall from him that is altogether neglected. In a great assembly he is the person upon whom all direct their eyes; it is upon him that their passions seem all to wait with expectation, in order to receive that movement and direction which he shall impress upon them; and if his behaviour is not altogether absurd, he has, every moment, an opportunity of interesting mankind, and of rendering himself the object of the observation and fellow-feeling of every body about him. (*TMS*, 64)[27]

This universal admiration of the rich, of course, can explain why the ambitious seek to attain these heights in the first place.

This is no mutual admiration society, however. The poor receive no such sympathy from the wealthy. Rather, they are subjected to indifference or worse. The reasons for this are evident in Smith's treatment of slavery in the *Lectures on Jurisprudence*. He notes there that relations between slaves and masters differ according to the relative wealth of the masters. Masters who possess no great financial wealth and are themselves "farmers" tend to be relatively humane: "The farmer generally works along with his servant; they eat together, and are little different. . . . [He] considers his servant as almost on an equal with himself, and is therefore the more capable of feeling with him" (*LJ*, 184).

By contrast, in more developed societies with wealthier slave owners, the master-slave relationship becomes antagonistic:

> In a rich country the disproportion betwixt them will be prodigious in all these respects. This disproportion will make the rich men much more severe to their slaves than the poorer ones. A man of great fortune, a nobleman, is much farther removed from the condition of his servant than a farmer. . . . The disproportion betwixt them, the condition of the nobleman and his servant, is so great that he will hardly look at him as being of the same kind; he thinks he has little title even to the ordinary enjoyments of life, and feel but little for his misfortunes. (*LJ*, 184)

In radically unequal societies, slaves receive harsher treatment. To illustrate, Smith cites Rome, "where the riches were immense." There "the slaves were treated with the utmost severity, and were put to death on the smallest transgressions" (*LJ*, 183). Inequality desensitizes the upper classes. Significant inequality severs the natural sentiments that foster sympathy.[28] As Smith explains in his *Theory of Moral Sentiments*, "men . . . feel so little for each other, with whom they have no particular connexion, in comparison of what they feel for themselves" (*TMS*, 105). This explains why, for example, the most powerful sentiments are directed toward family, friends, neighbors, colleagues, and the like. We incline to sympathize with those "whom we are obliged to live and converse a great deal with" (*TMS*, 265).[29] Along these lines, if the rich live only among the rich, the poor are not likely to stir much, if any, sympathy: "The mere want of fortune, mere poverty, excites little compassion. Its complaints are too apt to be the objects rather of contempt than of fellow-feeling" (*TMS*, 165). Often physically removed from other classes, the rich struggle to feel much of anything for the poor.

A passage from early in the *Theory of Moral Sentiments* clarifies this difficulty, where Smith notes that the "source of our fellow-feeling for the misery of others" is the ability "to conceive or be affected by what [man] feels." In this context, he observes, "persons of delicate fibers and a weak constitution" are particularly apt to feel sympathy for "the sores and ulcers which are exposed by beggars in the streets" (*TMS*, 14). This reference to a homeless beggar riddled with sores and ulcers recalls the story of Lazarus and Dives discussed in chapter 2 of this book and found in Luke 16:19–31. According to Smith, most naturally feel sympathy for the sore-laden pauper. But Smith's account illuminates why the affluent man is unmoved by flagrant spectacle of desperate poverty—it is because he cannot imagine himself suffering this fate. His wealth distances him from the beggar so that he cannot feel any hint of genuine sympathy.

A powerful example of this failure of sympathy can be found in Alexis de Tocqueville's *Democracy in America*, written several decades after Smith's *Moral Sentiments*. Providing fresh assessments of the relatively egalitarian culture in democratic America, Tocqueville notes that its "equality of conditions" produces a "greater gentleness of mores." He contrasts this gentle American egalitarianism with the aristocratic inequality found in France, where "each caste has its own opinions, feelings, rights, mores, and a whole separate existence." Consequently, he continues, aristocratic people "hardly manage to think of themselves as forming a part of the same humanity" as do the peasant and artisan classes. This breeds a "mutual insensibility" in which neither rich nor poor are capable of experiencing genuine sympathy for the other. The apogee of Tocqueville's discussion is in his reproduction of a letter written by an aristocrat, Madame de Sévigné, at a time when the local government was putting down a tax revolt by the poor. Sévigné describes the drawing and quartering of her poor neighbors as "a good example to the others" and then casually proceeds to note "the delightful weather."[30] This striking absence of Smithian sympathy is facilitated by conditions of extreme inequality. It is for this reason, the philosopher Samuel Fleischacker has suggested, that in order to foster "union and friendship" it is necessary that "our commerce with others needs . . . to be conducted under conditions of equality" and not where "one group dominates and exploits the other."[31]

The very nature of commercial society, Smith suggests, drives citizens apart in just this fashion:

> In commercial countries, where the authority of law is always perfectly sufficient to protect the meanest man in the state, the descendants of the same family, having no such motive for keeping together, naturally separate and disperse, as interest or inclination may direct. They soon cease to be of importance to one another; and, in a few generations, not only lose all care about one another, but all remembrance of their common origin, and of the connection which took place among their ancestors. (TMS, 263)

Distance mutes the beneficial effects of sympathy.[32] This applies not only geographically, but also economically. For Smith, the greater the inequality, the less sympathy; the less sympathy, the more harshness and violence. In the absence of sentiment, one imagines, that becomes the breeding ground for what he describes as an unfortunate desire in human nature to dominate others. He worries about a natural "love of domination and authority and the pleasure men take in having every (thing) done by their express orders" (LJ, 186). Loosening sympathetic bonds facilitates this alarming inclination. Where the wealthy cannot sympathize with the poor, they can dominate them with total disregard for their humanity.

In this vein, as did David Hume before him and James Madison afterward, Smith worries about the possibility of factions. Hume and Madison describe factions as emerging from the gulf between the rich and poor.[33] Although Smith is not quite that specific in attributing factions to economic inequality, this was a common assumption in the eighteenth century. He does not hesitate to observe that bitter divisions between wealthy capitalists and wage laborers can give rise to "shocking violence and outrage" (WN, 84). So it is possible and even likely that violent factions, on Smith's view, sometimes emerge from economic inequality. Given this, inequality poses serious problems for political stability: "The animosity of hostile factions . . . is often still more furious than that of hostile

nations" (*TMS*, 179). The fact that domestic factions are often "more furious" than those accompanying international conflict is serious indeed
since the latter is characterized by relatively casual violence, murder, and
"very little regard to the plainest and most obvious rules of justice" (*TMS*,
178).[34] In this context of a "nation distracted by faction," Smith observes,
"there are . . . always a few, though commonly but a very few, who preserve
their judgment untainted by the general contagion. They seldom amount
to more than, here and there, a solitary individual. . . . All such people are
held in contempt and derision . . . by the furious zealots of both parties"
(*TMS*, 179).[35] The opportunities to cultivate wisdom and virtue in unequal
and divided societies are, it seems, rare; even where isolated citizens overcome those odds, they will become ostracized and ineffectual agents of
social change.

Compounding this rich-poor divide, Smith observes in his *Wealth of
Nations* that the two classes are subjected to very different moral standards.
As he explains,

> in every society where the distinction of ranks has once been completely
> established, there have been always two different schemes or systems of
> morality current at the same time; of which the one may be called the
> strict or austere; the other the liberal, or, if you will, the loose system.
> The former is generally admired and revered by the common people:
> the latter is commonly more esteemed and adopted by what are called
> people of fashion. The degree of disapprobation with which we ought
> to mark the vices of levity, the vices which are apt to arise from great
> prosperity, and from the excess of gaiety and good humour, seems to
> constitute the principal distinction between those two opposite schemes
> or systems. In the liberal or loose system, luxury, wanton and even dis-
> orderly mirth, the pursuit of pleasure to some degree of intemperance,
> the breach of chastity, at least in one of the two sexes, &c. provided they
> are not accompanied with gross indecency, and do not lead to falsehood
> or injustice, are generally treated with a good deal of indulgence, and
> are easily either excused or pardoned altogether. In the austere system,
> on the contrary, those excesses are regarded with the utmost abhorrence
> and detestation. The vices of levity are always ruinous to the common
> people, and a single week's thoughtlessness and dissipation is often
> sufficient to undo a poor workman for ever, and to drive him through
> despair upon committing the most enormous crimes. (*WN*, 794)

For Smith, a regime of economic inequality imposes two very distinct
moral codes. The wealthy are subjected to the "loose" or "liberal" moral

code, which tolerates a vast array of behaviors often casually considered dissolute—the "the vices which are apt to arise from great prosperity." Transgressions of this moral code are largely dismissed with good humor and should not obstruct the transgressors' future success and happiness. The poor, by contrast, are subjected to an "austere" moral code in which the slightest violations are sanctioned with enduring "ruinous" consequences. What is striking in the obvious presence of double standards is how they violate Smith's own impulse toward "general" and "universal" moral rules (*TMS*, 184) and certainly the spirit of his "impartial spectator," who would employ the same rules and sanctions, regardless of class. In other words, it effectively institutes the very definition of Smithian injustice, whereby justice admits of "no exceptions or modifications" (*TMS*, 202) since the moral code operating in societies characterized by "distinction of ranks" applies the same rules differently according to social and economic class.[36] One might add, because for Smith the poor so admire the rich, the wealthy establish broader societal moral standards. The consequence is that while the poor model their behavior on the rich, they are punished like poor people. That is, a poor woman might violate chastity norms, but instead of being forgiven for the transgression, she is severely punished. Hence it is unsurprising that the poor find themselves in greater peril.

Smith's Solutions

As Smith understood the problems emanating from inequality, it is natural that his framework should also promise solutions. The overriding theme characterizing these answers, however, is that they are not solutions so much to the problems stemming from economic inequality as they are addressed to the problems of poverty. As such, even as Smith's understanding of the problems of inequality proves insightful, his suggestions are relatively modest. This is well-known to scholars who have written about Adam Smith and economic inequality. Samuel Fleischacker, for example, confesses that Smith's "positive programs" for alleviating poverty and inequality "seem a bit meager." And political theorist Dennis Rasmussen similarly observes, "it remains far from clear that Smith would approve of the state taking drastic steps to reduce—much less eliminate—economic inequality."[37] They are correct. This is not to say Smith offers readers nothing to address the problem of inequality. But it means that these measures are more modest than found elsewhere in this book.

Smith's primary solution to the problems associated with poverty is the power of the market itself to improve the conditions of everyone in society.[38]

This is undoubtedly one of his most broadly appealing remedies. For the most part, all one needs to do is to let the markets operate. It requires relatively few special governmental interventions. It places no special demands of individuals other than to do what comes naturally—pursuing their relatively unencumbered self-interest. At the end of the day, for Smith, despite his impassioned critiques of economic inequality, as political theorist Ryan Hanley observes, Smith "sides with commercial society," accepting its inequalities "on the grounds that poverty is a problem both more pressing and more capable of human alleviation than inequality."[39]

Smith outlines this solution in the introduction to his *Wealth of Nations*, where he compares "savage nations of hunters and fishers" with commercial societies. Nations of the former type require labor from all physically capable residents, but all

> are so miserably poor, that from mere want, they are frequently reduced, or, at least think themselves reduced, to the necessity sometimes of directly destroying, and sometimes of abandoning their infants, their old people, and those afflicted with lingering diseases, to perish with hunger, or to be devoured by wild beasts. (*WN*, 10)

By contrast, in "civilized" or "thriving" nations,

> though a great number of people do not labour at all, many of whom consume the produce of ten times, frequently of a hundred times more labour than the greater part of those who work; yet the produce of the whole labour of the society is so great, that all are often abundantly supplied, and a workman, even of the lowest and poorest order, if he is frugal and industrious, may enjoy a greater share of the necessities and conveniences of life than it is possible for any savage nation to acquire. (*WN*, 10)

"Savage" societies are frequently on the verge of starvation. Everyone is poor. The earliest societies of hunters "admit of no . . . inequality. Universal poverty establishes their universal equality" (*WN*, 713). Commercial society, by contrast, generates abundant wealth such that no one must starve. The great innovation and benefit of market society is its remarkable productivity. No infants should have to be abandoned. The aged can be supported. Expanding on Smith's arguments, one can observe that in commercial society today the American poor, for example, typically have access to cleaner water, better health care, superior nutrition, larger libraries, and more remarkable technologies than could have been conceived by the wealthiest members of any precommercial society.

One would have to be insensitive to the suffering and desperation of absolute poverty to be unsympathetic to Smith's argument. As many have noted,[40] Smith was genuinely concerned about the plight of poverty, and the market has proven to be useful in alleviating many of the concerns that plagued precommercial societies. The problem, however, is that it merely addresses poverty. It largely ignores inequality. And even though poverty and inequality are often linked, they are also importantly distinct. In this essential respect, then, Smith's appeal to the advantages of the market fails to address many of the problems he associated with inequality. The fact that the relatively poor—so long as they coexist in the same society inhabited with the fabulously wealthy—might have clean water, adequate food, and a roof over their heads does not in any substantial way resolve the social, moral, and psychic problems of inequality. Distinctions of rank and wealth thrive under conditions of economic inequality, along with pride, vanity, shame, injustice, class tensions, inadequate sympathy for the poor, and the lust for domination.[41] These problems are distinct from absolute poverty. They rather all stem from inequality. As such, the productivity of commercial society does not resolve the problems of inequality. If anything, insofar as commercial society expands the distance between rich and poor, it exacerbates them. The more advanced the economy and the greater the wealth, Smith notes, the greater the inequality (WN, 709-10).

A second possible Smithian solution to the problems associated with inequality can be located in his appeal to virtue. This is the view of Ryan Hanley, who has explored and revealed Smith's intentions in part 6 of the Moral Sentiments, "On the Character of Virtue." He argues that Smith added this section of his treatise in later editions precisely to address the problems introduced by commercial society. The Scottish philosopher characterizes the "wise and virtuous man" in terms that would indeed temper many of the worst moral and social problems resulting from economic inequality: he "is at all times willing that his own private interest should be sacrificed to the public interest of his own particular order or society" (TMS, 277). Smith elsewhere clarifies the importance of the conscience: "It is from him [the impartial spectator] only that we learn the real littleness of ourselves, and of whatever relates to ourselves, and the natural misrepresentations of self-love can be corrected only by the eye of this impartial spectator" (TMS, 159). If this disposition could be broadly cultivated, it would surely curb tendencies toward selfishness, pride, and domination. And if it could be nurtured in the context of commercial society, one could seemingly have it all—both the alluring wealth of market society and the social harmony of the virtuous.

Hanley confesses, however, that it is unclear this call to virtue effectively resolves the problems associated with inequality. "Is Smith's normative remedy capable of delivering the relief it promises?" he asks. "On the most obvious level, the answer has to be no."[42] Although genuine wisdom and virtue would surely curb some of the effects of economic inequality, just how would they come about? The cultivation of wisdom and virtue, among other things, presumably requires a degree of time, intelligence, resources, and conscious effort. In a commercial economy that relies heavily on the division of labor, however, these precious resources appear out of the reach for most. As suggested earlier, the division of labor denies the laboring class precisely these resources: "He [the wage laborer] naturally loses . . . the habit of such [mental] exertion, and generally becomes as stupid and ignorant as it is possible for a human creature to become. The torpor of his mind renders him not only incapable of relishing or bearing a part in any rational conversation, but of conceiving any generous, noble, or tender sentiment, and consequently of forming any just judgment concerning many even of the ordinary duties of private life" (WN, 782). These are not the qualities Smith associates with the cultivation of virtue. They almost fundamentally exclude their acquisition.

Wealthy classes, by contrast, would seem to have the resources for developing virtue. Anyone wealthy enough to forgo working for years would have abundant time to dedicate to the pursuit of wisdom and virtue. The problem, however, is that there is little incentive to do so. The great springs of human behavior—including self-interest and desire for public adulation—can be readily satisfied without virtue. As Smith observes, the rich are highly regarded *because they are wealthy*. It is possible to be admired for virtue, too, though he insists that this requires a wise and virtuous audience—and this audience is lamentably small:

> Two different models, two different pictures, are held out to us, according to which we may fashion our own character and behaviour; the one more gaudy and glittering in its colouring; the other more correct and more exquisitely beautiful in its outline: the one forcing itself upon the notice of every wandering eye; the other, attracting the attention of scarce any body but the most studious and careful observer. They are the wise and the virtuous chiefly, a select, though, I am afraid, but a small party, who are the real and steady admirers of wisdom and virtue. The great mob of mankind are the admirers and worshippers, and, what may seem more extraordinary, most frequently the disinterested admirers and worshippers, of wealth and greatness. (TMS, 74)[43]

Everyone, by nature, craves praise. We can win praise either through virtuous deeds or great wealth and ostentation. Those residing in wise and virtuous communities can earn public esteem with virtue. For those residing in "fallen" communities, public esteem is won with fortunes and opulence. Smith clarifies in this passage that wise and virtuous communities are rare. So most citizens lack incentive to pursue virtue. This is confirmed in his portrait of the moral rules actually governing the wealthy class. They are held to loose moral standards—much lower than the standards governing the poor: "luxury, wanton, and even disorderly mirth, the pursuit of pleasure to some degree of intemperance, the breach of chastity . . . are generally treated with a good deal of indulgence, and are easily either excused or pardoned altogether" (*WN*, 794). So long as the rules fail to change, there is no incentive to alter behavior.

Potential solutions to improve public morality might be found elsewhere in Smith's work. Foremost among these, he is keen to promote education for the poor, which is necessary to correct for the "gross ignorance and stupidity" that "so frequently benumb[s] the understandings of all the inferior ranks of people." Education promises, among other things, to curb "the delusions of enthusiasm and superstition." Such ambitions seem consistent with a general Enlightenment disposition to diffuse learning among the broad masses to promote greater democratic and meritocratic ends.[44] Yet Smith also insists in his discussion of education that it must promote order and respect for authority and "lawful superiors" and that it renders citizens "less apt to be misled into any wanton or unnecessary opposition to the measures of government" (*WN*, 788). Making a great deal of these passages and related ones, philosopher James A. Harris has argued, for Smith, "the goal of reformed education of the poor turns out to be nothing resembling enlightenment. The goal, rather, is to do better at keeping the poor orderly, respectful, and manageable."[45]

Although an orderly citizenry is necessary in important respects, Smith does not elaborate on how his educational reforms might improve the moral judgment of citizens to inspire broader wisdom and virtue. As such, he is vulnerable to Harris's claim that these amendments are largely aimed at making the poor more docile before the law, without suggesting how they might come to embrace wisdom and virtue—both as a personal guide and as a means by which to evaluate others. Further, without first achieving greater equality and reducing class tensions and faction, Smith suggests that it is difficult indeed to cultivate virtue: "in such situations, the strongest suggestions of humanity must frequently be stifled or neglected;

and every such neglect tends to weaken the principle of humanity" (*TMS*, 176).[46] So even though education can be a part of meaningful changes meant to combat inequality, as one finds in Plato, Hobbes, and Mill, for example, it is unclear whether Smith intends education to work in this same way.

Another recourse to temper the inconveniences of inequality is justice and the law. For Smith, justice is particularly necessary in commercial societies, where most citizens remain strangers to one another, in contrast with "pastoral societies" where everyone is known to one another.[47] Whereas pastoral societies can rely on love and benevolence to a great extent, commercial societies must employ government, laws, and rules since without them, selfishness and domination are free to wreak havoc.

> Society . . . cannot subsist among those who are at all times ready to hurt and injure one another. The moment that injury begins, the moment that mutual resentment and animosity take place, all the bands of it are broke asunder, and the different members of which it consisted are, as it were, dissipated and scattered abroad by the violence and opposition of their discordant affections. If there is any society among robbers and murderers, they must at least, according to the trite observation, abstain from robbing and murdering one another. Beneficence, therefore, is less essential to the existence of society than justice. Society may subsist, though not in the most comfortable state, without beneficence; but the prevalence of injustice must utterly destroy it.

To clarify, he continues, "Justice . . . is the main pillar that upholds the whole edifice. If it is removed, the great, the immense fabric of human society, that fabric which to raise and support seems in this world, if I may say so . . . must in a moment crumble into atoms" (*TMS*, 104). By "justice" Smith means the institution and enforcement of impartial laws,[48] or as Richard Boyd phrases it, "the disinterested application of common rules of title, transfer, and contract to all citizens alike."[49] More broadly understood by the philosopher Patricia Werhane, Smith's justice is the "virtue of impartial social interests," or "what an impartial spectator would deem to be appropriate and fair principles governing social relationships."[50] To be sure, Smith's hope is that the law is ultimately informed by "universally acknowledged" general rules, which represent "the ultimate foundations of what is just and unjust in human conduct" (*TMS*, 184).[51] He understands such a conception of justice to be the antidote to the natural "partial views" and "self-love" given to amplification in commercial society (*TMS*, 185).

Should just laws be enacted, one hopes, the regrettable elements of human nature might be repressed or channeled into more acceptable outlets.

The difficulty with Smith's appeal to justice is his own admission that government, laws, and justice have taken a very different shape. They have been, in reality, almost perfectly partial along class lines—emphatically by origin and design. Smith makes this exceptionally clear in his *Lectures on Jurisprudence* in describing the origins of government and laws in the earliest stages of propertied society. In this period, where

> some have great wealth and others nothing, it is necessary that the arm of society should be continually stretched forth, and permanent laws or regulations made which may ascertain [secure] the property of the rich from the inroads of the poor, who would otherwise continually make encroachments upon it. . . . Laws and government may [thus] be considered . . . in every case as a combination of the rich to oppress the poor, and preserve to themselves the inequality of the goods which would otherwise be soon destroyed by the attacks of the poor, who if not hindered by the government would soon reduce the others to an equality with themselves by open violence. The government and laws hinder the poor from ever acquiring the wealth by violence which they would otherwise exert on the rich; they tell them they must either continue poor or acquire them in the same manner as they have done. (*LJ*, 208)[52]

He elsewhere elaborates, "Civil government, so far as it is instituted for the security of property, is in reality instituted for the defense of the rich against the poor, or of those who have some property against those who have none at all" (*WN*, 715).[53] This oppression of the poor seems to violate his concern that "to hurt in any degree the interest of any one order of citizens, for no other purpose but to promote that of some other, is evidently *contrary to that justice and equality of treatment* which the sovereign owes to all the different orders of his subjects" (*WN*, 654; emphasis added). So although the ideal purpose of justice and the law is to institute impartial laws to govern a commercial society, the reality as Smith understands it, has been to preserve partiality, inequality, and injustice. Further, the very notion that institutionalized justice might be manifested in "oppression" runs contrary to Smith's insistence, in the words of Werhane, "that the laws of justice should protect every person equally from the harms of other persons."[54] Given this, unless accompanied by more ambitious institutional reforms, it is unclear that justice and the law might resolve inequality. Rather, they have traditionally preserved and extended inequality.[55]

To clarify, Smith indicates that hunting societies characterized by little private property and great equality are spared the tensions that necessitate the government and laws required for unequal societies. There may be disputes, of course, between individuals, but they resemble the spats one finds among "schoolboys" and can be resolved "by the interposition of the community" rather than through the institutionalization of laws and sanctions (*LJ*, 208). Serious and sustained conflict only emerges with the property itself, particularly the uneven distribution of property. Unequal property motivates the poor to raid the property of the rich; this, in turn, motivates the rich to establish a government to protect their holdings.

One might plausibly argue that it is easier to create genuinely just laws in democratic governments, as emerged in the years following Smith. Insofar as the laboring poor considerably outnumber the rich, they might easily reject the self-serving laws of the rich and establish rules more amenable to the general good. Yet there are reasons to be circumspect. As has already been mentioned, he doubts the ability of the working poor to reason thoughtfully about much of anything. This is not because they are naturally unintelligent. Quite to the contrary, he insists, "the difference of natural talents in different men is, in reality, much less than we are aware of; and the very different genius which appears to distinguish men of different professions, when grown up to maturity is not upon so many occasions so much the cause, as the effect of the division of labor. The difference between most of the dissimilar characters, between a philosopher and a common street porter, for example, seems to arise not so much from nature, as from habit, custom, and education" (*WN*, 28–29). Smith's observations here echo Hobbes's natural law of natural equality, which was required for peaceful commonwealths.[56]

The Smithian reason that workers are unlikely to become effective advocates for greater equality and better working conditions is instead because of their punishing, mind-numbing work. But the outcome, whether by nature or environment, is equally discouraging. The worker

> becomes stupid and ignorant as it is possible for a human creature to become. The torpor of his mind renders him, not only incapable of relishing or bearing a part in any rational conversation, but of conceiving any generous, noble, or tender sentiment, and consequently of forming any just judgment concerning many even of the ordinary duties of private life. (*WN*, 783)

Even though Smith undoubtedly feels great sympathy for those burdened with the hard work of commercial society, he offers little grounds for optimism regarding their ability to craft just social laws. In the absence of pressure from the poor to make reforms for just laws and given the "natural rapacity of the rich," one wonders where such laws might originate in Smith's system. Perhaps the most obvious source of such legal interventions would be the benevolence of the truly virtuous, whose natural sympathies and robust reason would foster the kinds of laws that would protect workers and offer opportunities to find better lives. But this presumes that they occupy positions of power and influence, which is not always the case. Indeed, the virtuous often shun power and influence precisely because of their corruptive tendencies.

Understanding the limits of earthly justice, Smith employs a further ultimate constraint on human behavior that might ameliorate the effects of economic inequality: divine justice. Insofar as the vices stemming from inequality cannot be controlled through virtue, education, laws, or the material rewards of the market, Smith hopes that contemplation of the hereafter might curb vice, including those vices stemming from economic inequality.[57]

> We are so far from imagining that injustice ought to be punished in this life, merely on account of the order of society, which cannot otherwise be maintained, that Nature teaches us to hope, and religion, we suppose, authorises us to expect, that it will be punished, even in a life to come. Our sense of its ill desert pursues it, if I may say so, even beyond the grave, though the example of its punishment there cannot serve to deter the rest of mankind, who see it not, who know it not, from being guilty of the like practices here. The justice of God, however, we think, still requires, that he should hereafter avenge the injuries of the widow and the fatherless, who are here so often insulted with impunity. In every religion, and in every superstition that the world has ever beheld, accordingly, there has been a Tartarus as well as an Elysium; a place provided for the punishment of the wicked, as well as one for the reward of the just. (*TMS*, 110)

Smith understands that earthly institutions often fail to embody and uphold justice. But where those institutions fail, he imagines, belief in divine sanctions might play some role in restraining the vices that might emerge from inequality. This is a theme to which he repeatedly returns (*TMS*, 154, 189, 195).

To be sure, insofar as citizens believe themselves subject to divine rewards and sanctions, these measures might moderate vice. This is likely why so many others, with otherwise relatively secular philosophies, have found themselves making similar appeals. Plato has his Myth of Er; Cicero has his dream of Scipio; Spinoza has his "universal faith"; Rousseau has his civil religion.[58] Smith's appeal to God's judgment similarly hopes to inspire civic-minded behavior.[59]

An obvious shortcoming with such promises, however, is that they only persuade the faithful. The faithless would be immune.[60] And the great irony in Smith's larger argument for divine justice for a world increasingly embracing commerce is the broad tendency of wealth and material comfort to suppress spiritual beliefs. Nietzsche's declaration of God's "death," after all, only comes late in the nineteenth century, concurrently with the Industrial Revolution and its riches.[61]

In defense of Smith's divine appeal as a means by which vice might be checked in advanced stages of capitalism, one could argue that by virtue of its very inequality, relatively few have attained the fortunes that would make spirituality dispensable. Perhaps the relative poverty of many in commercial societies might inspire them to resist vice. But this is cynical. Anytime the rules—in this case, of divine sanctions—apply to one group and not another, the rule-bound group is at the mercy of the lawless. In this instance, the rich could easily exploit the poor's religious sentiments to extract greater concessions and more wealth. This is, in fact, precisely Marx's criticism of religion. Religion is the "opiate of the masses" insofar as it exposes the laboring poor to their exploitation by the rich. But so conceived, it is also unjust by Smith's own standards—insofar, again, as justice requires that everyone play by the same rules. A "divine justice" that only constrains the poor is no justice at all in human terms.

Beyond divine appeals, there are more practical mechanisms in Smith's approach to taxation that would allow him to moderate inequality. In his discussion of toll roads, for example, Smith describes the "luxury" carriages of the rich that traverse these roads and endorses taxing them at higher rates insofar as "the indolence and vanity of the rich is made to contribute in a very easy manner to the relief of the poor" (WN, 725).[62] Similarly, Smith addresses house rent taxes, where he notes the difficulties faced by the poor in covering their basic expenses. They should be taxed very modestly on their homes. The "luxuries and vanities of life occasion the principal expense of the rich, and a magnificent house embellishes and sets off to the best advantage all the other luxuries and vanities which they possess." Therefore, he concludes, it is only right that rent taxes should fall heaviest on the wealthy since it is "not very unreasonable that the rich should contribute to the public expense, not only in proportion to their revenue, but something more than in that proportion" (*WN*, 842). Philosopher Eric Schliesser is right in calling this a "(mildly) progressive tax policy."[63] Even though this may not approach Rousseau's principle that taxes on the rich could "go up to the full amount that exceeds his necessities" (*PE*, 31), it is nevertheless a measure imposed on the rich to mitigate the most extreme inequalities burdening commercial societies.

Fleischacker and historian Gertrude Himmelfarb also observe that Smith never criticizes Britain's poor laws—a notable absence for a thinker associated with small-government philosophies.[64] This is a potentially significant omission in the *Wealth of Nations* insofar as the program elsewhere received significant criticism on the charge that it robbed the poor of their primary incentives to work.[65] Although John Stuart Mill also deeply sympathized with the poor, even he was ambivalent about the laws, which he feared could exacerbate poverty by incentivizing reproduction among the poor, resulting in a larger labor pool and, hence, downward pressure on wages.[66]

All of these approaches found in Smith suggest a palpable discomfort with economic inequality and some room around the edges for governments to use their limited authority to reduce the chasm between their wealthiest and poorest citizens. As noted earlier in this chapter, Smith was well aware of the dangers inequality posed for human relations and political societies. But there is an underlying ambiguity in Smith that is less prevalent or entirely absent in the thinkers treated elsewhere in this book.[67] Even though he was clearly aware of these dangers, he also saw certain advantages in maintaining a degree of inequality. This ambiguity is on display in his *Lectures on Jurisprudence* in which he insists,

> in the present state of things a man of great fortune is rather of advantage than disadvantage to the state, providing that there is a graduall descent of fortunes betwixt these great ones and others of the least and lowest fortunes.

Smith continues to assert that "this is not the case in England, where we have fortunes gradually descending from 40,000 to 2 or 300" (*LJ*, 196).[68] That is, Smith very much wants there to be rich people but without extreme inequality. How can this happen for the same philosopher who observed "wherever there is great property, there is great inequality. For one very rich man, there must be at least five hundred poor, and the affluence of the few supposes the indigence of the many" (*WN*, 709–10)? It is not entirely clear. But Smith has a possible argument in his defense. For him, the inequality specifically in commercial societies results from economic exchanges that also, to a degree, improved the standing of the poorest citizens. This is likely in contrast with the "great property" argument from the *Lectures on Jurisprudence*, which may presuppose a feudal or at least preindustrial economy. It is easy to see how, in an economy of that kind, that the wealth of one lord presupposes the existence of countless serfs. The economic growth brought about by market economies, by contrast, creates the need for more workers, which stimulates wage increases. As he argues in *Wealth of Nations*, amid economic growth, employers "bid against one another, in order to get them [workers], which sometimes raises both the real and the money price of their labour" (*WN*, 104). The market further incentivizes providing goods at the cheapest possible prices. And it also spurs innovations improving the lives of working people. For Smith, these are considerable benefits— benefits that will continue to lift the circumstances of the poor in every community that embraces the market.

Whether those improvements brought about by the market economy can lift the condition of workers such that there is "a graduall descent of fortunes betwixt these great ones and others of the least and lowest fortunes" is an open question. To be sure, the influential twentieth-century economist Simon Kuznets argued precisely this—that over time, capitalism would reduce inequality. Yet as already observed, the empirical evidence is mixed. And it may well be that Smith's solutions settle on the point that the market reduces poverty better than it solves inequality, as even most of Smith's defenders concede. As Rasmussen has noted, "whereas Rousseau condemns the intrinsic injustice of inequality, Smith concentrates more on providing for the poor."[69] Or as Smith himself acknowledges in his *Lectures on Jurisprudence*, "tho an agrarian law would render all on an equality, which has something very agreeable in it, yet a people who are all on an equality will necessarily be very poor" (*LJ*, 195).[70] Inequality is concerning, for him, to be sure. It is corrosive both morally and politically. Yet the dangers of poverty, it seems, are still more alarming to him. This is largely why he chose to invest greater effort in growing the economy than in addressing what he nevertheless admits are the real burdens of inequality.[71]

Conclusion

Where, then, does Adam Smith fit in the larger tradition of approaches to inequality? First, it is important to note that he, far more than anyone who preceded him, understood the problem of inequality as part of trade-off. One could achieve equality by returning to the hunter-gatherer societies that dominated early human civilization. There was scarcely any property, commerce, or money, so there was little wealth to be distributed unequally. Voltaire once quipped that Rousseau's *Discourse on Inequality* was an effort to restore such a world: "never has so much wit been used to seek to make us into animals; when one reads your work, one is seized with the desire to walk on all fours."[72] We could return to an earlier, more equal, stage of history but at what cost? We could make people more equal. But at the cost of depriving people of food, clothing, housing, medical, and other technological advances, is this really desirable? On this model of thinking, one can acknowledge that the inequality associated with capitalism is problematic and still prefer it to living with the material uncertainties experienced by early generations.

Smith's decision to prioritize economic growth and the material benefits it provides to the poorest citizens parallels Bernard Mandeville's argument for emphasizing economic growth decades earlier: "To such a Height, the very Poor / Liv'd better than the Rich before."[73] Stimulating the economy would create greater social wealth, the benefits of which would redound to the whole community, not just the rich. Everyone would benefit from scientific, technological, and material advances. And there is certainly truth in Mandeville's assertion that Smith, more than anyone, would advance. The economist Deirdre McCloskey has called this "the Great Enrichment":

> Poor people in the United States and other developed countries live better than 18th-century European monarchs. Today, supermarkets and other stores are stocked with an ever-growing variety of goods, lifespans have been extended by decades, and (in the past 40 years alone) billions of people have been lifted from poverty. These are just some of the amazing achievements that have come about as the result of the Great Enrichment, a flowering of opportunity and economic growth unparalleled in human history.[74]

This largely adheres to Mandeville's reasoning, and it is also found in thinkers like Steven Pinker, who has argued that even though inequality may be growing, this development is trivial in comparison to the gains made by unleashing the forces of capitalism and liberalism. Pinker specifically attributes the material gains of the past two centuries to Smith.[75] Both McCloskey and Pinker appear convinced that these gains can be sustained indefinitely by following the same policy of ignoring inequality and promoting economic growth through free markets.

It is difficult to deny the truth of Mandeville's thesis to a point. The pursuit of economic growth through free markets has done exactly what

McCloskey and Pinker have suggested—extended life spans, relieved suffering, provided abundant food, and rendered chores such as doing laundry and washing the dishes far more tolerable. It would seem ungrateful to deny this progress. Yet at the same time, these contemporary thinkers seem less aware than Smith that this progress has involved a trade-off. That is, unlike Smith, who emphasized the real moral, social, and political difficulties associated with inequality, McCloskey and Pinker instead dismiss inequality altogether. Inequality, if anything, is for them a blessing. Whereas, even though Smith prioritizes economic growth and poverty relief, no one can accuse him of embracing inequality as a blessing. It is, at best, a mixed blessing—a trade he makes with full awareness of its limitations and inconveniences.

A natural question in understanding Smith's trade-off of accepting inequality in exchange for economic growth is whether the benefits of growth extend indefinitely or whether they extend only so far, beyond which point the burdens of inequality are no longer compensated for by growth. The final two thinkers addressed in this book take on precisely this question. Both acknowledge Mandeville and Smith's presumption that growth brings valuable benefits that materially improve the human condition. And like Smith, they also worry about inequality. But what separates them from Smith is that they understand the benefits of economic growth to have natural limits. There is a point beyond which the benefits of economic growth no longer compensate for the burdens of inequality. For them, much of Europe had already reached that point by the mid-nineteenth century. Mill declared in his *Principles of Political Economy* that England had already secured the bulk of benefits to be acquired through economic growth: "It is only in the backward countries of the world that increased production is still an important object: in those most advanced, what is economically needed is a better distribution" (*Principles*, 755). For Marx, the economic growth associated with capitalism was a necessary stage of history but one that had already achieved its primary purpose of making socialism and communism possible. For Mill and Marx, Smith's markets had already achieved all the good they possibly could. It was now time to exchange the benefits of growth for those of greater equality.

CHAPTER SIX
John Stuart Mill

"THE WIDENING BREACH"

MUCH OF JOHN STUART MILL'S REPUTATION DERIVES from two works: *On Liberty* (1859) and *Utilitarianism* (1861). The former represents an extended defense of individual liberty, especially the freedoms of speech and of action, in which he articulates the principle that "the sole end for which mankind are warranted, individually or collectively, in interfering with the liberty of action of any of their number, is self-protection" (*Liberty*, 13). The latter presents his meta-ethical principle of utilitarianism—that actions are "right in proportion as they tend to promote happiness; wrong as they tend to produce the reverse" (*Utilitarianism*, 7). Yet there is a largely unknown undercurrent operating in both works—an underlying theme made explicit in other, less celebrated works: the persistent threat of economic inequality. In *On Liberty*, Mill expresses concern about an "ascendant class" that broadly imposes its views of morality on the basis of its "class interests, and its feelings of superiority," sentiments born of "self-interest" (*Liberty*, 10). He elaborates that such has been the case throughout much of history: between the Spartans and the Helots in the ancient world, plantation owners and Black slaves in the Americas, the nobles and the serfs in feudal Europe, and men and women throughout most of recorded history. In all such cases, "the moral feelings of the members of the ascendant class" have been established in law and opinion as the limits to individual liberty.

Mill expresses a related concern in *Utilitarianism* insofar as he attempts to establish a "feeling of unity" in moral communities. "Every step in political improvement," on his account, requires "removing the sources of opposition of interest and leveling of those inequalities of legal privilege between individuals or classes, owing to which there are large portions of mankind or happiness it is still practicable to disregard" (*Utilitarianism*, 33). For Mill, inequalities of opportunity, status, and economic condition tend to erode feelings of sympathy that might otherwise unite citizens and to which they naturally incline.

These concerns about the effects of class and of economic inequality are more suggested than elaborated in Mill's best-known works. But elsewhere he is more explicit. In his "Claims of Labour," he sketches the "rankling sense of injustice, which renders any approximation of feeling between the classes impossible" (Labour, 384). In his *Principles of Political Economy*, he castigates the British economy for having "not held the balance fairly between human beings, but have [rather] heaped impediments upon some, to give advantages to others; they have purposely fostered inequalities, and prevented all from starting fair in the race" (*Principles*, 207). And in his *Chapters on Socialism*, Mill laments that "a few are born to great riches, and the many to a penury, made only more grating by contrast." He equates extreme economic inequality to despotisms and slave societies, in which the wealthy seek to persuade the impoverished that their suffering, like the suffering of slaves and of oppressed victims of tyrants, is a "necessary evil" (*Socialism*, 227).

By his own account in his *Autobiography*, Mill always condemned concentrated wealth, poverty, and economic inequality. Relatively early in his career, he insisted that he was a "radical and democrat," who characterized the rich as guilty of "gross immorality," as those who would leverage their fortunes and power for the "predominance of [their] private over public interests in the State." His democratic inclinations at this stage suggested democratic solutions—that the poor might use universal suffrage to repair the social injustices associated with inequality. Further, he hoped that socialist experiments might emerge among the poor "in order that the higher classes might be made to see that they had more to fear from the poor when uneducated, than when educated" (*Autobiography*, 177–79). At this stage, he entertained socialism largely as a scarecrow with which to threaten the rich into curbing their selfish excesses. Later in his career he again characterizes himself, along with his wife, Harriet Taylor, as committed to "mitigating the inequalities" between rich and poor but now more "decidedly under the general designation of Socialists." But by this time, he was concerned that the social and economic system had also corrupted the working classes with "selfishness and brutality" equivalent to that which had long ago infected the wealthy (*Autobiography*, 239). More ambitious reforms would be required, including a genuine open-mindedness to socialism, as well as measures aimed at diminishing the damaging effects of selfishness bred by inequality.[1]

What emerges from a broad reading of Mill's corpus is that extreme and entrenched economic inequality is among the most disruptive forces in the social and political world. This much he shares with Plato, Jesus, Hobbes, Rousseau, Smith, and Marx. Further, like these others, he thought that something ought to be done about it: "I certainly think it fair and reasonable that the general policy of the State should favour the diffusion rather than the concentration of wealth" ("Income and Property," 569). Yet his solutions to the problems created by inequality are a curious blend of bits and pieces from his predecessors and other innovations relatively new in the nineteenth century. Like Smith, Mill is hopeful that inequality can be managed in a market economy through education and an improvement of public morals. Like Plato, Mill thinks the transition to a better public morality will be slow and gradual. Like Jesus and the Mosaic tradition of Jubilee as well as Hobbes, Mill is open to radical redistribution of private wealth. Like Rousseau, Mill is interested in ways in which this transfer of wealth can be achieved through taxation. But Mill's plan for educational reforms and wealth transfers are original in the details. His designs for the latter hinge significantly on ambitious *estate tax* reforms—and even more ambitiously on a massive one-generation land and wealth transfer. And his blueprints for the former include not only changes in primary and secondary education but also strategies to stimulate thinking outside of school, especially in the context of worker-owned cooperatives. Along the way, I argue that Mill's objections to economic inequality connect to his two most cherished principles: liberty and utility.

Before proceeding to Mill's texts, I would like to note a practice in at least some of the thinkers addressed in this book. I had noted earlier in my Plato chapter that whereas the Athenian philosopher was strikingly egalitarian in the economic realm, he was less so politically. Plato's Socrates in the *Republic* creates a state in which all power is concentrated in the hands of a few rulers, distinguished by their ability to discern abstract truths. When he has the opportunity to engage democracy, he is typically critical. For Plato, economic equality is one thing; political equality is another. Much the same holds in Thomas Hobbes. Although he was deeply concerned about economic inequality, his political preferences are decidedly inegalitarian. While he is willing to entertain democratic societies, he counsels against them, as they are prone to manipulation by skilled orators who can foster divisiveness. He prefers monarchy, or concentrated power in one set of hands, as the best way to preserve the peace.

Even though John Stuart Mill is complex in his feelings about democracy, one can certainly present him as conforming to the pattern established in Plato and furthered in Hobbes—as an egalitarian in economic terms but inegalitarian in political terms. The complexity here concerns Mill's advocacy of both democracy and representative government, on the one hand, but his simultaneous embrace of plural voting in his *Considerations on Representative Government*, on the other hand, in which the best-educated citizens have votes of greater weight than their lesser educated neighbors. In perhaps the most infamous passage from this work, Mill declares, "No one but a fool . . . feels offended by the acknowledgement that there are others whose opinion . . . is entitled to a greater amount of consideration than his" (*Considerations*, 181). Some have suggested that Mill's apparent elitism here reveals a deeper ambiguity about democracy,[2] while others have suggested that these passages must be contextualized as part of generally strong democratic commitments.[3] Since this book is less focused on political equality than economic equality, I note here that although Mill undeniably has elitist strands in his political thought, readers should not be tempted with him, any more so than with Plato or Hobbes, to conclude that he is an economic elitist. Indeed, in the same text where Mill defended his scheme of plural voting, he emphasized the democratic priority to "vote against the monster evil, the overruling influence of oligarchy" (*Considerations*, 211).

Inequality in Victorian Britain

Economic inequality was a defining feature of the larger social, political, and economic landscape of Victorian Britain. In many ways, the disparity characterizing this period carried over from earlier times. As Thomas Piketty has observed, there was a transformative process taking place in the British economy from the eighteenth to twentieth centuries, parallel to similar ones taking place throughout western Europe. This was the transition from ternary to proprietarian societies.[4] Ternary societies were distinguished by their division of power into three segments: the people, the clergy, and the nobles. This structure was firmly established in the Middle Ages, and elements of it extended into the nineteenth century. In 1500, approximately 3–4 percent of the British male population consisted of clerics of various descriptions including fully 2 percent of this population consisting of monks. Nobles constituted 1–2 percent of the British population at the same time. Extending back to the division of Parliament into the Houses of Lords and Commons in the fourteenth century, the House of Lords was constituted by both "lords spiritual" (clerics) and "lords temporal" (nobles). But the decisive moment in early modern British history was Henry VIII's dissolving of the monasteries in 1530, effectively reducing Britain to a two-class society: the nobles and everyone else. All the extensive property holdings of the British clerics would be sold to the nobles, who came to own virtually all of the land.

What was particularly distinctive about the nobles in early modern Britain, according to Piketty, was their relatively small numbers, especially in comparison with other Western countries, such as France or Spain. This had the effect of intensifying wealth concentration in a miniscule ruling class.[5] As Piketty notes, this meant for Britain and other similarly constituted nations at the time "the nobility had succeeded in constituting itself as a modest ownership elite, which held significant amounts of wealth and enjoyed considerable political and economic power."[6] The political power of the nobles was buttressed by the fact that they were now the sole source of members in the House of Lords and that the House of Commons was elected by a modest percentage of the wealthiest aristocrats. Their economic power was political power in the most traditionally oligarchic sense.

As Piketty describes, the landholding class evolved throughout modernity but without any significant losses to its financial and political powers. In the eighteenth and nineteenth centuries, aristocrats gradually began diversifying their portfolios to engage in mercantiles, colonial investments, and industry.[7] Meanwhile, commoners building their fortunes in the emerging market economy were able to convert their wealth into status and power, largely through marrying into aristocratic families. The combined forces of the traditional aristocracy and the emerging merchant fortunes largely excluded the putative third class of ternary societies—the people—from political life well into the nineteenth century. This would only begin to change with the Reform Acts of 1832 and 1867. The former, which would expand the franchise to small landowners, tenant farmers, and shopkeepers, was passed begrudgingly by Parliament only after a similar bill had failed a year earlier, resulting in widespread civil unrest with many buildings set ablaze and several deaths. This reform significantly expanded suffrage, yet still excluded most of the working poor—those who worked for wages and rented their dwellings. The 1867 Reform Law also represented an incremental expansion—now including those who paid rent of £10 or more a year as well as including agricultural landowners.[8]

Already significant by 1780, British inequality grew steadily through the end of the nineteenth century. In 1780, the top 1 percent of the British population owned 60 percent of the nation's financial property. The top

10 percent owned 90 percent. By 1900, the top 1 percent owned 70 percent, and the top 10 percent owned 92 percent of all British property.[9] This inequality endured right up until World War I, when extraordinary circumstances compelled radical policy changes. For the most part, nineteenth-century Britain was, per Eric Hobsbawm, characterized by a "stoic mass of those destined to live all their lives on a bare and uncertain subsistence," on the one hand, and "stream yachts and large racing stables, private trains, massacres of game-birds and opulent country house weekends stretching into weeks," on the other. It was largely defined by "the immensity of the gap between the top and bottom."[10]

For Piketty, this steadily growing inequality characterizing Britain throughout Mill's entire lifetime was buttressed by two important intellectual developments: the "sacralization of private property" and an increasingly influential doctrine of meritocracy.[11] The former was established as a source of certainty and stability in a world increasingly drifting from its old norms, both religious and social. That God would want property to be protected was a doctrine that extended back as far as John Locke, who viewed the purpose of government as protecting people's "Life, Health, Liberty, [and] Possessions." Such is the law of nature, as Locke understood it, and it was grounded in the "Workmanship of one Omnipotent, and infinitely wise Maker."[12] Once established, even in the face of declining religiosity in Europe, the sacralization of private property became increasingly secure as a public philosophy. This doctrine offered, according to Piketty, a "large dose of religious transcendence" to a world that was increasingly materialistic in orientation, filling the void left by the decline of the church.[13] Property rights came to assume a quasi-religious status for Western citizens, independent of religious beliefs and regardless of how unequally it might have been distributed.

Beyond this, not only was the protection of inequality a means of respecting an increasingly postreligious order against the chaos and instability of a world without a powerful church, protecting inequality was a moral obligation in a world where people had presumably earned their fortunes on the basis of their talent and efforts. That is, inequality came to be increasingly justified by the ideology of meritocracy. According to Piketty, "meritocratic discourse generally glorifies the winners in the economic system while stigmatizing the losers for their supposed lack of merit, virtue, and diligence."[14] As noted in chapter 4 of this book, meritocracy exploded in the Enlightenment, as Rousseau artfully described. The Genevan philosopher had arrived in Paris as meritocracy grew ascendent. As he recorded his personal ambitions in the *Confessions*, "Be first, then, in anything at all: I will be sought after; opportunities will present them-selves, and my merit will do the rest" (242). But soon after earning praise for his talents, he would question this very system: "What gives rise to all of these abuses, if not the fatal inequality introduced among men by the distinction of talents and the disparagement of virtues?" (*FD*, 24). While such distinctions, for Rousseau, were initially based on various talents, eventually they will be made exclusively on the basis of wealth, which will become the marker of talent and virtue (*SD*, 183–84). Unequal societies inevitably judge individual merit according to bank accounts. The wealth-ier people are, the greater their perceived talent and merit and, conse-quently, the greater their value *as human beings*.

Meritocracy's growth surely factored in justifying Victorian Britain's inequality. As we will see in chapter 7, Marx had given the matter sig-nificant thought.[15] But this seductive doctrine can also be found in Mill albeit with some ambiguity. Mill argues in *Utilitarianism* that merit was one of the operative factors informing most people's idea of justice. And everything else being equal, he was sympathetic to the idea that those who worked harder than others likely deserved more for their efforts. But at the same time, he was dubious that the unequal distribution of wealth found in his own society even remotely corresponded with merit, efforts, and justice (*Newman*, 444). Inequality in late-modern Britain mostly reflected the respective good or bad luck individuals had in the inheri-tance from their parents. Wealth for Mill did not signal talent; it signaled ancestry. The same was true of the poor. Thus, although the economic elite of his time wanted people to believe that their wealth reflected their great talent, effort, and persistence, for him it was nothing of the sort.

Needless to say, the condition of the working poor and unemployed in Britain throughout Mill's period was wretched, while those at the top of the economic ranks were enjoying unprecedented heights. There is much documentation of this contrast in contemporary accounts, includ-ing in journalist Henry Mayhew's *London Labour and the London Poor* (1850–1862). Mayhew interviewed and documented countless citizens working and residing in the city's poorest segments. He describes the coal-whippers—those who removed coal from ships—as covered in soot from head to toe. They regularly suffered workplace accidents, and when those accidents inevitably occurred, they lacked adequate nutrition and medi-cal treatment, as they typically lost their jobs, their incomes, and their homes. They frequently slipped into alcoholism and depression. The dock workers fared little better. Their incomes were subjected to wild fluctua-tions, depending on available work; and when jobs were unavailable, they fell into lives of petty crime. Mayhew reports that their "stomachs would be deprived of food by the mere chopping of the breeze." Dock workers typically arrived for work shoeless, coatless, and shirtless, stinking of foul odors from lack of bathing. The scene at the docks was one of "squalor and crime, and suffering, as oppress the mind even to a feeling of awe." But what made this worse, for Mayhew, was the juxtaposition of this squalor with the wealth this work generated for their employers.

> The docks of London are to a superficial observer the very focus of metropolitan wealth. The cranes creak with the mass of riches. In the warehouse are stored goods that are as it were ingots of untold gold. Above and below ground you see piles of treasure that the eye cannot compass. The wealth appears as boundless as the very sea it has traversed. The brain aches in an attempt to comprehend the amount of riches before, above, and beneath it. There are acres upon acres of treasure, more than enough, one would fancy, to stay the cravings of the whole world, and yet you have but to visit the hovels grouped round about all this amazing excess of riches to witness the same amazing excess of poverty. If the incomprehensibility of the wealth rises to sublimity, assuredly the want that co-exists with it is equally sublime. Pass from the quay and warehouses to the courts and alleys that surround them, and the mind is as bewildered with the destitution of the one place as it is with the superabundance of the other.[16]

The inequality characterizing London's docks and broader community were, as Piketty and others have demonstrated, typical of the larger inequality in the Victorian economy and society. And it was a disparity with which thinkers like John Stuart Mill and Karl Marx would be intimately acquainted.

Fundamental Principles:
On Liberty *and* Utilitarianism

John Stuart Mill is best known for his *On Liberty*, including its arguments for free speech and freedom of action. He outlines his principles with admirable clarity in chapter 1:

> The object of this essay is to assert one very simple principle, as entitled to govern absolutely the dealings of society with the individual in the way of compulsion and control, whether the means used be physical force in the form of legal penalties, or the moral coercion of public opinion. That

principle is, that the sole end for which mankind are warranted, individually or collectively, in interfering with the liberty of action of any of their number, is self-protection. That the only purpose for which power can be rightfully exercised over any member of a civilized community, against his will, is to prevent harm to others. His own good, either physical or moral, is not a sufficient warrant. . . . Over himself, over his own body and mind, the individual is sovereign. (*Liberty*, 13)

This defense of individual liberty has come to be known as the "harm principle"—that the only justifiable limits to personal liberty are where individual actions threaten to harm others. Insofar as individual actions are self-regarding, people should be free from state and societal interference.

Mill developed the harm principle to protect individuals against two threats. First, governments had in the Victorian age, according to Mill, overstepped their bounds in legislating matters of personal morality— imposing and enforcing standards of behavior, such as Sabbatarian laws, alcohol prohibition, and severe restrictions on divorce. Second, he worries about extralegal but powerful restrictions imposed on personal liberty by "opinion" or "custom," which impose conformity on individual behavior.[17] He points to occasions in which "society is itself the tyrant." As he elaborates, "there needs protection . . . against the tyranny of prevailing opinion and feeling; against the tendency of society to impose, by other means than civil penalties, its own ideas and practices as rules of conduct on those who dissent from them" (*Liberty*, 8). He defends the sanctity of the individual with the goal of cultivating an environment in which "human life . . . becomes rich, diversified, and animating" (*Liberty*, 63). Much of this progress, in the immediate term, is fueled by the experiments of "persons of genius," who must enjoy personal freedom to explore new thoughts, ideas, and lifestyles (*Liberty*, 65).

To be sure, Mill's commitment to the greatest possible personal liberty short of harming others is the late-modern foundation of the ethos of individualism. He celebrates individuals, particularly the "great geniuses," as "the salt of the earth," those who "set the example of more enlightened conduct." He emphasizes that "it is essential that different persons should be allowed to lead different lives." Indeed, insofar as society forecloses this personal space to cultivate and develop one's own personalities and talent, he calls it "despotism" (*Liberty*, 64). Along these lines, he has been criticized for fostering a culture of excessive individualism and selfishness. One nineteenth-century critic quipped, "The social science which starts with

Individuals . . . is based on a radical sophism."[18] Yet Mill was alert to the possibility of such objections when he drafted his essay, noting, "It would be a great misunderstanding of this doctrine to suppose that it is one of self-ish indifference." Indeed, he insists "there is a need of a great increase of disinterested exertion to promote the good of others" (Liberty, 76).

While Mill's principle of liberty is central to his political philosophy, he grounds his entire program on the higher principle of utility: "I regard utility as the ultimate appeal on all ethical questions; but," he continues, "it must be utility in the largest sense, grounded on the permanent interests of man as a progressive being" (Liberty, 14). He did not elaborate much on utility in the remainder of this work, but he would do so shortly thereafter in Utilitarianism. As already noted, utility, for Mill, "holds that actions are right in proportion as they tend to promote happiness; wrong as they tend to produce the opposite." This general statement of utility echoes his godfather, Jeremy Bentham. Yet Mill would develop this principle considerably beyond Bentham's account. Whereas Bentham was largely indifferent to the moral psychology of individual community members, Mill was highly attuned to their states of mind and how that might affect larger utilitarian considerations.

Among Mill's concerns was Bentham's relative indifference to the potentially damaging effects of self-interest. Bentham assumed that humanity was motivated—and only motivated—by "two sovereign masters, pain and pleasure."[19] These sovereign masters, for Bentham, were largely calculations of self-interest—what gives each individual pleasure or pain. As he would subsequently elaborate, "In every human breast . . . self-regarding interest is predominant over social interest; each person's own individual interest over the interests of all other persons taken together."[20] To the extent that calculations of self-interest can motivate people to pursue socially damaging courses of action, it is the state's responsibility to provide disincentives in the form of legal sanctions, hence appealing to individual self-interest to make the socially desirable choice. That is, on the Benthamite logic, bank robbers will be discouraged from robbing banks when the penalties for getting caught are sufficient to deter the robbery. But there is no grander appeal on this scheme to a deeper moral sense of communal bonds.

Bentham's extensive reliance on the cold logic of self-interest never sat well with Mill, who wrote in 1833:

There are, there have been, many human beings, in whom the motives of patriotism or of benevolence have been permanent steady principles of action, superior to any ordinary, and in not a few instances, to any possible, temptations of personal interest. There are, and have been, multitudes, in whom the motive of conscience or moral obligation has been thus paramount. There is nothing in the constitution of human nature to forbid its being so in all mankind. Until it is so, the race will never enjoy one-tenth part of the happiness which our nature is susceptible of. (*Remarks*, 15)

For Mill, Bentham had erred in his presuppositions about human nature. People are capable, and have at many moments in history, of acting on higher motives of patriotism, benevolence, and fellow-feeling. Bentham's mistake was consequential, as it stunted potential aggregate utility. Insofar as citizens only think in selfish terms, they lower—literally 90 percent by Mill's calculations—a community's utility. Those acting on pure selfishness diminish their own capacity for pleasure and happiness, not to mention their neighbors'.

This is why Mill repeatedly appeals in *Utilitarianism* to the need for transcending Bentham's egoism. Among the most-oft quoted excerpts from the essay is his rejection of the base pleasures that Bentham permitted or maybe even celebrated. For Bentham, when it comes to calculating utility, "pushpin is as good as poetry."[21] This was unacceptable to Mill since it undermined both human capacities and ultimately greater utility. This is the context in which he insisted, "It is better to be a human being dissatisfied than a pig satisfied; better to be Socrates dissatisfied than a fool satisfied." To understand Mill's declaration properly, however, one must press further. The reason that there are so many pigs is because their society has permitted or even encouraged them to sink "into indolence and selfishness" (*Utilitarianism*, 10). Contrary to Benthamite orthodoxy, Mill denies that selfishness is natural. He claims, to the contrary, that we have natural "social feelings" and even a fundamental "desire to be in unity with our fellow creatures."[22] As he presses, part of these natural social feelings includes a presumption of equality: "Society between human beings . . . is manifestly impossible on any other footing than the interests of all are to be consulted. Society between equals can only exist on the understanding that the interests of all are to be regarded equally" (*Utilitarianism*, 32). But these social feelings, without nurture and education, amount to very little. They are but a seed of what we might become. To achieve the greatest happiness possible, humanity must overcome its selfishness. Accomplishing this, for Mill, I argue, requires ameliorating inequality.[23]

Mill on the Dangers of Economic Inequality

Those dismissing concerns about inequality often proceed on two grounds. First, some argue that inequality does not actually exist or is at least exaggerated—that the economy is far more equal than "alarmists" suggest.[24] Second, others concede that although inequality exists, it is unproblematic. Neither of these can be said of Mill, who opposes both assertions. Regarding the first, he insisted that inequality is very real. To this extent, his sweeping review of Alexis de Tocqueville gets right to the point:

> The inequalities of property [in Britain] are apparently greater than in any former period of history. Nearly all the land is parcelled out in great estates, among comparatively few families; and it is not the large, but the small properties, which are in process of extinction. A hereditary and titled nobility, more potent by their vast possessions than by their social precedency, are constitutionally and really one of the great powers in the state. To form part of their order is that which every ambitious man aspires to, as the crowning glory of a successful career. The passion for equality of which M. de Tocqueville speaks almost as if it were the great moral lever of modern times, is hardly known in this country even by name. On the contrary, all ranks seem to have a passion for inequality. (*TOA*, II, 163)

He continues:

> Of all countries in a state of progressive commercial civilization, Great Britain is that in which the equalization of conditions has made least progress. The extremes of wealth and poverty are wider apart, and there is a more numerous body of persons at each extreme, than in any other commercial community. . . . Great fortunes are continually accumulated, and seldom redistributed. (*TOA*, II, 193)

For Mill, America's relative egalitarianism in the 1830s is exotic and deeply foreign to Victorians. England was historically unequal, and the underlying political culture at this time merely reaffirmed its inequality. This would, of course, only grow throughout Mill's life. Mill himself surely had no "passion for inequality" but rather a passion for equality, at least when compared to the economic disparities that dominated his world. He clarifies in the introduction to his *Chapters on Socialism* in which his egalitarian concerns are readily apparent.

> Notwithstanding all that has been done, and all that seems likely to be done, in the extension of franchises, a few are born to great riches,

and the many to a penury, made only more grating by contrast. No longer enslaved or made dependent by force of law, the great majority are so by force of poverty; they are still chained to a place, to an occupation, and to conformity with the will of an employer, and debarred by the accident of birth both from the enjoyments, and from the mental and moral advantages, which others inherit without exertion and independently of desert. That this is an evil equal to almost any of those against which mankind have hitherto struggled, the poor are not wrong in believing. (*Socialism*, 227)

There is much to unpack in this excerpt, which will happen in due course. But the immediate point is this: There can be no disputing that whatever advantages Mill might have attributed to market economies, inequality was not one of them. It is a problem with economic, moral, social, and political dimensions. As such, it demands the attention of legislators and reformers. This section sketches out the many reasons why economic inequality concerned Mill.

THE EFFECTS OF INEQUALITY ON THE RICH AND POOR AS INDIVIDUALS

Mill sketches the plight of the poor in his *Chapters on Socialism*, while sympathetically summarizing the socialist critiques of capitalism. He notes that defenders of capitalism argue that although there are indeed poor people, capitalism is the economic system that best enables the poor to rise. Unlike feudalism, it allows "mankind . . . to emerge from indigence" (230). It is not entirely clear whether Mill's imaginary interlocutor here is speaking of individuals or of the poor on the whole. But he seems to be speaking perhaps more of the latter—that a market economy lifts all boats in a high tide. The capitalists suggest, according to Mill, that money in the hands of the rich is what puts bread in the mouths of the poor. Yet he immediately notes that their "daily bread [is] . . . often in insufficient quantity; almost always of inferior quality" (230). Beyond this, even if poor workers under capitalism have bread today, there are no assurances that they will have it tomorrow. There is every chance, rather, that they will come to depend on either the government or on private charity. As such, Mill concludes, "the condition of numbers in civilized Europe, and even in England and France, is more wretched than that of most tribes of savages who are known to us" (230). All in all, as he reports in his *Principles*, there is among the poor a "wretchedness of a precarious subsistence" and a demoralization of those "who have been made reckless by always living from hand to mouth" (*Principles*, 375).

Among the reasons that the poor were suffering was the prevalence of adulterated foods. Sympathetically outlining what he takes to be the legitimate concerns of socialist Victor Prosper Considérant, Mill explains how competition among those in the food industry have incentivized finding the absolute cheapest ways in which to manufacture "food"—this included adulterated "foods," which replaced the natural elements of real food with ingredients like soap and sawdust. The natural market for these foodstuffs were the poor, who sought the cheapest groceries on their very modest budgets. As Mill laments, "the losses imposed on the consumers by the bad quality or the adulteration of goods are incalculable" (*Socialism*, 241).[25]

Beyond dietary concerns, however, he also worried about how poverty creates relationships of dependence. For much of history, according to Mill, dependence has been accepted as normal and even noble. This "theory of dependence," as he calls it, describes a condition in which the poor have their affairs "regulated *for* them, not *by* them." He continues that those embracing this position normatively, as some wealthy citizens have, hold that the poor "should not be required or encouraged to think for themselves, or give their own reflection or forecast an influential voice in the determination of their destiny. It is supposed to be the duty of the higher classes to think for them, and to take responsibility for their lot" (*Principles*, 759). This was standard under feudalism, where wealthy lords assumed responsibility for managing their serfs' affairs, providing room and board and tending to other needs. The serfs, in turn, received no serious education, rarely even learning how to read. Mill is indignant, however, in observing how the rich have failed to fulfill even these minimal duties to the poor: "No times can be pointed out in which the higher classes of this or any other country performed a part even distantly resembling the one assigned to them in this theory" (*Principles*, 760). In practice, the theory of dependence has rendered the working class not only reliant but desperately poor, uneducated, and directionless.[26] An illiterate and overworked laborer, for example, can scarcely notice the adulteration of her food, much less advocate for laws that might protect her from them. She largely depends on the goodwill of the rich to produce reliably healthy food, which as Mill has already suggested is a dubious assumption. Such is the poor's fate in this system of dependence.

Another striking consequence of poverty, for Mill, is its damage to the poor's moral lives. Because the indigent are preoccupied with finding a way to feed themselves, they have insufficient time for cultivation or education. "Education is not compatible with extreme poverty" (*Principles*, 375). Among other things, the poor cannot learn basic moral principles of self-control, particularly when it comes to reproduction.[27] So they thoughtlessly procreate without regard to its Malthusian implications—namely, their prolific reproduction will greatly expand the labor pool. This enlarged labor pool subsequently increases competition for scarce jobs. The increased competition for jobs ultimately suppresses wages. So "because men follow their brute instincts without due consideration" in the absence of education (*Principles*, 370), poverty grows still worse over generations.

Mill also suggests that great poverty compels desperate actions by the poor themselves. "Where there is no poverty, there will be a remarkable freedom from the vices and crimes which are the consequences of it" (*State of Society*, 98). The impoverished are frequently, to his mind, drawn to a life of petty crime. This is true for at least two reasons. First and most obvious, humanity is impelled to satisfy basic needs. If those needs cannot be satisfied through legal means, then the poor will satisfy them through criminal activity. As Mill elaborates elsewhere, "When, indeed, the poor are so poor that they can scarcely be worse off, respect on their part for rights of property which they cannot hope to share, is never safely to be calculated upon" (*TOA*, II, 176). Second, if they are poor because they are unemployed, they will have the time to devise and execute criminal schemes. This is an inconvenience for the rich in obvious ways, but it is also a serious problem for poor thieves when subjected to criminal sanctions.

Although Mill's treatment of the poor is relatively bleak, one might argue that his portrait of the rich is even bleaker. Just as he laments the lack of self-control among the poor, he finds a parallel problem among the rich. This is not so much self-control as regards procreative activities as it is a general characterological problem. It is the problem of *pleonexia*—a term we have seen in many chapters, going all the way back to Plato. Plato's Socrates identified *pleonexia* as the insatiable desire to have more—a desire that he characterized as fundamentally tyrannical. That is, for Socrates, to be in the grips of *pleonexia* is to be ruled by one's own desires, a condition fundamentally at odds with our prospects for true happiness. Mill is familiar with this ancient notion of *pleonexia* and even once spells it in Greek (πλεονεξία) in his *On Liberty*, amid a litany of undesirable character traits. There he speaks of "the desire to engross more than one's share of advantages (the *pleonexia* of the Greeks)" (*Liberty*, 79). But this is scarcely the only place where he cites the problem of *pleonexia*, especially as a problem plaguing the rich. In his "Notes on the Newspapers," Mill likens the rich to spoiled children. "A spoiled child is always dissatisfied. No spoiled child has all that it asks for, and the more [that] is bestowed, the more it is indignant that anything should be withheld. Distressed they are, for they never have so much money as they would like to have." He proceeds to label them as "always needy" (170–71). Subsequently in the same text, he speaks of an oligarchic class for whom its "wants . . . have become unconquerable" and who suffer under "the strongest temptations to find the means of supplying [their desires] at whatever cost" (185). This is especially important for Mill as a utilitarian philosopher since he is committed as a fundamental proposition as a moral thinker that "each person . . . desires his own happiness" (*Utilitarianism*, 35). If individuals, however, are in the grips of unquenchable desires and suffer from related "distress," the condition of *pleonexia* would be irrational and immoral in the strictest sense—namely, the rich conspire against their own happiness. This is why for Mill, "the best state for human nature is that in which . . . no one desires to be richer" (*Principles*, 754).

That the rich often seek more in the false belief that they will achieve greater happiness likely explains why Mill thought inequality—somewhat paradoxically—conspires against even its supposed beneficiaries. For him, "inequalities of wealth . . . have as pernicious an effect on those whom they seem to benefit, as upon those on whom they apparently press hardest" (*French News*, 674). So, from this perspective, it is irrational to be rich.

But irrationality is not in itself the kind of sin that Mill would proscribe according to the harm principle from *On Liberty*. Even though the quixotic pursuit of ever-greater wealth is foolish and self-destructive, *pleonexia* alone cannot be banished. So the question for Mill is how inequality and concentrated wealth might affect—and harm—others. It is only insofar as these conditions harm others that the government would be within its rights to address them.

The Social Effects of Economic Inequality and Concentrated Wealth

THE DANGERS OF SELFISHNESS

Any governmental intervention in the economy and personal lives of its citizens, according to *On Liberty*, requires that the actions under scrutiny harm other citizens or society itself. The relevant question for Mill is, thus, to what degree concentrated wealth and inequality harms them. As is clear from his *Autobiography*, Mill thought this harm was real and substantial:

> I was as much as ever a radical and democrat, for Europe, and especially for England. I thought the predominance of the aristocratic classes, the noble and the rich, in the English Constitution, an evil worth any struggle to get rid of; not on account of taxes, or any such comparatively small inconvenience, but as the great demoralizing agency in the country.[28] Demoralizing, first, because it made the conduct of the government an example of gross public immorality, through the predominance of private over public interests in the State, and the abuse of the powers of legislation for the advantage of classes. Secondly, and in a still greater degree, because the respect of the multitude always attaching itself principally to that which, in the existing state of society, is the chief passport to power; and under English institutions, riches, hereditary or acquired, being the almost exclusive source of political importance; riches, and the signs of riches, were almost the only things really respected, and the life of the people was mainly devoted to the pursuit of them. (*Autobiography*, 137)

There is much to unpack in Mill's assessment of the rich in a radically unequal society. The first problem is that the fabulously rich are exceptionally bad role models. He may be borrowing from Adam Smith, who understood that even the "vices and follies" of the rich are fashionable; "and the greater part of men are proud to imitate and resemble them in the very qualities which dishonor and degrade them" (*TMS*, 76). Mill finds similar depravity among the rich and is equally alarmed that the poor would imitate them to everyone's detriment.

Central to the flawed character Mill attaches to the rich is their tendency to elevate their private interests over public ones. The rich are dangerously selfish—a theme he explores later in the *Autobiography*, where he condemns the "deep rooted selfishness which forms the general character of the existing state of society" (176). But it is in his *Principles* that he elaborates most on selfishness of the wealthy:

> All privileged and powerful classes, as such, have used their power in the interest of their own selfishness, and have indulged their self-importance in despising, and not in lovingly caring for, those who were, in their estimation, degraded, by being under the necessity of working for their benefit. I do not affirm that what has always been must always be, or that human improvement has no tendency to

correct the intensely selfish feelings engendered by power; but though the evil may be lessened, it cannot be eradicated, until the power itself is withdrawn. (*Principles*, 760)

Mill understands the rich to be crudely selfish and almost cartoonishly harsh toward the lower classes. In fact, for him, it is often their willingness to be dangerously selfish that generates their fortunes in the first place. Fortunes, if not inherited, are built on "hard-hearted and close-fisted self-ishness, by the permitted tricks of trade, by gambling speculations, [and] not seldom by downright knavery" (*Socialism*, 232). Acquiring a massive fortune, for Mill, often requires venality. This tendency is not abandoned after acquiring one's fortune. Indeed, it merely transforms into *pleonexia*, which is the most pathological manifestation of selfishness.

Taking seriously the affluent's tendency to extreme selfishness and the poor's instinctive admiration for them as role models reveals much about Mill's concerns. This may confuse some readers, who only know Mill as the champion of individualism. Yet his celebration of individualism is by no means an embrace of uncouth selfishness. It is good to be an individual; it is socially destructive to be selfish. He expressly condemns "selfish indifference" in *On Liberty* (76). In *Utilitarianism*, he emphasizes that "selfishness [is] the principle cause which makes life unsatisfactory" (14). And in his *Considerations*, he similarly reports, "On the average, a person who cares for other people, for his country, or for mankind, is a happier man than one who does not" (137). So when the selfish rich man successfully models this behavior to the rest of society, he spreads misery broadly and conspires with others of his class against societal utility.

Mill contrasts this narrow selfishness with the positive value of fraternity, which, as political theorist Helen McCabe recently noted, "has been mostly ignored in Mill scholarship."[29] McCabe properly identifies fraternity as one of Mill's core moral principles, alongside liberty, equality, security, progress, and utility. For her, this commitment to fraternity was "instrumentally vital" to Mill, insofar as liberty, equality, progress, security, and utility are unattainable without it.[30] Her reading of Mill's commitment to fraternity is absolutely correct and grounded in one of the earliest readings of Mill via James Fitzjames Stephen, who similarly identifies this value as central to Mill's moral and political philosophy.[31] Yet it is worth adding two observations. First, fraternity is difficult to achieve without economic equality. That is, while McCabe rightly notes the instrumental value of fraternity to achieving greater equality, greater equality also fosters greater social harmony. Inequality can be a significant barrier to experiencing sympathetic feelings for fellow citizens. As Aristotle observes, even though there can be friends where economic inequality is modest, it is unlikely when "the separation is too large."[32] Second, this relationship of fraternity to equality persists throughout the history of political thought—most notably, including Plato, Rousseau, and Smith, who understand how economic inequality undermines the kind of moral community that characterizes healthy societies. It was in Plato's *Laws*, after all, where the Athenian Stranger declares the purpose of the laws to be but reconciling citizens "by laying down laws for them for the rest of time and securing their friendship with one another" (627e). The economic gap presents a real barrier to fraternity for Plato's Stranger, which is why he insists on equalizing wealth. For Rousseau, a healthy republic is one in which there are "so many reasons [for citizens] to like one another" and where there is a real prospect of them remaining "forever united." Inequality undermines this affection and unity (*d'Alembert*, 343). He writes in precisely this spirit in the *Social Contract* when he seeks to "bring the extremes as close together as possible." Similarly Smith notes, "The fortunate and the proud wonder at the insolence of human wretchedness, that it should dare to present itself before them, and with the loathsome aspect of its misery presume to disturb the serenity of their happiness" (*TMS*, 64). Whether Mill consciously borrows from Plato, Rousseau, or Smith in this respect, one cannot say. But he certainly resembles them.

Despite Mill's objections to selfishness, self-absorption in isolation cannot be legally prohibited on Mill's framework, or at least not with adults. It is only when selfishness inspires harmful acts against others that those acts can be outlawed. His legislative restriction, however, carries an important caveat. As Mill insists in *On Liberty*, society has "the whole period of nonage in which to try" to make children "capable of rational conduct in life" (82). And this is specifically why Mill's solution to the problem of selfishness is to be found in education.

CLASS LEGISLATION

Once selfishness takes root, it frequently manifests in what Mill calls "class legislation." Indeed, he alludes to this connection in the excerpted paragraph above from his *Autobiography* when he speaks of "the abuse of the powers of legislation for the advantage of classes" as one of the dangerous tendencies of the financial elite (137). But whereas it is a passing concern in his *Autobiography*, it becomes a dominant concern in his *Considerations on Representative Government*. Once selfishness takes root, according to the latter text, it has undeniable effects on legislation. This is because

> a selfish man will prefer even a trifling individual benefit, above his share of the advantage which his country would derive from a good law; because interests peculiar to himself are those which the habits of his mind both dispose him to dwell on, and make him best able to estimate. (218)

This is the very definition of the behavior that concerns Mill in the excerpted passage from his *Autobiography*—placing one's own private interests, even when "trifling," over the public interest. He explains,

> The moment a man, or a class of men, find themselves with power in their hands, the man's individual interest, or the class's separate interest, acquires an entirely new degree of importance in their eyes. Finding themselves worshiped by others, they become worshippers of themselves, and think themselves entitled to be counted at a hundred times the value of other people; while the facility they acquire of doing as they like without regard to consequences, insensibly weakens the habits which make men look forward even to such consequences as affect themselves. (*Considerations*, 137–38)

This selfishness, if allowed to persist, ultimately becomes a dominant legislative force, especially in democratic governments.

> One of the greatest dangers . . . of democracy, as of all other forms of government, lies in the sinister interest of the holders of power: it is the danger of class legislation, of government intended for . . . the immediate benefit of the dominant class, to the last detriment of the whole. (*Considerations*, 141)

This danger of class legislation recurs throughout the *Considerations* (e.g., 66, 122, 134, 141–43, 166, 170, 185, 216, 235, 248).[33] But it is not limited to this text. As he notes early in his *Principles*, "The greatest part of the utility of wealth, beyond a very moderate quantity, is not the indulgences it procures, but the reserved power which its possessor holds in his hands of attaining powers generally" (6). For Mill, money is power, and the most efficient way to exercise that power is to influence or shape legislation. As he subsequently elaborates, the wealthy "have used their power in the interest of their own selfishness" (760).[34] But perhaps his most dramatic account of this phenomenon comes in his *Condition of Ireland*, where he describes the plight of Irish governance after sustained oligarchic control:

> The root of this is deeply seated in the inveterate habits which were generated by a century and a half of oligarchical government, and which we have scarcely yet begun to shake off. To do anything for the poor by act of Parliament is a thing so unprecedented that it never presents itself in the light of a possibility. The machinery of legislation never suggests itself as an available means for such a purpose. When it is to make the rich richer, yes; that is an approved and a customary course: any project which assumes that form has a presumption in its favour. But to make the poor less poor, by exactly the same means, is a novelty to startle people. There have been in England plenty of inclosure bills, plenty of waste land brought under culture, and who ever heard of giving any of it to the poor? So far from it, that only after long struggles has the principle been conceded (and a most transcendent stretch of generosity was the concession thought), that compensation ought to be made to the poor for what they actually lose, the whole of the gain still going, as it has always gone, to swell the estates of the rich. (903)

As he further elaborates in his *Rationale of Representation*:

> In every country where there are rich and poor, the administration of public affairs would, even under the most democratic constitution, be mainly in the hands of the rich; as has been the case in all the republics of the old world, ancient and modern. (26)

The rich seize the mechanisms of government and then pursue a legislative agenda of enlarging their own fortunes at the expense of the poor. Henceforth, it is almost taken for granted that it is the business of legislation to protect the interests of its wealthiest citizens.

Mill concedes that if the poor were ever to take power from the rich, they might use their authority similarly—namely, punishing the rich mercilessly for their own benefit.[35] But this is only because they have learned their morals from the debased wealthy class. The rich are the "demoralizing agency," on his account, insofar as they model selfishness for everyone else. The poor learn their selfishness from the rich, according to Mill. So if and when tables should turn, the indigent would be as ruthlessly selfish as those they would have toppled.

INEQUALITY AND INJUSTICE

Inequality is problematic for Mill because it is a source of injustice. The closest he comes to defining justice is in chapter 5 of *Utilitarianism*, where he outlines the "various modes of action and arrangements of human affairs, which are classed, by universal or widely spread opinion, as just or unjust" (*Utilitarianism*, 43). He lists six such categories that spark people's sense of justice or injustice: (1) deprivations of liberty, (2) the enforcement of bad laws, (3) desert/merit, (4) breaking faith, (5) impartiality, and (6) equality. Several of these are threatened by significant economic inequality. Perhaps the most obvious one is desert or merit. He describes this as "the clearest and most emphatic form in which the idea of justice is conceived by the general mind," and he defines it thus: "a person is understood to deserve good if he does right, evil if he does wrong" (*Utilitarianism*, 45). Although he elaborates little on this mode of justice in *Utilitarianism*, he does so more extensively elsewhere, particularly regarding inequality. It is in this context that I return to the previously cited passage from his *Chapters on Socialism*:

> Notwithstanding all that has been done, and all that seems likely to be done, in the extension of franchises, a few are born to great riches, and the many to a penury, made only more grating by contrast. No longer enslaved or made dependent by force of law, the great majority are so by force of poverty; they are still chained to a place, to an occupation, and to conformity with the will of an employer, and debarred by the accident of birth both from the enjoyments, and from the mental and moral advantages, which others inherit without exertion and independently of desert. That this is an evil equal to almost any of those against which mankind have hitherto struggled, the poor are not wrong in believing. (227)

In describing inequality, Mill emphasizes its injustice. He stresses the main source of poverty is neither laziness nor a lack of intelligence but rather the "accident of birth"—that the poor do not deserve their poverty. Their destitution stems from the misfortune of having poor parents. And similarly, the affluent are rich not because of their extraordinary efforts and talents but rather because of their good fortune in parents. Inequality—combined with the practice of inheritance—is for Mill an engine of injustice in this sense. People are neither rewarded nor punished for their own virtues or vices. They are rewarded or punished for their ancestors' actions. And that should offend our sense of justice. Mill is even more explicit about the injustice of this arrangement of human affairs in "Newman's Political Economy":

> The distinction between rich and poor, so slightly connected as it is with merit and demerit, or even with exertion and want of exertion in the individual, *is obviously unjust*; such a feature could not be put into the rudest imaginings of a perfectly just state of society. (444; emphasis added)

Mill also condemns inequality by the "accident of birth" as offending an "acknowledged principle of justice" in his *Autobiography* (175). This is more than sufficient to demonstrate that great economic disparities—where sustained and extended by generations of inheritance—are deeply unjust by his standards.

But economic inequality offends more than Mill's principle of merit or desert. A second dimension in which inequality might upset justice concerns impartiality. For Mill, "it is, by universal admission, inconsistent with justice to be *partial*—to show favor or preference to one person over another in matters to which favor and preference do not properly apply" (*Utilitarianism*, 45; emphasis original). If it is, then, unjust to favor one person unduly over another, it is likewise unjust for institutions to favor one class over another. And this, of course, is the essence of class legislation. As already discussed, it is the tendency of institutions to favor the wealthy in its legislation. It is in this respect that Mill condemns the tendency of the "ruling class" to pursue "an endless variety of *unjust* privileges, sometimes benefitting their pockets at the expense of the people, sometimes merely tending to exalt them[selves] above others" (*Considerations*, 131–32; emphasis added). So class legislation, a nearly inevitable result of inequality, is by its very nature unjust.

A further respect in which economic inequality upsets Mill's understanding of justice regards *equality itself*,[36] although this is not as obvious as it first seems from the term "equality." This is because "equality," according to Mill, is applied in myriad ways and often means different things to different people. Yet he emphasizes that some notion of equality lurks in almost everyone's notion of justice. So what is equality? Its essence, for Mill, ultimately returns to the principle of utility itself.

> The equal claim of everybody to happiness, in the estimation of the moralist and of the legislator, involves an equal claim to all the means of happiness except in so far as the inevitable conditions of human life

and the general interest in which that of every individual is included set limits to the maxim. . . . But in whatever case it is deemed applicable at all, it is held to be the dictate of justice. All persons are deemed to have a *right* to equality of treatment, except when some recognized social expediency requires the reverse. And hence all social inequalities which have ceased to be considered expedient assume the character, not of simple inexpediency, but of injustice. (*Utilitarianism*, 62–63; emphasis original).

Most immediately, perhaps, Mill might have in mind social inequalities like sexism, which had been broadly assumed to be expedient. Unquestionably, he viewed these imbalances as unjust. But it is likely that he would have regarded radical economic inequalities to fall into the same category of a "social inequality" that was largely regarded as expedient. This, too, would be unjust.

It is easy to understand why he would have considered economic inequality problematic in this regard. This is because, following Rousseau and Smith, laws in economically imbalanced societies have historically favored the rich. In his essay *Ireland*, Mill approvingly quotes the Irish lord chancellor Redesdale, who castigated the Irish legal system as having "one law for the rich, and another for the poor" (*Ireland*, 71). Whereas some contemporaries criticized the chancellor for exciting animosities, Mill praises him for having the courage to "expose abuses" (*Ireland*, 72). Along these lines, he relates a story about a "certain Major Pitman," a magistrate from Devon County. Pitman reportedly "beat and kick[ed] his female servants to any pitch, short of danger to life and limb" and insulted them "with any degree of contumely." These abuses were horrific. Yet the courts dismissed these charges as not being "*of sufficient importance*" to merit prosecution. Mill posits, however, that had the same abuses been committed by a poor man, the courts would have certainly "inveigh[ed] against the insubordination and against the immorality of the poor." And when some speculated at the time that perhaps Major Pitman might lose his magistracy appointment, Mill incredulously asks, "Who ever heard of a magistrate dismissed for oppressing the poor, or tyrannizing over the weak?" ("Notes," 267).

Mill, in fact, had long harbored such concerns about equal treatment under the law. In his "Blessings of Equal Justice," he observed that Britain was particularly proud of its reputation of a legal system that was alone in the world as "pure and undefiled; that it gives ear alike to the rich and to the poor." Yet he found in practice that this was a lie.[37] He asks his readers to imagine a case, not unlike the case of Major Pitman, in which a rich man had harmed a poor woman. In such a case,

> it is only a rich man, it is only a member of the aristocracy, whose word is to be taken as conclusive evidence in his own cause. Thus then, whenever a rich individual and a poor one contradict each other on a matter of fact, the poor man is to be disbelieved, and the rich man suffered to carry off (perhaps) the wages of mendacity. And, to crown all, this inequity is to be covered with the veil of secrecy. ("Blessings," 44–45)

For Mill, in unequal societies, the laws and the decisions of judges will always favor the rich and powerful—a fact he describes repeatedly here as "injustice." This is an injustice at least twice over by utilitarian standards. Not only is it an injustice in violation of equal treatment; it is also a violation of impartiality. There is no good reason, for Mill, why the rich should be favored over the poor in legislation, much less in judicial decisions.

For Mill, unequal societies impose radically different moral and legal standards on the rich compared to the poor. Doing so violates his principle of equality as justice: that "all persons are deemed to have a *right* to equality of treatment." Given the radically different ways in which rich and poor are treated, this would constitute the very essence of inequality of treatment and, hence, injustice.

There is a final respect in which economic inequality, in the form of desperate poverty for some, threatens this equality of treatment dimension of justice insofar as it "involves an equal claim to all the means of happiness." Surely, for Mill, part of what it means to be happy is to satisfy basic needs. As he insists in his "Notes on the Newspapers," "poor laws are required by the plainest dictates of justice; since it is monstrous that human creatures, who exercised no choice in being born, should be starved for the fault of their progenitors. There is food enough on the earth for all." For this reason, Mill requires that "society may guarantee a subsistence to every one of its members" (266) since the famished cannot be happy on anyone's construction. An equal claim to happiness surely requires adequate provisions to all, where those supplies are sufficiently abundant.

This clarifies Mill's occasional sympathies for Rousseau. When Rousseau describes the appropriation of land, wealth, and resources by a small class of citizens and their subsequent efforts to establish a system meant to defend these resources against all others, Mill concedes that this argument has "satisfied [the] highest conceptions of justice and moral right, and [it] has the 'note' of intuitive truth." Mill's sympathy for Rousseau's arguments here undoubtedly rests at least partly on the fact that Rousseau was railing against the inequalities established in this process—because disparities are themselves, on his reasoning, inherently unjust. Thus, he presses further, "If there be in the natural constitution of things something patently unjust . . . do not these sentiments [of justice] impose on us the duty of striving, by all human means, to correct the injustice?" (*Thornton*, 651, 652). Inequality is frequently unjust, and injustice demands correction.

INEQUALITY AND THE PROBLEM OF SOCIAL TENSION

I have drawn attention to Mill's emphasis on social harmony. While he articulates a conception of humankind's natural "desire to be in unity with our fellow creatures" in *Utilitarianism*, he elaborates thoughtfully in his essay on *Coleridge*:

> The third essential condition of stability in political society, is a strong and active principle of cohesion among the members of the same community or states.[38] We need scarcely say that we do not mean nationality in the vulgar sense of the term; a senseless antipathy to foreigners; an indifference to the general welfare of the human race, or an unjust preference of the supposed interests of our own country; a cherishing of bad peculiarities because they are national; or a refusal to adopt what has been found good by other countries. We mean a principle of sympathy, not of hostility; of union, not of separation. We mean a feeling of common interest among those who live under the same government, and are contained within the same natural or historical boundaries. We mean, that one part of the community do not consider themselves as foreigners with regard to another part; that they set a value on their connexion; feel that they are one people, that their lot is cast together, that evil to any of their fellow-countrymen is evil to themselves; and do not desire selfishly to free themselves from their share of any common inconvenience by severing the connexion. (*Coleridge*, 134–35)

Stable, happy, and thriving political societies need citizens who enjoy mutual sympathy—they have common interests and understand that the common good takes precedence over self-interest. As Mill expressed in his *Autobiography*, thriving communities require that people consult the public good and not their individual self-concern.

As a thriving community is a cohesive community, for Mill, a troubled community is a divisive one. There is abundant evidence throughout his texts that such tensions commonly characterize radically unequal societies. This is clear as early as his essay "The Claims of Labour" in which he describes a society failing in this regard, where there is "no social or even physical welfare for the poor, where there is no relation between them and the rich except the payment of wages, and (we may add) the receipt of charity; no sense of co-operation and common interests between those associates who are now called the employers and the employed." Of course, the discussion thus far touches only the surface for Mill since it does not depict two classes as necessarily hostile but merely as lacking a common interest. But often in unequal societies the antipathy between the classes transcends mere indifference, becoming outright adversarial. As he elaborates later in the same paragraph, in the absence of shared interests, unequal societies commonly pit the classes against one another in "concealed enmity . . . [and] that *soured* animosity which is universal in this country towards the whole class of employers, in the class of the employed" (379; emphasis original).

Mill develops this theme in his *Principles*. Where inequality persists, the "rich regard the poor as, by a kind of natural law, their servants and dependents." The poor, in turn, regard their wealthy neighbors as "mere prey and pasture." Neither rich nor poor have anything resembling fellow-feeling across classes. Further, their relations are characterized, according to Mill, by the "total absence of regard for justice or fairness." So long as extreme inequality persists, it "will sooner or later become insupportable to the employing classes, to live in close and hourly contact with persons whose interests and feelings are in hostility to them" (*Principles*, 767). He further addresses the injustice in these relations in his "Claims of Labour," where the workers' inflamed sense of injustice fosters their hatred of their employers:

> Can they wonder that the people say—Instead of doling out to us a small fragment of what is rightfully our own, why do you not disgorge your *unjust* gains? One of the *evils* of the matter is, that the gains are so enormously exaggerated. Those who have studied the question know that the landlords gain very little by the Corn-Laws; and would soon have even that little restored to them by the indirect consequences of the abrogation. The rankling sense of *gross injustice*, which renders any approximation of feeling between the classes impossible while even the remembrance of it lasts, is inflicted for a quite insignificant pecuniary advantage. ("Claims of Labour," 383–84; emphases added)

Mill describes a subconscious utility calculation on behalf of the poor, who marvel at the scale of injustice their rich employers are willing to commit for the purpose of an "insignificant pecuniary advantage." The rich, to their minds, do not enjoy an appreciably better life with the money that they could be paying their workers. But they nevertheless hoard the money despite the fact that their employees would doubtless gain far greater pleasure from the same money, as a would-be utility monster, to borrow from Robert Nozick.[39] The lingering sense of injustice resulting from this "widening breach" between workers and their employees excludes the "fellow feeling and community of interest" found in thriving societies ("Claims of Labour," 382, 379).

Mill Addressing Inequality

Given that inequality inhibits or offends justice, utility, and general social flourishing, there can be no doubt that equality is a high priority for Mill. But it is always best to hear from the horse's mouth:

> In proportion to our distrust of the means which Socialists propose for correcting the unjust inequalities in the lot of mankind, do we deem it incumbent on philosophers and politicians to use their utmost endeavours for bringing about the same end by an adaptation of the existing machinery of society. We hold . . . that equality, though not the sole end, is one of the ends of good social arrangements; and that a system of institutions which does not make the scale turn in favour of equality, whenever this can be done without impairing the security of the property which is the product and reward of personal exertion, is essentially a bad government—a government for the few, to the injury of the many.
> (*Vindication*, 354)

Equality is indisputably important for Mill, though must be balanced with other values, including liberty, utility, and fraternity. It is likewise notable that he insists that something *can* be done to address it. Radical economic inequality is not a law of nature, akin to the other economic laws, such as the laws of production, trade, and the like. For him, the distribution of wealth reflects various causes, and those causes are largely up to societies to alter as they choose. Indeed, this point is important enough to Mill that the "preliminary remarks" from his *Principles* concludes with the following paragraph:

> Unlike the laws of Production, those of Distribution are partly of human institution: since the manner in which wealth is distributed in any given society depends on the statutes or usages therein obtaining.

But though governments or nations have the power of deciding what institutions shall exist, they cannot arbitrarily determine how those institutions shall work. The conditions on which the power they possess over the distribution of wealth is dependent, and the manner in which the distribution is effected by the various modes of conduct which society may think fit to adopt, are as much a subject for scientific inquiry as any of the physical laws of nature. (*Principles*, 21)[40]

So although the ways in which societies produce wealth might be constrained by economic laws akin to the laws of nature, the manners in which they distribute their resources are open to the free choice of those societies themselves. Societies only distribute wealth in radically unequal fashion because they have so chosen, either explicitly or tacitly. But they are also free to choose more egalitarian distributions.

This background assumption is essential in understanding the powerful introduction to Mill's *Chapters on Socialism*. There he emphasizes the growing suffrage of the British working class. This process, he notes, was already under way in other nations at this time, citing "the great country beyond the Atlantic," namely the United States. And even though it denied suffrage to large classes of citizens, such as women and slaves, it did tend to grant suffrage early on to most others. France enacted similar laws by 1848, as did many states of the German confederation. As Tocqueville observed in his *Democracy in America* in 1835, "a great democratic revolution is taking place in our midst."[41] Formerly aristocratic Europe was slowly becoming more American.

In Britain, the progress toward greater suffrage was progressing in fits and starts. Mill cites the Reform Acts of 1832 and 1867. The former was passed begrudgingly by Parliament only after a similar bill had failed a year earlier, resulting in riots and civil unrest throughout the country, with many buildings set on fire and at least twelve recorded deaths. The 1832 law would expand the franchise to small landowners, tenant farmers, and shopkeepers. It represented a significant expansion of suffrage, yet it also excluded most of the working poor—those who worked for wages and rented their dwellings. The 1867 Reform Law extended an incremental expansion—enfranchising those who paid rent of £10 or more a year as well as agricultural landowners. There would be two further Reform Acts in 1884 and 1918, with universal male suffrage only arriving by 1918. (Female suffrage would follow in 1928.)

Why did the suffrage movement matter to Mill? Because Tocqueville's message resonated with him—democracy was inevitably coming. And

Britain had to prepare for its effects. The most obvious of these was that the working poor were going to use their growing political power to address the imbalances of the British economy, as was their right, because contrary to elite opinion, "they have in reality the greatest stake [in politics], since their daily bread depends on" it (*Socialism*, 222). Among the most pressing matters for the working class at this time, according to Mill, were "inequalities of property." This inequality was significant in 1869 and still growing. The working class understood this much. Mill's sense was that as laborers acquired a greater political voice, they would pressure institutions to reduce inequality. This is all possible on Mill's presumption in the *Principles* that wealth distribution depends on legislative decisions. So long as the working poor have significant influence over these matters, they will press for greater equality.

If greater equality was inevitable, then, one of the key questions before Mill is what form it should take. How should the people use their growing power to promote equality? He considers multiple paths to greater equality outlined below. Broadly speaking, as with Plato and Rousseau, he entertained a wide range of avenues to greater equality—from relatively moderate ones working within the context of a commercial economy to more radical options bordering on socialism.

Before exploring Mill's strategies for addressing inequality, it is important to note one way in which he did *not* think it could be solved—namely, via individual works of charity or benevolence. Although he does not oppose acts of charity and thinks they are morally praiseworthy, by no means can anyone expect all the problems of inequality to be solved through them. As he insists in his "Claims of Labour":

> Justice is the one needful thing rather than kindness. We may at least say that kindness will be little appreciated, will have very little of the effect of kindness upon the objects of it, so long as injustice, or what they cannot but deem to be injustice, is preserved in. Apply this to several of the laws maintained by our legislature. Apply it, for example, to the Corn-Laws. Will the poor thank you for giving them money in alms; for subscribing to build baths and lay out parks for them, or, as Lord John Manners proposes, playing at cricket with them, if you are at the same time taxing their bread to swell your rents? We could understand persons who said—the people will not be better off whatever we do, and why should we sacrifice our rents or open our purses for so meagre a result. But we cannot understand men who give alms with one hand, and take away the bread of the labourer with the other. Can

they wonder that the people say—Instead of doling out to us a small fragment of what is rightfully our own, why do you not disgorge your unjust gains? One of the evils of the matter is, that the gains are so enormously exaggerated. ("Claims of Labour," 383)

In societies characterized by pervasive inequality and injustice, like the society Mill inhabited, it was not enough simply to engage in individual acts of charity, benevolence, or kindness. That on its own merely sustains the underlying injustices and inequalities. What is required, for Mill, are reforms promoting justice and equality.

Mill's Paths to Equality

Mill's paths to equality are characterized by his willingness to explore solutions within the system of private property and a commercial economy. But while he was more than willing to consider, at some stage, working with a system of private property, he did not want it remotely to resemble the Victorian economy. Indeed, so far as he was concerned, "the principle of private property has never yet had a fair trial in any country" because the national economies purporting to operate according to its principles were expressly committed to *inequality*. British capitalism was not born of genuine principles of market economies, nor "just partitions," but rather "of conquest and violence." People had not acquired their fortunes on the basis of "industry" and virtue but instead on vice and unearned inheritances. The system had been established and largely maintained, according to Mill, to "have purposely fostered inequalities, and prevent all from starting fair in the race." Leaning on the principle of justice that rewards merit, he insisted that even though perfect equality of opportunity may be unachievable, any reasonably just commercial economy would take measures to "temper that inequality by every means not subversive of the principle [of property] itself; if the tendency of legislation had been to favour the diffusion, instead of the concentration of wealth . . . the principle of individual property would have been found to have no necessary connexion with the physical and social evils which almost all Socialist writers assume to be inseparable from it" (*Principles*, 207–8).

We should also note, however, that although Mill certainly does not desire the radical inequality that characterizes Victorian Britain, neither does he think that a growing economy should have perfect equality: "a state of complete equality of fortunes would not be favourable to active exertion for the increase of wealth" (*Principles*, 891). The possibility of acquiring distinction—in wealth but also in realms like talent, knowledge, and virtue, according to Mill—is a positive stimulus in economies that need to grow. Complete equality would eliminate the motive of citizens to industry, which he views as necessary in growing economies.[42] This being said, even where he rejects perfect equality, Mill adds that "the diffusion of wealth, and not its concentration, is desirable, and that the more wholesome state of society is not that in which immense fortunes are possessed by a few and coveted by all" (*Principles*, 891).

REPRESENTATIVE GOVERNMENT

To be sure, Britain's democratizing context accounts for Mill's fascination with Tocqueville's two-volume *Democracy in America*. As he writes in his extended review of volume 1 of that work, "Eight centuries ago, society was divided into barons and serfs: the barons everything, the serfs nothing. At every succeeding epoch this inequality of condition is found to have somewhat abated." He continues,

> The many, for the first time, have now learned the lesson, which, once learned, is never forgotten—that their strength, when they choose to exert it, is invincible. And, for the first time, they have learned to unite for their own objects, without waiting for any section of the aristocracy to place itself at their head. The capacity of cooperation for a common purpose, heretofore a monopolized instrument of power in the hands of the higher classes, is now a most formidable one in those of the lowest. Under these influences it is not surprising that society makes greater strides in ten years, towards the levelling of inequalities, than lately in a century, or formerly in three or four. (*TOA*, I, 50, 51)

Mill learned from Tocqueville that greater democracy means greater equality, including economic equality. This had been known ever since the ancient Athenian Old Oligarch, who worried that whenever the poor seize power they would advance their own economic standing. As nations expanded suffrage, it seemed inevitable to Tocqueville and Mill that they would also become more equal.

Mill reasserts this principle as a selling point of representative government in his *Considerations on Representative Government*. For him, the "ideal" polity is one in which "the sovereignty, or supreme controlling power in the last resort, is vested in the entire aggregate of the community, every citizen . . . having a voice in the exercise of that sovereignty." He argues for popular sovereignty and universal suffrage based on two principles. First, that the rights and interests of all citizens will be far more jealously guarded by the people themselves. Second, and most relevant here, that "the general prosperity attains a greater height, and is more widely diffused" (*Considerations*, 64, 65). The more democratic the state, the more egalitarian its economy.

Mill's call for greater democratization is unquestionably part of his plan to address the problem of class legislation. In fact, just one page after asserting that more democratic nations are more economically equal, he explains that democratic nations need not worry so much about class legislation, which occurs "when power resides in an exclusive class" and that class "knowingly and deliberately sacrifices the other classes to themselves" (*Considerations*, 66). For Mill, widespread democratic suffrage and participation significantly reduces economic oppression.

ESTATE TAX REFORM

A key component of Mill's proposed reforms for systems of private property was his argument against large inheritances. Descendants' inheritance rights had simply been assumed for centuries as kind of a natural right. Among other things, it protected the large estates of the landed aristocracy. But it also fostered the indefinite growth of commercial elite wealth from one generation to the next, all while Britain's poor increasingly gravitated toward subsistence. Indeed, this is precisely why he condemns the dominant system that has "purposely fostered inequalities, and prevented all from starting fair in the race." The effect of the largest estates being passed down from one generation to the next was to create a radically unequal society with all its flaws. So any serious attempt to create a defensible system of private property requires careful scrutiny of inheritances.

Mill begins by distinguishing between the right of bequest versus the supposed right to inherit. These two "rights" have often been assumed to be synonymous. They are, however, distinct. The central right in a system of private property is the "right of producers to what they themselves have produced" (*Principles*, 215). But whereas the right to the wealth one has produced includes the right to dispose of it, or *bequest* it, it does not correspond to a right of others to inherit that money, at least to any substantial degree. The question of whether children[43] should inherit massive fortunes from their parents is fraught. To be sure, for Mill, children are entitled to the material comfort and education necessary to "start with a fair chance of achieving by their own exertions a successful life. To this every child has a claim." So if a parent has the financial means and dies before a child reaches maturity, that child is entitled to the inheritance that would provide a "fair chance" of a "successful life." This scarcely means, however, that children have the right to become "rich, without the necessity of any exertion" (*Principles*, 221).

In the absence of an inheritance right, then, the matter for Mill was to be decided by considerations of utility. Does the inheritance of enormous fortunes promote or inhibit "the permanent interests of the human race"?[44] He weighs the question carefully. On the one hand, he speculates that some might work especially hard throughout their lives with the express ambition of leaving their children a fortune. This hard work could potentially produce some social benefit. Yet on the other hand, "the mischiefs to society, of such perpetuities outweigh the value of this incentive to exertion, and the incentives in the case of those who have the opportunity of making large fortunes are strong enough without it" (*Principles*, 223). Among other "mischiefs," one presumes that Mill worries about the degree to which generational wealth exacerbates the gap between rich and poor and its attendant effects.[45] The inequality fostered by inheritances inflames selfishness, indolence, class tensions, and class legislation. These socially destabilizing effects are more than enough for Mill to dismiss any claims on behalf of the would-be beneficiaries of huge fortunes.

For all these reasons, Mill advocates an inheritance tax that would permit wealthy citizens to bequest their entire estates but "not to lavish it in enriching some one individual, beyond a certain maximum." That maximum is set by the amount it might take to afford "the means of a comfortable independence" (*Principles*, 225). He does not define "comfortable independence," but it is reasonable to assume the importance of the word "independence" here. Elsewhere in the *Principles* he speaks of a "theory of dependence" in which the poor are "not required or encouraged to think for themselves" and where it falls to others to "think for them, and to take the responsibility of their lot" (*Principles*, 759). In this context, to be independent means to have adequate resources to think for oneself and take responsibility for one's own affairs.[46] Beyond this, Mill recommends that the inheritance tax be imposed progressively, larger fortunes taxed at higher rates, with the highest set "as great as it can be made without giving rise to evasions" (*Principles*, 811).[47] Given his operational principles, one presumes that governments would likely tax the largest estates at comfortably over 90 percent.

Contrary to the claims of many,[48] Mill emphasizes that such taxes cannot be construed as unjust: "there is no injustice in taxing persons who have not acquired what they have by their own exertions, but have had it bestowed on them in free gift; and there are no reasons of justice or policy against taxing enormously large inheritances more highly than small inheritances" ("Income and Property," 491). The tax revenue has not been seized from the living who earned it themselves, so they cannot protest that their liberty has been infringed. And the beneficiaries cannot complain that they *deserve* their fortunes since they have not earned them. If anything, this tax promotes justice, as Mill understands it, since it promotes broader economic equality, along with the social, legal, and political benefits that flow from that.

Mill notes that Britain would not likely adopt such measures "unless the popular sentiment went energetically along with it" (*Principles*, 225).[49] He was not optimistic that it would happen soon. But he expected that, whenever it did, it would have profoundly beneficial effects.

> Wealth which could no longer be employed in over-enriching a few, would either be devoted to objects of public usefulness, or if bestowed on individuals, would be distributed among a larger number. While those enormous fortunes which no one needs for any personal purpose but ostentation or improper power, would become much less numerous, there would be a great multiplication of persons in easy circumstances, with the advantages of leisure, and all the real enjoyments which wealth can give, except those of vanity; a class by whom the services which a nation having leisured classes is entitled to expect from them, either by their direct exertions or by the tone they give to the feelings and tastes of the public, would be rendered in a much more beneficial manner than at present. A large portion also of the accumulations of successful industry would probably be devoted to public uses, either by direct bequests to the State, or by the endowment of institutions; as is already done very largely in the United States, where the ideas and practice in the matter of inheritance seem to be unusually rational and beneficial. (*Principles*, 226)

Mill's estate tax plan emphatically excludes the inheritance of large fortunes, which lack any social value. They are necessary only for "ostentation," "vanity,"[50] and the "improper power" that large fortunes often seek to exercise. Society is hindered, rather than advanced, by such accumulations of wealth. But if that wealth were instead broadly distributed or "devoted to public uses," it would serve a far greater good. Mill suggests that this can happen either via estate taxes, or private individuals can choose to give it away for these public purposes before they die. But in all cases, dynastic wealth must end.

The egalitarian effects of this policy cannot be exaggerated. Although Mill's proposal allows individuals to keep the lion's share of what they earn in a lifetime, the bulk of those earnings are returned to the larger society upon death, and the next generations will have to earn their own keep. One of Mill's earliest biographers, Alexander Bain, estimated that this policy alone would "pull down all large fortunes in two generations,"[51] which was especially radical in a society that had long protected dynastic wealth. On this basis alone, historian Gregory Claeys has concluded that for Mill "the state has as one basic aim rectifying social and economic inequalities."[52] To be sure, Mill's policy would mitigate many of the most dramatic inequalities of Victorian Britain. Yet it is also true that many enormous fortunes, such as Andrew Carnegie's and other industrialists', have been earned over the course of a single generation that would not be significantly affected by this policy alone. But this fact should not necessarily lead Mill's readers to conclude that he was comfortable even with these fortunes, as suggested by the myriad critiques of inequality outlined earlier. Hence the need for other measures discussed below.

BIRTH CONTROL AND AN EDUCATION AGAINST BRUTISH INSTINCTS

A primary source of poverty among the working poor, for Mill, was the large labor pool. The reason for its size was Britain's unsupportably high birth rate. Because wages "depend mainly upon the demand and supply of labour" (*Principles*, 337), a large population exercises downward pressures on compensation. It is no secret that Mill was highly influenced in this regard by Thomas Malthus, who had fervently warned in his *Essay on Population* about the dangers of unchecked population growth.[53] Mill's particular interest was in how his principles applied to wages. The greater the population, the greater the labor pool; the greater the labor pool, the lower the wages—wages that will ultimately drop "much too low for human happiness and dignity" ("Claims of Labour," 368). This means that the most direct measure for improving wages and working conditions is to reduce the workforce size: "The condition of the [laboring] class can be bettered in no other way than by altering that proportion to their advantage; and every scheme for their benefit, which does not proceed on this as its foundation, is, for all permanent purposes, a delusion" (*Principles*, 343).[54]

Mill insists that the fundamental cause of imprudent population in the working class was poor self-control. He emphatically insists in his *Principles*:

> Poverty, like most social evils, exists because men follow their brute instincts without due consideration. But society is possible, precisely because man is not necessarily a brute. Civilization in every one of its aspects is a struggle against the animal instincts. Over some even of the strongest of them, it has shown itself capable of acquiring abundant control. (*Principles*, 367)[55]

He stresses here that humanity's brute instincts, namely the sex drive, are to blame for excessive population. To this point in history, he continues, governments have largely encouraged people to act on these brute instincts. Religious and political institutions have sought to grow populations—encouraging citizens to procreate early and often. For that matter, the rich, sensing perhaps how a large working-class population serves their own self-interest in the form of lower compensation for their employees, have also taken up the cause of promoting greater reproduction among the poor (*Principles*, 368). That is, the working poor have largely been *taught* to reproduce indiscriminately. And because those lessons have been so friendly to the instincts, they have largely been heeded. Yet if people can be taught to procreate, they can also be taught, Mill reasons, to exercise greater self-control.

The working class, for Mill, needs to be taught in schools the most basic economic facts with profound consequences for their own well-being: the greater the population, the lower their wages. This education should be such "that every labourer looked . . . upon every other who had more than the number of children which the circumstances of society allowed to each, as doing him a wrong—as filling up the place which he was entitled to share" (*Principles*, 371). This simple lesson in economic reasoning, he posits, would alter family-planning decisions. He entertains the counterargument here that animal instincts will always defeat prudential reasoning but finds it unpersuasive. People have simply assumed this because prevailing public opinion—reinforced by religious and state teachings—have discouraged the kind of self-control that would be necessary to stabilize the population. So long as prevailing public opinion dismisses reproductive self-control as either blasphemous or unpatriotic, there can be little hope of managing population size. But if public opinion held it prudent to exercise reproductive self-control, Mill speculates, there would be a very different outcome. Public opinion is a powerful force, strong enough even to moderate those "brutish instincts," through a sustained program of prudential education.[56]

Beyond being taught the facts of supply and demand as applied to the labor pool, Mill also thought it necessary to teach the working class about developing birth control technologies. He had been committed to educating the people about birth control since his teenage years when he had stumbled across a strangled infant in St. James's Park, which he had surmised to have been killed because the parents had no means to provide for their child. Shortly thereafter, he and a friend were arrested for distributing birth control pamphlets authored by Francis Place, called "To Married Working People." The pamphlet, among other things, described sponge contraception as employed by women in France at the time, though largely unknown in Britain.[57]

Beyond education, Mill was serious enough about controlling the population size to improve wages among the working poor that he entertained a policy in *On Liberty* that would "forbid marriage unless the parties can show that they have the means of supporting a family" as "not exceed[ing] the legitimate powers of the State." This is potentially surprising to some readers of that text insofar as it may be difficult to identify the harms associated with the young and poor getting married. But for Mill, the matter is obvious. Excessive and early procreation without the means to support one's children is in its nature "an act injurious to others, which ought to be a subject of reprobation, and social stigma" (*Liberty*, 108). First, a parent who cannot provide for the basic needs of children is harming them. Second, those who procreate early and recklessly, to his mind, will reproduce often, and frequent breeding accelerates population growth at a rate harmful to wages.

EDUCATION AGAINST SELFISHNESS

Earlier, I argued that one of the great sources of inequality, for Mill, was the consuming selfishness of commercial citizens. The selfish citizen "never thinks of any collective interest, of any objects to be pursued jointly with others, but only in competition with them, and in some measure at their expense" (*Considerations*, 80). This selfishness, where tolerated or cultivated, inevitably leads those at the top of any hierarchy to advance their material interests, exacerbating economic inequality. But for Mill, unlike Thomas Hobbes or Jeremy Bentham, this selfishness is not hardwired. Humanity is not irredeemably or even naturally selfish. Selfishness only takes root in those societies that ignore its dangers. So for Mill, any

serious proposal for addressing inequality necessarily requires targeting
that egoism.

Reducing selfishness requires reforming education—among the most
powerful tools for shaping individual sentiments, feelings, and inclinations. As Mill would write in his *Three Essays on Religion*, the "power
of education is almost boundless" (*Religion*, 409). Perhaps nowhere is
the civic importance of education clearer than in his *Autobiography*. His
thoughts in one paragraph are so well developed that they are worth parsing in segments.

> To render any such social transformation either possible or desirable . . .
> [a] change of character must take place both in the uncultivated herd
> who now compose the labouring masses, and in the immense majority
> of their employers. Both these classes must learn by practice to labour
> and combine for generous, or at all events for public and social pur-
> poses, and not, as hitherto, solely for narrowly interested ones. But the
> capacity to do this has always existed in mankind, and is not, nor is
> ever likely to be, extinct. Education, habit, and the cultivation of the
> sentiments, will make a common man dig or weave for his country, as
> readily as fight for his country.

Mill opens this paragraph by stating the problem: that too many British
citizens are animated by "narrowly interested" motives. As noted earlier,
this was certainly true of the wealthiest citizens, whom he had described
as having "indulged their self-importance" (*Principles*, 760)—a point he
repeats here. But he also allows here that this narrow self-interest has likewise infected the poor who "compose the laboring masses." For Mill, self-
interest has contaminated the entire citizenry across the vast economic
spectrum. This being noted, however, he also allows that this is not a necessary condition. Again, contradicting Hobbes and Bentham, Mill denies
that human beings are forever destined to be ruled exclusively by their
own interests. They have the capacity to act on behalf of "public and social
purposes." This can be facilitated by improving education. Mill continues,
"True enough, it is only by slow degrees, and a system of culture prolonged
through successive generations, that men in general can be brought up
to this point." Just as the culture of selfishness pervading Victorian Britain took generations to build, replacing it with an ethos of "public and
social purpose" will likewise take generations. Transforming cultures
cannot happen overnight. It will take concerted and extended effort. In
doing so, Mill follows Plato's Athenian Stranger, who sought to address
inequality with "a small, careful transformation that gradually produces

a small result over a long period of time."[58] This is the nature of any serious program of education on Mill's account, especially moral education. For him, "the education of human beings is one of the most difficult of all arts, and this is one of the points in which it has hitherto been least successful; moreover improvements in general education are necessarily very gradual, because the future generation is educated by the present" (*Socialism*, 263–64). As the goal of moral education requires teachers with rare dispositions in existing society, the task of finding uncorrupted instructors is difficult. He fears that educators would be burdened with the same selfishness that must be rooted out from the students.

> But the hindrance is not in the essential constitution of human nature. Interest in the common good is at present so weak a motive in the generality not because it can never be otherwise, but because the mind is not accustomed to dwell on it as it dwells from morning till night on things which tend only to personal advantage. When called into activity, as only self-interest now is, by the daily course of life, and spurred from behind by the love of distinction and the fear of shame, it is capable of producing, even in common men, the most strenuous exertions as well as the most heroic sacrifices. The deep-rooted selfishness which forms the general character of the existing state of society, is *so* deeply rooted, only because the whole course of existing institutions tends to foster it; and modern institutions in some respects more than ancient, since the occasions on which the individual is called on to do anything for the public without receiving its pay, are far less frequent in modern life, than the smaller commonwealths of antiquity. (*Autobiography*, 241)

At this point, Mill returns to one of his core assumptions: that human nature is *not* fundamentally selfish. Not only is he here rejecting Bentham and Hobbes, but perhaps of greater consequence to his Victorian readers, he is also rejecting original sin. It had been the assumption of most Christians since Augustine that humanity is naturally and inescapably sinful. But Mill is more a student of Rousseau's doctrine of natural goodness than of Augustine's original sin. If our neighbors appear wicked, it is only because they have been poorly raised and educated and that society relentlessly reinforces this selfishness by encouraging and rewarding it. Selfishness, again, "is *so* deeply rooted, only because the whole course of existing institutions tends to foster it." As he elaborates in his *Chapters on Socialism*, selfishness results from "imperfect education" (269). Changing those institutions, including but not limited to schools, is required for uprooting it and the destructive inequality it engenders.

These considerations did not make us overlook the folly of premature attempts to dispense with the inducements of private interest in social affairs, while no substitute for them has been or can be provided: but we regarded all existing institutions and social arrangements as being (in a phrase I once heard from Austin) "merely provisional," and we welcomed with the greatest pleasure and interest all socialistic experiments by select individuals (such as the Co-operative Societies), which, whether they succeeded or failed, could not but operate as a most useful education of those who took part in them, by cultivating their capacity of acting upon motives pointing directly to the general good, or making them aware of the defects which render them and others incapable of doing so. (*Autobiography*, 176)

Mill allows that so long as people act selfishly, capitalism may offer the best available set of "merely provisional" institutions. But this is suboptimal from the broader perspective of what might be possible with educational reforms. And however corrupted a people might be, for Mill, they can always commence the process of self-improvement.

Given that Mill believes education to be the moral right of all children and the foundation for society's prospects for improvement and of transcending narrow self-interest, it may be surprising that he does not advocate a large system of public schools, established, funded, and maintained by governments.[59] He distrusts large, centralized school systems that might be "a mere contrivance for molding people to be exactly like one another" (*On Liberty*, 106). Or as he worries in his *Principles*, "a government which can mould the opinions and sentiments of the people from their youth upwards, can do with them whatever it pleases" (*Principles*, 950).[60] Societies should rather cultivate diverse schools, employing varied pedagogical approaches. They should be regarded as "competing experiments" in education (*On Liberty*, 106). This will not only avoid the problem of the state-created armies of like-minded automatons but will also provide the intellectually diverse citizenry that help societies thrive. The costs for private schooling should largely fall on the parents, excepting poorer families, who should receive public tuition assistance. The state will cover the entire schooling costs of the very poor. Mill refuses to let any child's life go to waste, whether it is an ignorant father standing in the way of his child's education or a family's poverty. Each child deserves an education, and society will benefit from the otherwise undiscovered talents of its poorer children, who may become great intellectuals, citizens, and leaders.

The culmination of Mill's education against selfishness is to be found in his "Religion of Humanity," as discussed in his *Three Essays on Religion*. Although Mill finds much to admire in religions, especially in the moral teachings of Jesus, he worries about how religions sometimes appeal to their adherents' selfish motives. Specifically, those promising divine rewards have the effect of tempting the believer "to regard the performance of his duties to others mainly as a means to his own personal salvation" and are, as such, "one of the most serious obstacles to the great purpose of moral culture, the strengthening of the unselfish and weakening of the selfish element in our nature" (*Religion*, 422). Insofar as religions cater to selfish motives, they undermine morality's mission of elevating the common good. To this extent, he proposes an alternative religion "grounded on large and wise views of the good of the whole" (*Religion*, 421). This religion would substitute fears of divine sanctions with aspirations for the approval of both the living and dead—including ancestors, friends, and the moral heroes of the past, such as Socrates, Jesus, Antonius, and even George Washington. There would be no material rewards for good deeds but only the satisfaction of having done something morally praiseworthy. The primary test of whether someone has done something good is if one has triumphed "over all selfish objects of desire" (*Religion*, 422). While Mill does not detail his pedagogy, his goal is to create a community in which selflessness is broadly shared and largely self-enforced through conscience and public opinion.[61] A society in which the Religion of Humanity is ascendant requires teachers, clergy, parents, neighbors, and political figures that profess and enforce a common-good orientation through praising or blaming *unselfish* and *selfish* acts, respectively. To be sure, this is a form of education—the kind that Mill prioritizes in those passages of his *Autobiography* cited above. Accomplishing this would take generations, but achieving this kind of community would be well worth the effort on his account. A community habitually orienting its citizens toward the common good, further, would surely be happier since selfishness undermines utility.

Finally and significantly, for Mill, taming selfishness means achieving a significant degree of sex equality. So many men are selfish, he observes, because they have been legally established as tyrannical rulers within their own households. Men have complete power over women—over their liberty, their property, their children, and even their bodies to the point that husbands can sexually assault their wives with complete immunity. When such despotic power is routinized and legally sanctioned, Mill reasons, it stimulates men's selfish inclinations. Sex equality, on his account, would produce men "much more unselfish and self-sacrificing than at present because they would no longer be taught to worship their own will." Once women are acknowledged as equals and there is a genuine "feeling of the equality of human beings," men will be freed from this temptation to self-admiration, as well as from the social ill-effects that stem from selfishness (*Subjection*, 158, 159).

WORKER COOPERATIVES

Since the rich have proven themselves to be poor stewards of the impoverished, the best prospects for improving the condition of the indigent is to stimulate their latent intelligence so they are empowered themselves to improve society: "The prospect of the future depends on the degree in which they [the poor] can be made rational beings" (*Principles*, 763). Much of this, Mill observes, is already in motion. They are increasingly reading newspapers, attending lectures, engaging in collective deliberations, joining trade unions, engaging in politics—"all serv[ing] to diffuse [the] variety of ideas among the mass, and to excite thought and reflection in the more intelligent" (*Principles*, 763–64; see also *TOA*, I, 50).[62] All of this can be accelerated with better schooling. The more education they get, the more intolerable will be the theory of dependence on which the wealthy justify their reign.

Beyond the need to enhance the working class's intelligence, for Mill, is the necessity of reducing the social tensions that accompany inequality in the Victorian economy. The social classes are increasingly hostile.

> The relation is nearly as unsatisfactory for the payer of wages as to the receiver. If the rich regard the poor as their servants and dependents, the rich in their turn are regarded as a mere prey and pasture for the poor; the subject of demands and expectations wholly indefinite, increasing in extent with every concession made to them. The total absence of regard for justice and fairness in the relations between the two, is as marked on the side of the employed as on that of the employers. We look in vain among the working classes in general for a just pride which will choose to give good work for good wages; for the most part, their sole endeavor is to receive as much, and return as little in the shape of service, as possible. It will sooner or later become insupportable to the employing classes, to live in close and hourly contact with persons whose interests and feelings are in hostility to them. (*Principles*, 767)

Employer-employee relationships in the Victorian economy are defined by their mutual hostility. The rich exploit the poor, deriving maximum profit from squeezing their employees. The employees, in return, distrust and detest their employers. Beyond this, employees work no more than the absolute minimum necessary to keep their jobs. This is scarcely a relationship defined by friendship or "justice and fairness" for Mill but rather one of mutual disdain and hostility.[63]

One possible solution to this problem would be to establish an economy of peasant proprietors, where individual farmers own and farm their own land. Mill had outlined and celebrated the virtues of this economy earlier in his *Principles*, where he praised this economic system for reducing poverty, promoting equality, improving intelligence, and fostering independence (*Principles*, 254–77). He celebrates its virtues over any form of hired labor for its "aggregate effects on human happiness" (*Principles*, 767), highlighting its elimination of the relationship of dependence that workers have on their employers. Yet he also identifies its primary drawback: inefficiency. As Mill insists, "labour is unquestionably more productive on the system of large industrial enterprises." This results in a "benefit to the whole" (*Principles*, 768). Further, he identifies a problem with the system of peasant proprietors in their relative isolation. There is no real "community of interest" or "mental communion" with fellow citizens. This burdens both the system of peasant proprietors and industrial capitalism. Neither promotes the broad community of interest capable of improving social relations.

Those seeking a morally superior economic arrangement that escapes the atomism of peasant proprietorship and the hostility of Victorian capitalism will need to cultivate a partnership—one motivated by "true justice and equality," where there is an "association, not isolation, of interests" (*Principles*, 768). This is the foundation on which Mill will build his case for an alternative mode of organizing a commercial economy. The remaining question concerns what kind of partnership—partnerships with capitalists or partnerships of workers among themselves? He sympathetically explores both.

The first of these partnership alternatives is profit sharing between capitalists and their employees. Under these arrangements, businesses are still owned by capitalists, but they do not hoard the profits for themselves. Rather, as in the case of the company operated by the Parisian tradesman M. Leclaire, which Mill describes at some length, workers have differentiated fixed wages or salaries, but at the end of the year, company profits are shared among all employees, proportionate to their wages or salaries.

Mill cites studies noting how profit sharing improves the intelligence and independence of laborers. It further stimulates their productivity since they are now compensated more for working harder. The greater their productivity, the more money they will receive at the end of the year. Although compensation is unequal, to be sure, it is less unequal than most companies operating at this time in which laborers worked for subsistence wages while the capitalists grew increasingly wealthy.

But the second alternative, worker co-ops, is clearly Mill's preferred alternative and the apple of his eye.[64] Worker co-ops are expressly more egalitarian in nature insofar as companies are not owned by capitalists but rather by "an association of the labourers themselves on terms of equality." He envisions ideally that these associations of workers would evolve spontaneously from the existing capital held by the savings of individual workers but also perhaps small loans from friends and neighbors or possibly by a "republican government." He expressly insists that it should not come, as more radical reforms might allow, by "robbing the capitalists of what they or their predecessors had acquired by labour and preserved by economy" (*Principles*, 775). By pooling their savings, the workers would not have to rely on a single or small group of wealthy capitalists to fund their business, nor would they have any partner in their venture with interests different from or opposed to their own. The capital would henceforth belong to the entire company and no single member of it. As such, it would be "indivisible property" (*Principles*, 783) where no member could request and receive a buyout. Unlike a joint-stock company, no portion of the company would be for sale. When workers quit, their original investment remains with the company and the continuing workers to develop as they see fit.

Worker co-ops, for Mill, retain all the virtues of profit-sharing businesses, but their benefits extend further. Because company rules are self-imposed by the workers, they have even greater discipline than profit-sharing ventures. As workers manage the company jointly, they naturally gravitate toward running it for "the manifest good of the community, and not for the convenience of an employer" (*Principles*, 780). Mill explains that these associations "do not exist for the mere private benefit of the individual members, but for the promotion of the co-operative cause" (*Principles*, 780). This suggests how co-ops help to break the cycle of selfishness typical in market economies. The self-interest plaguing industrial Britain, as Mill understands it, can be significantly transformed by increasing the number of worker cooperatives. As Mill describes cooperatives in his own time, the motives of workers transcend the "narrow selfishness" that dominate laborers at other companies and create greater "social sympathies" (*Principles*, 793, 792).

Companies failing to adopt this model, according to Mill, will find it increasingly difficult to hire dedicated employees. Workers will gravitate to cooperatives, knowing that they can earn more money, share in management, build a diverse set of skills, and avoid altogether the hostile work environment that dominates those other companies where employers and employees lack trust and assume polar opposition of interests. Given this, capitalists clinging to the old model where profits remain unshared will struggle to find competent labor, finding instead "work-people of only the worst description" (*Principles*, 793). And under these circumstances, they fail to compete in the marketplace with the worker co-ops in employing the best labor, which make presumably superior products, given that they are literally invested in doing so.

It is worth emphasizing that Mill does not envision anything like perfect economic equality resulting from the co-ops. The workers will not earn equal wages or salaries. Although all workers will be guaranteed a "fixed minimum, sufficient for subsistence" (*Principles*, 780), beyond that their equality will be proportionate—those who work more, earn more. This honors workers' freedom to decide how much money they want beyond that minimum. As with the profit-sharing model, proceeds will be shared at the end of the year according to the labor each worker contributed. Those who work harder will, at year's end, earn a greater percentage of the profits. But all workers will likely get something beyond subsistence, which was rarely true in most large-scale industries at this time.

While this, again, is not perfect economic equality, it would have significantly reduced Victorian Britain's massive inequality. Without a small number of investors to claim the lion's share of the company profits, those proceeds would be more broadly distributed. That would reduce or even eliminate the wealthiest classes, while raising workers to the middle class, who might have otherwise struggled on subsistence wages. As political theorist Michael B. Levy observes, in economies dominated by worker co-ops, "redistribution would be realized primarily through the spontaneous dissolution of a separate capitalist class and the emergence of a cooperative property, not an elaborate network of public services and social insurance plans."[65] Operative here also is the democratic nature of cooperatives. As cited earlier, democratic organizations promote conditions where "the general prosperity attains a greater height, and is more widely diffused" (*Considerations*, 65). Democratic cooperatives incline to relatively equal compensation, per Mill's own principles. Thus, an economy dominated by numerous competing cooperatives would be "the nearest approach to social justice and the most beneficial ordering of industrial affairs for the universal good, which it is possible at present to foresee" (*Principles*, 794).

This being acknowledged, the cooperative movement advances multiple goals for Mill: it (1) educates workers in how to run their own economic affairs, (2) respects their freedom and independence, (3) increases productivity, (4) reduces selfishness and promotes community sentiment, (5) reduces workplace and societal hostility between the working class and the capitalists by merging the classes, and (6) reduces inequality. Those are substantial benefits from a Millian perspective, worthy of earnest consideration by anyone attracted to his political philosophy.

REFORMED ENCLOSURE ACT

Mill's commitment to reducing selfishness, and ultimately inequality, through education has important implications he explores in his *Principles*. Namely, for him, that

> education is not compatible with extreme poverty. It is impossible effectually to teach an indigent population. And it is difficult to make those who feel the value of comfort who have never enjoyed it, or those appreciate the wretchedness of a precarious subsistence, who have been made reckless by always living from hand to mouth. (*Principles*, 375)

Given Mill's eagerness to root out selfishness, it is awfully difficult to teach people *not* to be self-centered when they have profound motives to hoard every meager advantage they have simply to survive. How effectively can one teach children on the verge of starvation to share their food with others? Perhaps it could be done, but it would be a challenge. Further, he presses, if another goal of education is to train students to strive to attain a higher station in life than that which they presently occupy, their imaginations can scarcely furnish the image of relative comfort or leisure. One can tell students, "Study if you want to succeed," but what does that mean to a child with no experience or image of what material "success" might resemble? The most natural thing for children to imagine is a continuation of their present environment and conditions. Rich kids will imagine themselves rich and the impoverished will imagine themselves poor.

So any truly effective educational reform that strives to create the possibility of transformational effects, much less even "diffuse good sense among the people," will require far more radical measures. Mill elaborates:

Individuals often struggle upwards into a condition of ease; but the utmost that can be expected from a whole people is to maintain themselves in it; and improvements in the habits and requirements of the mass of unskilled day-labourers will be difficult and tardy, unless means can be contrived of raising the entire body to a state of tolerable comfort, and maintaining them in it until a new generation grows up. (*Principles*, 375)

For Mill, the only way that progressive-minded reformers can reasonably expect education to succeed is by eliminating poverty.

He entertains at least two different means by which to furnish the poor with enough wealth to stimulate the imaginations of their children. The first would be to encourage the young and poor to go forth to Britain's colonies, where they could easily acquire the land and wealth that seems out of reach in their homeland (*Principles*, 376). He admires the United States' egalitarian ethos, which, in turn, stimulated a more productive economy (e.g., *Principles*, 890–91). The secret of early American success, for Mill, was "that there are not only no poor, there are scarcely any rich" (*State of Society*, 99).

A second means by which the poor might be provided with sufficient wealth for educating their children would be through a reformed enclosure act. Whereas in earlier generations, public land had been confiscated by the British government and transferred to wealthy citizens, Mill proposes that the government purchase land from existing landholders and then transfer that land to the working class in "sections of five acres or thereabouts, to be conferred in absolute property on individuals of the laboring class who would reclaim and bring them into cultivation by their own labour." This would alleviate desperate poverty and create an "intermediate class" (*Principles*, 377), which most resembles the "peasant proprietors" that he had praised for their hard work, intelligence, and independence. Children raised under these circumstances would have a real chance to absorb the education that is their natural right.

To this extent, Mill emphasizes that any program created along these lines should not adopt half measures—of giving land to only some of the very poor or of giving something less than a five-acre farmable plot: "feeble half-measures do but fritter away resources." Families must, on his account, have enough so as "to live and bring up their children in a degree of comfort and independence to which they have hitherto been strangers" (*Principles*, 378). It is only by adopting measures such as this that one can achieve the singular goal to facilitate a real education: to "extinguish extreme poverty for one whole generation" (*Principles*, 374).

THE STATIONARY STATE

Perhaps the most radical section in all of Mill's *Principles of Political Economy* outlines his stationary state. It also represents his most definitive statement promoting economic equality. As the political theorist Michael B. Levy has insisted, "the stationary state provided Mill with a set of economic and social conditions which logically completed his vision."[66] Mill's primary concern in these pages is how Adam Smith's advocacy of continuous economic growth has become a kind of Frankenstein's monster. As argued in chapter 5, Smith, like Mill, worried about poverty, and a significant part of his solution was to grow the economy indefinitely. As the economy grows, it produces more, such that "the produce of the whole labour of society is so great, that all are often abundantly supplied, and a workman, even of the lowest and poorer order . . . may enjoy a greater share of the necessities and conveniences of life than it is possible for any savage to acquire" (*WN*, 2). Growth means increased demand for goods, which in turn increases the demand for labor. This increased demand for labor in turn yields higher wages.

Yet Smith's system fails in this regard to control the dangers of inequality that accompany this growing economies. Although it may be true on his model that the poor in a growing economy have more of the "conveniences of life" than did tribal rulers in the days of hunting-and-fishing economies, they are often nevertheless much further behind their fellow citizens in relative terms. Put simply, Smith's poor are better off in absolute terms but worse off in relative ones. They might have working refrigerators, but their wealthy neighbors have private yachts. And because inequality is primarily a question of relative standing, Smith's growing economy offers limited solutions to the problems of inequality.

Mill observes that Smith's arguments for growth have become orthodoxy. Nineteenth-century economists had taken for granted that economies must grow at all costs. To illustrate this, Mill discusses John Ramsay M'Culloch, the first professor of political economy at the University of London, who insisted that the proper measure of a successful economy is not "a good distribution of wealth, but [rather] a rapid increase of it; his test of prosperity is high profits" (*Principles*, 752).

The dogma of economic growth may be helpful or even necessary for less developed economies, according to Mill. But even in conceding a period of growth as a necessary developmental stage, he can barely stomach its principles:

That the energies of mankind should be kept in employment by the struggle for riches, as they were formerly by the struggle of war, until the better minds succeed in educating the others into better things, is undoubtedly more desirable than that they should rust and stagnate. While minds are coarse they require coarse stimuli. (*Principles*, 754)

In early stages of development, economic growth is helpful—and even selfishness provides some benefits. "Coarse" minds require "coarse stimuli." But for Mill this phase has expired in most developed economies. Whatever gains were to be had have already been achieved. Continued growth and selfishness threaten much more harm than good—most notably to food supplies on Malthusian principles since the advocates of further growth presuppose greater population growth but also to the natural environment. The irrational drive to ceaselessly burgeon the economy will ultimately consume every corner of the globe:

> Nor is there much satisfaction in contemplating the world with nothing left to the spontaneous activity of nature; with every rood of land brought into cultivation, which is capable of growing food for human beings; every flowery waste or natural pasture ploughed up, all quadrupeds or birds which are not domesticated for man's use exterminated as his rivals for food, every hedgerow or superfluous tree rooted out, and scarcely a place left where a wild shrub or flower could grow without being eradicated as a weed in the name of improved agriculture. If the earth must lose that great portion of its pleasantness which it owes to things that the unlimited increase of wealth and population would extirpate from it, for the mere purpose of enabling it to support a larger, but not a better or a happier population, I sincerely hope, for the sake of posterity, that they will be content to be stationary, long before necessity compels them to it. (*Principles*, 756)

A growing economy consuming the natural world envelopes the space in which individuals might find solitude and contemplate "thoughts and aspirations which are not only good for the individual, but which society could ill do without" (*Principles*, 756).

Two further unfortunate elements of the growing economy are, of course, *pleonexia* and inequality. Mill speaks directly to the former in condemning *pleonexia* and those societies that celebrate the insatiable quest for wealth:

> I know not why it should be matter of congratulation that persons who are already richer than any one needs to be, should have doubled their

means of consuming things which give little or no pleasure except as representative of wealth; or that numbers of individuals should pass over, every year, from the middle classes into a richer class, or from the class of the occupied rich to that of the unoccupied. (*Principles*, 755)

For mature economies, Smith's moral justification for economic growth crumbles. Whereas Smith justified growth as a means of serving the poor, it now functions to further enrich the wealthy. Yet there is scarcely any further advantage available to them other than the satisfaction they take from their own vanity. For Mill, who stressed the distinction between the "higher" and "lower" pleasures, this clearly resembles a lower pleasure and one scarcely worth registering in his utility calculus.[67]

What would enhance utility in mature economies? His answer appears to be greater economic equality since, as intellectual historian Arthur O. Lovejoy has observed, "these [*pleonectic*] desires are essentially limitless, and . . . are obviously inconsistent with equality."[68]

It is only in the backward countries of the world that increased production is still an important object: in those most advanced, what is economically needed is a better distribution. (*Principles*, 755)[69]

By a "better distribution" Mill specifically means a more equal one. He clarifies in the next paragraph:

We may suppose this better distribution of property attained, by the joint effect of the prudence and frugality of individuals, and of a system of legislation favouring equality of fortunes, so far as is consistent with the just claim of the individual to the fruits, whether great or small, of his or her own industry. We may suppose, for instance . . . a limitation of the sum which any one person may acquire by gift or inheritance, to the amount sufficient to constitute a moderate independence. (*Principles*, 755)

This passage confirms that a "better distribution" of resources, for Mill, is one in which those assets are more equitably distributed. But there is much else transpiring here as well. For one thing, that equality should be fostered by appropriate legislation—that is, with the benefit of government intervention. This legislation would presumably include many of the measures already mentioned: estate taxes, education, birth control, property redistribution, and the promotion of worker cooperatives. But this passage, admittedly, also indicates Mill's comfort with a degree of inequality, so long as it corresponds with individual exertions. Inequality based on the accumulations of ancestors, however, is unacceptable. This reflects his principle of desert or merit. It seems perfectly fair and even proper for those willing to exert themselves more to earn greater rewards for their efforts. This also honors his principle of individual liberty. Those exerting themselves for extra compensation have this right as individuals. But it is important to recall at the same time, however, that even as Mill allows potentially significant wealth acquisition in a single lifetime, at life's end that wealth is returned to the society from which it originated. So there can be no dynastic wealth that takes generations to accumulate. He continues:

> Under this two-fold influence, society would exhibit these leading features: a well-paid and affluent body of labourers; no enormous fortunes, except what were earned and accumulated during a single lifetime; but a much larger body of persons than at present, not only exempt from the coarser toils, but with sufficient leisure, both physical and mental, from mechanical details, to cultivate freely the graces of life, and afford examples of them to the classes less favourably circumstanced for their growth. This condition of society, so greatly preferable to the present, is not only perfectly compatible with the stationary state, but, it would seem, more naturally allied with that state than with any other. (*Principles*, 755)

Again, Mill's vision of the stationary state is relatively egalitarian, especially in comparison to Victorian Britain. Workers cannot live on the edge of starvation, as was common practice at the time, but are rather to be "affluent." Further, there are to be no fortunes except for what can be earned in a single lifetime. In doing so, Mill combines two principles of justice he outlined in *Utilitarianism*: equality on the one hand and merit/desert on the other. Meanwhile, he is optimistic that in the context of the stationary state desperate poverty can be eliminated entirely.

Conclusion: A Progression toward Greater Equality

Mill's stationary state suggests a long progression of social and economic affairs. The "coarse minds" that populate the relatively coarse economies and societies are bound to be unattuned to the dangers of inequality that plague those communities, since for Mill, again, "it is only in the backward countries of the world that increased production is still an important object: in those most advanced, what is economically needed is a better distribution" (*Principles*, 755). Indeed, the very premise of progress is built into book 4 of the *Principles* in which the chapters on the stationary state and the worker cooperatives ("On the Probable Futurity of the Labouring Classes") are the natural culmination. Mill anticipates that progress toward greater equality advances utility "in the largest sense, grounded on the permanent interests of man as a progressive being" (*Liberty*, 14). Given that "a person who cares for other people, for his country, or for mankind, is a happier man than one who does not" (*Considerations*, 137), selfishness and inequality tend to conspire against human happiness. The animating goal is greater equality and greater fraternity, so that humanity can achieve greater happiness. This is his progressive vision of utilitarian success. As Helen McCabe has rightly insisted, "greater equality was for him a sign of greater progress."[70]

Despite his keen objective of achieving greater equality, however, Mill understands that it cannot be achieved overnight. There is no switch that can be flicked; there is no button that can be pressed; no sudden violent revolution can simply implement the stationary state or anything approaching it. This is one of the fundamental differences that distinguishes him from the revolutionary socialists of his day. Mill acknowledges as much in his *Chapters on Socialism*. The main ambition of the radical or revolutionary socialists is their promise to fix all the problems "quickly," but even as he says this, he is largely critical. The radicals would "plunge without any preparation" into dramatically new modes of social and economic organization (*Socialism*, 261). They also entertain violence, which holds no appeal to Mill's moderation. His moderate inclinations share little in common with radical means of social change.

This being said, for Mill, it is possible that communism might work "at some future time" when humanity is ready (*Socialism*, 270). What would this take? Mill answers, it "requires a high standard of both moral and intellectual education in all the members of the community" (*Socialism*, 271). By "moral" he means that people need to learn to do their work honestly and energetically. That is, there can be no free riders on the labor of their fellow citizens, who threaten to undermine the civil harmony to which he aspires. By "intellectual" he means the ability to estimate "distant interests"—those who can transcend short-term calculations of self-interest to grasp a larger vision of what might be achieved with social cooperation and cohesion. As things stood in 1869 when Mill drafted his *Chapters*, Britain was unprepared for communism. The state of education was sorely lacking, fraternal feelings were rare, and extreme inequality was the norm. Fixing all of this would take time. Those entertaining violent revolution before these social and economic changes occurred would inevitably find "disappointment" (*Socialism*, 271).

In promoting gradual change to greater equality, though perhaps never outright communism, Mill embraces the moderate tradition of Plato's Athenian Stranger in the *Laws*. Although the Stranger understood that extensive equality was ideal and best promoted the kind of fraternal bonds that characterized thriving societies, he also acknowledged that it could not be implemented suddenly or haphazardly. Achieving it would take generations—relying on education and altering long-standing social norms, by shaming selfishness, greed, and *pleonexia*. This gradual path to equality pursues egalitarian ends while acknowledging dangers in transitioning too quickly or violently. While Plato and Mill share a commitment to equality, they also share a commitment to fraternity. Fraternity is endangered, on their accounts, by seizing the property of one citizen and redistributing it to another. This is why even Mill's most ambitious plans for achieving equality never involve this kind of gesture. The steep inheritance tax involves taking the money only from deceased citizens rather than from living ones. The reformed enclosure laws include compensation for landowners. Worker cooperatives raise their own capital and seek to supplant traditional bourgeois-funded industries only by providing a superior business model, not by seizing bourgeois assets. In doing so, Mill's reasoning implies, fraternity can be promoted in a way that would be difficult on the radical approach, which exacerbates the festering mutual animosities of the classes and makes no pretense to ameliorate them. This perhaps above all makes Mill's approach to addressing inequality worthy of serious attention. Whether the wealthiest citizens would ever consent to these laws in the proper fraternal spirit, however, is another matter—one that Marx addresses squarely.

CHAPTER SEVEN

Karl Marx

"THE SOCIAL GULF"

SOME READERS MAY HAVE BEEN SURPRISED that certain figures in this book have expressed such strong egalitarian views. Neither in the public mind nor in the scholarly consensus are Plato and Hobbes, for example, considered to be economic egalitarians. I have made the case that they ought to be. There are others whose presence in this book will be unsurprising. Jean-Jacques Rousseau built his fame, in part, in writing his *Discourse on Inequality*, and he remains known to this day as a radical critic of social and economic inequality. To the extent that I have confirmed this will upset neither scholarly nor public consensus. One might think that much the same could be said of Karl Marx (1818–1883), who is certainly known to the public, like Rousseau, as a radical critic of inequality. His challenge to capitalist economies, characterized by striking divides between rich and poor, is unsubtle. He stridently demands that capitalism be dismantled and replaced with socialism and then eventually communism, defined by the principle, "From each according to his abilities, to each according to his needs" (*Gotha*, 321). On this basis, along with countless other commonly cited passages from the works of Marx and Engels, the public consensus is that Marx is perhaps the most egalitarian of all household-name philosophers.

Despite this reputation, there is a growing scholarly trend suggesting this publicly received view is either greatly exaggerated or simply false. Philosopher Richard W. Miller has, for example, suggested that Marx rejected egalitarianism as "utopian" because, on his reading of Marx, equality is "ephemeral, at best."[1] Even if equality could be momentarily established, it would be undermined by luck, market forces, natural differences, and other variables. For Miller's Marx, oppressed workers do not want equality so much as they seek the "goods of freedom and reciprocity."[2] Similarly, philosopher Allen W. Wood has argued that Marx participates in a tradition—established by Rousseau, Kant, and Johann Gottlieb Fichte— that values equality merely instrumentally. For Wood, Marx only occasionally embraces egalitarian principles insofar as they facilitate greater goods, especially freedom. Per Wood, "the wisest philosophers in this tradition . . . do not regard inequality in possessions . . . as bad in itself, but do think it necessary to limit it for other ends, especially freedom (independence of the arbitrary will of another). Marx disagrees with this bourgeois tradition on many points, but fundamentally agrees with it on this one."[3] For Wood's Marx, equality lacks intrinsic value; further, it is a distracting and defective concept. On this reading, insofar as proletarians embrace egalitarianism, they are conceptually confused.

For both Miller and Wood, further, since Marx denies the desirability of perfect equality, he cannot have been an egalitarian. Wood, for example, argues that "from each . . . to each" is decidedly *not* a principle of equality.[4] It is a principle of inequality, if anything, insofar as it insists that some are to get more than others, depending on their needs. Perfect equality where the needy and satisfied receive like shares, on this account, is simply unjust.

There is some truth in these readings of Marx. I do not question, for example, that Marx places a high value of freedom as he conceives it, and that equality serves this end. But to some degree, these newer readings of Marx overcorrect the earlier orthodoxy. Quite often, when Marx speaks of equality he means "equality," as advocated by bourgeois economies. I want the reader to take careful note of the scare quotes. There is *"equality"* and *equality* in Marx, and they are importantly distinct. "Equality" in the scare quotes is the belief in capitalistic economies that "each enters into relation with the other, as with a simple owner of commodities, and they exchange equivalent for equivalent" (*Capital*, 280) to the extent each partner in a work contract exchanges equally, labor for wages. Engels sometimes calls this "bourgeois equality" (e.g., *AD*, 118). This "equality," about which even Adam Smith was skeptical (*WN*, 83–84), is often celebrated as one of the greatest virtues of bourgeois societies. Miller and Wood are correct that achieving "equality," as understood, advocated, and employed by the bourgeois, is not among Marx's goals. The bourgeois value of equality here is an equality of exchange—giving and receiving goods and services of equal value, an equality as proprietors and as bearers of rights. This equality, for Marx, is realized in the exchange of commodities.

Yet beyond *"equality"* lies *equality*—a commitment to relative material equality underlying Marx and Engels's economic and political philosophy. And related to equality, of course, is *inequality*. As Marx observed once in the *New York Tribune*, "There is, perhaps, no better-established fact in British society than that of the corresponding growth of modern wealth and pauperism" ("Lunacy," 151). Inequality was real and growing, and its effects were, for him, indisputably corrosive. This is why, for example, he and Engels praised the reactionary socialists for correctly diagnosing "the disastrous effects of . . . the crying inequalities in the distribution of wealth" (*CM*, 178–79). It is why Marx decries "the social gulf that separates the worker from the capitalist" (*WLC*, 220). And it ultimately explains how, on Engels's account, "the spontaneous reaction against the crying social [and economic] inequalities" serve "as an agitational means in order to stir up the workers against the capitalists" (*AD*, 118–19). Economic inequality is not merely divisive for Marx and Engels; it eventually becomes the force that stirs the proletariat to pursue radical changes.[5]

Inequality in Nineteenth-Century Trier

Marx would write all three volumes of *Capital* while living in London—at the same time as John Stuart Mill was regularly revising his *Principles*. Because I have already discussed the economic conditions of nineteenth-century Britain in situating Mill, however, there is no need to repeat myself. Here we can explore Marx's origins. He was born and raised in Trier in 1818, a city now found in Germany a few kilometers from modern-day Luxembourg. Scholars have only recently begun to make earnest efforts at measuring inequality in Germany before the World Wars, but the evidence suggests a pattern of fluctuations.[6] Significant inequality persisted until the Black Death of 1347–1352, which had a powerful equalizing effect on the distribution of wealth. Inequality slowly crested thereafter for nearly three centuries until the Thirty Years War (1618–1648) and the plague that accompanied it (1627–1629). Inequality thereafter slowly grew again starting around 1700 throughout the rest of the modern period until the World Wars. This inequality was likely facilitated by population growth, increased industrial production, and a regressive tax system that transferred wealth from the poor to the affluent.[7] The city of Trier, for example, imposed a tax on milling and butchering that was passed on to consumers in the form of more expensive foodstuffs, especially burdening its poorest residents. Further, this inequality was more dramatic in rural areas, such as Trier, than in major cities. From 1700 to 1850, scholars estimate that the Gini index in rural Germany grew from 0.484 to 0.593. The latter figure resembles the inequality immediately preceding the Thirty Years War.

Trier itself was a provincial city of eleven thousand along the Moselle River in Eastern Prussia.[8] Founded by the Romans in 16 BCE, it would become solidly Catholic, remaining so even after the Reformation. Napoleon's 1794 invasion introduced a series of reforms known as the Napoleonic Code, which included the abolition of aristocratic privileges, the end of feudal serfdom, and the promise of equality before the law. Thereafter, Trier and the surrounding region became significantly more industrialized, including growing industries in wallpaper, porcelain, and cloth. Pockets of wealth could be found among merchants, bankers, and landowners.

French rule ended in 1815 and the city was absorbed into Prussia, but one important consequence of cutting its French ties was the loss of important markets for its goods—both cloth and porcelain companies were compelled to cease production soon thereafter resulting in unemployment and poverty. Although there remained wealthy merchants, bankers, and landowners, they encountered striking poverty in their midst—with significant growth in begging, the auctioning of household goods, liens, and prostitution. Increasing numbers came to rely on charity. By 1832, according to one study, 80 percent of the city's population earned less than 200 talers per year, placing them at or below the poverty level. Meanwhile, 1.2 percent of the city's residents earned more than 2,500 talers annually, distinguishing themselves as the city's financial elite. As a friend of Marx's father, Johann Heinrich Schlink, wrote in 1840, "pauperism is increasing everywhere to such a degree that it occasionally rises up as a threat, so that one will ultimately have to set a limit to the further expansion of the proletariat."[9] This "threat," of course, was directed at the wealthy residents of Trier, immune to the uncertainty and hunger that burdened 80 percent of the city's population. Although inequality was prevalent in much of Prussia throughout this period, as political scientist Daniel Ziblatt has observed, "the districts with the greatest concentration of landholding [and inequality] are found in the eastern parts of Prussia," which includes Trier.[10]

Marx and the Republican Freedom from Domination

There is a much debate about the first principles of Marx's political philosophy. But perhaps the best way to arrive at those principles is to reason backward from where he desires to conclude his economic history: communism. There is some debate about this, too, as his philosophy is subject to considerable contestation and internecine disputes. Much of this controversy about his understanding of communism reflects his own opacity. But Marx is clear about this much: communism frees people from the dominating forces of their employers, a government in which they have no real input, and the market itself. These forces are all predicated in capitalism on "the antagonism between the bourgeoisie and the proletariat" (*GI*, 87). For this reason, communism requires overturning the bourgeois order and replacing it with "the power of united individuals"—it "turns existing conditions into conditions of unity" (*GI*, 90).

Although Marx is notoriously vague about communism, one passage is particularly revealing. In the *German Ideology*, Marx (with Engels) notes that under communism, one can "hunt in the morning, fish in the afternoon, rear cattle in the evening, criticize after dinner." What makes this passage important, however, is not that anyone should be compelled to do any of these things but rather the absence of compulsion. In describing the day of a communist citizen, Marx and Engels contrast it with the lives of those lacking such choices. To live under capitalism is to have imposed activities and vocations. Before communism, one must be a "hunter, a fisherman, a shepherd, or a cultural critic, and must remain so if he does not want to lose his means of livelihood." His language throughout this discussion is evocative. He speaks of "alien power[s]" looming over workers that "enslave[s]" them (*GI*, 53). This is to say, capitalism effectively controls and dominates individuals so that they are entirely at the mercy of forces beyond their own control. Communism is, for Marx, freedom from this domination—from the compulsive forces of one's employer, from the bourgeoisie, from the system of private property, from a government directed by bourgeois forces.

Political theorist Frank Lovett has recently defined domination this way: "*A's* choice whether to *Φ* is dominated to the extent that some *B* has the uncontrolled ability to intentionally frustrate that choice." Further, he defines unfreedom: "*A* is not free to *Φ* to the extent that some *B* has the uncontrolled ability to intentionally frustrate *A's* choice whether to *Φ*."[11] Taken together, these two conditions of domination and unfreedom constitute the antithesis of republicanism, which valorizes freedom from domination. It is easy enough, as political theorist William Clare Roberts has persuasively argued, to understand Marx as a republican in these terms. Reading in Lovett's terms, a worker (*A*) is dominated to the extent that the bourgeoisie (*B*) has the ability to frustrate his choice to go hunting (*Φ*), for example, because his long hours and exhausting job leave him no energy or opportunity to do so. His lack of freedom is reinforced by related constraints. If he asks for more vacation time, he is fired. If he asks for shorter hours, he is fired. If he attempts to promote legislation that would address these constraints, he will find the legislature controlled by the bourgeoisie and, hence, obstructive. In all of these ways, Marx's workers are "dominated" and subjected to forces largely beyond their control.

Among those forces, I argue, is the economic inequality Marx identifies as a permanent feature of capitalism. This is for several reasons. Most obvious, the poverty often associated with inequality radically restricts the choices of workers who worry about where to find their next meal; they will not have the options available to republican citizens. But the great wealth on the other side of the economic divide creates its own forces of compulsion. The bourgeoisie, for Marx, controls economic and political institutions and then uses these institutions to dominate the proletariat. Communism, for Marx, is the condition of overthrowing this domination and its related forces. As such, communism requires dismantling the radical inequality that characterized capitalism through the nineteenth century.

Understanding Marx as a republican committed to a significant degree of economic equality places him in a tradition outlined in this book. This republican tradition can be traced all the way back to the mythical Spartan lawgiver, Lycurgus, who founded the ancient Greek republic on fairly strict terms of economic equality. Plato's Socrates would found the republican Kallipolis on similar terms of equality. And Rousseau would also expressly understand his ideal republic of the *Social Contract* as egalitarian. This association of republicanism and economic equality can also be found in figures not featured in this book, such as James Harrington, John Adams, and Frederick Douglass—all of whom worried about the power of concentrated wealth to dominate and oppress fellow citizens. All insisted that that wealth would have to be more broadly distributed to achieve their republican visions. This is not to say that they would have shared in Marx's communism. There are, naturally, many flavors of republicanism, but most all share a foundational assumption that inequality undermines republican principles.

"Equality" in Marx

Marx often speaks of "equality" pejoratively. "Equality" is not always good. And quite often it is pernicious on his account. Underlying its potential danger is the fact many, especially in bourgeois society, are inclined to view equality as a noble aspiration—an object of admiration. It is no accident, for Marx, that equality was one of the three fundamental objectives of the French Revolution, along with freedom and fraternity. Yet "equality" can, of course, assume countless interpretations and dimensions. For him, the bourgeois in capitalist economies is particularly committed to one particular conception of equality. Bourgeois "equality" is one of capitalism's core values, along with "freedom," "property," and "Bentham" (self-interest). By "equality," capitalist societies presuppose that "each enters into relation with the other, as with a simple owner of commodities, and they exchange equivalent for equivalent" (*Capital*, 280).[12] That is, capitalism recognizes all citizens as equals insofar as they can freely and equally contract with one another.

This conception of nefarious "equality" or bourgeois equality is not new with Marx. It can be found in Rousseau's *Discourse on Inequality*, where the rich and poor had come to loggerheads as the former had grown so wealthy and rapacious that they preyed on the poor for sport, "like those ravenous wolves which once they have tasted human flesh scorn all other food, and from then on want to devour only men" (*SD*, 171). Understanding that the rich were the only ones with something to lose, the poor responded violently. The twist in this story, however, is that the rich used this war to hatch an ingenious plan that would establish peace and legitimate their wealth. They proposed "rules of justice" that would "secure for everyone the possession of what belongs to him." This proposal of equal justice—whereby the "powerful and the weak alike" would be subjected to "mutual duties"—had the ring of fairness such that the poor quickly agreed to its terms. Yet in doing so, Rousseau argues, the contract gave "the weak new fetters, and the rich new forces," forever fixing "the Law of property and inequality" (*SD*, 172). This is why, as he elaborates in his *Emile*, that there is a "de jure equality that is chimerical and vain" in much of Europe, but that such "equality" in the modern state often serves as an instrument of violence and iniquity (*Emile*, 236). So for Rousseau, when the wealthy and powerful speak of the "equality" enjoyed in civil society, the majority should suspect that this "equality" is a weapon of the rich and powerful to maintain their privileges.

Engels would acknowledge Rousseau's discovery in which "each new advance of civilization is at the same time a new advance of inequality." For him, "in Rousseau . . . we find not only a line of thought which corresponds exactly to the one developed in Marx's *Capital*, but also, in details, a whole series of the same dialectical turns of speech as Marx used." He continues that the great error of Marx's opponents, such as Herr Eugen Dühring, was to employ a "shallow version of Rousseau's theory of equality," falsely taking legal equality alone to be sufficient without a corresponding economic equality (*AD*, 193–94). For Rousseau, such accounts of legal equality without economic equality are "only apparent and illusory," where equality "serves only to maintain the poor in his misery and the rich in his usurpation" (*SC*, 1.9, 58n).[13]

Returning to Marx, this dubious "equality" manifests in the labor contract. This is where two parties are said to be equal partners in a shared legal endeavor, yet where one party leverages its wealth to dominate the other. In the employment contract, the capitalist is said to be contractually equal to the worker. Neither party is formally recognized as having legal privilege or otherwise higher standing. As with Rousseau's narrative, achieving this "equality" of the labor contract took generations to accomplish. Per Marx, "centuries are required before the 'free' worker, owing to the greater development of the capitalist mode of production, makes a voluntary agreement, i.e., is compelled by social conditions to sell the whole of his active life, his very capacity for labour, in return for the price of his customary means of subsistence, to sell his birthright for a mess of pottage" (*Capital*, 382). In creating such disparate classes capitalism fashions a radical inequality with all the appearances of legitimacy. As Marx subsequently elaborates in *Capital*,

> all the notions of justice held by both the worker and the capitalist, all the mystifications of the capitalist mode of production, all capitalism's illusions about freedom, all the apologetic tricks of vulgar economics, have as their basis the form of appearance discussed above [concerning the supposed equal exchange of labor for wages], which makes the actual relation invisible, and indeed presents to the eye the precise opposition of that relation. (*Capital*, 680)

Namely, the ideas of justice and equality appear noble and legitimate. Yet the actual effect of those ideas as implemented in capitalist economies cuts against those very objectives.[14] "Equality," as Marx elaborates in his analysis on the French Declaration of the Rights of Man, "consists in the fact that the law is the same for all, whether it protects or whether it punishes" (*JQ*, 17). In the French Revolution, this most immediately meant terminating aristocratic and feudal rights and privileges, such as were mocked in Pierre Beaumarchais and Wolfgang Amadeus Mozart's *Marriage of Figaro*. This triumph over the old order, however, soon became for Marx the rights governing the labor contract between employer and employee, which are equal only in the relevant sense. And this bourgeois "equality" became the foundation of a material inequality. Perhaps the greatest champion of bourgeois equality might be Immanuel Kant, who expressly separates legal or "bourgeois" equality from economic equality:

"this thoroughgoing [legal] equality of individuals within a state, as its subjects, is quite consistent with the greatest inequality in terms of the quantity and degree of their possessions, whether in physical or mental superiority of others or in external goods."[15] For Kant, as with the revolution, the primary goal was to eliminate the legal inequalities that lingered from the feudal age. Economic inequalities emerging from a bourgeois system were to be accepted as just.

As Engels would insist, there is an important difference to be noted in "the equality of the bourgeoisie (abolition of class privileges)" from "that of the proletariat (abolition of the classes)" (AD, 478). Whereas the bourgeois sought to establish "equality" for themselves to ascend to unprecedented economic heights, the workers would evoke a proletarian, material equality that would ultimately abolish classes altogether. This reveals how they understand two different and often opposing conceptions of equality. As literary critic Terry Eagleton has observed, Marx "associated the notion of equality with what he saw as the abstract [bourgeois] equality of middle-class democracy, where our formal equality . . . serves to obscure real inequalities of wealth and class."[16]

The Origins of Inequality in Marx

The economic inequality that most interests Marx is found in capitalist economies. This is true both because Marx occupied this historical epoch but also because its inequality was in some ways the most dramatic. Yet he is fully aware that inequality has prevailed throughout recorded history: "The history of all hitherto existing society is the history of class struggle" (CM, 158). Societies have typically been organized by classes, and those classes are defined by economic divides. Marx and Engels continue, "Freeman and slave, patrician and plebeian, lord and serf, guild-master and journeyman, in a word, oppressor and oppressed, stood in constant opposition to one another." History, to their minds, has always been characterized by opposing classes, with the wealthy oppressing the poor. Furthermore, they observe that capitalism has emerged from the "ruins of feudal society," but it "has not done away with class antagonisms" (CM, 159). It has sustained the antagonisms characterizing earlier civilizations, only with modified rules that facilitate even greater inequalities.

Marx and Engels provide some explanation in the Manifesto of how this transition from feudal inequality to bourgeois inequality happened.[17] Among other things, the discovery of the Americas, along with increased engagement with East and South Asia created new commercial opportunities. But the *Manifesto* only really hints at how inequality evolved. For the longer answer, one must turn to volume 1 of *Capital*.

According to Marx, there is a distant past of inequality that explains its origins to all citizens of capitalist economies—a past as remote and mythical as the story of the Garden of Eden:

> Long, long ago there were two sorts of people: one, the diligent, intelligent, and above all the frugal élite; the other, lazy rascals, spending their substance, and more, in riotous living. The legend of theological original sin tells us certainly how man came to be condemned to eat his bread in the sweat of his brow; but the history of economic sin reveals to us that there are people to whom this is by no means essential. Never mind! Thus it came to pass that the former sort accumulated wealth and the latter sort finally had nothing to sell but their own skins. And from this original sin dates the poverty of the great majority who, despite all their labor, have up to now nothing to sell but themselves, and the wealth of the few that increases constantly, although they have long ceased to work. Such insipid childishness is every day preached to us in the defense of property. . . . [A]s soon as the question of property is at stake, it becomes a sacred duty to proclaim the standpoint of the nursery tale as the one thing fit for all age-groups and all stages of development. In actual history, it is a notorious fact that conquest, enslavement, robbery, murder, in short, force, play the greatest part. In the tender annals of political economy, the idyllic reigns from time immemorial. Right and 'labor' were from the beginning of time the sole means of enrichment, 'this year,' of course always excepted. As a matter of fact, the methods of primitive accumulation are anything but idyllic. (*Capital*, 873–74)[18]

This details what might be called the *myth of meritocracy*. The wealthy want to believe that their status resulted from their own intelligence, diligence, efforts, and frugality—the so-called bourgeois virtues—or at least the virtues of their ancestors. But perhaps even more important, they need the poor to believe the same. If the poor understand the rich to have earned their fortunes, they cannot begrudge them their rewards. It is simultaneously important that the poor understand their poverty reflects their own peculiar lack of talent and effort. Accepting their faults facilitates the acceptance of their fates.[19] This attribution of wealth and poverty to character and talents originates at least as far as the French economist Anne Robert Jacques Turgot, who in 1770 insisted that the "most powerful" of all causes of inequality is the "contrast between the intelligence, the activity, and above all the thrift of some with the indolence, inactivity, and extravagance of others."[20] Two decades later Kant would echo that the poor man must understand "the fault" for his condition "lies only in himself ([his lack of] ability or earnest will)."[21] If you are rich, it is because of your own extraordinary talents and efforts; if you are poor, it is because you are untalented and lazy. This underlying belief system validates the striking inequalities required in market economies, according to Marx.

Of course, for Marx, the myth of meritocracy is convenient—devised or at least promoted by those occupying society's top economic rungs. It is a form of ideology, a set of values established to protect the ruling order, just as bourgeois equality is itself a myth on his account. It helps the bourgeois to promote the myth that everyone is equal in a world where they factually are not, insofar as the poor believe they had an equal shot at success. They cannot complain about their poverty, so the reasoning goes, if they have been treated equally by the law. Insofar as the poor believe this, the bourgeois order has been effectively preserved. This is the function of ideology in Marx's understanding of bourgeois society.

This myth contradicts Marx's reality. The *real* source of inequality is "conquest, enslavement, robbery, murder, in short, force."[22] He sketches this process, at least from the discovery of the New World, in chapter 31 of *Capital*:

> The discovery of gold and silver in America, the extirpation, enslavement and entombment in mines of the indigenous population of the continent, the beginnings of the conquest and plunder of India, and the conversion of Africa into a preserve for the commercial hunting of blackskins, are all things which characterize the dawn of the era of capitalist production. These idyllic proceedings are the chief moments of primitive accumulation. (*Capital*, 915)

In describing how inequality emerged from the feudal world, he repeatedly emphasizes the role of violence and brutality. "Force," he insists, "is the midwife of every old society which is pregnant with a new one. It is itself an economic power." He recounts the Dutch republic's original sins in building its commercial empire—one built on "treachery, bribery, massacre, and meanness." He depicts the "victims of greed and tyranny, fettered in chains, forcibly torn from their families." The Dutch hollowed out countless villages in the East Indies condemning the inhabitants to generations of brutal slavery, all in the name of "*doux commerce*" (*Capital*, 916).[23] The pious English Puritans were little better in this regard "set[ting] a premium of £40 on every Indian scalp and every captured redskin," subsequently raising the bounty to £100 to accelerate the violence—all to make New England safe for commerce (*Capital*, 917–18).

The violence committed in Africa, Asia, and the Americas generated natural resources that would flow back to Europe. Manufacturing these resources into commodities facilitated, for Marx, "the concentration of capital" and a "vast increase in accumulation which was guaranteed by the mother country's monopoly of the market." As he summarizes his assessment of this "primitive accumulation," the "treasures captured outside Europe by undisguised looting, enslavement, and murder flowed back to the mother-country and were turned into capital there." And this concentration of capital in a small set of hands was the most proximate cause of modern inequality. In discussing early modern Holland, specifically in 1648, Marx cites the economic heights achieved by its bourgeois class, in a country with total capital "greater than that of all the rest of Europe put together," while its laborers were "more over-worked, poorer, and more brutally oppressed than those of all the rest of Europe put together" (*Capital*, 918). Theft, violence, and brutality generated massive wealth for a lucky few. But this is only the beginning of the story for Marx.

Once raw materials arrived from the New World to fashion into commodities, workers would be required. This is where his narrative gets more involved, not because the methods of further accumulation would be less violent and brutal but only because its methods would become subtler. The key is the ability of employers to extract uncompensated labor. They do this by paying workers considerably less than the value they add to the raw materials they fashion into commodities. The difference between these wages and the sale price of those commodities (minus the raw materials and other overhead costs) represents the employer's profit.[24] The more unpaid labor the employer extracts from the worker, everything else being equal, the greater the profit.

As market competition increases, capitalists are compelled to lower the costs of their commodities. These low prices are facilitated by decreasing the costs of production—namely, in reducing labor costs. Their wages can simply be lowered, they can be compelled to work for longer hours, or productivity can be increased through the further division of labor or technological advances, thus displacing numerous laborers, who then return to the "surplus army" of the unemployed. In all cases, the result is greater hardship and poverty for the workers, especially since the larger pool of unemployed workers further depresses wages. But beyond this, those able to win the greater share of the marketplace effectively also drive their competitors out of business. As Marx notes, marketplace competition "always ends in the ruin of many small capitalists, whose capital partly pass into the hands of their conquerors, and partly vanish completely" (*Capital*, 777). This is what Marx and Engels elsewhere describe as the gradual but almost inevitable descent of the middle class, who are "swamped in the competition with the large capitalists," into the proletariat (*CM*, 165). Engels describes this process in greater depth specifically in the context of industrial capitalism:

> We have seen how industry has been concentrated into fewer hands. Industry needs large amounts of capital in order to erect colossal factories which work so efficiently and cheaply that they drive the lower middle-class craftsmen out of business. The division of labour, the use of water power and steam power, and the introduction of modern machinery have been the three great forces which industry has used since the middle of the eighteenth century to upset the growth of the middle class. Large-scale industry, on the other hand, has created a class of propertyless wage earners and has raised a small number of the middle classes to position of great wealth and influence. This elevation of the chosen few has been spectacular, but their eventual downfall can be prophesied with certainty. No one can deny the obvious fact that the lower middle classes of the "good old days"—once quite a large section of the population— have been destroyed by the Industrial Revolution. It is equally obvious their place has been taken by the rich capitalists on the one hand and the poverty-stricken workers on the other. (*Condition*, 27–28)

The steady destruction of the middle class is central to the inequality distinctive to capitalism. As competition for market shares advances, those with resources to scale up production and reduce prices can seize a greater share of the market. Those with fewer resources descend into the ranks of the proletariat. As Marx would observe in his *German Ideology*, "Commerce and manufacturing created the big bourgeoisie; in the guilds was concentrated the petty bourgeoisie. . . . Hence the decline of the guilds, as soon as they came into contact with manufacturing" (*GI*, 78). And if some of the middle class can beat the odds and grab market shares through the force of their bourgeois virtues, they would then ascend to the bourgeois class themselves. The tendency of competition under capitalism is always that "the larger capital beats the smaller" (*Capital*, 777). In capitalist economies it is the fate of the middle class to dwindle continuously. And this is, of course, a formula for economic inequality since a society consisting only of the very rich, on the one hand, and "poverty-stricken workers," on the other, is necessarily unequal.

Marx further argues that capitalism requires its workers to be poor. That is, it only works in a context of economic inequality. To make this point, he references Bernard Mandeville, author of *Fable of the Bees* and broadly understood as the intellectual godfather of market economies. In his *Fable*, Mandeville assumes that most people are naturally lazy: "Man never exerts himself but when he is rous'd by his Desires" such that when his needs are met he never achieves his "Excellence and Abilities" but rather becomes a "lumpish Machine," who can "be justly compar'd to a huge Wind-mill without a breath of Air."[25] For some, according to Mandeville, the inspiration to work can come from vanity—the desire to be recognized for one's talents. But this is inapplicable to the working class. For them, the primary motivation to work comes from their "bellies." Because of their "extraordinary proclivity to Idleness, what reasons have we to think that they would ever work, unless they were oblig'd to it by immediate necessity?" As Mandeville asks, "Why should we imagine he would go to it at all, if he had fifteen or twenty pounds in his Pocket?" It is, thus, the civic duty of employers, on this reasoning, to pay low wages to ensure that laborers will return to work tomorrow and every day thereafter: "The only thing then that can render the laboring Man industrious, is a moderate quantity of Money; for as too little will, according as his Temper is, either dispirit or make him Desperate, so too much will make him Insolent and Lazy."[26]

Marx seizes on Mandeville's candor about this underlying assumption of bourgeois economies—that laborers must be poor to keep them working. Indeed, he praises Mandeville as "an honest man with a clear mind." What Mandeville admitted freely is, for Marx, the brutal assumption underlying the bourgeois economy: it can only be sustained on a policy of subsistence wages. As he subsequently elaborates, "everything therefore depends on making hunger permanent among the working class" (*Capital*, 800). But he adds something that he believes Mandeville missed: the more the laboring poor work for the bourgeois, the richer the bourgeoisie becomes. So inequality is not only created by impoverishing the workers but also by further enriching the capitalist class. Beyond this, pauperizing the working class creates, for Marx, an "eternal relation" of dependence of workers on their employees (*Capital*, 765), which turns out to be one of the most striking effects of inequality on his account.

Effects of Inequality in Marx

Inequality's persistence in industrial capitalism is inevitable for Marx. It remains to consider its individual and social effects. More so than perhaps anyone in this book, Marx is especially attuned to the effects of inequality on the working poor. These effects can be understood in both absolute and relative terms. That is, there are distinctive features of brute poverty in industrial capitalism, and there are the more psychological but still very real effects of poverty relative to the wealthy bourgeois. But I stress that Marx, even in speaking of poverty in absolute terms, is also addressing inequality. Capitalism, for him, requires both keeping workers on the edge of starvation and a bourgeoisie poised to exploit laborers' desperate circumstances. As Roberts has astutely noted, "vast inequality of wealth is, according to Marx, one of the essential conditions of capitalist production, and is constantly reproduced by capitalist production."[27]

EFFECTS ON THE POOR

When people read *Capital*, they generally focus on celebrated snippets, such as the passages on the fetishism of commodities or the origins and mechanics of surplus labor, since they are understood as Marx's original contributions to economics. While they are right to study these passages, what is often lost is his considerable attention to the laborers' working and living conditions. These passages reveal just how much Marx focused on their plight. By the time he turns to "The Working Day" in chapter 10 of *Capital*, their physical and mental suffering becomes his obsession.

At the outset, I emphasize that while Marx is discussing the condition of the poor, one must bear in mind that their suffering is borne out as part of a structural inequality. While they suffer in absolute terms, their poverty is facilitated and even mandated by a system defined by a chasm between rich and poor. And as Marx saw in Mandeville, the bourgeoisie *needs* the workers to be poor, desperately so, since any condition above this would undermine their incentive to work. The state of the poor is very much part of an essentially inegalitarian system. Marx explains in chapter 25. It follows from the "absolute general law of capitalist accumulation" that "in proportion as capital accumulates, the situation of the worker, be his payment high or low, must grow worse." It further follows that "it makes an accumulation of misery a necessary condition, corresponding to the accumulation of wealth. Accumulation of wealth at one pole, therefore, at the same time accumulation of misery, the torment of labour, slavery, ignorance, brutalization, and moral degradation at the opposite pole, i.e., on the side of the class that produces its own product as capital" (*Capital*, 799). Although wealth in capitalism may not be zero sum, where one person's economic gain was necessarily the loss of another, misery appears to be. The more suffering endured by the working class, the greater the pleasures enjoyed by the bourgeoisie.

Much of this attention is addressed to the poor's sheer physical suffering in industrial capitalism. Broadly speaking, on Marx's account, workplaces are "dens of misery where capitalist exploitation is given free rein to commit the most frightful iniquities" (*Capital*, 621). Quoting from a commissioned report in 1863, for example, he addresses the condition of workers in pottery factories:

> The potters as a class, both men and women, represent a degenerated population, both physically and morally. They are, as a rule, stunted in growth, ill-shaped, and frequently ill-formed in the chest; they become prematurely old, and are certainly short-lived; they are phlegmatic and bloodless, and exhibit their debility of constitution by obstinate attacks of dyspepsia, and disorders of the liver and kidneys, and by rheumatism. But of all diseases they are especially prone to chest-disease, to pneumonia, phthisis, bronchitis, and asthma. (*Capital*, 355)[28]

Citing available statistics, he notes that more than half of the deaths in the pottery district can be attributed to working conditions.

Among the most common health problems of the working poor, according to Marx, was insufficient and poor nutrition. Workers were undernourished, and what they ate was frequently malnourishing. He notes, with irony, that agricultural workers were among the "worst fed" (*Capital*, 809), with women and children being particularly malnourished. Among cotton workers, less than half had beer,[29] and more than a quarter lacked milk. Insufficient beer may seem a peculiar—or even amusing—problem to report from a twenty-first-century perspective, but beer was often a significant source of calories for the working class in the nineteenth century, not to mention it was typically freer from dangerous microorganisms in the water supply. Those deprived of beer often failed to reach adequate daily calorie needs. On multiple occasions, Marx notes the paucity of meat as a form of protein for the working poor (e.g., *Capital*, 827, 834, 835, 867, 902n). Citing a Dr. Simon, author of the "General Health Report," Marx notes that "cases are innumerable in which defective diet is the cause or aggravator of disease" among a large class of workers (*Capital*, 810). As also noted by Mill, one of the regular culprits in the malnutrition of laborers was adulteration of foods. "The adulteration of bread, and the formation of a class of bakers who sell bread for less than its full price, are developments which have taken place since the beginning of the eighteenth century" (*Capital*, 361). Adulteration was not limited to foods. It was also determined by a Parliamentary Commission that "the adulteration even of medicines is the rule, not the exception, in England" (*Capital*, 750n). The very existence of adulterated foods and medicines, of course, was incentivized by the market to sell to the poorest workers. At one point, Marx quotes the lamenting deposition of witnesses to the living conditions of the poor: "The diet of the English prisons is superior to that of ordinary labourers in England" (*Capital*, 834). The adulteration had measurable effects in childhood growth. In the 1870s, the average height of eleven- to twelve-year-old boys in upper-class schools was five inches taller than those of boys in working-class industrial schools.[30]

Beyond food, hygiene was also a persistent problem for the working poor. To illustrate this problem, Marx quotes at length Dr. Simon once again:

> Long before insufficiency of diet is a matter of hygienic concern, long before the physiologist would think of counting the grains of nitrogen and carbon which intervene between life and starvation, the household will have been utterly destitute of material comfort; clothing and fuel will have been scantier than food—against inclemencies of weather there will have been no adequate protection—dwelling space there will have been stinted to the degree in which over-crowding produces or increases disease; of household utensils and furniture there will have been scarcely any—even cleanliness will have been found costly and difficult, and if there still be self-respectful endeavors to maintain it, every such endeavor will represent additional pangs of hunger. The home, too, will be where shelter can be cheapest bought; in quarters where commonly there is least fruit of sanitary supervision, least drainage, least scavenging, least suppression of public nuisances, least or worst water supply, and, if in town, least light and air. Such are the sanitary dangers to which poverty is almost certainly exposed.

Marx emphasizes immediately after depicting the dietary and hygienic distress of the working poor its "intimate connection" with the "extravagant consumption, coarse or refined, of the rich" (*Capital*, 811). He continues, "The more quickly capitalist accumulation takes place, the more miserable the housing situation of the working class" (*Capital*, 812). The sufferings of the working poor are, for him, part of a larger structural inequality, where the bourgeoisie's luxurious lifestyle requires the deprivations of the working poor.

Poverty, malnutrition, dangerous working conditions, and poor hygiene among workers, of course, took a toll on working-class mortality rates. Quoting a medical health officer from Manchester, Marx[31] cites,

> The average age of death of the Manchester upper middle class was 38 years, while the average age of death of the laboring class was 17; while at Liverpool those figures were represented as 35 against 15. It

thus appeared that the well-to-do classes had a lease on life which was more than double the value of that which fell to the lot of the less favoured citizens. (*Capital*, 795)

These statistics are consistent with what Engels reports in his *Condition of the Working Class in England*. He found that whereas England's annual death rate in this period was one in every forty-five residents, the rates were much higher in industrial towns. Drawing on reports by G. Graham, he compares mortality rates between those living in "third class" homes versus those in the "first class," finding a death rate that is 78 percent higher for those in the third class (*Condition*, 121).

Beyond poverty's sheer physical toll on its workers for Marx, however, were its psychic costs. Foundational to understanding the psychic price of inequality on the working poor is his theory of alienation. Central to Marx's conception of alienation is the somewhat mystifying sentence, "The worker becomes poorer the more wealth he produces, the more his production increases in power and extent" (*EPM*, 59). Most immediately, this means modern wage laborers do not own the products they make. Whereas in earlier generations in different economic structures, those who made commodities were themselves their owners, free to use, sell, or barter as they saw fit, workers now owned only their wages. So the harder they work, the more commodities were owned by their employers—for *employers* to use, sell, or barter as they wished.

But this reading does not fully explain how the workers are "poorer" for having worked harder. Their wages are low—subsistence level, in fact. For the most part, they cannot drop lower than that for fear of triggering a class revolt. So in what sense is the worker poorer, as Marx insists they are? To answer this question, it is helpful to consider an underappreciated passage from his *Wage Labour and Capital*, written soon after his *Economic and Philosophic Manuscripts*:

A house may be large or small; as long as the surrounding houses are equally small it satisfies all social demands for a dwelling. But let a palace arise beside the little house, and it shrinks from a little house to a hut. The little house now that its owner has only very slight or no demands to make; and however high it may shoot up in the course of civilization, if the neighboring palace grows to an equal or even greater extent, the occupant of the relatively small house will feel more and more uncomfortable, dissatisfied, and cramped within its four walls. (*WLC*, 216)[32]

This description of inequality's psychic effects clarifies how the "worker becomes poorer the more wealth he produces." This is because he speaks of wealth and poverty in *relative* terms. As the worker creates greater wealth for his employer, he may not be poorer in absolute terms. But he becomes poorer in relative terms since his employer harvests all the fruits of the worker's additional exertions. With those results, the bourgeois can build or expand his palace. In witnessing the new economic heights of his employer, especially relative to his own poverty, the worker becomes increasingly "uncomfortable, dissatisfied, and cramped."

Marx insists this phenomenon is about inequality and not simply poverty. It is quite possible that workers' wages might grow incrementally, but so long as top fortunes grow disproportionately more, as he elaborates throughout section 4 of this essay, laborers become poorer in relative terms. As he continues:

> The rapid growth of productive capital brings about an equally rapid growth of wealth, luxury, social wants, social enjoyments. Thus although the enjoyments of the worker have risen, the social satisfaction that they give has fallen in comparison with the increased enjoyments of the capitalist, which are inaccessible to the worker, in comparison with the state of development of society in general. (*WLC*, 216)

He speaks here of the multiplication of desires, a theme also present in the *Manifesto* (*CM*, 162). Rousseau had expressed this particular concern almost a century earlier: "Nature gives us quite enough needs; and it is at the very least exceedingly imprudent to multiply them unnecessarily" (*Last Reply*, 84; see also Smith's *WN*, 181).[33] But what most interests Marx is how those needs are formed in relationship to the luxuries enjoyed by the rich. In witnessing the bourgeois enjoy their luxuries, the poor cannot but help to desire them. Yet their relative poverty pushes those luxuries out of reach. Hence the discomfort and dissatisfaction he describes.

This dissatisfaction exists in the context of rising absolute wages for the workers, since "wages are, above all, . . . determined by their relation to the gain, to the profit of the capitalist—comparative, relative wages" (*WLC*, 218). As Marx subsequently observes, the "material position of the worker" can improve "but at the cost of his social position. The social gulf that divides him from the capitalist has widened" (*WLC*, 221). He similarly comments in *Capital* that "in proportion as capital accumulates, the situation of the worker, be his payment high or low, must grow worse" (*Capital*, 799). And as he elaborates a few pages later, "if the extremes of poverty have not lessened, they have increased, because the extremes of wealth have"

(*Capital*, 806). It may be that as the wealth of nations grows, so grows the absolute wealth of the lower classes, but it continually grows worse in *relative* terms. This observation represents Marx's reply to Bernard Mandeville's *Fable of the Bees*, which opened with his poem "The Grumbling Hive."[34] A primary theme of the poem, and indeed the entire *Fable*, is the need to relax moral regulations to promote greater commerce, which would in turn promote the greater good of the community. That poem included the following stanza:

> Thus Vice nurs'd Ingenuity,
> Which join'd with Time and Industry
> Had carry'd Life's Coveniences,
> It's real Pleasures, Comforts, Ease,
> To such a Height, the very Poor
> Liv'd better than the Rich before,
> And nothing could be added more.[35]

Like Rousseau and Marx, Mandeville connects economic growth to the growing access to conveniences and luxuries. Also further, like them, he connects this growth to vice. But what is of particular interest here is the phrase, "To such a Height, the very Poor Liv'd better than the Rich before." He elaborates on this in Remark P later in the *Fables*:

> If we trace the most flourishing Nations in their Origin, we shall find that in the remote Beginnings of every Society, the richest and most considerable Men among them were a great while destitute of a great many Comforts of Life that are now enjoy'd by the meanest and must humble Wretches: So that many things which were once look'd upon as those that are so miserably poor as to be Objects of publick Charity, nay counted so necessary, that we think no Human Creature ought to want [for] them.[36]

For Mandeville, the growth of commerce and industry raises the living conditions of all in absolute terms. As Adam Smith would later echo, the growth of market economies "is so great, that all are often abundantly supplied, and a workman, even of the lowest and poorest order, if he is frugal and industrious, may enjoy a greater share of the necessities and conveniences of life than it is possible for any savage to acquire" (*WN*, 10). The point, for both Mandeville and Smith, is that while capitalism may not reduce inequality—which is not identified as problematic for Mandeville—it nevertheless improves the absolute living standards of all, especially the poor, such that "those who were once the greatest and richest of the Land would have Reason to envy the most reduced of our Species now."[37] And that seems to his mind to be of greater importance.

Marx does not expressly contest the argument that a rising tide of market economies lifts all boats, although some of his portraits of the conditions of the working poor in the nineteenth century suggest doubts. What he instead presses is that even where the conditions of the poor may be improving in absolute terms, inequality and its associated effects march forward.[38] Here, again, I flag inequality's psychic costs, such as dissatisfaction and depression, not to mention demoralization. Later I will address the further problems of inequality, especially dependence, antagonism, and the imbalances of power.

Many, of course, will dismiss this psychological experience as "envy" and unworthy of dignifying with philosophical, much less policy, attention. The philosopher John Rawls regarded envy as "something to be avoided and feared" and therefore simply assumed its absence in designing his principles of justice.[39] His colleague Robert Nozick referred to the "strangeness" of envy, asking, "Why don't they just shrug it off?" and concludes that little to nothing can be done about it.[40] Economists Deirdre McCloskey and Art Carden have commented, the "obsession with inequality walks with the soul-corroding sin of envy" and suggest that the relatively poor should be grateful that rich people are growing the economy and improving their lives thereby.[41] Steven Pinker dismisses "spiteful envy" as an unfortunate disposition that unfairly demonizes the successful. He recommends that the poor should embrace inequality as "heartening" insofar as it inspires their self-improvement. If anything, it is "a harbinger of opportunity."[42]

Yet these attitudes disregard Marx's myth of meritocracy and its associated psychic effects. This myth was unnecessary before industrial capitalism, even in the obviously unequal feudal era, because there was little pretense of justifying those inequalities. There was little to envy in feudalism because people's social status was not a reflection of their character. No one was personally responsible for their stations in life, as became the case in market societies. While feudal inequality was problematic in other respects, inequality assumed new complications. This is, again, why inequality engenders discomfort and dissatisfaction for Marx. This is almost confirmed by Pinker's optimism. For the Harvard professor, inequality should inspire hope since we, too, can aspire to be rich in an unequal society. Yet he fails to address what happens when people strive for wealth and fail, as so many do. Is it because they are stupid? Is it because they are lazy? Is it because they lack talent? These are the psychic and even existential questions that Marx provokes in *Wage Labour and Capital* with his story of the hut and the palace. In this context, envy is not so much "strange," as Nozick offers, as inevitable. In capitalism, the palace next door is a burning reminder of one's personal failures. And every time the mansion expands relative to the huts, for Marx, the poor feel smaller and increasingly worthless.

The psychic consequences of poverty in an unequal society are only one dimension of the nonphysical toll taken on the poor. The effects of the division of labor itself are also profoundly felt on the intellectual capacities of the working poor, as even Adam Smith knew. Marx is familiar with Smith's depiction of workers and quotes him extensively in *Capital*:

> The man whose whole life is spent in performing a few simple operations, of which the effects too are, perhaps, always the same, or very nearly the same, has no occasion to exert his understanding, or to exercise his invention in finding out expedients for removing difficulties which never occur. He naturally loses, therefore, the habit of such exertion, and generally becomes as stupid and ignorant as it is possible for a human creature to become. The torpor of his mind renders him, not only incapable of relishing or bearing a part in any rational conversation, but of conceiving any generous, noble, or tender sentiment, and consequently of forming any just judgment concerning many even of the ordinary duties of private life. (*Capital*, 483; *WN*, 781–82)

Smith's attention to the debilitating effects of the division of labor was not lost on Marx. On the Prussian's account, "a worker who performs the same simple operation for the whole of his life converts his body into the automatic, one-sided implement of that operation" (*Capital*, 458). He quotes Smith's Scottish predecessor, Adam Ferguson, that in so narrowing labor to such repeated discrete tasks, "We make a nation of Helots, and have no free citizens" (*Capital*, 474),[43] just as Smith had worried about workers in the division of labor, "Of the great and extensive interests of his country he is altogether incapable of judging" (*WN*, 782). But Marx expands, insisting the division of labor "converts the worker into a crippled monstrosity by furthering his particular skill as in a forcing-house through the suppression of a whole world of productive drives and inclinations" (*Capital*, 481). He expressly connects these abuses to inequality. The division of labor as it exists in industrial capitalism is a feature, not a bug, of its larger structural inequality: "In manufacture, the social productive power of the collective worker, hence of capital, is enriched through the impoverishment of the worker in individual productive power." The entire incentive for the division of labor is, of course, to increase profits—and those proceeds belong exclusively to the bourgeoisie. Further, he continues, it is to the factory owner's advantage to numb the minds of his workers as much as possible: "Manufacturers, accordingly, prosper most where the mind [of the worker] is least consulted." It benefits the bourgeoisie to "employ semi-idiots" so that the work can be performed most efficiently with minimal fuss (*Capital*, 483).

Marx passionately depicts these effects in the section on "Alienated Labor" from his *Economic and Philosophic Manuscripts*. The working poor are dispirited by their labor:

> The worker does not affirm himself in his work but denies himself, feels miserable and unhappy, develops no free physical and mental energy but mortifies his flesh and ruins his mind. The worker, therefore, feels at ease only outside work, and during work he is outside himself. . . . His work, therefore, is not voluntary, but coerced, *forced labor*. (*EPM*, 61–62; emphasis original)

This degrading work is "coerced," for Marx, because the poor man has nowhere else to turn to feed himself and his family. He must submit to dismal working conditions because he lacks options. Unable to stimulate his mind at work, the laborer eventually retreats to his more animal capacities—"eating, drinking, and procreating" (*EPM*, 62). Marx emphasizes throughout that the worker's conditions are absolutely tied to inequality:

> The more the worker produces, the less he has to consume; the more value he creates, the more worthless and unworthy he becomes; the better shaped his product, the more misshapen is he; the more civilized his product, the more barbaric is the worker; the more powerful the work, the more powerless becomes the worker; the more intelligence the work has, the more witless is the worker and the more he becomes a slave of nature.

Connecting this to *Wage Labour and Capital* and its discussion of inequality, Marx adds, capitalism "produces palaces" for the bourgeoisie "but hovels for the worker" (*EPM*, 61). The envy and resentment generated by this experience, of course, is only heightened when those in the hovels create the wealth that funds the palaces.

Marx expands on the punishing nature of labor in *Capital*, describing how "factory work exhausts the nervous system to the uttermost; at the same time, it does away with the many-sided play of the muscles, and confiscates every atom of freedom, both in bodily and in intellectual activity." He describes factory work as the "conversion" of the worker "into an automaton" (*Capital*, 548). Innovations in production, while enhancing productivity,

> distort the worker into a fragment of a man, they degrade him to the level of an appendage of a machine, they destroy the actual content of his labour by turning it into a torment; they alienate from him the intellectual potentialities of the labour process; . . . they deform the conditions under which he works, subject him during the labour process to a despotism the more hateful for its meanness; they transform his lifetime into working time, and drag his wife and child beneath the wheels of the juggernaut of capital.

It bears repeating, this process of degrading the working poor is intimately connected to the growing wealth of the bourgeoisie. He notes, "In proportion as capital accumulates, the situation of the worker, be his payment high or low, must grow worse" (*Capital*, 799). The fact that wages might increase yet his condition grows worse suggests that the problem, again, is inequality. This is why the solution is not higher wages, which amounts to little more than "a *better slave-salary*" (*CM*, 67, emphasis original). In a context where bourgeois wealth soars, token wage increases for workers do nothing to alter the exploitative economic structure. But even those gestures are not to be expected because of the "industrial reserve army" of the unemployed that can always replace those demanding better wages or working conditions. This reserve army

> rivets the worker to capital more firmly than the wedges of Hephaestus held Prometheus to the rock. It makes an accumulation of misery a necessary condition, corresponding to the accumulation of wealth. Accumulation of wealth at one pole is, therefore, at the same time accumulation of misery, the torment of labour, slavery, ignorance, brutalization and moral degradation at the opposite pole. (*Capital*, 799)

Thus the division of labor, innovations in production, the reserve army, and the general structure of the capitalist economy, on Marx's account, ensures inequality, envy, dissatisfaction, torment, ignorance, and misery.

Just above I quoted a passage from *Capital* that the economic structure drags the worker's "wife and child beneath the wheels of the juggernaut of capital." Before transitioning to the effects of inequality on the wealthy, then, it is worth considering its effects specifically on poor children. Most

striking is that during Marx's lifetime, many families in industrial capitalist economies were compelled to put their children to work in factories.
This is because when a breadwinner could not hope to earn more than
subsistence wages, the only way for a family to "get ahead," so to speak,
was to employ their children. This was true from the early days of the
market economy, according to Marx. He quotes Sir F. M. Eden to observe
these trends from the "birth" of large-scale industry:

> It may be worth the attention of the public to consider, whether
> any manufacture, which, in order to be carried on successfully,
> requires that cottages and workhouses should be ransacked for poor
> children; that they should be employed by turns during the greater part
> of the night and robbed of that rest which, though indispensable to
> all, is most required by the young; and that numbers of both sexes, of
> different ages and dispositions, should be collected together in such a
> manner that the contagion of example cannot but lead to profligacy
> and debauchery; will [it] add to the sum of individual or national felic-
> ity? (*Capital*, 922–23)

Of course, this is a rhetorical question for Marx, who makes this perfectly
clear in the very next extended quotation, this one from John Fielden,
concerning the demand in Derbyshire, Nottinghamshire, and Lancashire
for new hands to operate newly invented factory machines:

> Thousands of hands were suddenly required in these places, remote
> from towns; and Lancashire, in particular, being, till then, compara-
> tively thinly populated and barren, a population was all that she now
> wanted. The small and nimble fingers of little children being very
> far the most in request, the custom instantly sprang up of procuring
> apprentices (!) from the different parish workhouses of London, Bir-
> mingham, and elsewhere. Many, many thousands of these little, hap-
> less creatures were sent down into the north, being from the age of 7 to
> the age of 13 or 14 years old. The custom was for the master (i.e., the
> child-stealer) to clothe his apprentices and to feed and lodge them in
> an "apprentice house" near the factory; overseers were appointed to
> see the works, whose interest it was to work the children to the utmost,
> because their pay was in proportion to the quantity of work that they
> could exact. Cruelty was, of course, the consequence. . . . In many of
> the manufacturing districts, but particularly, I am afraid, in the guilty
> county to which I belong (Lancashire), cruelties of the most heart-
> rending were practiced upon the unoffending and friendless creatures

who were thus consigned to the charge of master-manufacturers; they were harassed to the brink of death by excess of labour . . . were flogged, fettered, and tortured in the most exquisite refinement of cruelty; . . . they were in many cases starved to the bone while flogged to their work and . . . even in some instances . . . were driven to commit suicide.

As Marx explains by extending his quotation from Fielden, "The profits of [these child-employing] manufacturers were enormous; but this only whetted the appetite that it should have satisfied" (*Capital*, 923). The entire reason why these abuses exist, for him, is because of the poverty of the working class and the bourgeoisie's eagerness for still-greater profits.

Another passage sketching the effects of child labor consists of an extended quotation from the *Daily Telegraph* in 1860, describing the working conditions of children in Nottingham:

Mr. Broughton Charlton, county magistrate, declared, as chairman of a meeting held at the Assembly Rooms, Nottingham, on 14 January 1860, that there was an amount of privation and suffering among that portion of the population connected with the lace trade, unknown in other parts of the kingdom, indeed, in the civilized world. . . . Children of nine or ten years are dragged from their squalid beds at two, three, or four o'clock in the morning and compelled to work for a bare subsistence, until ten, eleven, or twelve at night, their limbs wearing away, their frames dwindling, their faces whitening, and their humanity absolutely sinking into a stone-like torpor, utterly horrible to contemplate. . . . The system, as the Rev. Montagu Valpy describes it, is one of unmitigated slavery, socially, physically, morally, and spiritually. (*Capital*, 353)

In this period, fifteen-hour working days were not unusual for children, as were seventy-two-hour workweeks. Their life spans were cut dramatically short.

Child labor was so common, of course, because children were cheaper than adults (e.g., *Capital*, 372). Employing children meant lower wages, and lower wages meant cheaper commodities, hence greater market share and ultimately greater profits. In effect, child labor exacerbated inequality insofar as it allowed businesses to drop their workers' wages while growing profits.

Women were driven into factories for similar economic considerations. As Marx explains, this had broader effects on the whole family, especially the children. Child mortality rates in Marx's lifetime rose dramatically, largely from neglect:

As was shown by an official medical inquiry in the year 1861, the high death-rates are, apart from local causes, principally due to the employment of the mothers away from their home, and to the neglect and maltreatment arising from their absence, which consists in such things as insufficient nourishment, unsuitable food and dosing with opiates; beside this there arises an unnatural estrangement between mother and child, and as a consequence intentionally starving and poisoning of the children. (*Capital*, 521)

The poisoning of children with opiates is particularly striking as a depiction of the "moral degradation" (*Capital*, 522) central to this extreme inequality in industrial capitalism. As Engels would elaborate, "Women who have to work at home and have to look after their own children and other people's children dose them with this medicine [Godfrey's Cordial—an opiate], not only to keep them quiet but because of a widespread notion that it strengthens the child. Many women give the children this medicine while they are new-born infants." As children quickly developed greater tolerance of their opiate doses, those doses were increased until they "became pale, stunted and weak, generally dying before they are two years old" (*Working Class*, 118).

EFFECTS OF INEQUALITY ON THE
BOURGEOISIE: *PLEONEXIA*

While Marx's depiction of inequality's effects on the poor rank among the most dramatic passages in his vast oeuvre, there are corresponding effects on capitalism's primary beneficiaries—the bourgeoisie. But beyond the fact that both rich and poor simultaneously occupy places in the capitalistic order, they are at the same time intimately related. This begins with the very existence of private property itself. Prior to the age when property and wealth could be accumulated, for Marx, there was little reason to be greedy. Feudal lords surely had landed property and money but little chance of significantly expanding their wealth through effort, investment, or other means. It goes without saying, for the serfs, there was neither property nor any opportunity of acquiring it. So greed played little role in feudalism. It was only when private property and wealth became theoretically available to all and in potentially massive quantities that capitalism was born: the "wheels which political economy put in motion are *greed* [*die Habsucht*] and the *war among the greedy, competition*" (*EPM*, 59; emphases original). Marx's connection of property to greed parallels a similar passage from Rousseau, who had argued several decades earlier that money "is useful only as a sign of inequality" (*Corsica*, 140). It is only when people can begin to distinguish themselves by acquiring more than others that they begin to lust for it. This is the essence of property, inequality, and greed, as understood by both Rousseau and Marx.

Greed becomes a defining feature of the bourgeoisie in capitalist economies for Marx. Yet there is something in his account of greed that does not sit well with his critics. For him, avarice is not a natural component of human nature—something he, again, shares with Rousseau. Among the most celebrated critics of Marx's account of human nature is Sigmund Freud, who insisted that aggression, competition, selfishness, and greed are hardwired in human nature. Marx is naïve, on this account, to assume otherwise. Drawing on the latest trends in evolutionary science, which emphasized the "survival of the fittest," for Freud, it was obvious that human beings are competitive, greedy, and aggressive—they have been selected for these traits. The psychiatrist argues, "Aggressiveness was not created by property. It reigned almost without limit in primitive times, when property was still very scanty, and it already shows itself in the nursery."[44]

Yet for Marx, this accusation of naïveté would be misplaced. While the tradition of assuming natural selfishness extends at least as far as Augustine's doctrine of original sin, Marx attributes the most proximate source of bourgeois assumptions about natural greed and selfishness to Jeremy Bentham. For the communist, natural selfishness is not only one of the founding assumptions of modern capitalism, but it is also synonymous with Bentham, who had reduced all moral psychology to self-interested calculations. Capitalism assumes, like Bentham, that "each looks only to his own advantage" and further that the only thing that even loosely binds citizens together "is the selfishness, the gain and the private interest of each" (*Capital*, 280). Marx is unpersuaded by Bentham's mere assertions of selfishness. "Bentham," he writes, "is purely an English phenomenon." He continues, "With the driest naïveté he assumes that the modern petty bourgeois, especially the English petty bourgeois, is the normal man. Whatever is useful to this peculiar kind of normal man, and to his world, is useful in and for itself. He applies this yardstick to the past, the present, and the future." The reality is rather that "human nature [is] historically modified in each epoch" (*Capital*, 158–59n). This is why, for him, under feudalism "the concepts of honour, loyalty, etc., were dominant," whereas "during the dominance of the bourgeoisie [reigned] the concepts of freedom, equality, etc." (*GI*, 68).[45] On the Marxist reading, Freud is as naïve as Bentham insofar as he mistook the assumptions and preoccupations of his own culture for universal conditions of humanity.[46] At the end of the day, Marx rejects the notion that humanity is naturally greedy—rather insisting that avarice takes root only in a system of private property with opportunities to distinguish oneself in an unequal distribution of resources. Inequality, to be sure, is an essential element of this equation. Greed makes little sense where private property exists but is distributed in roughly equal amounts. It is rather activated by the possibility of accumulating radically unequal shares.[47]

But once greed has gained a foothold, for Marx, it becomes *pleonexia*, insatiable or compulsive desire. *Pleonexia* has been a leitmotiv throughout this book. Plato's Socrates characterized Thrasymachus as *pleonectic*. It was the major theme in the book of Ecclesiastes in which the restless rich are characterized as "chasing the wind," where "the surfeit of the rich will not let them sleep" (5:12). Hobbes cautioned against *pleonexia* as "a desire [of subjects] for more than their share" and as violative of the laws of nature (*Leviathan*, 15.22). Mill warned against those consumed with "the *desire to engross more than one's share of advantages* (the *pleonexia* of the Greeks)" (*Liberty*, 79; emphasis original). Yet perhaps no philosopher since Plato returns to this theme so often and with such vigor as does Marx. This is because bourgeois *pleonexia* is the animating force of capitalism as he conceived it.

Reviewing earlier discussions in this book, *pleonexia* is the ancient Greek word for "greed," but at the same time it is also more than greed. As depicted in the tyrannical soul of Plato's *Republic*, it is an all-consuming, insatiable greed. It is one thing to want, for example, an automobile to facilitate a commute. It is another thing to buy one car and then immediately lust for another. It is one thing to want to run for the school board. It is another thing to lust for power without end. It is one thing to desire financial comfort. It is another thing to be rich and still lust for greater wealth. It is the nature of *pleonexia* to want without ever having enough.

Certain objects of desire are most conducive to *pleonexia*—namely wealth, power, and public esteem. The hungry can become satiated in their desire for food. The *pleonectic* are never satisfied with their wealth. And what is distinctive about inequality under capitalism, for Marx, is the degree to which it nourishes this vice.

Perhaps nowhere is this clearer than in Marx's discussion of "hoarding" (*die Schatzbildung*) in chapter 3 of *Capital*, which briefly traces the history of this concept from antiquity to modernity. Hoarding's objects in antiquity, according to Marx, were precious metals, primarily gold and silver.

Gold and silver often took the form of currency but also had independent value as a marker of "superfluity or wealth." Unlike other commodities, because their primary value was in marking one's own distinction, there was no natural cap on the amount of gold or silver one could desire. In a society that grants individuals the right to accumulate private wealth, their "needs are ceaselessly renewed" (*Capital*, 228) since there is no ceiling to their desire for the distinction brought about by wealth. Beyond distinction, however, is the promise that wealth also brings power. As Marx observes, with the growth of commerce comes "an increase in the power of money, that absolutely social form of wealth which is always ready to be used. 'Gold is a wonderful thing! Its owner is master of all he desires." He continues to quote Columbus, who wrote in a letter from Jamaica in 1503, "Gold can even enable souls to enter Paradise" (*Capital*, 229).[48] As with the desire for distinction, there is no upper limit to the amount of power one might seek. Beyond the fact that the desires for distinction and wealth are theoretically boundless, what further unites them is the degree to which they can be purchased. This makes wealth a common denominator in the *pleonectic* quest. As Rousseau observed in his *Second Discourse*, of all the modes of inequality, wealth "is the last [object of desire] to which they are finally reduced," since for him, "it can easily be used to buy all the rest" (*SD*, 184).

The *pleonectic* nature of money in an economy that places no limits on wealth acquisition is perhaps most dramatic in this striking passage:

> But money is itself a commodity, an external object capable of becoming the private property of any individual. Thus the social power becomes the private power of private persons. Ancient society therefore denounced it as tending to destroy the economic and moral order. Modern society, which already in its infancy had pulled Pluto by the hair of his head from the bowels of the earth, greets gold as its Holy Grail, as the glittering incarnation of its innermost principle of life. (*Capital*, 229–30)

This is full of meaningful references to antiquity. The first is a footnote he adds after the words "moral order." Here he produces a passage from Sophocles's *Antigone*: "Nothing is so evil as money ever grew to be current among men. This lays cities low, this drives men from their homes, this trains and warps honest souls till they set themselves to works of shame; this still teaches folk to practice villainies, and to know every godless deed" (*Capital*, 230n43).

The second reference to antiquity comes in his mention of the origins of "modern society" in ancient Greece when Pluto[49] was pulled "by the hair of his head from the bowels of the earth." As Marx explains in a footnote, this is a reference to Athenaeus's *Deipnosophists*, which he quotes there: "*Pleonexia* hopes to drag Pluto himself out of the bowels of the earth" (*Capital*, 230n44).[50] I have substituted Marx's own word, *pleonexia*, in the original German edition for Fowkes's English translation of "avarice." That Marx did not translate the word into German as either "*die Habsucht*" or "*die Gier*" suggests a deliberate choice on his part. The entire section on "hoarding" aims at explaining the origins and nature of *pleonexia*. But beyond word choice is the historical reference itself. Athenaeus's text concerns the origins and uses of gold and silver in the ancient Greek world. The reference to Pluto being pulled from the bowels of the earth alludes to the ancient practice of mining, which he depicts as "delvings deep and painful."[51] Marx fails to note that Athenaeus himself is quoting another ancient source, Strabo, who describes the ancient mines as "inexhaustible treasuries of nature" such that the "subterraneous regions should not be regarded as the realms of Pluto, but of Plutus."[52] The mines' "inexhaustible" treasures correspond with Athenaeus's use of *pleonexia*'s inexhaustibility.[53]

Further, Athenaeus's paragraph on *pleonexia* and the mines references two figures discussed in chapter 1 of this book: Lycurgus and Plato. As noted there, both Lycurgus and Plato's Athenian Stranger banished gold and silver almost entirely from their respective cities. The point of gold and silver, for Plutarch's Lycurgus, was to foster "odious distinctions of inequality," so he required that all precious metals be surrendered to the state.[54] Plato's Stranger similarly banishes silver and gold to make "great money-making impossible," as the pursuit of large fortunes "can distort the character of a free man" (*Laws*, 741e–742a; see also 679e). For him, "neither the Silver nor the Golden Pluto [is] to have an established dwelling place in the city" (*Laws*, 801b). Both Plutarch's Lycurgus and Plato's Stranger understood something that Marx stresses here: that the ability to accumulate boundless fortunes stimulates the vice of *pleonexia* and, further, that the surest way of halting it is to shut off the faucet. The real difference between Lycurgus and Plato, on the one hand, and Marx, on the other, is the means of accomplishing this.

Marx details this species of greed in his chapter on the "General Formula for Capital" in *Capital*. In describing the formula for generating capital, $M-C-\Delta M$, where money (M) is exchanged for commodities (C), which are in turn exchanged for more money (profit, or ΔM), he repeatedly emphasizes that this process is "endless" (*Capital*, 252). One can buy in order to sell repeatedly and in perpetuity. This is to be contrasted with the opposite formula, C—M—C, in which one sells commodities in order to raise money to purchase other commodities. For example, I might sell my chickens to raise the money I need to fix my leaky roof. But that process has a concrete and obvious termination. The desire to fix my leaky roof is not susceptible to the same *pleonectic* nature that profit and wealth are. It is a discrete desire that can be completely and decisively satisfied. But the desire for greater profit cannot be, at least on Marx's understanding of the bourgeoisie. "The movement of capital is therefore limitless" (*Capital*, 253).

Marx dedicates an extended footnote in these pages to quoting Aristotle's *Politics* on the distinction between "economics" and "chrematistics." In the quoted passage, the ancient philosopher distinguishes between the two. For him, economics is the art of acquiring objects for their use value in Marxian terms. The acquisition of a tasty fig, for example, appeals to us because we are hungry for a sweet fruit. But chrematistics is different. It happens only after the invention of money when "wealth acquisition without limit" becomes possible. Whereas the desire for a fig is discrete and limited, the desire for wealth is potentially unlimited (*Capital*, 253–254n6).[55] Although this is not, strictly speaking, a discussion of *pleonexia*, it details the conditions that facilitate it. This is Marx's point: what capitalism does, par excellence, is to establish the conditions in which *pleonexia* thrives. It is only in a context of limitless acquisitional possibilities that one embraces the "boundless drive for enrichment, this passionate chase after value" insofar as capitalists can repeat the M—C—ΔM formula "again and again" (*Capital*, 254, 255). This is why political theorist William James Booth has correctly characterized the discussion of greed in these pages as "a theory of the modern equivalent of *pleonexia*."[56] Marx elaborates in his *Grundrisse*, "Greed as such [is] impossible without money; all other kinds of accumulation and of mania for accumulation appear as primitive, restricted by needs on the one hand and by the restricted nature of products on the other." He subsequently adds, "Greed . . . [is] distinct from the craving for a particular kind of wealth, e.g., for clothes, weapons, jewels, women, wine, etc. . . . Money is therefore not only the object but the fountainhead of greed." The lack of theoretical bounds to riches, first explored by Aristotle, inflames the "unlimited mania for wealth" (*Grundrisse*, 163, 222, 325). And just to emphasize the *pleonectic* nature of this species of greed, Marx adds, "The magnitude of the profit gives him [the bourgeois] hunger for yet more profit" (*Capital*, 530). This hunger is inherently insatiable.

At this juncture, however, Marx departs from his ancient predecessors. For ancient philosophers such as Plato, *pleonexia* is a disease of the soul. Plato's Socrates had likened the *pleonectic* individual in his *Gorgias* to a "leaking jar" (*Gorgias*, 493b). Just as those filling a leaky jar can never fill it, the moment *pleonectic* souls might think they have satisfied their desires, more desires, equally compelling, immediately follow. This desire never relents. They would therefore be, on his account, "the most miserable" because they lead an "insatiable, undisciplined life." Plato's Socrates returns to this theme again in the *Republic*, when he describes the tyrannical soul. The tyrant lives amid a "violent crowd of appetites" and must yield to them "or live in great suffering and pain." Each day tyrants awaken with many "terrible appetites," never truly able to satisfy them (573d–574a). They "live their entire lives without ever being friends with anyone" since they are untrustworthy, always preferring flattery to kinship (576a). This is why the tyrant, who is Socrates's archetype of the *pleonectic* soul, is *enslaved* to his own appetites and hence profoundly miserable. He is "poor and insatiable"—"poor" not in cash, of course, but in character and in happiness, ultimately reduced to "wailing, groaning, lamenting" and "painful suffering" (578a).

Yet while Plato's *pleonectic* soul is miserable, Marx paints a different picture. Because greed is so widespread and even celebrated in capitalist economies, the *pleonectic* individual is typically understood as "rational" (*Capital*, 254). This makes sense. The bourgeoisie failing to seek larger profits is at constant risk of economic annihilation. Businesses failing to pursue greater profits will only survive until others succeed in doing so. As soon as a competitor innovates with the division of labor, technology, marketing, outsourcing, or something else, the non-*pleonectic* individuals are undone, and failing heroic measures, they begin a painful descent into the working class. So under capitalism, the character trait that Plato, Aristotle, Hobbes, and Mill lament is absolutely necessary and indeed "rational" from a bourgeois point of view.

Thomas Hobbes had explained that equality creates competition (*Leviathan*, 13.3). In Marxian terms, in the context of capitalist economies, each business may be understood as equal in bourgeois terms: they have formal equality under the law to pursue the business model and strategies that suit them best. But as political theorist Michael Locke McLendon has commented, "while equality implies competition, the logic of competition is to annihilate equality. Competitions are designed to create winners and losers."[57] That is, under conditions of bourgeois equality, competition stimulates economic inequality in which some profit immensely, while others are driven to poverty. The competition to become a "winner" is sustained by *pleonexia*.

That *pleonexia* may be rational under capitalism does not mean that bourgeois life is pleasant or enjoyable. The psychic cost of *pleonexia* in capitalist economies is knowing that one is always on the precipice of economic ruin, even when occupying the top—just ask Blockbuster Video. *Pleonectic* capitalists are constantly plotting each other's demise. "Competition" for Marx is nothing more than the "war among the greedy" (*EPM*, 59). Although not quite a state of nature in Hobbes's sense, the process is similar in spirit. It is effectively a Hobbesian war of all against all among the bourgeois where, in Hobbes's terms, "there is no way for any man to secure himself so reasonable as anticipation, that is, by force or wiles" (*Leviathan*, 13.4). Marx insists in the same spirit that capitalism operates by "fraud, violence, etc." Just as for Hobbes there is no justice in the state of nature, for Marx under capitalism, "there are no absolute values." And just as competition is a defining feature of Hobbes's state of nature, so competition is "nothing other than the inner *nature of capital*, its essential character" (*Grundrisse*, 839, 414; emphasis original). And as with Hobbes's natural man, the life of Marx's bourgeoisie is often brutish and short-lived (*Capital*, 777).

Marx's conception of *pleonexia* also resembles Plato's in another respect—the degree to which *pleonectic* individuals are unfree. For Plato's Socrates, *pleonectic* souls are slaves to their appetites. The tyrant's soul is "full of slavery" (*Republic*, 577c), "never getting a taste of freedom" (*Republic*, 576a). This is because he "enslaves the best element in himself to the most wicked . . . ruthlessly enslav[ing] the most divine element in himself to the most godless and polluted" (*Republic*, 589de). Socrates describes tyrants as being "compelled" by forces beyond their control in the futile quest to satisfy their boundless appetites (*Republic*, 574a). These forces, for Socrates, transform "a man into a wolf" (*Republic*, 566a), unmoved by appeals to reason or justice, unconstrained, and compelled at all costs to satisfy his appetites.

In strikingly parallel terms, Marx describes the bourgeoisie as under similar forces of compulsion.

> In so far as he is capital personified, his motivating force is not the acquisition and enjoyment of use-values, but the acquisition and augmentation of exchange-values. He is fanatically intent on the valorization of value; consequently he ruthlessly forces the human race to produce for production's sake. In this way, he spurs on the development of society's

productive forces, and the creation of those martial conditions of production which alone can form the real basis of a higher form of society, a society in which the full and free development of every individual forms the ruling principle. Only as a personification of capital is the capitalist respectable. As such, he shares with the miser an absolute drive towards self-enrichment. But what appears in the miser as the mania of an individual is in the capitalist the effect of a social mechanism in which he is merely a cog. Moreover, the development of capitalist production makes it necessary constantly to increase the amount of capital laid out in a given industrial undertaking, and competition subordinates every individual capitalist to the immanent laws of capitalist production, as external and coercive laws. (*Capital*, 739)

Paralleling Plato's characterization of the appetites ruling over one's reason in *pleonectic* souls, for Marx greed and the imperatives of competition reign sovereign over the bourgeois psyche. The capitalist is unhesitatingly "ruthless," both to his workers and his competitors. Unlike Plato, for whom the appetites can take any number of undifferentiated forms, Marx's conception of the appetite is exceptionally specific: it is the "absolute drive towards self-enrichment." But its compulsive force is remarkably familiar—being entirely "subordinated" to the "immanent laws of capitalist production, as external and coercive laws."[58] The capitalist cannot do otherwise. In one memorable passage from the *Manifesto*, Marx and Engels speak of the bourgeois compulsion to drop wages below subsistence levels: the bourgeois is "unfit to rule because it is incompetent to assure an existence to its slave within his slavery, because *it cannot help* letting him sink into such a state, that it has to feed him, instead of being fed by him" (*CM*, 168–69; emphasis added). The bourgeoisie is powerless to resist surrounding economic forces that compel him to reduce wages to inhumane levels.

In one further parallel with Plato's tyrannical soul, the element of compulsivity, or enslavement to one's appetites, Marx describes the bourgeois as possessing a "werewolf-like hunger for surplus labour" in which the capitalist instinctively engages in "monstrous outrages" in a vain attempt to satisfy this ravenous impulse (*Capital*, 353), just as Plato explained that *pleonexia* turned "a man into a wolf."[59] Thus both Plato and Marx are so mortified by their respective subjects that they are driven to remove them from the ranks of humanity, likening them to fearsome beasts.

Biographer Michael Heinrich doubts that, for Marx, "the fact that the individual capitalist constantly attempts to increase his profit is . . .

rooted in any psychological trait like 'greed.'" Rather, for his Marx, "such behavior is *compelled* by the competitive struggle among capitalists."[60] Heinrich is not wrong to speak of this compulsion, which is surely a significant element of Marx's moral psychology as discussed above. But this dismissal of the role of greed is too hasty for at least two reasons. First and most obvious is because, as we have already seen, Marx himself repeatedly emphasizes the role of greed. The fact that he defines greed as an animating force of capitalism is not incidental. Greed's role is frequently emphasized throughout his *Grundrisse* and *Capital*. Second, if we understand greed as *pleonexia*, as suggested by Marx's own discussions, then greed is not inconsistent with compulsion. Compulsion is, from a certain point of view,[61] an essential feature of *pleonexia*, as has been the case ever since Plato and the ancients. Plato's tyrant is a "slave" and hence determined by his appetites. This does not mean he is not greedy. The same is true of Marx's bourgeoisie. He is both compelled by his economic system to exploit the working class and at the same time greedy. These are not mutually exclusive terms. Put otherwise, if it is wrong to speak of a role for greed in Marx, as Heinrich suggests, it would be equally wrong to speak of a role for greed in Plato.

The Social Costs of Inequality

The individual effects of inequality, for Marx, are tightly connected to their social effects. This is because *pleonexia* and competition are responsible for most of the injuries inflicted on the poor. When describing the sufferings of the working poor, he expressly connects them to the wealthy's greedy machinations. There is, for him, an "intimate connection between the pangs of hunger suffered by the most industrious layers of the working class, and the extravagant consumption, coarse or refined, of the rich, for which capitalist accumulation is the basis" (*Capital*, 811). In a footnote quoting F. D. Longe on the shoe trade:

> Great competition was shown between the different firms as to which could turn out the neatest article. Shortly afterwards, however, a worse kind of competition sprang up, namely, that of underselling one another in the market. The injurious consequences soon manifested themselves in reductions of wages, and so sweepingly quickly was the fall in the price of labour, that many first now pay only one half of the original wages. And yet, though wages sink lower and lower, profits appear, with each alteration in the scale of wages, to increase.

Marx proceeds in his own voice: "Even bad times are utilized by the manufacturers for making exceptional profits by excessive wage-reductions, i.e., by directly robbing the worker of his means of subsistence" (*Capital*, 582n57). He describes the bourgeois effort to extend the working day as long as possible:

> In its blind and measureless drive, its insatiable appetite for surplus labour, capital oversteps not only the moral but even the merely physical limits of the working day. It usurps the time for growth, development, and healthy maintenance of the body. It steals the time required for the consumption of fresh air and sunlight. . . . It reduces the sound sleep needed for the restoration, renewal and refreshment of the vital forces to exact the amount of torpor essential for the revival of an absolutely exhausted organism. It is not the normal maintenance of labour-power which determines the limits of the working day here, but rather the greatest possible daily expenditure of labour-power, no matter how diseased, compulsory and painful it may be, which determines the limits of the workers' period of rest. . . . It attains this objective by shortening the life of labour-power, in the same way as a greedy farmer snatches more produce from the soil by robbing it of its fertility.

Countless passages from *Capital* make the same point—there is a profound social cost to the greed and competition unleashed by capitalism. The cited passage is particularly apt in this respect. The "measureless drive, its insatiable appetite" is *pleonexia*. The bourgeoisie's boundless appetite compels him to rob his workers of their most essential of life needs—fresh air, sunlight, and sleep. Acting on this drive, he continues, yields the "premature exhaustion and death of this labour-power itself" (*Capital*, 375–76). And again, it bears emphasis: all of this is facilitated by radical inequality. Capitalism fosters the *pleonexia* that incentivizes low wages and poor living conditions. In a relatively equal society, or one that caps wealth, this drive would presumably be mitigated. The promise of enormous fortunes, for Marx, incentivizes capitalism's greatest abuses.

Marx notes other subtler, yet nevertheless consequential effects of extreme inequality. To appreciate this, it is useful to return to *Wage Labour and Capital*. He wrote section 4 of the essay in response to a major objection to socialist and communist movements—could not capitalism be salvaged and even embrace improved wages for the workers? He aims to consider "the most favourable case" for capitalism, "when productive capital grows, the demand for labour grows; consequently, the price of labour, wages, goes up" (*WLC*, 216). This is Adam Smith's justification of market economies, for whom "the demand for labour increases in years of sudden and extraordinary plenty." Consequently employers "who want more workmen, bid against one another, in order to get them, which sometimes raises both the real and the money price of their labour." By contrast, when the economy contracts, in periods of "sudden and extraordinary scarcity . . . [a] considerable number of people are thrown out of employment, who bid against one another, in order to get it, which sometimes lowers both the real and money price of labour" (*WN*, 103–4). Economic growth spurs the demand for workers and ultimately improved wages and well-being. This is arguably Smith's core moral defense of market economies.

Mill had challenged this orthodoxy in his discussion of the stationary state, insisting, "It is only in the backward countries of the world that increased production is still an important object: in those most advanced, what is economically needed is a better distribution" (*Principles*, 755). For him, economic growth in the developed world was an outmoded and even dangerous policy objective, threatening environmental destruction and social disharmony. Like Mill, Marx rejects the argument that economic growth can resolve most social problems, even where that growth might raise absolute wages. More specifically, he doubts that even higher wages in the context of a growing economy will improve the conditions for the working class. Earlier I cited material from *Wage Labour and Capital* that explored the psychic effects of economic inequality insofar as it results in dissatisfied workers compelled to witness the growing luxuries of the rich. This same essay further explores at least three more dimensions in which inequality threatens social relations: the growing power of the bourgeoisie, the domination and dependence of the workers, and the antagonism that characterizes the larger social milieu. It is now time to explore these.

The first argument regarding the social effects of inequality, according to Marx in *Wage Labour and Capital*, concerns the degree to which it amplifies bourgeois power. He suggests this at least twice:

> The division of social wealth between capital and labour has become still more unequal. With the same capital, the capitalist commands a greater quantity of labour. The *power of the capitalist class has grown*, the social position of the worker has deteriorated, has been depressed one step further below that of the capitalist. (*WLC*, 218–19; emphasis added)
>
> . . .
>
> Thus if the income of the worker increases with the rapid growth of capital, the social gulf that separates the worker from the capitalist

increases at the same time, and *the power of capital over labour*, the dependence of labour on capital, likewise increases at the same time. (*WLC*, 220; emphasis added)

Marx identifies Smith's moral defense of capitalism—that growing economies improve wages. Yet this wage increase is typically modest compared to simultaneous growth of bourgeois wealth. Even as workers earn more, capitalists are making proportionately much more. So economic growth actually exacerbates inequality. Beyond this, he emphasizes that with greater economic inequality comes greater social and political inequality—that economic inequality further empowers the bourgeoisie.

Marx elaborates on inequality and its relationship to domination in his *Grundrisse* when he approvingly quotes Robert Owen. It is worth excerpting this passage at length. Marx begins by describing the condition of pre-industrial workers, when the employers were small in scale, when "they usually fed at the same table, and lived together." In this period, "there prevailed a spirit and feeling of equality between them." As the economy advanced, however, all this changed:

Since the period when scientific power began to be largely applied to the business of manufacturing, a gradual change in these respects has taken place. Almost all manufacturers, to be successful, must now be carried on extensively and with a large capital; small masters with small capitals, have now very little chance of success, especially in the manufacture of the soft materials, such as cotton, wool, flax, silk, etc.; it is now indeed evident that so long as the present classification of society and mode of conducting the business of life shall continue, the small masters will be more and more superseded by those who possess large capitals, and that the former comparatively happier equality among the producers must give place to the greatest inequality between master and servant, that has yet occurred in the history of man. The large capitalist is now elevated to the position of an imperial lord, having the health, the life and death, indirectly, of his slaves, at his will. This power he obtains by combining with other large capitalists, engaged in the same interest with himself, and thus do they effectively coerce to their purpose those they employ. The large capitalist now wallows in wealth, the right use of which he has not been taught and knows not. He has acquired power by his riches. His riches and power blind his understanding; and when he most grievously oppresses, he believes he is conferring favours. (*Grundrisse*, 713–14)[62]

This excerpt threads together multiple themes. Before inequality, the workers and the relatively modest capitalist enjoyed harmonious relations. But once competition compelled industries to escalate their production, this "happy equality" was succeeded by the "greatest inequality," creating a fabulously wealthy and empowered bourgeoisie. Their boundless power extended to the life and death of the workers. Finally, it was unlikely to be used for humane purposes because wealth "blinds" the capitalist to humane sentiments.

For Marx, the bourgeois uses his wealth to shape laws and manipulate their implementation. He illustrates this in his discussion of laws passed in Britain ostensibly to protect workers' welfare. He finds the Factory Extension Act, for example, to be contaminated by "a mass of vicious exemptions and cowardly compromises," emasculating its supposedly good intentions. He characterizes the Workshops Regulation Act as "wretched as far as its detailed provisions were concerned" and remaining "a dead letter in the hands of the municipal and local authorities who were charged with its execution" (Capital, 625). The act was further weakened by transferring oversight of the factories to already overburdened factory inspectors, who lacked the time to perform their oversight functions. Marx explains precisely how these laws were rendered impotent:

> What strikes us, then, in the English legislation of 1867, is, on the one hand, the necessity imposed on Parliament of the ruling classes of adopting, in principle, such extraordinary and extensive measures against the excesses of capitalist exploitation; and, on the other hand, the hesitation, the unwillingness and the bad faith with which it actually put those measures into place. (Capital, 625-26)

On his reading, the capitalists wanted to appear concerned about the plight of the working class, all the while ensuring that those measures failed to accomplish their stated goals. The real purpose of these acts was never to improve working conditions; it was to assuage worker agitation by pretending that labor's grievances were being addressed.

Engels is sometimes more direct. For him, the bourgeois operate "as a united class and use the power of the State for their own ends." To this extent,

> it is obvious that the whole legal system has been devised to protect those who own property from those who do not. The laws are needed only because people exist who have no property. This aspect of the laws is admitted with brutal frankness in only a few cases. The laws against

vagrancy and being without visible means of support openly brand the proletariat as an illegal group in society. Nevertheless at the root of all laws lies the idea that the proletariat is an enemy which must be defeated. This can be seen from the way in which the law is administered by the judges. This is particularly true of the Justices of the Peace—themselves members of the middle class—and it is with these that the proletariat for the most part comes into contact. The Justices of the Peace have no hesitation in regarding the administration of the laws as a means of keeping the working classes down. Let a prosperous member of the middle classes be summoned—or rather, politely "invited to appear"—before a magistrate. The court naturally expresses regret that he should have been troubled to appear at all. The magistrate does everything in his power to smooth the path of the accused. And if the charges against the rich man are conclusively proved then the magistrate, with profuse apologies, merely imposes a trifling fine. The rich man flings the money contemptuously on the table and takes himself off. But if some poor devil of a worker appears before the magistrate it is quite a different story. He has nearly always had to spend the previous night—with other prisoners—in the lock-up. The magistrate shouts at him and assumes from the first that he is guilty. His defense is contemptuously brushed aside with the remark: "We have heard that sort of excuse before." (*Condition*, 317–18)

This passage recalls several themes addressed in earlier chapters of this book. Rousseau outlined how the laws have been constructed to benefit those of property and wealth, a point affirmed by Smith. Hobbes describes how the laws are lightly applied to the rich. Engels develops this line of eighteenth-century thought in building a case that the law is effectively a tool of the rich, especially in his treatment of the English enclosure laws:

The capitalists in Parliament are still trying—against the more enlightened views of those not wholly sunk in degrading selfishness—to keep the workers down as much as possible. One after another of the public commons are taken away from the workers and are used as building sites. The new houses may raise working-class living standards but they do the proletariat untold harm. A common was a place on which poor people could keep a donkey, a pig, or a few geese. There the young people could play and amuse themselves. But all this is being stopped. The workers lose a source of income when a common is taken away and the young people, having lost a playground, drift into public

houses. Every session of Parliament sees the passing of several Acts for
the enclosure of commons. (*Condition*, 318–19)

So not only does the law treat the wealthy favorably, for Engels, but it is
also their tool for confiscating public lands, which they, for their personal
enrichment, then rent to the poor. As Marx would explain in *Capital*, this
was nothing less than "the systematic theft of communal property" under
the guise of public law, a "whole series of thefts, outrages, and popular
misery that accompanied the forcible expropriation of the people" (*Capital*, 886, 889). Such is the power, according to Marx and Engels, of great
wealth amassed in unequal societies.

Marx illustrates this point in an article written for the *New York Tribune*
analyzing the 1856 Factory Act. Enacted, or as he characterizes it, "smuggled through," Parliament with the purported aim of protecting "the limbs
and lives" of mill workers, it included two components: (1) a law protecting worker safety, and (2) the establishment of courts that would handle
reported violations. In principle, of course, laws protecting mill worker
safety sound appealing. But in reality, Marx says quoting an inspection official, the laws exploited the "ignorance" of mill workers, who were unaware
of how the laws operated in practice. For one thing, he notes, all reports of
violations were heard by arbitrators "skilled in the construction" of the kind
of machinery used in this work. But, he continues, again quoting the inspector, those "engineers and machine-makers ought to be considered disqualified to act as factory arbitrators, by reason of their connection in trade
with the factory occupiers [owners], who are their customers." The law
stacked the deck in favor of the bourgeoisie. And even where arbitrators
discover violations, the fines imposed on factory owners were deliberately
"trifling" since the mill owners "took good care to have it so framed." These
laws in practice subverted their public purpose—and coincided with an
uptick in accidents, lacerations, contusions, amputations, and even death.
This all happened, for Marx, because factory owners themselves framed this
legislation—a privilege not extended to mill workers. Wealth is power, and
power advances still greater wealth and power. Thus it happens that "the
laws enacted for checking the cruel greediness of the mill-lords are a sham
and a delusion, being so worded as to baffle their own ostensible end and to
disarm the men entrusted with their execution" (*CFL*, 189–92).

Inequality, for Marx, also subjects the working poor to domination and
dependence. He dedicates a paragraph in *Wage Labour and Capital* to
sketching the problem:

To say that the worker has an interest in the rapid growth of capital is only to say that the more rapidly the worker increases the wealth of others, the richer will be the crumbs that fall to him, the greater is the number of workers that can be employed and called into existence, the more can the mass of slaves dependent on capital be increased. (*WLC*, 220)

This passage evokes several important themes. The idea that the workers are living off the crumbs of the rich evokes the parable of Lazarus and Dives from the book of Luke, discussed in chapter 2 of this book. Lazarus was a poor, desperately hungry man, covered in sores, who hoped for a few crumbs from a rich man's table. In the biblical narrative, Lazarus dies but is redeemed in the afterlife, while the rich man is condemned to torment in Hades. But when Marx evokes the story here, it has a different outcome. To be sure, the poor man seeks crumbs from the rich, but now he is condemned to permanent dependence on him with little hope of divine redemption.

Marx also evokes Lazarus in chapter 25 of *Capital*.[63] Here he details how the industrial reserve army of the unemployed enables the bourgeoisie in impoverishing the poor and enriching itself. "The relative mass of the industrial reserve army . . . increases with the potential energy of wealth." The immediate effect of this is to further impoverish the "*Lazarusschichte*," as he calls them. To be sure, the *Lazarusschichte* are the impoverished workers and reserve armies of capitalism. There is a sense in which Marx wants his readers to recall the conditions of Lazarus in the book of Luke. Just as Lazarus is poor, sick, sore-ridden, and desperately hungry, so are Marx's poor "degraded," "deformed," and "distorted." Marx shares this with the book of Luke. But Marx pushes further, modifying the old tale for modern times. According to theologian N. T. Wright, what the rich man most wants is "to keep the poor, ragged brother or neighbor out of sight and out of mind."[64] The begging is a nuisance. But whereas Lazarus is largely an annoyance to the wealthy, to be ignored as much as possible, the *Lazarusschichte* of *Capital* are the objects of "domination and exploitation" (*Capital*, 799). The point is to dominate them entirely and extract maximum cash value from their ragged bodies. The bourgeoisie has assumed the powers of an arbitrary despot for Marx. As an example, he notes that the capitalist can "annihilate all regularity of employment, and according to his own convenience, caprice [*Willkür*], and the interest of the moment, make the most frightful over-work alternate with relative or absolute cessation of work" (*Capital*, 686).

Marx depicts the domination of the poor dramatically in chapter 28 of *Capital*, "Bloody Legislation against the Expropriated," in which he reviews the history of monarchical domination of the poor. Under Henry VIII, for example, laws mandated the whipping and imprisonment of vagabonds. The king also had 72,000 vagabonds hanged.[65] Under Edward VI, those who refused to work were condemned to become the slaves of those who called out the idler in question. Elizabeth I had beggars flogged and branded on their ears if they were under age fourteen; those over eighteen were to be executed. James I had beggars and vagabonds publicly whipped and branded. There was a long history of violence against the poor before capitalism. But the peculiar inequality characterizing capitalism adds yet another dimension to the poor's misery according to Marx.

> The organization of the capitalist process of production, once it is fully developed, breaks down all resistance. The constant generation of a relative surplus population keeps the law of the supply and demand of labour, and therefore wages, within narrow limits, which correspond to capital's valorization requirements. The silent compulsion of economic relations sets the seal on the domination of the capitalist over the worker. Direct extra-economic force is still of course used, but only in exceptional cases. In the ordinary run of things, the worker can be left to the "natural laws of production," i.e., it is possible to rely on his dependence on capital, which springs from the conditions of production themselves. (*Capital*, 899)

Whereas in previous generations, the government did the oppressing, under capitalism it is delivered by the employers, who "dominate" their workers through "natural laws." Its material effect is to extract the most labor for the lowest possible wages. Much of this was facilitated by the "surplus population" willing to work for lower wages and under worse conditions. This provides the bourgeoisie their leverage to keep wages low and working conditions substandard, facilitating the relationship of "domination." As industry advances, for Marx, other innovations only enhance this domination—science, technology, machinery, and improvements in the division of labor all conspire to magnify "the power dominating over labour" (*Grundrisse*, 308).

Bourgeois domination over their workers establishes a relationship of complete dependence—where laborers are trapped in jobs with little hope of escape. Demands for higher wages or more humane working conditions can expect to be met with a pink slip. Laborers cannot simply quit their jobs either since their jobs are the source of their subsistence.[66] They depend on their employers entirely for feeding themselves and their families and, given the economic structure and the lack of better options, are entirely subject to their employers' whims.

As William Clare Roberts has persuasively argued in his brilliant *Marx's Inferno*, Marx's concern about domination reveals a republican strain in his thought insofar as republicanism rests on the principle of nondomination, where subjects are free from arbitrary power.[67] Marx's suggestion that workers are subject to the "caprice" of their employers certainly evokes this republican concern. For Roberts, it is the economic structure that dominates both the bourgeoisie and workers. This is surely true from a certain point of view. We have already seen how capitalism compels the bourgeois to embrace *pleonexia* as a way of life (e.g., *Capital*, 739). If they fail to be *pleonectic*, they lose and are thrust back into the working class. At the same time, the workers are clearly dominated by their employers, unable to make meaningful choices about their lives, jobs, and living conditions. In this sense, Roberts is right to speak of a "generalized form of domination" in capitalism, according to Marx.[68]

Roberts concludes that all parties are robbed of meaningful moral freedom: "market actors are not fit to be held responsible" due to their condition of domination by market forces. They are rather "playthings of alien forces."[69] While Marx certainly speaks this way sometimes, on other occasions he subjects the bourgeois to moral scrutiny. There is ample evidence of this in his abundant normative vocabulary. Comparing someone to a werewolf, for example, is a normative judgment about one's character, not merely a descriptive term. The same is true for the words "greedy" or *pleonectic*. To be greedy is to want more than what is appropriate. To have a sense of what is appropriate is to have a normative standard threatened or violated by greed. Marx employs (or approvingly quotes) words throughout *Capital* such as "ruthless," "degrading," "despotic," "disgusting," "corrupt," "heartless," "crooked," "sordid," "petty," "merciless," "barbarous," and the like. This language is inescapably normative.[70]

How should one interpret these moral judgments? It is best to understand Marx as adopting something resembling Kant's noumenal/phenomenal distinction.[71] The noumenal realm is where individuals are free and morally responsible for their choices. When students fail to submit an assignment, I may judge them irresponsible. The phenomenal realm, by contrast, understands the world as a large series of determined causal events—extending to human behavior. In this realm, I may well perceive my student's late paper as the result of working long hours outside of school to cover tuition and living expenses because of her own poverty and hence as beyond my moral judgment of these facts. Marx usually understands the economic world just the way that Roberts suggests—which would be the phenomenal perspective. This often extends to the machinations of the capitalists, whose behavior is, in the phenomenal sense, compelled by the economic system. Yet his moral judgments of the rich imply also a powerful noumenal dimension, which is clearly also a part of his work and in some ways animating its core. It is Marx's moral judgments of capitalism and the agents operating within it that stimulates his desire for something better.

A final social effect of inequality, according to Marx in *Wage Labour and Capital*, is the degree to which it fosters antagonism: "We see . . . that even if we remain *within the relation of capital and wage labour, the interests of capital and the interests of wage labour are diametrically opposed.*" He elaborates, "Even the *most favourable situation* for the working class, the *most rapid possible growth of capital,* however much it may improve the material existence of the worker, does not remove the antagonism between his interests and the interests of the bourgeois, the interest of the capitalist." He subsequently adds that as the wealth of the bourgeoisie grows, so grows "the power that is hostile" to the working class (*WLC*, 220–21; emphases original). This sentiment, of course, extends well beyond this essay. Hostile class relations are perhaps *the* defining feature of Marxian inequality, not limited to bourgeois inequality. After all, he and Engels open section 1 of the *Manifesto*, declaring, "The history of all hitherto existing society is the history of class struggles [*Klassenkämpfen*]" (*CM*, 158). They link classes and hostility in subsequent paragraphs, emphasizing the class divisions of each society, culminating in capitalism, itself characterized by "two great hostile camps" (*CM*, 159). As capitalism evolves, their relationship "take[s] more and more the character of collisions between two classes." In fact, they describe the bourgeoisie as finding itself "involved in a constant battle. At first with the aristocrats; later on, with those portions of the bourgeoisie itself, whose interests have become antagonistic to the progress of industry; at all times, with the bourgeoisie of foreign countries." At these stages, the bourgeoisie often recruits from the ranks of the workers to fight their battles. But eventually, "when the class struggle nears the decisive hour," the proletariat seizes bourgeois tools to combat the bourgeoisie itself (*CM*, 166–67).

Class antagonisms also manifest throughout *Capital*. Marx writes of the establishment of working hours, for example, as "the product of protracted and more or less concealed civil war between the capitalist class and the working class" (*Capital*, 413). In the same chapter, he identifies the "class antagonisms [that] had reached an unheard-of degree of tension" (*Capital*, 405). He twice raises the "antagonistic character of capitalist accumulation" in his chapter on "The General Law of Capitalist Accumulation" (*Capital*, 799, 812). And he describes the Luddites' "large-scale destruction of machinery," which occurred in response to the displacement of workers after mass layoffs.

Class antagonisms have become a familiar theme throughout this book. It is another leitmotiv in the history of political thought. Returning to Plato, excessive inequality fosters "enmities and civil strife both in cities and in private life" (*Laws*, 728e–729a). Jesus condemned the "house divided" (Matthew 12:22). Hobbes spoke of the "resentment and envy" resulting from extreme inequality as "the sources of sedition and war" (*Citizen*, 5.5). For Rousseau, extreme inequality in the state of nature eventually gives way to the "most horrible state of war" (*SD*, 172). Mill describes a "concealed enmity . . . [and] that soured animosity which is universal in this country towards the whole class of employers, in the class of the employed" ("Claims of Labour," 379). Class antagonism is a persistent theme in Western political thought. What is new in Marx, and what distinguishes him from his predecessors, is the degree to which he embraces this antagonism as a potentially useful resource in resolving the problem of inequality.

Solving the Problem of Inequality: Antagonism, Revolution, and Communism

The historian Walter Scheidel has observed, "high inequality has an extremely long pedigree."[72] It has persisted from prehistory into the present. Its trenchant persistence, for him, means that inequality is actually the norm. Equality is, by contrast, rare and fleeting, such as during the "great compression" of the American economy from roughly 1945–1980. The consensus cause of those decades of relative equality was its two world wars. To fund these wars, the United States found it necessary to raise the top marginal income tax rate to 91 percent, which predictably transferred significant wealth from the richest Americans to the poorest, hence dramatically reducing inequality. Scheidel observes that the wealthiest Americans—those at the top 0.01 percent—lost 40 percent of their share of national revenue.[73] Given this relatively recent history, many came to assume that *equality* was the norm rather than the exception. Yet Scheidel argues just the opposite: that *inequality* is the norm, equality the exception. In fact, inequality is so pertinacious that it can only be unseated or disrupted by what he calls the "four horsemen," which include mass-mobilization wars, transformative revolutions, state failure, and natural disasters such as plagues and pandemics. Of course, the four horsemen evoke the four horsemen of the apocalypse, as discussed in Revelation—associated with eschatology. In other words, these forces capable of disrupting inequality are so profound that they bring about a kind of end times—chaos, mass death, disorder, anarchy. So although they may bring equality, the costs are prohibitive. This is likely why there has traditionally been little appetite for the most radical means of reversing inequality, as discussed throughout this book. Plato's Athenian Stranger is perhaps the closest to entertaining the beneficial effects of radical change when he speculates about a great flood wiping out most of civilization, along with its stores of gold and silver, imparting survivors with "the most well-bred dispositions," burdened by "neither wealth nor poverty." In the absence of wealth and poverty, the Stranger reasons, there is "neither insolence nor injustice, nor again jealousies and ill will" (*Laws*, 679bc).

Even understanding the potential for profound economic transformation through radical measures, Plato's Stranger ultimately prefers incremental reforms, concerned about safeguarding the civic harmony central to his political theory. A republic can only thrive where citizens share fraternal sentiments, and that kind of goodwill is undermined by confiscating and redistributing wealth on a large scale. It instead creates lingering resentments stifling affective bonds.

Marx, however, approaches this differently. He is the sole figure in this book who cautiously invites one of those "four horsemen"—revolution. And although he acknowledges the discomforts and inconveniences associated with class antagonisms and civil war, he is more open to using those antagonisms for necessary economic and social transformations, rather than merely quelling them by moderating inequality under capitalism.

Marx and Engels open the *Manifesto* by describing a long-enduring "antagonism of oppressing and oppressed classes [*Klassengegensätzen*]" (*CM*, 168). This oppression continues provided that "certain conditions" can be met, including subsistence wages for workers. But equally important are bourgeois measures that prevent the workers from realizing their status as oppressed victims. This is why the doctrine of "bourgeois equality" is so important. So long as workers understand themselves to be *equal* to their employers both in legal rights and as contractual partners, their concerns about of oppression can largely be suppressed. Supporting this effort also is the myth of meritocracy—that the economic world has been justly sorted into a frugal and virtuous elite, on the one hand, and lazy rascals, on the other. So long as workers believe their fate reflects their own personal inadequacies, they accept their oppression as legitimate.

But every system has a breaking point, according to Marx. For capitalism, this occurs when inequality reaches its extreme limits. We can deduce this from remarks in *Capital* and the *Manifesto*. In the former, Marx speaks of "the constant decrease in the number of capitalist magnates, who usurp and monopolize all the advantages of this process of transformation," combined with the growing "mass of misery, oppression, slavery, degradation, and exploitation" of the workers (*Capital*, 929). The *Manifesto* depicts the modern laborer as sinking "deeper and deeper below the conditions of his own class. He becomes a pauper, and pauperism develops more rapidly than population and wealth" (*CM*, 168). In both cases, Marx understands the outer limits of inequality to highlight the antagonisms that have long persisted beneath the surface. The hidden hostility underlying capitalism has become the open hostility of class war.[74] The embrace of radical change and revolution is a defining feature of Marxian social reform: "In a state of society founded on antagonism of classes, if we want to prevent slavery in fact as well as in name, we must accept war" (*Chartism*, 131).

In this sense, the antagonisms that worried the likes of Plato, Hobbes, Rousseau, Smith, and Mill are not merely concerning to Marx. They are *absolutely essential*. As he famously insists in his *Poverty of Philosophy*, "No antagonism, no progress. That is the law which civilization has followed down to our day. Up to the present the productive forces have been developed thanks to this *régime* of the antagonism of classes" (*Poverty*, 65–66). This is why he rejects the more moderate socialists, such as Pierre-Joseph Proudhon, whom he labels a "bourgeois socialist." As Marx and Engels complain in the *Manifesto*, such reformers "want all the advantages of modern social conditions without the struggles and dangers necessarily resulting therefrom. They desire the existing state of society minus its revolutionary and disintegrating elements" (*Manifesto*, 182). For this reason, Marx would also likely object to many of the reforms for reducing inequality considered throughout this book.

There is some dispute among Marx's readers on whether the proletariat must employ violence to overturn the bourgeois economy and establish a new regime. In some cases, on his account, violence appears necessary. For much of continental Europe, according to Marx in an 1872 speech, "the level of our revolution must be force; it is a force to which we must someday appeal in order to erect the rule of labor." But in the very same speech, he allows that there are other places—namely, the United States and the United Kingdom—"where the workers can attain their goal by peaceful means" (*Possibility*, 523).

Marx might have thought that these countries were candidates for nonviolent change because of their relatively advanced democratization. The United States was born in the eighteenth century with greater opportunity for small farmers, for example, to have a meaningful political voice than anywhere in Europe. The most striking exception to this, of course, was the institution of slavery. Yet by the time Marx delivered this 1872 speech, the Civil War had been concluded, abolishing slavery, and the Fifteenth Amendment to the Constitution had been ratified, guaranteeing the freed slaves the right to vote. Although the struggle for suffrage was to extend much longer, he was likely optimistic that the democratic struggle against oppression could be repeated against other oppressive forces in America, especially against exploitative labor in the North. Less dramatically but equally important in the United Kingdom, the movement to extend the franchise had begun in earnest in Britain. In 1832, a law would expand the franchise to small landowners, tenant farmers, and shopkeepers. And the 1867 Reform Law also represented an incremental expansion—now including those who paid rent of £10 or more a year and agricultural landowners. To be sure, these measures did not enfranchise the entire British working class any more than the Fifteenth Amendment fully guaranteed Blacks the right to vote. But these measures likely encouraged Marx to entertain real nonviolent change.

But what about societies lacking this hope? Of those where democratic movements were stunted or altogether absent? A useful example here might be France, where workers made at least two serious attempts to advance egalitarian political and economic goals in Marx's lifetime—the first in the 1848 Revolution and the second in the ill-fated Paris Commune of 1871. As Engels reports concerning the former, the workers were originally optimistic that the revolution would establish a "social republic," yet just as soon as they tasted success, they were violently suppressed by the bourgeois. Per Engels, the "government had taken care to have an overwhelming superiority of force. After five days' heroic struggle, the workers were defeated. And then followed a blood-bath among the defenseless" (*Introduction*, 620).

The events surrounding the Paris Commune of 1871 were even more dramatic. Following the loss of the Franco-Prussian War, members of the French National Guard seized a portion of Paris to govern for the benefit of the working classes. The commune's reforms included a strict separation of church and state, forgiveness of rent debts, salary caps on the highest paid offices, the closing of pawn shops, and an end to the death penalty symbolized in the public burning of a guillotine. But this attempt to establish a "social republic" met with state violence culminating in "the massacre of defenseless men, women, and children" (*Introduction*, 625). Marx responds to the violence by insisting that the commune members were engaged in a just war—a "war of the enslaved against their enslavers, the only justifiable war in history." As a defensive war, the commune "used fire strictly as a means of defense" (*Civil War*, 648). The French government had evolved, for Marx, into nothing less than "the national power of capital over labor, of a public force organized for social enslavement, of an engine of class despotism" (*Civil War*, 630). On such terms, the outlook for genuinely peaceable evolution to socialism and greater equality appeared, to Marx, foreclosed. The government responded to this uprising with crushing violence. And on the principle of self-defense, the workers had the right to fight back.

Marx's underlying assumption is that in such places, the rich will not freely surrender any significant portion of their property. To illustrate, he alludes to the fate of the Gracchi brothers in ancient Rome (*GI*, 93). Born into aristocratic families, Tiberius and Gaius Gracchus worried about the increasing concentration of landed property in the hands of a small elite, worked by day laborers and slaves, which were replacing the small farms that used to dominate the Roman countryside. In response, Tiberius introduced an agrarian reform act, which would confiscate lands from wealthy Romans and redistribute them to landless ones. He began implementing the laws but was then clubbed to death by his wealthy opponents, his body dumped in the Tiber. About a decade later, his brother, Gaius, ascended to power and sought to resume the agrarian reforms, meeting with a similar fate. The moral of the story, for someone like Marx, is that working through the system, as it were, is not always going to solve the problem of inequality. A further lesson is that the wealthy are perfectly prepared to use violence whenever they sense their property is threatened. If the poor are unwilling to meet force with force, so the reasoning goes, they will meet the same fate as the Gracchi. In fact, as Marx often argues, the wealthy do not even need to be threatened with property loss to employ violence—they use it routinely in maintaining bourgeois society. "Force," as noted earlier, is for him "the midwife of every old society which is pregnant with a new one. It is itself an economic power."

One can propose luxury taxes, estate taxes, education reforms, commercial reforms, and so forth, but if any of these threaten accumulated fortunes, the rich will deploy their resources to resist them. Consider how much, for example, they employ lobbyists, political action committees, advertising campaigns, and other techniques to resist even modest raises of marginal tax rates. Imagine how they would respond, for example, to Mill's steep estate tax. Most politicians intuitively understand this, which is why they rarely pursue such legislation.

For Marx, in some societies, the only way the rich will part with their money is with violent revolution. This is surely not to everyone's taste. It is not the preferred path to equality of anyone else addressed in this book. It is not even Marx's preferred path. The resistance to violence can be partly attributed to the fact that many of his predecessors had personally endured violent revolutions or civil wars, such as Plato and Hobbes. Others assume that revolutions or civil wars create more problems than they solve. But for Marx, under certain conditions there is no alternative. Violence is sometimes the only language the recalcitrant and violently exploitative rich can understand. In technical terms, he calls this the "negation of the negation" in which the "expropriators are expropriated." More directly, he calls it a "violent and difficult process" (*Capital*, 929).

This raises questions about what transpires after capitalism. And even where many accept Marx's criticisms of capitalism in broad terms, they are underwhelmed by his ultimate replacement for it: communism. There is no need here to engage in a full-scale analysis of the communism's practical realizability. Others have done so. My emphasis is understanding its egalitarian dimensions.

At this point, I want to recall that for an important school of Marx scholarship, including Miller and Wood, Marx is *not* an egalitarian. According to Miller, equality is, for Marx, "inappropriate as the main standard for judging social arrangements." For Wood, Marx denies "there is any equal standard that could be used to formulate some ideal demand of justice." Darrin McMahon has relatedly observed, "Marx's emphasis on individual self-realization makes no mention of equality, and in fact it presupposes inequalities insofar as individual abilities, needs, and conditions will necessarily vary." [75]

To evaluate the claim that Marx is not egalitarian, it is helpful to examine the central text outlining Marx's conception of communist justice: *The Critique of the Gotha Program*. This text features the celebrated line, "from each according to their abilities, to each according to their needs." He wrote this originally as "Marginal Notes on the Program of the German Workers' Party" in response to a compromise reached by two German leftist parties in 1875, rejecting their consensus—that in communism, the labor's proceeds would be subject to a "fair distribution." Much, of course, hinges on the meaning of "fair distribution." For the Gotha Program, this meant "the individual producer receives back from society—after the deductions have been made—exactly what he gives to it." Marx seizes on this as the principle of "equal right," which is effectively equivalent to "bourgeois right." As observed earlier, "equality" for Marx often amounts to "bourgeois" equality. He adds here that this is also apparently true in early communism, "still stamped with the birth-marks of the old society from whose womb it emerges." But for most who have lived under capitalism, this conception of "fair distribution" has an intuitively appealing ring.

Yet Marx further interrogates this notion of equality. "This equal right," he notes, "is an unequal right for unequal labour" since different workers have "unequal individuals endowment[s]"—some are stronger or smarter than others. "It is, therefore, a right of inequality" since those with greater natural attributes can work harder and reap the rewards. Further, he continues, this principle of "fair distribution" ignores the varying needs of individuals. Some are married; others are not. Some have children; others do not. Some are disabled; others are not. So strict equality represents a kind of inequality since the single man, for example, will be "richer" than those married with children drawing the same salary. For all these reasons, Marx notes, bourgeois equality is a misguided standard. It is a principle of equality in theory that actually promotes material inequality. This is how he arrives at his own principle of fair distribution for a "higher phase of communist society," a stage only attainable once production has crossed a high threshold and "all of the springs of common wealth flow more abundantly." That principle is, of course, "From each according to their abilities, to each according to his needs" (*Gotha*, 318–21).[76]

Allen Wood has argued that Marx arrived at this maxim "precisely because it is *not* a principle of equal right in any sense: neither people's abilities nor their needs are equal."[77] This is true in two respects. First, Marx considers "equal rights" to be ideology in bourgeois society—used to cement the privileges of the wealthy and trap the poor in the lowest rungs of the social ladder. Second, Wood correctly observes unequal abilities and needs. But he draws the wrong conclusions in suggesting Marx broadly dismisses egalitarianism. We can know this from considering why bourgeois equality is wrong for Marx. It is wrong because it sustains a system of material inequality. This is why, I argue, Marx and Engels carefully distinguish bourgeois equality from material equality. Bourgeois equality's failings do not render material or economic inequality irrelevant. We know this from Marx's alarm at the "social gulf that separates the worker from the capitalist." The Prussian political economist worries about inequality because he seeks some degree of material quality. As Marx and Engels specify in the *German Ideology*, "one of the most vital principles of communism" is the equality of "the *stomach* and of physical *needs*." This brute physical equality is an underlying justification for "to each according to his need." Any departure from this principle, on their account, is to "justify *inequality*" (*GI*, 566; emphases original).

Finally, I want to connect Marx's communist egalitarianism to his republicanism. Liberating people from domination means relieving their economic domination. That domination is expressed through extreme inequality. This republican concern also animates Rousseau. The historian of political thought Maurizio Viroli has written of Rousseau, "He takes his concept of liberty from the republican writers," which prominently includes prioritizing "the *preservation* of the just political order."[78] Rousseau indeed emphasizes both liberty and the preservation of just political orders. But economic equality is central to this republican vision. In his *Social Contract*, Rousseau identifies the aim of all republican legislation as "freedom and equality. Freedom because any individual dependence is that much force taken away from the State; equality because freedom cannot subsist without it." He then clarifies by asking, "Do you, then, want to give the State stability? bring the extremes as close together as possible; tolerate neither very rich people nor beggars. These two states, which are naturally inseparable, are equally fatal to the common good" (2.11, 80n).[79] He connects the republican goal of liberty with stability, which can only be achieved with significant economic equality. The point is, if we are to read Marx as a republican, like Rousseau or still others,[80] then we must understand the intimate relationship of liberty and economic equality. No equality, no liberty. So while it is appropriate to stress Marx's republicanism as grounded in nondomination, part of what it means to be free from arbitrary authority, for Marx as with many other republicans, is dismantling the vast inequalities that support economic, social, and political domination.

Wood could respond to this reading of Marx as consistent with his claim that it is "necessary to limit it [inequality] for other ends, especially freedom (independence from the arbitrary will of another)."[81] This much is true. Marx does not insist on precise economic equality, whatever that might entail. But Wood implies that equality is somehow incidental to Marx's political theory rather than essential. Such readings miss the forest among the trees. Even if one were to grant that equality is merely of "instrumental" value in service of other principles, it is at the same time essential to the realization of those values. It is the same with human life, which requires delivering oxygenated blood cells to the brain. Breathing is instrumentally necessary for this process. This does not render breathing incidental to human life. It is a core feature of sustaining life even though it is in some sense instrumental. This is the case with equality in Marx. His critique of capitalism is literally inconceivable without his critique of inequality. His principle of communist justice would likewise be inconceivable when paired with radical economic inequality. These considerations demonstrate, I hope, that the efforts to disentangle Marx from fundamental considerations of equality and inequality are misleading. To this extent, the public understanding of Marx as an egalitarian, though sometimes wrong in details, is not wrong in spirit.

Conclusion: Radical Inequality Demands Systemic Changes

There is an important lesson to be learned from Marx about inequality. The problems stemming from radical inequality cannot be resolved with modest or cosmetic gestures. For him, inequality comes from economic systems designed to create widely separated winners and losers. The only solution is to abandon the system and replace it with one prioritizing greater equality. This is why he and Engels condemned the "bourgeois socialists" in their midst, including "economists, philanthropists, humanitarians, improvers of the condition of the working class, organizers of charity," and the like. The defining feature of bourgeois socialism, on their account, is the desire to maintain the status quo as much as possible. For Marx and Engels, bourgeois socialists desire that "the proletariat should remain within the bounds of existing society, but should cast away all its hateful ideas concerning the bourgeoisie" (*CM*, 181, 182). They offer modest gestures, like acts of charity and improved wages, to quell the proletariat and forestall bolder economic and social transformations that would require significant financial sacrifices of the rich.

Public displays of charity are very much in vogue today. As inequality in the United States has grown over recent decades, so too have conspicuous charitable displays from billionaires. Such gestures have incontestably improved many lives. Yet Marx would urge a more skeptical lens. The point of grandiose charity, for him, is more fundamentally about forestalling systemic change and protecting the lion's share of bourgeois assets. Perhaps the proof in this is that few of these gestures have fully embraced

Jesus's conception of charity: "Sell your possessions, and give alms" (Luke 12:33). Rarely, if ever, have even outsized charitable gestures by billionaires required donors to make lifestyle sacrifices. When the poor or their advocates complain about inequality and concentrated wealth, the rich are often quick to retort with a long list of charitable deeds. As the journalist Anand Giridharadas has observed, the effect of such charity is, "those at greatest risk of being resented in an age of inequality are . . . recast as our saviors from an age of inequality."[82] The political theorist Rob Reich has similarly cautioned, "Philanthropy can be the pursuit of self-interest, . . . or an exercise of power, sometimes an objectionable exercise of power; when undertaken by the wealthy it can be the expression of a plutocratic voice in a democratic society."[83] The concern for Marx, Giridharadas, and Reich is that charity is deployed as a means of maintaining underlying structural inequalities that made charity necessary in the first place.

It is worth emphasizing that no figure addressed in this book suggests that charity is a primary solution to the problem of inequality. If the problems of inequality are structural, so must also be the reforms. As with Marx, Plato does not think that inequality can be resolved by the rich donating to the poor. The rich are, for him, a part of the problem. And even where they can be brought to understand their role in maintaining inequality, the solution is not almsgiving. The solution, rather, is to embrace fundamental changes in the laws bringing about greater equality. Even Jesus, who celebrates almsgiving more than anyone, invokes the structural reform of Sabbatical and Jubilee laws requiring the regular forgiveness of all debts and the redistribution of property. The solutions to inequality, if anything is to be learned from these texts, are to come from laws more than ad hoc charity. As Mill insisted, when it comes to inequality, "justice is the one needful thing rather than kindness" (*Labour*, 383).

Conclusion

THE LESSONS OF CANONICAL
WISDOM ON INEQUALITY

MORE THAN A CENTURY AGO, at the peak of the Gilded Age, political scientist and social Darwinist William Graham Sumner observed that while he often heard complaints about economic inequality, those critics never spelled out the reasons for their objections. "What law of nature, religion, ethics, or the state is violated by inequalities of fortune?" he asked, implying that he had never encountered serious arguments to this effect.[1] Sumner's incredulity is remarkable, however, as those religious, ethical, and political objections to inequality were there already in books he had surely studied throughout his long career as a political theorist. Indeed, he taught an entire course on Plato at Yale, yet seemed entirely unaware of Plato's principled objections to the "inequalities of fortune."[2] He had read and somehow either forgotten or skipped over Plato's description of a city characterized by inequality as effectively "two [cities] . . . which are at war with one another: the city of the poor and that of the rich" (*Republic*, 422e–423a).

While Sumner's social Darwinism may no longer be fashionable, his neglect of these arguments against inequality in familiar texts remains common. More than a century after Sumner, Steven Pinker has praised wealth and inequality in his best-selling *Enlightenment Now*, a book that purports to honor the wisdom of the seventeenth and eighteenth centuries. For him, significant economic inequality "is almost a mathematical necessity" in thriving societies and is "a harbinger of opportunity" in developing ones. He confidently insists that the economic growth accompanying this equality has improved the lives of everyone, not just the rich.

Economic growth, he observes, has brought air-conditioning to even the poor.[3] This is surely a great comfort to the poor in warm climates. Given his celebration of inequality, it is perhaps unsurprising that Bill Gates, one of the wealthiest men in the world, championed Pinker's book as his "new favorite book of all time."[4] As the most prominent work in recent decades to confirm to the rich that inequality is more a social blessing than a burden, Pinker's arguments surely soothe billionaires much better than James's disconcerting warning, "You rich people, weep and wail for the miseries that are coming to you" (James 5:1). That aside, over the course of a long book dedicated to lionizing the wisdom of seventeenth- and eighteenth-century thinkers, Pinker fails to acknowledge even in passing that several of the most celebrated intellectuals of that period, including Hobbes, Rousseau, and Smith, registered serious objections to inequality. It may well be that delivering air-conditioning to the masses is worth risking the potential dangers of inequality, but how does one draw inspiration from the Enlightenment and come away with such a constricted view of its concerns? The arguments against inequality found in historical texts are hardly peripheral; they emphatically deserve to be as prominent a feature of these thinkers' thought as any other part of their work.

Although Pinker does not use the term, his emphasis on addressing absolute poverty rather than inequality suggests that he embraces *sufficientarianism*. This doctrine posits that even though poverty is a legitimate concern, inequality is not. The primary moral imperative is to relieve poverty where it exists. The philosopher Harry Frankfurt has been among its most prominent advocates: "Economic equality is not, as such, of particular moral importance. With respect to the distribution of economic assets, what is important from the point of view of morality is not that everyone should have the same but that each should have enough."[5] Economist Deirdre McCloskey is equally clear: "It doesn't matter ethically whether the poor have the same number of diamond watches and Porsche automobiles as do the owners of hedge funds. It does, however, matter ethically whether they have the same opportunities to vote or to learn to read or to have a roof over their heads."[6]

No one should dispute the importance of improving the absolute condition of the poor. Sufficientarianism's reduction of all social, political, and moral questions to poverty alleviation, however, severely constrains the moral imagination as it has been expressed throughout history. Consider, for example, McCloskey's suggestion that the "opportunity to vote" represents meaningful political equality. This fails to grasp the multidimensionality of democratic citizenship. While voting is surely important, it is among the least consequential ways in which the wealthy exercise their democratic citizenship, which can include, among other things, making large campaign donations, forming and funding political action committees, purchasing political advertising, and schmoozing with political elites. The suffrage of the poor is important and obviously requires protection. But one cannot assume that this right alone protects against oligarchic control over putatively democratic institutions. Such oversights are common in the sufficientarian literature that dismisses inequality as "ethically irrelevant."[7] But these considerations are not overlooked by Rousseau or Mill who, for example, understand the myriad ways in which inequality subverts democratic institutions.

To be sure, sufficientarians do not deny the importance of housing the poor. Nor do they deny an obligation to educate them. But they emphatically deny that extreme inequality represents a legitimate social problem. The real problem, which is absolute rather than relative poverty, can be solved by "growing the pie," as it were—that is, promoting economic growth. McCloskey notes that the emergence of the "bourgeois virtues" had the effect of lifting 90–95 percent of the world's population out of absolute poverty.[8] And that is something to feel triumphant about—a vindication of those values.

The growing appeal of sufficientarianism has paralleled both economic growth as well as growth inequality—to levels rivaling the Gilded Age. It is appropriate now to take stock and ask whether these trends are an unmixed blessing, as we have been assured. The history of political thought is useful for just such purposes. Mill implored in his discussion of the stationary state, for example, "It is only in the backward countries of the world that increased production is still an important object: in those most advanced, what is economically needed is a better distribution" (*Principles*, 755). For him, there comes a time when the blessings of economic growth might pose a real danger. Yet McCloskey politely dismisses the worries of her "amiable" and "sweet Mill," whom she otherwise admires. For her, his misguided egalitarianism emerged from "a growing list of imagined but unmeasured imperfections" falsely attributed to capitalist economies.[9] It obviously betrays the limits of Mill's imagination, in other words, to hold that any society could fail to savor the benefits of boundless economic growth and inequality, especially as those benefits are enjoyed by the lowest rungs of society. McCloskey dismisses Mill's arguments but never pauses to carefully weigh, much less refute, them.

For McCloskey, one reason that earlier generations mistakenly cautioned against inequality is because they embraced a zero-sum economic framework in which one person's financial gain is another's loss. To be sure, this assumption was dominant before Adam Smith all the way up through Jean-Jacques Rousseau, who once asked someone with aspirations to become rich, "How is it possible to become wealthy without contributing to impoverishing someone else?" (*WFT*, 9). Mandeville began challenging this orthodoxy in the early eighteenth century. For him, a commercial economy improves the condition of all at the same time, including the poorest: "we shall find that in the remote Beginnings of every Society, the richest and most considerable Men among them were a great while destitute of a great many Comforts of Life that are now enjoy'd by the meanest and must humble Wretches."[10] Smith affirms that the poor in market economies "may enjoy a greater share of the necessities and conveniences of life than it is possible for any savage to acquire" (*WN*, 10). Joseph Schumpeter similarly comments in the twentieth century, "There are no doubt some things available to the modern workman that Louis XIV himself would have been delighted to have yet was unable."[11] McCloskey thus follows established precedent in emphasizing that by virtue of the market economy, to be sure, "the rich got richer" while "the poor [got] richer, much richer." This "Great Enrichment," as she calls it, has buried zero-sum conceptions of economics in favor of one that is "distinctly positive-sum" or "win-win."[12]

One wonders, however, why was Adam Smith less confident about this? If he was so confident about unmitigated triumph of economic growth, why then was he at pains to detail the moral and political costs of inequality? Even in prioritizing economic growth over reducing inequality, there is no sense in which this growth, for him, can be characterized as "win-win." For him, economic inequality always entails winners and losers. The material improvements of the downtrodden do not solve all the problems associated with myriad forms of inequality. Even Winston Smith in *1984* had the material benefits of a desk job and a television—advantages of a productive economy largely unavailable to his ancestors. It would be strange, however, to insist that he therefore has no right to complain about his predicament.

Another problem of inequality ignored by the sufficientarians but well understood by the figures treated throughout this book is the corrupting effect of inequality on the rich themselves. Whether one characterizes this as the corruption of souls or the debasing of character, there is striking unanimity that great fortunes tend to inflame the worst elements of human nature. I have emphasized this concern throughout. This assessment of inequality's effects on character has been confirmed by the psychologist Dacher Keltner, who has found that the wealthy tend to act in "self-gratifying and often greedy ways," becoming increasingly "rude and offensive" and delighting in stories that "divide and demean."[13] He finds, among other things, that the wealthy are significantly more likely to shoplift, have affairs, drive through a crosswalk while ignoring pedestrians, and seize for themselves the last remaining cookie off a serving dish. They are also more likely to avoid paying their taxes and to invent elaborate justifications for doing so. In fact, according to Keltner, justifying bad behavior is among the favorite pastimes among the ill-behaved rich—they show "no shortage of imagination when it comes to explaining away [their own] injustices." When shown graphs depicting widening inequality gaps in the American economy, "those from upper-class backgrounds were more likely to attribute the income gap to talent, genius, effort, and hard work."[14] The rich, that is, have persuaded themselves that they have deserved their fortunes. This sense of entitlement, on Keltner's account, emboldens further presumptuous behavior.

Another compelling study, conducted by the scholars Katherine DeCelles and Michael Norton, finds a striking correlation between the presence of first-class sections on airplanes and air-rage events. Specifically, they find that airplanes including a first-class section are four times more likely to experience these episodes than those lacking a first-class cabin. Although other factors, such as extended delays, generate similar effects, the very presence of a first-class cabin was found to have the same effect on air-rage incidents as a nine-and-a-half-hour delay. As the psychologist Keith Payne has aptly noted in commenting on this study, "What makes it fascinating . . . is that incidents of rage take place even when there are no true have-nots on a flight."[15] That is, rarely is an airline passenger poor in the absolute sense that concerns sufficientarians. Yet the inequality between the fabulously rich and everyone else, who would not likely even interact on a flight, remains a highly significant independent variable stimulating anger, arguments, and even physical violence.

Such lines of research are important for many reasons. I raise two of them here. First, they confirm much of what has been understood by philosophers starting with Plato. The sense of natural superiority and immunity to the law and moral scrutiny has long been understood as dangerous in unequal societies. Similarly, the awareness of inequalities has long been a source of discontent, discord, and even violence, as philosophers from Plato to Marx have repeatedly emphasized. Second, the studies reveal the obvious shortcomings of theories dismissive of inequality. In focusing almost exclusively on poverty alleviation and economic growth, sufficientarians lack the moral infrastructure to confront long-identified problems increasingly confirmed by contemporary research. One can, of course, ignore the effects of inequality on society and individual character, but the Western tradition emphatically counsels otherwise. If people claim to revere this tradition, they should heed its warnings.

There is an additional problem burdening many sufficientarians—the assumption that the problems of poverty and inequality can be reduced to the dollar amount required to satisfy the basic needs of the poor. Elizabeth Popp Berman refers to this approach as "thinking like an economist,"— where social problems are reduced to simplistic mathematical elements without consideration of their intricate moral complexities. As Berman notes, as recently as the early 1970s, lawmakers were receptive to antipollution policies that shamed polluters. But by the 1980s, "environmental policy turned away from a moral framework that stigmatized polluters and toward the position that pollution was simply an externality to be priced."[16] Emerging cap and trade proposals dismissed the deeper moral concerns inevitably intertwined with matters like environmental destruction or economic inequality. Reducing everything to easily measured numbers, like efficiency, GDP, or absolute poverty levels, is attractive to a certain mindset, while ignoring the moral questions that transcend simple mathematical reductionism. This sort of thinking is represented by Richard Posner, who has gone so far as to merge GDP and morality: "the criterion for judging whether acts and institutions are just and good is whether they maximize the wealth of society."[17] In a similar spirit, David Dollar and Aart Kraay have argued that economic growth is "good for the poor," regardless of whether it is accompanied by greater inequality.[18] Perhaps the peak of this kind of thinking is summarized by Margaret Thatcher's adviser Keith Joseph: "If we are to reduce poverty in this country and to raise our standard of living, we need more inequality than we have now."[19] The values expressed here are inattentive to inequality's complex psychological, moral, social, and political effects. Suffice it to say, this mode of thinking is alien to the figures addressed throughout this book, who are among the most insightful moral psychologists in Western civilization.

There is a Benthamite quality to this—in assuming that moral and political problems have elegantly simple mathematical solutions. But we should recall how Mill distanced himself from Bentham, not only from his godfather's myopic insistence that every person has always been and will forever be egoistic but also from his mathematical reductionism. This criticism is to be found more between the lines of Mill's *Utilitarianism* than in his express arguments. Unlike his explicit rejections of Bentham's trenchant egoism, Mill rebukes Bentham in this respect by refusing to reduce his moral philosophy to mathematical formulas. Yes, Mill wants the greatest happiness. But there is no suggestion on his part that we can actually *quantify* that. Rather, for Mill, we know that happiness consists in successfully fostering healthy human relationships—in nudging people to embrace the interests of their fellow citizens as their own. We desire nothing more, he finds, than "to be in unity with our fellow creatures" (*Utilitarianism*, 32). And we know that we have promoted utility, by extension, when this sense of unity is enhanced rather than undermined.

Economic inequality poses one of the most formidable barriers to achieving this unity. This is why reducing inequality and not mere poverty alleviation, for Mill, is among the most pressing tasks of governments. Much the same operates in other thinkers treated in this book. But my immediate point is this: simple numbers like GDP and economic growth rate do not effectively replace considerations of unity and solidarity. We cannot achieve these ends simply by deriving some fixed number of how much money to throw at the poor.[20] The indigent in democratic societies fully deserve equal concern and respect. They have hopes and dreams; they have loves and fears; they have anxieties and envies. Addressing our social problems involves the careful work of moral psychology and political theory, not simple mathematical formulas. We need to understand how inequality affects psyches, social relationships, laws, policies, and institutions. To this extent, the vast majority of thinking in this book dispenses with mathematical solutions to the problem of inequality. There are no simple formulas delineating the *right degree* of inequality.[21] We can only know whether we have ameliorated the problem of inequality by the degree to which we perceive citizens care more about, and are inclined less to exploit, one another. This is not to dismiss mathematics, which plays an important role in describing the degree and trajectory of inequality over time. But we ought to be cautious in assuming that the solutions to inequality's problems can be reduced to simple mathematical formulas or gestures, like calculations of GDP or the poverty line.

The sufficientarians have certainly evolved beyond the social Darwinists, like Sumner, who insisted that a "drunkard in the gutter is just where he should be."[22] They have committed to feeding and housing the poor. But they still fail to weigh the many other dangers attached to unequal societies—perils known since Plato. This failure sometimes carries the seeds of social Darwinism and leads to a lamentable failure of imagination in addressing inequality. Former Bain Capital executive Edward Conard speaks the sufficientarian language when acknowledging moral obligations to help the "less fortunate." For him, those with low IQ scores are destined to end up poor, and they "need help." At the same time, however, he cautions, "Our compassion can lead us to do more harm than good."[23] His preferred solutions to help the needy, rather, include facilitating the immigration of high-skilled foreigners, radically reducing the number of college students majoring in the humanities, reducing marginal corporate tax rates, and resisting the temptation to lower taxes on the middle class. In short, these measures, to his mind, promote economic growth, which he believes is the best way to promote the welfare of those with low IQ scores.[24] Conard's solution to the problem of inequality, in other words, is to presume the poor's intellectual deficiencies, repeal existing social programs intended to assist them, and provide tax breaks to wealthy citizens. Although most sufficientarians are not so callous as this, Conard's approach to inequality is nevertheless precisely sufficientarian—growing the economy will provide benefits to all, even those burdened by low IQ scores.

Perhaps the single most common theme uniting thinkers in this book regarding the problem of inequality is the degree to which inequality divides political communities. For Plato's Athenian Stranger, for example, economic inequality "breed[s] both civil war and faction" (*Laws*, 744d). For Jesus, "every kingdom divided against itself is laid to waste, and no city or house divided against itself will stand" (Matthew 12:22). For Hobbes, inequality is a source of faction, and "factions are the source of sedition and civil war" (*Citizen*, 10.12). For Rousseau, inequality inflames the "citizens' hatred of one another" (*PE*, 20). Smith describes how in unequal societies, the "disproportion betwixt them [rich and poor] . . . is so great that he [the wealthy man] will hardly look at him [the poor] as being of the same kind" (*LJ*, 184). Mill observes that unequal societies commonly pit the classes against one another in "concealed enmity . . . [and] soured animosity" (*Labour*, 379). And for Marx, the inequalities required by capitalism stimulate "antagonisms" between the classes culminating in class war.

This reveals a persistent theme that colors inequality today: that radical inequality, everything else being equal, fosters hostility. As the political theorist Anne Phillips has cautioned, "Living in a world of stark economic inequalities erodes our ability to see others as people like ourselves," producing "hatreds" for members of opposing classes but often even more viscerally directed to those occupying the same economic rungs as themselves, such as the working poor against minorities, refugees, and asylum seekers.[25] In so cautioning, she confirms what we should have noted in the history of political thought all along. As Rousseau observed more than two centuries ago, inequality "weaken[s] assembled men by disuniting them" and "sow[s] the seeds of real division" (*SD*, 185). His concern about inequality's divisive effects remains relevantly ominous.

Sufficientarians' impulse to dismiss economic inequality and communal solidarity represents an attempt, in important respects, to subvert much of political philosophy itself. They have similarly sought to reduce complex questions of moral and political theory to simple mathematical and economic ones. If only economic growth can achieve a certain threshold, we have been assured that justice will be served. That is admittedly one way to do political theory, but it is largely inconsistent with political theory's traditions, and it should be acknowledged as a radical departure. I have endeavored to demonstrate that the most celebrated political theory, historically speaking, involves more than boosting economic productivity. It demands more than even ensuring that the poor have the right to vote, enough to eat, a roof over their heads, and air-conditioning. Political theory has traditionally involved addressing the thorny matters of human nature, social theory, moral psychology, and moral philosophy. What the history of political thought reveals, and what is lacking in influential segments of the inequality debate today, is the understanding that inequality is intrinsically connected to all of these matters. There is no magic GDP figure, no target economic growth rate, or even a Gini coefficient number that can replace the task of carefully thinking through how inequality affects human nature, moral psychology, moral philosophy, and political institutions. There are no shortcuts to a more perfect union.

Judith Shklar once observed that among Rousseau's distinguishing features was his eagerness to borrow from the ancient philosophers Plato and Aristotle, whose social philosophies were integrated with psychology, ethics, religion, myth, history, and natural science. The breadth of their thought informed his own deployment of "psychological, pedagogic, artistic, ethical, and religious ideas," all of which would play a role in what she called his "philosophical ensemble."[26] Like many of the most compelling thinkers in the Western tradition, Rousseau resisted simple answers to vexing social problems and understood matters like inequality to operate in relation to a complex web of ideas. The Nobel laureate economist Angus Deaton has echoed almost precisely this sentiment: "economics has been very narrow in its focus compared with its origins. . . . If you read Adam Smith, or Karl Marx, . . . or John Stuart Mill . . . there's a very broad set of issues including philosophy, some psychology, serious contemplation of the human condition in all its strengths and weaknesses and in all its dimensions—whereas a lot of economics over the last 20 or 30 years has become obsessed with efficiency."[27] He laments that economics has simply ignored these larger questions that rightly concerned earlier generations of economists and philosophers—a disposition that compelled them to take inequality seriously. It is no coincidence that Deaton cites these particular thinkers, as they represent precisely the rich tradition of political and economic thinking highlighted in this book. As these figures intuitively know, justice and the common good are not reducible to efficiency, economic growth, or poverty vouchers. A degree of economic equality is admittedly far from sufficient to ensure thriving political communities. But if we can learn anything from giants on whose shoulders we stand, it is almost certainly a component of it. Political thought cannot be entirely extricated from questions of equality and inequality. These matters inevitably shape our social world. We ignore them only at our peril.

NOTES

Introduction

1. Blanchet, Saez, and Zucman 2022.
2. Oxfam 2022.
3. Dolan and Petterson-Withorn 2022.
4. Beer 2020.
5. See Piketty 2014; 2020.
6. Wolff 2017, xiii.
7. Sommeiller and Price 2018, 13.
8. Scheidel 2017, 21.
9. Lindblom 1977, 44.
10. Freud (1927) 1961, 15.
11. Douglass (1856) 2020.
12. Plutarch 2001, 1:145.
13. I note here that the historical character of Jesus was not "Western" in the sense that he was European. He obviously was not. He was, rather, a Jewish man from Roman Palestine. He is included in the "Western canon" here because of the Bible's central role in the development of that tradition.
14. This book ends with Marx not because he was the last notable philosopher to address and criticize inequality. There would be many important critics of inequality in the twentieth century, including but not limited to Keynes, Kuznets, Pareto, Galbraith, and Rawls (some of these figures are discussed in Milanovic 2023 and McMahon 2023). It ends with Marx in the nineteenth century rather because Marx's radical solution to the problem of inequality represents a kind of culmination of the longer history. These twentieth-century critics of inequality deserve to be studied—and they are. But in many ways, they deserve a book of their own.
15. Piketty 2014, 444, 567, 443, 571, 514, 537.
16. For example, Cowen 2011; McCloskey 2016, 52, 637–38; 2016b; 2019, 147–48; Pinker 2018, 98.
17. McCloskey 2016, 52. To be sure, this reasoning is already present in Willam Graham Sumner in the late nineteenth century, who wrote, "The yearning after equality is the offspring of envy and covetousness" (Sumner [1883] 1989, 145).
18. Cowen 2010; 2022.
19. Brooks, 2014 (italics in original); 2013.
20. Friedman 1962, 161. See also Cowen (2019), who scoffs at the notion that there are egalitarian dimensions in Plato and Hobbes, for example.
21. Hayek (1944) 1972, 13.
22. See Phillips 2021.
23. The recent *Oxford Handbook to Economic Inequality* (2011) includes thirty-seven essays by social scientists and one by a political theorist.
24. Stuurman 2017, 5.

25. To be sure, I take some inspiration in the fact, as Mike Savage (2021, 8) has observed, that there has increasingly been "intense cross disciplinary synergy" to be found among the various social sciences, such that "the issue of inequality has come to straddle specific disciplines and has inspired social scientists to work together in an unprecedented way," insofar as political scientists and sociologists, for example, work with economists. My own study pushes these interdisciplinary engagements to consider political theory, philosophy, and history to be in dialogue with the social sciences.

26. Piketty 2014, 3.

27. Confucius 1979, 138; Lao Tzu 1963, 60; Gandhi (1909) 1996, 140.

28. Relatedly, Adam Smith asks why do people "pursue riches and avoid poverty"? The answer is not to be found, he suggests, in supplying the "necessities of nature" but rather in satisfying "vanity and distinction." There is no boost to "vanity" or "distinction" in wealth unless there is inequality. This is how, he argues, the rich succeed in their goal of drawing to themselves the "attention of the world" (TMS, 62–63).

29. Shklar 1969, 195. Even Milton Friedman (1962, 190) acknowledges, "poverty is in part a relative matter."

30. To be sure, whereas some will attribute this drop in absolute poverty to Johnson's anti-poverty measures, others have attributed these to economic growth resulting from deregulation, lower taxes, and the like.

31. Mishel and Kandra 2021.

32. D. Markovits 2019, 78.

33. See Mills 1997, 37–39.

34. All references to the *Social Contract* are to book and chapter numbers, followed by page numbers.

35. Although this is what the political scientist and social Darwinist William Graham Sumner ([1883] 1989, 39) suggests at one point in reducing critiques of inequality to "an old Ecclesiastical prejudice in favor of the poor and against the rich," a prejudice of "ludicrous contradictions," he argues, that threatens to "replunge Europe into barbarism."

Chapter One

1. This reputation has been most insistently affirmed by Leo Strauss, who observes, in writing about the *Republic*, "we never see or hear him [Socrates] speak to shoemakers or the like. He converses . . . only with people who are not common people—who belong in one way or the other to an elite" (Strauss 1964, 57).

2. To be sure, some scholars suggest that the *Republic* depicts as many as three different conceptions of "philosopher rulers," including philosophers by design, philosophers by nature, and philosophical erotics. Roslyn Weiss describes the first two in her *Philosophers in the Republic*, whereas Jill Frank has drawn attention to a version of philosopher rulers defined by their *eros* for truth (Frank 2018, chap. 5).

3. Popper [1945] 1971, 152; see also Andrew 1989.

4. Crossman 1959, 180.

5. As S. Sara Monoson has correctly insisted, "it is essential to identify his [Plato's] distance from the contemporary ideology of oligarchy as well as aristocracy" (Monoson 2000, 118). For Monoson, many facile readers of Plato assume that his conception

of aristocracy—where political power rests with those characterized by exceptional wisdom and virtue—implies a broader embrace of elitism, extending to the rule of the rich.

6. Existing accounts can be found in Morrow 1960, 101–12; Strauss (1973) 1998, 77–79; Stalley 1983, 97–98; McWilliams 1986; Bernadete 2001, 168; Wallach 2001, 378–80; Bobonich 2002, 375–76; Fleischacker 2004a, 42–43; Garnsey 2007, 7; Thompson 2007, 32–35; Vaughan 2008, 10–22; Zuckert 2009, 94; Santas 2010, 159–65; Annas 2017, 85; Santas 2018; and Kramm and Robeyns 2020. Of these treatments of Plato on inequality, Morrow, Vaughan, and Santas are the most substantial. Morrow's important reading interprets Plato's treatment of inequality in the *Laws* as a response to Athenian circumstances. Vaughan's thoughtful analysis has a specific interest in the problem of poverty in the *Republic* and *Laws* and includes in her analysis a conception of "relative" poverty, which is a marker of inequality. Santas (2018) provides the most thorough account of Plato on equality. But his approach differs from mine. First, Santas explores several modes of inequality in Plato's dialogues, not just economic. So he dedicates relatively little space specifically to economic issues in comparison with my chapter. Second, Santas's approach to inequality in Plato is more concerned with connecting it to his idea of justice, whereas my approach here, while not inattentive to justice, places more emphasis on Plato's attention to civic harmony and, subsequently, the ways inequality upsets that harmony.

7. For more on ancient Greek oligarchy, see Simonton 2018.

8. In this section and in the following one on Lycurgus, I rely extensively on Plutarch's *Lives*, which is not understood to be always historically accurate. Among the challenges, it is uncertain that Solon and Lycurgus were actual historical persons (see McMahon 2023, 100). To mitigate these questions, I draw on Aristotle's *Constitution of Athens* where it tends to affirm elements of Plutarch's account. As for whether they were real people, it does not matter so much as the stories that were told about him to educated Greeks of Plato's day. What is important is that Plato likely heard the stories about Lycurgus in Sparta and borrowed generously from them in his political theory.

9. Plutarch's *Lives*, 114. John Stuart Mill would later comment on such practices in the ancient world: the "law of most countries were all severity to the debtor. They invested the creditor with a power of coercion, more or less tyrannical. . . . This arbitrary power has extended, in some countries, to making the insolvent debtor serve the creditor as his slave" (Mill, *Principles*, 5.9.8). See also Scheidel 2017, 192.

10. Aristotle, *Constitution of Athens*, 214.

11. Plutarch, *Lives*, 114.

12. Plutarch, *Lives*, 116. See also Aristotle, *Constitution of Athens*, 214, 217.

13. Plutarch 2001, 115.

14. Plutarch 2001, 145.

15. Although I have noted above that Plutarch's account of the ancient lawgivers has been questioned on its historical accuracy, it is worth observing that in his *Politics*, Aristotle praises moderate states in which wealth is relatively equal so that the rich do not "grow into violent and great criminals" and the poor do not grow "into rogues and petty rascals." Cities must rather consist, "as far as possible, of equals and similars and these are generally the middle classes." To this end, he specifically praises Lycurgus for having originated from a "middle condition" (*Politics*, 4.11, 1295b,

1296a). To the extent Lycurgus was mythical, stories about him were nevertheless widely shared throughout Greece and accepted as important history.

16. Plutarch, *Lives*, 59.

17. Plutarch, *Lives*, 54. The Spartan inequality described by Plutarch here echoes that outlined much earlier by Aristotle: "The mention of avarice naturally suggests a criticism [of Sparta] on the inequality of property. While some of the Spartan citizens had quite small properties, others have very large ones; hence the land passed into the hands of the few" (*Politics*, 2.6, 1270a).

18. To be fair, according to Plutarch, Solon was "no admirer of riches." This being said, he objects less to wealth than Lycurgus insofar as that wealth was justly procured (2001, 1:107). For this reason, perhaps among others, his economic reforms for Athens were more moderate than Lycurgus's.

19. Plutarch, *Lives*, 59.

20. Plutarch, *Lives*, 59.

21. Plutarch, *Lives*, 60. For similar reasons, and likely inspired by Plutarch's account of Lycurgus, Rousseau bans currency in his constitutional project for Corsica since "it is useful only as a sign of inequality" (*Corsica*, 140).

22. Plutarch, *Lives*, 60.

23. Plutarch, *Lives*, 60–61. I note here that Thomas More adopted common meals likely for similar reasons in his *Utopia* (42–43).

24. As Matthew W. Maguire has noted of Plutarch's reforms, "meals . . . in common kept inequality and fractiousness from impinging on the unity of the state" (Maguire 2006, 65).

25. Plutarch, *Lives*, 61.

26. Aristotle, *Politics*, 1266b.

27. Plutarch, *Lives*, 79.

28. Plutarch, *Lives*, 596.

29. Plutarch, *Lives*, 699.

30. Ober 1989, 192.

31. Old Oligarch, 1.4.

32. Old Oligarch, 1.13.

33. Old Oligarch, 1.14.

34. Balot 2001, 187.

35. Balot 2001, 216.

36. Antiphon 2011, 114.

37. Wolpert 2002, 22.

38. McCormick 2018, 51.

39. Or one might alternatively read the *Republic* as a warning against the atrocities that might be required by a blind pursuit of justice.

40. This office is commonly translated as "philosopher king," which is somewhat misleading since Plato's Socrates insists that women can serve in this office as well as men (*Republic*, 456a).

41. Although Plato generally employs the word "*sophrosune*" when speaking of self-control or self-mastery, here he uses *kosmiotes*, which emphasizes orderliness. Many thanks here to Jill Frank for noting this exception.

42. Previous scholars have observed and commented on the role of fraternal love in Plato's *Republic* (e.g., Vlastos 1981, 11–19; Seung 1996, 99–106; Schofield 2009).

43. Plato sometimes explains the priority of this fraternal love by warning against its opposite: "Do we know of any greater evil for a city than what tears it apart and makes it many instead of one?" (*Republic*, 462ab).

44. Scholars have generally been aware of this myth's relationship to the formation of fraternal bonds. See, for example, Vlastos 1981, 11–12; Strauss 1964, 102–3; Konstan 2018, 167. On the myth of autochthony more generally, see E. Markovits 2008, 139–42.

45. Spartan inequality had no doubt grown considerably since Lycurgus, but Athens's commercial society had likely even greater inequality in the fifth century BCE.

46. To be sure, Plato has in mind here the fact that the Athenian oligarchs' greed led them to seize power in two revolutions during his lifetime, and the second revolution (of 404) resulted in a successful counterrevolution by the poor. Plato's lesson from Athenian events is that both wealth and poverty ultimately fuel revolution. Ryan Balot details these revolutions and their relationship to both wealth and poverty (Balot 2001, chap. 6).

47. The definitive work on *pleonexia* in the ancient world is Balot 2001. But see also Frank 2018, in which she describes *pleonexia* as "the signal feature" of "an unjust soul" (141).

48. One might argue that the theory of *pleonexia* is partly a response to Cephalus's assertion that wealth leads to virtue since it represents a polar opposite view of the relationship of wealth and virtue (*Republic*, 331ab).

49. An excellent account of how money and greed distort the Platonic soul can be found in Schofield 2006, chap. 6. Similar arguments can be found in Kramm and Robeyns 2020, who characterize these as Plato's "intrinsic arguments" against excessive wealth (958).

50. See Balot 2001, 10.

51. Plato subsequently emphasizes this very point—that the oligarch is "terrified of losing his . . . possessions" (*Republic*, 554d).

52. Those who elevate the unnecessary or lawless appetites have "tyrannical souls," a diseased soul on a different order for Plato. See *Republic*, 571a–576b.

53. This is certainly true of the character of Cephalus, a wealthy metic (resident alien) depicted in book 1 (*Republic*, 329e–331d).

54. As Jeffrey Green has observed, "Plato's scheme for a ruling elite of philosopher-kings required, he understood, that there be no property, and thus no economic inequality, among this class, because Plato accepted that economic divisions otherwise would interfere with the rule of reason and virtue" (Green 2015, 88).

55. On this point, see Lemoine 2020, 100.

56. Jonathan Lear (2006) has previously connected Cephalus's fear of Hades with the Myth of Er. There is a substantial literature on Plato's use of myth in the *Republic* and his other dialogues. For treatments of Plato's myths and the surrounding debates, see Keum 2020; Partenie 2009; and Kirkland 2012, 38–41.

57. As Tae-Yeoun Keum has characterized this portion of the myth, "Choosing well would require the capacity to resist packing one's subsequent life with superficial advantages" (Keum 2020, 60).

58. See Reeve (1988) 2006, 156; Roochnik 2003, 99; and Ferrari 2005, 70.

59. The Stranger repeatedly stresses the fundamental nature of friendship and harmony for legislation and political flourishing, including, 697d, 698c, 738d, 743c, 771b, 837a, 843c, 862a–c, and 880e. Plato's emphasis on friendship in the *Laws* has

led T. K. Seung to conclude that it is "the ultimate end of Magnesia" (Seung 1996, 255). As Balot has observed, the question of social harmony was particularly acute in Athens during Plato's lifetime, when divisiveness was peaking (Balot 2001, 180–211).

60. For an account stressing the centrality of virtue in Plato's *Laws*, see Bobonich 2002, 90–91, 416–17.

61. Plato wrote this letter to Dionysius as a warning that he was failing precisely this test of just laws and was hence subject to the "destruction" Plato outlines in his *Laws*. See Morrow (1940) 1971. Some question the authenticity of this letter (see Aalders 1969).

62. This again echoes comments he makes in his Eighth Letter, specifically with regard to Argos and Messene (354b).

63. See Wallach 2001, 380.

64. It is important to acknowledge per this book's title that the Athenian Stranger references civil war as the "greatest of all plagues" here. But I think this title is nevertheless justified insofar as the kind of dissention that arises from significant inequality is the one identifiable and necessary source of this plague per the *Laws*. To affirm this association of inequality and the "greatest of all plagues," I appeal to the sixteenth-century French philosopher Jean Bodin, who notes, "THE commonest cause of disorders and revolutions in commonwealths has always been the too great wealth of a handful of citizens, and the too great poverty of the rest. The histories are full of occasions on which those who have given all sorts of reasons for their discontents have taken the first opportunity that offered of despoiling the rich of their possessions. . . . For this reason Plato called riches and poverty the two original plagues of the commonwealth, not only because of the misery that hunger occasions, but the shame, and shame is a very evil and dangerous malady" (*Six Books of the Commonwealth*, 5.2, 161–62).

65. Plato's suggestion that a natural disaster brought about conditions of economic equality anticipate the more recent arguments of Walter Scheidel that natural disasters have historically been, in fact, one of the "great levelers" ending periods of extreme inequality (Scheidel 2017).

66. In his *Social Contract*, Rousseau will echo the Stranger's observation especially with regard to being raised in the position of presumptive power: "Everything combines to remove justice and reason from a man who has been brought up to command others" (*SC*, 3, 6, 100). It is quite possible that Rousseau adopted this position upon reading Plato's *Laws*, which Rousseau owned and read carefully. See Silverthorne 1973.

67. Josiah Ober has observed that Darius Xerxes's extreme wealth imparted a sense of poverty and deprivation among all of his subjects (Ober 2015, 76–77).

68. See also *Laws*, 743a, 743c.

69. See also *Laws*, 837a and Seung 1996, 254.

70. I rely here on Seung 1996, 233–35.

71. Although one cannot be certain about Plato's sources here, it is possible that he might have had in mind Phaleas of Chalcedon, whom Aristotle describes in *Politics*, 2.7. Like Plato's Stranger, Phaleas was a radical egalitarian, who acknowledges that his egalitarianism is much easier to achieve at the founding of a state than after some time has elapsed. His egalitarianism, however, is even more radical than the Stranger's insofar as he insists "that the property of the citizens should be equal" (*Politics*,

1266a40). Aristotle acknowledges Plato's inequality ratio, though describes it as 5:1, the richest to the poorest (*Politics*, 1266b6–7).

72. It is worth noting here that maintenance of these property laws is the very first duty outlined for the guardians of the laws, perhaps the most important public office in the city of Magnesia.

73. According to Aristotle, Lycurgus's failure to address inheritances was ultimately the cause of great economic inequality in Sparta and led to its undoing (*Politics*, 2.9, 1270a15–23). In this respect, Plato's Stranger here is correcting one of Lycurgus's greatest oversights.

74. It is now generally accepted that one of the greatest factors promoting extensive economic inequality is the "ability to transmit wealth from one generation to the next" (Scheidel 2017, 37).

75. See, for example, Putnam 2015, 41–42.

76. Along these lines, Phaleas of Chalcedon is reputed to have been attentive to marriages and the practice of dowries specifically to avoid the problem of economic inequality "by the rich giving but not receiving dowries, and the poor receiving but not giving them" (Aristotle, *Politics*, 1266b3–5).

77. Plato's discussion of marriage in the *Laws* is surprising for those who only know his *Republic*. In the *Republic*, Plato arranges marriages very carefully through "mating lotteries" with the purpose of matching elite citizens with each other (459c–460a). The concern in the *Laws* is not so much to create elite citizens who might one day be fit to serve as philosopher rulers but rather to avoid the concentration of wealth and the vices that engenders.

78. As Glenn Morrow observes, this currency policy was common in the ancient Greek world. The one exception was Plato's home of Athens. As such, Morrow argues, Plato is singling out Athens as unusually corrupt in facilitating this mode of wealth accumulation. See Morrow (1960) 1993, 140.

79. The Athenian Stranger's fairly extensive regulation of the marketplace here differs considerably with Socrates's approach in the *Republic*, who employs a light hand with regard to economic regulations (425cd). This is because he is dubious about whether laws can be efficacious in the absence of virtue. Namely, without a virtuous citizenry, we can expect that citizens will simply find ways around laws and regulations to pursue their individual selfish or *pleonectic* agendas, just as corporations today sometimes pay extravagant sums to lawyers who can help them avoid sanctions against, for example, environmental protection legislation. Socrates's solution in the *Republic* is to emphasize virtue, where citizens are trained to think more instinctively about what serves the good of the community. The approach Plato's Stranger takes in the *Laws*, by contrast, suggests that even though virtue can and must be taught, it is naïve to assume that education alone can solve the problem. Some will ignore the lessons they have been taught, and others ought not to be left prey to their appetites.

80. See Zuckert 2009, 94.

81. Seung 1996, 233.

82. Indeed, as already mentioned, a wealthy Spartan gouged out one of Lycurgus's eyes in response to his radical economic reforms.

83. Calls for higher taxes on the wealthy by the wealthy themselves seem to be growing in recent times. Consider, for example, Eli Broad's appeal for a wealth tax on the wealthiest Americans, which, he argues, will "start to address the economic inequality

eroding the soul of our country's strength" (Broad 2019). See also P. Cohen 2019. Mill seems to have something like this in mind when he speaks of reducing inequality through the "better feelings of the powerful" (Mill [1879] 1989, 227).

84. Aristotle acknowledges this difficulty in imposing equality on those accustomed to inequality in *Politics*, 5.3, and James Harrington cites Aristotle to make precisely this point in his *Commonwealth of Oceana*, 14. Finally, John P. McCormick notes a similar principle operating in Machiavelli's response to the Roman agrarian laws: "One cannot expect to take property away from those who have managed and benefited from it for an extended period of time without provoking them into uncivil behavior" (McCormick 2018, 57; see Machiavelli, *Discourses*, 1.37).

85. Montesquieu, *Spirit of the Laws*, 7.2.

86. This principle of expanding inequality over time is implied by Plato's recounting of the transition from oligarchy to democracy in book 8 of the *Republic* (555c). It is also the thesis of Thomas Piketty's *Capital in the 21st Century*.

87. Plato, *Statesman*, 284b–e.

88. DeCelles and Norton 2016.

89. In this spirit, see Andrew 1989.

90. Williams 2013.

91. Although there were some working in industry as well. Kitto 1951, 131–32.

92. Morrow 1939, 123.

93. Morrow (1960) 1993, 149.

94. The same reading also applies to Thomas More's *Utopia*, like Plato's *Laws*, an egalitarian regime among citizens that nevertheless presumes slavery.

95. Kitto 1951, 134.

96. Diogenes Laertius, *Lives*, 299.

97. Plutarch 2001, 1:661.

98. See Ober 2015, 80 and Winters 2011, 84. I note here that even where a society is relatively equal in comparison to its peers does not mean that its inequality is unproblematic. South Korea, for example, compares favorably to other developed nations according to the Gini coefficient, yet recent cinema (e.g., *Parasite*) and television (e.g., *Squid Game*) suggests that inequality is on the minds of many citizens and a defining part of what it means to be a Korean today.

99. Aristotle, *Politics*, 2.9, 1270a. See Gottlieb 2018.

Chapter Two

1. Pope Francis Twitter account, September 14, 2014, https://twitter.com/Pontifex /status/460697074585980928. See also Bergoglio 2013, 104. The passage from 1 Timothy reads, "For the love of money is a root of all kinds of evil, and in their eagerness to be rich some have wandered away from the faith and pierced themselves with many pains." The pope also echoes Rousseau, who similarly posited, "The first source of evil is inequality" (*Observations*, 45).

2. Bergoglio 2013, 28, 29.

3. The Latin title, *Laudato Si'*, is commonly cited in theological circles. The cited edition was published as *Encyclical on Climate Change and Inequality*.

4. Bergoglio 2015, 29–30.

5. Bergoglio 2013, 103–4.

6. Ratzinger 2009, 72, 77. It is worth mentioning here that there is a strong tradition among twentieth-century Catholic writings, such as the *Quadragesimo Anno* and *Laborem Exercens*, that has been amplified by writers such as G. K. Chesterton and Hilaire Belloc.

7. Barton (1925) 2000, chap. 6.

8. Quoted in B. Friedman 2021, 300, 298 (emphasis original), 296, 295.

9. Van Biema and Chu 2006.

10. It should be said that I am reading these texts *as texts* in historical context as a historian of political thought rather than as representing the word of God. The latter would be theology. This is instead an attempt to contextualize and clarify the thought of the figures as they occur in a particularly central and formative text in the Western tradition. Among other things, this means I do not attempt here to synthesize the entire Bible as one coherent text, as is common among theologians. I rather work, insofar as it is possible, to treat each relevant *character* of the Bible as having his own relatively coherent themes.

11. Much of this description over the next few paragraphs is drawn from chapters 3–4 of Aslan 2013.

12. See Beaudoin 2007, 17; Hamel 2010, 309; and Horsley (1985) 1999, 61.

13. See Hamel 2010, 311. Of course, there is ample testimony of a regional viticulture in the Gospels (e.g., Matthew 20:1–16; 21:28, 33–46).

14. See Horsely (1985) 1999, 56.

15. Goodman 1987, 57–58. See also Horsley (1985) 1999, 58–61.

16. Exemptions from this law were secured from rabbis at the time issuing a *prosbul*, which authorized creditors to loan with interest, even with the right to demand payment during Sabbatical years (Yoder [1972] 1994, 64–65). I will say more on Sabbatical and Jubilee years shortly.

17. Such practices help contextualize the parable of the tenants in Mark 12:1–9 in which clearly disgruntled tenants end up killing a series of slaves sent to collect rent on behalf of an absent and wealthy landowner.

18. As Thomas Carney has observed, this practice was considered normal, even if irksome: "Wealth was just as avariciously sought as in any capitalist society, but on a 'seize or squeeze' principle, not by generating it through increased production. Capital was formed in antiquity by taking it from someone else, either as booty in war or as taxes squeezed out of a toiling peasant population" (Carney 1975, 93). See also Piketty 2020, 220.

19. Crossan 1991, 222.

20. Hamel 2010, 317–18.

21. Josephus, *Antiquities*, 18.2. It is worth noting here that Sepphoris needed to be rebuilt after a tax revolt in 6 CE. The Jews of Sepphoris had rejected direct rule by Rome and its imposition of taxes, which Jewish residents viewed as Caesar's claim to divine status. To teach the poor revolutionaries a lesson, the Romans responded by burning the city to the ground, enslaving thousands, and crucifying still thousands more. This provided Antipas—a Jew appointed by the Romans—the opportunity to rebuild the city. All this would have been fresh in the minds of Jesus's early followers.

22. See Aslan 2013, 21–24.

23. Horsley (1985) 1999, 56, 60.

24. In periods of Gentile rule, it was common for kings to appoint and dismiss high priests.

25. Goodman 1987, 34–36, 44.

26. See Horsley 1986, 27, 30. As N. T. Wright has commented, "The guardians of the Temple were notorious for their rich and oppressive lifestyle" (N. T. Wright 2001b, 152).

27. Goodman (1997) 2013, 280.

28. Paul 1991, 2.

29. All biblical citations are to Harold W. Attridge, ed., *Harper Collins Study Bible* (New York: Harper Collins, 2006).

30. See also Amos 6.11.

31. This passage continues to make exceptions for strangers or foreigners.

32. See also Exodus 21:2–6. This provision obviously neither freed non-Jewish slaves nor treated freed women to the same benefits bestowed on freed men.

33. Aristotle references a practice of the ancient world that resembles this where "no one should possess more than a certain quantity of land. . . . Formerly in many states there was a law forbidding anyone to sell his original allotment of land" (*Politics*, 6.4, 1319a7–11). Beyond Aristotle, Babylonian and Assyrian cultures were known to practice something like Sabbatical and Jubilee laws. It was not uncommon when new kings ascended to the throne for them to call for the remittance of debts, the manumission of slaves, and to return property to its original owners. What distinguishes Jewish law from other cultures in this regard is mandating these measures on a fixed schedule. See Barton and Muddiman 2001, 106–7. See also Hudson 2018, 173–74.

34. For the original, equitable, distribution, see Numbers 26:52–54.

35. As N. T. Wright notes, "Money is not a possession, it's a trust" (2001a, 196). To be sure, one can find secular echoes of this doctrine in early modernity, where all property ultimately belongs to the sovereign and the people are but temporary stewards. See Hobbes, *Leviathan*, 24.4–5 and Rousseau, *Social Contract*, 1.9.

36. For example, Solomon 1997, 151; Bruno 2010, 88.

37. This is a brief excerpt of the extensive passage concerning divine retribution that continues through Leviticus 26:33. It is worth adding that although these punishments are for violating any of God's laws, God is reported by Moses to specify violation of Sabbatical laws at Leviticus 26:34. Further, the entire section of divine sanctions is sandwiched between two discussions of Jubilee years (Leviticus 25; 27:17–25). So it is safe to assume that these punishments apply to those bold enough to violate the Mosaic Jubilee mandate to return property to the initial equitable distribution.

38. Josephus notes, for example, that during the reign of Julius Gaius Caesar, the Romans honored the Sabbatical laws with regard to the Jews by exempting them from taxes one out of every seven years (*Antiquities*, 14.202–3).

39. Notably, Deuteronomy anticipates the concerns the wealthy subsequently outline to Hillel: "If there is among you anyone in need, a member of your community in any of your towns within the land that the Lord your God is giving you, do not be hard-hearted or tight-fisted toward your needy neighbor. You should rather open your hand, willingly lending enough to meet the need, whatever it be. *Be careful that you do not entertain a mean thought thinking, 'The seventh year, the year of remission, is*

near,' and therefore view your needy neighbor with hostility and give nothing; your neighbor might cry to the Lord against you, and you would incur guilt" (Deuteronomy 15:7-9; emphasis added).

40. See Horsley (1985) 1999, 59. Further, as Scott Korb has remarked, what made the Jubilee laws "less important to a wealthy landowner than dietary law against eating pork is anybody's guess" (Korb 2010, 91).

41. Bergsma 2007, chap. 7. It is important to note that this tradition found in the Pentateuch and Amos does not suggest that the Hebrew Bible is uniform on matters of wealth, poverty, and inequality. The most obvious exception to the skeptical view of wealth can be found repeatedly in Proverbs, which according to Richard Coggins, "represents a distinctly prosperous and upper-class viewpoint" (Coggins 1987, 11). Although the book repeatedly acknowledges that true wealth is wisdom (e.g., Proverbs, 2:1-5; 3:13-16; 8:10, 18-21), it does not demonize material wealth, much less does it have God target the wealthy for vengeful destruction. Specifically, it speaks of God providing material rewards for pious deeds (11:24-25), whereas the impious are met with poverty (13:18). And it even speaks of the poor being disliked by their neighbors, while the wealthy acquire many friends (14:20).

42. The other two were the Sadducees and the Pharisees.

43. *Jewish War*, 2.7.125.

44. *Antiquities*, 18.19-20. The Essenes' radically egalitarian economic doctrines parallel some of the economic principles and policies employed by Plato's Athenian Stranger in the *Laws*. Betz notes these but thinks they represent parallels more than influence, suggesting that the principles of the Essenes are derived from the more culturally specific texts and traditions of the Jewish world. See Betz 1999, 467.

45. Betz 1999, 458. With regard to the Dead Sea, the Dead Sea scrolls are thought to be the works of Essenes from this period. They address wealth and economic matters in some detail. As Catherine M. Murphy has observed in her comprehensive study of these materials, "concern for inequities of income and distribution and the arrogance presumed to motivate them are prominent" (Murphy 2002, 447).

46. See Brownlee 1955, 73 and Aslan 2013, 84-85. At least one commentator has gone so far as to suggest in an extended argument that Jesus himself was an Essene (Nesbit 1895). Further, Ratzinger also speculates that it appears that "not only John the Baptist, but possibly Jesus and his family as well, were close to the Qumran community" (Ratzinger 2008, 14). The Qumrans were the particularly strident Essenes responsible for writing the Dead Sea scrolls.

47. Matthews 2015, 61.

48. Josephus, *Antiquities*, 20.180. Also see Horsley (1985) 1999, 2.

49. Horsley (1985) 1999, 3, 27.

50. See Hobsbawm (1969) 1981, 19-20. I am here following Horsley (1985) 1999, 48-51.

51. *Jewish War*, 1.1204.

52. Aslan 2013, 18.

53. Horsley (1985) 1999, 72.

54. *Antiquities*, 20.124.

55. S. Cohen 1988, 222; 1979, 189n9.

56. *Jewish War*, 2.425.

57. *Jewish War*, 2.269.

58. *Jewish War*, 2.430.

59. *Jewish War*, 6.258.

60. There is a striking exception to this pattern: the Gospel of John hardly addresses these issues at all.

61. Augustine, *City of God*, 10.3.

62. Augustine, Homily 10 on the First Epistle of John, quoting John 13:34; emphasis original.

63. Here is a notable difference between Matthew and Mark, on the one hand, and Luke, on the other. For the former, when the rich man presses Jesus here, Jesus prefaces his follow-up with "If you wish to be perfect," which has subsequently been taken by many to be a "counsel of perfection," applicable to monks, nuns, and the like. But in Luke, there is no such preface, suggesting that this advice to surrender all property is not a mere counsel of perfection but rather a necessary condition for all who wish to attain eternal life. Further, as Barton and Muddiman (2001, 870) have observed, the "counsel of perfection" reading is strained in light of Matthew 19:23–26.

64. For example, see Attridge 1989, 1701; Wright 2001c, 53; Barton and Muddiman 2001, 870; Crossan 1991, 275.

65. In some commentaries the rich man is identified as "Dives," which is simply Latin for "rich."

66. William Clare Roberts has noted Karl Marx's own interest in this tale and how its lessons are echoed in his account of capital. See Marx, *Capital*, 798 (though Marx's German term *Lazarusschichte* [Lazarus layer] is rendered in the English translation as "pauperized"); Roberts 2017, 184–86. Marx also suggestively references a theory among some capitalists that in a growing market economy, "the richer will be the crumbs that fall" to the poor (*WLC*, 220), evoking Lazarus and Dives for the industrial age.

67. See chapter 1 of this book for a detailed account.

68. At the same time Zaccheus does this, he also promises to Jesus that he will correct the sins of his ill-gotten gains by refunding those he had defrauded four times over (Luke 19:8).

69. Jesus repeats the dictum "You cannot serve God and wealth" in a different context in Luke 16:13.

70. This is, to be sure, why Jesus insists that his apostles have no money (Matthew 9:8–9; Mark 6:8; Luke 9:3).

71. Drawing on John Wesley, the German sociologist Max Weber points to this separation of wealth and the actual teachings of the Gospels. As the West grew wealthier, "the search for the Kingdom of God commenced gradually to pass over into sober economic virtue; the religious roots died out slowly, giving way to utilitarian worldliness." Even more dramatically, he adds that greater wealth effectively perverted the teachings of the Gospels with regard to wealth and inequality. Rather than condemning inequality, the increased wealth of the bourgeoisie in the eighteenth and nineteenth centuries "gave him the comforting assurance that the unequal distribution of the goods of this world was a special dispensation of Divine Providence" (Weber [1904] 2001, 119, 120).

72. See Balot 2001, 28 and Reeve (1988) 2006, 47.

73. See also Ecclesiastes 5:10: "The lover of money will not be satisfied with money; nor the lover of wealth, with gain. This is also vanity."

74. Seung 1962, 262. Rousseau similarly suggests that the presence of luxury "corrupts rich and poor simultaneously, the former by possession and the latter by covetousness" (*SC*, 3.4, 93).

75. *Jewish War*, 2.160. Josephus himself was a Pharisee, which might have prejudiced this assessment (Goodman 1987, 82).

76. Horsley 1995, 151.

77. Goodman 1987, 74.

78. In noting Jesus's case against the Pharisees here, one must acknowledge the abuse of this critique by subsequent Christians for violently anti-Semitic purposes, such as in inquisitions, pogroms, and the Holocaust. Amy Levine has outlined that attacks on the Pharisees often either extend or even accidentally imply "anti-Jewish tropes" (A.-J. Levine 2021, 404). As she notes, discussions of the Pharisees, as depicted in the New Testament, require contextualization and an acknowledgment of how these passages have been employed by anti-Semites. Along these lines, Levine and Brettler observe that "Matthew's Pharisees may represent rival Jewish scribes competing for community loyalty following the Roman war, and thus Matthew's Gospel may provide a look into the tensions existing between Jesus' followers and other Jews in the late first century. . . . Adherents of a particular group or set of beliefs often polemicize most strongly against those who share similar, but not identical, beliefs; this may be responsible for some of the strong anti-Pharisaic rhetoric in Matthew" (Levine and Brettler 2017, 41).

79. Beelzebul was an ancient synonym for the devil employed by those unwilling to utter his name.

80. I do not mean to suggest that there are not other divisions between the Pharisees and the others that might have concerned Jesus.

81. Matthew's Jesus here even references the banditry that plagued the Jewish world in this period by comparing his debate with the Pharisees with "plunder[ing] the property" of others (Matthew 12:29).

82. As New Testament scholar N. T. Wright has summarized, Jesus "had announced the jubilee, the great release from debt, for which God's people had longed" (N. T. Wright 2001d, 34). See also Attridge 1989, 1769; Barton and Muddiman 2001, 481; and Hudson 2018, 224.

83. There is some discrepancy among Christians on the use of "debts" versus "trespasses." The Greek, however, literally employs "debts" (*aphiemi* or ὀφειλήματα). This term is ambiguous enough in Greek to cover many vices, including financial debts. See Yoder (1972) 1994, 62. Lyndon Drake (2014) has argued that Jesus was specifically demanding the elimination of financial debts in the Lord's Prayer.

84. Hudson 2018, 225.

85. Rousseau, *Emile*, 313n.

86. This passage most immediately recalls Leviticus 19:18: Do "not hate in your heart anyone of your kin; you shall reprove your neighbor, or you will incur guilt yourself. You shall not take vengeance or bear a grudge against any of your people, but you shall love your neighbor as yourself."

87. See Barton and Muddiman 2001, 874.

88. See chapter 13, especially 510–11.

89. Derrett 1961, 367.

90. Wright, 2001c, 51.

91. Rousseau, *Emile*, 313n. A century later, American Quakers had expected that the Civil War would culminate with a Jubilee—the freeing of slaves to be combined with redistribution of land from the former slave owners to the former slaves. As Daniel Mandell has noted, members of Congress at this time, including Thaddeus Stevens and Charles Sumner, "considered land confiscation and slave emancipation as two aspects of the same goal" (Mandell 2020, 223). Around the same time, John Stuart Mill was interested in the Jubilee insofar as it returned property "to the common stock to be redistributed" (*Socialism*, 277), a principle reflected in his own suggestion that inheritances be radically scaled back with the bulk of large estates being broadly distributed (*Principles*, 2.2.4, 5.2.3).

92. See Attridge 1989, 2052.

93. For example, Davids 1982.

94. See Josephus, *Antiquities*, 20.9.1.

95. Aslan 2013, 212.

96. Cited in Barton and Muddiman 2001, 1257.

97. I elaborate substantially on the role of the general will in Rousseau's approach to the problem of inequality in chapter 4. See Rousseau, *Social Contract*, 4.1, 122.

98. For example, see Meister and Stump 2010, 56. I note that others still have contested that there are significant differences between the two.

99. I draw here significantly from Harrill 2012, 23–31.

100. See Harrill 2012, 25.

101. Paul likely brought uncircumcised Gentiles with him into the sacred Jewish Temple, which would have been received as an act of provocation. This led to a riot. Scholars generally agree that this precipitated his execution. See Harrill 2012, 70–74.

102. Paul here is citing Exodus 16.18, where Moses is frustrated by the fact that some of his tribe have accumulated much bread and others none, where those with ample supplies were reluctant to share with the deprived.

103. Barton and Muddiman 2001, 1143.

104. This can be contrasted with Jesus praising the "widow's offering"—an impoverished woman who gives away the little money she had—which extended far beyond giving "according to your means."

105. Judge 1960, 60.

106. Bart D. Ehrman (2018, 133), for example, has argued that most of Paul's converts "would have been lower-class and uneducated." Although this remains possible, Ehrman's interpretation does not exclude the presence of wealthy and educated congregants, which would be enough to support my interpretation here that Paul was careful not to offend that portion of his congregations.

107. For example, Harrill 2012, 62 and Theissen 1979, 69.

108. Theissen 1979, 95.

109. Paul's condemnation of greed but not wealth is common in contemporary Western culture. As I write this note, an entry into the 2020 contest for the Democratic presidential nomination, Deval Patrick, has argued against Elizabeth Warren's and Bernie Sanders's wealth tax thus: "My idea would be a much, much simpler tax system for everyone," he said. "I don't think that wealth is the problem. I think greed is the problem." Like Paul, he does not elaborate on the reasons greed can be effectively separated from wealth. See Viser and Weigel 2019.

110. It is worth mentioning here that Seneca's brother, Novatus Gallio, was a Roman magistrate who personally dismissed charges against Paul (Acts 18:12–17). So it is certain that Paul would have known of Seneca.

111. See E. Wilson 2014, 127–41.

112. *On the Happy Life*, 20.3.

113. *On the Happy Life*, 21.4.

114. See Riley 1986, 4–5.

115. See Plato, *Republic*, 462c–e.

116. Basil 2009, 43.

117. Basil 2009, 50.

118. Basil 2009, 51.

119. Basil 2009, 53.

120. Basil 2009, 79.

121. Basil 2009, 66.

122. See Schroeder 2009, 33–38.

123. Brown 2012, 315.

124. Rees 2004, 194.

125. Although an argument can be made that Marx's influence mirrors that of religious figures.

126. Strauss 1967. Steven B. Smith has argued that the contest for authority between Jerusalem and Athens constitutes "the core of Strauss's thought" (S. Smith 2007, 26).

127. Habermas 2010, 18–19; see also Habermas 2007, 42.

128. Ratzinger 2007, 77.

129. Habermas 2007, 51.

Chapter Three

1. All references to Hobbes's works, save *Behemoth*, are to chapter and paragraph numbers.

2. Recent exceptions include Labiano 2000, Josephson 2016, Apeldoorn 2018, and Blau 2019.

3. Macpherson 1945, 528.

4. Macpherson 1987, 663.

5. Levin 1982.

6. Kavka 1986, 210.

7. Kavka 1986, 214.

8. Macpherson 1945, 528.

9. Istvan Hont (2005, 17–20) and Richard Tuck (2002, 81–83) come the closest to understanding Hobbes along the lines discussed in this essay, but neither substantially elaborates on Hobbes's economic egalitarianism. Christopher Brooke (2020, 1408–9) suggests that Hobbes sets the stage for Rousseau's "non-intrinsic egalitarianism" but does not spell out Hobbes's economic views.

10. Along these lines, one might recall Richard Whatmore's critique of Quentin Skinner for ignoring contexts of political economy (Whatmore 2006, 121–26).

11. Tocqueville (1835/40) 1988, 11.

12. For insights on Hobbes and anxiety, see Botting 2017.

13. For example, see C. Hill (1961) 1980, 20; (1967) 1969, 65, 87. It should be noted, however, that this inflation was largely limited to essentials, such as food and lodging. Curiously, inflationary trends did not apply to luxuries items and other goods typically purchased by the well-to-do. See Hoffman et al. 2002, 323, 330–34.

14. Wrightson 2000, 118.

15. Such notions were not unique to the English of the sixteenth and seventeenth centuries and typically inform accusations of "price gouging," such as Plato's Athenian Stranger sought to prohibit in Magnesia (see *Laws*, 921c).

16. Wrightson 2000, 121.

17. Mandeville, *Fable*, 301.

18. Hill (1967) 1969, 85.

19. P. Bowden, quoted in Wrightson 2000, 184.

20. C. Hill (1961) 1980, 18.

21. C. Hill (1961) 1980, 19.

22. C. Hill (1967) 1969, 57–58.

23. Wrightson 2000, 194.

24. Martinich 1999, 357. Deborah Baumgold (1988, 124) emphasizes that "Hobbes identifies with, and appeals to, ordinary subjects." See also Kapust and Turner (2013, 668) along these lines.

25. Martinich 1999, 72.

26. Andy Wood (2002, 82) has commented, "Probably the most common cause of riots during the sixteenth and early seventeenth centuries was the enclosure of common land." Though, to be sure, there were uprisings predating even this. Francis Bacon treated these in his *History of the Reign of King Henry VII*, and Hobbes was intimately familiar with this work.

27. For more on Kett's Rebellion, see Dauber 2016.

28. Hill (1961) 1980, 21.

29. Cornwall 1977, 23.

30. See Alford 2017 and Schmitt (1942) 2015.

31. Ryrie 2017, 110.

32. Hill (1967) 1969, 85.

33. Hill (1961) 1980, 15–16.

34. Wrightson 2000, 193.

35. Hill (1961) 1980, 31.

36. Aquinas, q. 78, art. 1. See Thomas 1965, 225.

37. Bacon (1597–1625) 2002, 411.

38. Wrightson 2000, 205–9; Grassby 1970, 98.

39. Hill (1967) 1969, 45; (1961) 1980, 16–17.

40. Grassby 1970, 91.

41. Hill (1967) 1969, 87.

42. Broadberry et al. 2015, 308.

43. Wrightson 2000, 200.

44. Hill (1961) 1980, 36–37.

45. Hill (1961) 1980, 21–27.

46. Hill (1967) 1969, 106.

47. Stone 1958, 52.

48. Hill (1961) 1980, 46.

49. It is worth noting here that scholars have already rightfully drawn attention to the religious dimensions of this conflict, which also significantly occupied Hobbes's mind in developing his political theory (e.g., Collins 2005). Yet even these religious dimensions of the tensions leading to the English Civil War had an economic context.

50. This doctrine in Hobbes has been explored and developed by Gregory Kavka (1986, chap. 2). But see also Wootton 2018, chap. 4.

51. Hobbes is apparently referencing the Eighty Years War, or the Dutch War of Independence.

52. Holmes 1990, xxn25.

53. To be sure, Hobbes himself located other indignities that were more inescapable: "Want is less a disgrace than stupidity; for the former can be attributed to the inequity of fortune; the latter is attributable to nature alone" (Man, 11.8).

54. This passage alone is enough to refute Levin's claim that "it is no part of the Hobbesian bargain to gain security against hunger, cold, ignorance, or poverty" (Levin 1982, 341).

55. Thucydides (1629) 1989, 3.45.

56. Hobbes may have been influenced in this regard by his one-time employer, Francis Bacon, who wrote, "The matter of seditions is of two kinds: much poverty and much discontentment. . . . And if this poverty and broken estate in the better sort be joined with a want and necessity in the mean people, the danger is imminent and great. For the rebellions of the belly are the worst" (Bacon [1597–1625] 2002, 367). I was alerted to this and other relevant passages from Bacon cited here by Samuel Zeitlin.

57. Thomas Aquinas, q. 66, art. 7 (p. 140).

58. What he will not tolerate, however, is its opposite—the rich stealing from the poor: "To rob a poor man is a greater crime than to rob a rich man, because it is to the poor a more sensible damage" (Leviathan, 28.51).

59. See, for example, Leviathan, 3.12, 5.15, 8.27, 12.31, 46.13–32. Exceptions to this rule are noted in more detail in Leijenhorst 2001. For Hobbes's relationship to Scholasticism more generally, see Brett 1997 and 2011.

60. It should be said somewhere that not all of Hobbes's remarks about the poor are entirely sympathetic. Like many in his day (and other epochs), he assumed that at least some poverty was attributable to bad habits. For example, "although everyone knows that wealth is got by industry and kept by thrift, the poor always shift the blame from their own idleness and extravagance onto the government of the commonwealth, as if their private property was exhausted by public exactions" (Citizen, 12.9). This being noted, he neither denies the fact of their poverty nor the dangerous passions that accompany it. These are concrete facts that a successful and enduring commonwealth must acknowledge and address.

61. There have been some questions raised about Hobbes's authorship of this work, but I am persuaded by Timothy Raylor that it is authentically Hobbes. See Raylor 2019, 281–92.

62. Aristotle 2018, 2.16, 1390b31–1391a15.

63. To be sure, Aristotle's account of the wealthy bears some resemblance to that sketched by his teacher, Plato, especially in his Laws.

64. This has previously been noted in Strauss (1936) 1996, 40–41.

65. See Thomas 1965, 199–200.

66. Hobbes, *Tacitus*, 49. Thanks to Graeme Garrard for drawing my attention to this passage.

67. Wootton (2018, 101) addresses Hobbes's conception of greed in his *Power, Pleasure, and Profit*.

68. Balot 2001, chap. 5.

69. Thucydides (1629) 1989, 3.82.

70. Thucydides (1629) 1989, 3.45.

71. The fact that Hobbes twice uses the word *"pleonexia,"* once in Greek (*Elements*) and once in its Romanized spelling (*Leviathan*) lends to the suggestion that Hobbes is deeply informed by one or both of the accounts of Thucydides and the Greek New Testament. He also would have encountered this word in reading Plato and Aristotle.

72. Caesar 1578, 4.

73. Harrington (1656) 1992, 111. See 1 Timothy 6:10.

74. See Thomas 1965, 216–18.

75. Adrian Blau (2009) has added, along these lines, that for Hobbes, greed is a source of corruption that threatens the commonwealth.

76. Boyd 2004, 56–57.

77. Hobbes's critique of the pursuit of private over public or common ends is also a religious critique, as he argues in his section "On Religion," "That which taketh away the reputation of love is the being detected of private ends, as when the belief they require of others conduceth or seemeth to conduce to the acquiring of dominion, riches, dignity, or secure pleasure to themselves only or specially. For that which men reap benefit by to themselves they are thought to do for their own sake, and not for love of others" (*Leviathan*, 12.27). For Hobbes, the pursuit of private ends undermines the Christian duty of love or mutual charity, summed up in the commandment, "Thou shalt love thy neighbor as thyself" (*Leviathan*, 30.13). He emphasizes that it is one of the sovereign's most important responsibilities that this maxim be taught to all subjects.

78. Madison (1787–89) 2003, 42.

79. See chapter 1 for discussions of Plato on factions. Aristotle would similarly observe in his *Politics*, "That the middle constitution [with neither rich nor poor] is best is evident, since it alone is free from faction" (1296a).

80. See Thomas 1965, 220.

81. In *Leviathan*, he defines it as "Grief for the success of a competitor in wealth, honour, or other good . . . joined with endeavor to supplant or hinder a competitor" (*Leviathan*, 6.48). Also worth noting is a passage from Thucydides's *History of the Peloponnesian War*: "Without the destructive force of envy . . . people would not value revenge over piety, or profits over justice" (3.84).

82. Pinker 2018, 98–99; but see also Frankfurt 2015, 10–11 and McCloskey 2016, 46, 50.

83. Tuck (2002, 83) mentions the ship money taxes in a similar context.

84. Again here, Hobbes may well be informed by Bacon's similar observation: "Above all things, good policy is to be used that the treasure and monies in a state be not gathered into few hands. For otherwise a state may have a great stock, and yet starve. And money is like muck, not good except that it be spread. This is done chiefly by suppressing, or at least keeping a straight hand upon the devouring trades of usury,

ingrossing, great pasturages, and the like." Bacon later attributes the concentration of wealth to the growing prevalence of usury. For Bacon, "a state flourisheth when wealth is more equally spread" (Bacon [1597–1625] 2002, 369).

85. Richard Tuck (2002, 81–83) has also argued along these lines regarding chapter 24 of *Leviathan*.

86. This practice of redistributing land also has an English precedent in William's seizure of all land upon his invasion of England in 1066 on the presumption of sovereign authority upon conquering. See A. Levy 1954, 594. Hobbes expressly cites this precedent at *Leviathan*, 24.6.

87. In fact, the parallels might begin at least one step earlier than this insofar as Hobbes speaks of "that *mortal god* to which we owe, under the *immortal God*, our peace and defence" (*Leviathan*, 17.13). It is worth adding here that the notion of all property belonging to either a god or the sovereign is subsequently adopted by Rousseau for similar purposes in his *Social Contract*, 1.9.

88. See, for example, Holmes 1990, 13n16.

89. Larry May (1987, 241) has argued that "equity . . . is the dominant moral category in Hobbes's political and legal philosophy." Tom Sorell (2016) also acknowledges that equity is an important moral category for Hobbes but finds that it is subordinate to justice.

90. In his *Elements*, by contrast, Hobbes defines the opposite of equity to be *pleonexia* or greed, "which is commonly rendered as covetousness, but seemeth to be more precisely expressed by the word ENCROACHING" (*Elements*, 17.2). In this case, as with partiality, the effect is the same since for Hobbes greed is a primary source of war and sedition (*Leviathan*, 11.4). Partiality also, as Blau (2009) notes, undermines the rule of law.

91. Hobbes also strongly implies that the absence of equity in a commonwealth fuels the "hope for impunity" that one finds among "the rich and mighty" (*Leviathan*, 30.15).

92. One might argue that the forced redistribution of property would create new problems that would undermine peace—namely, that those losing their property would develop resentments that undermine the public peace.

93. Hoekstra (2012) is particularly insightful on Hobbes, egalitarianism, and pride, yet does not connect these concepts to wealth distribution.

94. As Steven B. Smith (2012, 152) has summarized Hobbes on this point, "His critique of pride is not religious—'pride goeth before the fall'—but political. Pride is dangerous because it causes conflict and war."

95. The fact that Hobbes insists on equal tax liabilities may not seem progressive, but bear in mind the context in which the poor were carrying a substantial tax burden in this time when wealthy merchants were routinely refusing to pay their ship money taxes. In context, the argument for equal liability would have likely offended many of Hobbes's readers in the merchant class. The equal liability to taxes, for Hobbes, amounts to a rejection of the doctrine ultimately embraced by Leona Helmsley, the New York real estate heiress, who is reported to have uttered, "We [the rich] don't pay taxes. The little people pay taxes" (Goldman 1992).

96. For an insightful accounting of Hobbes's biblical source here, see Baumgold 1988, 122–23. See also Cooke 1996, 43; R. Harrison 2003, 44–45; and Stauffer 2018, 205–6.

97. Brooke 2012, 74; 2017, xxvii.

98. Indeed, as previously cited, this view expressly echoes his summary of Aristotle's *Rhetoric* with similar language: "Rich men are contumelious, and proud; this they have from their riches" (*Rhetoric*, 2.18).

99. As Teresa Bejan (2010, 609) has observed about Hobbes, "popular education was of paramount political importance."

100. As Devin Stauffer has observed, "this is one of the chief purposes of Hobbes's state of nature teaching: to sober men up, and in particular to convince those who are capable of a sensible sobriety of the necessity of uniting in a rational commonwealth that can protect them against those who remain *intoxicated by pride*" (2018, 206; emphasis added).

101. Locke (1690) 1988, §13.

102. I should add here that this is at least one clear advantage to Plato's system in which philosopher rulers are denied the right to any private wealth.

Chapter Four

1. Cranston 1984, 121.

2. Weirich's argument is particularly confusing on at least three levels. First, he does not spell out Aristotle's principle of justice as resulting in significant economic inequality. Second, it is even more vexing because Aristotle himself is often highly critical of economic inequality, such as in his *Politics*, where he counsels "to try to mix the multitude of the poor with that of the rich or to increase the middle class, since this dissolves the faction caused by inequality" (*Politics*, 5.8, 1308b29–30). Third, it is even more confusing because he attributes to Rousseau a commitment to meritocracy that Rousseau himself dedicated much of his career to rebuking, such as in his first two *Discourses*. As Michael Locke McLendon (2018, 104) has argued, just because Rousseau acknowledges distinctions in natural talents does not suggest in any way that those of greater talents should receive greater material rewards in a just society. Fourth, although Weirich acknowledges that Rousseau allows for "some restrictions" of economic inequality, he does not attempt to explain in any detail why Rousseau should desire that inequality should be so restricted—or to what extent. See Weirich 1992, 193–194.

3. McCormick 2007, 116; emphasis added. But see also McCormick 2016 and 2018.

4. Vaughan 2008, 79–80.

5. Scholz 2012, 16–19.

6. Neuhouser 2013, 2014.

7. An excellent, extended treatment of the role of *amour-propre* in Rousseau's political philosophy can be found in Neuhouser's earlier book *Rousseau's Theodicy of Self-Love* (2008). See also O'Hagan 1999, 112–23; Cooper 1999, 115–82; and McLendon 2018.

8. Starobinski (1971) 1988, 282.

9. Rosenblatt 1997, 19–20.

10. Micheli du Crest, cited in Rosenblatt 1997, 64; emphasis original. Such evidence contradicts Cranston's (1984, 121) assertion that Geneva's elite "were not conspicuously rich."

11. Rosenblatt 1997, 21.

12. Helpful studies on this history include Mason 1993, Rosenblatt 1997, and J. Miller 1984.

13. It should be noted here that by virtue of citizenship qualifications pertaining to sex, moral fitness, and financial solvency, only about 1,500 of the 25,000 Genevan inhabitants qualified for citizenship. It should also be noted that Genevan citizenship in the eighteenth century was for sale—immigrants could purchase it at a price (Rosenblatt 1997, 17).

14. Rosenblatt 1997, 25.

15. Quoted in Rosenblatt 1997, 23.

16. Rosenblatt 1997, 26.

17. For more on how Rousseau's experiences in St. Gervais contributed to his subsequent political ideas, consult Rosenblatt 1997, 29–34 and McLendon 2009, 509.

18. By contrast, his wealthy cousin (his uncle's son) was tracked for a career as a military engineer.

19. Cited in Starobinski (1971) 1988, 284.

20. Shklar 1998, 277.

21. Mandeville, *Fable*, 8, 4.

22. Mandeville, *Fable*, 169.

23. Mandeville, *Fable*, 194.

24. Mandeville, *Fable*, 124.

25. Hume, *Political Essays*, 150–53; Montesquieu, *Spirit of the Laws*, 338.

26. See Warner 2015, 47.

27. John Rawls cites Rousseau's observation when addressing the effects of inequality in *Justice as Fairness*: "Significant political and economic inequalities" are associated with "a will to dominate and arrogance on the part of the rich." He continues, "These effects of social and economic inequalities can be serious evils and the attitudes they engender great vices" (Rawls 2001, 131).

28. In this passage, Rousseau is quoting the fictional young man who has written him.

29. As Rousseau writes in his *Second Discourse*, socialized man has the following trajectory: "First necessities have to be provided for, and then superfluities; next come delicacies, and then immense wealth, and then subjects and then Slaves; he has not a moment's respite. . . . My hero will end up by cutting every throat until he is sole master of the Universe. Such, in brief, is the moral picture if not of human life, at least of the secret aspirations of every Civilized man's heart" (*SD*, 199).

30. Rousseau develops these observations in his *Emile*, where he speculates on the moral psychology of the wealthy. "If I were rich, I would have done everything necessary to become so. I would therefore be insolent and low, sensitive and delicate toward myself alone, pitiless and hard toward everyone else, a disdainful spectator of the miseries of the rabble—for I would no longer give any other name to the indigent, in order to make people forget that I once belonged to their class. Finally, I would make my fortune the instrument of my pleasures, with which I would be wholly occupied" (*Emile*, 345). See Rasmussen 2015 for an extended discussion of this passage. Elsewhere in *Emile*, he observes, for the "powerful and rich," religious faith constitutes "the only brake on their passions" (312).

31. As Joseph Reisert (2003, 85) has noted in his fine treatment of Rousseau and friendship, the inequality of fortunes "will always be a potential sore spot in the relationship" between rich and poor.

32. See, for example, Fleischacker 2004a, 55–61.

33. See his *Corsica*, 124.

34. This passage is important enough to Rousseau that he would quote it in full almost twenty years later in his *Dialogues* (203–4).

35. Rousseau's analysis of the effects of poverty on moral decision making persists to this day. Joshua Hunt describes his youth defined by poverty in which habitual lying became second nature and for whom deception "doesn't feel dishonest because its falsehoods recognize the deeper truth that many of society's institutions are hostile to the poor. Lying to the landlord keeps a roof over our head. Lying to the social worker keeps our family together" (Hunt 2022).

36. Neuhouser 2014, 26n6.

37. Shklar 1969, 184.

38. See, for example, Riley 1986; A. Levine 1993; Neidleman 2001; and Farr and Williams 2015.

39. As he posits in his *Political Economy*, "one has to be free in order to will" (9).

40. In this claim, I deviate from many other established scholars, including Masters 1968, Melzer 1983, Scott 1994, and Simpson 2006. I defend this interpretation at length in Williams 2007 and 2014.

41. See also 231, 249.

42. For example, *SC*, 2.1, 59; 2.6, 69; 3.15, 117; *PE*, 9; *Mountain*, 232.

43. This conception of the general will has been contested by Jason S. Canon (2022).

44. Shklar 1969, 185. She subsequently elaborates, "The whole aim of the general will is to prevent inequality" (Shklar 1969, 190).

45. See Williams 2024 for a discussion of how Rousseau borrows from Plutarch in developing his conception of economic inequality.

46. See Scheidel 2017, 43.

47. See J. Miller 1984, 105–22.

48. Per Shklar (1969, 191), "The people is sovereign only as long as it can and does prevent institutionalized inequality." To the best of my knowledge, Rousseau is the first major political philosopher to articulate the argument that extreme inequality undermines democratic sovereignty. This argument is now common among critics of economic inequality. Thomas Piketty (2014, 464), for example, comments, "The main reason for the feeling of dispossession that grips the rich countries today is this loss of democratic sovereignty." See also Bartels (2008) 2017, 345; Hacker and Pierson 2010, 110–12; Gilens 2012, 234; Stiglitz 2012, 148–82; and Gilens and Page 2014.

49. This very much anticipates what Winters (2011, 22–25) calls the "wealth-defense industry" insofar as one of the first tasks of oligarchs is to marshal their resources into protecting and advancing their personal fortunes, largely by co-opting the political system.

50. Rousseau allows in this passage that "inequality, carried to a point, can have its advantages" but then immediately follows with, "you will certainly grant that it ought to have limits" (*d'Alembert*, 336). The main advantage it has, as discussed in Rousseau's text here, is the fact that one no longer has to worry as much about corruption

from the theater. It is already corrupted. As is clear from the overall discussion of inequality in these paragraphs from the *Letter*, Rousseau thinks inequality entirely inappropriate for any state aspiring to be a republic or democracy. Inequality is least damaging in large monarchical states.

51. As Daniel Markovits (2019, 60) has written that the elites have become "immodestly sure of their own virtues."

52. Again, Markovits aptly observes, "meritocracy purports to construct a social order that is not simply unequal but *justly* unequal" (D. Markovits 2019, 73; emphasis added).

53. Rousseau's insights here cut against F. A. Hayek's celebration of meritocratic inequality in his *Road to Serfdom*. Hayek argued that inequality is much easier to bear in meritocratic and market-based societies specifically because one's status and wealth is "determined by impersonal forces" rather than the "design" of social institutions. For the Austrian economist, there is "no slight to a person, no offense to his dignity" to fail in market society. The impersonal nature of the market is such that, Hayek reasons, people can slough off their failures (Hayek [1944] 1972, 106). But his analysis minimizes the degree to which (1) the "winners" will be emboldened by their victories to take more than their fair share and (2) the "losers" will become demoralized. For this and many other reasons, Rousseau is the more keen psychologist of inequality.

54. Vaughan 2008, 22.

55. Walker et al. 2013, 224, 230.

56. Wilkinson and Pickett 2018, 150.

57. Sandel 2020, 14. As Wilkinson and Pickett (2018, 162) have summarized the phenomenon as it applies across the classes, "Those at the top often believe they are there because they were naturally endowed with plenty of 'the right stuff,' just as those near the bottom often think that their low status reflects a lack of ability."

58. Rousseau likely absorbed this reform from his careful reading of Plutarch's "Life of Lycurgus" in which the Spartan lawgiver is praised for banishing gold and silver currency, which is the source of "odious distinction or inequality" (Plutarch, *Lives*, 60). In his *Emile*, Rousseau notes that "iron was money in Sparta" (189).

59. As he writes in his *Political Economy*, the "love of fatherland . . . combines the force of amour propre with all the beauty of virtue" (16).

60. Rousseau favorably cites a practice in the Roman Republic of paying taxes in produce (*Corsica*, 147).

61. Rousseau also cites tithes as a possible source of government revenue, which might suggest the presence of currency. It is likely, however, that he conceives of tithes in the form of produce. This was, in fact, the original understanding of tithes as found in Deuteronomy 14:22–23. Rousseau expressly states that taxes should be paid in produce in his *Government of Poland* (237).

62. Rousseau also considered establishing laws restricting inheritances, such as to "bring things back to equality, so that each might have something and no one have anything in excess" (*SF*, 160). Rousseau evidently included this in an earlier draft of *Corsica*, only to remove it from the final version. I speculate that he did so not because he retracted his egalitarianism but rather because his laws against commerce largely eliminated concerns about accumulations of private wealth.

63. In this aim, Rousseau borrows from one of his legislative heroes, Lycurgus, who similarly sought to devalue the social status attached to wealth. As Plutarch

summarizes, the Spartans "had no need at all [of the money-making pursuits] in a state where wealth obtained no honor or respect" (Plutarch 2001, 1:74).

64. For discussion of these issues in some detail, see Williams 2014, 171–204.

65. To be sure, there are many contemporary rebukes to this kind of call to greater patriotism. See Johnston 2007 and Kateb 2008. For a defense of patriotism, see S. Smith 2012, chap. 12.

66. Piketty 2020, 83.

67. See Montesquieu, *Spirit of the Laws*, 13.14.

68. See Tocqueville, *Old Regime*, 86–87. As Tocqueville continues, "Of all the various ways of making men conscious of their differences and of stressing class distinctions unequal taxation is the most pernicious, since it creates a permanent estrangement between those who benefit and those who suffer by it" (88).

69. See Piketty 2020, 76.

70. Tocqueville, *Old Regime*, 258. See also Behrens 1963, 461. As Adam Smith would observe soon after Rousseau, capitation taxes were popular "where the ease, comfort, and security of the inferior ranks of people are little attended to" (*WN*, 869).

71. Mill worries about the income tax for similar reasons, given "the impossibility of ascertaining the real incomes of the contributors," rendering it effectively "in practice unequal in one of the worst ways, falling heavily on the most conscientious" (*Principles*, 831, 832).

72. This willingness to entertain taxing the wealthiest citizens to the level of subsistence is the closest Rousseau gets to describing a progressive tax system (rates increasing according to the wealth of individual taxpayers). Readers might be surprised that his tax structure did not make a more explicit case for progressive income tax rates. There are two factors that might explain this since I do not think his failure to make that case is based on sympathy for an overtaxed elite. First, the immediate problem in eighteenth-century France was that the rich were hardly paying any taxes at all—by a combination of legal exemptions and routine fraud. So Rousseau's insistence that they pay taxes at the same rate as the poor (and hence far more actual money than the poor) would have been received as outrageous by the privileged elites of this time. Second, progressive tax rates were largely unconceived when Rousseau wrote his *Discourse on Political Economy* in 1755. The first proposal for progressive tax rates in France of which I am aware came in 1767 from Louis Graslin (1728–1790), who suggested a progressive scale ranging from 5 percent to 75 percent, depending on income. It was not until the twentieth century that France actually adopted a progressive tax rate. See Piketty 2020, 110–11, 142–43. Rousseau's inclination to adopt a "proportionate" tax system resembles that found in Thomas Hobbes's *Leviathan* (30.17). Finally, Rousseau's tax proposal here would still be far more progressive than that of many US states, such as Washington, in which the poorest 20 percent of citizens pay 17.8 percent of their income in taxes and the wealthiest 1 percent, including Jeff Bezos and Bill Gates, pay around 3 percent (Harris and Appelbaum 2021).

73. Rosenblatt 1997, 202; emphasis original.

74. This echoes *SD*, 184.

75. Rousseau subsequently notes that democratic governments can only exist where there is "little or no luxury; for luxury is either the effect of riches, or makes them necessary; it corrupts rich and poor alike, the one by possession, the other by

covetousness; it sells out the fatherland to laxity, to vanity; it deprives the State of all its Citizens by making them slaves to one another and all of them to opinion" (*SC*, 3.4, 93).

76. Although it must be acknowledged that this has been subjected to serious questioning. See, for example, Saxonhouse 1976.

77. Wollstonecraft (1791) 1995, 110; emphasis original.

78. See, for example, Okin 1979, chaps. 5–8; Pateman 1988, 96–103; and Lange 2002.

79. For a more skeptical reading of Rousseau on this passage, see Klausen 2014, 84.

80. See Muthu 2003, 31–46 for a detailed account of Rousseau's fondness of native cultures.

81. Mills 1997, 5.

82. Gordon 2015, 42. But see also Gordon 2014, chap. 3, especially 108–9.

83. Cited by Riley 1986, 9.

84. Technically, this actually begins with David Hume in his essay "Of Commerce" ([1752] 1994, see especially 98–101). But it is worth adding that he closes this same essay by warning his readers against a "too great disproportion of wealth," which oppresses the poor and discourages industry (102).

Chapter Five

1. See Fleischacker 2004a, 62–68; 2004b, 110–11, 205–8, 223–26; Vaughan 2008, 81–95; Hanley 2009a, 15–52; Rasmussen 2008, 72–73, 96–97, 105–6; 2016; Boucayannis 2013; Schliesser 2017.

2. Again, I am not alone in finding this in Smith's work. See especially Hanley 2009a; Boucayannis 2013; Rasmussen 2016; Schliesser 2017; and Liu 2022.

3. Boucayannis 2013 suggests otherwise.

4. These statistics are found in Hobsbawm 1968, 31. I draw much of this section from the same text as well as C. Hill (1967) 1969.

5. Piketty 2020, 165. See also Hobsbawm 1968, 26, 31 and Hill (1967) 1969, 213.

6. Hill (1967) 1969, 229.

7. Phillips 2021, 27, 29.

8. Hill (1967) 1969, 237.

9. Locke (1697) 1997, 183; see Vaughan 2008, 53.

10. Hill (1967) 1969, 262.

11. Phillipson 2012, 26.

12. Lindert 2000; Hoffman et al. 2002.

13. Soltow 1990, 42. The Gini coefficient measures inequality, whereby a score of 0 represents a society with perfectly equal wealth across all peoples and a score of 1 represents the most extreme inequality. For comparison of the Scottish case, in 2010 Norway scored .268, the United States scored .411, and Zambia scored .575 on the Gini coefficient for overall wealth. See the World Bank, n.d.

14. Piketty 2020, 195.

15. Hobsbawm 1952, 59.

16. It appears earlier, however, in his "Astronomy" (49) and *Theory of Moral Sentiments* (215). All citations hereafter to this text will be abbreviated as *TMS*, followed by

book, chapter, and section numbers where applicable, and finally page number. See also the celebrated passage from *WN*, 26–27: "It is not from the benevolence of the butcher, the brewer, or the baker that we expect our dinner, but from their regard to their own interest. We address ourselves, not to their humanity but to their self-love, and never talk to them of our own necessities but of their advantages. Nobody but a beggar chooses to depend chiefly upon the benevolence of his fellow-citizens."

17. The complexities of Smith's approach to human nature is a common theme in much of the literature. See Haakonssen 1981; Winch 1978; Morrow (1926) 1969; Lindgren 1973; Werhane 1991; Fleischacker 2005b; Rasmussen 2008; Hanley 2009a; and Schwarze and Scott 2019.

18. For a thorough accounting of these virtues, see Hanley 2009a, chap. 4.

19. Stigler 1975, 237. This passage has been cited in Fleischacker 2004b, 84 and Fleischhacker 2023. Glory Liu (2022, 2) has traced this account to the "Chicago School's distillation of Smith's ideas into a popular and powerful myth: that rational self-interest is the only valid premise for the analysis of human behavior, and that only the invisible hand of the market, not the heavy hand of government, could guarantee personal and political freedom."

20. *TMS*, 62.

21. *TMS*, 63.

22. In this Smith departs from Rousseau, who observed that the poor despise the rich (*SD*, 187).

23. As Levy and Peart (2013, 384) have indicated, the vast majority of citizens have a natural inclination to place their confidence in the wealthy. The authors cite the following passage from *TMS*: "Nature has wisely judged that the distinction of ranks, the peace and order of society, would rest more securely upon the plain and palpable difference of birth and fortune, than upon the invisible and often uncertain difference of wisdom and virtue"—since presumably being able to identify true wisdom and virtue requires rare skills of discernment (*TMS*, 267).

24. *TMS*, 300.

25. As a contemporary economist remarks, "Much of what has gone on [in recent economic history] can only be described by the words 'moral deprivation.' Something wrong happened to the moral compass of so many people working in the financial sector and elsewhere. When the norms of a society change in a way that so many have lost their moral compass, it says something significant about the society." He continues one page later that the market has evolved to the point where "everything is acceptable and no one is accountable" (Stiglitz 2012, xvii, xviii).

26. See Hanley 2009a, 50.

27. Smith frequently repeats this theme throughout *TMS* at 75, 77, 138, 235, 266–67, 294, and 297.

28. Why does this only work in one direction for Smith? Namely, why do the poor admire and feel sympathy for the wealthy while the wealthy feel contempt for the poor? It would seem to follow logically from his observation that it is much easier for people to feel sympathy for the joys of others rather than their sorrows: "I will venture to affirm, that, when there is no envy in the case, our propensity to sympathize with joy is much stronger than our propensity to sympathize with sorrow" (*TMS*, 56).

29. As Fonna Forman-Barzilai (2005) has argued, Smith inherited this spatial conception of sympathy from David Hume. Although Forman-Barzilai brings

NOTES TO CHAPTER FIVE

considerable insight into how Smith's treatment of proximity might inform his conception of moral judgment across cultures, she does not explore how distance might affect sympathy across widely divergent social and economic classes within the same society.

30. Tocqueville (1835/40) 1988, 2.3.1. For discussion of this passage, see Storey and Storey 2021, 148–50.

31. Fleischacker 2019, 98.

32. As Richard Boyd (2013, 458) has also observed with regard to Smith, "Once human beings become so radically differentiated that they are unrecognizable to one another, they cease to be able to feel sympathy for their fellow citizens."

33. Hume (1741–1742) 1994, 34; Madison (1787–89) 2003, 41; see also Machiavelli (1531) 1998, 111; Ferguson (1766) 1996, 93; and Rousseau (1755) 2019, 171–72.

34. *TMS*, 178.

35. See Boyd 2013, 460.

36. In arguing that inequality in this way can violate the Smithian conception of justice, I counter the view of Rasmussen (2016, 346) that "the mere act of becoming spectacularly wealthy oneself, and thereby increasing economic inequality, clearly does not cause an 'real and positive hurt' to others in Smith's sense." This may be true in the strictest sense, but if we take seriously his suggestion that a wealthy class establishes and enforces separate moral and legal codes for rich and poor, as a result of inequality, then a real Smithian injustice has occurred.

37. Fleischacker 2004b, 205; Rasmussen 2016, 351. See also McMahon 2023, 176.

38. See Rasmussen 2008, 9; Hanley 2009a, 15–19; and Aspromourgas 2013, 274.

39. Hanley 2009a, 17.

40. See Fleischacker 2004a, 2004b; Vaughan 2008.

41. As Chrystia Freeland (2012, 79–84) has observed, these tensions frequently exist in the enormous gap between the top 0.1 percent and the top 1 percent.

42. Hanley 2009a, 210.

43. Smith also subsequently observes that "very few men" are comfortable in appealing primarily to their consciences rather than public applause as a guiding standard for their moral behavior.

44. For example, see Himmelfarb 1985, 59–60.

45. Harris 2020, 146. For a contrary view, see Oprea 2022 and Frame and Schwarze 2023.

46. As Richard Boyd (2013, 453) has emphasized, for Smith "civility is increasingly difficult under conditions of real or presumed inequality."

47. Werhane (1991) has argued that justice is, in fact, the preeminent virtue required in commercial society for Smith.

48. Smith stresses that justice must be impartial in *TMS*, 107.

49. Boyd 2013, 451.

50. Werhane 1991, 43.

51. He subsequently insists on a "sacred regard [for] general rules" since they are "the commands and laws of the Deity, who will finally reward the obedient, and punish the transgressors" (*TMS*, 188, 189).

52. While Smith here addresses the possibility of acquiring private wealth through personal industry, he subsequently comments, "A porter or day labourer must continue poor forever" (*LJ*, 521). In providing this account of the origins of government,

he closely follows Rousseau's *Discourse on the Origin of Inequality*, a text he knew very well. There Rousseau describes "the origin of Society and of the Laws" as having "forever fixed the Law of property and inequality" ([1755] 2019, 173). This view is repeated in Rousseau's *Emile*: "The universal spirit of the laws of every country is always to favor the strong against the weak and those who have against those who have not. This difficulty is inevitable and it is without exception" (*Emile*, 236n). See also Lomonaco 2002; Rasmussen 2008; and Stimson 2015. Rousseau also employs the word "oppression" (*l'oppression*) in a similar context in his *Discourse*, as Smith does in his *LJ* (177).

53. Smith's words here are echoed less than a century later by Friedrich Engels: the "legal system has been devised to protect those who own property from those who do not" (Engels, *Condition*, 317).

54. Werhane 1991, 85.

55. It is worth noting that insofar as Smith envisions the existence of an abstract, more universal conception of justice independent of the origins described here, it is unclear that it would be employed in practice to evaluate the wealthy: "Success covers from his [the spectator's] eyes, not only the great imprudence, but frequently the great injustice of their enterprises; and, far from blaming this defective part of their character, he often views it with the most enthusiastic admiration" (*TMS*, 295–96). Along these lines, at one point, Smith seems to suggest that the wealthy stand above the laws, wherever those laws do not operate in their favor, insofar as he notes that "men in the inferior and middling stations in life . . . can never be great enough to be above the law" (*TMS*, 75). As Stiglitz (2012, 37) has echoed, "Those who win at it [modern capitalism] often possess less admirable characteristics as well: the ability to skirt the law, or to shape them in their own favor."

56. "The ninth law of nature . . . *that every man acknowledge another for his equal by nature*. The breach of this precept is *pride*" (*Leviathan*, 15.21; emphases original).

57. I am arguing here that divine justice *might* be intended by Smith as a last line of defense to enforce virtuous behavior in a world prone to moral corruption. An alternative, and not mutually exclusive, interpretation offered by Michelle Schwarze and John T. Scott (2015) is that Smith intends these appeals to have more the effect of consolation in the face of moral insult and disappointment (see also Lindgren 1973, 150).

58. In his notes to *TMS*, Ryan Hanley (2009b, 460n14) observes Smith's affinity to Plato and Rousseau along precisely these lines.

59. I do not make any claims about the sincerity of Smith's religious appeals here since Smith is notoriously vague about his personal commitments. See Lindgren 1973, 132–52 and Kennedy 2013, 473–81.

60. One may also plausibly argue that the effects are also limited among the faithful. A central teaching in the Christian tradition, for example, is the persistence of vice as a result of original sin—which necessarily implies a failure of sanction to restrain human behavior.

61. Nietzsche merely confirms what worried John Wesley more than a century earlier: "I fear, where riches have increased, the essence of religion has decreased in the same proportion" (Wesley, quoted in Weber [1904] 2001, 118). As Weber notes, Wesley's assumption that great wealth threatens religious faith and morality was indeed the consensus view in early modernity: "No one in the seventeenth century

doubted the existence of these relationships. . . . [They] assumed them as obvious" (Weber [1904] 2001, 256n96). Along these lines, see Pascal (1670) 1995, 218–19.

62. See Fleischacker 2004b, 205 and Schliesser 2017, 200.

63. Schliesser 2017, 200.

64. Fleischacker 2004a, 63 and Himmelfarb 1985, 61.

65. Along these lines, see Mandeville, *Fable*, 183–85. For Mandeville, poverty is perhaps the greatest of all incentives to work. Poor laws, on this logic, deprive the laborers of this motive and encourage idleness.

66. See Persky 2016, 109, 118–21.

67. See Fleischacker 2013, 498 and Rasmussen 2016, 343–44.

68. This passage has been cited in Winch 1996, 83 and J. Hill 2016, 74.

69. Rasmussen 2008, 103.

70. Deborah Boucoyannis (2013) offers a robust and compelling account of Smith as committed to equality. Her Smith has designed an economy of high wages and low profits that, when well regulated, promotes extensive economic equality. Although I have often been tempted by her reading of Smith, I am reminded by passages like the one just cited that Smith apparently abandons the effort for greater equality in favor of reducing poverty.

71. An alternative account of how to make sense of Smith's apparent tension can be found in Boucoyannis 2013, which rejects the idea that Smith tolerates inequality at all. For a different view of Smith, James A. Harris (2020) has argued that although Smith is a perceptive and sensitive critic of economic inequality, he is ultimately informed by "Whiggish" commitments that led him to protect inequality for the sake of political stability. Or as Eric Schliesser (2017, 373) has characterized Smith, "Some social hierarchy, while founded on original injustices, turns out to be useful."

72. Voltaire (1755) 2018, 341.

73. Mandeville, *Fable*, 26.

74. McCloskey 2020.

75. Pinker 2018, 83.

Chapter Six

1. The evolution of Mill's views being noted here, I will not make too much of it in this chapter. The fact of his concern about inequality is consistent throughout his career.

2. For example, Villa 2017.

3. For example, McCabe 2021 and Arlen 2022.

4. I borrow in this section significantly from Piketty 2020, chap. 5.

5. For example, in 1800 less than 2 percent of the British population consisted of nobles, whereas in Portugal in the same year, it was greater than 6 percent. See Piketty 2020, 161.

6. Piketty 2020, 162.

7. Piketty 2020, 168.

8. There would be two further Reform Acts in 1884 and 1918, with universal male suffrage only arriving by the end of World War I in 1918. (Female suffrage would finally arrive in 1928.)

9. In fact, inequality grew slightly over this period, such that by 1900, the top 1 percent owned 70 percent and the top 10 percent owned 92 percent of all British property. See Piketty 2020, 195.

10. Hobsbawm 1968, 165, 166.

11. Piketty 2020, 123. Piketty suggests that the meritocracy arguments only began to predominate in the twentieth century, though for reasons covered in my chapter on Rousseau, I think the arguments were present much earlier. (See also McLendon 2018.) In this section, I depart from Piketty mainly on the arrival time of meritocracy's sway, not in its potency as ideology.

12. Locke, *Second Treatise*, 2.6.

13. Piketty 2020, 123.

14. Piketty 2020, 710.

15. See *Capital*, 873–74.

16. Mayhew (1850–1862) 2020, 277–78.

17. Jennie Ikuta (2020, 73) has characterized conformity to be "the main problem of the text."

18. F. Harrison 1896, 496. Similar readings persist today. My reading of Mill here is very much at odds with that offered by Patrick J. Deneen. Deneen has argued that Mill, in fact, sought to foster a community in which "the 'best' would dominate the 'ordinary.'" Mill's ideal community, according to Deneen, is "organized for the benefit of the strong" (Deneen 2018, 146, 148). His reading of Mill is hindered by (1) inattention to Mill's economic writings, (2) failure to recognize Mill's concern for the conditions of ordinary people, (3) failure to observe Mill's concern about the problems associated with the rich and powerful, and (4) failure to note the pattern of Mill's concern for building a sense of community. I hope in this chapter to draw needed attention to all of these dimensions of Mill's thought so that scholars like Deneen might avoid the trap of mischaracterizing him as a proto-Randian champion of the rich and powerful.

19. Bentham (1789) 2003, 1.1; emphasis original.

20. Bentham 1824, 392–93; emphasis original.

21. This is actually Mill's paraphrase of Bentham from section 4 of his essay, *Bentham* (113). Bentham's original defense of pushpin being as good as poetry from a utilitarian perspective can be found in his *Rationale of Reward* (206–7).

22. Mill repeatedly emphasizes the need for a sense of "unity" among citizens throughout *Utilitarianism* (27, 32) as well as his *Principles of Political Economy* (205) and *Coleridge* (135).

23. As the philosopher Henry R. West (2004, 98–99) has observed, "Mill . . . thinks that these feelings [of unity] can be reinforced by external sanctions, and that as civilization goes on and improvements in political life remove inequalities of legal privilege between individuals or classes, there is an increasing tendency for each individual to feel a unity with all the rest." This assessment is correct, only it does not go far enough. It is insufficient, for Mill, that the legal privileges of the classes are equalized—the classes themselves must be more equal. This is partly because legal privileges tend to correspond to wealth in unequal societies, where wealthy citizens control the political institutions and reinforce their legal and economic privileges through "class legislation," as Mill outlines in his *Considerations on Representative Government*, chapter 6. As he elaborates, "In all countries, there is a majority of poor, a minority who, in contradistinction, may be called rich. Between these two classes,

on many questions, there is complete opposition of apparent interest" (chap. 6). For Mill, the path to a "sense of unity" requires reducing inequality.

24. See, for example, Gramm, Ekelund, and Early 2022.

25. See also Marx, *Capital*, 1:358.

26. As McCabe (2021, 168) has observed, Mill "associated 'dependence' with inequality and independence with equality."

27. See Vaughan 2008, 123–27 and Rauhut 2021, 77–80.

28. Mill describes "the demoralizing effect of great inequalities of wealth and social rank" as the legitimate concern of pessimists—expressly like Rousseau—in *Coleridge* (123).

29. McCabe 2021, 183.

30. McCabe 2021, 185.

31. Stephen ([1873] 1992, 198, 169) was no fan of Mill's fraternity, insisting that the desire for social harmony is a "baseless and presumptuous dream," and that "between all classes of men there are and always will be real occasions of enmity and strife."

32. Aristotle, *Ethics*, 8.7.

33. As Dana Villa (2017, 233) has observed, Mill was "all too aware of the sinister [partial and class-bound] interests that impede both progress and reform."

34. John Rawls credits Mill with understanding this problem in his *Justice as Fairness*: A "reason for controlling economic and social inequalities is to prevent one part of society from dominating the rest. When those kinds of inequalities are large, they tend to support political inequality. As Mill said, the bases of political power are (educated) intelligence, property, and the power of combination, by which he meant the ability to cooperate in pursuing one's political interests" (Rawls 2001, 130–31). The combination of the economically advantaged in the pursuit of "one's political interests" is the problem posed by what Mill calls "class legislation."

35. This is precisely what Old Oligarch argued, as discussed in chapter 1 of this book.

36. McCabe (2021, 160–83) correctly identifies equality as one of Mill's core moral principles.

37. It could easily be argued that instances like this, where societies promise equal consideration but instead deliver inequality, violate the fourth conception of justice outlined by Mill in *Utilitarianism*: breaking faith. Insofar as a society promises one set of (equal) legal standards but it actually enforces a very different (unequal) one, citizens would not be wrong in supposing they have been unjustly deceived.

38. The first two conditions are education and a sense of national loyalty.

39. Robert Nozick (1974, 41) describes individuals who purportedly gain so much pleasure from seemingly trivial matters that a strictly utilitarian society would be morally compelled to satisfy those individuals above all other policy goals. For Nozick, this is evidence of utilitarianism's failure as a moral philosophy. My point is not to demonstrate any weaknesses in utilitarianism per se since it is clear that Mill thinks the workers would, in fact, get greater pleasure from the money than their employers. My point is that the employers fail to appreciate this fact.

40. Charles Lindblom (1977, 44) echoes Mill a century later: "In principle, governments can redistribute income and wealth and repeat the redistribution as frequently as wished. Their disinclination to do so requires a political explanation." A generation thereafter, Hacker and Pierson (2010) similarly argue that American economic

inequality resulted from deliberate policy choices, not as the inevitable result of quasi-natural forces.

41. Tocqueville (1835/40) 1988, 9.

42. This raises the question of whether equality would be problematic in economies that *do not* need to grow. This is not a category that Smith considers, but it is an active possibility for Mill—even an ultimate goal of all moral economies. I will say more about this "stationary state" later.

43. Following Bentham, Mill quickly dismisses the idea that anyone who is not a "direct heir" deserves any inheritance whatsoever (*Principles*, 220).

44. Students of Mill will recognize this phrase for its resemblance to *On Liberty*'s characterization of utility as concerned with the "permanent interests of man as a progressive being" (*On Liberty*, 14).

45. Here I agree with Joseph Persky, who describes Mill's estate tax reforms to be aimed at checking "the intergenerational concentration of wealth" and "guarantee[ing] against the unattractive concentration of wealth" (Persky 2016, 96). But Persky limits his analysis of Mill's utility calculus for the tax reform's effects on incentives to work—that the inheritance of large estates discourages heirs to adopt a work ethic, leaving them indolent (97). Although this is true, I would argue that these other considerations—in the form of class legislation, social tensions, injustice, and the like—constitute greater considerations from Mill's utilitarian perspective. It is unlikely that a small handful of lazy heirs would inflict nearly as much pain on society than would, for example, an increasingly hostile social and economic environment.

46. I should also add that although Mill wants heirs to be "independent," he does not want them to be independent without having to work for it: "I do not recognise as just or salutary, a state of society in which there is any 'class' which is not labouring" (*Principles*, 758). So the amount one inherits should not be enough to be independent without working. It is to be able to achieve independence through working.

47. It is worth noting that Mill is skeptical of income taxes, among other reasons, because it is so easy for clever rich people to hide their incomes. Estate taxes are less easy to hide on his account. Although it should be noted that Donald Trump's top economic adviser, Gary Cohn, has insisted that "only morons pay the estate tax" (quoted in D. Markovits 2019, 58). Whether this is because Mill overestimated the degree to which estate taxes would be easy to collect or because estate taxes and finance in the United States evolved to be so baroque as to facilitate such evasions is an open question.

48. See, for example, Holcombe 2000 and Bakst 2017. Angus Deaton (2023a, 94) traces modern opposition to the estate tax to Milton Friedman, noting that 727 economists have signed a letter opposing this tax.

49. Britain would finally pass an estate tax in the Finance Act of 1894, but initially its maximum rate was a mere 8 percent on estates valued at over £1 million. It was not until World War I that it was substantially raised to 40 percent, eventually growing to 80 percent shortly after the conclusion of World War II.

50. Regarding vanity, as Mill notes elsewhere in the *Principles*, "government ought to set an example of rating all things at their true value, and riches, therefore, at the worth, for comfort or pleasure, of the things which they will buy: and ought not to sanction the vulgarity of prizing them for the pitiful vanity of being known to possess them, or the paltry shame of being suspected to be without them" (*Principles*, 810).

51. Bain 1882, 89.

52. Claeys 2013, 75.

53. See, for example, Capaldi 2004, 41, 336.

54. Marx would subsequently label this advocacy of birth control the "*humanitarian* school," which he admits, "sincerely deplores the distress of the proletariat" (*Poverty*, 135).

55. See Vaughan 2008, 124–27.

56. It is worth noting here that Marx was extremely dubious about such a plan. He noted that reformers like Mill had suggested procuring "the best possible education for themselves and their children," yet lamented that the "schools have seldom been so ill attended, or school fees so ill paid." For Marx, these plans were a mockery of the poor insofar as increasingly more women and children were being compelled to work in factories "with prolonged hours of work." And even if they had managed to attend their school lessons, "the opportunity of learning how to keep population at the pace prescribed by Malthus" would be nothing but truisms, equivalent to pretending to "save a man from starving by telling him that the laws of Nature demand a perpetual supply of food for the human body" (*LQ*, 165).

57. Capaldi 2004, 41.

58. Plato, *Laws*, 736d.

59. I here gently challenge Hans Jensen's (2001, 504) suggestion that Mill proposed establishing "a state-supported system of 'national education.'" Jensen does not consult Mill's extensive thoughts about education as outlined in *On Liberty*.

60. Persky (2016, 125) explains how Mill's worries about the dangers of indoctrination is largely following the concerns of both James Mill and Jeremy Bentham.

61. It is reasonable to ask whether the sanctions of public opinion that Mill appears to lean on here are inconsistent with his concerns about the tyrannical tendencies of public opinion.

62. See Persky 2016, 129–31.

63. Mill emphasizes just a couple of pages later, the goal of economic reforms should be to avoid dividing the classes into "two parties with hostile interests and feelings" (*Principles*, 769).

64. Gregory Claeys (1987, 124–26) and Helen McCabe (2021, 20–23) have demonstrated that while Mill was initially skeptical of such co-ops as a youth, he gradually embraced them enthusiastically.

65. M. Levy 1981, 292.

66. M. Levy 1981, 275.

67. Recalling the distinction in *Utilitarianism* between the dissatisfied Socrates and the satisfied pig, Mill's condemnation of the *pleonectic* capitalist here gives special meaning to the term "bourgeois pig." The bourgeois pig is understood in Millian terms as the capitalists who can only enjoy themselves in the "low" pleasures of unnecessary wealth, conspicuous consumption, and pointless distinction.

68. Lovejoy 1961, 210.

69. He elaborates in the next sentence that part of this plan includes population control already discussed above. One finds Émile Durkheim coming to similar conclusions toward the end of his career (see Mergy 2009, 8–9).

70. McCabe 2021, 162.

Chapter Seven

1. R. Miller 1984, 21.

2. R. Miller 1984, 19.

3. Allen Wood 2014, 256. William Clare Roberts (2017, 180) agrees with Wood that freedom from arbitrary will is indeed one of Marx's highest priorities, yet disagrees about his assessment of equality in Marx.

4. Allen Wood 2014, 259.

5. Along these lines, Terrell Carver (2018, 35–49) has noted extensive parallels between Marx's treatment of class and inequality with the political and economic goals of the Occupy Wall Street movement.

6. Here I draw on Alfari, Gierok, and Schaff 2022.

7. See Alfani, Gierok, and Schaff 2022, 111. The fact of this regressive tax scheme was surely in the minds of Marx and Engels when they included in the *Communist Manifesto* a provision for a "heavy progressive or graduated income tax" (*CM*, 175).

8. Much of what follows here is drawn from Heinrich 2019.

9. Quoted in Heinrich 2019, 46.

10. Ziblatt 2008, 625.

11. Lovett 2022, 26.

12. Unless otherwise noted, all references to *Capital* are to volume 1.

13. As Hont (2015, 72) would characterize Rousseau on this point, "The poor were sold on the advantages of legal equality, which were quite real, without understanding the consequences of superimposing it on a system of unregulated private property."

14. There is a significant debate among Marx scholars on whether he holds a rich and metaphysically vested understanding of ideas like justice and equality. Richard Miller and Allen Wood believe he does not. Kai Nielsen (1988) believes he does. I have sided with Nielsen on this debate. See Williams 2007, 249–59.

15. Kant (1793) 1996, 292.

16. Eagleton 2011, 103.

17. As Terrell Carver (2018, 74) has noted, one of the major themes of the *Manifesto* is that "inequalities of wealth and power are becoming more, rather than less, extreme."

18. It is worth noting that this myth, as Marx acknowledges, decidedly does not originate with Adam Smith, who was at pains to emphasize that "the difference of natural talents between individuals is much less than what is supposed," as Marx himself acknowledges (*Poverty*, 140). Smith continues, "The difference between the most dissimilar characters, between a philosopher and a common street porter, for example, seems to arise not so much from nature, as from habit, custom, and education" (*WN*, 17).

19. This effect is amplified by multimillionaires, for example, who portray the working poor as possessing "low IQ's" (Conard 2016, 196).

20. Turgot (1770) 1973, 125.

21. Kant (1793) 1996, 294. According to one study, this belief that poverty is largely attributable to laziness is more common in the United States than in Europe: "54 percent of Europeans believe the poor are unlucky, whereas only 30 percent of Americans share the belief" (Alesia, Glaser, and Sacerdote 2001, 242).

22. It is worth noting that even though Marx's judgment may seem stern to some, it actually differs little from the moderate Scottish Enlightenment philosopher David Hume, who wrote, "Almost all the governments, which exist at present, or of which there are remains any record in story, have been founded originally, either on usurpation or conquest, or both, without any pretense of a fair consent, or voluntary subjection of the people" (Hume [1748] 1994, 189–90).

23. This was the belief that commerce inclines nations to peaceful and harmonious relations. Per Helena Rosenblatt (1997, 52–53), *doux commerce* was the belief that "through economic trade, man's material life is sweetened" and further "that through social interaction man becomes more gentle, that is, humane and polite." The French word *doux* is derived from *douceur*, which means "peacefulness," among other related notions. Born largely from Bernard Mandeville's *Fable of the Bees*, this doctrine, which endorsed the role of self-interest in bringing about peace and social harmony, would find advocates among subsequent figures such Montesquieu and Hume. Marx may well be subtly drawing the reader's attention to the fact that although Hume was clever enough to understand the brutal nature of how states were formed, he failed to understand how that brutality persisted thereafter through the operations of commerce. Before Marx, Rousseau likewise attacked this doctrine in his "Preface to Narcissus" in which he describes the reality of *doux commerce* as men living together "by obstructing, supplanting, deceiving, betraying, destroying one another." Rather than promoting peace and harmony, the doctrine of *doux commerce* is, for the Genevan, "the fatal source of the violence, the betrayals, the treacheries and all the horrors necessarily required by a state of affairs in which everyone pretends to be working for the profit or reputation of the rest, while only seeking to raise his own above theirs and at their expense" (*Narcissus*, 102–3).

24. Marx details the economics of this process in chapter 4 of *Capital*.

25. Mandeville, *Fable of the Bees*, 184 (remark Q). David Hume would echo Mandeville a half century later: "We see, that, in years of scarcity, the weaver either consumes less or labours more, or employs both these expedients of frugality and industry" (Hume [1758] 1994, 163). Gertrude Himmelfarb (1985, 51) has suggested that Mandeville's theory here was the "consensus view at the time."

26. Mandeville, *Fable of the Bees*, 1:192 (remark Q). Marx discusses these pages in *Capital*, 754–65.

27. Roberts 2017, 180n138. See also Galbraith 2016, 22.

28. Marx quoting Dr. J. T. Arledge, senior physician at the North Staffordshire Infirmary.

29. See Dingle 1972. It is not for nothing that Bavarians sometimes call beer *flüssiges Brot*, or "liquid bread."

30. Hobsbawm 1968, 164.

31. This quotation was actually inserted by Engels in the third German edition of *Capital*.

32. This passage has been cited for relatively similar purposes in Vaughan 2008, 153. This phenomenon has been empirically confirmed by the economist Clement Bellet (2020). Marx repeats this sentiment later in his *Civil War in France*, where he notes the "misery of the masses was set off by a shameless display of gorgeous, meretricious and debased luxury" (631).

33. See Rasmussen 2008, 35–40.

34. Although not cited *by* Marx in this tradition, John Locke describes the same phenomenon in his *Second Treatise on Government* a generation earlier than Mandeville: "There cannot be a clearer demonstration of any thing, than several nations of the Americans are of this, who are rich in land, and poor in all the Comforts of Life; whom Nature having furnished as liberally as any other people, with the materials of Plenty, i.e. a fruitful Soil, apt to produce in abundance, what might serve for food, raiment, and delight; yet for want of improving it by labour, have not one hundredth part of the Conveniencies we enjoy: And a King of a large and fruitful Territory there, feeds, lodges, and is clad worse than a day Labourer in *England*" (5.41; emphasis original).

35. Mandeville, *Fable*, 26.

36. Mandeville, *Fable*, 169.

37. Mandeville, *Fable*, 172.

38. Along these lines, Marx importantly notes that the economist David Ricardo understood individual wealth is a relative or social phenomenon, most meaningful when compared with others. On this point, see Roberts 2017, 179–80.

39. Rawls 1971, 530.

40. Nozick 1974, 240.

41. McCloskey and Carden 2020, 63.

42. Pinker 2018, 98, 101.

43. See Ferguson (1766) 1996, 177.

44. Freud, *Civilization and Its Discontents*, 97–98.

45. It naturally bears emphasizing that by "equality" here, Marx means bourgeois equality, the equality of rights or legal equality, as opposed to economic equality, which is decidedly *not* part the bourgeois ideology.

46. T. K. Seung (1982, 164) criticizes Freud on similar grounds, who had, in his estimation, generalized unreasonably "from the Viennese leisure class" in a "relatively opulent bourgeois" society.

47. Compare with Mill's criticism of Bentham's doctrine of natural selfishness in chapter 6 of this book.

48. Given the sale of indulgences by the Church in this period, it was not unreasonable for orthodox Catholics to believe that they could purchase salvation through the acquisition of great wealth and the subsequent donation of a portion of it to the Church for its various construction projects.

49. Pluto was the ancient Greek god of wealth and the underworld.

50. Athenaeus's passage here reveals how he was the god of these two otherwise disconnected artifacts. Since wealth was literally mined from mines below the surface, Pluto came to be the god of both.

51. Athenaeus 1929, 52.

52. Strabo, 3.2. The lineage of quotations has even one further intermediary, Poseidonius, whom Athenaeus is quoting at length from a text that exists now only in fragments. So technically, Marx is quoting Athenaeus, who is quoting Poseidonius, who is quoting Strabo.

53. Marx drawing attention to the mines with this quote provides an opportunity to reflect on the fact that more than one thousand British miners died in accidents

annually in the 1850s due to the "owners' gross neglect of the men's safety and health in that dark and murderous occupation" (Hobsbawm 1968, 116).

54. Plutarch, *Lives*, 1:60. Marx addresses similar reforms as proposed by the nineteenth-century French politician Alfred Darimon (1819–1902). In the spirit of Plutarch's Lycurgus and Plato's Athenian Stranger, Darimon proposes abolishing the "privilege of gold and silver" by degrading them "to the rank of all other commodities" (as paraphrased by Marx). Yet Marx is ultimately dubious about the efficacy of this as a solution to the problems of greed and exploitation because it does not abolish currency generally, much less exchanges where one party retains incentives to better the other party. He mocks Darimon on this point: "Abolish money and don't abolish money!" (*Grundrisse*, 126, 127).

55. See Aristotle, *Politics*, 1.8.

56. Booth 1993, 247.

57. McLendon 2018, 139.

58. Much of the compulsion is in the effort to produce the cheapest possible commodities, as Marx observes "the profit-mania and competition which compel commodities to be produced as cheaply as possible" (*Capital 3*, 179). This passage, in fact, points to the compulsion of both forces under discussion here: competition and greed ("profit-mania").

59. The same point could be made, I think, regarding Marx's multiple comparisons of the bourgeoisie to vampires (e.g., *Capital*, 342, 367, 416, 598; *CFL*, 191), who similarly act on compulsion rather than from rational reflection.

60. Heinrich 2012, 88; emphasis original.

61. By a "certain point of view," I mean the phenomenal point of view.

62. See Owen 1837, 56–57. I have substituted Owen's original English here rather than using Nicolaus's English translation of Marx's translated German. Marx's use of Owen here is with his obvious endorsement, as he was perhaps his favorite of all the nineteenth-century socialists (see Roberts 2017, 244–46).

63. I am not the first to note Marx's attention to Lazarus in *Capital*. See Roberts (2017, 184–85), who discusses Marx's reference to Lazarus with a slightly different emphasis.

64. Wright 2001a, 201.

65. In *Capital*, Marx notes that vagabonds were executed for a third offense of beggary. It is in the *German Ideology* that he cites the number of hangings (*Capital*, 896–97; *GI*, 77).

66. As Engels notes, given the conditions of the workhouses, quitting one's job in this period and choosing to live on public assistance was no option (Engels, *Condition*, 324–31).

67. Roberts 2017, 62–70, 82–103.

68. Roberts 2017, 85.

69. Roberts 2017, 82.

70. See Seung 1994, 221. See also Hasamyi 1980 and Nielsen 1988. As Carver (2018, 139) notes, Marx "used morally referential terminology because he had very strong opinions on class-divided social system through which—for woefully insufficient reasons, so he argued—some people labour for the benefit of other, or simply languish in poverty, as do their children."

71. See Kant, *Critique of Pure Reason*, 467–79.

72. Scheidel 2017, 4.

· 73. Scheidel 2017, 149.

74. I am adapting these terms invented by T. K. Seung (1993, 135).

75. R. Miller 1984, 20; Allen Wood 2014, 258; McMahon 2023, 265. See also Milanovic 2023, 120–21.

76. As Wood correctly notes, this phrase was most immediately associated with Louis Blanc (1811–1882) in his *Plus de Girondins* (1851) but traceable back to the book of Acts (2:44–45). See Allen Wood 2014, 259.

77. Allen Wood 2014, 259; emphasis original.

78. Viroli 1988, 213.

79. Arturo Chang and I have written on this passage from the *Social Contract* in Chang and Williams 2024.

80. The same point can be made in addressing the work of Harrington or the sections on republicanism in Montesquieu's *Spirit of the Laws*.

81. Allen Wood 2014, 256.

82. Giridharadas 2018, 6.

83. Reich 2018, 18.

Conclusion

1. Sumner (1902) 1914.

2. Starr 1925, 78.

3. Pinker 2018, 103, 101, 117.

4. Gates 2018.

5. Frankfurt 2015, 7.

6. McCloskey resembles Michael Walzer, who similarly insists that inequality is a "question of culture, not of distributive justice." Therefore, he concludes, "so long as yachts and hi-fi sets and rugs have only use value and individualized symbolic value, their unequal distribution doesn't matter" (Walzer 1983, 108). But an important difference is that Walzer provides an extensive list of "blocked exchanges," or things that money cannot buy, including political influence, political offices, privileged speech, and legal privileges. So although Walzer seems, in principle, sympathetic to McCloskey, he actively seeks to isolate the material privileges enjoyed by the wealthy in unequal societies.

7. As Ingrid Robeyns (2019, 256) has observed, "rich people can give up their right to vote; however, if they can still set up and fund think tanks that produce ideologically driven research or if they still have direct private access to government officials, then they will still have asymmetrical powers."

8. McCloskey 2016, 46, 48.

9. McCloskey 2018, 64; 2016a, 648.

10. Mandeville, *Fable*, 169.

11. Schumpeter (1942) 1950, 67.

12. McCloskey 2016, 38, 39.

13. Keltner 2016, 100.

14. Keltner 2016, 132.

15. Payne 2017, 3.

16. Berman 2022, 9.

17. Posner 1983, 115.

18. Dollar and Kraay 2002.

19. Quoted in Appelbaum 2019, 7.

20. This attitude is perhaps best expressed by McCloskey (2017, 7), who quips, "Give the poor cash subsides, and quit worrying about them spending it on booze." Although I am sure McCloskey's attitude toward the poor is not as callous as this sounds, there is a disposition revealed in this remark. The problem is to be solved, the conscience is to be cleaned, by simply giving subsidies to the poor. When she says to "quit worrying," one can almost finish the thought for her. Quit worrying whether the poor spend their money on booze, but also quit worrying if they suffer from anxieties related to their relative poverty. Quit worrying whether they are made to feel small or morally and politically irrelevant. Quit worrying if the rich use their money to cement political and legal advantages. "Quit worrying" is the mantra of those who deny that inequality is a phenomenon of *moral psychology*. It is the mantra of those indifferent to its social, political, and psychic effects.

21. The exception here, Plato, proves the rule. Plato's Stranger does, in fact, propose a mathematical formula for ideal equality—the 4:1 ratio discussed in chapter 1. Yet Plato acknowledges that this formula only applies to the founding of new territories for new peoples who have never before had a government or even any prior history. Given the rarity of such opportunities, the Stranger insists, we rather typically nudge our actual existing republics in the direction of greater equality, without insisting on a numerical goal.

22. Sumner (1883) 1989, 114.

23. Conard 2016, 196, 197. Notably, Anne Phillips has commented on such observations: "Differences in intelligence" are now "projected onto differences in social class, generating categories of the 'smart' and the 'stupid' that attribute social inequalities to individuals' own lack of ability." For the poor, according to this philosophy, there is nothing left but to "face the unpalatable truth of their stupidity." This, on her reasoned account, results in "destroying the very belief in human equality that supposedly underpins democracy" (Phillips 2021, 4, 5).

24. Conard's insistence that the large number of college humanities majors endangers the public good borders on comical since (1) the number of humanities students has been in precipitous decline for decades (without the associated social benefits anticipated by Conard) but more significantly because (2) it is precisely in the humanities that students can learn to be critical of the kinds of arguments Conard offers.

25. Phillips 2021, 13.

26. Shklar 1969, 225.

27. Deaton 2023b.

BIBLIOGRAPHY

Aalders, G.J.D. 1969. "The Authenticity of the Eighth Platonic Epistle Reconsidered." *Mnemosyne*, 4th ser., 22 (3): 233–57.

Alesia, Alberto, Edward Glaeser, and Bruce Sacerdote. 2001. "Why Doesn't the United States Have a European-Style Welfare State?" *Brookings Papers on Economic Activity* 2: 187–277.

Alfani, Guido, Victoria Gierok, and Felix Schaff. 2022. "Economic Inequality in Preindustrial Germany, ca. 1300–1850." *Journal of Economic History* 82 (1): 87–125.

Alford, Stephen. 2017. *London's Triumph: Merchant Adventurers and the Tudor City*. London: Allen Lane.

Andrew, Edward. 1989. "Equality of Opportunity as the Noble Lie." *History of Political Thought* 10 (4): 577–95.

Annas, Julia. 2010. "Virtue and Law in Plato." In *Plato's "Laws": A Critical Guide*, edited by Christopher Bobonich, 71–91. Cambridge: Cambridge University Press.

Annas, Julia. 2017. *Virtue and Law in Plato and Beyond*. Oxford: Oxford University Press.

Antiphon. 2011. Excerpted in *Readings in Ancient Greek Philosophy: From Thales to Aristotle*, edited by S. Marc Cohen, Patricia Curd, and C.D.C. Reeve. Indianapolis: Hackett.

Apeldoorn, Laurens van. 2018. "'The Nutrition of a Commonwealth': On Hobbes's Economic Thought." In *History of Economic Rationalities: Economic Reasoning as Knowledge and Practice Authority*, edited by Jakob Bek-Thomsen, Christian Olaf Christiansen, Stefan Gaarsmand Jacobsen, and Mikkel Thorup, 21–30. Dortmund: Springer.

Appelbaum, Binyamin. 2019. *The Economists' Hour: False Prophets, Free Markets, and the Fracture of Society*. New York: Little, Brown.

Aquinas, Thomas. (1265–73) 2003. *On Law, Morality, and Politics*. 2nd ed. Indianapolis: Hackett.

Aristotle. 1996a. *Constitution of Athens*. In *Politics*, edited by Stephen Everson, 209–63. Cambridge: Cambridge University Press.

Aristotle. 1996b. *Politics*. Edited by Stephen Everson. Cambridge: Cambridge University Press.

Aristotle. 1998. *Politics*. Translated by C.D.C. Reeve. Indianapolis: Hackett.

Aristotle. 2014. *Nicomachean Ethics*. Translated by C.D.C. Reeve. Indianapolis: Hackett.

Aristotle. 2018. *Rhetoric*. Translated by C.D.C. Reeve. Indianapolis: Hackett.

Arlen, Gordon. 2022. "Liberal Plebeianism: John Stuart Mill on Democracy, Oligarchy, and Working-Class Mobilization." *American Political Science Review* 117 (1): 249–62.

Aslan, Reza. 2013. *Zealot: The Life and Times of Jesus of Nazareth*. New York: Random House.

Aspromourgas, Tony. 2013. "Adam Smith on Labor and Capital." In *The Oxford Handbook of Adam Smith*, edited by Christopher J. Berry, Maria Pia Paganelli, and Craig Smith, 267–89. Oxford: Oxford University Press.

Athenaeus. 1929. *The Deipnosophists*. Translated by Charles Burton Gulick. Cambridge, MA: Loeb Classical Library.

Attridge, Harold W. 1989. *The Harper Collins Study Bible*, new rev. stand. ed. New York: Harper Collins.

Augustine. 1951. *Commentary on the Lord's Sermon on the Mount with Seventeen Related Sermons*. Edited by Denis J. Kavanagh. Washington, DC: Catholic University of America Press.

Augustine. 1998. *The City of God against the Pagans*. Edited by R. W. Dyson. Cambridge: Cambridge University Press.

Bacon, Francis. (1597–1625) 2002. *Essays*. In *The Major Works*. Edited by Brian Vickers. Oxford: Oxford University Press.

Bacon, Francis. (1622) 1998. *History of the Reign of King Henry VII*. Edited by Brian Vickers. Cambridge: Cambridge University Press.

Bain, Alexander. 1882. *John Stuart Mill: A Criticism. With Personal Reflections*. London: Longmans.

Bakst, Daren. 2017. "It's Time to Fully Repeal the Unjust and Immoral Death Tax." *Daily Signal*, December 12. https://www.dailysignal.com/2017/12/12/tax-legislation -must-repeal-death-tax/.

Balot, Ryan K. 2001. *Greed and Injustice in Classical Athens*. Princeton: Princeton University Press.

Bartels, Larry M. (2008) 2017. *Unequal Democracy: The Political Economy of the New Gilded Age*. 2nd ed. Princeton: Princeton University Press.

Barton, Bruce. (1925) 2000. *The Man Nobody Knows*. Chicago: Ivan R. Dee.

Barton, John, and John Muddiman. 2001. *The Oxford Bible Commentary*. Edited by John Barton and John Muddiman. Oxford: Oxford University Press.

Basil of Caesarea. 2009. *On Social Justice*. Translated by C. Paul Schroeder. Crestwood, NY: St. Vladimir's Seminar Press.

Baumgold, Deborah. 1988. *Hobbes's Political Theory*. Cambridge: Cambridge University Press.

Beaudoin. Steven M. 2007. *Poverty in World History*. London: Routledge.

Beer, Tommy. 2020. "Top 1% of U.S. Households Hold 15 Times More Wealth than Bottom 50% Combined." *Forbes*, October 8. https://www.forbes.com/sites/tommybeer /2020/10/08/top-1-of-us-households-hold-15-times-more-wealth-than-bottom -50-combined/?sh=1ff8f14b5179.

Behrens, Betty. 1963. "Nobles, Privileges, and Taxes in France at the End of the Ancien Régime." *Economic History Review* 15 (3): 451–75.

Bejan, Teresa M. 2010. "Teaching the *Leviathan:* Thomas Hobbes on Education." *Oxford Review of Education* 36 (5): 607–26.

Bejan, Teresa M. 2018. "First Impressions: Hobbes on Religion, Education, and the Metaphor of Imprinting." In *Hobbes on Politics and Religion*, edited by Laurens van Apeldoorn and Robin Douglass, 45–62. Oxford: Oxford University Press.

Bellet, Clemente. 2020. "The McMansion Effect: Top House Size and Positional Externalities in U.S. Suburbs." *SSRN*. https://papers.ssrn.com/sol3/papers.cfm?abstract _id=3378131.

Bentham, Jeremy. (1789) 2003. *The Principles of Morals and Legislation.* In *The Classical Utilitarians,* edited by John Troyer. Indianapolis: Hackett.

Bentham, Jeremy. 1824. *Book of Fallacies.* London: John & H. L. Hunt.

Bentham, Jeremy. 1825. *The Rationale of Reward.* London: John & H. L. Hunt.

Bergoglio, Jorge Mario [Pope Francis]. 2013. *The Joy of the Gospel* (Evangelii Gaudium). Washington, DC: United States Conference of Catholic Bishops.

Bergoglio, Jorge Mario [Pope Francis]. 2015. *Encyclical on Climate Change and Inequality: On Care for Our Common Hope.* Brooklyn: Melville House.

Bergsma, John Sietze. 2007. *The Jubilee from Leviticus to Qumran.* Leiden: Brill.

Berman, Elizabeth Popp. 2022. *Thinking like an Economist: How Efficiency Replaced Equality in U.S. Public Policy.* Princeton: Princeton University Press.

Bernadete, Seth. 2001. *Plato's "Laws": The Discovery of Being.* Chicago: University of Chicago Press.

Betz, Otto. 1999. *The Cambridge History of Judaism, Vol. 3: The Early Roman Period.* Edited by William Horbury, W. D. Davies, and John Sturdy. Cambridge: Cambridge University Press.

Bevan, David, and Patricia Werhane. 2015. "The Inexorable Sociality of Commerce: The Individual and Others in Adam Smith." *Journal of Business Ethics* 127: 327–35.

Blanchet, Thomas, Emmanuel Saez, and Gabriel Zucman. 2022. "Who Benefits from Income and Wealth Growth in the United States?" https://realtimeinequality.org.

Blau, Adrian. 2009. "Hobbes on Corruption." *History of Political Thought* 30 (4): 596–616.

Blau, Adrian. 2019. "Hobbes's Practical Politics: Political, Sociological, and Economistic Ways of Avoiding a State of Nature." *Hobbes Studies* 33 (2): 109–34.

Bobonich, Christopher. 2002. *Plato's Utopia Recast: His Later Ethics and Politics.* Oxford: Oxford University Press.

Bodin, Jean. (1576) 1955. *Six Books of the Commonwealth.* Edited by M. J. Tooley. Oxford: Basil Blackwell.

Booth, William James. 1993. *Households: On the Moral Architecture of the Economy.* Cambridge: Cambridge University Press.

Botting, Eileen Hunt. 2017. "Wollstonecraft, Hobbes, and the Rationality of Women's Anxiety." In *Disability and Political Theory,* edited by Barbara Arneil and Nancy J. Hirschmann, 123–43. Cambridge: Cambridge University Press.

Boucoyannis, Deborah. 2013. "The Equalizing Hand: Why Adam Smith Expected the Market to Produce Wealth without Steep Inequality." *Perspectives on Politics* 11 (4): 1051–70.

Boyd, Richard. 2004. *Uncivil Society: The Perils of Pluralism and the Making of Modern Liberalism.* Lanham, MD: Lexington Books.

Boyd, Richard. 2013. "Adam Smith on Civility and Civil Society." In *The Oxford Handbook of Adam Smith,* edited by Christopher J. Berry, Maria Pia Paganelli, and Craig Smith, 443–63. Oxford: Oxford University Press.

Bray, Michael. 2007. "Macpherson Restored? Hobbes and the Question of Social Origins." *History of Political Thought* 28 (2): 56–90.

Brett, Annabel A. 1997. *Liberty, Right, and Nature.* Cambridge: Cambridge University Press.

Brett, Annabel A. 2011. *Changes of State: Nature and the Limits of the City in Early Modern Natural Law.* Princeton: Princeton University Press.

Broad, Eli. 2019. "I'm in the 1 Percent. Please, Raise My Taxes." *New York Times*, June 25.

Broadberry, Stephen, Bruce M. S. Campbell, Alexander Klein, Mark Overton, and Bas van Leeuwen. 2015. *British Economic Growth, 1270–1870*. Cambridge: Cambridge University Press.

Brooke, Christopher. 2012. *Philosophic Pride: Stoicism and Political Thought from Lipsius to Rousseau*. Princeton: Princeton University Press.

Brooke, Christopher. 2017. Introduction to *Leviathan*, by Thomas Hobbes, ix–xxxvi. London: Penguin Books.

Brooke, Christopher. 2020. "Nonintrinsic Egalitarianism, from Hobbes to Rousseau." *Journal of Politics* 82 (4): 1406–17.

Brooks, David. 2013. "Who Would Plutarch Write about Today?" Speech at Yale University's Jackson Institute for Global Affairs, February 26.

Brooks, David. 2014. "The Inequality Problem." *New York Times*, January 16.

Brown, Peter. 2012. *Through the Eye of a Needle: Wealth, the Fall of Rome, and the Making of Christianity in the West, 350–550 AD*. Princeton: Princeton University Press.

Brownlee, W. H. 1955. "John the Baptist in the New Light of Ancient Scrolls." *Interpretation: A Journal of Bible and Theology* 9 (1): 71–90.

Bruno, Christopher R. 2010. "'Jesus Is our Jubilee' . . . But How? The Background and Lukan Fulfillment of the Ethics of Jubilee." *Journal of the Evangelical Theological Society* 53 (1): 81–101.

Brunt, Peter A. 1977. "Josephus on Social Conflicts in Roman Judaea." *Kilo: Beiträge zur alten Geschichte* 59 (1–2): 149–52.

Caesar, Philipp. 1578. *General Discourse against the Damnable Sect of Usurers*. London: Iohn Kyngston for Andrevv Maunsell in Paules Church-yard at the signe of the Parret.

Canon, Jason S. 2022. "Three General Wills in Rousseau." *Review of Politics* 84 (3): 350–71.

Capaldi, Thomas. 2004. *John Stuart Mill: A Biography*. Cambridge: Cambridge University Press.

Carney, Thomas F. 1975. *The Shape of the Past: Models and Antiquity*. Lawrence: University of Kansas Press.

Carver, Terrell. 2018. *Marx*. Cambridge: Polity.

Chang, Arturo, and David Lay Williams. 2024. "Rousseau and Tlaxcala: Indigenous Transfigurations, Republican Liberty, and the Trans-Imperial Politics of the New World." *Polity*, forthcoming.

Cicero. 1999. *Letters to Atticus*. Translated by D. R. Shackleton Bailey. Cambridge, MA: Harvard University Press.

Claeys, Gregory. 1987. "Justice, Independence, and Industrial Democracy: The Development of John Stuart Mill's Thoughts on Socialism." *Journal of Politics* 41 (1): 122–47.

Claeys, Gregory. 2013. *Mill and Paternalism*. Cambridge: Cambridge University Press.

Coggins, Richard J. 1987. "The Old Testament and the Poor." *Expository Times* 99 (1): 11–14.

Cohen, G. A. 2000. *If You're an Egalitarian, How Come You're So Rich?* Cambridge, MA: Harvard University Press.

Cohen, Patricia. 2019. "A Message from the Billionaire's Club: Tax Us." *New York Times*, June 24.

Cohen, Shaye. 1979. *Josephus in Galilee and Rome: His Vita and Development as a Historian*. Leiden: Brill.

Cohen, Shaye. 1988. "Roman Domination. The Jewish Revolt and the Destruction of the Second Temple." In *Ancient Israel: A Short Introduction from Abraham to the Roman Destruction of the Temple*, edited by Hershel Shanks, 205–35. Washington, DC: Biblical Archeological Society.

Collins, Jeffrey R. 2005. *The Allegiance of Thomas Hobbes*. Oxford: Oxford University Press.

Conard, Edward. 2016. *The Upside of Inequality: How Good Intentions Undermine the Middle Class*. New York: Penguin.

Confucius. 1979. *The Analects*. Translated by D. C. Lau. London: Penguin.

Conwell, Russell H. 1915. *Acres of Diamonds*. New York: Harper.

Cooke, Paul D. 1996. *Hobbes and Christianity: Reassessing the Bible in Leviathan*. Lanham, MD: Rowman & Littlefield.

Cooper, Laurence D. 1999. *Rousseau, Nature, and the Problem of the Good Life*. University Park: Pennsylvania State University Press.

Cornwall, Julius. 1977. *Revolt of the Peasantry, 1549*. London: Routledge.

Cowen, Tyler. 2010. "Books which Have Influenced Me Most." *Marginal Revolution: Small Steps to a Much Better World* (blog), March 16. https://marginalrevolution .com/marginalrevolution/2010/03/books-which-have-influenced-me-most.html.

Cowen, Tyler. 2011. "Keeping Envy Local in Income Disparity." *New York Times*, April 18.

Cowen, Tyler. 2019. "Thursday Assorted Links." *Marginal Revolution: Small Steps toward a Much Better World* (blog), March 28. https://marginalrevolution.com /marginalrevolution/2019/03/thursday-assorted-links-200.html.

Cowen, Tyler. 2022. "Fight Poverty, Not Income Inequality." *Washington Post*, November 2022.

Cranston, Maurice. 1984. "Rousseau on Equality." *Social Philosophy & Policy* 2 (1): 115–24.

Crossan, John Dominic. 1991. *The Historical Jesus: The Life of a Mediterranean Jewish Peasant*. New York: Harper Collins.

Crossman, R.H.S. 1959. *Plato Today*. Oxford: Oxford University Press.

Daly, Eoin. 2017. *Rousseau's Constitutionalism: Austerity and Republican Freedom*. London: Bloomsbury.

Dauber, Noah. 2016. *State and Commonwealth: The Theory of the State in Early Modern England, 1559–1640*. Princeton: Princeton University Press.

Davids, P. H. 1982. *The Epistle of James*. Exeter: Paternoster.

Deaton, Angus. 2023a. *Economics in America: An Immigrant Economist Explores the Land of Inequality*. Princeton: Princeton University Press.

Deaton, Angus. 2023b. "Exploring American Inequality." *Pitchfork Economics* (podcast), November 24.

DeCelles, Katherine A., and Michael I. Norton. 2016. "Physical and Situational Inequality on Airplanes Predicts Air Rage." *Psychological and Cognitive Sciences* 113 (20): 5588–91.

Deneen, Patrick J. 2018. *Why Liberalism Failed*. New Haven: Yale University Press.

Derrett, J. Duncan M. 1961. "Fresh Light on St Luke xvi: Dives and Lazarus and the Proceding Sayings." *New Testament Studies* 7: 364–80.

Destri, Chiara. 2016. "Rousseau's (Not-So) Oligarchic Republicanism: Reflections on McCormick's *Rousseau's Rome and the Repudiation of Populist Republicanism.*" *Critical Review of International and Political Philosophy* 19 (2): 206–16.

Dingle, A. E. 1972. "Drink and Working-Class Living Standards in Britain, 1870–1914." *Economic History Review* 25 (4): 608–22.

Dolan, Kerry A., and Chase Petterson-Withorn. 2022. "World's Billionaire List: The Richest in 2022." *Forbes.* https://www.forbes.com/billionaires.

Dollar, David, and Aart Kraay. 2002. "Growth Is Good for the Poor." *Journal of Economic Growth* 7 (3): 195–225.

Douglass, Frederick. (1856) 2020. "The Accumulation of Wealth." In *The Jacobin,* edited by Matt Karp. https://jacobinmag.com/2020/02/frederick-douglass -accumulation-wealth-land-reformer.

Drake, Lyndon. 2014. "Did Jesus Oppose the *Prosbul* in the Forgiveness Provision of the Lord's Prayer?" *Novum Testamentum* 56 (3): 233–44.

Eagleton, Terry. 2011. *Why Marx Was Right.* New Haven: Yale University Press.

Ehrman, Bart D. 2018. *The Triumph of Christianity: How a Forbidden Religion Swept the World.* New York: Simon & Schuster.

Engels, Friedrich. (1845) 1958. *The Condition of the Working Class in England.* Translated by W. O. Henderson and W. H. Chaloner. Stanford: Stanford University Press.

Engels, Friedrich. (1878–94) 1954. *Anti-Dühring: Herr Eugen Dühring's Revolution in Science.* Moscow: Foreign Languages Publishing House.

Engels, Friedrich. (1891) 1978. Introduction to *The Civil War in France* in *The Marx-Engels Reader,* 2nd ed., edited by Robert C. Tucker, 618–29. New York: Norton.

Farr, James, and David Lay Williams. 2015. *The General Will: The Evolution of a Concept.* Cambridge: Cambridge University Press.

Ferguson, Adam. (1766) 1996. *An Essay on the History of Civil Society.* Edited by Fania Oz-Salzberger. Cambridge: Cambridge University Press.

Ferrari, G.R.F. 2005. *City and Soul in Plato's "Republic."* Chicago: University of Chicago Press.

Fleischacker, Samuel. 2004a. *A Short History of Distributive Justice.* Cambridge, MA: Harvard University Press.

Fleischacker, Samuel. 2004b. *On Adam Smith's "Wealth of Nations": A Philosophical Companion.* Princeton: Princeton University Press.

Fleischacker, Samuel. 2013. "Adam Smith on Equality." In *The Oxford Handbook of Adam Smith,* edited by Christopher J. Berry, Maria Pia Paganelli, and Craig Smith, 485–500. Oxford: Oxford University Press.

Fleischacker, Samuel. 2019. *Being Me, Being You: Adam Smith & Empathy.* Chicago: University of Chicago Press.

Fleischacker, Samuel. 2023. "Talking to My Butcher: Self-Interest, Exchange, and Freedom in the *Wealth of Nations.*" In *Interpreting Adam Smith: Critical Essays,* edited by Paul Sagar, 62–76. Cambridge: Cambridge University Press.

Forman-Barzilai, Fonna. 2005. "Sympathy in Space(s): Adam Smith on Proximity." *Political Theory* 33 (2): 189–217.

Frame, Edward, and Michelle Schwarze. 2023. "Adam Smith on Education as a Means to Political Judgment." *Political Research Quarterly* 76 (3): 1224–34.

Frank, Jill. 2018. *Poetic Justice: Re-reading Plato's "Republic."* Chicago: University of Chicago Press.

Frankfurt, Harry. 2015. *Inequality*. Princeton: Princeton University Press.

Freeland, Chrystia. 2012. *Plutocrats: The Rise of the New Global Super-rich and the Fall of Everyone Else*. New York: Penguin.

Freud, Sigmund. (1927) 1961. *The Future of an Illusion*. Translated by James Strachey. New York: Norton.

Freud, Sigmund. (1930) 2010. *Civilization and Its Discontents*. Translated by James Strachey. New York: Norton.

Friedman, Benjamin M. 2021. *Religion and the Rise of Capitalism*. New York: Vintage Books.

Friedman, Milton. 1962. *Capitalism and Freedom*. Chicago: University of Chicago Press.

Galbraith, James K. 2016. *Inequality: What Everyone Needs to Know*. Oxford: Oxford University Press.

Gandhi, Mahatma. (1909) 1996. *Swaraj*. In *Selected Political Writings*, edited by Dennis Dalton. Indianapolis: Hackett.

Gates, Bill. 2018. "My New Favorite Book of All Time." *Gates Notes: The Blog of Bill Gates*, January 26. https://www.gatesnotes.com/Enlightenment-Now.

Gilens, Martin. 2012. *Affluence and Influence: Economic Inequality and Political Power in America*. Princeton: Princeton University Press.

Gilens, Martin, and Benjamin I. Page. 2014. "Testing Theories of American Politics: Elites, Interest Groups, and Average Citizens." *Perspectives on Politics* 12 (3): 563–81.

Goldman, John J. 1992. "Leona Helmsley Sentenced to 4 Years in Prison: Taxes: The Hotel Queen Must Surrender on April 15. Her Plea to Remain Free to Care for Her Ailing Husband Is Rejected." *Los Angeles Times*, March 19.

Goodman, Martin. 1987. *The Ruling Class of Judaea: The Origins of the Jewish Revolt against Rome, A.D. 66–70*. Cambridge: Cambridge University Press.

Goodman, Martin. (1997) 2013. *The Roman World 44 BC–AD 180*, 2nd ed. London: Routledge.

Gordon, Jane Anna. 2014. *Creolizing Rousseau: Reading Rousseau through Fanon*. New York: Fordham University Press.

Gordon, Jane Anna. 2015. "Comparative Political Theory, Creolization, and Reading Rousseau through Fanon." In *Creolizing Rousseau*, edited by Jane Anna Gordon and Neil Roberts, 19–60. London: Rowman & Littlefield.

Gottlieb, Paul. 2018. "Aristotle on Inequality of Wealth." In *Democracy, Justice, and Equality in Ancient Greece: Historical and Philosophical Perspectives*, edited by Georgios Anagnostopoulos and Gerasimos Santas, 257–68. Cham: Springer.

Garnsey, Peter. 2007. *Thinking about Property: From Antiquity to the Age of Revolution*. Cambridge: Cambridge University Press.

Giridharadas, Anand. 2018. *Winners Take All: The Elite Charge of Changing the World*. New York: Knopf.

Gramm, Phil, Robert Eklelund, and John Early. 2022. *The Myth of American Inequality: How Government Biases Policy Debate*. Lanham, MD: Rowman & Littlefield.

Grassby, Richard. 1970. "English Merchant Capitalism in the Late Seventeenth Century: The Composition of Business Fortunes." *Past and Present* 46 (February): 87–107.

Green, Jeffrey Edward. 2015. "Liberalism and the Problem of Plutocracy." *Constellations* 23 (2): 84–95.

Griswold, Charles. 1999. *Adam Smith and the Virtues of the Enlightenment*. Cambridge: Cambridge University Press.

Griswold, Charles. 2018. *Jean-Jacques Rousseau and Adam Smith: A Philosophical Encounter*. London: Routledge.

Haakonssen, Knud. 1981. *The Science of a Legislator*. Cambridge: Cambridge University Press.

Habermas, Jürgen. 2007. "Pre-political Foundations of the Democratic Constitutional State." In *The Dialectics of Secularization: On Reason and Religion*, 21–52. San Francisco: Ignatius Press.

Habermas, Jürgen. 2010. *An Awareness of What Is Missing: Faith and Reason in a Post-secular Age*. Cambridge: Polity Press.

Hacker, Jacob S., and Paul Pierson. 2010. *Winner-Take-All Politics: How Washington Made the Rich Richer and Turned Its Back on the Middle Class*. New York: Simon & Schuster.

Hamel, Gildas. 2010. "Poverty and Charity." In *Jewish Daily Life in Roman Palestine*, edited by Catherine Hezsner, 308–25. Oxford: Oxford University Press.

Hanley, Ryan Patrick. 2009a. *Adam Smith and the Character of Virtue*. Cambridge: Cambridge University Press.

Hanley, Ryan Patrick. 2009b. "Textual Notes." In *Theory of Moral Sentiments*, edited by Ryan Patrick Hanley. New York: Penguin.

Hanley, Ryan Patrick. 2019. *Our Great Purpose: Adam Smith on Living a Better Life*. Princeton: Princeton University Press.

Harrill, J. Albert. 2012. *Paul the Apostle: His Life and Legacy in their Roman Context*. Cambridge: Cambridge University Press.

Harrington, James. (1656) 1992. *The Commonwealth of Oceana*. Edited by J.G.A. Pocock. Cambridge: Cambridge University Press.

Harris, James A. 2020. "The Protection of the Rich against the Poor: The Politics of Adam Smith's Political Economy." *Social Philosophy & Policy* 37 (1): 138–58.

Harris, Johnny, and Binyamin Appelbaum. 2021. "Blue States, You're the Problem." *New York Times*, November 9.

Harrison, Frederic. 1896. "John Stuart Mill." *The Nineteenth Century* (September): 487–508.

Harrison, Ross. 2003. *Hobbes, Locke, and Confusion's Masterpiece: An Examination of Seventeenth-Century Political Philosophy*. Cambridge: Cambridge University Press.

Hasamyi, Ziyad I. 1980. "Marx on Distributive Justice." In *Marx, Justice, and History*, edited by Marshall Cohen, Thomas Nagel, and Thomas Scanlon, 27–64. Princeton: Princeton University Press.

Hayek, Friedrich A. (1944) 1972. *The Road to Serfdom*. Chicago: University of Chicago Press.

Heinrich, Michael. 2012. *An Introduction to the Three Volumes of Karl Marx's "Capital."* Translated by Alexander Locasio. New York: Monthly Review Press.

Heinrich, Michael. 2019. *Karl Marx and the Birth of Modern Society: The Life of Marx and the Development of His Work, Volume 1: 1818–1841*. Translated by Alexander Locasio. New York: Monthly Review Press.

Hill, Christopher. (1961) 1980. *A Century of Revolution, 1603–1714*. New York: Norton.

Hill, Christopher. (1967) 1969. *The Pelican Economic History of Britain, Vol. 2, 1530–1780: Reformation to Industrial Revolution*. London: Penguin.

Hill, John E. 2016. *Adam Smith's Equality and the Pursuit of Happiness*. London: Palgrave Macmillan.

Himmelfarb, Gertrude. 1985. *The Idea of Poverty: England in the Early Industrial Age*. New York: Vintage Books.

Hobbes, Thomas. (1620) 1995. "Discourse upon the Beginning of Tacitus." In *Three Discourses: A Critical Modern Edition of Newly Identified Works of the Young Hobbes*, edited by Noel B. Reynolds and Arlene Saxonhouse, 31–67. Chicago: University of Chicago Press.

Hobbes, Thomas. (1637) 1839. *The Whole Art of Rhetoric*. In *The English Works of Thomas Hobbes of Malmesbury*, vol. 6. London: John Bohn.

Hobbes, Thomas. (1640) 1994. *Elements of Law: Human Nature and De Corpore Politico*. Edited by J.C.A. Gaskin. Oxford: Oxford University Press.

Hobbes, Thomas. (1642) 1998. *On the Citizen*. Edited by Richard Tuck and Michael Silverthorne. Cambridge: Cambridge University Press.

Hobbes, Thomas. (1651) 2011. *Leviathan, or the Matter, Form, and Power of a Commonwealth Ecclesiastical and Civil*. Rev. ed. Edited by A. P. Martinich and Brian Battiste. Peterborough, ON: Broadview Press.

Hobbes, Thomas. (1658) 1991. *On Man*. In *Man and Citizen (De Homine and De Cive)*. Edited by Bernard Gert. Indianapolis: Hackett.

Hobbes, Thomas. (1688) 1990. *Behemoth, or the Long Parliament*. Edited by Ferdinand Tönnies. Chicago: University of Chicago Press.

Hobsbawm, E. J. 1952. "The Machine Breakers." *Past & Present* 1 (1): 57–70.

Hobsbawm, E. J. 1968. *Industry and Empire: From 1750 to the Present Day*. London: Penguin.

Hobsbawm, E. J. (1969) 1981. *Bandits*. Rev. ed. New York: Pantheon.

Hoekstra, Kinch. 2005. "The End of Philosophy (The Case of Hobbes)." *Proceedings of the Aristotelean Society* 106: 25–62.

Hoekstra, Kinch. 2006. "A Lion in the House: Hobbes and Democracy." In *Rethinking the Foundations of Modern Thought*, edited by Annabel Brett and James Tully with Holly Hamilton-Bleakley. Cambridge: Cambridge University Press.

Hoekstra, Kinch. 2012. "Hobbesian Equality." In *Hobbes Today*, edited by S. A. Lloyd, 76–112. Cambridge: Cambridge University Press.

Hoffman, Philip T., David S. Jacks, Patricia A. Levin, and Peter H. Lindert. 2002. "Real Inequality in Europe since 1500." *Journal of Economic History* 62 (2): 322–55.

Holcombe, Richard G. 2000. "The Death Tax Is Fair?" Foundation for Economic Education, October 1. https://fee.org/articles/the-death-tax-is-fair/.

Holmes, Stephen. 1990. Introduction to *Behemoth*, by Thomas Hobbes, vii–l. Chicago: University of Chicago Press.

Hont, Istvan. 2005. *Jealousy of Trade: International Competition and the Nation-State in Historical Perspective*. Cambridge, MA: Belknap.

Hont, Istvan. 2015. *Politics in Commercial Society: Jean-Jacques Rousseau and Adam Smith*. Cambridge, MA: Harvard University Press.

Horsley, Richard A. (1985) 1999. *Bandits, Prophets, and Messiahs: Popular Movements in the Times of Jesus*. Harrisburg, PA: Trinity Press.

Horsley, Richard A. 1986. "High Priests and the Politics of Roman Palestine." *Journal for the Study of Judaism* 17 (1): 23–55.

Horsley, Richard A. 1995. *Galilee: History, Politics, People.* Valley Forge, PA: Trinity Press International.

Horsley, Richard A. 2009. *Covenant Economics: A Biblical Vision of Justice for All.* Louisville: Westminster John Knox Press.

Hudson, Michael. 2018. *And Forgive Them Their Debts: Lending, Foreclosure, and the Redemption from Bronze Age Finance to the Jubilee Year.* Dresden: Islet-Verlag.

Hume, David. (1741–42) 1994. "Of Parties in General." In *David Hume: Political Essays*, edited by Knud Haakonssen, 33–39. Cambridge: Cambridge University Press.

Hume, David. (1748) 1994. "Of the Original Contract." In *David Hume: Political Essays*, edited by Knud Haakonssen, 186–201. Cambridge: Cambridge University Press.

Hume, David. (1752) 1994. "Of Commerce." In *David Hume: Political Essays*, edited by Knud Haakonssen, 93–104. Cambridge: Cambridge University Press.

Hume, David. (1758) 1994. *Political Essays.* Edited by Knud Haakonssen. Cambridge: Cambridge University Press.

Hunt, Joshua. 2022. "How I Became a Pathological Liar." *New York Times*, July 13.

Ikuta, Jennie. 2020. *Contesting Conformity: Democracy and the Paradox of Belonging.* Oxford: Oxford University Press.

Jefferson, Thomas. (1785) 2006. "Letter to James Madison, October 28, 1785." In *The Essential Jefferson*, edited by Jean M. Yarbrough, 395–98. Indianapolis: Hackett.

Jensen, Hans E. 2001. "John Stuart Mill's Theories of Wealth and Income Distribution." *Review of Social Economy* 59 (4): 491–507.

Johnston, Steven. 2007. *The Truth about Patriotism.* Durham, NC: Duke University Press.

Josephson, Peter B. 2016. "Hobbes, Locke, and the Problems of Political Economy." In *Economic Freedom and Human Flourishing: Perspectives from Political Philosophy*, edited by Michael R. Strain and Stan A. Veuger, 9–29. Washington, DC: American Enterprise Institute.

Josephus, Flavius. 1965. *Jewish Antiquities*, vols. 1–13. Translated by Louis H. Feldman. Cambridge, MA: Harvard University Press.

Josephus, Flavius. 1981. *The Jewish War.* Translated by G. A. Williamson. London: Penguin.

Judge, E. A. 1960. *The Social Pattern of Christian Groups in the First Century: Some Prolegomena to the Study of New Testament Ideas of Social Obligation.* London: Tynedale.

Kant, Immanuel. (1781/87) 1929. *Critique of Pure Reason.* Translated by Norman Kemp Smith. New York: St. Martin's.

Kant, Immanuel. (1793) 1996. "On the Common Saying: That May Be True in Theory, but It Is of No Use in Practice." In *Practical Philosophy*, edited by Mary J. Gregor, 273–310. Cambridge: Cambridge University Press.

Kapust, Daniel J., and Brandon P. Turner. 2013. "Democratical Gentlemen and the Lust for Mastery: Status, Ambition, and the Language of Liberty in Hobbes's Political Thought." *Political Theory* 41 (4): 648–75.

Kateb, George. 2008. *Patriotism and Other Mistakes.* New Haven: Yale University Press.

Kavka, Gregory S. 1986. *Hobbesian Moral and Political Theory*. Princeton: Princeton University Press.

Keltner, Dacher. 2016. *The Power Paradox: How We Gain and Lose Influence*. New York: Penguin.

Kennedy, Adam. 2013. "Adam Smith on Religion." In *The Oxford Handbook of Adam Smith*, edited by Christopher J. Berry, Maria Pia Paganelli, and Craig Smith, 464–84. Oxford: Oxford University Press.

Keum, Tae-Yeoum. 2020. *Plato and the Mythic Tradition in Political Thought*. Cambridge, MA: Belknap.

Kitto, H.D.F. 1951. *The Greeks*. London: Penguin.

Kirkland, Sean. 2012. *The Ontology of Socratic Questioning in Plato's Early Dialogues*. Albany: Status University of New York Press.

Klausen, Jimmy Casas. 2014. *Fugitive Rousseau: Slavery, Primitivism, and Political Freedom*. New York: Fordham University Press.

Konstan, David. 2018. *In the Orbit of Love: Affection in Ancient Greece and Rome*. Oxford: Oxford University Press.

Korb, Scott. 2010. *Life in Year One: What the World Was Like in First-Century Palestine*. New York: Riverhead Books.

Kramm, Mattias, and Ingrid Robeyns. 2020. "Limits to Wealth in the History of Western Philosophy." *European Journal of Philosophy* 28 (4): 954–69.

Krohn, Marvin D. 1976. "Inequality, Unemployment, and Crime: A Cross-National Analysis." *Sociological Quarterly* 17 (4): 303–13.

Kuznets, Simon. 1955. "Economic Growth and Income Inequality." *American Economic Review* 45 (1): 1–18.

Labiano, Jesus M. Zaratiegui. 2000. "A Reading of Hobbes' *Leviathan* with Economists' Glasses." *International Journal of Social Economics* 27 (2): 134–46.

Laertius, Diogenes. 1972. *Lives of the Eminent Philosophers*. Translated by R. D. Hicks. Cambridge, MA: Harvard University Press.

Lange, Linda. 2002. *Feminist Interpretations of Jean-Jacques Rousseau*. University Park: Pennsylvania State University Press.

Lao Tzu. 1963. *Tao Te Ching*. Translated by D. C. Lau. London: Penguin.

Lear, Jonathan. 2006. "Allegory and Myth in Plato's *Republic*." In *The Blackwell Guide to Plato's "Republic,"* edited by Gerasimos Santas, 25–43. Oxford: Blackwell.

Leijenhorst, Cornelis Hendrik. 2001. *The Mechanisation of Aristotelianism: The Late Aristotelian Setting of Thomas Hobbes' Natural Philosophy*. Leiden: Brill.

Lemoine, Rebecca. 2020. *Plato's Caves: The Liberating Sting of Cultural Diversity*. Oxford: Oxford University Press.

Letwin, William. 1972. "The Economic Foundations of Hobbes's Politics." In *Hobbes and Rousseau: A Collection of Critical Essays*, edited by Maurice Cranston and Richard S. Peters, 143–65. Garden City, NY: Anchor Books.

Levin, Michael. 1982. "A Hobbesian Minimal State." *Philosophy & Public Affairs* 11 (4): 338–53.

Levine, Amy-Jill. 2021. "Preaching and Teaching the Pharisees." In *The Pharisees*, edited by Joseph Sievers and Amy-Jill Levine, 403–27. Grand Rapids: Eerdmans.

Levine, Amy-Jill, and Marc Z. Brettler. 2017. *The Jewish Annotated New Testament: New Revised Standard Version*. Oxford: Oxford University Press.

Levine, Andrew. 1993. *The General Will: Rousseau, Marx, Communism*. Cambridge: Cambridge University Press.

Levy, Aaron. 1954. "Economic Views of Thomas Hobbes." *Journal of the History of Ideas* 15 (4): 589–95.

Levy, David M., and Sandra J. Peart. 2013. "Adam Smith and the State: Language and Reform." In *The Oxford Handbook of Adam Smith*, edited by Christopher J. Berry, Maria Pia Paganelli, and Craig Smith, 372–92. Oxford: Oxford University Press.

Levy, Michael B. 1981. "Mill's Stationary State and the Transcendence of Liberalism." *Polity* 14 (2): 273–93.

Lindblom, Charles. 1977. *Politics and Markets: The World's Political Economic Systems*. New York: Basic Books.

Lindert, Peter H. 2000. "When Did Inequality Rise in Britain and America?" *Journal of Income Distribution* 9: 11–27.

Lindgren, J. R. 1973. *The Social Philosophy of Adam Smith*. The Hague: Nijhoff.

Liu, Glory M. 2022. *Adam Smith's America: How a Scottish Philosopher Became an Icon of American Capitalism*. Princeton: Princeton University Press.

Locke, John. (1690) 1988. *Two Treatises on Government*. Edited by Peter Laslett. Cambridge: Cambridge University Press.

Locke, John. (1697) 1997. "An Essay on the Poor Law." In *Political Essays*, edited Mark Goldie, 182–99. Cambridge: Cambridge University Press.

Lomonaco, Jeffrey. 2002. "Adam Smith's 'Letter to the Authors of the *Edinburgh Review*.'" *Journal of the History of Ideas* 63 (4): 659–76.

Lovejoy, Arthur O. 1961. *Reflections on Human Nature*. Baltimore: Johns Hopkins University Press.

Lovett, Frank. 2022. *The Well-Ordered Republic*. Oxford: Oxford University Press.

Machiavelli, Niccolò. (1531) 1998. *Discourses on Livy*. Translated by Harvey C. Mansfield and Nathan Tarcov. Chicago: University of Chicago Press.

Macpherson, C. B. 1945. "Hobbes Today." *Canadian Journal of Economics and Political Science* 11 (4): 524–34.

Macpherson, C. B. 1962. *The Political Theory of Possessive Individualism: Hobbes to Locke*. Oxford: Oxford University Press.

Macpherson, C. B. 1982. Introduction to *Leviathan*, by Thomas Hobbes, 9–63. New York: Penguin.

Macpherson, C. B. 1987. "Thomas Hobbes." In *The New Palgrave Dictionary of Economics*, edited by John Eatwell, Baron Eatwell, Murray Milgate, and Peter Kenneth Newman, 2:663–64. London: Macmillan.

Madison, James. (1787–89) 2003. *The Federalist with the Letters of Brutus*. Edited by Terence Ball. Cambridge: Cambridge University Press.

Maguire, Matthew W. 2006. *The Conversion of the Imagination: From Pascal to Rousseau to Tocqueville*. Cambridge, MA: Harvard University Press.

Mandell, Daniel R. 2020. *The Lost Tradition of Economic Equality in America, 1600–1870*. Baltimore: Johns Hopkins University Press.

Mandeville, Bernard. (1723) 1997. *The Fable of the Bees and Other Writings*. Edited by E. J. Hundert. Indianapolis: Hackett.

Markovits, Daniel A. 2019. *The Meritocracy Trap: How America's Foundational Myth Feeds Inequality, Dismantles the Middle Class, and Devours the Elite*. New York: Penguin.

Markovits, Elizabeth. 2008. *The Politics of Sincerity: Plato, Frank Speech, and Democratic Judgment*. University Park: Pennsylvania State University Press.

Martinich, A. P. 1999. *Hobbes: A Biography*. Cambridge: Cambridge University Press.

Marx, Karl. (1843) 1994. *On the Jewish Question*. In *Selected Writings*, edited by Lawrence H. Simon. Indianapolis: Hackett.

Marx, Karl. (1844) 1994. *Economic and Philosophic Manuscripts*. Edited by Lawrence H. Simon. Indianapolis: Hackett.

Marx, Karl. (1847) 1910. *The Poverty of Philosophy*. Translated by H. Quelch. Chicago: Charles H. Kerr.

Marx, Karl. (1849) 1977. *Wage Labour and Capital*. In *Collected Works of Karl Marx and Friedrich Engels*, vol. 9. New York: International Publishers.

Marx, Karl. (1853a) 2007a. "Chartism." In *Dispatches from the* New York Tribune*: Selected Journalism of Karl Marx*, edited by James Ledbetter, 129–38. London: Penguin.

Marx, Karl. (1853b) 2007b. "The Labor Question." In *Dispatches from the* New York Tribune*: Selected Journalism of Karl Marx*, edited by James Ledbetter, 163–66. London: Penguin.

Marx, Karl. (1857) 2007. "Condition of Factory Laborers." In *Dispatches from the* New York Tribune*: Selected Journalism of Karl Marx*, edited by James Ledbetter, 189–97. London: Penguin.

Marx, Karl. (1858) 2007. "The Increase of Lunacy in Great Britain." In *Dispatches from the* New York Tribune*: Selected Journalism of Karl Marx*, edited by James Ledbetter, 151–60. London: Penguin.

Marx, Karl. (1857–58) 1973. *Grundrisse: Foundations of the Critique of Political Economy*. Translated by Martin Nicolaus. London: Penguin.

Marx, Karl. (1867) 1976. *Capital: A Critique of Political Economy*, vol. 1. Translated by Ben Fowkes. London: Penguin.

Marx, Karl. (1871) 1978. *The Civil War in France*. In *The Marx-Engels Reader*, 2nd ed., edited by Robert C. Tucker. New York: Norton.

Marx, Karl. (1872) 1978. "The Possibility of Non-violent Revolution." In *The Marx-Engels Reader*, 2nd ed., edited by Robert C. Tucker, 522–24. New York: Norton.

Marx, Karl. (1875) 1994. "Critique of the Gotha Program." In *Selected Writings*, edited by Lawrence H. Simon. Indianapolis: Hackett.

Marx, Karl. (1894) 1981. *Capital*, vol. 3. Translated by David Fernbach. London: Penguin.

Marx, Karl, with Friedrich Engels. (1845) 1998. *The German Ideology*. Amherst, NY: Prometheus Books.

Marx, Karl, and Friedrich Engels. (1848) 1994. *The Communist Manifesto*. In *Selected Writings*, ed. Lawrence H. Simon, 157–86. Indianapolis: Hackett.

Mason, Pamela A. 1993. "The Genevan Background to Rousseau's *Social Contract*." *History of Political Thought* 14 (4): 547–72.

Masters, Roger D. 1968. *The Political Philosophy of Rousseau*. Princeton: Princeton University Press.

Matthews, Mark C. 2015. *Riches, Poverty, and the Faithful: Perspectives on Wealth in the Second Temple Period and the Apocalypse of John*. Cambridge: Cambridge University Press.

May, Larry. 1987. "Hobbes on Equity and Justice." In Hobbes's "Science of Natural Justice," edited by C. Walton and P. J. Johnson, 241–52. Dordrecht: Nijhoff.

Mayhew, Henry. (1850–62) 2020. London Labour and the London Poor: Selections. Edited by Janice Schoeder and Barbara Leckie. Peterborough, ON: Broadview Press.

McCabe, Helen. 2021. John Stuart Mill, Socialist. Montreal: McGill-Queen's University Press.

McCloskey, Deirdre Nansen. 2014. "Equality Lacks Relevance if the Poor Are Growing Richer." Financial Times, August 11.

McCloskey, Deirdre Nansen. 2016. Bourgeois Equality: How Ideas, Not Capital or Institutions, Enriched the World. Chicago: University of Chicago Press.

McCloskey, Deirdre Nansen. 2017. "Notes towards an Essay on Illiberalism in Economics." Handout for the Session, "On Ignorance in Economics," Chicago, January 6.

McCloskey, Deirdre Nansen. 2018. "The Two Movements in Economic Thought, 1700–2000: Empty Economic Boxes Revisited." History of Economic Ideas 26 (1): 63–96.

McCloskey, Deirdre Nansen. 2019. Why Liberalism Works: How True Liberal Values Produce a Freer, More Equal, Prosperous World for All. New Haven: Yale University Press.

McCloskey, Deirdre Nansen. 2020. "The Great Enrichment." Discourse, July 13. https://www.discoursemagazine.com/p/the-great-enrichment.

McCloskey, Deirdre N., and Art Carden. 2020. Leave Me Alone and I'll Make You Rich: How the Bourgeois Deal Enriched the World. Chicago: University of Chicago Press.

McCormick, John. P. 2007. "Rousseau's Rome and the Repudiation of Populist Republicanism." Critical Review of International and Political Philosophy 10 (1): 3–27.

McCormick, John. P. 2016. "Response to Destri." Critical Review of International and Political Philosophy 19 (2): 217–30.

McCormick, John P. 2018. Reading Machiavelli: Scandalous Books, Suspect Engagement, and the Virtue of Populist Politics. Princeton: Princeton University Press.

McLendon, Michael Locke. 2009. "Rousseau, Amour-Propre, and Intellectual Celebrity." Journal of Politics 71 (2): 506–19.

McLendon, Michael Locke. 2018. The Psychology of Inequality: Rousseau's Amour-Propre. Philadelphia: University of Pennsylvania Press.

McMahon, Darrin M. 2023. Equality: The History of an Elusive Idea. New York: Basic Books.

McWilliams, Wilson Carey. 1986. "On Equality as the Moral Foundation for Community." In The Moral Foundation of the American Republic, edited by Robert H. Horwitz, 183–213. Charlottesville: University of Virginia Press.

Meister, Chad, and J. B. Stump. 2010. Christian Thought: A Historical Introduction. London: Routledge.

Melzer, Arthur M. 1983. "Rousseau's Moral Realism: Replacing Natural Law with the General Will." American Political Science Review 77 (3): 633–51.

Mergy, Jennifer. 2009. "'The Politics of the Future': An Unknown Text by Émile Durkheim." Durkheimian Studies/Études Durkheimiennes 15: 7–14.

Milanovic, Branko. 2023. Visions of Inequality: From the French Revolution to the End of the Cold War. Cambridge, MA: Belknap.

Milanovic, Branko, Peter H. Lindert, and Jeffery G. Williamson. 2007. "Pre-industrial Inequality." Economic Journal 121 (551): 255–72.

Mill, John Stuart. (1823) 1986. "Blessings of Equal Justice." In *Newspaper Writings, Collected Works of John Stuart Mill*, vol. 22, edited by John M. Robson. Toronto: University of Toronto Press.

Mill, John Stuart. (1833) 2006. *Remarks on Bentham's Philosophy*. In *Collected Works of John Stuart Mill: Essays on Ethics, Religion, and Society*, vol. 10, edited by J. M. Robson. Indianapolis: Liberty Fund.

Mill, John Stuart. (1834) 1982. "Notes on the Newspapers." In *Essays on England, Ireland, and the Empire, Collected Works of John Stuart Mill*, edited by John M. Robson, 23: 149–280. Toronto: University of Toronto Press.

Mill, John Stuart. (1834) 1986. "French News." In *Newspaper Writings, Collected Works of John Stuart Mill*, edited by John M. Robson, 22: 670–74. Toronto: University of Toronto Press.

Mill, John Stuart. (1835a) 1977a. *M. de Tocqueville on Democracy in America*, I. In *Essays on Politics and Society, Collected Works of John Stuart Mill*, vol. 18, edited by John M. Robson. Toronto: University of Toronto Press.

Mill, John Stuart. (1835b) 1977b. *Rationale of Representation*. In *Essays on Politics and Society, Collected Works of John Stuart Mill*, vol. 18, edited by John M. Robson. Toronto: University of Toronto Press.

Mill, John Stuart. (1836) 1977. *State of Society in America*. In *Essays on Politics and Society, Collected Works of John Stuart Mill*, vol. 18, edited by John M. Robson. Toronto: University of Toronto Press.

Mill, John Stuart. (1838) 2006. *Bentham*. In *Collected Works of John Stuart Mill: Essays on Ethics, Religion, and Society*, vol. 10, edited by J. M. Robson. Indianapolis: Liberty Fund.

Mill, John Stuart. (1840) 1977. *M. de Tocqueville on Democracy in America*, II. In *Essays on Politics and Society, Collected Works of John Stuart Mill*, vol. 18, edited by John M. Robson. Toronto: University of Toronto Press.

Mill, John Stuart. (1840) 2006. *Coleridge*. In *Collected Works of John Stuart Mill: Essays on Ethics, Religion, and Society*, vol. 10, edited by J. M. Robson. Indianapolis: Liberty Fund.

Mill, John Stuart. (1845) 2006. "The Claims of Labour." In *The Collected Works of John Stuart Mill, Vol. 4: Essays on Economics and Society*, edited by J. M. Robson, 363–89. Indianapolis: Liberty Fund.

Mill, John Stuart. (1845–71) 2006. *Principles of Political Economy*. In *The Collected Works of John Stuart Mill*, vols. 2–3, edited by J. M. Robson. Indianapolis: Liberty Fund.

Mill, John Stuart. (1849) 1985. *Vindication of the French Revolution of February 1848, Essays on French History and Historians*. In *The Collected Works of John Stuart Mill*, vol. 20, edited by J. M. Robson. Toronto: University of Toronto Press.

Mill, John Stuart. (1849–71) 2006. *Principles of Political Economy*. In *The Collected Works of John Stuart Mill*, vols. 2–3, edited by J. M. Robson. Indianapolis: Liberty Fund.

Mill, John Stuart. (1851) 2006. "Newman's Political Economy." In *The Collected Works of John Stuart Mill, Vol. 5: Essays on Economics and Society*, edited by J. M. Robson, 439–57. Indianapolis: Liberty Fund.

Mill, John Stuart. (1852) 2006. "The Income and Property Tax." In *The Collected Works of John Stuart Mill, Vol. 5: Essays on Economics and Society*, edited by J. M. Robson, 463–98. Indianapolis: Liberty Fund.

Mill, John Stuart. (1859) 1989. *On Liberty*. In *On Liberty and Other Writings*, edited by Stefan Collini. Cambridge: Cambridge University Press.

Mill, John Stuart. (1861) 1991. *Considerations on Representative Government*. Buffalo: Prometheus Books.

Mill, John Stuart. (1861) 2001. *Utilitarianism*. 2nd ed. Edited by George Sher. Indianapolis: Hackett.

Mill, John Stuart. (1869) 1989. *The Subjection of Women*. In *On Liberty and Other Writings*, edited by Stefan Collini. Cambridge: Cambridge University Press.

Mill, John Stuart. (1869) 2006. "Thornton on Labour and Its Claims." In *The Collected Works of John Stuart Mill, Vol. 5: Essays on Economics and Society*, edited by J. M. Robson, 631–68. Indianapolis: Liberty Fund.

Mill, John Stuart. (1873) 1990. *Autobiography*. London: Penguin.

Mill, John Stuart. (1874a) 2006a. *Autobiography*. In *The Collected Works of John Stuart Mill, Vol. 1: Autobiography and Literary Essays*, edited by J. M. Robson. Indianapolis: Liberty Fund.

Mill, John Stuart. (1874b) 2006b. *Three Essays on Religion*. In *The Collected Works of John Stuart Mill, Vol. 10: Essays on Ethics, Religion, and Society*, edited by J. M. Robson. Indianapolis: Liberty Fund.

Mill, John Stuart. (1879) 1989. *Chapters on Socialism*. In *On Liberty and Other Writings*, edited by Stefan Collini. Cambridge: Cambridge University Press.

Miller, James. 1984. *Rousseau: Dreamer of Democracy*. New Haven: Yale University Press.

Miller, Richard W. 1984. *Analyzing Marx: Morality, Power, and History*. Princeton: Princeton University Press.

Mills, Charles. 1997. *The Racial Contract*. Ithaca: Cornell University Press.

Mishel, Lawrence, and Jori Kandra. 2021. "CEO Pay Has Skyrocketed 1,322% since 1978." *Economic Policy Institute*, August 21.

Monoson, S. Sara 2000. *Plato's Democratic Entanglements: Athenian Politics and the Practice of Philosophy*. Princeton: Princeton University Press.

Montesquieu, Baron de. (1748) 1989. *Spirit of the Laws*. Translated by Anne M. Cohler, Basia Carolyn Miller, and Harold Samuel Stone. Cambridge: Cambridge University Press.

More, Thomas. (1516) 1992. *Utopia*. 2nd ed. Translated by Robert M. Adams. New York: Norton.

Morrow, Glenn R. (1926) 1969. *The Ethical and Economic Theories of Adam Smith*. New York: A. M. Kelly.

Morrow, Glenn R. 1939. *Plato's Law of Slavery in Its Relation to Greek Law*. Urbana: University of Illinois Press.

Morrow, Glenn R. (1940) 1971. "Plato and the Rule of Law." In *Plato II: Ethics, Politics, and Philosophy of Art and Religion*, edited by Gregory Vlastos, 144–65. Garden City, NY: Anchor Books.

Morrow, Glenn R. (1960) 1993. *Plato's Cretan City: A Historical Interpretation of the "Laws."* Princeton: Princeton University Press.

Murphy, Catherine. 2002. *Wealth in the Dead Sea Scrolls and in the Qumran Community*. Leiden: Brill.

Muthu, Sankar. 2003. *Enlightenment against Empire*. Princeton: Princeton University Press.

Neidleman, Jason. 2001. *The General Will Is Citizenship: Inquiries into French Political Thought.* Lanham, MD: Rowman & Littlefield.

Nesbit, Edward Planta. 1895. *Christ, Christians, Christianity.* London: Simpkin, Marshall, Hamilton, Kent.

Neuhouser, Frederick. 2008. *Rousseau's Theodicy of Self-Love: Evil, Rationality, and the Drive for Recognition.* Oxford: Oxford University Press.

Neuhouser, Frederick. 2013. "Rousseau's Critique of Economic Inequality." *Philosophy and Public Affairs* 41 (3): 193–225.

Neuhouser, Frederick. 2014. *Rousseau's Critique of Inequality: Reconstructing the Second Discourse.* Cambridge: Cambridge University Press.

Nielsen, Kai. 1988. "On Marx Not Being an Egalitarian." *Studies in Soviet Thought* 35 (4): 287–326.

Nolan, Brian, Wiemer Salverda, and Timothy M. Smeeding. 2011. *The Oxford Handbook of Economic Inequality.* Oxford: Oxford University Press.

Nozick, Robert. 1974. *Anarchy, State, and Utopia.* New York: Basic Books.

Ober, Josiah. 1989. *Mass and Elite in Democratic Athens.* Princeton: Princeton University Press.

Ober, Josiah. 2015. *The Rise and Fall of Classical Greece.* Princeton: Princeton University Press.

O'Hagan, Timothy. 1999. *Rousseau.* London: Routledge.

Okin, Susan Moller. 1979. *Women in Western Political Thought.* Princeton: Princeton University Press.

Oprea, Alexandra. 2022. "Adam Smith on Political Judgment: Revisiting the Political Theory of the Wealth of Nations." *Journal of Politics* 84 (1): 18–32.

Owen, Robert. 1837. *Six Lectures Delivered in Manchester.* Manchester, UK.

Oxfam. 2022. "Profiting from Pain: The Urgency of Taxing the Rich amid a Surge in Billionaire Wealth and a Global Cost-of-Living Crisis." https://www.oxfamamerica .org/explore/research-publications/profiting-from-pain/.

Pack, Spencer J. 1996. "Slavery, Adam Smith's Economic Vision, and the Invisible Hand." *History of Economic Ideas* 4 (1–2): 253–69.

Partenie, Catalin. 2009. *Plato's Myths.* Cambridge: Cambridge University Press.

Pascal, Blaise. (1670) 1995. *Pensées.* Translated by A. J. Krailsheimer. London: Penguin.

Pateman, Carole. 1988. *The Sexual Contract.* Stanford: Stanford University Press.

Paul, Shalom M. 1991. *Amos: A Commentary on the Book of Amos.* Edited by Frank Moore Cross. Minneapolis: Augsburg Fortress.

Payne, Keith. 2017. *Broken Ladder: How Inequality Affects the Way We Live, Think, and Die.* New York: Viking.

Persky, Joseph. 2016. *The Political Economy of Progress: John Stuart Mill and Modern Radicalism.* Oxford: Oxford University Press.

Phillips, Anne. 2021. *Unconditional Equals.* Princeton: Princeton University Press.

Piketty, Thomas. 2014. *Capital in the 21st Century.* Translated by Arthur Goldhammer. Cambridge, MA: Belknap.

Piketty, Thomas. 2020. *Capital and Ideology.* Translated by Arthur Goldhammer. Cambridge, MA: Harvard University Press.

Piketty, Thomas. 2021. *Brief History of Equality.* Translated by Steven Rendall. Cambridge, MA: Belknap.

Pinker, Steven. 2018. *Enlightenment Now: The Case for Reason, Science, Humanism, and Progress*. New York: Viking.

Plato. 1961a. *Eighth Letter*. In *The Collected Dialogues of Plato*, edited by Edith Hamilton and Huntington Cairns. Princeton: Princeton University Press.

Plato. 1961b. *Gorgias*. In *The Collected Dialogues of Plato*, edited by Edith Hamilton and Huntington Cairns. Princeton: Princeton University Press.

Plato. 1961c. *Seventh Letter*. In *The Collected Dialogues of Plato*, edited by Edith Hamilton and Huntington Cairns. Princeton, NJ: Princeton University Press.

Plato. 1979. *The Laws of Plato*. Translated by Thomas L. Pangle. Chicago: University of Chicago Press.

Plato. 2004. *Republic*. Translated by C.D.C. Reeve. Indianapolis: Hackett.

Plutarch. 2001. *Lives*. 2 vols. Translated by Arthur Hugh Clough. New York: Modern Library.

Plutarch. 2019. "To an Uneducated Leader." In *How to Be a Leader*, translated by Jeffrey Beneker, 41–190. Princeton: Princeton University Press.

Popper, Karl. (1945) 1971. *The Open Society and Its Enemies, Volume I: The Spell of Plato*. Princeton: Princeton University Press.

Posner, Richard A. 1983. *The Economics of Justice*. Cambridge, MA: Harvard University Press.

Postan, M. M. 1972. *The Medieval Economy and Society: An Economic History of Britain, 1100–1500*. Berkeley: University of California Press.

Putnam, Robert. 2015. *Our Kids: The American Dream in Crisis*. New York: Simon & Schuster.

Rasmussen, Dennis C. 2008. *The Problems and Promise of Commercial Society: Adam Smith's Response to Rousseau*. University Park: Pennsylvania State University Press.

Rasmussen, Dennis C. 2015. "If Rousseau Were Rich: Another Model of the Good Life." *History of Political Thought* 36 (3): 499–520.

Rasmussen, Dennis C. 2016. "Adam Smith on What Is Wrong with Economic Inequality." *American Political Science Review* 110 (2): 342–52.

Ratzinger, Joseph [Pope Benedict XVI]. 2007. "That Which Holds the World Together: The Pre-political Moral Foundations of a Free State." In *The Dialectics of Secularization: On Reason and Religion*, 53–80. San Francisco: Ignatius Press.

Ratzinger, Joseph [Pope Benedict XVI]. 2008. *Jesus of Nazareth: From the Baptism in the Jordan to the Transfiguration*. Translated by Adrian J. Walker. San Francisco: Ignatius Press.

Ratzinger, Joseph [Pope Benedict XVI]. 2009. *Charity in Truth (Caritas in Veritate)*. San Francisco: Ignatius Press.

Rauhut, Daniel. 2021. "Saving the Poor: John Stuart Mill on Poverty and the Poor." In *Poverty in the History of Economic Thought: From Mercantilism to Neoclassical Economics*, edited by Mats Lundahl, Daniel Rauhut, and Neelambar Hatti, 76–88. London: Routledge.

Rawls, John. 1971. *A Theory of Justice*. Cambridge, MA: Belknap.

Rawls, John. 2001. *Justice as Fairness: A Restatement*. Edited by Erin Kelly. Cambridge, MA: Belknap.

Raylor, Timothy. 2019. *Philosophy, Rhetoric, and Thomas Hobbes*. Oxford: Oxford University Press.

Rees, B. R. 2004. *Pelagius: Life and Letters*. Edited by B. R. Reeve. Martlesham, UK: Boydell.

Reeve, C.D.C. (1988) 2006. *Philosopher-Kings: The Argument of Plato's "Republic."* Indianapolis: Hackett.

Reich, Rob. 2018. *Just Giving: Why Philanthropy Is Failing Democracy and How It Can Do Better*. Princeton: Princeton University Press.

Reisert, Joseph R. 2003. *Jean-Jacques Rousseau: A Friend of Virtue*. Ithaca: Cornell University Press.

Riley, Patrick. 1986. *The General Will before Rousseau: The Transformation of the Divine into the Civic*. Princeton: Princeton University Press.

Roberts, William Clare. 2017. *Marx's Inferno: The Political Theory of "Capital."* Princeton: Princeton University Press.

Robeyns, Ingrid. 2019. "What, if Anything, Is Wrong with Extreme Wealth?" *Journal of Human Development and Capabilities* 20 (3): 251–66.

Roochnik, David. 2003. *Beautiful City: The Dialectical Character of Plato's "Republic."* Ithaca: Cornell University Press.

Rosenblatt, Helena. 1997. *Rousseau and Geneva: From the "First Discourse" to the "Social Contract," 1749–1762*. Cambridge: Cambridge University Press.

Rousseau, Jean-Jacques. (1749–56) 2005. "On Wealth and Fragments on Taste." In *The Plan for Perpetual Peace, On the Government of Poland, and Other Writings on History and Politics, The Collected Writings of Rousseau*, vol. 11, edited by Christopher Kelly, 6–18. Hanover, NH: University Press of New England.

Rousseau, Jean-Jacques. (1751) 2019. *Discourse on the Sciences and Arts*. In *The Discourses and Other Early Political Writings*, edited by Victor Gourevitch. Cambridge: Cambridge University Press.

Rousseau, Jean-Jacques. (1751) 2019. *Observations by Jean-Jacques Rousseau of Geneva*. In *The Discourses and Other Early Political Writings*, edited by Victor Gourevitch. Cambridge: Cambridge University Press.

Rousseau, Jean-Jacques. (1752) 2019. *Last Reply*. In *The Discourses and Other Early Political Writings*, edited by Victor Gourevitch. Cambridge: Cambridge University Press.

Rousseau, Jean-Jacques. (1752–53) 2019. "Preface to Narcissus." In *The Discourses and Other Early Political Writings*, edited by Victor Gourevitch, 94–108. Cambridge: Cambridge University Press.

Rousseau, Jean-Jacques. (1755) 2019. *Discourse on the Origin and the Foundations of Inequality among Men or Second Discourse*. In *The Discourses and Other Political Writings*, edited by Victor Gourevitch. Cambridge: Cambridge University Press.

Rousseau, Jean-Jacques. (1756) 2019. *Discourse on Political Economy*. In *The Social Contract and Other Later Political Writings*. 2nd ed. Edited by Victor Gourevitch. Cambridge: Cambridge University Press.

Rousseau, Jean-Jacques. (1758) 1937. "Letter to Robert Tronchin, November 26, 1758." In *Citizen of Geneva: Selections from the Letters of J. J. R.*, edited by Charles Hendel, 159–61. Oxford: Oxford University Press.

Rousseau, Jean-Jacques. (1758) 2004. *Letter to d'Alembert on the Theater*. In *Letter to d'Alembert and Writings for the Theater, The Collected Writings of Rousseau*, vol. 10, edited by Allan Bloom, Charles Butterworth, and Christopher Kelly. Hanover, NH: University Press of New England.

Rousseau, Jean-Jacques. (1761) 1997. *Julie, or the New Heloise*. Translated by Philip Stewart and Jean Vache. Vol. 6 of *The Collected Writings of Rousseau*. Hanover, NH: University Press of New England.

Rousseau, Jean-Jacques. (1762) 1979. *Emile, or On Education*. Translated by Allan Bloom. New York: Basic Books.

Rousseau, Jean-Jacques. (1762) 2019. *The Social Contract*. In *The Social Contract and Other Later Political Writings*. 2nd ed. Edited by Victor Gourevitch. Cambridge: Cambridge University Press.

Rousseau, Jean-Jacques. (1764) 2001. *Letters Written from the Mountain*. In *Letter to Beaumont, Letters Written from the Mountain, and Related Writings, The Collected Writings of Rousseau*, vol. 9, edited by Christopher Kelly and Eve Grace. Hanover, NH: University Press of New England.

Rousseau, Jean-Jacques. (1767) 1997. *Plan for a Constitutional Project for Corsica*. In *The Plan for Perpetual Peace, On the Government of Poland, and Other Writings on History and Politics, The Collected Writings of Rousseau*, vol. 11, edited by Christopher Kelly. Hanover, NH: Dartmouth College Press.

Rousseau, Jean-Jacques. (1767) 1997. "Separate Fragments" from *Plan for a Constitutional Project for Corsica*. In *The Plan for Perpetual Peace, On the Government of Poland, and Other Writings on History and Politics, The Collected Writings of Rousseau*, vol. 11, edited by Christopher Kelly. Hanover, NH: Dartmouth College Press.

Rousseau, Jean-Jacques. (1769) 2019. "Letter from J. J. Rousseau to M. de Franquières, 25 March 1769." In *The Social Contract and Other Later Political Writings*. 2nd ed. Edited by Victor Gourevitch, 277–90. Cambridge: Cambridge University Press.

Rousseau, Jean-Jacques. (1772) 2019. *Considerations on the Government of Poland*. In *The Social Contract and Other Later Political Writings*. 2nd ed. Edited by Victor Gourevitch. Cambridge: Cambridge University Press.

Rousseau, Jean-Jacques. (1772–76) 1990. *Rousseau, Judge of Jean-Jacques: Dialogues*. In *The Collected Writings of Rousseau*, vol. 1, edited by Roger D. Masters and Christopher Kelly. Hanover, NH: Dartmouth College Press.

Rousseau, Jean-Jacques. (1781) 2019. *Essay on the Origins of Languages*. In *The Discourses and Other Political Writings*, edited by Victor Gourevitch. Cambridge: Cambridge University Press.

Rousseau, Jean-Jacques. 1994. "Political Fragments." In *Social Contract, Discourse on the Virtue Most Necessary for a Hero, Political Fragments, and Geneva Manuscript, The Collected Writings of Rousseau*, vol. 4, edited by Roger D. Masters and Christopher Kelly. Hanover, NH: University Press of New England.

Ryrie, Alec. 2017. "Reformation." In *A Social History of England, 1500–1750*, edited by Keith Wrightson, 107–28. Cambridge: Cambridge University Press.

Saez, Emmanuel, and Gabriel Zucman. 2016. "Wealth Inequality in the United States since 1913: Evidence from Capitalized Income Tax Data." *Quarterly Journal of Economics* 131 (2): 519–78.

Sandel, Michael. 2020. *The Tyranny of Merit: What's Become of the Common Good?* New York: Farrar, Straus and Giroux.

Sanders, E. P. 1983. *The Historical Figure of Jesus*. London: Allen Lane.

Santas, Gerasimos. 2010. *Understanding Plato's "Republic."* Oxford: Wiley-Blackwell.

Santas, Gerasimos. 2018. "Plato on Inequalities, Justice, and Democracy." In *Democracy, Justice, and Equality in Ancient Greece: Historical and Philosophical*

Perspectives, edited by Georgios Anagnostopoulos and Gerasimos Santas, 161–78. Cham: Springer.

Savage, Mike. 2021. *The Return of Inequality: Social Change and the Weight of the Past*. Cambridge, MA: Harvard University Press.

Saxonhouse, Arlene. 1976. "The Philosopher and the Female in the Political Thought of Plato." *Political Theory* 4 (2): 195–212.

Scheidel, Walter. 2017. *The Great Leveler: Violence and the History of Inequality from the Stone Age to the Twenty-First Century*. Princeton: Princeton University Press.

Schliesser, Eric. 2017. *Adam Smith: Systematic Philosophy and Public Thinker*. Oxford: Oxford University Press.

Schmitt, Carl. (1942) 2015. *Land and Sea*. Translated by Samuel Garrett Zeitlin. Candor, NY: Telos Press.

Schofield, Malcolm. 2006. *Plato: Political Philosophy*. Oxford: Oxford University Press.

Schofield, Malcolm. 2009. "*Fraternité, Inégalité, la parole de Dieu*: Plato's Authoritarian Myth of Political Legitimation." In *Plato's Myths*, edited by Catalin Partenie, 101–15. Cambridge: Cambridge University Press.

Scholz, Sally. 2012. "Rousseau on Poverty." In *Economic Justice: Philosophical and Legal Perspectives*, edited by Helen Stacy and Win-Chiat Lee, 13–28. Dordrecht: Springer.

Schroeder, C. Paul. 2009. Introduction to *On Social Justice*, by Saint Basil the Great, 15–39. Translated by C. Paul Schroeder. Crestwood, NY: St. Vladimir's Seminar Press.

Schumpeter, Joseph A. (1942) 1950. *Capitalism, Socialism, and Democracy*. New York: Harper.

Schwarze, Michelle A., and John T. Scott. 2015. "Spontaneous Disorder in Adam Smith's *Theory of Moral Sentiments*: Resentment, Injustice, and the Appeal to Providence." *Journal of Politics* 77 (2): 463–76.

Schwarze, Michelle A., and John T. Scott. 2019. "Mutual Sympathy and the Moral Economy: Adam Smith Reviews Rousseau." *Journal of Politics* 8 (1): 66–80.

Scott, John T. 1994. "Politics as an Imitation of the Divine in Rousseau's *Social Contract*." *Polity* 26 (3): 473–501.

Seneca the Younger. 1932. *On the Happy Life*. In *Seneca: Moral Letters*, vol. 2, translated by John W. Basore. Cambridge, MA: Harvard University Press.

Seung, T. K. 1962. *The Fragile Leaves of the Sibyl: Dante's Master Plan*. Westminster, MD: Newman Press.

Seung, T. K. 1993. *Intuition and Construction: The Foundation of Normative Theory*. New Haven: Yale University Press.

Seung, T. K. 1994. *Kant's Platonic Revolution in Moral and Political Philosophy*. Baltimore: Johns Hopkins University Press.

Seung, T. K. 1996. *Plato Rediscovered: Human Value and Social Order*. Lanham, MD: Rowman & Littlefield.

Sherwin-White, A. N. 1963. *Roman Law and Roman Society in the New Testament*. Oxford: Oxford University Press.

Shklar, Judith N. 1969. *Men and Citizens: A Study of Rousseau's Social Theory*. Cambridge: Cambridge University Press.

Shklar, Judith N. 1998. "Jean-Jacques Rousseau and Equality." In *Political Thought and Political Thinkers*, edited by Stanley Hoffmann, 276–93. Chicago: University of Chicago Press.

Silverthorne, M. J. 1973. "Rousseau's Plato." *Studies on Voltaire and the Eighteenth Century*, no. 116, 235–49.

Simonton, Matthew. 2018. *Classical Greek Oligarchy: A Political History*. Princeton: Princeton University Press.

Simpson, Matthew. 2006. *Rousseau's Theory of Freedom*. London: Continuum.

Smith, Adam. (1759–90) 2009. *Theory of Moral Sentiments*. Edited by Ryan Patrick Hanley. New York: Penguin.

Smith, Adam. (1763) 1978. *Lectures on Jurisprudence*. Edited by R. L. Meek, D. D. Raphael, and P. G. Stein. Oxford: Oxford University Press.

Smith, Adam. (1776) 1982. *An Inquiry into the Nature and Causes of the Wealth of Nations*. Edited by R. H. Campbell and A. S. Skinner. Indianapolis: Liberty Fund.

Smith, Adam. (1795) 1980. "History of Astronomy." In *Essays on Philosophical Subjects*, edited by I. S. Ross, 33–105. Oxford: Clarendon.

Smith, Steven B. 2007. *Reading Leo Strauss: Politics, Philosophy, Judaism*. Chicago: University of Chicago Press.

Smith, Steven B. 2012. *Political Philosophy*. New Haven: Yale University Press.

Solomon, Norman. 1997. "Economics of the Jubilee." In *The Jubilee Challenge: Utopia or Possibility?* edited by Hans Ucko. Geneva: WCC Publications.

Soltow, Lee. 1990. "Inequality of Wealth in Land in Scotland in the Eighteenth Century." *Scottish Economic and Social History* 10 (1): 38–60.

Sommeiller, Estelle, and Mark Price. 2018. "The New Gilded Age: Income Inequality in the U.S. by State, Metropolitan Area, and County." Economic Policy Institute, July 19. https://files.epi.org/pdf/147963.pdf.

Sorell, Tom. 2016. "Law and Equity in Hobbes." *Critical Review of International Social and Political Philosophy* 19 (1): 29–46.

Spinoza, Benedict. (1670) 2002. *Theological-Political Treatise*. In *Spinoza: Complete Works*, translated by Samuel Shirley. Indianapolis: Hackett.

Starobinski, Jean. (1971) 1988. *Jean-Jacques Rousseau: Transparency and Obstruction*. Translated by Arthur Goldhammer. Chicago: University of Chicago Press.

Stalley, R. F. 1983. *An Introduction to Plato's "Laws."* Indianapolis: Hackett.

Starr, Harris E. 1925. *William Graham Sumner*. New York: Holt.

Stauffer, Devin. 2018. *Hobbes's Kingdom of Light: A Study of the Foundations of Modern Political Philosophy*. Cambridge: Cambridge University Press.

Stephen, James Fitzjames. (1873) 1992. *Liberty, Equality, Fraternity*. Edited by Stuart D. Warner. Indianapolis: Liberty Fund.

Stigler, George. 1975. "Smith's Travels on the Ship of State." In *Essays on Adam Smith*, edited by Andrew Skinner and Thomas Wilson, 265–77. Oxford: Clarendon.

Stiglitz, Joseph E. 2012. *The Price of Inequality: How Today's Divided Society Endangers Our Future*. New York: Norton.

Stimson, Shannon. 2015. "The General Will after Rousseau: Smith and Rousseau on Sociability and Inequality." In *The General Will: The Evolution of a Concept*, edited by James Farr and David Lay Williams, 350–81. Cambridge: Cambridge University Press.

Stone, Lawrence. 1958. "The Inflation of Honors 1558–1641." *Past and Present* 14:45–70.

Storey, Benjamin, and Jenna Silber Storey. 2021. *Why We Are Restless: On the Modern Quest for Contentment*. Princeton: Princeton University Press.

Strabo. 1924. *Geography.* Translated by Horace Leonard Jones. Cambridge, MA: Loeb Classical Library.

Strauss, Leo. (1936) 1996. *The Political Philosophy of Hobbes: Its Basis and Its Genesis.* Chicago: University of Chicago Press.

Strauss, Leo. 1964. *The City and Man.* Chicago: University of Chicago Press.

Strauss, Leo. 1967. "Jerusalem and Athens: Some Introductory Remarks." *Commentary,* June, 45–57.

Strauss, Leo. (1973) 1998. *The Argument and Action of Plato's "Laws."* Chicago: University of Chicago Press.

Stuurman, Siep. 2000. "The Canon of the History of Political Thought: Its Critique and a Proposed Alternative." *History and Theory* 39 (2): 147–66.

Stuurman, Siep. 2017. *The Invention of Humanity: Equality and Cultural Difference in World History.* Cambridge, MA: Harvard University Press.

Sumner, William Graham. (1883) 1989. *What the Social Classes Owe Each Other.* Caldwell, ID: Caxton Printers.

Sumner, William Graham. (1902) 1914. *The Challenge of Facts and Other Essays.* New Haven: Yale University Press.

Theissen, Gerd. 1979. *The Social Setting of Pauline Christianity.* Philadelphia: Fortress.

Thomas, Keith. 1965. "The Social Origins of Hobbes's Political Thought." In *Hobbes Studies,* edited by K. C. Brown, 185–236. Oxford: Blackwell.

Thompson, Michael J. 2007. *The Politics of Inequality: A Political History of the Idea of Economic Inequality in America.* New York: Columbia University Press.

Thucydides. (1629) 1989. *The Peloponnesian War.* Translated by Thomas Hobbes. Chicago: University of Chicago Press.

Tocqueville, Alexis de. (1835) 2006. *Memoir on Pauperism: Does Public Charity Produce an Idle and Dependent Class of Society?* New York: Cosimo Classics.

Tocqueville, Alexis de. (1835/40). 1988. *Democracy in America.* Translated by George Lawrence. New York: Harper Perennial.

Tocqueville, Alexis de. (1856) 1983. *The Old Regime and the French Revolution.* Translated by Stuart Gilbert. New York: Anchor Books.

Tuck, Richard. 2002. *Hobbes: A Very Short Introduction.* Oxford: Oxford University Press.

Turgot, Anne Robert Jacques. (1770) 1973. *Reflections on the Formation and the Distribution of Wealth.* In *On Progress, Sociology, and Economic: Three Major Texts,* edited by Ronald L. Meek. Cambridge: Cambridge University Press.

Van Biema, David, and Jeff Chu. 2006. "Does God Want You to Be Rich?" *Time,* September 10.

Vartija, Devin. 2021. *The Color of Equality: Race and Common Humanity in Enlightenment Thought.* Philadelphia: University of Pennsylvania Press.

Vaughan, Sharon. 2008. *Poverty, Justice, and Western Political Thought.* Lanham, MD: Lexington Books.

Villa, Dana. 2017. *Teachers of the People: Political Education in Rousseau, Hegel, Tocqueville, and Mill.* Chicago: University of Chicago Press.

Viroli, Maurizio. 1988. *Jean-Jacques Rousseau and the "Well-Ordered Society."* Translated by Derek Hanson. Cambridge: Cambridge University Press.

Viser, Matt, and David Weigel. 2019. "Deval Patrick Has No Money and Not Much Staff. He's Counting on Optimism." *Washington Post,* November 14. https://www

.washingtonpost.com/politics/deval-patrick-has-no-money-and-not-much-staff
-hes-counting-on-optimism/2019/11/14/801e8fb8-067c-11ea-b17d-8b867891d39d
_story.html.

Vlastos, Gregory. 1941. "Slavery in Plato's Thought." *Philosophical Review* 50 (3): 289–304.

Vlastos, Gregory. 1981. *Platonic Studies*. 2nd ed. Princeton: Princeton University Press.

Voltaire. (1755) 2018. "Letter to Rousseau" (August 30). In *Jean-Jacques Rousseau: Fundamental Political Writings*, edited by Matthew W. Maguire and David Lay Williams, 341–44. Peterborough, ON: Broadview Press.

Walker, Robert, Grace Bantebya Kyomuhendo, Elaine Chase, Sohail Choudry, Erika K. Bumbrium, Jo Yongmie Nicola, Ivar Lodemel, Leemamol Mathew, Amon Mwiine, Sony Pellisserty, and Yan Ming. 2013. "Poverty in Global Perspective: Is Shame a Common Denominator?" *Journal of Social Policy* 42 (2): 215–33.

Wallach, John. 2001. *The Platonic Political Art: A Study of Critical Reason and Democracy*. University Park: Pennsylvania State University Press.

Walzer, Michael. 1983. *Spheres of Justice: A Defense of Pluralism and Equality*. New York: Basic Books.

Warner, John M. 2015. *Rousseau and the Problem of Human Relations*. University Park: Pennsylvania State University Press.

Weber, Max. (1904) 2001. *The Protestant Ethic and the Spirit of Capitalism*. Translated by Talcott Parsons. London: Routledge.

Weirich, Paul. 1992. "Rousseau on Equality." *History of Philosophy Quarterly* 9 (2): 191–98.

Weiss, Roslyn. 2012. *Philosophers in the Republic: Plato's Two Paradigms*. Ithaca: Cornell University Press.

Werhane, Patricia H. 1989. "The Role of Self-Interest in Adam Smith's *Wealth of Nations*." *Journal of Philosophy* 86 (11): 669–80.

Werhane, Patricia H. 1991. *Adam Smith and His Legacy for Modern Capitalism*. Oxford: Oxford University Press.

West, Henry R. 2004. *An Introduction to Mill's Utilitarian Ethics*. Cambridge: Cambridge University Press.

Whatmore, Richard. 2006. "Intellectual History and the History of Political Thought." In *Palgrave Advances in Intellectual History*, edited by Richard Whatmore and Brian Young, 109–29. Basingstoke: Palgrave Macmillan.

Wilkinson, Richard, and Kate Pickett. 2018. *The Inner Level: How More Equal Societies Reduce Stress, Restore Sanity, and Improve Everyone's Well-Being*. New York: Penguin.

Williams, David Lay. 2007. *Rousseau's Platonic Enlightenment*. University Park: Pennsylvania State University Press.

Williams, David Lay. 2010. "Political Ontology and Institutional Design in Montesquieu and Rousseau." *American Journal of Political Science* 54 (2): 525–42.

Williams, David Lay. 2013. "Plato's Noble Lie: From Kallipolis to Magnesia." *History of Political Thought* 34 (3): 363–92.

Williams, David Lay. 2014. *Rousseau's "Social Contract": An Introduction*. Cambridge: Cambridge University Press.

Williams, David Lay. 2017. "Rousseau on Inequality and Free Will." *Political Theory* 45 (4): 552–65.

Williams, David Lay. 2024. "Rousseau's Ancient Ends of Legislation: Liberty, Equality (& Fraternity)." In *Cambridge Companion to Rousseau's "Social Contract,"* edited by Matthew W. Maguire and David Lay Williams, 113–37. Cambridge: Cambridge University Press.

Wilson, Emily. 2014. *The Greatest Empire: The Life of Seneca.* Oxford: Oxford University Press.

Wilson, James Lindley. 2019. *Democratic Equality.* Princeton: Princeton University Press.

Winch, Donald. 1978. *Adam Smith's Politics.* Cambridge: Cambridge University Press.

Winch, Donald. 1996. *Riches and Poverty: An Intellectual History of Political Economy in Britain, 1750–1834.* Cambridge: Cambridge University Press.

Winters, Jeffrey. 2011. *Oligarchy.* Cambridge: Cambridge University Press.

Wolff, Edward N. 2017. *A Century of Wealth in America.* Cambridge, MA: Belknap.

Wollstonecraft, Mary. (1791) 1995. *A Vindication of the Rights of Woman.* In *A Vindication of the Rights of Man and a Vindication of the Rights of Woman,* edited by Sylvana Tomaselli. Cambridge: Cambridge University Press.

Wolpert, Andrew. 2002. *Remembering Defeat: Civil War and Civic Memory in Ancient Athens.* Baltimore: Johns Hopkins University Press.

Wood, Allen W. 2014. "Marx on Equality." In *The Free Development of Each: Studies on Freedom, Right, and Ethics in Classical German Philosophy,* 252–73. Oxford: Oxford University Press.

Wood, Andy. 2002. *Riot, Rebellion, and Popular Politics in Early Modern England.* New York: Palgrave Macmillan.

Wootton, David. 2018. *Power, Pleasure, and Profit: Insatiable Appetites from Machiavelli to Madison.* Cambridge, MA: Belknap.

World Bank. "Gini Index." Accessed May 5, 2015. http://data.worldbank.org/indicator/SI.POV.GINI.

Wright, Archie T. 2017. "Social and Economic Injustice: Apocalyptic Themes in the Epistles of Enoch and the Apostle of John." In *The Blessings of Enoch: 1 Enoch and Contemporary Theology,* edited by Philip F. Esler. Eugene: Cascade Books.

Wright, N. T. 2001a. *Luke for Everyone.* Louisville: Westminster John Knox Press.

Wright, N. T. 2001b. *Mark for Everyone.* Louisville: Westminster John Knox Press.

Wright, N. T. 2001c. *Matthew for Everyone.* Louisville: Westminster John Knox Press.

Wright, N. T. 2001d. *The Early Christian Letters for Everyone.* Louisville: Westminster John Knox Press.

Wrightson, Keith. 2000. *Earthly Necessities: Economic Lives in Early Modern Britain.* New Haven: Yale University Press.

Yoder, John Howard. (1972) 1994. *The Politics of Jesus: Vicit Agnus Noster.* 2nd ed. Grand Rapids: Eerdmans.

Young, Michael. (1958) 1994. *The Rise of Meritocracy.* New Brunswick, NJ: Transaction.

Zeitlin, Samuel G. 2021. "'The Heat of a Feaver': Francis Bacon on Civil War, Sedition, and Rebellion." *History of European Ideas* 47 (5): 643–63.

Ziblatt, Daniel. 2008. "Does Landholding Inequality Block Democratization?" *World Politics* 60: 610–41.

Zuckert, Catherine H. 2009. *Plato's Philosophers: The Coherence of the Dialogues.* Chicago: University of Chicago Press.

INDEX

144, 160, 170, 315, 357n23; Smith on, 170–73, 188–90, 199–201, 250, 252, 275, 293–94, 315; universal standards of living improved by, 141, 189, 199–201, 214, 250, 275–76, 293, 312–15, 317, 357n23; zero-sum conception of, 97, 107, 144, 170, 314–15

common good: ancient Greek thought and, 29, 39, 46; Hobbes and, 120–21, 126; private vices and enterprise resulting in, 140–42; racial inequality and, 168; Rousseau and, 165. *See also* general will

common meals, 23

communism. *See* socialism/communism

community. *See* civic harmony

Conard, Edward, 318–19, 361n24

concentrated wealth, 9–11. *See also* economic inequality; wealth and the rich

concord. *See* mutual sympathy

Confucius, 9

Considérant, Victor Prosper, 215

Consistory of Pastors, 139

contumely, 131–32

Conwell, Russell, 56

Cornwall, Julian, 104

Corsica, 9, 15, 147, 156, 160–61, 326n21

COVID-19 pandemic, 11–12

Cowen, Tyler, 5, 323n20

Cranston, Maurice, 135–36

Crossan, John Dominic, 59

Crossman, R.H.S., 18

currency. *See* money

Cyrus, 37–38

Daily Telegraph (newspaper), 281

Darby, Abraham, 174

Darimon, Alfred, 359n54

Darius, 38

Darius Xerxes, 38–39, 44, 328n67

Deaton, Angus, 320–21

debt forgiveness: the Jews, Jesus, and, 13–14, 61–62, 65–66, 79–81; Plato and, 41, 47; social benefits of, 81; Solon and, 20, 41. *See also* loans and interest

DeCelles, Katherine, 316

Declaration of the Rights of Man (France), 263

De divitiis (*On Riches*), 97

democracy: Athens and, 21, 25; Geneva and, 138; Hobbes and, 204; Mill and, 203, 205, 230, 233–34, 247–48, 314; Plato and, 204; Rousseau and, 154–56, 314, 344n48, 346n75; United States and, 305. *See also* political equality; republicanism

Deneen, Patrick J., 352n18

dependence of the poor on the rich: Marx on, 16, 297–301; Mill on, 214–15; Rousseau on, 150, 156

Derrett, J. Duncan M., 83

desire: insatiable, 5, 17, 53, 74, 76, 81, 97, 146, 216, 251, 284–88, 292; moderation of, 52. *See also* greed

despotism, 135, 169

Dionysius, 54

distribution/redistribution of wealth/property: Aristotle on, 332n33; among biblical Jews, 62; in biblical times, 13–14, 61–62, 64, 66, 69, 78–82, 84, 90, 332n33; Hobbes on, 14, 100, 121, 125–27, 341n86; Marx on, 308; Mill on, 16, 204, 208, 229–31, 233, 236–37, 247, 252, 255; Plato on, 13, 41–43, 46–48; political nature of, 353n40; in Rome, 306; Rousseau on, 14–15, 137, 160; in Sparta, 22. *See also* property

division of labor, 105, 183, 191, 195, 277–78

Dollar, David, 317

Douglass, Frederick, 3, 5, 261

doux commerce, 140–42, 266, 357n23

Dühring, Eugen, 262

Durkheim, Émile, 355n69

Eagleton, Terry, 264

Eastern Church, 96

East India Company, 105, 106, 174

economic equality/egalitarianism: Douglass and, 3; historical instances of, 6; Hobbes and, 99; inequalities coexisting with, 165–66; Jubilee laws and, 85; Mill and, 250–53; Plato and, 18–19, 37–44, 47–49, 53; republicanism linked to, 261; Rousseau and, 135–36, 154, 165, 169; Smith and, 351n70; Solon and, 20–21, 24; in United States, 302. *See also* economic inequality

85–86, 96–97; Hobbes on, 113, 115–22; Mill on, 213–20; Plato on, 16, 30–31, 33–34, 38, 45; Rousseau on, 145–50, 157–59, 343n27; Smith on, 179–88. *See also* morality; psychology

industry, 176–77

inequality. *See* economic inequality; income inequality; racial inequality; wealth inequality

inflation, 102, 338n13

inheritance: Jesus and, 75; Lycurgus and, 329n73; Mill and, 16, 234–37, 354nn45–47; Plato and, 43; Rousseau and, 345n62

interest. *See* loans and interest

invisible hand, 177

Isaiah, 62

James, 57, 85–89, 93, 96, 313

James I, King, 108, 299

Jensen, Hans, 355n59

Jerusalem, 59–60, 62, 73, 77–78, 86–87, 89

Jesus, 67–88; and almsgiving/charity, 70–71, 95–96, 311; ambitions and goals in teachings of, 67–69, 81–85; audience for, 57, 67, 91; and bandits, 65, 70; Beatitudes, 70, 85; on economic inequality, 6, 10, 79, 302, 319; on greed, 74–78; historical context of, 67; on inheritance, 75; love of God as highest good for, 13–14; Mill and, 243; Nazareth as birthplace of, 58; Parable of the Rich Fool, 75; Parable of the Sower, 74, 85; Parable of the Unforgiving Servant, 80; Paul compared to, 88–96; and the Pharisees, 77–85; and poverty/the poor, 14, 69–71, 86; Sermon on the Mount, 83–84; suggestions for reducing inequality, 14, 79–81; on wealth and the rich, 57, 71–75, 78, 93. *See also* New Testament

Job, 130–31

Johnson, Lyndon, 10, 324n30

John the Baptist, 63

Joseph, Keith, 317

Josephus, 63, 64–66, 77

Jubilee laws, 13–14, 61–62, 64, 69, 78–82, 84–85, 90, 125–26, 332n33

Judas, 77

Judge, E. A., 91

justice: economic inequality as threat to, 5, 223–29; Mill and, 208, 223–29, 231–32, 353n37; Plato and, 35–36, 39; Rousseau and, 150–54; Smith and, 193–95, 350n55. *See also* impartiality; law and legislation; morality

justification by works, 87

Kant, Immanuel, 98, 257, 263–64, 266, 300

Kavka, Gregory, 100

Kay, John, 176

Keltner, Dacher, 316

Kett, Robert, and Kett's Rebellion, 104

Kitto, H.D.F., 51–52

Kraay, Aart, 317

Kuznets, Simon, 199

labor: contract between employer and worker, 263; division of, 105, 183, 191, 195, 277–78; in eighteenth-century Britain, 175–77, 182–83, 191; Marx on, 263, 265–82, 297–301; in mercantilist England, 102–5, 107; at origins of inequality, 265–69; Smith on, 183, 191, 277; supply and demand of, 198, 216, 237–39, 279, 299; working and living conditions of, 196, 267, 270–73, 278–81, 294–95. *See also* proletariat; worker cooperatives

Laertius, Diogenes, 52–53

Lao Tzu, 9

law and legislation: in ancient Greece, 19–23, 41; class advantage as foundation of, 135, 148–49, 155, 169–70, 194–96, 202, 218, 221–22, 224–26, 234, 262, 295–97; general will as basis for, 151–52, 154–55; Hobbes and, 111, 120, 134, 296; Marx on, 295–97; Mill on, 202, 218, 221–22, 224–26, 234; Plato on, 34–37, 42–46, 48–49; the rich's disregard for, 117–18, 316 (*see also* impunity, presumed by the rich); Rousseau on, 135, 148–49, 151–52, 154–55, 169, 296; Smith on, 169–70, 192–96, 296. *See also* Jubilee laws; justice; natural laws; Sabbatical laws

Lawrence, William, 56

Leclaire (Parisian tradesman), 245

factions in, 121; inheritance in, 236; Mill and, 213, 230, 236, 249; political effects of economic inequality in, 12; poverty in, 10, 189, 200, 356n21; slavery in, 3, 174, 202, 305; suffrage in, 230; taxation in, 302
usury, 105–6, 119
utility, as Mill's highest political value, 15–16, 171, 202, 211, 254

Valpy, Montagu, 281
vanity. *See* pride/vanity
Vaughan, Sharon, 137, 158, 325n6
Villa, Dana, 353n33
Viroli, Maurizio, 309
virtue: associated with the bourgeois, 105, 265, 268, 314; *doux commerce* theory and, 140; in mercantilist England, 105; Plato on, 27, 29–31, 35–36; Rousseau on, 145–47, 149, 154; Seneca on, 93; Smith on, 190–92. *See also* morality
Voltaire, 200
voting rights. *See* suffrage

wages, 103, 182, 237, 294
Walzer, Michael, 360n6
War of Spanish Succession, 138
War on Poverty, 10, 324n30
wealth and the rich: Aristotle and, 115, 325n15; in Athens and Sparta, 23; attitudes toward, 16; among biblical Jews, 60–64, 73; Catholic Church and, 358n48; Christian attitudes about, 55–57, 71–75, 78, 85–87, 90–93, 95–97; concept of, 10; effects of economic inequality on, 282–91, 315–16; in eighteenth-century Britain, 173–74; generational, 11, 81, 105, 224, 234–37, 253, 329n74, 354n45; greed compared to, 74–75; Hobbes and, 14, 114–24, 127, 133–34; impunity presumed by, 14, 100, 118, 122, 131–32, 134, 316 (*see also* law and legislation: the rich's disregard for); James on, 85–87, 93; Jesus's critique of, 57, 71–75, 78, 93; Marx and, 282–91; Marx on myths and stereotypes of, 16; in mercantilist England, 105–7, 116–17; Mill and, 15, 216–19, 221–22; and morality, 39–40,

63, 86, 90, 94–95, 115–18, 187–88, 192, 216–17; as obstacles to love of God, 14; Paul and, 90–93, 96; Plato and, 20, 29–34, 37–40, 286, 327n46; Pope Francis and, 55; power connected to, 121, 124, 144–45, 156, 186, 344n49; pride and arrogance linked to, 131; psychology of, 33–34, 100, 114–20, 157, 170, 180–82, 315–16; ratio of possessions of the rich and the poor, 10, 13, 42–43, 273–76, 279, 294; in Roman Palestine, 73, 76, 83, 86, 88; Rousseau and, 10, 15, 143–47, 157–58, 285, 343n30; Sadducees and, 78; Seneca and, 92–93; Smith and, 15, 179–80, 184–88, 191–92, 218, 324n28; of the sovereign, 133–34. *See also* aristocracy; bourgeoisie; class; concentrated wealth; dependence of the poor on the rich; distribution/redistribution of wealth/property; luxuries; money; politics; property
wealth inequality, 11
Weirich, Paul, 136, 342n2
Weiss, Roslyn, 324n2
Werhane, Patricia, 193, 194, 349n47
Wesley, John, 350n61
West, Henry R., 352n23
Wilkinson, Richard, 158, 345n57
will. *See* free will; general will; private wills
Winters, Jeffrey, 344n49
Wollstonecraft, Mary, 8, 166
Wolpert, Andrew, 26
women, effects of industrial capitalism on, 281–82. *See also* gender equality
Wood, Allen W., 257, 307–9, 356n14
Wood, Andy, 338n26
worker cooperatives, 244–48
workers. *See* labor
works, justification by, 87
Workshops Regulation Act (Britain), 295
Wright, N. T., 83–85, 298
Wrightson, Keith, 102, 103, 106–7

Zacchaeus, 73
zero-sum conception of the economy, 97, 107, 144, 170, 314–15
Ziblatt, Daniel, 259
Zucman, Gabriel, 1

A NOTE ON THE TYPE

THIS BOOK has been composed in Miller, a Scotch Roman typeface designed by Matthew Carter and first released by Font Bureau in 1997. It resembles Monticello, the typeface developed for The Papers of Thomas Jefferson in the 1940s by C. H. Griffith and P. J. Conkwright and reinterpreted in digital form by Carter in 2003.

Pleasant Jefferson ("P. J.") Conkwright (1905–1986) was Typographer at Princeton University Press from 1939 to 1970. He was an acclaimed book designer and AIGA Medalist.

The ornament used throughout this book was designed by Pierre Simon Fournier (1712–1768) and was a favorite of Conkwright's, used in his design of the *Princeton University Library Chronicle*.